The Digital Folklore of Cyberculture and Digital Humanities

Stamatis Papadakis
University of Crete, Greece

Alexandros Kapaniaris
Hellenic Open University, Greece

IGI Global
PUBLISHER of TIMELY KNOWLEDGE

A volume in the Advances in Human and Social Aspects of Technology (AHSAT) Book Series

Published in the United States of America by
IGI Global
Information Science Reference (an imprint of IGI Global)
701 E. Chocolate Avenue
Hershey PA, USA 17033
Tel: 717-533-8845
Fax: 717-533-8661
E-mail: cust@igi-global.com
Web site: http://www.igi-global.com

Library of Congress Cataloging-in-Publication Data

Names: Papadakis, Stamatios, 1974- editor. | Kapaniaris, Alexandros Georgios, 1971- editor.
Title: The digital folklore of cyberculture and digital humanities / Stamatis Papadakis, and Alexandros Kapaniaris, editors.
Description: Hershey PA : Information Science Reference, [2022] | Includes bibliographical references and index. | Summary: "This book investigates digital folklore, archival ethnography and digital humanities are generally of particular interest and are in the process of being developed and established internationally, attempting to balance between the national needs and the rapid changes and peculiarities of cutting-edge technologies, standards and noted in the international community"-- Provided by publisher.
Identifiers: LCCN 2022012082 (print) | LCCN 2022012083 (ebook) | ISBN 9781668444610 (hardcover) | ISBN 9781668444627 (paperback) | ISBN 9781668444634 (ebook)
Subjects: LCSH: Folklore and the Internet. | Folklore archives--Technological innovations. | Archival materials--Digitization. | Digital humanities. | Information society.
Classification: LCC GR44.E43 .D54 2022 (print) | LCC GR44.E43 (ebook) | DDC 398.0285--dc23/eng/20220420
LC record available at https://lccn.loc.gov/2022012082
LC ebook record available at https://lccn.loc.gov/2022012083

This book is published in the IGI Global book series Advances in Human and Social Aspects of Technology (AHSAT) (ISSN: 2328-1316; eISSN: 2328-1324)

British Cataloguing in Publication Data
A Cataloguing in Publication record for this book is available from the British Library.

All work contributed to this book is new, previously-unpublished material. The views expressed in this book are those of the authors, but not necessarily of the publisher.

For electronic access to this publication, please contact: eresources@igi-global.com.

Advances in Human and Social Aspects of Technology (AHSAT) Book Series

Mehdi Khosrow-Pour, D.B.A.
Information Resources Management Association, USA

ISSN:2328-1316
EISSN:2328-1324

Mission

In recent years, the societal impact of technology has been noted as we become increasingly more connected and are presented with more digital tools and devices. With the popularity of digital devices such as cell phones and tablets, it is crucial to consider the implications of our digital dependence and the presence of technology in our everyday lives.

The **Advances in Human and Social Aspects of Technology (AHSAT) Book Series** seeks to explore the ways in which society and human beings have been affected by technology and how the technological revolution has changed the way we conduct our lives as well as our behavior. The AHSAT book series aims to publish the most cutting-edge research on human behavior and interaction with technology and the ways in which the digital age is changing society.

Coverage

- Activism and ICTs
- Digital Identity
- Information ethics
- Public Access to ICTs
- Philosophy of technology
- Cyber Behavior
- Gender and Technology
- Human-Computer Interaction
- Human Development and Technology
- Technoself

IGI Global is currently accepting manuscripts for publication within this series. To submit a proposal for a volume in this series, please contact our Acquisition Editors at Acquisitions@igi-global.com or visit: http://www.igi-global.com/publish/.

The Advances in Human and Social Aspects of Technology (AHSAT) Book Series (ISSN 2328-1316) is published by IGI Global, 701 E. Chocolate Avenue, Hershey, PA 17033-1240, USA, www.igi-global.com. This series is composed of titles available for purchase individually; each title is edited to be contextually exclusive from any other title within the series. For pricing and ordering information please visit http://www.igi-global.com/book-series/advances-human-social-aspects-technology/37145. Postmaster: Send all address changes to above address.

Titles in this Series

For a list of additional titles in this series, please visit: www.igi-global.com/book-series/advances-human-social-aspects-technology/37145

Analyzing Multidisciplinary Uses and Impact of Innovative Technologies
Emiliano Marchisio (Giustino Fortunato University, Italy)
Information Science Reference • © 2022 • 320pp • H/C (ISBN: 9781668460153) • US $240.00

Handbook of Research on Applying Emerging Technologies Across Multiple Disciplines
Emiliano Marchisio (Giustino Fortunato University, Italy)
Information Science Reference • © 2022 • 548pp • H/C (ISBN: 9781799884767) • US $270.00

Handbook of Research on Digital Violence and Discrimination Studies
Fahri Özsungur (Mersin University, Turkey)
Information Science Reference • © 2022 • 837pp • H/C (ISBN: 9781799891871) • US $270.00

Opportunities and Challenges for Computational Social Science Methods
Enes Abanoz (Ondokuz Mayıs University, Turkey)
Information Science Reference • © 2022 • 277pp • H/C (ISBN: 9781799885535) • US $215.00

Handbook of Research on Promoting Economic and Social Development Through Serious Games
Oscar Bernardes (ISCAP, ISEP, Polytechnic Institute of Porto, Portugal & University of Aveiro, Portugal) and Vanessa Amorim (Porto Accounting and Business School, Polytechnic Institute of Porto, Portugal)
Information Science Reference • © 2022 • 665pp • H/C (ISBN: 9781799897323) • US $270.00

Impact and Role of Digital Technologies in Adolescent Lives
Shaveta Malik (Terna Engineering College, India) Rohit Bansal (Department of Management Studies, Vaish College of Engineering, Rohtak, India) and Amit Kumar Tyagi (Vellore Institute of Technology, Chennai, India)
Information Science Reference • © 2022 • 313pp • H/C (ISBN: 9781799883180) • US $215.00

Applied Ethics in a Digital World
Ingrid Vasiliu-Feltes (University of Miami, USA) and Jane Thomason (University College London, UK)
Information Science Reference • © 2022 • 316pp • H/C (ISBN: 9781799884675) • US $215.00

Multidisciplinary Perspectives on Diversity and Equity in a Virtual World
Emily K. Reeves (Midwestern State University, USA) and Christina Janise McIntyre (Midwestern State University, USA)
Information Science Reference • © 2022 • 317pp • H/C (ISBN: 9781799880288) • US $215.00

IGI Global
PUBLISHER of TIMELY KNOWLEDGE

701 East Chocolate Avenue, Hershey, PA 17033, USA
Tel: 717-533-8845 x100 • Fax: 717-533-8661
E-Mail: cust@igi-global.com • www.igi-global.com

List of Reviewers

Zoi Arvanitidou, *University of Malta, Malta*
Anastasios K. Barianos, *Hellenic Mediterranean University, Greece*
Tharrenos Bratitsis, *University of Western Macedonia, Greece*
Cheuk Ting Chan, *Independent Researcher, China*
Orestis Charalampakos, *Hellenic Mediterranean University, Greece*
Dickson K. W. Chiu, *University of Hong Kong, China*
Eirini Christinaki, *KU Leuven, Belgium*
Alkistis Dalkavouki, *National Technical University of Athens, Greece*
Maria Gasouka, *University of the Aegean, Greece*
Rea Kakampoura, *National and Kapodistrian University of Athens, Greece*
Michail Kalogiannakis, *University of Crete, Greece*
Nikolaos Karantalis, *University of Patras, Greece*
Iraklis Katsaris, *Hellenic Mediterranean University, Greece*
Georgios Katsadoros, *University of the Aegean, Greece*
Dimitrios Koukopoulos, *University of Patras, Greece*
George Koutromanos, *National and Kapodistrian University of Athens, Greece*
Ilias Logothetis, *Hellenic Mediterranean University, Greece*
Myra Yi Ching Mak, *University of Hong Kong, China*
Jose A. Marquez-Dominguez, *Universidad de la Cañada, Mexico*
Carmen C. Martinez-Gil, *Universidad de la Cañada, Mexico*
Evangelia Moula, *Hellenic Open University, Greece*
Aphrodite L. Nounanaki, *National and Kapodistrian University of Athens, Greece*
Alexandros Papadakis, *Hellenic Mediterranean University, Greece*
Georgios Pasiopoulos, *University of the Aegean, Greece*
Ada Yuen Mei Poon, *University of Hong Kong, China*
Beatriz A. Sabino-Moxo, *Universidad de la Cañada, Mexico*
Miguel A. Sanchez-Acevedo, *Universidad de la Cañada, Mexico*
Eirini Sifaki, *University of Thessaly, Greece*
Xin Sun, *University of Hong Kong, China*
Manolis G. Varvounis, *Democritus University of Thrace, Greece*
Nikolas Vidakis, *Hellenic Mediterranean University, Greece*

Table of Contents

Section 2
Digital Humanities, Education, Gamification, and Applications

Section 3
Digital Humanities: Online Communities, Digital Storytelling, Libraries, and Museums

Detailed Table of Contents

The evaluation of the three-year e-learning program "Introduction to the Science of Folk Culture" is the subject of this chapter. In particular, the research aimed at evaluating six semester courses conducted under the scientific supervision of the Laboratory of Folklore and Social Anthropology of the Department of History and Ethnology of Democritus University of Thrace with the collaboration of the Department of Preschool Sciences Education and Educational Planning of the University of the Aegean. The whole project was supported by the Academy of Folk Culture and Local History of the Cultural Organization "Magniton Kivotos" in aid of the rescue of the cultural inventory of the Holy Metropolis of Demetrias and Almiros. The aim of the research is to investigate whether the trainees in the three-year program understood the introductory knowledge of folklore in order to acquire a theoretical background as well as other useful skills so that they could continue and understand other, more specialized subjects related to the science of folklore science.

Conspiracy theories are a folk narrative genre that tends to arise whenever crises occur; thus, inevitably, these kinds of theories appeared on the pandemic of COVID-19 as well. Their spread used to be done through magazines with relevant subject matter and through the word of mouth. The internet has changed this treaty because, by giving space in the dissemination of any information, it seems to have enhanced the widest spread of this narrative genre too. So, in this chapter, the impact of the internet on the genre will be highlighted through a long-term digital folklore research on the Greek internet. Through the case study of conspiracy theories about the COVID-19 pandemic, in the context of digital folklore, this chapter intents to highlight the impact of the internet on the genre, its spread, and its function, as well as the way the internet users' uptake the genre.

A summary of the museum and archival practices related to the digital humanities should investigate whether they have promoted the digitization of clothing and fashion archives. At the time of the COVID-19 pandemic, widespread internet use was observed, and augmented reality technologies were applied. Since March 2020, fashion collection owners have intensified their digitization. There is a comprehensive discussion about virtual reports, which, using the tools provided by modern technology, create new forms of knowledge. Contemporary art is increasingly using folklore material as a source of inspiration to explore the relationships between tradition and innovation. All over the world, artists, scholars, and curators of exhibitions try to exhibit folklore archives. In this way, the curators experiment with new, participatory, collaborative, and visual representation methods, breathing new life into traditional and folklore objects.

study is presented to evaluate the proposed methodology.

This chapter presents action research based on the transformational design of a young adult novel (Υ.A.) into an alternate reality game (ARG) on Instagram and its implementation as an extra-curricular activity. The Y.A. novel, The Deer of Rhodes, by K. Stoforos, was selected according to specific criteria, among which of major importance was the smooth integration of local history elements in it. The action research explored the relationship between students' participation in the activity and their attitudes toward literature, their acquisition of certain historical knowledge, and the strengthening of their computational thinking. The assessment of the action research was based on the monitoring of the students' engagement during the implementation, the recording of their performance in embedded tests, and the statistical analysis of their responses in the questionnaire that was handed out after the implementation.

Chinese martial arts (Kungfu) is a popular cultural heritage, but its teaching and learning is very traditional. Social media have been increasingly used in education. The use of social media fosters a virtual learning environment for better interaction and helps effective and efficient learning. This research investigates how social media aids Kungfu learning and preservation and the factors affecting learners' behavioral intention. Semi-structured interviews with learners were conducted to obtain qualitative data. Many learners are currently using YouTube, Facebook, and WhatsApp to share videos, exchange learning materials, and communicate with teachers and classmates. Using social media helps preserve Kungfu in two ways—heritage protection and interest arousal—while face-to-face lessons are still highly valued. Recommendations are suggested to teachers, learners, martial arts associations, and the Hong Kong government accordingly.

Serious games are increasingly integrated into official learning settings due to their effectiveness as teaching tools, especially in cultural heritance. Despite extensive research on the field and a consensus on their value, there are few meticulous studies that evaluate serious games and their effect on knowledge in the long term. Literature describes a lot of games and their innovations, but few go on to perform a retrospective analysis to locate areas that should be solved in future games. In this chapter, a retrospective analysis of a serious game teaching about Ancient Greek Theater is performed, utilizing study results from experiments conducted with the game. The authors describe the experiments and the results procedures and present them along with their conclusions on how game design and development decisions affected those results. With the work presented in this chapter, the authors expect valuable insight to be unlocked for the improvement of future game designs for education.

Teachers incorporate gamification techniques and game-based learning (GBL) into the learning material rapidly. Technological advancements on the world wide web have essentially assisted GBL as it has allowed the creation of many educational platforms and applications. Despite these web applications' advancements, technology has more to offer than a just website, moving into virtual worlds, enhancing the real world with digital content and artefacts, using users' geolocation to navigate them into learning material around their physical world, and gathering, processing, and analysing information about the users with the purpose to better adjust the information provided to them. The collaboration between gamification techniques and modern technologies are explored to showcase the possibilities this merger can give. Applications using state-of-the-art technologies and gamification techniques tend to increase engagement and motivation of students, increase their soft skills, and develop a positive perspective towards learning and education.

The chapter will instruct readers into the fundamentals of online social research, filling a vital, instructional gap in the literature. After a summary of the theoretical path towards digital ethnography and a description of the discipline's overall strengths, the chapter will begin a practical breakdown of the research planning and execution processes. This will follow the following steps: preparation and entrée, sample design, quantitative and qualitative methods of data collection, and ethical considerations. All the above will be informed by the researcher's own experience and will be geared towards under- or post-grad anthropology and ethnography students with some experience with online spaces.

This study investigates the adaption and digitalization development of Buddhist libraries in the current mobile computing age and proposes a three-level pyramid model of Buddhist library digitalization. The cases studied include the functions, missions, and objectives of the Yunlin Buddhist Library in Lingyin Temple, Mainland China; the Luminary Buddhist Institute Library in Taiwan; and the Buddhist Digital Resource Center (BDRC) in America. In particular, their path of development, objectives, achievements, and obstacles are analyzed. This case study provide some examples for maintaining digital Buddhist databases and physical Buddhist libraries in these temples for sustainable development.

The COVID-19 pandemic and the consequent instability of the health crisis rapidly transformed the cultural landscape and the way the public experiences the museum. Recent research suggests that museums saw a rise in online activity, shifting traditional audience proðles and challenging museums to ðnd ways of accommodating new forms of engagement. This chapter highlights the central role of online cultural content in broadening social access, enhancing the museum experience, and consolidating a new form of communication with audiences in the digital environment. Building from cultural theory, the author then focus on cultural creation during the COVID-19 pandemic confinement focusing on an innovative, creative project organized by the National Museum of Contemporary Art in Athens (EMST). Finally, these vernacular forms of cultural expression converse with digital folklore research, hoping to fuel the discussions within the digital humanities related to the worlds of art, its social influences, and reception.

In this chapter, digital storytelling is examined as means of cultural heritage preservation by focusing on personal attachment to stories themselves. In the contemporary digital society, stories are being told and they are being told differently. Thus, digital storytelling is becoming a significant part of social life and seems to be imposing a trend in humanitarian issues. This chapter attempts to examine the issue through a brief literature review on the connection of digital storytelling and cultural heritage. Examples of small-scale studies conducted within academic theses (mainly postgraduate) or funded projects are utilized in order to record the telling or retelling cultural stories, whether in everyday life or in more formal contexts, such as museum visits. Overall, the aim of the chapter is to reach an understanding of how short stories can redefine the way we perceive cultural elements, following the current societal trends for speed and increased interaction.

Preface

INTRODUCTION

The publication focuses on the definition of the meaning of Digital folk culture, on contributing to the comprehension of the content and its internal divisions, on suggesting a classification of internet tools which, in the end, on making it a privileged field of production, development, rescue and dissemination of various kinds of folk culture.

In addition, the publication will focus in particular on a) opportunities and chances for folklore research online, b) research challenges for online folk groups (electronic folklore groups, e-groups and online communities, and c) opportunities for production of digital internet material from items and research in the field of folk culture, d) opportunities provided for digitization, documentation and promotion of elements related to folk culture and e) challenges which are in progress and concern the creation of enriched didactic interventions in the context of the teaching of folk culture through digital media. Moreover, it will include relevant chapters with suggestions to the community of Folklore (which may be helpful, more broadly, in the digital humanities). Furthermore, in our estimation, it is possible to strengthen Digital Folklore internationally, which is currently forming and establishing, balancing national needs and the rapid changes and peculiarities of cutting-edge technologies and standard methods noted within the international community.

At the same time, the publication includes relevant chapters for the Digital Humanities, i.e. the traditional humanities, enlarged and enriched digitally, to focus and develop their theoretical, research, teaching, writing, etc., objects in a new digital, technological environment. After all, we must not forget that this is a rapidly evolving process due to the new ways of communication and changes in the mind (artificial intelligence). Also, the acceleration of the digital transformation that is taking place lately (and due to the covid-19 pandemic) has significantly influenced humanities studies in general and Folklore in particular. In this context, Digital Folklore (e-folklore or digital Folklore) stands out with its critical, innovative elements, among others, information and communication technologies, interactive internet media and enriched digital activities.

OVERVIEW

In the first chapter, entitled "Folk Culture and cutting-Edge Technologies," of the first unit, "The Digital Folklore of Cyberculture: Theoretical Framework and Applications," Alexandros G. Kapaniaris focuses on a new field of folklore research, that of digital Folklore (e-folklore or digital Folklore) as well as on issues related to research and popular culture, education and the production of digital folklore material, tools of distance education (e-learning), digital storytelling and in general the tools of ICT (Digital Humanities). The article seeks to define the concept of Digital Folklore, contribute to understanding its content and internal divisions, and propose a classification of internet tools, making it a privileged field of production, development, rescue and dissemination of various kinds of folk culture.

The second chapter, entitled "The Gender Dimension of Digital Folklore," by Maria Gasouka and Zoi Arvanitidou, refers to gender and the Internet. As the social environment of Folklore Studies is digitized, women and men folklorists realize that they can no longer ignore the Internet and other forms of mediation associated with New Technologies. As digital Folklore develops, it is evident that Digital Gender Folklore, the feminist Folklore of the Internet, is also growing in its context. The chapter also focuses on using ICT, which requires the redefinition of terms and concepts related to culture, group, community, and gender in their modern dimension, directly related to information technology and the Internet.

The evaluation of the three-year e-learning program "Introduction to the Science of Folk Culture" is the subject of the second chapter entitled "E-Learning Program Introduction to the Science of Folk Culture" by authors Alexandros G. Kapaniaris and Manolis G. Varvounis. The chapter describes the research on whether the trainees in the three-year program folklore understood the introductory knowledge of Folklore to acquire theoretical background and other valuable skills so that they could continue and understand other, more specialized subjects related to the science of folklore science.

The fourth chapter, entitled "Conspiracy Theories about the Pandemic of COVID-19 and Their Function on the Greek Internet," by authors Rea Kakampoura and Aphrodite L. Nounanaki, focuses on conspiracy theories as a folk narrative genre. It tends to arise whenever crises occur; thus, this kind of theory appeared during the pandemic of Covid-19. Their spread was done through magazines with the relevant subject matter and word of mouth. So, in this chapter, the impact of the Internet on the genre will be highlighted through long-term digital folklore research on the Greek internet.

The fifth chapter with the title "Digitization of Costume and Fashion Archives" by the author Zoi Arvanitidou summarises the museum and archival practices related to the digital humanities, which should investigate whether they have promoted the digitization of clothing and fashion archives. During the Covid-19 pandemic, widespread Internet use was observed and augmented reality technologies were applied. Since March 2020, fashion collection owners have intensified their digitization. Through digital exhibitions, the role of collections. There is a comprehensive discussion about virtual reports, which, using the tools provided by modern technology, create new forms of knowledge. Contemporary art is increasingly using folklore material as a source of inspiration to explore the relationships between tradition and innovation. All over the world, artists, scholars, and curators of exhibitions try to show folklore archives. The curators experiment with new, participatory, collaborative, visual representation methods, breathing new life into traditional and Folklore objects.

The sixth chapter is entitled "Hip Hop-Low Bap-Killah P. Songs Written for Fyssas Without Pavlos: A Critical Review" of the author Georgios Pasiopoulos and Georgios Katsadoros. One of the leading research interests of modern folklore science concerns data related to the social, economic, political, and cultural contexts of certain groups whose members maintain a sense of community. Music has always provided such groups with a means of expression and collectivities, and communication between artists and the public, like song lyrics, depict social realities and representations. Low bap and Hip-hop music have not been yet analyzed and studied from a folkloristic point of view. The assassination of Pavlos Fyssas, a member of a Low bap band, brought Low bap and Hip-hop music again to the fore. Its impact on the Greek music scene, in general, can be seen through songs written primarily about this incident and captured on social media. This study presents research and analysis of these songs' lyrics and the audience's responses to them. This collective way of responding to a particular event indicates the presence of a group, a folk one in essence, which expresses itself, demonstrating its members' common traits, in a digital, folk environment.

In the second unit entitled "Digital Humanities, Education, Gamification, and Applications," the seventh chapter has the title "Digital Narrative as an Educational Tool for Cultural Heritage Teaching" by Nikolaos Karantalis, Dimitrios Koukopoulos, and George Koutromanos. Our age is unquestionably characterized by the dominance of technology and digital media in all manifestations of human action. Inevitably, the debate over the use of these media becomes increasingly intense in areas that are extremely important for the intellectual development of men, such as the field of culture and education. This reality leads educational systems to adapt curricula to new developments so that digital media is now a critical educational tool for many courses. Especially in the subject of history and especially local history and Folklore, digital storytelling can be the connecting link between the old and the new. This can be immensely helpful when the lesson plans aim to bring students in touch with cultural heritage, both material and intangible. The present study shows that digital storytelling can be used creatively in teaching a local history and folklore course.

In the eighth chapter titled "Digital Media in Indigenous Language Education," Miguel A. Sanchez-Acevedo, Beatriz A. Sabino-Moxo, Jose A. Marquez-Dominguez, and Carmen C. Martinez-Gil present the following ideas: Education has started a transformation by including digital media technologies to enhance the learning process. This transformation was accelerated by the COVID-19 pandemic, which paralyzed face-to-face classes and switched to distance education modalities through various platforms. Animation and storytelling have been the most effective digital tools to transmit knowledge; also, augmented reality has gained popularity in education. Indigenous languages are a cultural wealth and provide a tremendous philosophical and cultural value associated with linguistic diversity. This chapter describes different digital tools developed to teach Cuicateco, Mazateco, and Nahuatl. Three indigenous languages are spoken in Mexico; then, a usability study is described to evaluate the effectiveness of digital tools; finally, a case study is presented to evaluate the proposed methodology.

In the ninth chapter with the title "Enlivening a Young Adult Novel on Instagram: Fostering Reading for Pleasure and Interest in Local History," the author Evangelia Moula presents action research based on the transformational design of a young adult novel (Υ.A.) into an Alternate Reality Game (ARG) on Instagram and its implementation as an extra-curricular activity. The Y.A. novel: The Deer of Rhodes by K. Stoforos was selected according to specific criteria, and it was of significant importance to the smooth integration of local historical elements. The action research explored the relationship between students' participation in the activity and their attitude toward literature, their acquisition of specific historical knowledge, and the strengthening of their computational thinking. A significant challenge was proving that digital environments, including social networks, can be an alternative tool to promote specific educational goals and improve school life. The assessment of the action research was based on the monitoring of the students' engagement during the implementation, the recording of their performance in embedded tests, and the statistical analysis of their responses in the questionnaire that was handed out after the implementation.

In the tenth chapter with the title "Using Social Media as Learning Aids and Preservation," the author Myra Yi Ching Mak, Ada Yuen Mei Poon and Dickson K. W. Chiu present Chinese martial arts (Kungfu) as a famous cultural heritage, but its teaching and learning are very traditional. Social media have been increasingly used in education. The use of social media fosters a virtual learning environment for better interaction and helps effective and efficient learning. This research investigates how social media aids Kungfu learning and preservation and the factors affecting learners' behavioural intention. Semi-structured interviews with learners were conducted to obtain qualitative data. Many learners are currently using YouTube, Facebook, and WhatsApp to share videos, exchange learning materials, and communicate with teachers and classmates. Using social media helps preserve Kungfu in two ways: heritage protection and interest arousal, while face-to-face lessons are still highly valued. Accordingly, recommendations are suggested to teachers, learners, martial arts associations, and the Hong Kong government.

The eleventh chapter has the title "Teaching Ancient Greek Theatre Through In-Game Exploration" of the Anastasios K. Barianos, Ilias Logothetis, Michail Kalogiannakis end Nikolas Vidakis. Serious games are increasingly integrated into official learning settings, due to their effectiveness as teaching tools, especially in cultural heritage. Despite extensive research on the field and a consensus on their value, few meticulous studies evaluate challenging games and their effect on knowledge in the long term. The literature describes a lot of games and their innovations, but few go on to perform a retrospective analysis to locate areas that should be solved in future games. In this chapter, a retrospective analysis of a severe game teaching about Ancient Greek Theater is performed, utilizing study results from experiments conducted with the game. We describe the experiments and the results procedures and present their conclusions on how game design and development decisions affected those results. With the work presented in this chapter, the authors expect valuable insight to be unlocked to improve future game designs for education.

The twelfth chapter with the title "Gamification Techniques Capitalizing on State-of-the-Art Technologies" of the Ilias Logothetis, Anastasios Kristofer Barianos, Alexandros Papadakis, Eirini Christinaki, Orestis Charalampakos, and Michail Kalogiannakis focus on the fact that nowadays, teachers incorporate gamification techniques and game-based learning (GBL) into the learning material rapidly. Technological advancements on the world wide web have essentially assisted GBL as it has allowed the creation of many educational platforms and applications. Despite these web applications' advancements, technology has more to offer than a just website, moving into virtual worlds, and enhancing the real world with digital content and artefacts, using users' geolocation to navigate them into learning material around their physical world. Furthermore, by gathering, processing, and analyzing information about the users to adjust better the information provided to them. The collaboration between gamification techniques and modern technologies is explored to showcase the possibilities this merger can give. Applications using state-of-the-art technologies and gamification techniques tend to increase the engagement and motivation of students, increase their soft skills, and develop a positive perspective toward learning and education.

In the third unit entitled "Digital Humanities: Online Communities, Libraries, and Museum," the thirteenth chapter entitled "A Methodological Guide for the Study of Online Communities," Alkistis Dalkavouki describes the fundamentals of online social research, filling a vital, instructional gap in the literature. After a summary of the theoretical path toward digital ethnography and a description of the discipline's overall strengths, the chapter will begin with a practical breakdown of the research planning and execution processes. This will follow the following steps: preparation and entrée, sample design, quantitative and qualitative methods of data collection, and ethical considerations. All the above will be informed by the researcher's own experience and geared towards under- or postgraduate anthropology and ethnography students with some experience with online spaces.

The fourteenth chapter with the title "Recent Digitalization Development of Buddhist Libraries: A Comparative Case Study" by Xin Sun, Dickson K. W. Chiu, and Cheuk Ting Chan. They present the adaption and digitalization development of Buddhist libraries in the current mobile computing age and propose a three-level pyramid model of Buddhist library digitalization. The cases studied include the functions, missions, and objectives of the Yunlin Buddhist Library in Lingyin Temple, Mainland China, the Luminary Buddhist Institute Library in Taiwan and the Buddhist Digital Resource Center (BDRC) in America. In particular, their path of development, objectives, achievements, and obstacles are analyzed. This case study provides examples of maintaining digital Buddhist databases and physical Buddhist libraries in these temples for sustainable development.

The fifteenth chapter is entitled "Museum Digital Activities During the Pandemic: Art as Communicative Experience" by Eirini Sifaki. This chapter highlights the central role of online cultural content in broadening social access, enhancing the museum experience, and consolidating a new form of communication with audiences. Unlike most communication, which occurs through discourse, art communicates through felt experience, offering a vision of our world. Building from cultural theory, we aim to examine cultural creation during the confinement period focusing on an innovative, creative project organized by the National Museum of Contemporary Art in Athens. (EMST) "EMST for Health" is intended to bring health professionals into a creative dialogue with contemporary art. Their involvement with different works of art resulted in producing rich textual and visual material (short texts, poems, photographs, paintings, objects, and artefacts), which comprises their thoughts, feelings, and experience with the work of art in that particular period. In this light, we consider this specific collection of artistic/cultural creations the repository of recorded communication that allows us to access that period's structure of feeling through a pure, multimodal living material, seeing unconscious realities.

The sixteenth chapter is entitled "Cultural Heritage Redesigned Through Digital Storytelling" by Tharrenos Bratitsis. In this chapter, Digital Storytelling is examined as means of cultural heritage preservation by focusing on personal attachment to the stories themselves. In the contemporary digital society, stories are being told differently. Thus, digital storytelling is becoming a significant part of social life and seems to be imposing a trend on humanitarian issues. This chapter examines the issue through a brief literature review on the connection between digital storytelling and cultural heritage. Examples of small scale studies conducted within academic theses (mainly postgraduate) or funded projects are utilized to record telling or retelling cultural stories, whether in everyday life or more formal contexts, such as museum visits. Overall, the chapter aims to reach an understanding of how short stories can redefine the way we perceive cultural elements, following the current societal trends for speed and increased interaction.

CONCLUSION

The publication *The Digital Folklore of Cyberculture and Digital Humanities* tries to contribute to the issues of digital Folklore and those of the digital humanities. The authors explore this field of humanities (Folklore, history, anthropology, education, theatre, and social sciences) based on the Internet and Information and Communication Technologies. In addition, the digital humanities are of particular interest due to the rapid changes and peculiarities of cutting-edge technologies, standards, and methodologies emerging within the international community.

The publication can be used as a teaching manual or enrichment at the postgraduate level. It can cover courses in university departments of history, Folklore, anthropology, primary education, preschool education, communication, and digital media. Postgraduate students and PhD candidates can also use it. In higher education, there are not enough sources, articles and books that focus on digital humanities studies, digital Folklore and archival ethnography using digital media.

Stamatis Papadakis
University of Crete, Greece

Alexandros Kapaniaris
Hellenic Open University, Greece

Acknowledgment

The authors of this volume acknowledge the significant contribution of the editorial advisory board and express our warm thanks for their substantial contributions to the chapters of authors who are university professors, researchers and educators, folklorists, and scientists.

The publication focuses on the definition of the meaning of Digital folk culture to contribute to the comprehension of the content and its internal divisions and to suggest a classification of internet tools which, in the end, make it a privileged field of production, development, rescue and dissemination of various kinds of folk culture.

At the same time, the publication includes relevant chapters for the Digital Humanities, in the traditional humanities, enlarged and enriched digitally to focus and develop their theoretical, research, teaching, writing, etc., objects in a new digital, technological environment. After all, we must not forget that this is a rapidly evolving process, as new ways of communication change the mind (artificial intelligence). Furthermore, the acceleration of the digital transformation that is taking place lately (and due to the covid-19 pandemic) has significantly influenced humanities studies in general and Folklore in particular.

There are several members of the editorial advisory board that we should be incredibly grateful for so eagerly commenting on more than one chapter to support this collective volume.

In addition, a special thank you to all the authors and members of the editorial advisory committee who devoted their time and know-how to supporting this collective volume.

There are several members of the editorial advisory board that we should be incredibly grateful for so eagerly commenting on more than one chapter to support this collective volume.

We also wish to thank Lindsay Wertman, Managing Director IGI Global, Jan Travers, Director of Intellectual Property & Contracts IGI Global; Brittany Haynes, Editorial Assistant, IGI Global; Caroline Campbell, Marketing Manager, IGI Global; Charlie Mercer, PsycINFO Book Content Coordinator and Maria Rohde, Assistant Development Editors, IGI Global for their extensive (and good-natured) editing support in the preparation of the final manuscript and for their support in managing the many details associated with publishing a book.

We want to thank our families for their ongoing help, support, and encouragement.

Stamatios Papadakis
University of Crete, Greece

Acknowledgment

Alexandros Kapaniaris
Hellenic Open University, Greece

Section 1

The Digital Folklore of Cyberculture: Theoretical Framework and Applications

Chapter 1
Folk Culture and Cutting-Edge Technologies:
Digital Folklore

Alexandros Georgios Kapaniaris
Hellenic Open University, Greece

ABSTRACT

One of the fields of popular culture science is digital folklore. The field of science also focuses on a new field of folklore research, that of digital folklore (e-folklore or digital folklore) as well as on issues related to research and popular culture, education, and the production of digital folklore material, tools of distance education (e-learning), digital storytelling, and in general, the tools of ICT (digital humanities). The chapter seeks to define the concept of digital folklore, to contribute to the understanding of its content and its internal divisions, to propose a classification of internet tools, which finally make it a privileged field of production, development, rescue, and dissemination of various kinds of folk culture.

INTRODUCTION

Since 2000, there has been a worldwide scientific dialogue on what we mean by digital folklore. There is also scientific research concerning the digital practices, methods, and technologies with which modern digital studies interact. Another field of study is the "conversation" of traditional folklore methods with digital technology. So today's folklorists are called upon to take a stand on a range of digital internet technologies and folklore theory issues. A vital issue in the above questions and the searches of folklorists is how digital technologies mediate in folklore research. That is, what and what kind of analysis can be implemented in digital cultural environments.

DOI: 10.4018/978-1-6684-4461-0.ch001

DIGITAL FOLKLORE: CONCEPTUAL FRAMEWORK, CLARIFICATIONS

Trying to decipher the relationship of folklore with new technologies, we will conclude that a large volume of editing, searching, presenting, researching and interacting logographic material with digital environments occurs on the internet (Papadakis, 2021). Thus, the view that the internet has become a privileged place for spreading and disseminating popular culture seems to be supported by many folklorists and scientists (Kapaniaris, 2020: 48).

McClelland (2000: 182) states that "the internet functions as a folklore conductor…" Howard (2008: 99) argues that the internet functions as a "powerful, new channel" that ensures the rapid transmission of various types of folk culture, Katsadoros (2013: 99) emphasizes that the internet appears as a "space for free movement and development of folk culture", while Blank (2013: 5) considers that "technology is a conduit for expression, a fertile ground, enabling users to participate in the circulation and dissemination of traditional forms of expression in new ways ". Blank (2016: 162) also, in a recent article, argues that the internet is a new opportunity to study urban legends and their derivatives, which may be chain mail and fraudulent emails. At the same time, he believes that the internet is ideal for transmitting folk narratives due to its anonymity and effectiveness in rapidly disseminating ideas.

Blank (2009), having thoroughly studied the relationship between the internet and folklore, defines the latter as the external expression of creativity by individuals and their communities in innumerable forms and interactions.

Hubert (2003: 151), when referring to the people of the internet, refers to the "internet browser" for whom information gathering has become a way of life, highlighting another area of digital folklore at the research level.

Michael (2009) perceives the world of the internet as a world par excellence folkloric. He talks about homo internetcus that creates a peculiar culture, the "internet culture". He presents this culture as a new need, a new tendency for individual and community life.

Oring (2013) puts another dimension to the study of popular culture as a field of digital folklore by stating that popular culture, with its traditional creations resulting from face-to-face social interactions, is now transmitted over the internet. So the informal or folk culture of the World Wide Web is folk culture indeed.

To this international dialogue on the internet as a field of reproduction and dissemination of popular culture, the views on the oral tradition on the internet can be added, which works, as Katsadoros (2013: 99) points out, as "… electronic orality…", as well as the views of Bacon (2011: 60) and Blank (2009), who consider those elements of digital popular culture that are transmitted and disseminated on the internet as "digital vernacular", characterizing them as a direct descendant of the oral tradition.

Dundes (2005) also claim that urban folklore allows the coexistence of the individual with the collective identity of the specific folk group. Thus, a new type of folk wisdom and knowledge is developed on the internet in a cultural environment without specific limits, such as that of the internet (online discussions, chat, blogs, fora, etc.), creating new traditions and new folk groups (Kapaniaris, 2020: 46).

Today, humanity studies, and folklore, are confronted with new research environments that are evolving as new research fields with the corresponding new terms, such as cyber ethnography, netography, virtual communities, cyber people, indigenous digital, digital immigrants, etc., making the ethnography of digital life an essential aspect of modern social research that uses and studies internet and ICT tools. (Gasouka & Foulidi, 2012: 102). Blank (2013: 163) urges folklorists to become more actively involved in internet field research and to lead the emerging field of cyber ethnography because the internet facilitates human interactions that interest folklorists over time. He even claims that folk groups are easily recognized on the internet, as evidenced by chat forums, blogs, online political activity and other forms of communication and interaction. In particular, Blank argues that it is an ideal place for folklorists to conduct their studies in terms of human interaction on the internet. The anonymity of online interactions allows them to maintain their professional distance from their subjects and, at the same time to participate in an online community (Blank 2013: 170).

Another critical issue in digital folklore is what we mean by the term "folk group" on the internet. Furthermore, while the term "folk group" in the classical sense means, principally, an original social group whose members share a traditional culture, it is well known that the definition of "popular group" is a complex and multidimensional concept, including any group that is distinguished by a common characteristic or behaviour (Katsadoros, Gotzageorgiou 2010). However, in the case of digital folk groups (digital folk groups or e-groups), we refer to the groups created on the world wide web's websites, in the electronic addresses, as essential sources of research data for digital folklore (Foulidi, 2015).

Diamantaki (2013: 4) typically mentions digital groups: "These new co-op formations are, therefore, fewer communities in the traditional sense and more social networks, more or Less loose, built based on 'common interests." "Ideas", "cooperation" or "feelings" and not based on direct relations of kinship, history and neighbourhood "(Diamantaki 2013: 4). The number of digital groups is exceptionally high, and their form varies considerably. They operate in social networks, forums, blogging, and virtual worlds and communicate synchronously and asynchronously (by email, listserv email, newsgroup, discussion fora, chat, bulletin boards, newsletters).

Another interesting issue is the relationship of folk culture in the internet environment concerning the concept of tradition, belief, legend and narrative. As is well known, the above elements of folk culture stem from symbiotic relationships, such as emotional engagement between people, use of the body with all its positive forces, possibly from risky commitments that give meaning to life or from assumptions in front of images created by the use of hearing, touch and smell. However, will it be interesting to clarify what the internet is helpful for in this case? How can we use it in the different fields of folk culture, utilizing its remarkable ability to store and provide access to large amounts of information? (Hubert, 2003: 170).

The internet can be used effectively to store and display information material of folk culture with great success, as long as the information is processed and classified for immediate access and retrieval (Papadakis, Kalogiannakis, Sifaki & Vidakis, 2018; Vidakis et al., 2020). Catalogues of fairy tales, collections of riddles, collections of photographs, and series of folk songs and customs can be stored and redistributed regardless of volume and variety of information (audio, image, video, text), assisting both researchers and students. Students in the educational process and research. The management and display of Folk Culture Archives through databases can be done internally on an intranet or publicly via the internet. More specifically, the storage, systematization, and efficient and rapid retrieval of the material of folklore collections are an essential priority for the permanent preservation of cultural heritage with the help of technology and the internet (Kapaniaris, 2008).

Another issue in digital folklore is the internet as a field for reproducing and disseminating folk culture. Thus interesting are the views on the oral tradition on the internet expressed by various researchers such as Katsadoros (2013: 99), who talks about "... electronic orality...", as well as the views of Bacon (2011: 60) and Blank (2009), who consider as "digital vernacular" those elements of digital folk culture, which are transmitted and disseminated on the internet, characterizing them as a direct descendant of the oral tradition.

Of course, the internet cannot replace the emotional engagement between the narrator or the creator and the participants in the narrative or the event or the narration. The use of the body, the assumptions, the thoughts and the emotions that develop each time are unique and are not easy to transfer with the help of new technologies. Of course, in cases where the rescue, promotion and documentation of folklore material can enhance new forms of expression at the urban, local, ethnic or even individual level, combined with efforts to record, store and retrieve remotely, the internet offers space and step into material and expression of folk culture. Therefore, the internet can become the conduit of folklore material that can be used for various uses such as education, with the appropriate transformation into an educational or research context, applying the respective principles and regulations of the pedagogical - teaching and research approach and ethics. Also, the internet can be used as a tool for transportation and dissemination, through the posting on popular websites of elements of popular culture by institutions (archives, organizations, collections), and respectively retrieval of folklore material by users, for instance, by general population groups, if previously the respective curators have chosen the forms and the extent of the material that they will publish, with the respective metadata and their descriptions (Kapaniaris, 2020: 45-46).

What is Digital Folklore?

Defining the concept of digital folklore or e-folklore1 It is not an easy task because the term "internet culture" is used flexibly, and its application in specific circumstances can be controversial. On the contrary, folklorists today realize that they cannot ignore the internet and other forms of mediation associated with new technologies. What is certain is that folklore has been renewed and is now found on the web of our digital age. We must also not forget that a fundamental feature of digital folklore is the transcendence of the concept of space and time due to the widespread use of the internet and wireless communication devices.

Therefore, as digital folklore, we can define the meeting point of folk culture with the internet and new technologies aimed at the study, research, development and dissemination of any form of expression of folk culture. More specifically, digital folklore focuses on a) the possibilities and opportunities for folklore research through the internet, b) research challenges of online groups (digital folk groups, electronic folklore groups, e-groups), social media and online communities, and c) opportunities for the production of digital online material from evidence and research in the field of folk culture; d) opportunities provided for the digitization, documentation and promotion of elements related to folk culture; interventions in the context of the teaching of popular culture through digital media, f) distance education challenges concerning folk culture.

FOLK CULTURE, EDUCATION AND DIGITAL STORYTELLING: CHALLENGES AND OPPORTUNITIES FOR THE SPREAD OF FOLKLORE

Folk culture in all its forms and folklore material can be the "basic material", the content that can often be transformed into a digital narrative when specially integrated into an educational script in the respective activity sheets. Also, material from possible on-site folklore research of students / three or trainees (folklore tiles), in the context of a research project, may provide evidence that by itself (fragmented) may not have the same educational value as they would have if it were presented as complete learning objects. The collection, distribution and processing of photographs, sounds, folk songs, narratives, fairy tales, riddles, folk paintings, and folk art items is possible with appropriate digitization techniques to "bring to life" a story, a legend, a memory, an event and to be used as a primary material for the creation of complex and straightforward learning objects which in turn can be the first preparation for a digital narrative (Kapaniaris & Gasouka, 2016).

The use of digital storytelling and other multimedia books (e.g. enriched digital books) offers the ability to act as conduits that can transmit folk culture to education and other groups of people in museums and cultural venues. In particular, digital storytelling, when connected to folk culture, is another tool of digital folklore and enables students to come into contact with fairy tales, myths, riddles, folk songs, folk art and traditional professions in an entirely interactive a way in which the participation and the unique learning path of the students are constructed by themselves, in a somewhat constructive way. As a result, students do not become passive recipients by watching a conventional video but can interact with a multitude of multimedia elements and informative texts and, in parallel with the use of the internet, participate in activities and games of folk culture (Kapaniaris, 2022).

The opportunities that digital storytelling can offer both to education and especially to students or learners are their involvement in the design, thus mobilizing their imagination and creativity. Especially in the field of popular culture, which is so rich in visual and verbal stimuli and material (riddles, proverbs, folk myths and legends, fairy tales, narratives, supernatural elements, folk songs, folk painting, etc.), students or learners learn to systematize their thinking, analyze and transform a large amount of information. Respectively, however, the challenges created by the coexistence of folklore and digital storytelling in the field of digital folklore are many and are related to the expansion of folklore studies with education, acting not only as a digital tool but also as a learning process, in content quite attractive environment, such as that of folk culture. The penetration of technology and the internet in our time has created a narrative that can be characterized as digital and thus highlights our folk culture to students and other categories of trainees (Kapaniaris, 2022).

DISTANCE EDUCATION AS A TOOL FOR DISSEMINATION AND EDUCATION IN FOLKLORE

For several years now, the science of folklore and other sciences related to cultural studies has been using ICT tools emphasising the internet (Poultsakis, Papadakis, Kalogiannakis, & Psycharis, 2021). However, in distance education (e-learning), we do not have enough bibliographic references in Greece and internationally, for organized long-term efforts of programs for folklore, by higher education institutions or other scientific and social institutions. Exceptions are the distance learning programs (e-learning) of the National and Kapodistrian University of Athens (Vocational Training Center) with the program "Folklore: Contemporary Folk Culture."2 Moreover, the design of a distance learning program for folk culture from the University of the Aegean (University Aegean: e-Programs for Lifelong Learning) entitled "Folk Culture & Education using Information & Communication Technologies."3 Which was designed in 2014 but ultimately did not materialize. As far as the offered program of the National and Kapodistrian University of Athens is concerned, it is for three months and is offered for a fee, while that of the University of the Aegean has not yet been implemented beyond the design stage. We have not also found Massive Open Online Courses for the science of folklore that offer free organized and long-term study programs in Greece or internationally (Varvounis & Kapaniaris, 2021: 76).

Also, an exciting and long-term distance education program for folklore, a three-year distance and living program (mixed program), is the program entitled "Introduction to the Science of Popular Culture" implemented by the Academy of Popular Culture & Local History.4, the educational section of the cultural institution "Magniton Kivotos, for the rescue of the cultural reserve" Ecclesiastical Foundation of the Holy Diocese of Demitriados & Almyros with the scientific supervision of the "Laboratory of Folklore & Social Anthropology" of the Department of History & Ethnology of the School of Classical & Humanities Studies of the Democritus University Design of the University of the Aegean. The semester courses of the three-year program "Introduction to the Science of Popular Culture" were: 1) "Introduction to Folklore", 2) "Modern Horizons of Folklore Studies (Folklore and Gender, Internet and education)", 3) Literary Folklore, 4) Digital Folklore, c) Religious Folklore, d) Contemporary Folk Culture and Local cultural / tourist development (Kapaniaris & Varvounis, 2019 a, b, c, d; Kapaniaris, Gasouka & Varvounis, 2019).

The purpose of the innovative blended learning distance learning program was to educate participants in areas of folk culture and to confirm the fact that the science of Folklore is not static but constantly evolving, which records and interprets the new aspects and manifestations of social life and folk creation (Vidakis et al., 2019). The three-year course of the six-semester folklore courses is indicative so that the trainee cannot exhaust the subject of the science of folklore; however, he can provide introductory studies in order for the trainees to understand as well as possible the folklore phenomena as well as to connect them with the local cultural development and the promotion of the cultural stock. The educational program started with an extensive introduction to folklore, where the terms and concepts of the subject of folklore were studied. The issues of gender, the internet and school were developed in the next section, thus delimiting the modern horizons of folklore studies. In the third section, digital folk culture was presented in combination with education and how the internet and new technologies are invading popular culture, thus studying the new field of Digital Folklore. Religious Folklore was the third subject of this three-year curriculum, focusing on the study of widespread religious behaviour and the Greek folklore reality of the field of "religious folklore". Then the fourth section was the Philological Folklore which included the view of some types of the famous speech, in their "traditional" form and their modern forms, where and how they appear. The last section of the program dealt with the topic of modern folk culture and local cultural-tourism development with topics related to the issues of the contribution of folk culture to local development and the promotion of cultural stock (Kapaniaris & Varvounis, 2019 a,b,c,d · Kapaniaris, Gasouka & Varvounis, 2019 · Kapaniaris & Varvounis, 2022).

CONCLUSION

Digital Folklore, internationally, is shaping and establishing itself, trying to balance national needs and the rapid changes and peculiarities of cutting-edge technologies, standards, and methodologies noted within the international community (Papadakis, Trampas, Barianos, Kalogiannakis, & Vidakis, 2020).)

At the same time, digital folklore, a field of folklore, is part of the Digital Humanities, for instance, the traditional humanity studies, enlarged and enriched digitally, focusing and developing their theoretical, research, teaching, writing, etc. objects in a new technological art environment.

We must also realize that the digital humanities, as well as digital folklore, are a rapidly evolving process, as are new ways of communicating, changes in mind (artificial intelligence), and the acceleration of the recent digital transformation (and due to the covid-19 pandemic) have significantly influenced humanities studies in general and Folklore in particular (Katsaris & Vidakis, 2021; Lazarinis, Boididis, Kozanidis & Kanellopoulos, 2022). In this context, digital folklore (or e-folklore) stands out with its critical, innovative elements, including information and communication technologies, interactive internet media and enriched digital activities (Barianos, Papadakis & Vidakis, 2022).

Thus, we conclude that digital folklore is a future path in the evolution of the science of folklore. However, at the same time, to date, we do not have complete answers to the number of questions that arise concerning folk culture and the internet. As folklorists, we are in the phase of collective reflection and exchange of views.

It is also essential that in Greece and internationally, a dialogue on digital folklore has long since begun and is constantly evolving, focusing on the traditional interaction with the digital. Today, traditional folklore has to re-examine a significant part of the available folklore material as concerns and objections develop that form new research data. Tools of this new orientation are web 3.0 tools, augmented reality, social media, digital storytelling, distance learning, databases and the internet.

REFERENCES

Bacon, J. (2011). *The Digital Folklore Project: Tracking the Oral Tradition on the World Wide Web* (MA thesis). East Tennessee State University. https://dc.etsu.edu/etd/1398

Blank, T. J. (2009). *Folklore and Internet: Vernacular Expression in the Digital World*. State University Press Logan. doi:10.2307/j.ctt4cgrx5

Blank, T. J. (2013). *The Last Laugh: Folk Humor, Celebrity Culture, and Mass-Mediated Disasters, in the Digital Age*. University of Wisconsin Press.

Diamantaki, K. (2003). Internet Communities. An electronic public sphere? In *The digital challenge: Media and democracy*. Academic Press.

Dundes, A. (2005). Folkloristics in the Twenty-First Century (AFS Invited Presidential Plenary Address, 2004). *Journal of American Folklore*, *118*, 385–408.

Foulidis, X. (2015). *New horizons in Greek Folklore Studies: The internet as a field of production, dissemination and educational utilization of Popular Culture* [Doctoral Thesis]. University of the Aegean.

Gasouka, M., & Foulidi, X. (2012). *New horizons of folklore studies - Conceptual framework, research, gender, internet, school*. Sideris Publications.

Howard, R. G. (2008). Electronic Hybridity: The Persistent Processes of the Vernacular Web. *Journal of American Folklore*, *121*(480), 192–218. doi:10.1353/jaf.0.0012

Hubert, L. D. (2003). *The Internet*. Kritiki Publications.

Kapaniaris, A. (2008). *Digitization, Documentation and Promotion of Greek Culture: The Case of the Archive "Dimitrios G. Kaslas"* [Diploma Thesis]. Hellenic Open University.

Kapaniaris, A. (2020). *Digital Folklore and Education: Enriched Media and Innovative Approaches to the Teaching of Popular Culture*. Pedio.

Kapaniaris, A. (2022). The meeting of digital storytelling with popular culture and education in the field of digital folklore. In M. Varvounis, G. Katsadoros, & A. Kapaniaris (Eds.), *People, genders, identities, cultures. Folklore and gender approaches*. Gonis.

Kapaniaris, A., & Gasouka, M. (2016). Folk culture and digitally enriched books (Enriched e-books): Designing learning resources for education using the internet. In Internet cultures. Pedio.

Kapaniaris, A., Gasouka, M., & Varvounis, M. (2019). E-learning program: «Introduction to the science of Folk Culture»: Evaluation of the semester course. *World Wide Journal of Multidisciplinary Research and Development*, *5*(5), 24–34.

Kapaniaris, A., & Varvounis, M. (2019a). Design and implementation of e-learning programs in folklore, ethnography and history: Following the Logic of the Mass Open Internet Courses (MOOC). *World Wide Journal of Multidisciplinary Research and Development*, *5*(1), 22–29.

Kapaniaris, A., & Varvounis, M. (2019b). E-Learning Program «Introduction to the Science of Folk Culture»: Evaluation of the course. *World Wide Journal of Multidisciplinary Research and Development*, *5*(5), 1–10.

Kapaniaris, A., & Varvounis, M. (2019c). Folklore on the road to distance education (e-learning). *Folklore, Bulletin of the Hellenic Folklore Society*, *44*.

Kapaniaris, A., & Varvounis, M. (2019d). The experience of distance education (e-learning) in the field of Folklore: The evaluation, the first conclusions, the proposals and the new developments. *Folklore, Bulletin of the Hellenic Folklore Society*, *44*.

Kapaniaris, A., & Varvounis, M. (2022). E-Learning program "Introduction to the Science of Folk Culture": Evaluation of the three-year program. In S. Papadakis & A. Kapaniaris (Eds.), *The Digital Folklore of Cyberculture and Digital Humanities*. IGI Global.

Katsadoros, G. (2013). The science of folklore in the modern technological age. *Electronic Orality. Education Sciences. From the weak classification of Pedagogy to interdisciplinarity and scientific hybridization*, 99-122.

Katsadoros, G., & Gotzageorgiou, A. (2010). Primary education and folklore. The collection of cultural material through the school practice. An example from Kremasti, Rhodes. *Proceedings of the* 1st Panhellenic Conference with international participation, Local Communities & Higher Education Institutions: Coexistence for Sustainable Development.

Katsaris, I., & Vidakis, N. (2021). Adaptive e-learning systems through learning styles: A review of the literature. *Advances in Mobile Learning Educational Research*, *1*(2), 124–145. doi:10.25082/AMLER.2021.02.007

Lazarinis, F., Boididis, I., Kozanidis, L., & Kanellopoulos, D. (2022). An adaptable multi-learner serious game for learning cultural heritage. *Advances in Mobile Learning Educational Research*, *2*(1), 201–215. doi:10.25082/AMLER.2022.01.004

McClelland, Br. (2000). Online Orality: The Internet, Folklore, and Culture in Russia. In L. B. Lengel (Ed.), *Culture and Technology in New Europe: Civic Discourse in Transformation in Post-Communist Nations* (pp. 179–191). Ablex.

Michael, G. V. (2009). Homo Interneticus or Folklore and the Internet. Folklore, Bulletin of the Hellenic Folklore Society, 291-305.

Oring, E. (2013). Thinking through Tradition. In Tradition in the Twenty-First Century: Locating the Role of the Past in the Present. Utah State University Press. doi:10.7330/9780874218992.c01

Papadakis, S. (2021). Advances in Mobile Learning Educational Research (A.M.L.E.R.): Mobile learning as an educational reform. *Advances in Mobile Learning Educational Research, 1*(1), 1–4. doi:10.25082/AMLER.2021.01.001

Papadakis, S., Kalogiannakis, M., Sifaki, E., & Vidakis, N. (2018). Evaluating Moodle use via Smart Mobile Phones. A case study in a Greek University. *EAI Endorsed Transactions on Creative Technologies, 5*(16).

Papadakis, S., Trampas, A., Barianos, A., Kalogiannakis, M., & Vidakis, N. (2020). Evaluating the Learning Process: The "ThimelEdu" Educational Game Case Study. *Proceedings of the 12th International Conference on Computer Supported Education, 2*, 290-298. https://www.scitepress.org/Link.aspx?doi=10.5220/0009379902900298

Papadimitriou, E., Kapaniaris, A., Zisiadis, D., & Kalogirou, E. (2013). *Digital Storytelling in Kindergarten: An alternative tool in children's way of expression.* Mediterranean Center of Social and Educational Research, MCSER Publishing.

Poultsakis, S., Papadakis, S., Kalogiannakis, M., & Psycharis, S. (2021). The management of Digital Learning Objects of Natural Sciences and Digital Experiment Simulation Tools by teachers. *Advances in Mobile Learning Educational Research, 1*(2), 58–71. doi:10.25082/AMLER.2021.02.002

Varvounis, A., & Kapaniaris, A. (2021). Folklore on the road to distance education (e-learning). *Folklore, 44*(4), 75–96.

Vidakis, N., Barianos, A., Trampas, A., Papadakis, S., Kalogiannakis, M., & Vassilakis, K. (2019). Generating Education in-Game Data: The Case of an Ancient Theatre Serious Game. *Proceedings of the 11th International Conference on Computer Supported Education, 1*, 36-43. https://link.springer.com/chapter/10.1007/978-3-030-58459-7_30

Vidakis, N., Barianos, A. K., Trampas, A. M., Papadakis, S., Kalogiannakis, M., & Vassilakis, K. (2020). Game Raw Data Collection and Visualization in the Context of the "ThimelEdu" Educational Game. In H. C. Lane, S. Zvacek, & J. Uhomoibhi (Eds.), *Computer Supported Education. CSEDU 2019. Communications in Computer and Information Science* (Vol. 1220). Springer. doi:10.1007/978-3-030-58459-7_30

ADDITIONAL READING

Barianos, A., Papadakis, A., & Vidakis, N. (2022). Content manager for serious games: Theoretical framework and digital platform. *Advances in Mobile Learning Educational Research*, *2*(1), 251–262. doi:10.25082/AMLER.2022.01.009

Gasouka, M., Kapaniaris, A., Arvanitidou, Z., Foulidi, X., & Raptou, E. (2013). Halk Kültürü ve Zenginleştirilmiş Kitaplar: Digital Araçlarla Zenginleştirme Araçlarını Örneklerle Değerlendirme "E-Anagnosis". Çeviren: A. Serdar ARSLAN. *Journal Karatekin Edebiyat Fakültesi Dergisi*, *4*(1), 87–102.

Kalogiannakis, M., & Papadakis, S., (2008). Hybrid learning for women and socially sensitive groups for the promotion of digital literacy. *Training, 6*, 2.

Kalogiannakis, M., Vassilakis, K., Alafodimos, C., Papadakis, S., Papachristos, D., & Zafeiri, E. (2009). Adult Education and Lifelong Learning. The case of GSAE (General Secretary for Adult Education) in Greece. *International Journal of Advanced Corporate Learning*, *2*(4), 15–20. doi:10.3991/ijac.v2i4.981

Kapaniaris, A., & Zampetoglou, G. (2021). Visual programming for the creation of digital shadow play performance using mobile devices in times of Covid-19. *Advances in Mobile Learning Educational Research, 1*(2), 162–170. doi:10.25082/AMLER.2021.02.010

Kapaniaris, G. A. (2020). Folk Culture and Education: The Role of Information Technology and Information and Communication Technologies in the Production of Digital Educational Materials. In M. Kalogiannakis & S. Papadakis (Eds.), *Handbook of Research on Tools for Teaching Computational Thinking in P-12 Education* (pp. 456–479). IGI Global. doi:10.4018/978-1-7998-4576-8.ch018

Kapaniaris, G. A. (2020). Folk Culture and Enriched Digital Teaching: Designing Educational Scenarios With the Use of ICT. In M. Kalogiannakis & S. Papadakis (Eds.), *Handbook of Research on Tools for Teaching Computational Thinking in P-12 Education* (pp. 480–501). IGI Global. doi:10.4018/978-1-7998-4576-8.ch019

Papadakis, S., & Kalogiannakis, M. (2019). Evaluating the effectiveness of a game-based learning approach in modifying students' behavioural outcomes and competence, in an introductory programming course. A case study in Greece. *International Journal of Teaching and Case Studies*, *10*(3), 235–250. doi:10.1504/IJTCS.2019.102760

ENDNOTES

1 The following researchers have been involved in the definition of digital folklore (Digital folklore, e-folklore): Aldred, B., Gr. (2010), «Identity in 10,000 Pixels: LiveJournal Userpics and Fractured Selves in Web 2.0», in New Directions in Folklore 8 (1/2), pp: 6-35, Ashton, C. (2007), «Folklore and the Internet: From the Editor », in Folklore Forum 37, (1) pp: 2-4, Bacon, J. (2011),« The Digital Folklore Project: Tracking the Oral Tradition on the World Wide Web », in Electronic Theses and Dissertations. Paper 1398. A thesis presented to the Department of Literature and Language faculty at East Tennessee State University partially fulfils the requirements for a Master of Arts in English. Retrieved February 10, 2016, from https://dc.etsu.edu/etd/1398, Baym, N., K. (1993),

"Interpreting Soap Operas and Creating Community", in The Journal of Folklore Research 30 (2 / 3), pp: 143-77, Blank, T., J. (2009a), Folklore and the Internet: vernacular expression in a digital world, Logan, Utah: Utah State University Press, Boellstorff, T. (2008), Coming of Age in Second Life: An Anthropologist Explores the Virtually, Human Princeton: Princeton University Press, Bronner, S., J. (2009), «Digitizing and Virtualizing Folklore», in Blank, T., J. (ed), Folklore and the Internet: Vernacular Expression in a Digital World, Logan: Utah State University Press, pp: 21—66, Bronner, S., J. (2011), Explaining Traditions: Folk Behavior in Modern Culture. Lexington: The University Press of Kentucky, Dorst, J. (1990), «Tags and Burners, Cycles and Networks: Folklore in the Telectronic Age», in Journal of Folklore Research 27, pp: 179-190, Ellis, B. (2003), «Making a Big Apple Crumble: The Role of Humor in Constructing a Global Response to Disaster», in Narvaez, P. (ed), Of Corpse: Death and Humor in Folklore and Popular Culture, Logan: Utah State University Press. Earlier pp: 35–82. The version was published in New Directions in Folklore on June 6 2002. Retrieved October 14, 2015, from https://scholarworks.iu.edu/dspace/handle/2022/6911, Foote, M. (2007), «User picks: Cyber Folk Art in the Early 21st Century », in Folklore Forum 37, pp: 27-38, Frank, R. (2004),« When the Going Gets Tough, the Tough Go Photoshopping: September 11 and the Newslore of Vengeance and Victimization. », in New Media & Society 6 (5), pp: 633-658. Retrieved May 18, 2015, from https://dx.doi.org/10.1177/146144804047084, Frank, R. (2011), Newslore: Contemporary Folklore on the Internet. Jackson: University Press of Mississippi, Gray, M. (2009), Out in the Country: Youth, Media, and Queer Visibility in Rural America, New York: New York University Press, Howard, R., G. (1998), «Researching Folk Rhetoric: The Case of Apocalyptic Techno-Gaianism on the Worldwide Web», in Folklore Forum 29 (2), pp: 53-73, Kirshenblatt-Gimblett, B. (1995), «From the Paperwork Empire to the Paperless Office: Testing the Limits of the Science of Tradition », in Bendix, R. Zumwalt, R., L. (eds), Folklore Interpreted: Essays in Honor of Alan Dundes, New York: Garland, pp: 69-92, Moore, R., J., E., Hankinson, C., G., Ducheneau, N. (2009), «From 3D Space to Third Place: The Social Life of Small Virtual Spaces», in Human Organization 68 (2), pp: 230–240.

2 The distance (e-learning) program "Folklore: Contemporary Popular Culture" of the National & Kapodistrian University of Athens (https://elearn.elke.uoa.gr), according to the study program ",... aims to highlight its relationship with traditional press (newspapers, magazines, etc.) with modern folk culture. Thus, after a general but concise introduction to the science of folk culture, the new subject, its relevant terminology, and its subject matter will be presented. There will also be a talk on proverbs in journalism and politics and anything else relevant to research in the press. The program will present a sample and new customary phenomena that entered the celebration (e.g. St. Valentine), while there is rich, relevant literature. In this way, it will be demonstrated that Folklore is not a static science but is constantly evolving as it monitors, examines and interprets new aspects of social life and folk creation. " The duration of the program is three months, and the estimated duration in hours is 70. The program is offered for a fee, and the Academic Manager is the Folklore Professor Minas Alexiadis. In more detail, the program has the following structure: Didactic Unit 1: Brief Introduction to the Science of Folk Culture and Didactic Unit 2: Modern Greek Folklore. Terminology and topic, Didactic Unit 3: Written and Oral Speech in Folk Literature and Tradition, Didactic Unit 4: Greek Folklore and Printed Sources, Didactic Unit 5: Journalistic Speech and Proverb, Didactic Unit 6: Letters to Newspapers, Didactic Unit 7: Printed Folk Poetry in the Islands of the Archipelagos, Didactic Unit 8: The Western Valentine's Day in Greece / Booklets of love and affection, Didactic Unit 9: Greek Hopeful Modern Folk Books. Special reference to

Kazamias, Didactic Unit 11: Proverbial and Opinion Speech of Greek Politicians. Samples from the Athenian Press, Teaching Module 12: Anti-proverbs in Athenian Newspapers, Teaching Module 13: Illustrations of Folk Professions in Old Postcards ("Postcards") and Photographs, Teaching Module 14: Fairy Tale and News.

3 The program "Folk Culture & Education using Information & Communication Technologies" of the University of the Aegean (e-Programs for Lifelong Learning, https://e-epimorfosi.aegean.gr/) its design is aimed to help those interested in getting acquainted with folk culture, education in combination with the integration of tools and environments ICT which can be used to teach folk culture. The program also offers topics related to qualitative research methods, redefining contemporary data on folk culture, tradition and modern folklore studies. At the same time, the importance of folk culture for education is highlighted by creating educational scenarios for its teaching through ICT. Finally, the relationship between folk culture and the internet is clarified.

4 The website "http://learn.cultureacademy.gr" is the website of the Academy of Folk Culture & Local History. The website contains reports on the curriculum and other activities of the institution.

Chapter 2
The Gender Dimension of Digital Folklore

Maria Gasouka
University of the Aegean, Greece

Zoi Arvanitidou
University of Malta, Malta

ABSTRACT

Internet folklore explores popular digital cultures. As the social environment of folklore studies is digitized, women and men folklorists realize that they can no longer ignore the internet and other forms of mediation associated with new technologies. Thus, in the age of postmodernism, which is inconceivable without technology and information technology, the science of folklore redefines cultural terms and concepts in their modern dimension, directly intertwined with information technology and the internet. As digital folklore develops, it is evident that digital gender folklore, the feminist folklore of the internet, is also growing in its context.

INTRODUCTION

All the evidence points to the exciting development of the feminist dimension of the Digital Humanities and historical encounters between traditional Humanities and digital technologies. The result of this meeting is the formation of a new reality, characterized by the systematic use of digital resources and the analysis of their application, by different methods of research, teaching, and publishing, with the main characteristics of interdisciplinarity, synergy, digital tools, but also the realization that the printed on the paper word is no longer the primary means of production and distribution of knowledge (Risam, 2015).[1] The fact is confirmed in Digital Folklore, where here, too, the gender mediates the research process. There is already a serious debate, for example, about whether, in these new contexts, the problems often faced by researchers during their traditional research often make them "vulnerable" due to deep-rooted gender prejudices and their sexuality (Gasouka and Foulidi, 2017), as some claim. This is a view that most active folklorists do not seem willing to accept, at least in the current period. In

DOI: 10.4018/978-1-6684-4461-0.ch002

any case, their main goal, among other things, is the formation of models, which involve the synthesis of text technology, digital conditions, and analysis of folklore, while trying to highlight the extent of the female folklore research presence in the online world and at the same time, compiling and delimiting the field of Digital Gender Folklore. At the same time, they formulate the much-needed theoretical frameworks concerning the meaning and content of Cyberfeminism and its relation to Digital Folklore[2]. And it is there that they point out the absence of women, essentially their exclusion, not only from the use of technology but also from its history (Wernimont & Losh, 2018). However, the feminist dimension of Digital Folklore allows, on the one hand, to make women and the folklore knowledge that concerns them visible on the Internet and especially in digital groups and communities, and on the other hand, to highlight the research of gender-conscious folklorists and the pursuit of to go beyond phenomena that wronged and altered women and their worlds in the context of traditional folklore.

And women folklorists point out that, starting to work scientifically and research on the Internet, they found that since its inception, it was formed both in terms of its use and the reasons articulated within it, in a patriarchal way. Today the issue raises the question of the gender dimension of the relationship between cyberspace, cutting-edge technologies, and the Internet. This dimension calls for new theoretical elaborations across the spectrum of the Digital Humanities, a strong critique of the exclusion of women from the debate for technology and redefinition from the perspective of women, and not only the Internet and cyberspace and technologies (Bailey-Moya, 2011)[3]. Of particular interest to gender-conscious folklorists is the impact of new technologies on the lives of women researchers on the self-image of these women. In the way they perceive and interpret the world. Therefore, they participate in the broader effort in feminist Digital Humanities, always with a detailed category of gender, to identify and deconstruct gender stereotypes and prejudices in cyberspace and explore relationships between the sexes. Within the sexes in its context, explore the relationship between women and technology, etc. Also, make effective use of feminist theory and its respective tools to address sexism, racism, and militarism found in the digital material of the Internet (Bailey-Moya, 2011), a fact that also concerns the science of Digital Folklore. And based on this logic, authors should not miss the fact that the Internet is a transformative public and political space (Gasouka, 2017). Facilitates new forms of citizenship, which allow people to claim, construct and express themselves, their genders, and their sexualities. This includes the connection between the various digital areas, the requirement of accountability and transparency, and essential opportunities for building a new type of feminist movement, after all[4].

FOR A DIGITAL GENDER FOLKLORE

The gender analytical category highlights and validates the social dimension of popular cultures and the Internet (Brown, 1989) while at the same time validating the necessity and importance of Digital Gender Folklore. As mentioned above (Gasouka and Foulidi, 2012, 2017), the Internet is a field of culture and a cultural tool. It allows new social formations, virtual communities, and groups as a cultural space. At the same time, it is offered a new type of folklore / ethnographic gender research (Gasouka and Foulidis, 2017). Thus, many gender-conscious researchers are now studying the social, cultural, and other formations they encounter on the Internet. Feminists look from a gender perspective at the aspects of popular cultures that permeate the Internet, their research genres, the content, and ultimately, the new generation of popular cultures in the internet environment. They focus on the performance issues, the role of the individual within this new type of community or popular group (Gasouka and Foulidi, 2012), and the meaning and content of the exchanges, competitions, and negotiations that take place within it. They also focus on issues related to gender identities and how relations of power are formed. At the same time, they are constantly interested in the way associations and hierarchies are included within the sexes in these digital cultural environments, simultaneously as the differences identified (if any) between women in the same digital community or group (Strathern, 1987). The research of feminist folklorists on the Internet maintains their analytical purposes. They are governed by the same fundamental principles and conceptual frameworks that characterize traditional gendered folklore research to formulate their questions. The study approaches the members of the specific electronic group each time as expressions and carriers of a -often developing- culture, who tacitly share common meanings in their habits and behaviours, in their beliefs and value systems, in their symbols, in that in two words it composes its culture in the context of the Internet (Gasouka et al., 2012). In turn, gender-conscious folklorists are asked to answer essential questions such as how digital technologies and their worlds affect feminist folklore theory? What methods and tools need to be developed and utilized in this regard? How does the female experience mediate digital folklore research? What kind of gender analysis can take place in digital cultural environments? How are issues of race, gender, sexuality, etc., and other types of identities related to Digital Gender Folklore, and to what extent is it still influenced by the "fear of the other," as is often the case in traditional folklore? In this case, it is worth noting that the importance of gender research is that it offers[5] essential knowledge about the "Other," especially in digital symbolic systems and behaviors while contributing to the revelation of new types. Structures and records the new kind of heterogeneity (Dimitriou 2017). They focus again on the re-examination of the life and world of women, trying to make them visible in the new conditions, having their voice heard, revealing their hidden forces, and, most importantly, highlighting their contribution to the creation of culture in general and widespread culture in particular, what cyberculture[6] and even cyber folklore is called (Gasouka and Foulidi, 2017). In addition, they are interested in where all this is gathered and how it is interpreted. The interpretation of expressive motifs is an essential element of this research, according to Blank (2012), and determines the differences between traditional and Digital Folklore.

The fact is that most of the above issues have not yet been fully clarified. However, some elements of traditional Gender Folklore are certainly used appropriately to contribute to the understanding of the content of Digital Folklore more broadly and to its definition as a science with a gender dimension[7]. Feminist folklorists also recognize that a fundamental feature of Digital Gender Folklore is the transcendence of space and time. Due to the widespread use of the Internet and wireless devices, they need to revise definitions of place and, in fact, the area, the private one, that is, the space of the house, which is the space where women were found and operated for thousands of years (Gasouka and Foulidi, 2017). And in the case of Digital Gender Folklore[8], many of the topics traditionally explored by folklorists with a gender consciousness, such as female expression, female tradition, the process of female narration and memory, the rituals of women, etc., have taken on new, modified forms in the digital world.

In contrast, with the development of technology and its evolution, new digital data emerge about the position of women in the popular cultures of the Internet. At the same time, although they cannot be naturally connected to the subjects of their research - an element crucial for feminist researchers - in this case, there are digitized creative outlets with which data are collected, analyzed, and interpreted[9]. Apart from anonymity, collectivity, repetition, and variation are also visible in Digital Gender Folklore. Also, there is the belief that the social formations of spaces do not have physicality identified and the manifestations of digital cultures in their context[10]. Also, although the geographical position of the researcher and research subject is rated as less critical than that of traditional surveys, given that physical proximity is not a prerequisite for participating in a virtual community, the Internet is an element of real life, with the dominant feature of interaction (Gasouka, 2017). The digital popular groups and communities studied by feminist folklorists constantly evolve gender relations and repetitive, active contacts. Popular internet groups are easily recognizable, as shown by fora, chats, blogs, etc. New female traditions are forming in online communities and web dialects. A new type of popular wisdom and knowledge of women emerges from many online discussions between different communities and groups. The uniqueness of the Internet's expression allows confirmed based on the above. The researchers, among other things, are particularly interested in balancing the friendly self with the collective identity of the specific popular group they study each time. The conditions of this kind of knowledge production are fascinating, and the code of gender behavior develops in the group and the organized subgroups, which operate within a larger community (Carter, 2005). Feminist folklorists recognize the lack of empirical data today and the connection between researcher and informant, as already mentioned. They are still studying how gender mediates access to these new communities, accessed using a keyboard instead of face-to-face. Whether the communication is only through cables and fiber optics highlights women's real needs and expectations (Gasouka and Foulidi, 2017).

At the same time as the above, feminist folklorists certainly understand that their boundaries are somewhat blurred. They consider it necessary for their research to confirm the self-identification of the participants in the study as members of the group or community, their mutual acquaintance, information, which is related to the female self, as well as rituals, habits, beliefs, behaviors, as well as emotions after all (Gasouka, 2017). In particular, concerning their femininity, the issues of identity and self-determination of these women, desires, expectations, aspirations, etc., are taken seriously into account in the context of the social and cultural practices observed in cyberspace, especially women. Thus, folklorists realize that this is significantly related to the different traditions and developments in computer cultures[11]. And it is worth noting that the dissemination of information, a fundamental feature of the Internet, has never been a purely technological issue. It has always been related to social transformation, as it is a process of social change. It is also an element inextricably linked to women's social, economic, cultural, and political situation, with the formation of power and power relations always having a strong gender dimension. Authors note that the ongoing debate over gender and the Internet tend to focus on gendered facts, absent from internet-governing policies, violations due to this treaty, and the need for increased participation of women in decision-making forums.

Consequently, the question naturally arises for the research folklorists: "As feminist researchers, what kind of internet do we want, and how do we have to act to achieve it?". However, what is certain is that the spread of the Internet and the new forms of knowledge and communication that are emerging for women are changing not only the way information is used, science, art, and politics, but also society itself. Finally, the digital communities and groups themselves, primarily called upon to study by gender-conscious folklorists, are merely places of female activity in the broader computer cultures, the router cultures[12]. The popular groups on the Internet, one way or another, are important sources of research data for the Digital Folklore of the Gender, just as it happens with the various popular groups in the context of traditional Folklore. And the digital team has recognizable, predictable, analytical features of shared traditions and the identities of its members (Turkle, 1995)[13]. In fact, given that online communities are developing multipurpose virtual environments (Economou 2006), which shape the virtual places where social interaction and collaboration are developed, in these environments, the development of research, and folklore or ethnography, produces new terms, such as netnography, cyber-ethnography, cyber-folk indigenous, digital settlers, etc. It is a process that utilizes the potential of digital technology in new research areas, and gender-conscious folklorists benefit from it in their research (Gasouka and Foulidis, 2012) since the specific terms have a strong gender dimension. It is a fact that virtual communities and networks are unique challenges and opportunities for gender folklore / ethnographic research, as it is a massive archive of human activities, unprecedented and changeable (Jones, 1999). It is about searching for real women who live in the most remote areas, connected by an ever-growing variety of web databases, who sit behind the controls and are more identified by common interests and computer-related purposes than by their nation or geography.

The concepts of "representation," "deconstruction," "narrative," "transition," "diversity," "symbolic sphere," etc., are being explored and negotiated within the new digital contexts, always in the light of feminist theory. These unique digital formations are communities in the traditional sense and social networks, built based on shared interests, ideas, collaboration, or feelings rather than immediate kinship, history, and the neighborhood, which is a significant challenge for feminist researchers[14]. What is certain is that the Internet does not limit the activity of the presence of women in its popular groups; on the contrary, it acts as a folklore conductor for women as well. After all, women's presence in popular internet communities will exist regardless of the researchers' intentions. Consequently, this presence has developed the relevant gender research in an online context. All these, without ignoring the difficulties that arise from the loss of essential details, such as the social and ethnic origin of the research subjects, marital status, education, sexual orientation, religion, etc. These components may not be accessible and easily concealed or altered. The difficulties also include the fact that the establishment of scientific criteria for archiving information has not been completed yet (Gasouka and Foulidis, 2017).

In any case, internet feminist folklore research takes place in fields such as recognition of gender diversity, necessity, and the importance of research focuses on women from their perspective; the beginning of research with an in-depth study of the social status of women and the dominant gender culture of each community or group. It even insists on exploring those factors that explain the inferiority and subjugation of women, the forms of power and empowerment they may possess, the historical development and differences in the sexes' social roles, and their relations to critical evaluation data from a gender perspective. Folklorists also seek new contexts to study the invisible, examine the unpretentious and find out whether, even in internet conditions, a series of events related to gender are still systematically ignored. And of course, to confirm that Digital Gender Folklore, which seeks to make the invisible visible, to turn insignificant into the important, places women on the "stage" like worthy "actors," approaches them as subjects and not as objects. It insists on concentrating and hearing loudly, and on the Internet, the individual and collective female voices, since women do not have one but many voices, which they want to express themselves in the new technological environments.

CONCLUSION

As mentioned above, ICT requires the redefinition of terms and concepts related to culture, group, community, and gender in their modern dimension, directly related to information technology and the Internet. Thus, an interesting discussion has arisen, among other things, about the need to overcome the new technological conditions of gender, ethnicity, sexuality, and other divisions and obstacles, also as the need to use new languages and codes[15]. All of this can be found in different forms of online communities and groups with standard practices, ideological coherence, and intra-community language communication, which are, among other things, in forming habits, customs, traditions, and sometimes generally not gender-neutral. Consequently, it becomes evident that this leads to a redefinition of the term "society," which transcends physical boundaries, but also of the word "identity," whose content and fluidity are expanded and often mediated by the imagination of the user and the user, their innermost desires and lies that can easily be used in the communication process (Poster, 1995). It is no coincidence that authors often refer to the Internet as "fragmented identities," which, for many folklorists, differ from the user's real life. However, the authors of this article insist that gender and electronic environments are perhaps the most exciting component of any identity and any new type of cultural classification. What is certain is that gender is still ultimately a web of relationships of duality and difference, that is, the primary parameter of the construction of all kinds of cultural concepts, and feminists seek to highlight the fact as convincingly as possible in the context of the popular Internet cultures (Gasouka and Foulidi, 2017).

REFERENCES

Bailey, M. Z. (2011). All the Digital Humanists Are White, All the Nerds Are Men, but Some of Us Are Brave. *Journal of Digital Humanities*, *1*(1), 9-12.

Blank, T. J. (2009b). Toward a Conceptual Framework for the Study of Folklore and the Internet. In T. J. Blank (Ed.), *Folklore and the Internet: Vernacular Expression in a Digital World* (pp. 1–20). Utah State University Press. doi:10.2307/j.ctt4cgrx5.4

Blank, T. J. (2012). *Folk Culture in the Digital Age: The Emergent Dynamics of Human Interaction*. Utah State University Press. doi:10.7330/9780874218909

Bronner, S. J. (2009). Digitizing and Virtualizing Folklore. In Folklore and the Internet: Vernacular Expression in α Digital World. Utah State University Press. doi:10.2307/j.ctt4cgrx5.5

Brown, M. (1989). Women, Folklore and Feminism. *Journal of Folklore Research*, *26*(3), 259–264.

Dimitriou, S. (2017). Social Development and Power Relations. The Methodology of the Human Sciences. Athens: Alexandria.

Dundes, A. (1980). *Interpreting Folklore*. Indiana University Press.

Escobar, A., Hess, D., Licha, I., Sibley, W., Strathern, M., & Sutz, J. (1994). Welcome To Cyberia: Notes on the Anthropology of Cyberculture. *Current Anthropology*, *35*(June), 211–231. doi:10.1086/204266

Gasouka, M. (2017). *Ethnography, Internet and Folklore Studies. European Journal of Social Sciences*. Available online at www.oapub.org/soc

Gasouka, M., Arvanitidou, Z., Foulidi, X., & Raptou, E. (2012). Folklore Research and its New Challenges: From the Ethnography to Netnografy. *Mediterranean Journal of Social Sciences*, *3*(8), 111–116.

Gasouka, M., & Foulidi, X. (2012). *Contemporary Horizons of Folklore Studies-Conceptual Framework, Research, Gender, Internet, School*. Sideris.

Gasouka, M., & Foulidi, X. (2017). *Aspects of Ethnographic Research in Folklore Studies. Feminist Ethnography, Internet Ethnography*. Papazisis.

Jones, S. (1997). *Virtual Culture*. Sage Publications.

Liu, A. (2012). Where is Cultural Criticism in the Digital Humanities? In M. K. Gold (Ed.), *Debates in the Digital Humanities*. U of Minnesota P. doi:10.5749/minnesota/9780816677948.003.0049

Macek, J. (2005). Defining Cyberculture. In P. Binková, J. Volek, & N. Masaryk (Eds.), *Média a realita* (Vol. 2, pp. 35–65). University Press.

Petridis, P. A. (2011). *Digital Records and Exchange Practices: An Anthropological Approach to Peer-to-Peer Networks*. Panteion University of Social and Political Sciences.

Porter, C. (2006). A Typology of Virtual Communities: A Multi-Disciplinary Foundation for Future Research. *Journal of Computer-Mediated Communication*, *10*(1), 3. doi:10.1111/j.1083-6101.2004.tb00228.x

Risam, R. (2019). Beyond the margins: Intersectionality and the digital humanities. In B. Bordalejo & R. Risam (Eds.), *Intersectionality in Digital Humanities*. Arc Humanities Press. doi:10.2307/j.ctvs32szz.7

Strathern, M. (1987). An Awkward Relationship: The Case of Feminism and Anthropology. *Journal of Women in Culture and Society*, *12*(2), 288–292. doi:10.1086/494321

Turkle, S. (1995). Life on the screen: identity in the age of the Internet. New York: Simon & Schuster.

Wernimont, J., & Losh, E. (2018). Introduction. In Bodies of Information: Intersectional Feminism and the Digital Humanities (pp. ix-xxvi). University of Minnesota Press.

ENDNOTES

1. Gender is an analytical scientific category that allows us to understand, both from a methodological and theoretical point of view, the inherent gender dimension of digital technology and the worlds and cultures developing on the Internet.
2. Today, the world wide web is a field of feminist expression, both scientific and cinematic, as it is a way of online mobilizations through hashtags and organizing demonstrations in the streets. And it is at the same time the field of formulating new ideas and producing a feminist anti-community, which challenges the dominant male-centred discourse of the public sphere. Through the internet, feminists have revived the debate on the issue of gender equality and renewed their practices. At the same time, they succeeded in forcing the mainstream media to focus on their claims (Wernimont and Losh, 2018).
3. It also urges the motivation of mainly young women to use new technologies and actively participate in their creation and calls for their disclosure of the interconnection of these technologies with the gender systemic hierarchy and its structures in internet research and science. At the same time, they oppose the masculine nature of technology and seek to make it widely accepted that gender, sexuality, race or religion, etc., have no place in the internet's culturally / socially free field.
4. Authors should point out that for most feminist internet researchers, the dichotomy "virtual world or "cyberspace" / "real world" that prevailed for the first time no longer exists. As almost all of our lives and their communication aspects are flooded with technology, sometimes "unconsciously,"

this dualism seems obsolete. And this is not only in science and research but also in politics, movements, etc., which manage to harmonize their claims and struggles between non-virtual and virtual worlds, often with remarkable success (Gasouka et al., 2012).

5 In contrast to what has been happening for a long time with traditional folklore research in the past.

6 Defined as culture, the culture that results from the use of computers and multiple purposes. The term cyberculture has been used since the '90s, attributed as cyberculture, cyberculture, internet culture (Petridis, 2011). They are "the cultural constructions on which the new technologies are based and which in turn help in the formation of the cultural constructions" (Escobar, 1994: 211). In short, the term cyberculture can be used as a descriptive, analytical or ideological concept to convey the political and ideological dimensions of ICT (Macek, 2005).

7 Feminists even believe that they can research and interpret gender aspects of the digital world because in Digital Folklore, women, their lives, and their works can be studied in the same way that any female group in the real world is studied.

8 Confirming similarly broader views of Blank (2009b).

9 For example, avatars, videos, chat in online communities, etc.

10 Probably, more extensively than in traditional Folklore, in terms of women in the various digital groups, there is a kind of inconsistency in the interaction experienced by many researchers, who communicate only through text, concerning several researchers who are wary of. A point of view that supports this inconsistency is the lack of proximity or overlap of exchanges and the delay. Researchers who are critical of the prospect of the development of Digital Gender Folklore disagree with this view. They insist that electronic coexistence does not always ensure the formation and cohesion of the community and women (Gasouka and Foulidi, 2017).

11 Who are not united in their manifestations, which is why authors are talking about popular cultures and not popular culture.

12 Most feminist internet folklorists believe that any folklorist can research and interpret aspects of the digital world. In Digital Folklore, the group study, e.g., is done in the same way that every real-world group is studied.

13 According to Dundes (1980), a famous group has at least one common element, which can be associated, e.g., with language, culture, education, politics, professional and sports, religion, etc. This group, as a rule, during its existence, builds traditions, acquires repetitive habits, articulates its speech, while a sense of "belonging" develops in its members. Dundes even predicted the future close relationship of folklore science with technology. They argued that technology would eventually shape the study of folklore and create new forms of communication that might produce different folklore criteria and motivations. At the same time, it did not seem apprehensive about the fact.

14 For many authors, such as Porter (2004) or Jones (1997), communities are just one of the many metaphors on the Internet, and the narrative about them is also one of many related online narratives.

15 Which can be based on animations, abbreviations, tricks, videos, memes, etc.

Chapter 3
E-Learning Program "Introduction to the Science of Folk Culture": Evaluation of the Three-Year Program

Alexandors Georgios Kapaniaris
Hellenic Open University, Greece

Manolis Georgios Varvounis
Democritus University of Thrace, Greece

ABSTRACT

The evaluation of the three-year e-learning program "Introduction to the Science of Folk Culture" is the subject of this chapter. In particular, the research aimed at evaluating six semester courses conducted under the scientific supervision of the Laboratory of Folklore and Social Anthropology of the Department of History and Ethnology of Democritus University of Thrace with the collaboration of the Department of Preschool Sciences Education and Educational Planning of the University of the Aegean. The whole project was supported by the Academy of Folk Culture and Local History of the Cultural Organization "Magniton Kivotos" in aid of the rescue of the cultural inventory of the Holy Metropolis of Demetrias and Almiros. The aim of the research is to investigate whether the trainees in the three-year program understood the introductory knowledge of folklore in order to acquire a theoretical background as well as other useful skills so that they could continue and understand other, more specialized subjects related to the science of folklore science.

INTRODUCTION

The implementation of the remote program titled "Introduction to the Science of Folk Culture" began in the spring semester of 2017-18 and was completed in the Spring Semester of 2020-21. The program was implemented during this period in two cycles of training, and the total duration of a training cycle

DOI: 10.4018/978-1-6684-4461-0.ch003

was three years (six semesters). The training program was offered free of charge by the Academy of Folk Culture & Local History of the Cultural Organization "Magniton Kivotos, for the "Preservation of the Cultural Reserve" of the Holy Metropolis of Demetrias & Almyros (http://learn.cultureacademy.gr) under the scientific supervision of the Laboratory of Folklore and Social Anthropology, Department of History & Ethnology, of the Democritus University of Thrace and the Department of Early Childhood Education and Educational Planning Sciences of the University of the Aegean in Greece.

The six-monthly courses of the three-year program "Introduction to the Science of Folk Culture" were: 1) "Introduction to Folklore", 2) "Contemporary Horizons of Folklore Studies (Folklore and Gender, Internet and Education)", 3) Philological Folklore, 4) Digital Folklore, c) Religious Folklore, d) Contemporary Folk Culture and Local Cultural / Tourist Development.

Finally, this Academy of Folk Culture and Local History project for free cultural studies to adults showed that citizens embraced all this effort in Magnesia, the Region of Thessaly, and various cities of Greece. It is also noteworthy that the scientific committee, the rapporteurs, and professors of the university institutions, combined with the administrative staff, have voluntarily offered their services with great consistency and quality.

PURPOSE OF THE PROGRAM

The aim of the innovative program that was conducted with the blended learning model of distance education was to educate the participants in the fields of folk culture but also to confirm the fact that the science of folklore is not static but constantly evolving, which records and interprets the new aspects and expressions of social life and famous creation.

This three-year circle of six-semester folklore courses indicates that the trainee cannot exhaust the topic of the science of folklore. However, it can provide introductory studies for the trainees to understand folklore phenomena as best as possible and connect them with the local cultural development and the promotion of the cultural reserve.

The educational program began with an extensive introduction to folklore, where the terms and concepts of the subject of folklore were studied. The issues of gender, the internet, and school were developed in the following section, thus delimiting the modern horizons of folklore studies. In the third unit, digital folk culture was presented in combination with education and how the internet and new technologies invade the field of folk culture, thus studying the new field of Digital Folklore. Religious folklore was the third subject of this three-year curriculum, focusing on the study of folk religious behaviour and the Greek folklore reality of the field of "religious folklore". Subsequently, the fourth object was Philological Folklore, which included considering some kinds of folk discourse in their "traditional" form and in their modern manifestations, where and as they appear. The last section of the program dealt with the issue of contemporary folk culture and local cultural - tourism development with themes related to the issues of the contribution of popular culture to local development and the promotion of the cultural reserve.

THE STRUCTURE AND CHARACTERISTICS OF THE PROGRAM

Each semester course was structured into six subsections with fifteen days (fortnight). The Scientific Coordinator defines the organization of the program's structure for each semester course. For each subsection, there was the primary study material, a relevant presentation in PowerPoint form, suggested articles from the relevant bibliography, additionally suggested optional bibliography, a video lesson with a duration of an hour, discussion groups in which the trainees participated, and quizzes of ten multiple-choice questions as well as right-wrong questions.

The evaluation of each semester course initially presupposed the successful completion of multiple-choice question quizzes and right-wrong questions for each subsection (fortnight). Of these six quizzes of the subsections, it is mandatory that the trainees should have completed three of the six quizzes. The final evaluation of each semester course took place after the end of the sixth subsection with thirty multiple-choice and right-wrong questions. It should also be mentioned that there were also optional activities in selected fortnights for each semester course. In addition to the above educational material, the trainees had the opportunity to watch the video lessons of the subsections of each lesson on the particular channel of the program on YouTube that functioned as a video case.

The authors of the educational material were the members of the Scientific Committee, the Scientific Coordinators of each semester course, external collaborators, digital educational books from the University Repository "Greek Academic Electronic Textbooks and Aids / Kallipos" as well as the publications of the Academy of Popular Culture and Local History.

The trainees had the opportunity to attend the entire program that led to a relevant certificate or select as many of the program's modules as they wanted and thus obtain a relevant certificate of participation and successful completion. Those trainees who completed the courses and the assessment tests in each semester course (out of a total of six semesters) in one of the two circles of the three-year program participated in the final evaluation (certification process) by completing an automated test of sixty multiple-choice questions and right-wrong questions from the entire three-year program of study.

The ways of e-learning that were followed in the programs that were developed on a case-by-case basis were: a) asynchronous e-learning (Moodle platform), b) synchronous e-learning (live YouTube transmission during face-to-face teaching in the first three semesters), and c) a combination of the blending learning for the first three semesters. So gradually, we were led to Massive Open Online Courses (MOOC) logic.

THE THREE-YEAR DISTANCE PROGRAM "INTRODUCTION TO THE SCIENCE OF FOLK CULTURE" AS A MASSIVE OPEN ONLINE COURSE (MOOC)

The main features of a Massive Open Online Courses (MOOC), as its name suggests, are massiveness, openness, and the use of internet technologies. Specifically, according to Fini (2009) and McAuley et al. (2010), these are:

1. Massive: without restrictions on the number of people who can attend.
2. Open: accessible to anyone who has a computer with an internet connection and, usually, not always free of charge.
3. Online: accessible via the internet.
4. Lessons: structured around a set of purposes of a particular study area.

Concerning the categories of MOOCs, the distinction proposed by Tzimogiannis (2017:393) has to do with the pedagogical approach used each time.

So the first category is called cMOOCs (connective MOOCs) and was started by Siemens and Downes based on the theory of connectivism. In this model, the trainees develop knowledge networks, having an active role in regulating their learning and collaboration.

The second category, xMOOCs (extended MOOCs), work closer to traditional education philosophy, focusing on the content and adopting behavioural models, knowledge transfer, learning limits, and assessment tests. This category was created against the need for more and more people to obtain some certification from higher education institutions and other official bodies (Barianos, Papadakis, & Vidakis, 2022; Lazarinis, Boididis, Kozanidis, & Kanellopoulos, 2022). It can serve, in some cases, even hundreds of thousands of trainees (Karsenti, 2013).

Finally, there is also a hybrid category, the bMOOCs (blended MOOCs), which combine the above methods or even face-to-face teaching, having, on the one hand, closed content but seeking, on the other hand, the cooperation and interaction between the participants.

In addition to the above basic MOOC categories, new mixed forms of open courses have been created. Many designers and trainers are experimenting with new ways to enhance learning and improve the learners' experience. These forms are: a) the pMOOCs, in which learning is based on project-based learning and problem-based learning, b) the pdMOOCs (professional development MOOCs), which are designed for the professional development of individuals in different areas of work, and c) the sMOOCs (social MOOCs), in which the design is based on social media and mobile technologies while adopting ubiquitous learning approaches in virtual communities, to enhance learning motivation and interaction between participants (Tzimogiannis, 2017:394).

The basic philosophy on which the design of the three-year program "Introduction to the Science of Folk Culture" and other programs that were later implemented by the Academy of Folk Culture & Local History were based has many features in common with the axes and design factors of Massive Open Online Courses (MOOCs). In particular, the distance learning program "Introduction to the Science of Folk Culture" has the following characteristics: a) Tuition is free, b) Massive participation (for Greece and other countries), c) No special conditions and restrictions, d) Second chance for adults, e) Democratization, f) Learning communities (debates on every separate unit and the whole program).

As far as the free attendance is concerned, as mentioned above, the attendance of the courses was free of charge, without any charge for the participants. The only burden on the participants, including at a voluntary level, is the purchase of a parallel textbook related to the thematic unit to enrich their library. Besides, the digital material provided free of charge covers the needs of each semester course that functions as a unit in the program. Concerning massive participation, it should be mentioned that there was no restriction on the registration and monitoring of the three-year program. The program was attended by many regions of Greece, America, Germany, and Cyprus. The only prerequisite for participation in the program was knowledge of the Greek language and basic computer handling knowledge (use of mail, browser) (Kapaniaris & Varvounis, 2019a:23-24).

Especially on the issue of participation, apart from the above technical requirements, it should be noted that there were no special conditions and restrictions (Vidakis et al., 2019, 2020). Thus, there was no specific condition or restriction (e.g. limited positions). In particular, while designing the programs, no restrictions were placed concerning the level of studies, profession, or other special skills the trainee should have. Also, each interested party had the opportunity to choose and enrol in more than one offered program at the Academy of Folk Culture & Local History. Also, the program was not funded by a European public or private body or enterprise (Kapaniaris & Varvounis, 2019a:24).

The issue of a second chance for adults was also one of the critical points of the philosophy of programs' design. Many adult people have not had the opportunity to study due to social and economic factors (Papadakis, Trampas, Barianos, Kalogiannakis, & Vidakis, 2020). For this reason, they often expressed this desire in public. The fact that the offered non-formal studies are carried out in collaboration with two academic institutions of Greece (the Democritus University of Thrace and the University of the Aegean), in combination with the systematic organization that converges on formal university studies (curriculum, semester courses, examination procedure, exercises, educational material, certification, etc.) was another incentive and opportunity for those interested. In addition, in order to ensure to the greatest possible extent that citizens are informed about these programs during the registration period, there have been announcements on local social media, through the YouTube channel (relevant promotional video), on Facebook (relevant page of the organization) and finally on a website of the Hellenic Folklore Society, which is accessible to all and especially those interested in the field of folk culture (Kapaniaris & Varvounis, 2019a:24).

However, the democratization of education and training was another issue during the program's design. Besides, the concept of open education is inextricably linked to the democratization of society, which should support the right of people to develop within the framework of lifelong learning. At the same time, they work, thus making the world in which they live more transparent and fair (Sofos, Kostas & Parashou 2015). Through the programs of the Academy of Folk Culture and Local History, any citizen, man, or woman was allowed to come into contact with academic units in the field of cultural studies that would probably help him/her to cope better in his/her place of work (professional needs). Also, the participation of each citizen in such programs can cover personal needs or personal interests in the context of lifelong learning (Kapaniaris & Varvounis, 2019a:24).

Finally, the contribution to the development of learning communities (debates on every separate unit and the whole program) (Papadakis, Kalogiannakis, Sifaki, & Vidakis, 2018) was another primary objective of both the teachers and the scientific team of the Academy of Folk Culture & Local History, to gradually create a learning community in the field of cultural studies using the tools of the discussions that exist in every fortnight or every general discussion concerning the semester course. Other strategies used were face-to-face workshops with parallel discussions related to the subjects of the semester courses. Additionally, through face-to-face courses and graduation ceremonies with lectures that have already taken place, an effort was launched to build a closer relationship between the trainees so that later, more efficiently, they can converse (remotely) within the discussion areas of the e-learning platform (Kapaniaris & Varvounis, 2019a:25).

THE CONTENT OF THE SEMESTER COURSE "INTRODUCTION TO FOLKLORE"

The first semester of the annual distance program "Introduction to Folklore" was preparatory, aiming to help students acquire a theoretical framework to understand the following teaching units of the three-year program. The content of the first semester concerned the following teaching subjects every fortnight: a) The genesis of a new science: The social and ideological context. The German Romanticism and the specific corresponding Greek themes of Greek folklore, b) A brief retrospection (milestones) in the "history" of Greek Folklore: Sources of folklore news from Homer to Nikolaos Politis, c) Historical-Comparative and historical-social methods of folklore, "tools" of the historical-social method, orality, and literacy in popular culture, d) From the people of German Romanticism to the Greek terms people, famous, from folk culture to popular culture; the magical character of popular thought, e) Manners, customs, survival, and revival of customs, folklorism, characteristics of folklore phenomena; problems during revivals; new-fests and other new hybrid forms of customs, f) Relations of Folklore with other humanities. Her "special" relationship with Philology, especially literature (Kapaniaris & Varvounis, 2019b:2).

THE CONTENT OF THE SEMESTER COURSE "MODERN HORIZONS OF FOLKLORE STUDIES (FOLKLORE AND GENDER, INTERNET AND EDUCATION)"

The second semester of the distance program "Introduction to the Science of Folk Culture" concerned the distance learning course entitled "Modern Horizons of Folklore Studies (Gender, Internet, School)", which aimed to help and strengthen students to acquire a theoretical framework with emphasis on contemporary pursuits and the redefinition of the goals and tools of folklore science, but also in relationships and the influences it receives from currents, such as postmodernism, feminism, postcolonial theories, theories of sexuality, etc. In particular, the course highlights the study of the contribution of the analytical category "Gender" to the renewal, modernization, and democratization of folklore studies, the internet and its ethnography, the new quests of folklore research, and the approach to folklore, in contrast to the dominant perceptions until recently, as a means and a vehicle for approaching and accepting diversity in the relations between cultures, ethnicities, various popular groups, social classes and strata, social genders, sexuality, religion, etc. The content of the first semester was related to the following teaching subjects: a) New data in folkloric studies: the contemporary people of folklore, ethnography as a research method, and the redefinition of the notion of "tradition", b) Popular culture and gender. The representation of women in folk fairytales, c) From ancient therapists to women of folk medicine and colloquial medicine, d) Modern aspects of folk culture: Gender, body and fashion, e) Folk culture and Education, f) Folklore and Digital Ethnography (Kapaniaris & Varvounis, 2019d:78).

THE CONTENT OF THE SEMESTER COURSE "LITERARY FOLKLORE"

The second semester of the distance program "Introduction to the Science of Folk Culture" concerned the distance course entitled "Literary Folklore", which aimed to help and strengthen students to acquire a theoretical framework for the field of folklore science that studies the genres of folk literature concerning social life, the institutions and the folk groups of their creation. The content of the first semester concerned the following teaching subjects every fortnight: a) Folk traditions, b) Folk song (as text), unique references to rebetiko, predatory song and contemporary printed folk poetry, c) Narration - Fairytale and jocular narrations, d) Proverbial speech, e) The magical power of the name - Baptismal names, surnames, nicknames, place names, f) Enigma, incantation, password languages.

THE CONTENT OF THE SEMESTER COURSE "DIGITAL FOLKLORE"

The second semester of the distance program "Introduction to the Science of Folk Culture", concerned the distance learning course entitled "Digital Folklore", which aimed to help and strengthen students to acquire a theoretical and practical framework for the new subject of digital folklore, its relationship with education and the study of online groups (digital folk groups, electronic folklore groups, e-groups) and digital communities. The digital folklore course comes to study the "people" on the internet (Kapaniaris, 2020). The content of the first semester concerned the following teaching subjects every fortnight: a) Introduction to Digital Folklore, b) Folk Culture and Internet - The teaching of folk culture, c) Digital Learning Objects: Creating Enriched Digital Books on Folk Culture, d) Digital Storytelling and Folk Culture - Educational m-scenarios, e) Digital groups and online communities as a field of Digital Folklore, f) Gender relations, cultural practices, and symbolisms in a virtual religious community.

THE CONTENT OF THE SEMESTER COURSE "RELIGIOUS FOLKLORE"

The fourth semester of the distance program "Introduction to the Science of Folk Culture", concerned the distance course entitled "Religious Folklore with emphasis on Orthodoxy", which aimed to help and strengthen students to acquire a theoretical framework of the basic theoretical principles and methodological tools of the field of "Religious Folklore", and the presentation of the main events of Greek folk religiosity in the customary ceremonial events of the "circle of life" (birth – marriage – death) and the "circle of time" (annual festive circle), as well as the contemporary and modern religious events, their literary representations, the forms of folk religious art and the manifestations of folk religiosity through modern cutting-edge technologies and Social Media. Thus, the trainees will acquire as much as possible a complete knowledge of the subject and the ability to recognize, record and study – interpret the important traditional and modern events. The content of the first semester concerned the following teaching subjects every fortnight: a) Introduction to Religious Folklore (theory, methodology, basic concepts). Customs and rituals of the "circle of life", b) Modern and contemporary "urban" forms of Greek folk religiosity (theoretical approaches – examples), c) Greek folk religious art (traditional forms and modern survivals and adaptations), d) Literary representations of ritual forms of Greek traditional religious behaviour, e) The internet, cutting-edge technologies, and Social Media as sources for the study of modern folk religious phenomena, f) Customs and rituals of the annual festive circle – public ritual. Recapitulation of the unit.

THE CONTENT OF THE SEMESTER COURSE "CONTEMPORARY FOLK CULTURE AND LOCAL CULTURAL/TOURISM DEVELOPMENT"

The sixth semester of the distance program "Introduction to the Science of Folk Culture" concerned the distance course entitled "Contemporary Folk Culture and Local Cultural / Tourism Development", which aimed to help and strengthen students to acquire a theoretical framework for the subject of popular culture concerning local and tourist development. In particular, the semester course investigated the relationship of tourism and new technologies with folk culture and their relationship with the local - tourist development. The content of the first semester concerned the following teaching subjects every fortnight: a)

Local cultural development and ICT tools: the case of popular culture, b) Local Participatory Cultural Development Plans, c) Exploitation of social media as tools of cultural - tourism development, d) Traditional arts and techniques and sustainable development, e) Folk culture and tourism, f) Excursions of cultural associations: Analysis of their social and economic functions.

REVIEW OF SURVEYS FOR THE EVALUATION OF SEMESTER COURSES

For the semester courses: 1) "Introduction to Folklore" and 2) "Modern Horizons of Folklore Studies (Folklore and Gender, Internet and Education)", relevant research was carried out and published in a scientific journal (Kapaniaris & Varvounis, 2019b:1-10; Kapaniaris, Varvounis, Gasouka 2019:24-34).

The first evaluation survey of the first-semester course titled "Introduction to Folklore" took place from March 1, 2018, to May 2018. The survey's target population was 31 people who attended the semester in the first semester (Spring Semester 2017-18) and who completed the questionnaire before and after the attendance of the course.

For the tool to be distributed to the participants (target group of the research), Google forms were used in two separate stages. A) initial stage (pre-test), i.e., before attending the course to capture the expectations and opinions of the participants on several issues; b)final (post-test), i.e., after the completion of the course to capture the final opinion after the completion of the participation. The questionnaire consists of three question sets. The questions are grouped as follows: A. Demographic data reported, B. Aim and expectations, C. Knowledge, skills, and competencies in ICT. Questions were scored using a 4-point Likert scale where the value 1 corresponds to the selection I AM VERY INTERESTED and the value 4 to NOT INTERESTED AT ALL. The section is completed with an open question OTHER (Kapaniaris & Varvounis, 2019b:2)

Unit A included: a) Age, b) Gender, c) Education, d) Occupation, and e) Residence. The B section included: a) A group of questions where objectives are recorded - data obtained. (b) A group of questions where expectations are recorded- elements that have been improved. Section C included: a) A group of questions where the experience of participation is evaluated and mainly in the thematic content. b) A group of questions where the knowledge and skills of the participants are evaluated. (Kapaniaris & Varvounis, 2019b:2).

From the research results, we will focus on the investigation concerning the cognitive object of the course. This part of the research was investigated (pre-post), the teaching objects of the six fortnights of the cognitive subject related to "Introduction to Folklore" and are reported in Table 1and the bar chart below in detail.

The tendency is similar to the overall picture of the survey and concerns a high concentration of responses to the "advanced" or "good" options, which means that in both phases, the initial and final attitude to the subject matter and the content was positive. All the unit elements show average ratings indicating an improvement in the initial very positive values. These changes are statistically significant in 5 out of 6 cases, resulting in very positive initial evaluations improving significantly further. The only non-statistically significant change concerns the relationship of folklore with the rest of the sciences, where there, too, from the comparison of average values, the tendency that appears concerns an improvement in the initial values (Kapaniaris & Varvounis, 2019b:8).

The second evaluation survey of the second-semester course titled "Modern Horizons of Folklore Studies (Gender, Internet, School)" took place from October 1 2018, to January 2019. The target popula-

Table 1. Distribution of frequencies and percentages of individual variables at the initial and final moment regarding the cognitive subjects

	Advanced		Good		Neutral		Not Good	
	N	%	N	%	N	%	N	%
11.a. Content of Greek folklore	9	29,0%	19	61,3%	1	3,2%	2	6,5%
post	15	48,4%	16	51,6%	0	0,0%	0	0,0%
11.b. Milestones in Greek Folklore	7	22,6%	16	51,6%	5	16,1%	3	9,7%
post	15	48,4%	14	45,2%	1	3,2%	1	3,2%
11.c. Methods and Tools of Folklore	7	22,6%	15	48,4%	8	25,8%	1	3,2%
post	14	45,2%	16	51,6%	1	3,2%	0	0,0%
11.d. Issues concerning the people of German Romanticism concerning Greek terms	6	19,4%	12	38,7%	10	32,3%	3	9,7%
post	12	38,7%	17	54,8%	2	6,5%	0	0,0%
11.e. Mores, customs, survival and revival of customs, folklorists, etc	10	32,3%	15	48,4%	5	16,1%	1	3,2%
post	17	54,8%	13	41,9%	1	3,2%	0	0,0%
11. f. Relationship between folklore and other humanities	13	41,9%	13	41,9%	5	16,1%	0	0,0%
post	16	51,6%	13	41,9%	2	6,5%	0	0,0%

Figure 1. Investigating aims and expectations regarding the cognitive subject of the course

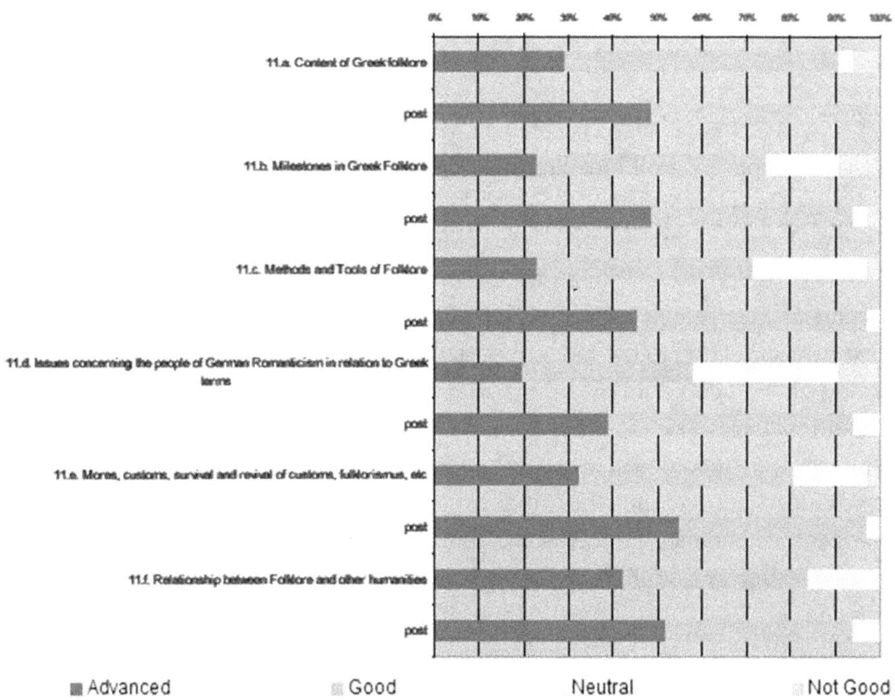

Table 2. Distribution of frequencies and percentages of individual variables at the initial and final moment regarding the cognitive subjects of the course

	Advanced		Good		Neutral		Not good	
	N	%	N	%	N	%	N	%
11.a. New data in folkloric studies: the contemporary people	6	14,6%	22	53,7%	10	24,4%	3	7,3%
post	27	65,9%	14	34,1%	0	0,0%	0	0,0%
11.b. Ethnography as a research method and the redefinition of the notion "tradition"	4	9,8%	19	46,3%	16	39,0%	2	4,9%
post	0	0,0%	0	0,0%	0	0,0%	0	0,0%
11.c. Methods and tools of Folklore	8	19,5%	20	48,8%	11	26,8%	2	4,9%
post	0	0,0%	0	0,0%	0	0,0%	0	0,0%
11.d. Popular culture and gender. The representation of women in folk fairytales	6	14,6%	14	34,1%	15	36,6%	6	14,6%
post	27	64,3%	15	35,7%	0	0,0%	0	0,0%
11. e. From ancient therapists to women of folk medicine and colloquial medicine	3	7,3%	15	36,6%	14	34,1%	9	22,0%
post	31	73,8%	11	26,2%	0	0,0%	0	0,0%
11. f. Modern aspects of folk culture: Gender, Body, and Fashion	4	9,8%	19	46,3%	14	34,1%	4	9,8%
post	27	64,3%	15	35,7%	0	0,0%	0	0,0%
11. g. Folk culture and Education	7	17,1%	17	41,5%	15	36,6%	2	4,9%
post	27	64,3%	15	35,7%	0	0,0%	0	0,0%
11. h. Folklore and Digital Ethnography	3	7,3%	17	41,5%	13	31,7%	8	19,5%
post	28	66,7%	14	33,3%	0	0,0%	0	0,0%

tion of the survey was 42 people who completed the questionnaire both times and attended the semester course "Modern Horizons of Folklore Studies (Gender, Internet, School)" second semester (Spring Semester 2018-19). The survey methodology is the same as mentioned above during the evaluation of the first semi-annual course (Introduction to Folklore).

From the survey results, we will focus on the investigation concerning the cognitive subject of the course. In this part of the research were investigated (pre-post), the teaching objects of the six fortnights of the cognitive subject related to the modern horizons of folklore studies and are mentioned in table 2 and the bar chart below in detail. In the case of additional categories, the central tendency concerns no statement of additional answers.

Where responses were recorded at the 'after' time, these responses showed an equally high concentration in the same categories, and thus the initial expectations were maintained. In the case of additional categories, the central tendency concerns the failure to provide additional replies. Finally, by self-evaluating the knowledge and skills in the proposed categories, individuals initially declare mainly the answers "advanced" or "good". At the same time, after the intervention, the highest percentages appear in the first two choices, which are increased compared to the initial moment. Therefore, an improvement in knowledge and skills was observed (Kapaniaris, Gasouka & Varvounis, 2019:28-29).

Figure 2. Exploring aims and expectations regarding the cognitive subject of the course

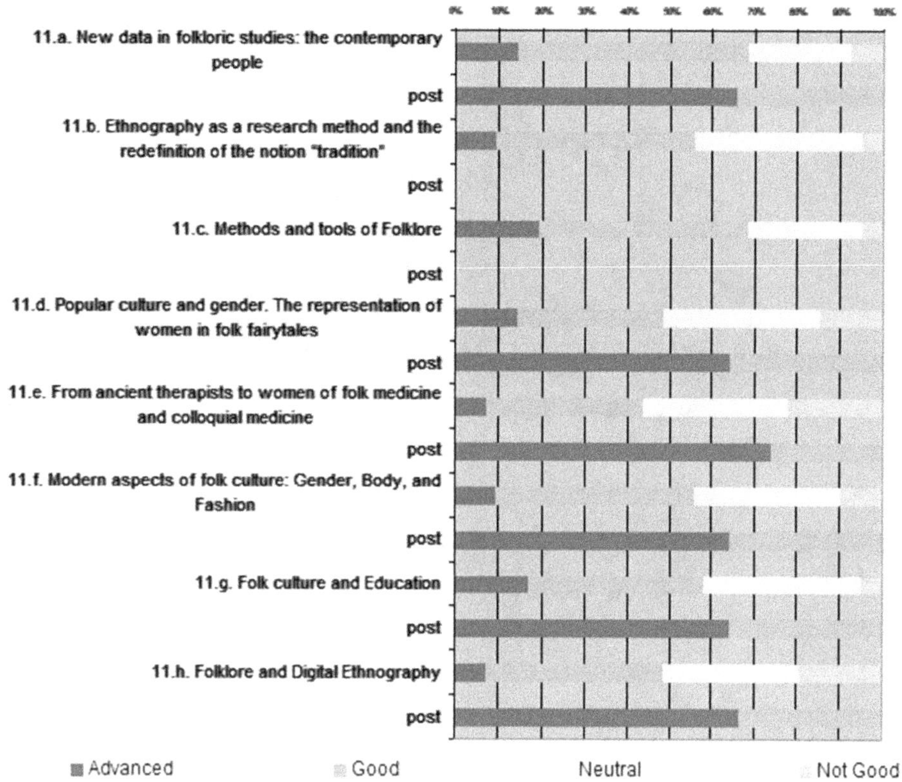

OVERALL EVALUATION OF THE THREE-YEAR PROGRAM "INTRODUCTION OF THE SCIENCE OF FOLK CULTURE"

The overall evaluation research of the program titled "Introduction to the Science of Folklore" took place from 3-10 October 2021. The survey's target population was 83 people who attended all six-semester courses and who completed the questionnaire after the end of the course.

In order to distribute the tool to the target population, the Google form was used to capture the final point of view after the completion of the participation. The questionnaire consists of three sections of questions. The questions are grouped as follows: A. Demographic data reported, B. Aim and expectations, C. Knowledge, skills, and competencies in ICT. Questions were scored using a 4-point Likert scale where the value 1 corresponds to the selection I AM VERY INTERESTED and the value 4 to NOT INTERESTED AT ALL. The section is completed with an open question OTHER.

Demographic Data

In demographic data and more specifically in the first question, "What is your age" we observe that 6.1% were between 18-24, 17.1% between 25-34 years old, 17.1% from 35-44 years old, 45.1% between 45-54

Figure 3. What is your age?

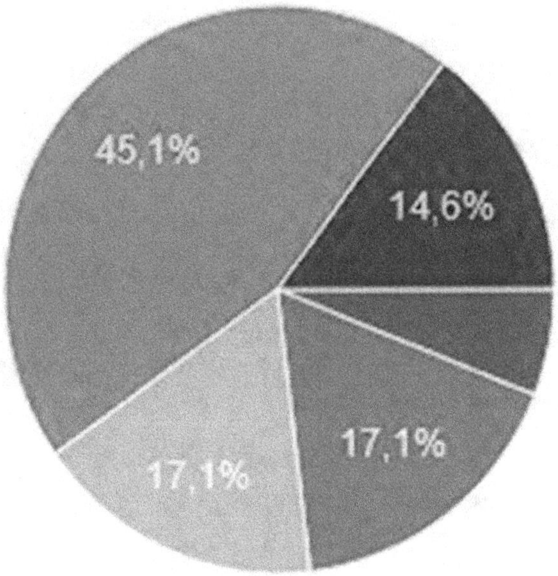

years old and 14.6% over 55 years old. Cumulatively over 45 years old was 59.7%, a percentage quite large, whereas from 25 to 44 years old, it was 34.2%. Just 6.1% were between the ages of 18 and 24.

In conclusion, it follows that the distance learning program students for folklore are adults in middle age and middle-aged adults. However, a percentage of 34.3 is more youthful (25-44 years old).

Gender

Concerning gender, the students who attended the program were 73.2%, while men were 26.8%. This percentage may be justified because women have a greater interest in folklore. Perhaps some are unemployed and thus have more time to attend and study the material.

EDUCATIONAL LEVEL

The educational level in the three-year distance free program for folklore shows that only 14.6% hold a high school diploma or an equivalent secondary-school leaving certificate, 39% of the participants hold an essential degree in higher and technical education (AEIs-TEIs), 43.9% hold a master's degree in education and 3.1% a doctoral degree. In conclusion, 47% hold a master's degree (43.9%) and a doctoral degree (3.1%). This percentage is very high and probably shows the need for young scientists to attend specialized training programs that are entirely free of charge and without having to attend them in person, in their personalized way. The percentage of participants who hold a primary degree in higher

Figure 4. What is your gender?

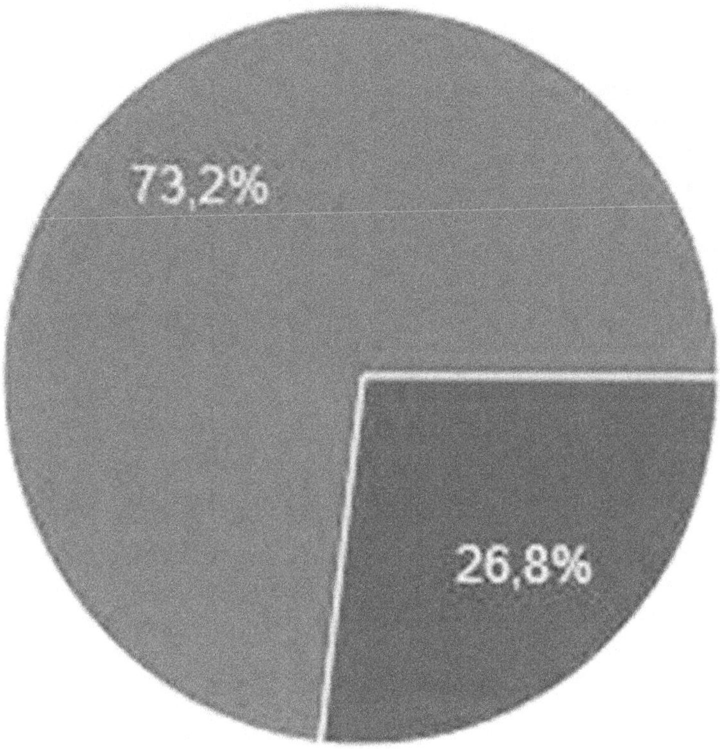

and technical education (39%), who are also looking for specialized training programs that are entirely free of charge and without having to attend them in person in their personalized way, is also impressive.

CURRENT PROFESSION

The participants' employment during the three-year program is recorded in the question "What is your current profession?" where 13% were Primary Education teachers, and 19.5% were Secondary Education teachers. 32.5% who attended the three-year demanding program were teachers resulting from that. They needed training on issues related to popular culture. 2.6% were employees in structures with young people, 6.5% were employees with young people, 1.3% performed internships or voluntary training, 3.9 were unemployed, 2.6% were civil servants, 2.6% were private employees, 1.3% were students and the remaining percentage of various declared professions of the private and public sector.

Figure 5. What is your educational level?

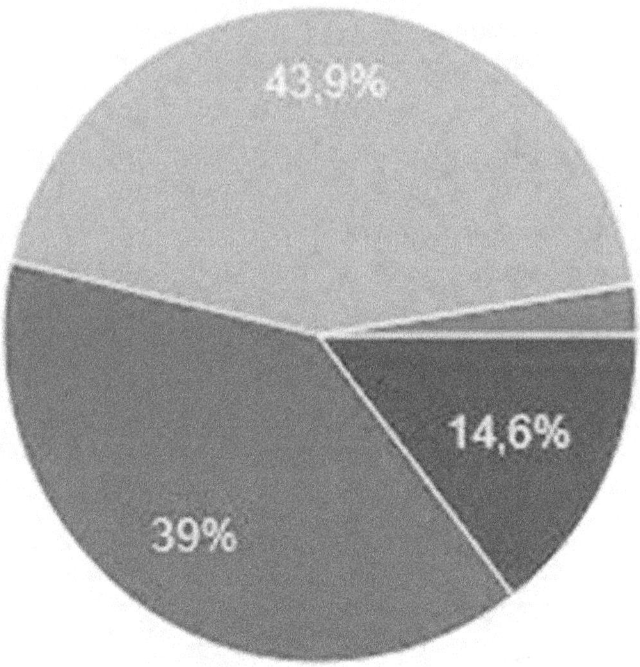

OBJECTIVES AND EXPECTATIONS

Part B' of the research was about the goals and expectations of the participants in the three-year training program. The first question that was asked was, "After you participated in the program "Introduction to the Science of Popular Culture", what did you get?" with alternative answers:

1. I have acquired new skills
2. I have acquired new knowledge
3. I have been in contact with experts in the field
4. I have worked with people with whom I share the same interests on the subject
5. I have developed new abilities
6. I will get the certificate that interests me
7. I have gained a competitive advantage
8. I have gained access to educational resources related to the topic

In the sub-question "a. I have acquired new skills", 71.96% of the participants replied "I am very interested", a percentage of 26.82% replied "I am interested", a percentage of 1.22% said "I am neutral", and in a percentage of 0% they replied, "I am not interested".

Figure 6. What is your current profession?

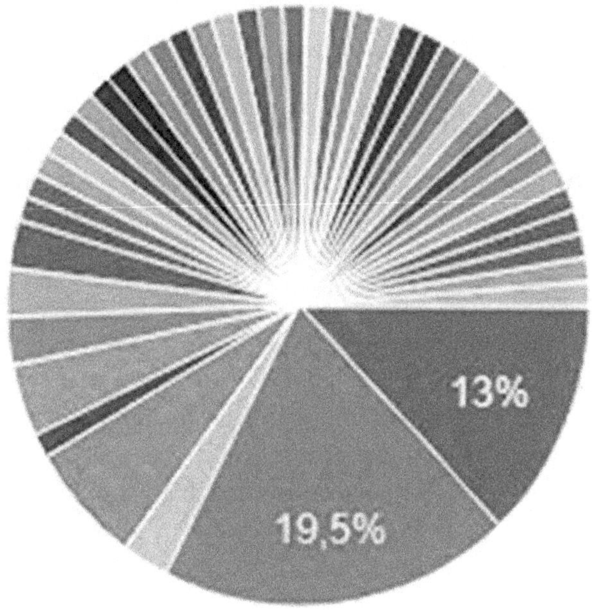

In the sub-question "b. I have acquired new knowledge", the participants answered a percentage of 82.93% "I am very interested", in a percentage of 13% they replied "I am interested", in a percentage of 1.2% ", I am neutral", and in a percentage of 0% they replied, "I am not interested".

In the sub-question "c. I have been in contact with experts in the field", the participants answered a percentage of 50% "I am very interested", a percentage of 39.02% answered "I am interested", a percentage of 10.98%, they answered "I am neutral", in a percentage of 0% they answered, "I am not interested".

In the sub-question "d. I have worked with people with whom I share the same interests on the subject" 39.02% answered "I am very interested", a percentage of 40.24% answered "I am interested", a percentage of 19.52% said, "I am neutral." In a percentage of 1.22%, they answered, "I am not interested".

In the sub-question "e. I have developed new skills" 62.20% answered "I am very interested", a percentage of 31.71% replied "I am interested", in a percentage of 6.09% said "I am neutral", and a percentage of 0% replied, "I am not interested".

In the sub-question "f. I will get the certificate that interests me" 48.78% answered "I am very interested", in a percentage of 29.26% answered "I am interested", in a percentage of 18.29% said "I am neutral", and a percentage of 3.65% answered, "I do not care".

In the sub-question "g I have gained a competitive advantage", 36.58% answered "I am very interested", in a percentage of 32.93% answered "I am interested", in a percentage of 24.40% answered, "I am neutral." In a percentage of 6.09%, they replied, "I do not care".

Figure 7. After you participated in the "Introduction to the Science of Folk Culture" project, what did you gain?

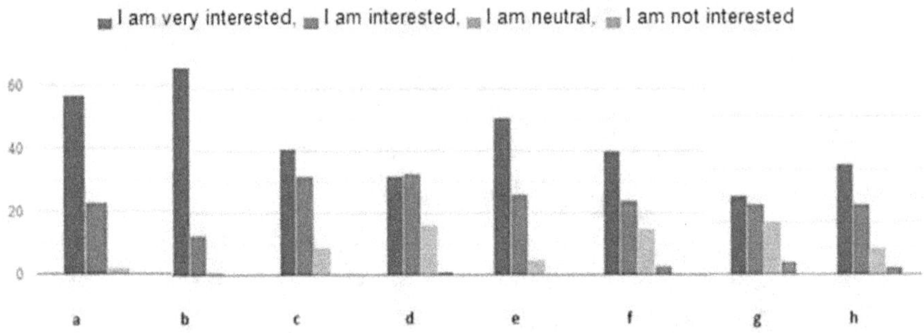

To the sub-question "h. gain access to educational resources related to the subject" 51.21% answered "I am very interested", a percentage of 32.93% replied "I am interested", 12.20% said "I am neutral", and a percentage of 3.66% replied, "I am not interested".

From the answers given by the respondents, it is recorded that the primary motivation for attending the three-year program for folk culture was the knowledge, skills, and competencies acquired from participation in the educational program. However, a high percentage of the trainees' interest (48.78% "I am very interested" and 29.26% answered "I am interested") concerning the question "f. I will get the certificate that interests me" indicates the need and also the connection of learning with documentary evidence of this new knowledge.

The second question of part B' of the research was: "After the completion of the program, what do you think you have gained?" with alternative answers:

1. I will be able to apply what I will have learned in my work
2. I will be able to change the way things work in my institution/organization
3. I will be able to influence the policies on the subject in the institutions and workplaces (cultural/educational institutions, etc.)
4. I will be able to get a better job
5. I will be able to improve my current work
6. I will be able to get more professional opportunities
7. I will gain a competitive advantage
8. I will gain access to educational resources related to the topic

In the sub-question "a. Will I be able to apply what I will have learned in my work", the participants answered a percentage of 41.86% "I am very interested", in a percentage of 36.05% they replied "I am interested", in a percentage of 15.12% "I am neutral" and in a percentage of 6.97% they replied, "I am not interested".

In the sub-question "b. Will I be able to change the way things work in my institution/ organization", the participants replied at a rate of 28.04% "I am very interested", in a percentage of 34.15% they replied

"I am interested", in a percentage of 30.49% "I am neutral" and in a percentage of 7.32% they replied, "I do not care".

In the sub-question "c. Will I be able to influence policies on the subject in institutions and workplaces (cultural/educational institutions, etc.)", the participants replied with a percentage of 25.60% "I am very interested", in a percentage of 42.69% they replied "I am interested", in a percentage of 26.83% "I am neutral" and in a percentage of 4.88% they replied, "I am not interested".

In the sub-question "d. Will I be able to get a better job", the participants answered a percentage of 23.17% "I am very interested", a percentage of 28.04% they answered "I am interested", a percentage of 34.15% ", I am neutral" and in a percentage of 14.64% they replied, "I am not interested".

In the sub-question "e. Will I be able to improve my current work", 34.14% of the participants answered "I am very interested", 37.80% answered "I am interested", 23.18% "I am neutral", and 4.88% answered, "I am not interested".

In the sub-question "f. Will I be able to get more professional opportunities", the participants answered a percentage of 34.14% "I am very interested", a percentage of 34.14% they answered "I am interested", a percentage of 23.18% ", I am neutral" and in a percentage of 8.54% they replied, "I am not interested".

In the sub-question "g. I will gain a competitive advantage", the participants answered a percentage of 36.59% "I am very interested", a percentage of 36.59% answered "I am interested", a percentage of 19.29% "I am neutral" and in a percentage of 8.53% they replied, "I am not interested".

In the sub-question "h. I will gain access to educational resources related to the topic", the participants replied a percentage of 54.88% "I am very interested", in a percentage of 30.48% they replied "I am interested", in a percentage of 10.98% "I am neutral" and in a percentage of 3.65% they replied, "I am not interested".

Overall, of the above questions, the highest percentages concerning the interest of the participants are occupied by the questions "a. I will be able to apply what I will have learned in my work" with a percentage of 41.86% "I am very interested", and 36.05% "I am interested" and to the question "h. I will gain access to educational resources related to the subject" the participants answered at a rate of 54.88% "I am very interested", and with 30.48% they answered, "I am interested". These answers indicate that the program graduates are thinking of applying to their work knowledge and skills that they learned and knew during the three-year program for folk culture. There is also a strong interest in gaining access to references, resources, and material for the folk culture they will probably use for their professional development and service/work needs.

Your Knowledge, Skills, and Competences

In part C of the research, "Your Knowledge, Skills, and Competencies", and in the first question ", How do you evaluate your knowledge/experience in the following subjects after the completion of the program?" with alternative answers concerning the semester courses of the three-year program "Introduction to the Science of Popular Culture":

1. Introduction to Folklore
2. Modern Horizons of Folklore Studies (Gender, Internet, School)
3. Digital Folklore (Education, Internet, New Technologies)
4. Religious Folklore
5. Philological Folklore

Figure 8. After completing the program, what do you think you have gained?

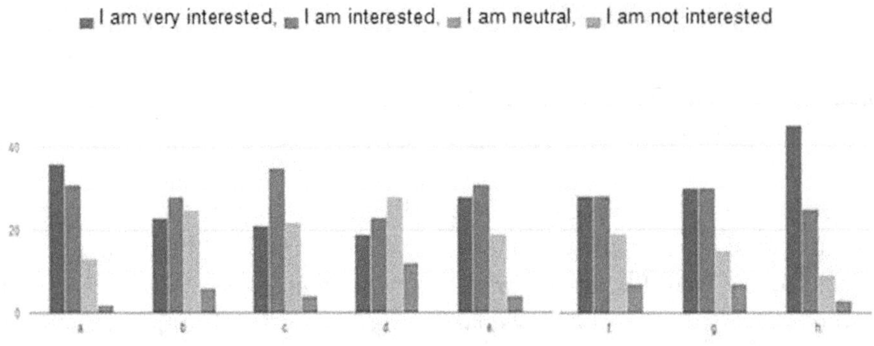

6. Contemporary Folk Culture and Local Cultural / Tourism Development

Table 3 distinguished the distribution of frequencies and percentages of individual variables for the cognitive objects of the course (units of each fortnight).

Table 3. Distribution of frequencies and percentages of individual variables for the cognitive objects of the course

Semester courses of the three-year program "Introduction to the Science of Folk Culture."	Very Good		Good		Neutral		Not good	
	N	%	N	%	N	%	N	%
Introduction to Folklore	67	81,7	15	18,3	0	0	0	0
Contemporary Horizons of Folklore Studies (Gender, Internet, School)	56	68,29	25	30,49	1	1,22	0	0
Digital Folklore (Education, Internet, New Technologies)	50	60,97	31	37,81	1	1,22	0	0
Religious Folklore	55	67,07	25	38,49	2	2,49	0	0
Philological Folklore	61	73,17	20	24,41	1	1,22	0	0
Contemporary Popular Culture and Local Cultural/Tourism Development	60	73,17	22	26,83	0	0	0	0

Interpreting the above results, we conclude that the six-month course "Introduction to Folklore" managed to gain the participants' most significant preference and interest by following with a slight difference, in order of preference, the sections: e. Philological Folklore, f. Contemporary Folk Culture, and Local Cultural/Tourism Development, b. Modern Horizons of Folklore Studies (Gender, Internet, School), d. Religious folklore, c. Digital Folklore (Education, Internet, New Technologies). It is possible that the course "Digital Folklore" was more difficult for them because it also required practical activities (creation of a virtual museum and digital storytelling, creation of groups on social media, etc.). Finally, there were no significant percentages for the answers "I am neutral" and "I do not care" in all six-semester courses.

Figure 9. How do you assess your knowledge/experience in the following topics after completing the program?

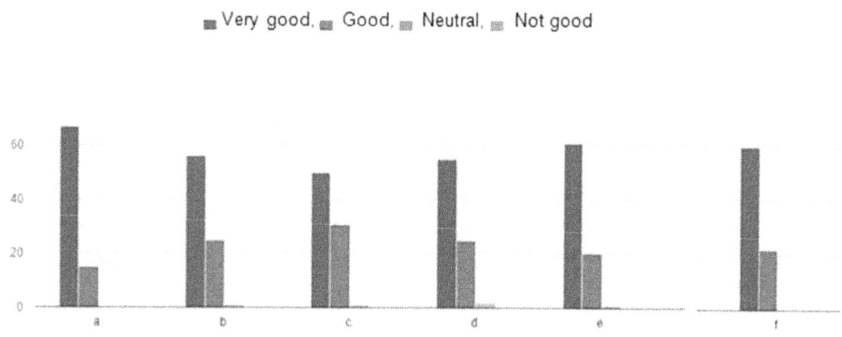

The second question of the research of part C was: "How do you evaluate your knowledge/experience in the following subjects after completing the program? with alternative answers:

1. Digital literacy (the ability to use computers and other technologies to improve learning, productivity, and performance)
2. Visual literacy (the ability to understand, produce and communicate through visual images)
3. Information literacy (the ability to find, evaluate, and compile information)
4. Presentation skills (the decision of the best way to present a story/research/literature review through a paper)
5. Assessment skills (the acquisition of know-how in the evaluation/criticism of the work of others, as well as their own)

In the sub-question "a. Digital literacy (the ability to use computers and other technologies to improve learning, productivity, and performance)", the participants answered a percentage of 58.54% "I am very interested", in a percentage of 37.81% they replied "I am interested", in 3.65% "I am neutral" and in a percentage of 0% they replied, "I am not interested".

In the sub-question "b. Visual literacy (the ability to understand, produce and communicate through visual images)," the participants answered a percentage of 63.42% "I am very interested", a percentage of 30.49% replied "I am interested" in a percentage of 6.09% "I am neutral" and in a percentage of 0% they replied, "I am not interested".

In the sub-question "c. Information literacy (the ability to find, evaluate and compile information)", the participants replied at a rate of 62.19% "I am very interested", in a percentage of 32.93% they replied "I am interested", in a percentage of 3.66% "I am neutral" and in a percentage of 1.22% they replied, "I am not interested".

In the sub-question "d. Presentation skills (the decision on the best way to present a story/research/literature review through work)", the participants replied at a rate of 53.66% "I am very interested", 41.47% answered "I am interested", 4.87% "I am neutral" and 0% answered, "I do not care".

In the sub-question "e. Evaluation skills (the acquisition of know-how in the evaluation/criticism of the work of others, as well as their own)", the participants answered at a rate of 51.22% "I am very

Figure 10. How do you assess your knowledge/skills in the following topics after completing the program?

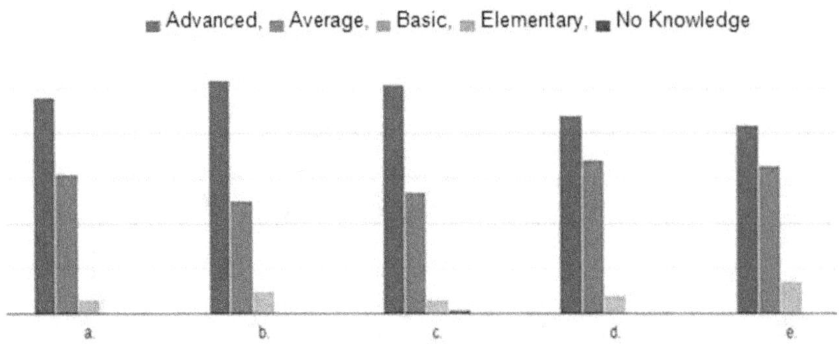

interested" in a percentage of 40.25% they replied "I am interested", in a percentage of 8.53% "I am neutral" and in a percentage of 0% they answered, "I am not interested".

From the above answers to the sub-questions that concern mainly issues of digital literacy, which require the primary use of ICT tools, it is recorded that the three-year distance program for folk culture contributed substantially to the development of digital skills of the participants. This is because the trainees daily came into contact with the free Moodle course management software, i.e. a Learning Management System, where they had to respond to automated quizzes, post their viewpoints in the discussion groups, post papers, communicate via email, retrieve digital material and bibliography, search for video lessons on the YouTube channel and other more specialized ICT tool handling tasks in the framework of the semester course "Digital Folklore".

In addition to the above questions in the survey for evaluating the three-year program for folk culture, there were also open questions that the trainees answered with a short text. Typically, the trainees to the open question "There are other expectations from the program", some answered: a) "Grateful to have attended the three-year program. I will not just talk to you about "expectations", but something real has already happened: I helped in the registration of my association-organization "Active Citizens" https://epfarsalon.gr/ in the Registry of Cultural Institutions of the Ministry of Culture and Sports and then a grant request was submitted for the digitization of the School Museum. I also really like the research and the recording.... and now I know the way to do it", b) "To enrich my knowledge", c) "The opportunity to participate in a doctorate related to folklore", d) "Enrichment of knowledge about folklore relics and monuments", c) "Supplies for a better and permanent job ".

To the open question, "Is there another goal that you would like the program to cover?" some trainees replied as follows: a) "To help us obtain a master's degree that would be recognized and be awarded points in teachers' notices", b) "Deepening in the science of Greek folklore, interest in the proposed bibliography, study for further personal spiritual development".

During the six semesters of implementing the three-year program that evaluated the above quantitative research, a combination and on-site monitoring were carried out with keeping a diary of teaching interventions (qualitative research). From the notes kept in a detailed diary, the statistics of the platforms for the participation of the trainees, as well as from the comments on videos of the teachings, it emerged that the trainees actively participated in the educational process following the program. This is recorded by the detailed statistics for their participation on the platform, their participation in the discussion groups, and their attendance of the course videos on the platform. The participants reacted positively to the alternation of teachers every fortnight, the alternative enriched educational material, and the possibility that one could attend the two-hour lesson in person or remotely through YouTube live with the possibility of intervention (online chat) or on YouTube later with a link that existed on the moodle platform. Another important event for the trainees was the opportunity given at the end of the semester to be examined in the final test in three examination periods. All those thematic modules required by the curriculum were taught with the cognitive subject. In the on-site monitoring of face-to-face teachings, there was constant participation. Regarding the digital participation of the trainees (discussions on the moodle platform, monitoring statistics, statics on YouTube, discussions in the Online chat of YouTube) recorded more minor but steady participation in the discussions compared to the face-to-face meetings. It is possible that mandatory participation activities in the discussions increased the participation of the trainees as the mandatory participation in the completion of the quizzes every fortnight.

CONCLUSIONS – PROPOSALS

In conclusion, the three-year educational program "Introduction to the science of Folk Culture", which was carried out mainly remotely and face-to-face, was an ambitious program. Initially, there was a concern about whether it would be completed due to its extended duration. The six-semester courses, the number of modules of each semester course (fortnight), the number of teachers who supported the courses, the number of videos, the extensive free bibliography as well as the management of the channel on YouTube, but on moodle were the main components that had to be carried out at the right time. At the same time, the management team and the communication team had to continuously support the participants by mail. Also another additional difficulty was the operation of a parallel second circle of the implementation of the three-year program. So, when the training program was in the implementation of the second-semester course, at the same time, it was in operation and the first semester of the second circle and so on.

In addition, the production and configuration of the educational material (learning resources) was another challenge, aiming at the final educational material to be quite user-friendly while at the same time being revealed every fortnight. The operation of the discussion groups that added interactivity and inclusiveness to the training program presupposed that someone had to check the discussion groups daily (Katsaris & Vidakis, 2021; Poultsakis, Papadakis, Kalogiannakis, & Psycharis, 2021).)

However, the evaluation of the project showed that teachers, and adults over the age of 35, are seeking with great interest scientific programs in the digital humanities, especially in history and folklore. A key issue is also the free access to such adult programs. The element of massiveness, i.e. the available number of people who can attend a program, has also been a positive element highlighted by the survey. Participants choose open programs, i.e. accessible to anyone who has a computer with an internet connection, structured around a set of purposes of a specific study area. Thus, the basic philosophy on which based the design of the three-year program "Introduction to the Science of Folk Culture" and other programs that were subsequently implemented by the Academy of Popular Culture and Local History was confirmed to have many features in common with the axes and design factors of Massive Open Online Courses (MOOCs) (Papadakis, 2021).

The research (quantitative-qualitative) evaluation of the three-year program "Introduction to the Science of Folklore" leads us to consider that the new designs of similar programs should take into account that such programs should have a comprehensive certification from corresponding Lifelong Learning Centers as well as access to scientific libraries and free textbooks.

Another proposal is the additional design of interactive activities and learning objects specific to each program. In addition, the creation of a video course archive may work in new programs as complementary audiovisual sources. Finally, the efforts made by cultural and self-administrative bodies at the level of adult education could be linked even more with undergraduate programs of study at universities and Lifelong Learning Centers.

The experience of our effort for the implementation of the three-year program in collaboration with the Laboratory of Folklore and Social Anthropology of the Department of History & Ethnology of the Democritus University of Thrace and the collaboration with the Department of Early Childhood Education and Educational Planning Sciences of the University of the Aegean in Greece gave the program an additional added scientific value and prestige in combination with the services offered by the professors of the respective Universities.

ACKNOWLEDGMENT

We would like to thank the following teachers: Dr. Emmanuel Sergis, Professor of Folklore of the Department of Language, Philology and Culture of the Black Sea Countries of the Democritus University of Thrace, Dr. Nikos Karpouzis, Collaborating Scientific Staff of the Hellenic Open University of Patras (HAP), Garyfalia Theodoridou, Dr. of Folklore of the Democritus University of Thrace, Elpiniki Tastani, Dr. of Folklore of the Democritus University of Thrace and Anagnostis Papakyparissis, PhD candidate of the University of Athens, Despina Damianou, former Assistant Professor at the Democritus University of Thrace, Thanasis Kougoulos, Member of the Special Scientific Staff at the Department of History and Ethnology of the Democritus University of Thrace, Lecturer at the Hellenic Open University, George Kouzas, Assistant Professor of Urban Folklore at the Philosophical School of the National and Kapodistrian University of Athens, Nadia Macha - Bizoumi, Assistant Professor of Folklore at the Department of History and Ethnology of the Democritus University of Thrace.

We would also like to thank the following teachers: Maria Gasouka, Professor of Folklore and Gender of the Department of Early Childhood Education and Educational Design sciences of the University of the Aegean and Scientific Coordinator of the program "Introduction to the Science of Popular Culture", Evangelia Raptou, Doctor of the University of the Aegean, Zoe Arvanitidou, Postdoctoral researcher of the University of the Aegean, Lecturer of the University of Malta and Xanthippi Fulidi Postdoctoral researcher of the University of the Aegean.

REFERENCES

Barianos, A., Papadakis, A., & Vidakis, N. (2022). Content manager for serious games: Theoretical framework and digital platform. *Advances in Mobile Learning Educational Research*, *2*(1), 251–262. doi:10.25082/AMLER.2022.01.009

Fini, A. (2019). The technological dimension of a Massive Open Online Course: The case of the CCK08 course tools. *International Review of Research in Open and Distance Learning*, *10*(5). Advance online publication. doi:10.19173/irrodl.v10i5.643

Kapaniaris, A., Gasouka, M., & Varvounis, M. (2019). E-learning program: «Introduction to the science of Folk Culture»: Evaluation of the semester course: «Contemporary Horizons of Folklore Studies, (Gender, Internet, and Education). *World Wide Journal of Multidisciplinary Research and Development*, *5*(5), 24–34.

Kapaniaris, A., & Varvounis, M. (2019a). Design and implementation of e-learning programs in folklore, ethnography, and history: Following the Logic of the Mass Open Internet Courses (MOOC). *World Wide Journal of Multidisciplinary Research and Development*, *5*(1), 22–29.

Kapaniaris, A., & Varvounis, M. (2019b). E-Learning Program «Introduction to the Science of Folk Culture»: Evaluation of the course: «Introduction to the Science of Folk Culture. *World Wide Journal of Multidisciplinary Research and Development*, *5*(5), 1–10.

Kapaniaris, A., Varvounis, M. (2019c). Folklore on the road to distance education (e-learning). *Folklore, Bulletin of the Greek Folklore Society*, *44*.

Kapaniaris, A., Varvounis, M. (2019d). The experience of distance education (e-learning) in the field of Folklore: The evaluation, the first conclusions, the proposals and the new developments. *Folklore, Bulletin of the Greek Folklore Society*, *44*.

Kapaniaris, A., & Zampetoglou, G. (2021). Visual programming for the greation of digital shadow play performance using mobile devices in times of Covid-19. *Advances in Mobile Learning Educational Research*, *1*(2), 162–170. doi:10.25082/AMLER.2021.02.010

Kapaniaris, G. A. (2020). *Digital Folklore and Education, Enriched Media and Innovative Approaches to the Didactics of Folk Culture*. Pedio.

Karsenti, T. (2013). What the research says. *International Journal of Technologies in Higher Education*.

Katsaris, I., & Vidakis, N. (2021). Adaptive e-learning systems through learning styles: A review of the literature. *Advances in Mobile Learning Educational Research*, *1*(2), 124–145. doi:10.25082/AMLER.2021.02.007

Lazarinis, F., Boididis, I., Kozanidis, L., & Kanellopoulos, D. (2022). An adaptable multi-learner serious game for learning cultural heritage. *Advances in Mobile Learning Educational Research*, *2*(1), 201–215. doi:10.25082/AMLER.2022.01.004

McAuley, A., Stewart, B., Siemens, G., & Cormier, D. (2010). *The MOOC model for digital practice*. University of Prince Edward Island through the Social Sciences and Humanities Research Council's "Knowledge Synthesis Grants on the Digital Economy".

Papadakis, S. (2021). Advances in Mobile Learning Educational Research (A.M.L.E.R.): Mobile learning as an educational reform. *Advances in Mobile Learning Educational Research*, *1*(1), 1–4. doi:10.25082/AMLER.2021.01.001

Papadakis, S., Kalogiannakis, M., Sifaki, E., & Vidakis, N. (2018). Evaluating Moodle use via Smart Mobile Phones. A case study in a Greek University. *EAI Endorsed Transactions on Creative Technologies, 5*(16).

Papadakis, S., Trampas, A., Barianos, A., Kalogiannakis, M., & Vidakis, N. (2020). Evaluating the Learning Process: The "ThimelEdu" Educational Game Case Study. *Proceedings of the 12th International Conference on Computer Supported Education*, 2, 290-298. 10.5220/0009379902900298

Poultsakis, S., Papadakis, S., Kalogiannakis, M., & Psycharis, S. (2021). The management of Digital Learning Objects of Natural Sciences and Digital Experiment Simulation Tools by teachers. *Advances in Mobile Learning Educational Research, 1*(2), 58–71. doi:10.25082/AMLER.2021.02.002

Sofos, A., Kostas, A., & Parashou, V. (2015). *Online distance learning - From theory to practice*. Association of Greek Academic Libraries – National Technical University of Athens.

Tzimogiannis, A. (2017). *E-Learning, Theoretical Approaches, and Educational Designs*. Athens: Kritiki Publication.

Vidakis, N., Barianos, A., Trampas, A., Papadakis, S., Kalogiannakis, M., & Vassilakis, K. (2019). Generating Education in-Game Data: The Case of an Ancient Theatre Serious Game. *Proceedings of the 11th International Conference on Computer Supported Education, 1*, 36-43. doi:10.5220/0007810800360043

Vidakis, N., Barianos, A. K., Trampas, A. M., Papadakis, S., Kalogiannakis, M., & Vassilakis, K. (2020). Game Raw Data Collection and Visualization in the Context of the "ThimelEdu" Educational Game. In H. C. Lane, S. Zvacek, & J. Uhomoibhi (Eds.), *Computer Supported Education. CSEDU 2019. Communications in Computer and Information Science* (Vol. 1220). Springer. doi:10.1007/978-3-030-58459-7_30

ADDITIONAL READING

Kalogiannakis, M., & Papadakis, S., (2008). Hybrid learning for women and socially sensitive groups for the promotion of digital literacy. *Training, 6*, 2.

Kalogiannakis, M., Vassilakis, K., Alafodimos, C., Papadakis, S., Papachristos, D., & Zafeiri, E. (2009). Adult Education and Lifelong Learning. The case of GSAE (General Secretary for Adult Education) in Greece. *International Journal of Advanced Corporate Learning, 2*(4), 15–20. doi:10.3991/ijac.v2i4.981

Kapaniaris, A., & Zampetoglou, G. (2021). Visual programming for the creation of digital shadow play performance using mobile devices in times of Covid-19. *Advances in Mobile Learning Educational Research, 1*(2), 162–170. doi:10.25082/AMLER.2021.02.010

Kapaniaris, G. A. (2020). Folk Culture and Education: The Role of Information Technology and Information and Communication Technologies in the Production of Digital Educational Materials. In M. Kalogiannakis & S. Papadakis (Eds.), *Handbook of Research on Tools for Teaching Computational Thinking in P-12 Education* (pp. 456–479). IGI Global. doi:10.4018/978-1-7998-4576-8.ch018

Kapaniaris, G. A. (2020). Folk Culture and Enriched Digital Teaching: Designing Educational Scenarios With the Use of ICT. In M. Kalogiannakis & S. Papadakis (Eds.), *Handbook of Research on Tools for Teaching Computational Thinking in P-12 Education* (pp. 480–501). IGI Global. doi:10.4018/978-1-7998-4576-8.ch019

Papadakis, S., & Kalogiannakis, M. (2019). Evaluating the effectiveness of a game-based learning approach in modifying students' behavioural outcomes and competence, in an introductory programming course. A case study in Greece. *International Journal of Teaching and Case Studies*, *10*(3), 235–250. doi:10.1504/IJTCS.2019.102760

Chapter 4
Conspiracy Theories About the Pandemic of COVID-19 and Their Function on the Greek Internet

Rea Kakampoura
National and Kapodistrian University of Athens, Greece

Aphrodite Lidia Nounanaki
National and Kapodistrian University of Athens, Greece

ABSTRACT

Conspiracy theories are a folk narrative genre that tends to arise whenever crises occur; thus, inevitably, these kinds of theories appeared on the pandemic of COVID-19 as well. Their spread used to be done through magazines with relevant subject matter and through the word of mouth. The internet has changed this treaty because, by giving space in the dissemination of any information, it seems to have enhanced the widest spread of this narrative genre too. So, in this chapter, the impact of the internet on the genre will be highlighted through a long-term digital folklore research on the Greek internet. Through the case study of conspiracy theories about the COVID-19 pandemic, in the context of digital folklore, this chapter intents to highlight the impact of the internet on the genre, its spread, and its function, as well as the way the internet users' uptake the genre.

INTRODUCTION

Conspiracy theories (CTs) are a folk narrative genre that tends to emerge whenever crises causing uncertainty occur. A pandemic is definitely such an event. Although they seem to form a new narrative genre, CTs date back to the early twentieth century (Butter &Knight, 2018, pp.33-46). Therefore, long before Covid-19, the 1918 'Spanish flu' pandemic brought to light its own CTs. They tended to spread, mainly, as rumours through word of mouth and journalism. That was the primary means of disseminat-

DOI: 10.4018/978-1-6684-4461-0.ch004

ing the genre. The internet, though, enhanced the proliferation of CTs, as it did to the widest spread of any information. In fact, since the COVID-19 pandemic is the first of the internet and social media era, its related theories spread faster than at any other moment in history (Bodner, Welch & Brodie, 2021, p. 6). This alone reinforces the importance of delving into the genre.

This paper intends to highlight the impact of the internet on the genre, its spread and function, as well as its uptake by internet users, through a case study of CTs on the Covid-19 pandemic, in the context of digital folklore, and through long-term research on the Greek internet. In order to conduct a definition, a literature review is offered in this chapter to describe the genre. The field on which the research was held is also defined and described through digital folklore literature, along with related methodological issues. The chapter's main focus is on the case of CTs during the COVID-19 pandemic and their appearance on the Greek internet. As a result, these theories are examined by presenting them following the chronological order in which they appeared online. The way these theories are discussed, adopted and replicated, or rejected and criticized by internet users is also approached. The research fills a gap in both the literature of digital folklore studies in Greece and the study of the spread of CTs regarding the pandemic of COVID-19 on the internet.

CONSPIRACY THEORIES: DEFINITIONS AND RESEARCH ISSUES

Before looking into the characteristics of their internet spread, it is necessary to analyse how these theories can be described, what they are about, when they occur and what their function is.

CTs are being studied by a wide range of fields as are political science (interested in achieving political objectives or studying the expression of criticism within foreign or domestic policy and international relations), psychology (researching the relationships between susceptibility to CTs and other psychological patterns), history (seeking to map development lines and megatrends), and media studies are among the fields studying CTs (as discourse that is represented through films and literature, but is often linked to politics) (Önnerfors, 2021, p. 24). In fact, a large European network named Comparative Analysis of Conspiracy Theories (COMPACT, https://conspiracytheories.eu/) was established from 2016 to 2020 to bring together researchers from several disciplines to explore these phenomena (Önnerfors, 2021, p. 24). Folklore studies look into the cultural characteristics of these theories as folk groups narratives while they study also their connection to other similar genres, such as rumours or urban legends (Campion-Vincent, 2007, pp. 162-199).

CTs have the ability to make events or sequences of occurrences 'legible,' giving them meaning. They aim to reveal the hidden truth behind contemporary and historical events, (Van Prooijen & Douglas 2017, pp.323–333) or even natural disasters (bad weather, tsunamis, epidemics, and so on) (Taguieff, 2016, p.50). They explain the world by proposing alternative interpretations for unexpected and catastrophic events with primarily economic and political implications, which are frequently accidental, unintentional or unpretentious (Aeronovitch, 2010, p.6). They attain their purpose by assuming that dark forces (individuals or groups, Taguieff, 2016, p.25) are secretly controlling political and social order (Fenster, 2008, p.1), plotting to harm a group of people or even humanity as a whole (Douglas, 2021: 270-217; see also Douglas et al. 2016, pp.57-77, 2017, pp.3-35). Thus, coincidences cannot be random, but are taken as clues that divulge underlying connections and provide models for interpreting facts, compatible with their supporters' way of thinking and cognitive level (Taguieff, 2016, p.13-15). As a result, social, economic, political, religious and moral issues are being comprehensively interpreted (Goldzwig, 2002, p.492).

The unexpected and unexplained shifts that occurred in late modernity, especially during times of crisis or major upheavals that disrupt social values and prevailing norms (Taguieff, 2016, p.163), prompted fear and suspicion that 'invisible forces' ruled the world. This is also aided by "negative globalization," as defined by Bauman (2007, p.129). CTs, a genre of contemporary folk narratives[1], represent all of these fears. Nevertheless, the human impulse to create stories appears to be the driving force behind CTs' popularity (Aeronovitch 2010, p.349, p.354).

However, rejection of official information, which is perceived as inaccurate and deceptive, is a pre-condition for the emergence of CTs (Taguieff, 2015, p.81). So, people create narratives (theories) as explanations for their fears, or hunt for answers elsewhere in new types of informational media, such as the internet, because there is a dearth of trustworthy information or the current information does not make much sense. Their spread used to be done through magazines with relevant subject matter and thus, was relatively restricted. The oral transmission of this kind of topics limited the transferability of evidence. So, the genre was more often shared as a fluid rumour than as reliable information. As a matter of fact, folklorists classified narratives of this kind into the category of 'rumours', as, for instance, Fine & Ellis did in their 2010 book *The Global Grapevine: Why Rumours of Terrorism, Immigration and Trade Matter.* Nowadays they have been restored as a separate narrative genre which has distinct morphological and thematical qualities.

THE INTERNET AS THE RESEARCH FIELD FOR THE SPREAD OF THE GENRE. METHODOLOCICAL ISSUES

Internet has altered this treaty by allowing the dissemination of any information, enhancing the popularity of the genre while also allowing its transmission in its entirety, without any simplifications or omissions.

Technology has emerged as a field in which folklore could evolve (Dégh, 1994), especially since the appearance of the internet, being a promising field for the spread of CTs too. It should be highlighted, however, that this new digital field cannot be isolated from the "physical" one, which is well-established in folkloristic, ethnological, and anthropological studies. As Budka (2011, p.12) points out, this does not imply the abandonment of conventional methods (e.g., ethnographic method or field research), but rather a critical elaboration of some of their aspects.

Internet can be seen as a new data of this era that facilitates the diffusion of popular culture more widely - even globally – and, also, quickly but it cannot be separated from the field of folkloristic and anthropological studies. Of course, one fundamental difference is their substance/materiality –being one digital and the other physical- yet they both relate to common similar issues that are inextricably linked. Moreover, many subjects that fall within the folklore and anthropological themes (Ellis, 2001, pp.1-10) have taken on new dimensions or have been modified through the digital world (Blank, 2009, pp.9-13). This applies also to the genre of CTs.

Folklore appeared online and began to spread in such a clear and recognisable way, as Blank (2009, p.2-9) mentions, by the time the internet became a method of easier communication, as it did in the offline world. Internet thus, turned into a perfect route for the transmission of folk narratives and other folkloristic genres, because anonymity and efficiency were ensured. The field of Digital Folklore is the one dealing with all these aspects. More precisely, digital folklore studies the messages of various contents that circulate widely on the internet, which has evolved into a new, flexible and widely used method of information exchange[2] (Katsadoros, 2013, p.107). In more details, digital folklore explores and examines customs, traditions and cultural elements of visual, textual and aural performance that resulted from the user's involvement in personal computer applications (Lialina & Espenschied, 2009, Krawczyk-Wasilewska, 2016, p.27). It is the externalization of creativity through the numerous forms and interactions that users and their communities engage in on the internet (Blank, 2009, p.6).

The distribution of folkloristic material on the internet follows the axes below. On the one hand, "traditional" folk culture is transmitted, disseminated, but also preserved on the Internet (e.g., *mantinades*, jokes, etc.). Modern forms of popular culture, on the other hand, are generated primarily for online usage, although many of them go beyond this environment and are integrated into the offline domain (Katsadoros, 2013, pp.109-111) (e.g., the internet memes that can be, also, verbally transmitted). Internet and, especially, social media, can also be preserved as a field of archival digital ethnography due to the various archives that are being uploaded (for instance, the archives of the "Pelioritians in Egypt", Kapaniaris & Varvounis, 2019, pp.11-18).

How can this material be located and collected on the internet? The research methods employed in this 'new' field are the same as those used in the offline world, but by critically processing some of their aspects and adapting them to the new environment. So, folklore material from the internet environment arises using distinct methods depending on the target of the respective research. Long-term online folklore study can be applied to investigate, for example, the dissemination of a particular kind of popular culture in the new environment. Digital ethnographic research, that is netnography, is used to explore digital communities, interactions, and relationships among website users (Kozinets, 2020). Of course, internet archives can be reviewed and technology can be employed as a projection and decryption tool for a digital archive, but, also, as a tool for collecting new data (Varvounis & Kapaniaris, 2019, p.114).

Still, which part of the chaotic space of the internet is going to be examined? The internet is one of the most visible manifestations of globalization, making all cultural products fabricated by smaller or larger groups accessible and allowing their interaction with those produced by other groups (Thompson, 2012, p.49). Part of the internet is becoming 'local', due to the activity of users who transfer their cultural characteristics to it. Nonetheless, on account of the worldwide nature of the field and globalization, many items of popular culture often cease to contain only the features of a local tradition and follow the new path of a multimodal spread that is now global, due to high mobility across national borders (Brednich, 2001, p.7). The spoken language is one of the most distinguishing cultural features, therefore this 'national' internet can be identified, in most cases, by the functional use of national languages on it. As will be seen below, the 'Greek internet' is the one where the Greek language is employed, because the CTs that are situated on it are not only small-scale local ones, but are also connected to each other in a wider narrative with a long duration of even worldwide dissemination and influence.

So, in the context of digital folklore and using the example of the dispersal of CTs associated to the COVID-19 pandemic, we intend to highlight the impact of the environment of the Greek internet on the genre itself, as well as its perception and dissemination by the Greek internet users. The impact of the internet on the genre will be underlined by analysing data obtained through a long-term digital folklore research (which lasted from 2/2020 to 2/2022) on the Greek internet and through digital ethnographic research for the analysis of online subgroups. Therefore, this study significantly relies on samples from both the surface and deep web with relevant topics, such as blogs, websites, social media (primarily Facebook), and YouTube. In fact, material has been collected from a sample of two hundred and thirty-eight (238) webpages (websites and open blogs), twenty-two (22) YouTube channels and twenty-four (24) Facebook pages/groups. The vast majority of these websites promote conspiracy-based interpretations on any given issue out of conviction, not by chance or ignorance. Thus, we conducted a combination between *actor-based* and *topic-based* approach (Heft & Buehling, 2022, p. 4). On the one hand, users, websites and social media accounts recognised for their active engagement in such narratives and dissemination on the internet have been approached. On the other hand, case-specific key terms have been searched to locate more related posts[3].

For the uptake of the narrations by the internet users, their comments and related posts will be analysed. To this approach several memes are going to be presented as well (collected mainly from twenty Facebook pages). Names have been removed from the samples taken from social media posts, but the majority are posts that have been converted into memes. By using memes, the 'burden' of 'exposing' users while presenting their opinions is lifted. Eventually, the influence of the internet on the genre, its spread, and function, as well as the way internet users perceive and reinterpret the genre, will be illustrated through a case study of CTs about the Covid-19 pandemic.

THE COVID-19 PANDEMIC IN GREECE

CTs tend to arise with greater intensity and frequency whenever crises occur. The Covid-19 pandemic is a global health crisis that has complicated many social, economic, and cultural issues. They do appear in doubtful situations, such as when people are unable to explain why things are going wrong, but also when the gathered information is deemed untrustworthy (Shahsavari, et a., 2020, p.280). In the present case, information about the pandemic includes medical terminology -hard to be followed by the majority of people-, extreme protection measures had to be implemented rather quickly -both globally and locally- and all the death and fear that ensued appear to be the reasons why mainstream information, that is, information presented by the media, was considered unreliable.

The first infection of the COVID-19 virus in Greece was detected on the 26th of February 2020. According to official figures, the number of cases was kept low during the first variations of the virus (around two thousand per day) but when the omicron variation (located in Greece in December 2021) was discovered, the cases increased dramatically (reaching 50.126 on 4/1/22 and ranging around 20.000 daily ever since). The number of deaths from the virus' adverse effects increased in Greece as everywhere else due to the delta variant (located in Greece in June 2020). The vaccination campaign began on December 27, 2020, and was treated by the Greek population in various ways[4].

CTs appeared on the internet and especially on social media immediately after the first news about COVID-19. Following the progression of the pandemic, these theories started by denying at first the pandemic's existence, then attempting to explain its creation and, then, concentrating on the 'latest developments'. As the pandemic progressed, many events sparked the development of these theories whose aspects could be grouped into the following broader topics:

- Existence and origin: the virus does not exist (e.g. is a Hoax) or is human made (e.g., in a laboratory).
- Secret agendas: The virus has been deliberately spread or its natural spread has been artificially augmented (e.g., via 5G signals) so that the virus can be used as an excuse to alter humanity (e.g., reducing the world's population, modifying human DNA through vaccines, and making the blood of the unvaccinated priceless).

- Pseudo-scientific reasoning: The vaccine is harmful, as all the health measures are, both for the body and the 'soul' (e.g., masks reduce the percentage of oxygen inhaled, the vaccine and the QR codes are 'the mark of the beast').
- Political reasoning: Health measures to combat the spread of the virus are implemented to intentionally harm or bring society under control and can pose a serious threat to democracy (e.g., new world order theories).
- The scale of the conspiracy (e.g., theories explaining local or global events).

CONSPIRACY THEORIES REGARDING THE PANDEMIC ON THE INTERNET

CTs related to the pandemic will be approached in the sequence in which they first appeared on the internet as the pandemic evolved. We attempt to evaluate and analyse their diffusion on the field by scrutinising their content. However, due to their proclivity to produce patterns even when none exist, these CTs can be divided into two categories based on their reference and impact factor (van Prooijen et al., 2018, pp.320-335). On the one hand, such limited or local schemes are identified, and, on the other, multinational conspiracies are classified as large-scale ones. A mega-conspiracy, also known as a super-conspiracy, is a collection of conspiracies that extend to a global scale and interpret a malignant force's plan. The concept of the mega-conspiracy is that it is associated with history itself driven by forces with almost transcendent power (Taguieff, 2016, p.26, p.37, p.89).

These countless CTs are all fictitious (because plots do happen, for instance, in politics and business). Micro-conspiracies are sometimes created ephemerally, based on some arbitrary connection between unrelated events, having a short-term influence. One such example is the connection between the vaccination and the fire that erupted in Athens in the summer of 2021. According to this 'interpretation' the fire was set intentionally to contain the vaccine, so that anyone who refused the immunization would inhale the vaccine's contents through evaporation (figure 2).

Since the Attica region has the highest number of unvaccinated individuals, they ignited a fire to burn the vaccine mixture from the vaccines at a specific time, so that it will be dispersed into the air and vaccinate us. Put wet towels on the face and do not go out for 48 hours.

In some cases, they are connected to each other in a wider narrative with a long duration of dissemination and influence. One such example is the interrelation of the pandemic to The New World Order theory[5]. The pandemic, according to this theory, does not exist. It is a ruse to implant microchips into people in order to make them obedient to the conspirators. Such examples refer to the large-scale uptake of the pandemic and the goal of reducing the world's population by the master-mind Bill Gates[6], who is often regarded as a conspirator.

Other such theories connect the pandemic to several known CTs, as are those about masonry controlling the world combined with the prevailing of Satan through the new-world-order-theory, 5g, the microchip, turning man into artificial intelligence (as shown in figure 4), or they are linked to political or other prominent personalities who seem to have foreseen the fall of humanity. Kissinger, for instance, is supposed to have predicted in 2009 that people will be forced to receive mandatory vaccinations which would be the end of mankind: "*(...) when the herd receives mandatory vaccinations, the game ends. they will accept anything. (...) Check the flock of sheep and control the flock. (...)*" (https://rb.gy/gkrn34).

Figure 1. The entire pandemic conspiracy story condensed into a single image that depicts the new 'normality' and its adherents, who lack critical thinking and blindly accept all new norms they hear from the media like obedient sheep (that are for example social distancing, the mask-gag, the implanted microchip through vaccine that is remotely activated, and so on). (https://rb.gy/nlleqv).

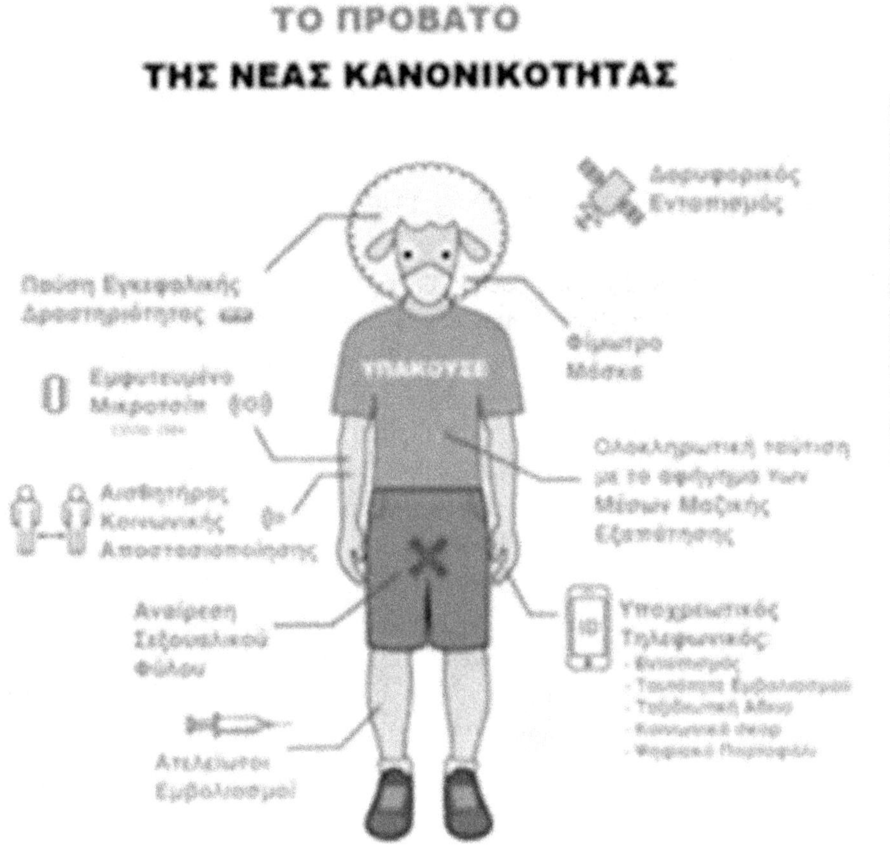

The local CTs focused on the mistreatment of patients in local hospitals, who are treated as experimental animals, so in case they die, the pandemic can be used as an excuse[7]. They bring real examples of people who, despite appearing to be healthy, died while hospitalised. They exhibit specific examples of such situations, generally with the patient's personal data and images, in order to illustrate the truth of the given facts[8].

Nonetheless, the CTs found on the Greek internet, concern every reported development of the pandemic, as well as a heavy focus on its control (both locally and globally). The pandemic, initially, was considered a hoax[9], a ploy to generate fear and gain control over those being afraid[10]. Those who refused to believe the deception and did not get afraid, appeared as revolutionaries seeking to uncover the hidden truth.

The next step was to accept the existence of the pandemic, which was regarded as human-made, a laboratory product, prepared as a weapon against humanity, as a means of population reduction, as can be seen in an article titled *Coronavirus: The secret plan for population reduction in the entire world?*[11]

Figure 2.

(https://rb.gy/xlvw2c), in which an attempt is made to provide a plausible reasoning that will show that such a scenario does not seem to be all that utopian after all.

The same perception of the pandemic appears to prevail, as seen by countless internet posts and even Facebook groups. Such one is titled: *Coronavirus; The plan of the World Government* (https://rb.gy/nkbwtv). On that page, in which the description is the following: *Coronavirus is the great plan for the imposition of Global Governance and Slavery on the Planet*, all posts refer to the pandemic with scepticism based on conspiracies.

However, while trying to cooperate with the idea of a pandemic spreading worldwide, the first governmental attempts to control it emerged. The first lockdown (13/5-1/6/2020) was imposed. So, fears of being controlled acquired fertile ground. In that framework the control is intensively connected to the New World Order theory, as referred on the video *All the things they don't want you to understand:*

Figure 3. Have you ever wondered why Bill Gates, a software developer, ended up as a Covid expert? Because the Covid vaccination is an 'operating system' designed to program humans and hack their biological functions

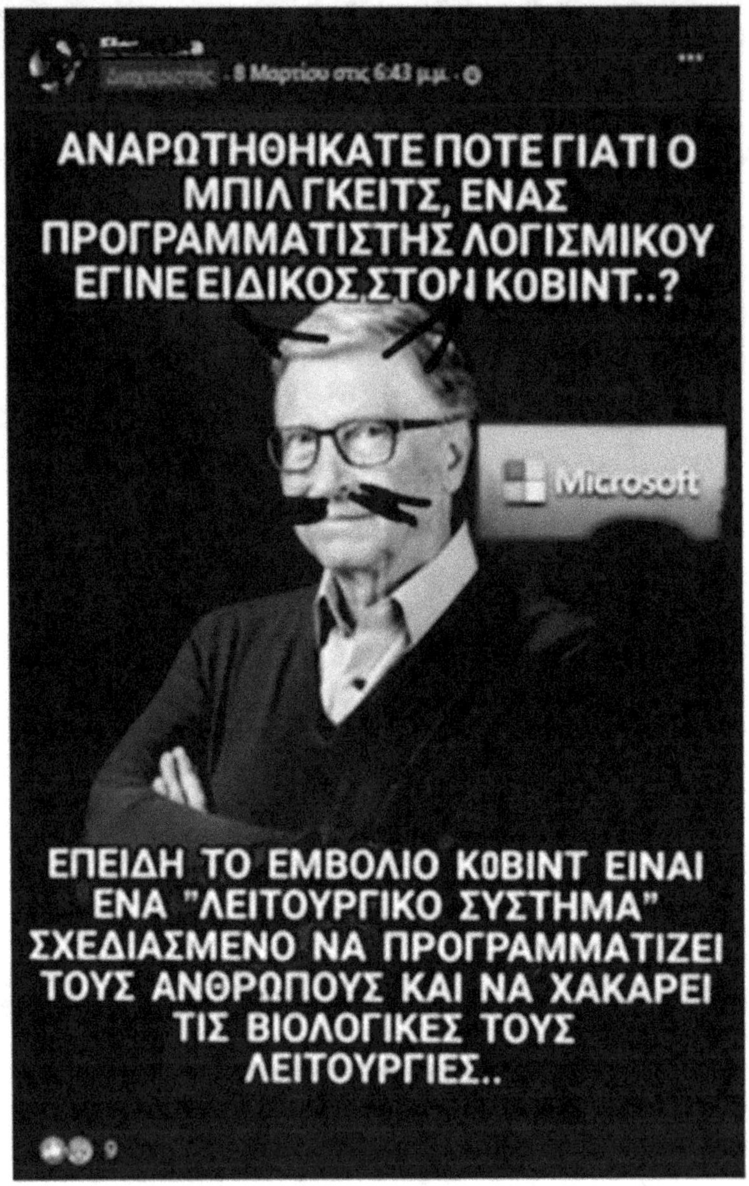

*Nowadays the word control has taken on frightening proportions ... in the following video we will see together why and how they control us. But, also, what is the New Order of Things (*https://rb.gy/7zmfk5).

The usage of facemasks, initially only in interior places but soon everywhere, was the next 'strike'. A complete pseudo-scientific argument evolved against the usage of facemasks, which concerned the detrimental implications of their use (i.e., the user is supposed to be inhaling fumes causing fainting, germs grow, freedom of speech is deprived). Two relevant Facebook pages (*NO to facemasks, NO to the microchip-vaccine,* https://rb.gy/0ikuy4 and *No to facemasks,* https://rb.gy/pljuck) are located on which

Figure 4. Write the word CORONAVIRUS upside down and translate it from Hindi to English. It brings out: the rising of the omniscient, i.e., Satan. Now you know who directs the Masonic prime minister. Now you know that 5g is the transponder. The chip of the vaccine is the transmitter that will make you a robot https://rb.gy/oeujrx.

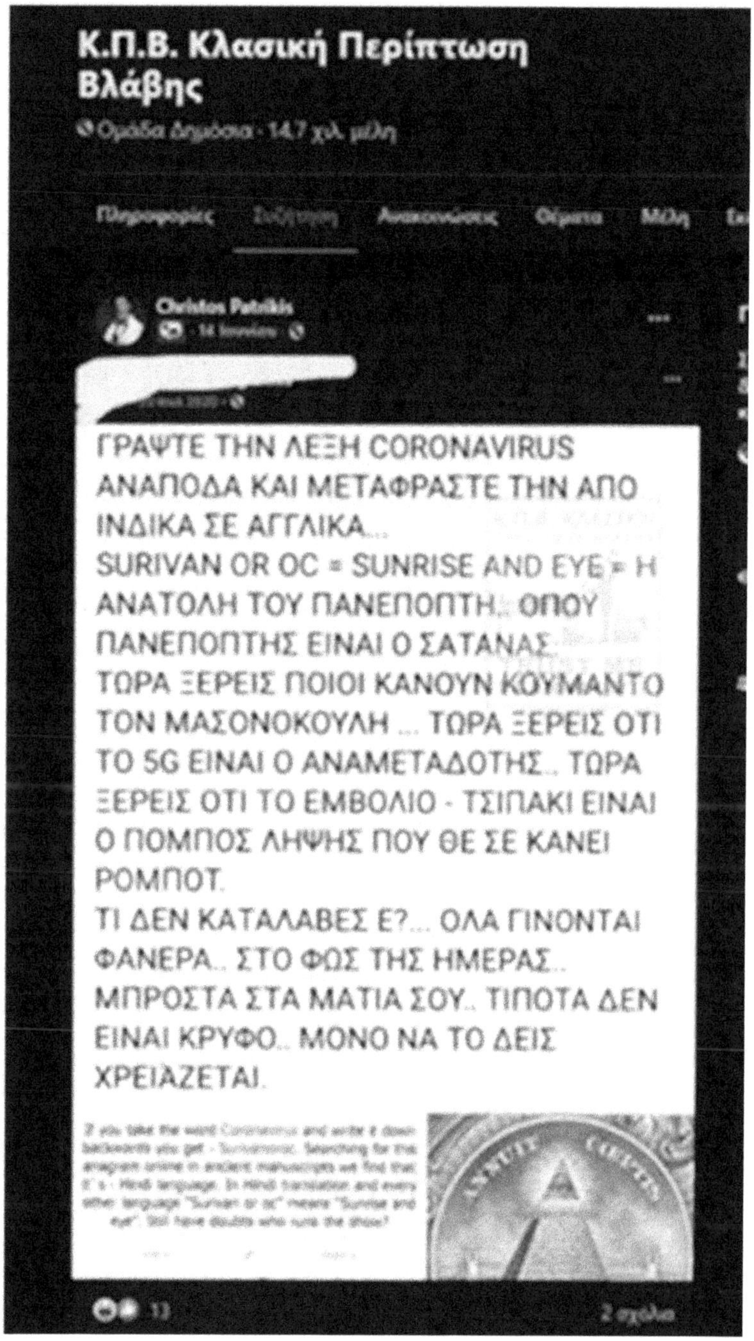

the reasoning of the denial is defended with enraged posts on the harmful effects of the mask, as well as one on the denning parents who refuse to impose the use of facemask on their children at school (*No child with a mask at school,* https://rb.gy/00xgpe), who, in the meantime, have returned to school, after months of distance learning.

Fear of something is a vulnerability that can be exploited. In the context of CTs, some people present themselves as 'experts' on the secrets of a -global- scene. They claim to carry the knowledge that emerged from personal 'research' or knowledge on a professional level and present themselves as the ones who 'demystify', expose and reveal hidden aspects on the matter they are experts (Taguieff, 2016, p.153). So, in this case several doctors are the 'brave insiders' who have figured out the way to decipher the plot and are thus, aggressively expressing their thoughts online about the usage of facemasks, mainly by children, and complementing their remarks with dramatic images (as shown in figure 7).

Another distinguishing element of these ideas is that they are written in the form of a scientific document, which includes a wealth of data and information in the form of (pseudo)scientific[12] research (Aeronovitch, 2010, pp.11-13). The indication becomes evidence in these theories and it is what makes the "experts'" argumentation almost rational or even scientifically evident. In their interpretive narratives, therefore, the irrational is intertwined with the rational in a way that makes them almost plausible (Taguieff, 2015, p.39). However, the leap into the imaginary, which always happens at some point in the description of events, ultimately turns the narrative to a paranoid one (Hofstadter, 1996 [1965], p.83, cf. Taguieff, 2015, p.43). Nonetheless, advocates of the conspiracy regard denunciation of the conspiracy as an action against it, rather than a simple description of it, since by revealing the expediencies it contains, it weakens them. In other words, when the content of a conspiracy is revealed, it loses its power because it ceases to be disguised (Taguieff, 2015, p.45).

Thus, the fundamental aim of such ideas is to capture the truth and establish it through audio-visual data in order to evince the positions they promote, and the internet is the appropriate venue for spreading the 'truth'. Nevertheless, their purpose always remains the same: to unveil and 'awaken' the world.

Several theories arose about the content of the masks as well as numerous 'experiments' proving there is something terrifying hidden inside or on them, which were recorded and presented as facts. The masks supposedly contained sim cards giving signals of the location of the user, or they had small worm-like microchips on them meant to be inhaled by the user, revealed only when placed over boiling water making them move. Inevitably several such experiments proving their existence were uploaded online as evidence[13].

The next scientific method of dealing with the pandemic was to conduct tests. These were, of course, also, fought against with scientific-like argumentation. The purpose of placing the cotton swab in people's nostrils was considered to be a way to 'reset' their brains and make them obedient by pressing firmly on a spot behind the sinusitis. This is the epiphysis, a real endocrine gland, but with different functions than the ones supposed. The use of this practice is known to mankind, so evidences are drowned from historic sources (as shown in figure 9).

When the vaccination was introduced, however, things evolved radically. Even the beginning of the debate over developing a vaccine provoked a variety of reactions. Although rational-looking reservations about the vaccinations continued to circulate online[14], based on scattered and unrelated medical terminology (i.e., its consistence and the mRNA[15], magnetism generated by the vaccine, and so on[16]), a connection to religious matters arouse, also, rapidly.

The concept of "conspiracy theories" begins with Popper's studies on the "conspiracy theory of society". He associates this position with the results of the secularization of religious prejudices. According to Popper (1945), modern conspiracy discourse is a consequence of the magical and religious thought that emerged through the secularization process. It is the outcome of the reinvestment of aspects

Figure 5. The masks are killing!!!! German scientific research on 22,930 students confirms. The average time of using the mask was 270 minutes a day. Diseases caused by the usage of the mask were reported by 68% of parents. Symptoms included headache (53%), difficulty in concentrating (50%), less euphoria (49%), discomfort (42%), learning disabilities (38%) and drowsiness or fatigue (37%).

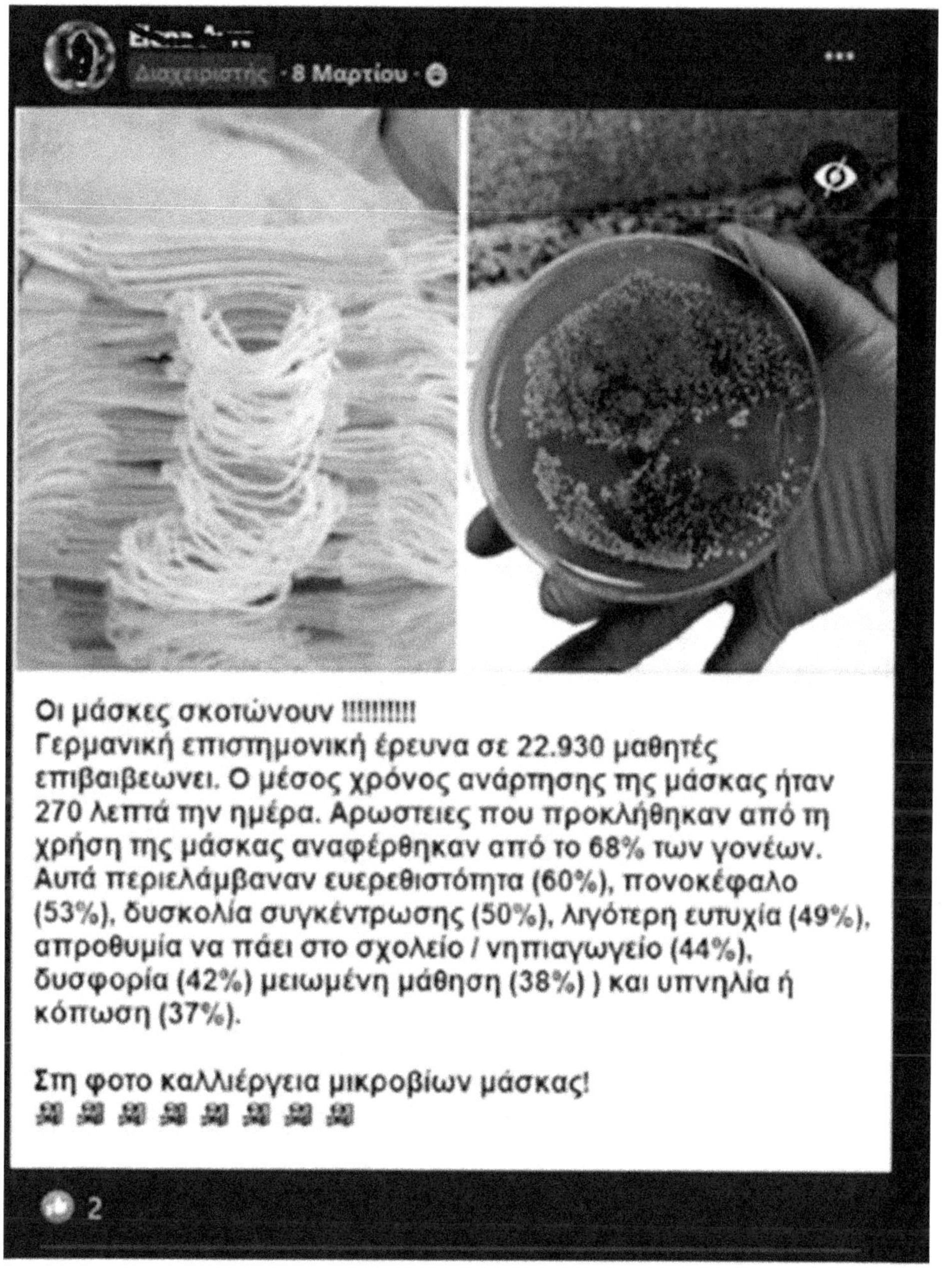

of the Christian symbolic system and the weakening of religion as a method of social control (Taguieff, 2016, pp.115-116). The connection of CTs with religious reason, though, is the result of yet another cause. In the -negatively- globalized society, non-religious issues are frequently expressed in terms of

Figure 6. A text that was posted largely on Facebook by those who denied the use of facemasks explaining the reasons: I'm not sick. Masks reduce oxygen uptake. Germs are trapped near the nose and mouth. There is no scientific evidence to suggest that healthy people should wear masks. Wearing a mask is a sign of submission and deprivation of freedom. https://rb.gy/4o3w3j.

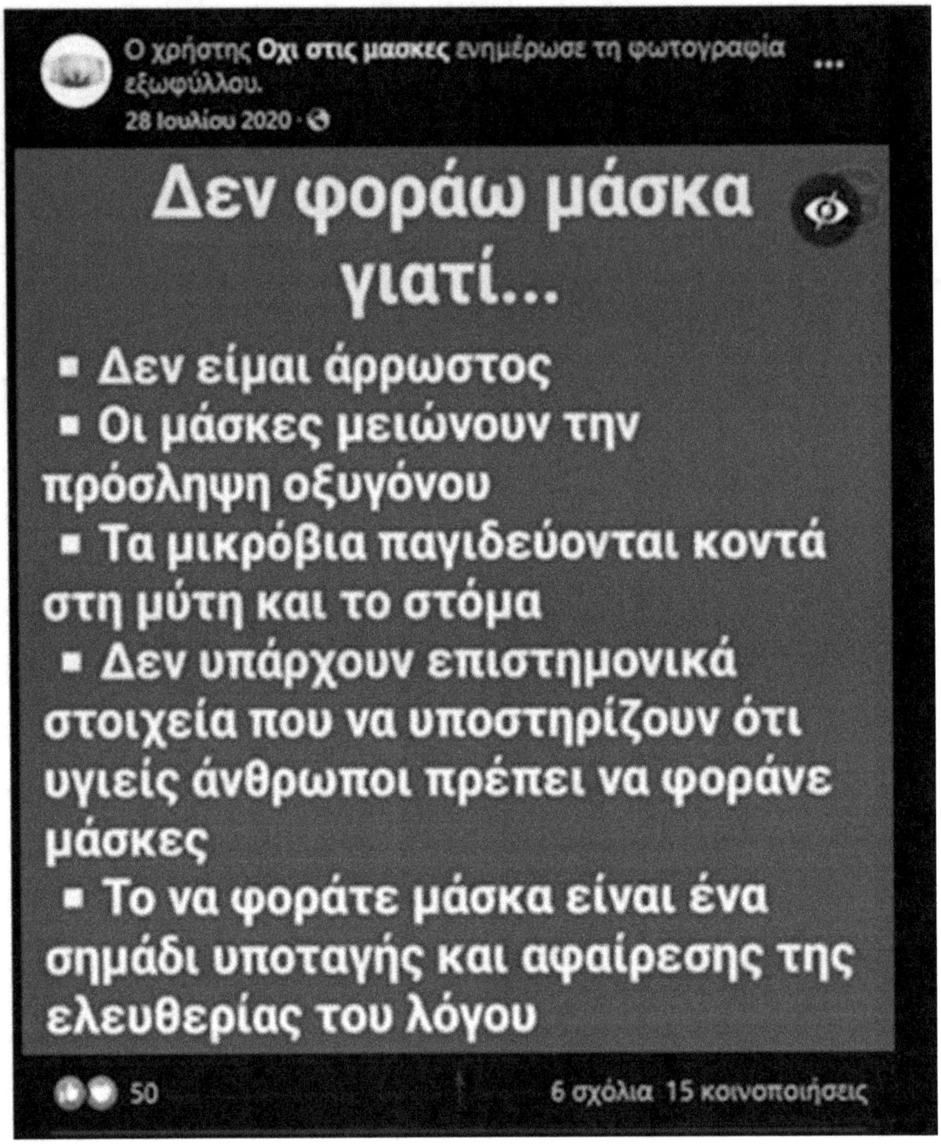

"religious awakening," and secular ideological manifestations of resistance have been substituted by religious ideological formulations. Political discourse, therefore, flows towards the Manichaean call to arms against fraudulent - almost satanic - forces that threaten the world and force humanity to confront good and evil, life and death (Bauman, 2007, pp.150-152).

This 'position' resulting from the literal interpretation of some religious texts has taken on great proportions in the collective fantasy and has been combined with CTs about reality. The 'mark of the beast' is one like this. In the book of *Revelation* there is the prophecy that before the return of Jesus, a

Figure 7. The 'I do not know why my baby has respiratory problems' now has an explanation. https://rb.gy/dkez8i.

world dictator known as the Antichrist will rise to power and reign for seven years. He will overthrow all religions and impose on the world the worship of himself. In order to wield complete economic and political dominance, he and his prime minister, whom the book of *Revelation* refers to as a "false prophet," will apply the "mark of the beast."

The connection, therefore, with the 'mark of the beast[17]' (which in Greek is the 'mark of antichrist' and is called *'haragma'- engraving*) prevails amongst their subjects and is explained through prophecies

Figure 8. What does the vaccine cause to people according to a doctor from the USA, who is recognised as an expert only by being a doctor https://rb.gy/mgnndx

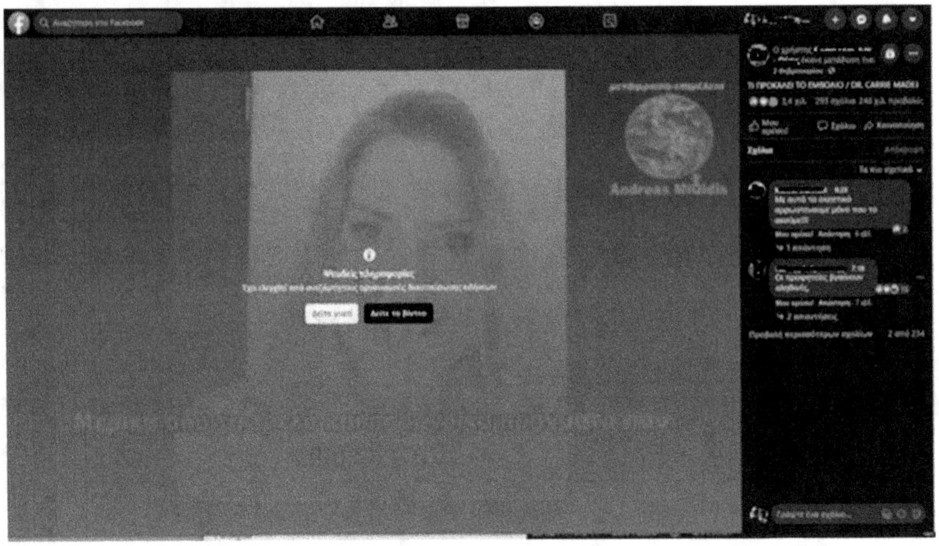

Figure 9. The suppression of the epiphyseal gland (Epiphysis) of slaves to remain submissive has been a known practice for thousands of years. Those who do not remember, the past will be repeated. The use of the cotton swab in the nose comes from ancient times where the Egyptians did exactly the same to the slaves to always keep them faithful without revolting .... what exactly happens in the year 2021 .... the cotton of the swab used in the COVID-tests is impregnated with epoxy caustic substance which burns the most important point of the encephalitis the neutral pituitary gland ... it is located in the centre of the forehead in between and a little above the eyebrows ... the so-called third eye .... (https://rb.gy/wjmgla)

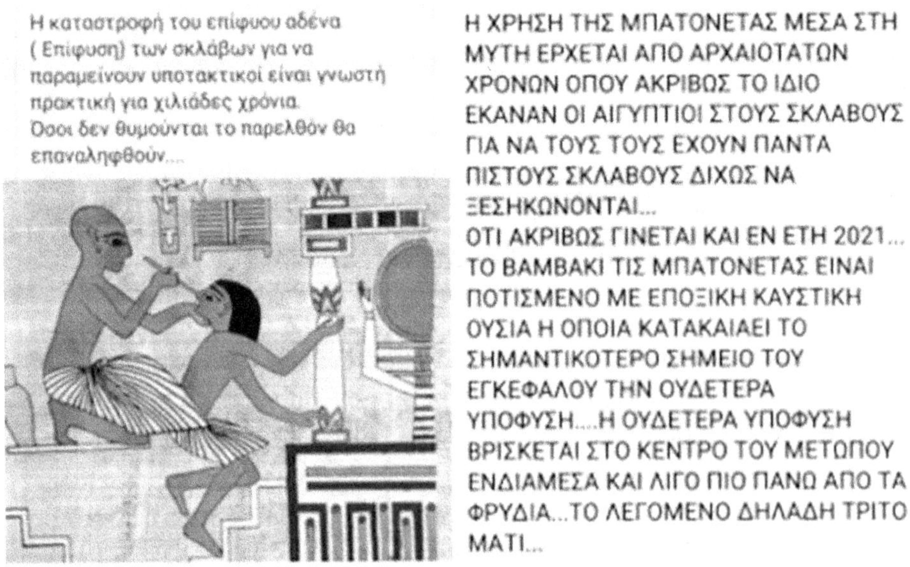

Figure 10. A post describing that in Italy vaccinated people who died have turned into zombies.

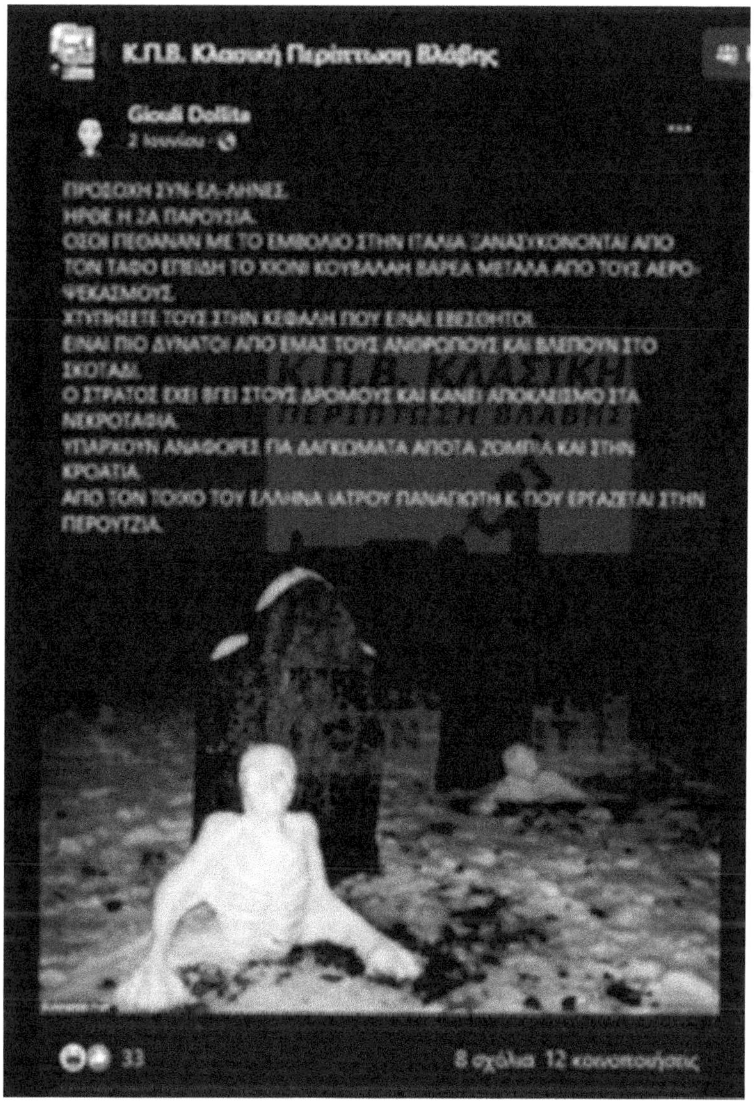

given by ‘new saints’, and low-ranking or even some high-ranking clergy and monks[18]. In fact, according to a recent study by one of the doctors from the National Pandemic Management Committee (N. Tzanakis, https://rb.gy/dgep4l), 11% of those who are not vaccinated and refuse to do so cite religious reasons for their refusal.

Taguieff (2015, pp.67-68) incorporates these CTs into the man’s attempt to interpret the unknown or what is not easily comprehended and approached. In this endeavour, loans from the magical-religious way of thinking are utilised- since they are familiar to people. As a result, CTs can be viewed as a continuation of magic, which has been adapted to the attributes of modernity.

There were objections against the masks as well, particularly when they were required to be worn within churches, or when the state required priests to use separate spoons for Holy Communion. These

Figure 11. Revelation of John: (13-17) 'and that no one can sell anything apart from Him who has the mark or the name of the beast or the number of his name'

acts, however, were considered as an attack to the church by the state and an attempt to impose itself, using the pandemic as an excuse.

The attack against the vaccine, though, had nothing to do with the issues of 'earthly' power and control. It was immediately perceived as the Evil's newest attempt to enslave the masses. Thus, the new way to be 'marked by the beast'.

What looks to be the menacing feature of the vaccine, the source of this worry, is most likely the fact that it is something injected into the body. It is conceded unnatural to interfere with the body, which must be kept as 'pure' as possible, closer to its genuine form[19].

The explanations given regarding the negative effects of vaccines focus mainly on the loss of human quantities[20]. If mankind was made in image and likeness of God, it loses its connection to its creator when it transforms into something else (according to some ideas, 'into a machine,') and becomes therefore, pray to His opponent. According to one idea, there will be seven vaccine shots, each of which will strike a significant blow to humanity. In Greek folklore, the number seven is said to be 'magical,' and in this case, it is a clear analogy to the seven 'sacraments of the church' (see figure 14). So, it seems that even

Figure 12. 'We refuse the use of masks!! They closed down the churches before, but now we will not allow them to even humiliate them.' A poster circulating the internet referring to the first lockdown, when all temples were closed along with any other place related to commercial or other kind of activity.

- or especially – unproven matters of faith and religion are isolated from the context in which they are placed and incorporated into theories that are believed to exist. They are warped or distorting theories that turn into a 'realistic' interpretation of historical events, with which they are connected, combined

Figure 13. In the vaccination certificate there is the number of the beast....666 !!!The marking of Anti-christ!!!! (https://rb.gy/m0k99j)

and they, ultimately, advocate a new causality in the world's historical trajectory. This interpretive method tends to produce narrative structures that stem from contemporary cultural beliefs combined with previously held beliefs and values that are constantly renegotiated. So, the resulting narrative forms (rumours, legends, and CTs) incorporate patterns that are already present in folk narratives, preserving the pre-existing value system or key features (Konstantopoulou, 2011, pp. 24-28).

These are not accepted by the official Greek Christian Orthodox church because they are folk beliefs (*lore*). Therefore, the church reacted by printing a flier (figure 15) supporting the vaccination program

Figure 14. The first and second vaccine-dose is about tracing the one that got it. The third and forth is to get the person tuned to a specific frequency. 5G will help in this. The fifth and sixth dose is to direct the person to specific actions. The seventh dose is a DNA change. The installments are seven like the ecclesiastical sacraments, this is not accidental! (https://rb.gy/lqm4so)

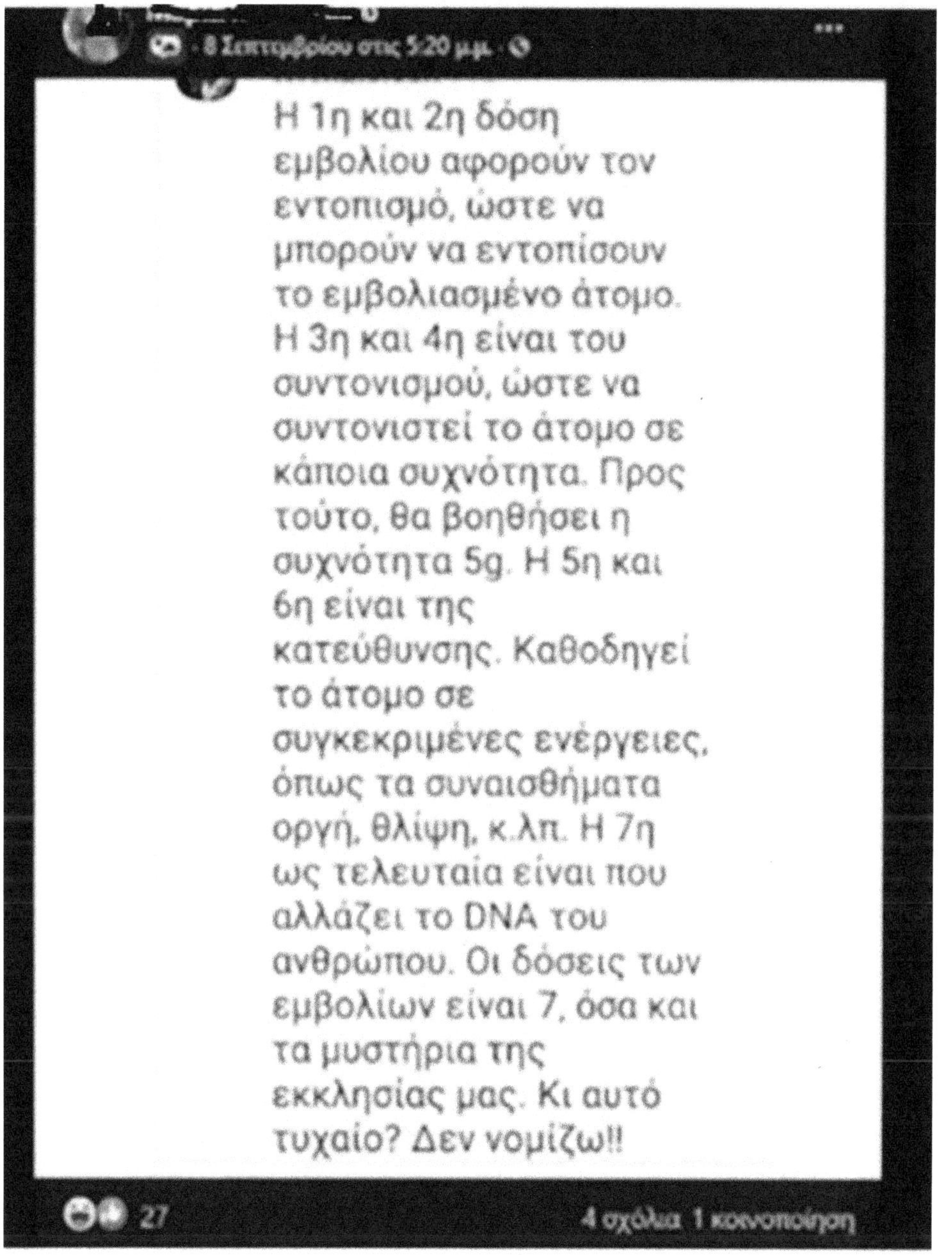

and encouraging religious people to get vaccinated, as an attempt to clarify that there is no connection between vaccination and faith.

Despite the antivaccine movement connected to religious matters, another explanation for what triggered these theories seems to be the way the pandemic was fought against through political decisions

Figure 15. This is the text the church issued to promote and support the vaccination; it came out on July 2021

ΙΕΡΑ ΣΥΝΟΔΟΣ ΤΗΣ ΕΚΚΛΗΣΙΑΣ ΤΗΣ ΕΛΛΑΔΟΣ

ΠΡΟΣ ΤΟΝ ΛΑΟ

ΟΙ ΧΡΙΣΤΙΑΝΟΙ ΜΑΣ ΡΩΤΟΥΝ
ΓΙΑ ΤΟ ΕΜΒΟΛΙΟ
ΚΑΙ ΟΙ ΓΙΑΤΡΟΙ ΜΑΣ ΑΠΑΝΤΟΥΝ

Κατά τή συνεδρίαση τῆς Διαρκοῦς Ἱερᾶς Συνόδου τῆς Τρίτης 13ης Ἰουλίου 2021 προσῆλθαν ὁ Ὑπουργός Ὑγείας κ. Βασίλειος Κικίλιας καί ὁ Καθηγητής τῆς Ἰατρικῆς Σχολῆς κ. Σωτήριος Τσιόδρας, πρός τούς ὁποίους ὁ Μακαριώτατος Ἀρχιεπίσκοπος Ἀθηνῶν καί πάσης Ἑλλάδος κ. Ἱερώνυμος καί οἱ Σεβασμιώτατοι Συνοδικοί Ἀρχιερεῖς ἔθεσαν πολλά ἐρωτήματα τόσο γιά τήν πορεία τῆς πανδημίας, ὅσο καί γιά τή χρήση τῶν νέων ἐμβολίων κατά τῆς COVID-19, ἐκφράζοντας προβληματισμούς καί ἀπορίες Κληρικῶν καί λαϊκῶν χριστιανῶν, μελῶν τῆς Ἐκκλησίας τῆς Ἑλλάδος.

Τά ἐρωτήματα ἐστάλησαν καί γραπτῶς καί ἀπαντήθηκαν ἀρμοδίως. Ὡς ἐκ τούτου, ἀποστέλλονται ἀκολούθως πρός ἐνημέρωση τοῦ ἱεροῦ Κλήρου καί τοῦ πιστοῦ Λαοῦ τῆς Ἐκκλησίας τῆς Ἑλλάδος:

1 *Ἔχω κάνει καί τίς δύο δόσεις τοῦ ἐμβολίου. Στήν περίπτωση αὐτή, τί προστασία ἔχω ἀπό τή μετάλλαξη «Δέλτα»;*

Ὅλα τά ἐμβόλια (Pfizer, Moderna, Astra Zeneca, Johnson & Johnson) προσφέρουν ὑψηλή προστασία γιά τήν ἀποφυγή σοβαρῆς νόσησης, διασωλήνωσης καί θανάτου, ὅπως καί γιά τήν πιθανότητα νά νοσήσει κάποιος καί νά μπεῖ στό νοσοκομεῖο. Ἡ ὑψηλή αὐτή προστασία ἰσχύει καί γιά τή μετάλλαξη «Δέλτα».

2 *Ἐφόσον ἔχω κάνει καί τίς δύο δόσεις τοῦ ἐμβολίου, θά χρειαστεῖ ὕστερα*

Ἡ Ἐκκλησία μιλάει στά παιδιά της μέ τήν γλώσσα τῆς Εὐθύνης, τῆς Ἀληθείας καί τῆς Ἀγάπης

53

that were imposed abruptly and strictly. Thus, some people already feeling marginalised or ignored by their governments appear to have found an easy way to express their frustration. They do not oppose significant political decisions made by these governments, such as labour rights, since they feel powerless. They retaliate for all the mistreatment by refusing to support their government when asking for their 'assistance' (Douglas, 2021, p.271). That means, they refuse to get vaccinated as a means of resistance.

Nevertheless, using the internet to promote these views seems to have been difficult, as every post on the surface and deep web containing phrases related to the pandemic, such as the word "vaccine", were automatically censored. However, such reports are 'censored' in the internet environment and were either downloaded or negatively characterized by it as fake news. Consequently, to avoid the internet's censorship, the words used in these posts had to be disconnected from the pandemic terminology, thus, for instance, several letters were substituted by symbols in the term 'vaccine'[21] and the word 'graft' (boli[22]) was subsequently used instead the word vaccine. This, however, could be, also, interpreted as an attempt to underestimate it or demonstrate its nefarious intent to modify mankind, similar to what happens when a tree is grafted.

Figure 16 Chats amongst members of anti-vaccine Facebook groups, in which the opposing opinion to the vaccine is promoted as the prevailing feature that binds them together. (https://rb.gy/bi3s5f, https://rb.gy/fvd9ax)

THE INTERNET USERS' PERCEPTION OF THESE THEORIES

The subject matters of these theories have been disgusted, adopted and reproduced, or rejected and criticised by the internet users, transferring the polarization that prevails in every sector of social interaction on the topic of the pandemic to the internet. Those who believe in, defend and reproduce the content of pandemic CTs frequently remark in groups or websites where these subjects are commonly accepted. Thus, they share or repost them in order to become or remain a part of a broader group in which they belong and feel secure (Douglas, 2021, p.271, Graeupner & Coman, 2017, pp.218-222), and which they feed back with information on concerns already known and commonly accepted. People are more likely to believe in CTs if they need to stand out from the crowd (Lantian et al., 2017), have a strong desire to belong somewhere (Graeupner & Coman, 2017), or sense their group is underappreciated (Cichocka et al., 2016) or threatened (Jolley et al., 2018).

In this way not only they reinforce their own belief, but the link they form by banding together behind e.g. vaccination opposition, also serves as the connecting point needed to form a group (Dundes, 1980, p.6). The public and open promotion of such ideas is done with full awareness that it will cause a rift with other users who discard them. Despite the risk, however, is it carried out with rather an altruistic purpose. So, these theories are communicated by their supporters in order to awaken other deceived human beings to recognise the lies and become part of the 'resistance'. CTs assume their position in politics

Figure 17. There is no virus

by clearly distinguishing between the identities attributed to 'friend' (i.e., 'us') and 'enemy' (threatening 'other'), resulting in either oversimplified or misconstrued perceptions of events (Taguieff, 2016, p.61).

There are two types of reactions to these notions: Either they are attacked as dangerous or they are derided for being insane.

It's just a flue

Only vaccinated people are getting it

I am dead

How does a person believing in CTs sees himself/ How the rest of the world sees them..

CONSPIRACY THEORIES AS INTERNET MEMES

The most intense and creative reaction to the radical opinions of those promoting the CTs among the internet users is reacting to them through memes.

It is not uncommon for narrative genres that elicit belief in their material (e.g., urban legends) to change function depending on whether or not the 'narrator' believes in it. As a result, they are easily turned into jokes (Smith, 1997, p.494, Clarke, 2008, 2002, pp.131-150). This seems to be yet another such example. Therefore, various posts or comments by internet users expressing conspiracies as personal opinions or supporting them as facts are transmitted and reposted as memes by other users who do not believe those theories are true.

As a kind of multimedia digital popular lore, memes tend to emerge in online environments, criticizing or commenting on attitudes and behaviours, as well as current issues (Blank, 2012, pp.1-24.

Figure 18. Memes out of posts on the theories for the vaccine (https://rb.gy/x9qaap)

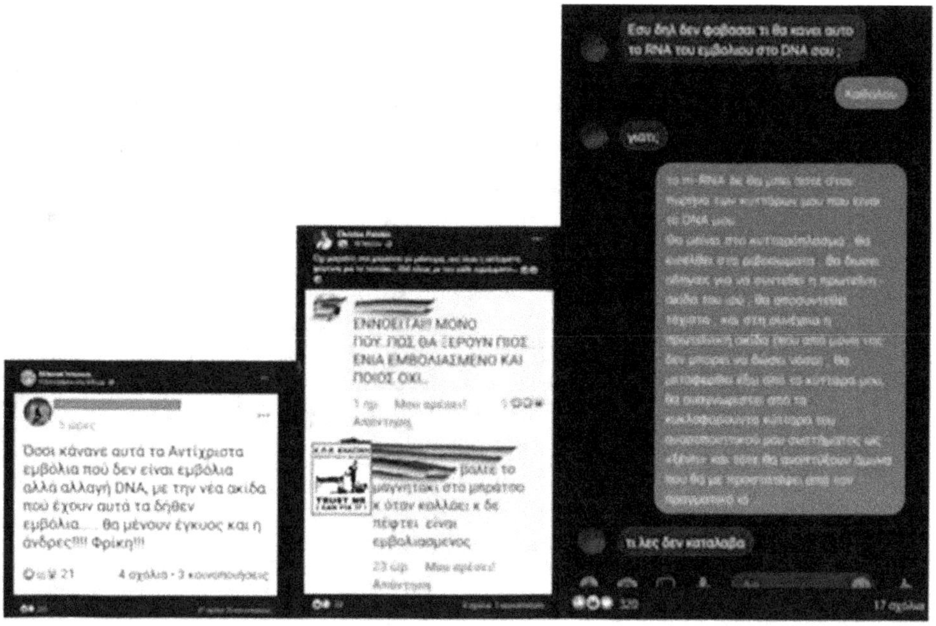

Katsadoros & Nounanaki, 2021, pp.389-432). In fact, not many conditions need to be met for a digital item to be called a meme. Essentially, the term "meme" tends to be used for any specimen of online humour (Dynel, 2021, p.179).

Making a meme by publishing a chat topic that appears 'worthy' of becoming a meme, or simply a comment that internet users have put somewhere online, has become a widespread activity. In fact, the names and avatars of users are sometimes being erased or hidden, so that no one gets stigmatised for their opinions, but nothing else gets censored.

Turning this kind of posts into memes is the most straight forward way to express opposition to the opinions expressed in those chats and comments.

These kind of chats and posts that were turned into memes are sometimes labelled by those who post them. For example, you can see here (figure 19) a post by a woman, 'famous' on social media for her edgy opinions, being labelled 'high priestess of the *pseks*' (this is short for '*ψεκασμένοι*', 'sprayed', a 'name' that is given to those who believe in CTs since the most well-known and common one is about *Chemtrails*[23]).

But it is not just the uptake of these conspiracies that is being sharply rendered. The CTs themselves are also being commented on through memes, as, for example, the constructed 'image' (figure 20) in which several different theories are combined. More precisely, it is a plane belonging to Bill Gates that has a 5G antenna on it, with an immigrant pilot, 'spraying' Chemtrails and vaccine ingredients, including, of course, microchips, while flying over flat Earth.

Figure 19. "The high priestess of the 'pseks' strikes again with a new Facebook profile" (https://rb.gy/62nyco)

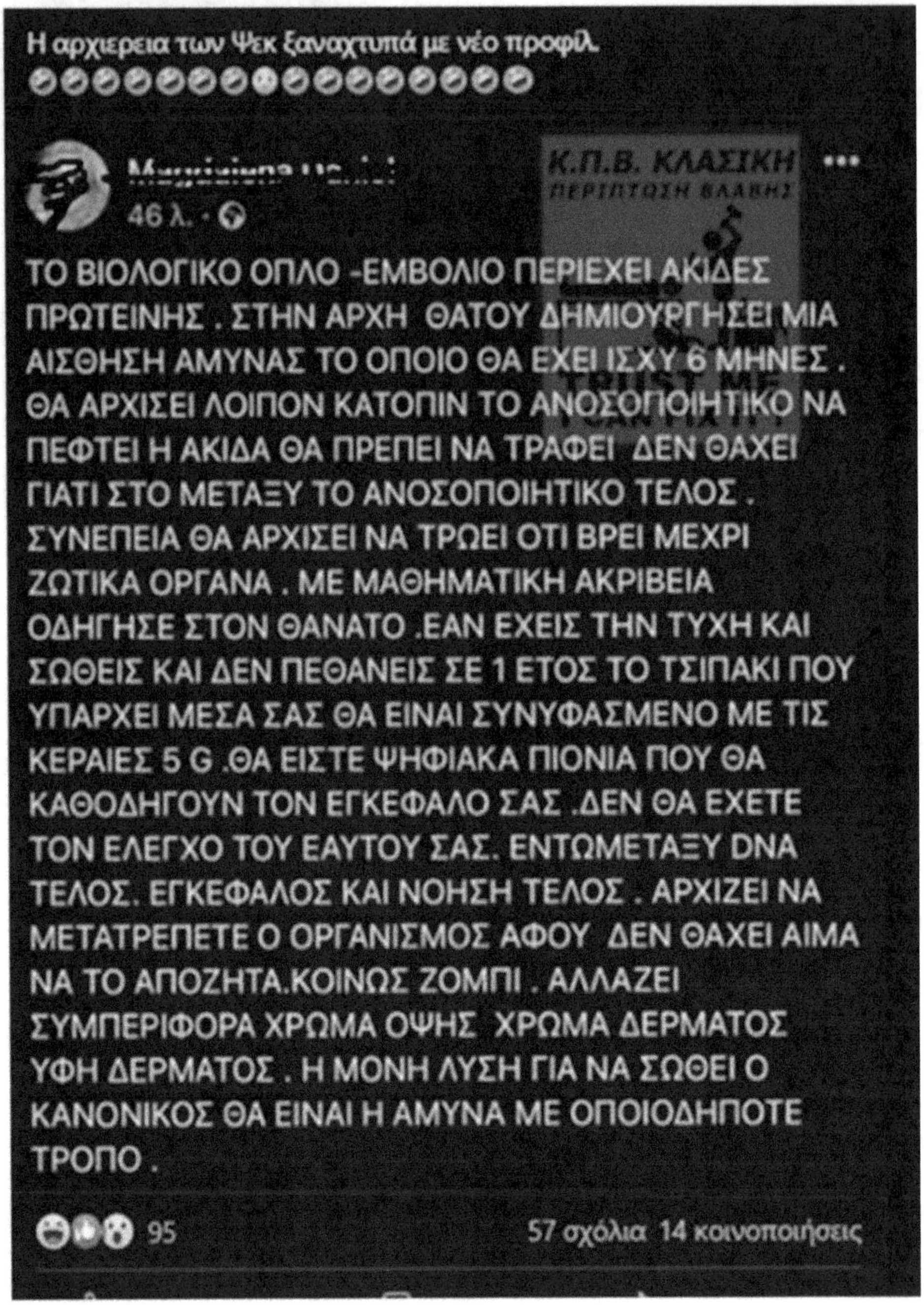

Figure 20. 5G flying antennas driven by migrant pilots' spraying aluminium, barium and ilithium (a pun with the word lithium that carries an 'I' in front, which turns into the Greek word meaning 'idiot') and launching chips in all directions, while flying over flat terrain. Of course, it is owned by Bill Gates. (https://rb.gy/4dry1t)

CONCLUSION

The purpose of the present paper was to highlight the spread of CTs on the COVID-19 pandemic through the internet and their uptake by the internet users. The internet provides endless opportunities to express opinions and draw conclusions based on personal 'research' into a wide range of information. It provides a wealth of information and the facility to accompany every opinion with 'proof' that verifies it too. CTs are thus pushed as established facts and accurate information.

The examination of the topic content, substance, and structure of CTs yielded several conclusions. They seem to incorporate themes, concepts and feelings from a peculiar modern fantasy, such as the quest for supremacy, the fear of lacking social and political control in everyday life, the future of religion, and the inability to regulate and predict destructive impulses, among others. Their topics ultimately reflect the diverse ways in which some people perceive and intend to comprehend the world (Thomas, 1979: pp.83-88). CTs are, in the end, man's simplistic attempt to explain the 'dark course' of the world he lives, despite the fact it leads to a 'chimerical' reality (Taguieff, 2015, pp.175-176).

In terms of the influence of Coronavirus CTs and their intake by internet users, it has emerged that, despite the fears that are promoted via those on the internet, a loud voice of opposition to CTs and reason is, also, bursting out of the interaction among internet users. Users contribute to the pluralism of the internet (also described as 'democracy') by sharing humorous memes that satirize CTs, expressing their views on current events through public discourse on socio-political problems. Memes, which in this case focus on contemporary social and political topics, are thus a way of communicating important knowledge and viewpoints on the subject. This condition demonstrates the creation of 'groups' by internet users, which are largely driven by a shared value system. As a consequence, turning conspiracy-related posts into memes reflects a dismissive attitude toward their original content (Dynel, 2021, pp.175-179).

In a nutshell, CTs thrive on the internet due to the facilities the latter provides to its users, both as an endless source of information but, also, as a platform for free expression. It is also a 'place' where users can connect with others who share the same worldview or fears, but, also, with people who reject the same modern attitudes. As a result, groups are formed both by users who react positively towards the CTs on the pandemic, and those who respond negatively to them.

REFERENCES

Aeronovitch, D. (2010). *Voodoo Histories: The role of the Conspiracy Theory in Shaping Modern History*. Riverhead Books.

Bauman, Z. (2006). *Liquid Fear*. Polity Press.

Blank, T. (2009). *Folklore and the Internet: Vernacular Expression in the Digital World*. Utah State University Press. doi:10.2307/j.ctt4cgrx5

Blank, T. (2012). Pattern in the Virtual Folk Culture of Computer-Mediated Communication. In T. Blank (Ed.), *Folk Culture in the Digital Age* (pp. 1–24). Utah State University Press. doi:10.7330/9780874218909.c00

Bodner, J., Welch, W., & Brodie, I. (2021). *COVID-19 Conspiracy Theories QAnon, 5G, the New World Order and Other Viral Ideas*. McFarland & Company, Inc., Publishers Press.

Brednich, R. (2001). *Where They Originated... Some Contemporary Legends and Their Literary Origins.* Paper presented at ISCLR Congress, Melbourne, Australia. https://www.folklore.ee/folklore/vol20/legends.pdf

Budka, Ph. (2011). *From Cyber to Digital Anthropology to an Anthropology of the Contemporary?* https://pdfs.semanticscholar.org/ac2c/2652a560a824eb5c1a919058e13154382376.pdf

Butter, M., & Knight, P. (2018). The History of Conspiracy Theory Research. A Review and Commentary. In J. E. Uscinski (Ed.), *Conspiracy Theories and the People Who Believe Them.* Oxford University. doi:10.1093/oso/9780190844073.003.0002

Campion-Vincent, V. (2007). Rumors and Urban Legends. *Diogenes, 54*(1), 162–199. doi:10.1177/0392192107073437

Cichocka, A., Marchlewska, M., & Golec de Zavala, A. (2016). Does self-love or self-hate predict conspiracy beliefs? Narcissism, self-esteem and the endorsement of conspiracy theories. *Social Psychological & Personality Science, 7*(2), 157–166. doi:10.1177/1948550615616170

Clarke, St. (2002). Conspiracy Theories and Conspiracy Theorising. *Philosophy of the Social Sciences, 32*(2), 131–150. doi:10.1177/004931032002001

Dégh, L. (1994). *American Folklore and the Mass Media.* Indiana University Press.

Douglas, K. (2021). COVID-19 conspiracy theories. *Group Processes & Intergroup Relations, 24*(2), 270–275. doi:10.1177/1368430220982068

Douglas, K. M., Sutton, R. M., Callan, M., Dawtry, R., & Harvey, A. (2016). Someone is pulling the strings: Hypersensitive agency detection and belief in conspiracy theories. *Thinking & Reasoning, 22*(1), 57–77. doi:10.1080/13546783.2015.1051586

Douglas, K. M., Sutton, R. M., & Cichocka, A. (2017). The psychology of conspiracy theories. *Current Directions in Psychological Science, 26*(6), 538–542. doi:10.1177/0963721417718261 PMID:29276345

Douglas, K. M., Uscinski, J. E., Sutton, R. M., Cichocka, A., Nefes, T., Ang, C. S., & Deravi, F. (2019). Understanding conspiracy theories. *Political Psychology, 40*(S1), 3–35. doi:10.1111/pops.12568

Dundes, A. (1980). *Interpreting Folklore.* Indiana University Press.

Dynel, M. (2021). COVID-19 memes going viral: On the multiple multimodal voices behind face masks. *Discourse & Society, 32*(2), 175–195. doi:10.1177/0957926520970385

Ellis, B. (2001). A Model for Collecting and Interpreting World Trade Centre Disaster Jokes. *Newfolk: New Directions in Folklore, 5*, 1-10. https://scholarworks.iu.edu/journals/index.php/ndif/article/view/19881/25963

Fenster, M. (2008). Conspiracy Theories: Secrecy and Power in American Culture. University of Minneapolis Press.

Fine, G. A., & Ellis, B. (2010). *The Global Grapevine: Why Rumors of Terrorisms, Immigration and Trade Matter.* Oxford University Press. doi:10.1093/acprof:oso/9780199736317.001.0001

Fuchs, C. (2021). *Bill Gates Conspiracy Theories as Ideology in the Context of the COVID-19 Crisis. In Communicating COVID-19*. Emerald Publishing Limited. doi:10.1108/978-1-80117-720-720211007

Gasouka, M., & Foulidi, X. (2012). *Contemporary Horizons of Folklore Studies. Conceptual Framework, Research, Gender, Internet, School [Σύγχρονοι ορίζοντες των λαογραφικών σπουδών. Εννοιολογικό πλαίσιο, έρευνα, φύλο, διαδίκτυο, σχολείο]*. I. Sideris.

Gasouka, M., & Foulidi, X. (2017). *Aspects of ethnographic research in folklore studies. Feminist Ethnography - Internet Ethnography [Όψεις Εθνογραφικής Έρευνας στις Λαογραφικές Σπουδές. Φεμινιστική Εθνογραφία- Διαδικτυακή Εθνογραφία]*. Papazisis.

Goldzwig, S. R. (2002). Conspiracy Rhetoric at the Dawn of New Millennium: A Response. *Western Journal of Communication*, *66*(4), 492–506. doi:10.1080/10570310209374751

Graeupner, D., & Coman, A. (2017). The dark side of meaning-making: How social exclusion leads to superstitious thinking. *Journal of Experimental Social Psychology*, *69*, 218–222. doi:10.1016/j.jesp.2016.10.003

Heft, A., & Buehling, K. (2022). Measuring the diffusion of conspiracy theories in digital information ecologies. *Convergence*, 1–22. doi:10.1177/13548565221091809

Hofstadter, R. (1996). *The Paranoid Style in American Politics and Other Essays*. Harvard University Press. (Original work published 1965)

Jolley, D., Douglas, K. M., & Sutton, R. M. (2018). Blaming a few bad apples to save a threatened barrel: The system-justifying function of conspiracy theories. *Political Psychology*, *39*(2), 465–478. doi:10.1111/pops.12404

Kapaniaris, A., & Varvounis, M. (2019). Social networking and communication tools in archive ethnography: Tools for collecting, displaying and recording material or digital research notebooks? *WWJMRD*, *5*(5), 11–18.

Katsadoros, G. (2013). The science of folklore in the modern technological age. Electronic orality [Η επιστήμη της λαογραφίας στη σύγχρονη τεχνολογική εποχή. Η ηλεκτρονική προφορικότητα]. In Education Sciences. From the weak classification of Pedagogy to interdisciplinarity and scientific hybridization [Επιστήμες της εκπαίδευσης. Από την ασθενή ταξινόμηση της Παιδαγωγικής στη διεπιστημονικότητα και στον επιστημονικό υβριδισμό]. Αθήνα: Παιδαγωγικό Τμήμα Δημοτικής Εκπαίδευσης Πανεπιστημίου Αιγαίου και Ταξιδευτής.

Katsadoros, G., & Nounanaki, A. (2021). The image of the Pontians in digital folklore: The case of memes. *Popular Tradition of Pontus: from the Past to the Present. Proceedings of the International Scientific Conference of Folklore*, 389-432.

Konstantopoulou, Ch. (2011). *Symbols, Archetypes and phobias. Introduction to the sociology of the imaginary* [Σύμβολα, Αρχέτυπα και φοβίες. Εισαγωγή στην κοινωνιολογία του φαντασιακού]. Αθήνα: Εκδόσεις Παπαζήση.

Kozinets, R. V. (2020). *Netnography: The Essential Guide to Qualitative Social Media Research*. Sage. doi:10.4324/9781003001430

Krawczyk-Wasilewska, V. (2016). *Folklore in the Digital Age: Collected Essays*. University of Łodź.

Lantian, A., Muller, D., Nurra, C., & Douglas, K. M. (2017). "I know things they don't know!": The role of need for uniqueness in belief in conspiracy theories. *Social Psychology, 48*(3), 160–173. doi:10.1027/1864-9335/a000306

Lialina, O., & Espenschied, D. (Eds.). (2009). *Digital Folklore. To Computers Users with Love and Respect*. Merz & Solitude.

Önnerfors, A. (2021). Conspiracy theories and COVID-19: The mechanisms behind a rapidly growing societal challenge. The Swedish Civil Contingencies Agency (MSB).

Popper, K. R. (1945). *The open society & its enemies*. Routledge.

Shahsavari, S., Holur, P., Tangherlini, T. R., & Roychowdhury, V. (2020). Conspiracy in the time of corona: Automatic detection of covid-19 conspiracy theories in social media and the news. *Journal of Computational Social Science, 3*(2), 279–317. doi:10.100742001-020-00086-5 PMID:33134595

Smith, P. (1997). Contemporary Legend. In Th. A. Green (Ed.), *Folklore: An Encyclopedia of belief, customs, tales, music and art* (pp. 493–495). ABC-CLIO.

Taguieff, P. A. (2016). Court traité de complotologie. Paris: Fayard.

Thomas, L. V. (1978). *Civilisation et Divagation*. Payot.

Thompson, T. (2012). Netizens, Revolutionaries, and the Inalienable Right to the Internet. In T. Blank (Ed.), *Folk Culture in the Digital Age* (pp. 46–59). Utah State University Press. doi:10.7330/9780874218909.c02

Van Prooijen, J.-W., & Douglas, K. M. (2017). Conspiracy theories as a part of history: The role of societal crisis situations. *Memory Studies, 10*(3), 323–333. doi:10.1177/1750698017701615 PMID:29081831

Van Prooijen, J.-W., Douglas, K. M., & de Inocencio, C. (2018). Connecting the dots: Pattern perception predicts belief in conspiracies and the supernatural. *European Journal of Social Psychology, 48*(3), 320–335. doi:10.1002/ejsp.2331 PMID:29695889

Varvounis, M., & Kapaniaris, A. (2019). Archival ethnography & interpretations in the digital environment: 'conversing' with the archives of the 'Pelioritians in Egypt': The planning of a long-term research [Αρχειακή εθνογραφία & αναγνώσεις σε ψηφιακό περιβάλλον: «συνομιλώντας» με τα αρχεία των «Πηλιορειτών εν Αιγύπτω»: Ο σχεδιασμός μιας μακροχρόνιας έρευνας]. *Εκκλησιαστικός Φάρος Επιστημονικόν Θεολογικόν Περιοδικόν Σύγγραμμα του Πατριαρχείου Αλεξάνδρας και πάσης Αφρικής. Τόμος ΠΖ΄-ΠΗ΄*, (2018-2019), 113–146.

ENDNOTES

1 Therefore, their subject matter changed following and interpreting historical and political developments. That is, until World War II, imaginary conspiracies were launched against religious and political figures. After the War, conspirators were located within or behind governments, while their victims were the manipulative masses (Taguieff, 2015, p.61). Since the 1990s, a new con-

spiracy theory has been developed against the so-called "New World Order" or, as the emic term is, the "New Order of Things". So, their themes revolve eventually around anti-globalization and the devilishness of international financial capital (Taguieff, 2015, p.62). Towards the middle of the 20th century the delinquent or criminal groups, which were the main perpetrators of the conspiracy theories, were gradually replaced by governments, their secret services and the media that are considered to be at the service of governments for the manipulation of the masses (Taguieff, 2015, p.118).

2 Several Greek scholars started researching this field. See, as an example, Gasouka & Foulidi (2012), (2017).

3 Some of the keywords searched are: *theories + conspiracy + pandemic, coronavirus, real+ pandemic, vaccine, vaccine +haragma, boli, masks, dangerous + facemasks, what + are+they + hiding + coronavirus, population + reduction + pandemic, faith+pandemic.*

4 For all data about the pandemic see the official governmental webpage about the pandemic https://covid19.gov.gr/covid19-live-analytics/.
All webpages listed in this chapter have been last accessed on 28/4/2022.

5 The new world order, also known as the (emic) 'New Order of Things', is a controversial concept that was coined in the early 1990s. A conspiracy theorist views it as a "new form of the devil" or in general as the entanglement of the absolute evil that plots against human existence. This globalization is denounced as an inherently destructive process - that is why it finds a great response in nationalist circles and is integrated into their theory - which can be controlled by revealing those who conspire against 'us' (Taguieff, 2016, p.159). For this reason, nationalist politicians or 'orators' are attracted to the anti-global rhetoric of these theories and reproduce them (Taguieff, 2015, p.82).

6 See the article entitled: Pseudo-Messiah Bill Gates will save us from the pandemic! https://rb.gy/iykdcd
On this topic, see Fuchs (2021, pp.99-144).

7 See e.g., the article entitled Nurse crying: COVID does NOT kill people, people are killed in hospitals https://rb.gy/kvdrjb, and the one that states that: THEY KILL PEOPLE IN "ATTIKON" AND IN THE "COVID" INTENSIVE CARE UNITS AND TAKE 33,000+ EUROS FROM THE STATE FOR EACH KILLING. INCREDIBLE COMPLAINTS TO THE EARS OF "DEAF" PROSECUTORS. (https://rb.gy/aazaiv)

8 See e.g., a post that shows the picture of a woman and states that the woman on it died last night (January 9, 2021) at the hospital of Trikala. Relatives complain doctors were the ones killing her. There is a recording from a telephone communication as she secretly had a mobile phone with her. She can be clearly heard saying to her daughter: 'come and take me. They weighed me, they beat me and they tied me to the bed and they forcibly inject me against my will.' The relatives took the recording to the Sofades' police station where they were advised to go to a lawyer. (https://rb.gy/ibzwuf).

9 See for example the article entitled: HOAX KORONVIRUS: FALSE PANDEMIC VIRUS TO COVER THE GLOBAL SPREAD OF THE 5G SYNDROME (Video) (https://rb.gy/leyavy), or the one entitled: *the pandemic control of the masses*(https://rb.gy/etkvqs) Coronavirus: Another "pandemic" scam like the H1N1 in 2009 or are they going for population reduction"? "With this TERRORISM that they spread, it is certain that they are preparing a very fast MASS VACCINATION" (https://rb.gy/ogsvgc).

10 As referred to in the articles Snowden: The pandemic is a ploy to impose permanent surveillance measures (https://rb.gy/rgsgco), or Do we live in a worldwide biological war? Are we participating in a social engineering experiment? (hhttps://rb.gy/leyavy)

11 See also the video on YouTube entitled The morbid goal of cutting from the source https://rb.gy/ynrqdy, or the one entitled Coronavirus- goal is the reduction of the world population before the Global Government of the modern elite (https://rb.gy/cpf3hn).

12 They are also functioning as pseudo-sociologically, even as a corresponding pseudo-political science (Taguieff, 2016, p.16) that interprets conjunctural sequences at a social, historical or political level.

13 Such are, for example, videos uploaded mainly on YouTube that record every step of opening a mask and revealing its contents, like: *WHAT ARE THEY HIDDING INSIDE THE MASK!!!* (https://rb.gy/slidee) *Microchip in the masks...see what they are hiding from us!!!* (https://rb.gy/vdjfvu), P*ests on the masks* (https://rb.gy/w4haoc), M*orgellons in medical masks and PCR tests for Covid 19* (https://rb.gy/dp8h2s), M*orgellons and Morgellons fibres in medical masks. Worms (h*ttps://rb.gy/r1hwnn), D*O NOT WEAR A MASK AGAIN!!! Morgellons-parasites are hidden inside the masks!!!* (https://rb.gy/mpxt8d), experiment: showing the 'worms' move on a medical mask (https://rb.gy/fucgdg).

14 A short text that was posted from several users on the reason why people are asked to have a vaccination certificate, asking: Since it is a given that the vaccine does not stop the transmission of the virus, what exactly does the vaccination certificate certify? (https://rb.gy/dpxwn5).

15 See, RNA Technology of Nanovaccines (https://rb.gy/hhtn7h), Dr. Tal Zaks by MODERNA: How MRNA Works in the Human Body - Why It Is Called "The Software of Life" and How It Is "Hacked" (Video) (https://rb.gy/s9a1m5), etc.

16 People vaccinated against coronavirus are magnetizing objects (https://rb.gy/ujp9xy), and so on.

17 Religious way of thinking and cosmology actually feed conspiracy theories based on the 'reason' of such a religion and distort it by adapting it to specific current events or dystopian scenarios. A relevant example that flourished around 2017 on the Greek internet is the lore about the '*Haragma*'.

18 The connection of the vaccine to religious aspects is circulating both as personal opinions amongst internet users as well as 'facts' presented by some bigot webpages. See e.g., The Bishop of Morphou strikes again: The vaccine, the neo-taxis and the antichrist (https://rb.gy/bmg2v1), Ambrosios: The vaccine will be accompanied by the chip and the number 666 of the Antichrist (https://rb.gy/vx4b2b), Elder Efthymios: The compulsory vaccination (https://rb.gy/hxjnrq), Saint Paisios warns: Epidemics and vaccines will be used to impose a global anti-Christian government! (https://rb.gy/nem602), The carving (Haragma) of the Antichrist (by P. Elpidios) (https://rb.gy/70jequ), Saint Morphou: vaccine and Antichrist (https://rb.gy/ynam3o), "Confession of faith" in Agrinio: "Resist the Antichrist - Do not get any vaccine" (video) (https://rb.gy/kqi9oc), Path to the dawn - path to freedom in Christ and the Kingdom of God (https://rb.gy/hx7eaf), and so on.

19 Thus, the thing that was considered the 'haragma' before the vaccine were the tattoos. The negative reception to tattoos is also framed by social issues despite the religious ones.

20 See, for instance. the article on a Facebook page called *I choose NO in the Haragma of Revelation* (https://rb.gy/aa0g66) on which several aspects of this reasoning are being described.

21 See as an example the article titled *He got vaccinated and a few days later the Greek medicine student left his last breath*, where the word vaccinated is written using several symbols instead of letters like: Emβ%λι@στηκε (https://rb.gy/fc0nzh),

22 See the Facebook group *Fuck your vaccines...We are not getting the shot* ('boli') (https://rb.gy/rbp86g)

23 The theory that refers to governments, or other parties engaged in a secret program, adding toxic chemicals to the atmosphere from an aircraft in a way that forms visible plumes in the sky, somewhat similar to contrails. Various different motivations for this alleged spraying are speculated, including sterilization, reduction of life expectancy, mind control or weather control. See https://rb.gy/mkqkij.

Chapter 5
Digitization of Costume and Fashion Archives

Zoi Arvanitidou
University of Malta, Malta

ABSTRACT

A summary of the museum and archival practices related to the digital humanities should investigate whether they have promoted the digitization of clothing and fashion archives. At the time of the COVID-19 pandemic, widespread internet use was observed, and augmented reality technologies were applied. Since March 2020, fashion collection owners have intensified their digitization. There is a comprehensive discussion about virtual reports, which, using the tools provided by modern technology, create new forms of knowledge. Contemporary art is increasingly using folklore material as a source of inspiration to explore the relationships between tradition and innovation. All over the world, artists, scholars, and curators of exhibitions try to exhibit folklore archives. In this way, the curators experiment with new, participatory, collaborative, and visual representation methods, breathing new life into traditional and folklore objects.

INTRODUCTION

The digitization of cultural heritage is gaining ground between museums and individual collections. On the other hand, most individual costume collectors believe that sharing theirs leads to wear and tear. Digitization expands their accessibility, giving everyone access to any valuable cultural heritage, which leads to interest in it and helps produce identity (Buchyczyk, Nicolescu, & Urdea, 2017).

Contemporary art is increasingly using folklore material as a source of inspiration to explore the relationships between tradition and innovation. All over the world, artists, scholars, and curators of exhibitions try to exhibit folklore archives. In this way, the curators experiment with new, participatory, collaborative, and visual representation methods, breathing new life into traditional and folklore objects (Buchyczyk, Nicolescu, & Urdea, 2017).

An overview of the digital humanities-related museum and archival activities should look at whether they have fostered the digitization of clothes and fashion archives. At the time of the Covid-19 pandemic

DOI: 10.4018/978-1-6684-4461-0.ch005

(which began in early 2020), widespread Internet use was observed and augmented reality technologies were applied. Since March 2020, fashion collection owners have intensified their digitization. Through digital exhibitions (which are not intended to replace authentic archives), they have redefined the role of their collections to read at a different level. Their digital version is designed to be used by the extended network of Humanities Sciences researchers and academics. There is a comprehensive discussion about virtual reports, which, using the tools provided by modern technology, create new forms of knowledge (Rossi, 2020).

Recently there has been an increase in digital costume folklore archives, which has given researchers an increase in their sources of information. From a technological point of view, the best of these sources facilitated their users and their different and specific needs. There are other needs for those who organize and introduce new material (internal users) and those looking for information (external users). The concerns of all of them and the possible solutions that will address them must be considered. There is rapid technological development, but digitized clothing archives usually have limited funding and available completion time. Technology can evolve and, in some cases, be withdrawn due to age (Kirkland, Martin, Schoeny, Smith, & Strege, 2015). Clothes are historical and folklore documents imbued with the user's identity and personal history. Therefore, they convey individual but transient narratives and are quickly forgotten. Other details, such as leaflets or accessories (gloves, hats, scarves), can give the folklorists valuable cultural elements, helping them understand their time better, providing more complete interpretations, inspiring designs, and regenerative clothing versions.

However, the digitization of costume and fashion archives has its peculiarities. It differs from the traditional archives (such as manuscripts, letters, advertisements, prints), which are very well represented on a screen due to their two-dimensional form. The garment as a 3D object is complicated to digitize. Clothes, costumes, and fabrics can be photographed, but their digital image remains an incomplete representation of reality. This issue is partially offset by including garment details and their unwritten history. Costumes and fashion archives also collect and edit these individual stories, and their digitization provides opportunities to become more widely known. For example, the Yorkshire Fashion Archive, in digitizing its costume and fashion archives, not only focused on each of these garments but sought to revitalize local, social, and cultural history by including individual oral narratives and photographs of their use of clothing from their former owners. This information helps preserve the history of Yorkshire memorized by the people and accompanies the objects of the collection as a rich text file (Hall, 2017).

The fashion items (clothes and accessories) during the 19th - 20th centuries were not considered worthy of being kept in museums due to their perishability and connection with the shallow pleasures of low culture and women. Today they have been re-evaluated and are now considered worthy of preservation to study, as the tremendous social, cultural, historical, and economic value of these natural remnants of fashion was recognized. This approach changed archivists' attitudes and museum curators. They realized that fashion is a realistic everyday experience reflecting social and cultural change. Their importance goes beyond the traditional circle of fashion; it reflects collective, social, and cultural values because fashion is the expression and property of large social groups.

THE CULTURAL HERITAGE OF THE FASHION SECTOR

From 2000 until today, fashion has developed and mutated intensely. The emergence of fast fashion that is accessible to the younger generation has increased consumers, and at the same time, high fashion consumption is expanding into the economic downturn. Fashion has also been "democratized" on the Internet due to bloggers' work and the digital presentations of museums, specialists, and fashion houses such as Prada, Louis Vuitton, and Hermes. The application "The Museum System" was widely used to store and distribute the Internet of fashion clothing collections. Museums and fashion houses have attracted visitors by digitizing their archives in new ways. Haute couture houses try to promote their brand, highlighting their design heritage and thus lead to increased collaboration between the marketing and image-making departments. The digitization of their collections offers new tools to study traditions and memories related to clothing. In fashion, as the number of brands and consumers increases, the sense of belonging becomes more and more critical through access to the heritage of every fashion house. The digital presence makes these houses known to more and more people in new ways while maintaining an aura of exclusivity. Technology helps spread the tradition, merging old and new, making fashion accessible to a broader audience (Martin & Vacca, 2018).

Commitment to a brand is key to the relationship between heritage, records, and fashion knowledge. As the number of brands and consumers increases, the sense of participation in high fashion houses' legacy becomes more critical. The big haute couture houses and smaller ones realize that their collections are valuable by transferring knowledge about their heritage. This issue of origin is firmly integrated into the strategy of promoting their brand, which increases the need for archivists. By digitally presenting the corporate collections, these fashion houses become known to a broader audience in new ways while at the same time retaining a glamour of exclusivity. Online archives and interactive applications in their live exhibition space are vital to creating and transferring new knowledge to visitors to the collections and essential research tools for scholars. Thus, technology is a more comprehensive transfer of tradition, mixing the old (collections) with the new (digital technology) so fashion knowledge becomes accessible to ever-larger layers. As a result of the digitization of fashion archives, the fashion system is undergoing a radical transformation in heritage presentation, research, and the construction and transfer of new knowledge. A radical rethinking of how the cultural heritage of fashion archives will be preserved and enhanced is required because points and values take on different meanings depending on the socio-cultural context in which fashion is used, consumed, and interpreted (Steele, 1998). The increasing integration of digital media that allows high-speed access to and transfer information has allowed museums and fashion companies to increase cultural expansion (Martin & Vacca, 2018).

The Evolution of Digital Collections

Initially, digital technologies were used as a means of communication and a vehicle for transmitting cultural content to a larger audience. Still, today it is possible to use fashion archives collaboratively, which increases knowledge creation. Over time, museums and fashion houses have created websites designed to be used directly and exclusively on the Internet to communicate their archival heritage, interpretation, and more people's participation through active collective applications (Schnapp, 2015). Recently, archives have been transformed into interactive ones to allow the collections to be explored without time constraints; they can interact with other files, documentation, and the possibility of creating a personalized collection of information. In such "augmented" archives, each piece of the material collection is accompanied by detailed digital information that interprets the framework and facilitates the interaction between the users of the digital display (Martin & Vacca, 2018).

Fashion collections began to be created around 1850. Initially, non-western garments were collected due to their exotic hue. At the same time, used dresses were considered unworthy of salvation (Lou,

1998). Today fashion has become a valuable resource in museums' exhibition agendas due to the financial gains of attending large crowds. That is why museums that do not have a historical costume department want to host fashion clothing exhibitions. Specialized fashion museums, such as the Costume Institute at the Metropolitan Museum of Art, or the Fashion Institute of Technology Museum, invest money and time to digitize their archives. Among the reasons for these actions are a) the benefits for the physical condition of the clothes, as the digital database contributes to their preservation since there is no direct physical handling, and b) the increase of accessibility since the physical presence is not required of the designer in the exhibition space, and there is no time limit for access (Martin & Vacca, 2018).

Digitization Techniques

Various software such as Museum System or Past Perfect catalogs and manages fashion collections. These organize items based on type, manufacturer, date of creation or acquisition, country of origin, and designer. The integration of digital images allows exhibitors to recognize an element without physical handling, which is very important for delicate old clothes or designs that any handling could wear out. The collection can be accessed easily without unnecessary pressure on the objects. The most crucial element in these digital archives is the photos. Clothing photography is expensive, time-consuming, and constantly evolving. In the past, they photographed the front and back of the garment. Still, today the standards require the garments to be worn in figures and photographed from many angles or create 360-degree videos. At the same time, the users can focus on details at very high magnification. Fashion students and lecturers experimented with a three-dimensional clothes representation at the Drexel Digital Museum Project of the Drexel Foundation. The Internet is available with image libraries, such as Shared-self and Artstor, accompanied by information about each outfit and where a keyword can be searched. Digital fashion archives allow the accurate study of clothing and democratize the history of fashion and apparel, allow comprehensive research into a particular designer, trend, or period, and have changed how fashion is researched. Digital photography allows for a parallel, unlimited life for natural clothing that is rarely exposed and, at the same time, provides accurate and accessible documentation. Websites like Polyvore and Pinterest allow users to build a personal collection of clothing photos, although not all details are documented. While the physical fashion archive is a highly restricted access space, where only a handful of trusted researchers and designers are accepted, its digital copy is entirely democratic and accessible to everyone for an unlimited time to become a source of knowledge and participatory experience (Martin & Vacca, 2018).

Examples of Using Digital Technology in Fashion Exhibitions

Initially, fashion clothes museum exhibitions were frozen presentations of upper-class women put on lifelike mannequins (Steele, 2008). The first use of technology was the video screens that presented the production process of the exposed clothes, their presentation on the Catwalk, etc. Today the technology allows for interaction with the exhibition's visitors with smartphone applications, which with QR codes carry additional information about exhibits, even in experiences plus exhibition curation. A prime example is the 2014 exhibition of Charles James: Beyond Fashion at the Metropolitan Museum of Art (MET), which used active screens featuring designs of James's clothing. Charles James was a famous Anglo-American fashion designer of the 1950s, and the MET show featured fifteen of his most distinctive and iconic dresses. Each garment was in the center of a circular black platform with cameras on robotic arms all around, scanning the garments and displaying them on adjacent screens to understand each garment's conceptual intent and constructional details (Healy, 2016). The software could deconstruct each garment and present it as a technical design (pattern) to reveal the intricate details of James's clothing. The 3D display enabled direct virtual interaction with the garment when projected on the screen. Thus, the technology of 2010 enabled the analysis of historical costumes, revealing interior details and their function, transmitted the technique of a couturier who acted 60 years ago to the modern visitors of the exhibition, and helped in a deeper understanding of the construction of the clothing. (Healy, 2016; Martin & Vacca, 2018).

Other similar examples are the items Items: Is Fashion Modern? At the New York Museum of Modern Art (2017-2018), The Fashion World of Jean Paul Gaultier: From the Sidewalk to the Catwalk at the Brooklyn Museum in New York (2014), where talking mannequins and interactive screens overwhelmed visitors in the magical world of the designer, presenting in detail all the materials used and the working hours required to make each garment and finally the Miyake Issey Exhibition: The Work of Miyake Issey at the Tokyo National Art Center (2016), where an augmented reality application for smartphones was used so that visitors could interact with digital designs by Miyake Issey. Also, the exhibition Dressing Room: Archiving Fashion at the Museum of New York City shows through video and timelapse some internal, invisible to the public, maintenance procedures of the textile and clothing collections, presenting the work of the conservators and curators (Martin & Vacca, 2018). All the examples show that in modern fashion shows, technology promotes the balancing and utilization of free time for learning inside the museum while facilitating the transfer of meaning and historical knowledge (Capacete-Caballero, Caulfield-Sriklad, & McKay, 2013).

The Archives of Fashion Houses

Contrary to the practices of museums, fashion houses jealously guard and protect their records, which are a valuable resource of each house's history and contain extensive knowledge of their interests and practices while also being of great value to designers. They are characterized by a wide variety of materials that accumulate for years. Most of them are documents (fashion designs) that concern draft fashion designs, studies of forms, silhouette and functionality, original clothes, studies of colour variations, design details, research findings on materials, patents, brochures from advertisements, press releases, and mainly photos. Their digitization is crucial for transmitting the heritage and traditions of the fashion houses. The main goal of digitization is the democratization of cultural heritage and knowledge. The first example is the Valentino Garavani Virtual Museum. The Valentino House decided to digitize its archive while not creating a traditional museum. From the contents of the archives, it seems that software requires everything from documents and photos to video fashion shows with the soundtrack. It was introduced in 2011, with the designer's retirement to present his fifty-year career. It contains about 300 garments, divided into thematic sections concerning the periods of Valentino design and designed and created in collaboration with Novacom Associes (Paris) and Kinmonth - Monfreda Design Project (London). Each item is accompanied by digital references to its history, biographies of clothing users, design sketches, digital images of fabrics and precious materials used, and photos of women with them at events. Also, the archive contains a digital library with over 5000 clothing images and about 100 videos from Valentino fashion shows. The Virtual Museum uses an open-source application and 3D technology in real-time and is accessible at www.valentino-garavani-archives.org. The house used the digital presentation to achieve permanent and increasing attention to its activities.

Another example is the fashion house Channel, which tries to communicate its legacy with a live digital archive, Paraffection, by founding a subsidiary in 2002. It aims to promote and retain the high-level artisans of the craft workshops that work with the house, which are gradually disappearing for financial reasons or due to the non-attendance of new artisans. Paraffection presents 12 top Maison crafts whose techniques are vital for the operation of the French fashion system (Pacault & Patchett, 2018). The aim of Paraffection, apart from highlighting the craftsmanship of the artisans of these houses, is to transit this heritage into modern design approaches. Digital technology favours the preservation and dissemination of know-how, facilitating the work of newer artificial ones without replacing them. The archives that have been hiding secrets of artisans for 100 years are becoming more organized, more functional, and, above all, accessible. Thus, the digital presentation of heritage highlights the cultural identity of a product, technique, or knowledge as a critical part of a collective culture and history, with the immediate benefit of a growing emotional impact on the consumer imagination, creating an intangible value for the home (Martin & Vacca, 2018).

Several Italian houses have archives and showrooms, such as the Armani/Silos, the Salvatore Ferragamo Museum, Gianfranco Ferre Foundation, the Gucci Garden, the Ottavio and Rita Missoni Foundation, the Micol Fontana Foundation, the Roberto Capucci Foundation, the Emilio Pucci Foundation, and the Valentino Garavani Virtual Museum mentioned earlier. Armani/Silos allows researchers to browse its digital archive, mainly fashion clothing designs and videos from fashion shows, but this can only be done through terminals located at its headquarters in Silos (Franceschini, 2019). Similarly, the Salvatore Ferragamo Museum allows digital browsing only in its museum space at its headquarters in Florence. The Gianfranco Ferre Foundation has digitized some of its collections available online. Although it has a showroom, Gucci Garden is not interesting enough for its archival heritage. The Ottavio and Rita Missoni Foundation digitized most of its archive and continue to complete it and post it online. The Micol Fontana Foundation archive is maintained at the institution of the same name. It is only accessible on-site, although part of it was posted on the CSAC website (discussed below). The Roberto Capucci Foundation has digitized its archives; they are available online and organized periodically but purely photographic. Digital documents or inventory cards do not accompany the clothes. The Emilio Pucci Foundation was commissioned to run Promemoria, which used the Archives platform but did not post it online. Finally, the Valentino Garavani Virtual Museum has a website with a 3D Virtual gallery, but its use is complicated, and the archives are not easy to read. As it turns out, all of these digital archives do not have context cards and need a lot of extra work to deepen and complete. Another project that could achieve direct collaboration between a digital application and a designer's files, although in its infancy, is Kara Chung's Instagram account, where celebrity designer virtual clothes are worn and advertised by an avatar (Rossi, 2020).

TECHNICAL ISSUES AND TERMINOLOGY

For users to have easy access to the images and information through the search engines, the data must be entered in a standard format. In digital applications, the information that accompanies the idea of an object or document as a directory entry is called metadata. A metadata format is the set of rules followed for cataloging that clears the form of the directory entry contents and its structure. If the metadata format follows specific standard layouts, it allows search engines to detect it on the Internet. For data to be shared by a community, it must be agreed upon which data and image templates to use. The Dublin Core (DC) standard for metadata design works well in historical costumes. Contains rules for creating data fields of an archive, which allow the optimal description of the elements of a historical garment, such as title, creator, category, date, etc. DC can be used for any object, e.g., photo, document, 3D objects such as garments, audio recording, or video. This allows the users to integrate archival materials and clothing and search for clothes from other collections. The most commonly used databases are based on DC. To this were added many more elements specifically for clothing collections, giving it advanced sorting capabilities and ease of search for the user. The Drexel Digital Museum Project uses the Open Archive Initiative Protocol for Metadata Harvesting, which incorporates DC standards but extends to new ones, to include clothing from multiple collections to coexist in a standard digital display. It allows descriptive search of a garment, i.e., by title, creator, or the collection's name to which it belongs (Kirkland, Martin, Schoeny, Smith, & Strege, 2015).

Language and Terminology of Description of Clothing Collections

The garment's description is understandable for the catalog (it must contain the keyword), and the user must access a digital collection. Vocabularies are closely monitored to reduce ambiguities and ambiguities and inconsistencies in spoken languages. It was initially agreed to use the definitions of the Fairchild fashion dictionary. Still, inconsistencies were found with other known fashion dictionaries, improvements were made, and more objective terms were sought. When specific data structures are used correctly, users talk about linked data. When controlled vocabularies are used, and users choose a particular keyword, the search engine focuses more on users' requirements. For historical clothing, it allows searching through structural elements of the garment, such as the shape of the neckline and the waist level, which enables the examination of patterns over time. In well-known historical clothing terms, many historical clothing sites use alphabetical catalogs to classify data entry correctly, but it may be problematic for ordinary fashionistas, anthropologists, and sociologists. The Drexel Digital Museum Project uses the vocabulary of the International Museum Committee, which contains basic terms for clothing classification. It starts with the general terms (men, women, children, babies), then underwear or outerwear, after the part of the body they cover, and finally the historical name of the garment. This allows users of different specialties to access. The Historic Dress website adds visual representations. The user who does not know the garment's name or the style can recognize it among some photos while quoting synonymous terms (Kirkland, Martin, Schoeny, Smith, & Strege, 2015).

Digital Image Templates

Given the considerable time and amount of money spent on photography, the captured images must be of high definition for the accurate capture of the garments because time irreversibly degrades them. Follow the Museum Online California Archive (MOAC) for clothing photography, where a mannequin dressed in clothing is placed on a rotating base and photographed by 18 cameras. All these photos are combined in a Quick Time Virtual Reality file. The interactive digital video obtained allows panoramic rotation and magnification of construction details and fabrics (Kirkland, Martin, Schoeny, Smith, & Strege, 2015).

Garments and fabrics are expensive to store, and there are difficulties exposing them. The limited space may force museums to sell a batch of clothing that is too "simple" to maintain or too expensive to maintain. But if they are photographed and posted on the Internet, there is a chance that a researcher will draw valuable conclusions and find more importance (Kirkland, Martin, Schoeny, Smith, & Strege,

2015). The Historic Dress website creates links to digitized publications such as Godey's Lady Book to build a platform to store them and old catalogs, photos, and technical textbooks to showcase the production process.

In 2003 Dr. Kathryn Jakes, Professor of Textile Science at Ohio State University, started a library of fiber reference images and developed the Media Manager software, which uses Gold Fusion as its web development platform. The latter was initially designed to link simple web pages, HTML based, to a single database. The Media Manager can also display metadata and house photos of the historical costume collection on a simple website. But when Ohio State University stopped funding Media Manager upgrades in 2012, open-source software was sought. The Historic Dress website also uses OmeKa open-source software for website creation and content management, which is free but requires staff to enter data, maintain and subscribe to a hosting provider. Omeka is based on Dublin Core but can integrate several costumes' primary fields and accept all audio, video, and video formats. As users examine the digital photo of the garment in multiple contexts and draw conclusions, digitization externalizes the interpretation (Kirkland, Martin, Schoeny, Smith, & Strege, 2015).

CLOTHES COLLECTIONS DIGITIZATION INITIATIVES IN USA UNIVERSITIES

The Drexel Digital Museum (DDM), curated by Associate Professor Cathy Martin, contains images and text from historical costumes from the Robert and Penny Fox Collection at Drexel University in Philadelphia, USA, and selections from private collections. Since 1999, Martin has experimented with image templates for garments and their electronic storage and explanatory text (Kirkland, Martin, Schoeny, Smith, & Strege, 2015). Until 2000 archiving was done with paper cards and minimal access to the collection. There were sporadic exhibitions, lending to other institutions, and short appointments of students and teachers with a part-time curator to examine specific, predefined pieces. The Drexel Digital Museum Project was created to allow unobstructed access and avoid stress on the exhibits (Martin & Ko, 2011).

The first necessary step in creating a severe digital archive is to properly delineate its mission and purpose and explore future users' operational and quality needs. Students, designers, teachers, fashion designers, and members of the Costume Society of America were interviewed and researched, and the desired features of the digital archive were decided. The data from the research identified groups of potential users, their work environments, the technological means they would use, the frequency of internet fashion searches, and a list of desirable features of the archive. It was found that the functional requirements of external users coincided with the most basic desires for high-definition images, multi-angle shots, the ability to focus on details of garments, and multiple alternative ways of accessing them in search. For in-house users, the claims stemmed from publications related to similar digitization efforts by Kent State University, the New York Institute of Fashion Technology, the MET Costume Institute, and the University of Texas Fashion Collection (Kirkland, Martin, Schoeny, Smith, & Strege, 2015). The Drexel Digital Museum Project allows users to explore the clothes in ways not allowed in their actual exhibition. So, since 2000, the Drexel Digital Museum Project has video, quick time virtual reality (QTVR), rotation of clothes by 360 degrees, focus on construction details and decorations, and the ability to create virtual catwalk fashion shows. Existing open-source digital software enables these capabilities. In addition to the rotation, the coats can be removed, the skirts can be lifted, and all this any day of the year, any time of the day or night, regardless of the opening hours of the actual museum. Drexel fashion design students use it to draw inspiration for their designs. The active participation of users involves many different perspectives and promotes learning teaching (Martin & Ko, 2011).

To fully appreciate a garment, it must be observed worn on a living, moving body, and indeed, in the past, historical clothes were presented in vivid models. Still, today this is not acceptable because it strains these fragile objects. To address the problem, the Digital Clothing Centre of Seoul University has created an application that can adapt clothing to every body type and body movement and realistically produce its vigorous activities. This application, The Digital Clothing Suite, uses 82 landmark points in a body, where the dimensions of the body are loaded and create a virtual body. The measurements are also entered from the garment, and a virtual miniature is created. Physical parameters of the garment material (such as rigidity, density, texture), printed designs, and decorations can also be loaded. So, fashion design students have a unique tool to experiment with design. The final virtual garment wears the virtual model giving life to the historical clothes; due to the ease of use of the Digital Clothing Suite, the taught CAD course for fashion was integrated (Martin & Ko, 2011). Another effort is that of Gayle Strege, curator of the University of Ohio Historic Costume and Textiles Collection, who created the Fashion2Fiber database to include digital photos of clothing that were not posted in a digital collection needs Fashion History students. At the Vassar College Drama Department, Arden Kirkland, Costume Design Assistant of the small collection of historical clothing (650 pieces), digitized it in 2002 to increase user access to it. Students of the theatre department mainly use the archive for inspiration for producing theatrical costumes, who need a high-definition image and access to the details of the construction of each outfit. At the same time, Kiki Smith, a Professor of Theatre at Smith College in Massachusetts, convened a team of librarians, computer software development engineers, archivists, curators, and historians from 2013 to 2014 to develop Historical Dress: The Centre for the Study of Clothing, Costume (Kirkland, Martin, Schoeny, Smith, & Strege, 2015).

CLOTHES COLLECTIONS DIGITIZATION PROJECT IN EUROPE

Digitization of the Victoria and Albert Museum Fashion Archives

In the era of COVId - 19 emergency health and the consequent restrictions on human movement, the Victoria and Albert Museum in London presented its collections remotely in a variety of ways:

- A Google Art deal
- A Youtube channel
- A TV series on the BBC (Secret of the Museum)

In May 2020, Victoria and Albert Museum published a press release mentioning his presence on the Internet. It is estimated that 80% of his collections have already been digitized. Using 3D Sketchfab software, it can present clothes in 3D. Among the modules offered, the Online Interaction offers high-definition photos to focus on details and information about the exhibit. The Further Highlights section presents conferences and events, such as Fashion in Motion. Part of the site contains wallpapers offered for download and even an index of fashion publications. Using 3D Sketchfab software, it can present clothes in 3D. Among the modules offered, the Online Interaction offers high-definition photos to focus on details and information about the exhibit. The Further Highlights section presents conferences and events, such as Fashion in Motion. Part of the site contains wallpapers offered for download and even an index of fashion publications. The latest posts are interactive, and all of its pages are shared via Facebook, Twitter, Instagram, and Pinterest.

All this leads to new user experiences, different reading levels, and unprecedented possibilities for research and learning. The main features of digital V&A are the persistence in interactivity with the participation of users and the possibility of sharing digital objects (Rossi, 2020). New approaches to archiving and preservation aim to increase access to remnants of the past, participatory forms of content production and research, and informal education that transforms traditional libraries and museums (Schnapp, 2008). With WEB 2.0, data has been introduced, a key parameter for the promotion of digital Humanities, which allows the social production of quality content and the possibility of its use by any non-profit organization while remaining dynamically open to new updates and additions of recent archives (Fiormonte, Numerico, & Tomasi, 2015).

The Italian "Culturaitalia"

The Italian Culturaitalia is a Project of the Ministry of Cultural Heritage and Activities, under the scientific supervision of the Scuola Normale Superiore di Pisa, and accumulates the Italian national cultural heritage. It includes various Italian archives and has many portals in operation, such as the 20th Century Fashion Archives Portal. The portal collects digital content from public and private collections such as the Textile Museum of Prato and the Emilio Pucci Foundation (Rossi, 2020). The Italian NAtional Archival Association 2009 built the portal Twentieth Century Fashion Archives and inventoried, cataloged, and digitized material of the most important Italian fashion houses.

CSAC Archive Digitization

The Centre for Archives and Communication (CSAC) of Parma was founded in 1968 and became a museum in 2015. It contains 12 million art, fashion, theatre, cinema, and photography objects. The fashion department was founded in 1976 and had 80,000 pieces, including sketches by Micol Fontana and Brunetta Mateldi. The digitization of CSAC started in 2017 with the activation of its website that used the Omeka application. In virtual exhibitions, it is possible to enrich the content with the users' posts while the management costs are less than those of the traditional museums. In 2017, directory cards were increased load on the SAMIRA platform that fully manages digital archives and contains three parts: management, directory, and search. The list is divided into "Sections" and "Funds."

The "Sections" section is divided into five sections: Art, Media, Project, Photography, and Show, where the digitized material is available. The "Funds" contain the names of the archives. Each page includes the archive's name, title, date, background, material, construction technique, preservation status, comments, digital photos of the garment, and its copyright. CSAC has recently launched efforts to make metadata available through the Culturaitalia and Europeana portals. It also promotes research in digital humanities, such as the 2018 research program, Socialising the Archive, which aimed to find digital tools and strategies to enhance archive accessibility. It was an attempt to start a dialogue with the research community, spread some knowledge, and measure the users' liking. In 2019, the project Ettore Sottsass Virtual Exhibition developed products useful for educational purposes, integrated digital archives and other museum activities, and increased accessibility to different audiences. In this way, they would achieve a collection upgrade and access to items that the traditional exhibition would avoid presenting to protect them. Finally, during the Covid-19 pandemic, CSAS archives were linked to companies in the textile chain of the greater Parma area (Rossi, 2020).

Yorkshire Fashion Archive Digitization

However, the digitization of costume and fashion archives has its peculiarities. It differs from the traditional archives (such as manuscripts, letters, advertisements, prints), which are very well represented on a screen due to their two-dimensional form. The garment as a 3D object is complicated to digitize. Clothes, costumes, and fabrics can be photographed, but their digital image remains an incomplete representation of reality. This is partially offset by including garment details and their unwritten history. Costumes and fashion archives also collect and edit these individual stories, and their digitization provides opportunities to become more widely known. For example, the Yorkshire Fashion Archive, in digitizing its costume and fashion archives, not only focused on each of these garments but sought to revitalize local, social, and cultural history by including individual oral narratives and photographs of their use of clothing from their former owners. This information helps preserve the history of Yorkshire memorized by the people and accompanies the objects of the collection as a rich text file (Hall, 2017).

The Yorkshire Fashion Archive of the University of Leeds School of Design was founded in 1990 to archive clothing sold or used in Yorkshire during the 19th and 20th centuries. It includes mainly women's clothing, a few men's, fabrics, books, fashion magazines, advertisements, etc. The archive aims to detect changing social behaviours and cultural influences and use Modes Complete, a collection management software implemented by many museums. Through this software, they upload to each recording a series of photos together with the relevant metadata for the depicted clothes that include the memories - experiences from their previous owners.

EUROPEANA AND GOOGLE WEAR CULTURE

The digitization of cultural heritage is increasingly the concern of various museums. This need is guided by the general rule that sharing means caring. The significant increase in accessibility to the cultural heritage brought by digitization activates the production of identities and interests and care for it. The pan-European project Europeana Fashion (2015) and the international project Wear Culture (2017) by Google Cultural Institute are the most important platforms for promoting and distributing the fashion heritage. Today, fashion as an economic activity and cultural event is digitally distributed on multiple levels, access to a vast audience. There is a considerable difference when only a few wealthy people buy fashionable clothes or attend the colorful monthly fashion magazines. Due to the development of communication technologies (Internet, smartphones, etc.) and fashion's great resonance and popularity, fashion communication has been democratized and reached a large audience. Museums collect and preserve fashion items and possess their essence, regardless of the digitization of their collections. The progress of digitization depends on the relevant funding, which is not inexhaustible, so museums must cooperate with larger organizations, e.g., the European Union (Melchior, 2019).

Europeana Fashion

Europeana is a European Commission-funded digital project by the European Union that aims to enhance the memory of Europe's cultural heritage by using culture as a shared resource for education and research. In 2005 the European Library Initiative launched a search engine with access to all European Union countries (around 4000 libraries) and posted them on the Internet through the Europeana.eu website, containing over 50 million archives. It has been in Creative Commons mode since 2012; Europeana data is available for free. Of course, it is guided by the philosophy of "sharing is caring" (Sanderhoff, 2014). The Europeana Fashion Heritage Association (EFHA) was founded in 2014 as a non-profit organization based in Florence, Italy, and has been responsible for introducing new data to the Europeana Fashion collection. EFHA has 20 public and private organizations and 42 content providers and contains fashion and digital heritage management content through its www.fashionheritage.eu platform, while collaborating with schools such as the Parsons School of Design in Paris. It caters to many different users, from the researcher and the professional designer looking for something specific to the occasional user who wants to relax looking for fashion images. EFHA is an international hub where galleries, libraries, museums, and fashion archives share its digital heritage best practices for digitization and exploitation. It acts as a link between all cultural heritage institutions (Melchior, 2019).

Europe's public and private fashion archives share a legacy of stories, costumes, fashion designs, fashion magazine sketches, photo catalogs, and videos from fashion shows. EFHA acts as a collector of fashion material as it interfaces files and databases. EFHA creates an interconnection between archives of different forms, such as scientific, essential, monothematic, and multidimensional archives enabling communication. The EFHA digital database contains around one million digital images of fashion items for use by any user who must follow the rules for the benefit of digital material, such as copyright rules. (Rossi, 2020).

The EFHA website is structured through stories and narratives. When users visit www.fashionheritage.eu the categories "Designers" and "Fashion and History" appear, and there are different fashion stories in each category. For example, in the "Designers" section, there are subsections for various European fashion designers, modern and older. There are other sections/content categories on the EFHA website, such as "Object Focus," "Runway Archive," "EFHA World," "Events," and "Exhibitions." The category "Object Focus" presents individual garments accompanied by an informative text about their creation. For example, in this category, the narrative "Object Voices/A Rich Evening Cape from Southern Germany" presents the material and how to build an evening cape from Southern Germany. In the "Exhibitions" category, there is information about recent fashion shows. In the "Runway Archive" category, there are archives of fashion shows of various designers. In the "Events" and "EFHA World" categories, the latest fashion stories about clothes, exhibitions, publications in scientific journals, and fashion shows are presented. As it seems, the website's main content is fashion stories edited by various experts. Reports can be found in different categories, i.e., they "circulate" in different types, and there are several entry points in each category, but the search algorithm is complicated. More entry points for www.fashionheritage.eu can be found on Facebook, Twitter, Instagram, Pinterest, and LinkedIn. There is even room for in-depth research for researchers, fashion professionals, and designers, who even indirectly meet through the platform and share ideas (Melchior, 2019; Rossi, 2020).

The Europeana Fashion website differs somewhat from that of EFHA. Its structure follows most museums' encyclopaedic organization that considers the material object to be evidence of the past and that museums are empowered to preserve and use it. The initial classification categories are: "Designers," "Technique," "Material," "Item type," "Type of media," With subcategories in each easily accessible. Each item displayed on the Europeana Fashion website is accompanied by an explanatory text, information about its creator and the type of item, metadata, and location. Exhibitions curated by experts directly showcase designer fashion and include iconic fashion designers based in 20th-century Paris, such as Vionnet, Dior, and Balenciaga. The "Past to Present" exhibition shows how designers use fashion history archives to draw new inspiration. Europeana Fashion is, therefore, a place for curated thematic exhibitions of fashion collections with pedagogical purposes to promote the understanding of fashion as a European cultural heritage. Fashion generally has a small share in traditional museum collections, and only social history museums are interested in it. Still, Europeana Fashion highlights that clothing is part of individual identity and incorporates social class and cultural norms, leading to official recognition that fashion has a legal place in the cultural sphere (Melchior, 2019).

We Wear Culture by Google

In 2011, the Google Cultural Institute was founded as a non-profit organization to digitize the world's cultural heritage. This institute owned Google Arts and Culture, which in 2017 presented We Wear Culture, which initially included 30,000 fashion projects. Google Arts and Culture have 183 partners in 40 countries. Google's, We Wear Culture project presents the 3000 years of fashion history in a digital exhibition, free access to all. It is a global project involving 180 organizations worldwide, coordinated by the Salvatore Ferragamo Museum, and it was presented on June 8, 2017, at the Metropolitan Museum of Art (MET). Museum curator Andrew Bolton said it was challenging to maintain a permanent clothing exhibition because of their fragility. Google's platform offers profound democratization of fashion, offering free access to all.

The project allows researchers to zoom in on details that are not visible with a simple glance at the clothes, leading to a perfect investigation. Over 400 sections were created by curators of archives of the largest museums and fashion houses worldwide. These archives present details of the garments that are not visible to the naked eye. The history and the silk road, the Versailles fashion, the British Punk style, the story of Kimono and Sari, the little black dress of the Coco Channel, and traditional clothing-making techniques are presented. The project is structured in various fashion stories - fashion narratives, to catch the world's attention. Kate Lauterbach (2017), program manager of We Wear Culture, states that conventional museums hold archives and contribute to the project. Google converts them into stories and provides them to the public. Google owns and implements technological tools such as art cameras, street view, and virtual reality. Therefore, it can provide technical support to partners to present the fashion stories they have edited. There is video, audio, photos, and texts on each level. There is no limit to texts' length or videos and images' numbers that each curator wants to include in their narrative. Google does not interfere with or validate fashion stories; it just uploads them. Of course, it suggests to the curators the required structure for easy access and recognition by the public. Eventually, Google will provide the technological tools and partners to contribute to the content (Lauterbach, 2017).

The We Wear Culture website introduces a collection of fashion stories edited by specialized fashion experts and shared by a technology-commercial company that wants to save anyone's knowledge about the arts and culture. So, the essential value of digitizing clothes and fashion designs is the huge accessibility (Melchior, 2019). The website includes some primary sections. All of these sections are featured on the We Wear Culture homepage. The first section is "Wearing culture, in detail." It is divided into four main areas: "The Icons" (fashion designers from around the world), "The movements" (fashion trends and historical periods), "The making of" (the technique of making clothes), and "The arts" (fashion relationship with arts). In the second section of "Wear Culture," a series of videos presented some modern clothing and fashion items (the bikini, ripped jeans, the Choker, etc.) by Ingrid Nilsen. The third section is related to art and fashion. It is called "Fashion + Art: a collaboration as old as time" and shows how the meeting of fashion and visual arts creates inspiration for designers. This section presents in detail museum exhibitions related to fashion and art. The work of the curators is severe, it aims at the transfer of knowledge, and there are no objects that are not accompanied by interpretive texts. We Wear Culture does not promote research; users can not download images or comment on them. There is no active participation, but they can access and collect information about interesting fashion stories (Melchior, 2019). Google says it was motivated to create the project through many searches for fashion clothes and shows (Martin & Vacca, 2018).

Fashion means any adornment and shaping of the body and the way it is placed (Melchior, 2019). We Wear Culture and Europeana Fashion use stories to showcase fashion broadly, including everything from haute couture to street fashion. Some criticize these two isotopes, blaming them for failing to promote the idea of a single European or world cultural heritage, nor its interconnections, despite the bright, flawless high-definition image. No sharing or exchange of knowledge is promoted, as new knowledge does not arise from the listing of garments but requires an exploration of the environment in which these garments were born, created, used, and preserved. Thus the two sites fail to retain a broader knowledge of the overall social context to promote historical research (Calanca, 2020).

REASONS WHY GOOGLE AND THE EUROPEAN UNION HAVE PROMOTED THE DIGITIZATION OF FASHION HERITAGE

When asked why these two organizations promoted the digitization of fashion archives, they both answered that it helps their core values of increasing accessibility, which is a strategy that legitimizes the Wear Culture and Europeana Fashion projects. This, in turn, convinces project partners to contribute to the fashion heritage they hold. Associate professor Bjarki Valtysson (2011) of the University of Copenhagen, studying the official documents of the European Union for the creation of Europeana Fashion, concluded that the purpose of its design was ideological. But such ideological movements did not exist in the technology company Google. In this case, providing accessibility encourages major cultural institutions to work with it on things that can leverage power games locally and more widely. But Google may want to take advantage of digital search tracks that such companies quickly detect for commercial purposes (Melchior, 2019).

On the other hand, according to the technical directors, a different parameter arouses the interest of the two organizations in the digitization of the fashion heritage. This stems from the uniqueness of fashion archives that are varied in structure and classification, which poses an exciting challenge for technicians who have to devise new metadata formats. Indeed, fashion is complicated. Created by different designers, there are many techniques and materials of construction. There are various aesthetic styles, many brands, and corporate names, and it is addressed to men, women, and children. There are also different clothes with different uses (pants, jackets, shirts, etc.). This requires a lot of various search engine keywords (Lauterbach, 2017). Content providers (museums, archives) believe that by partnering with Google and giving access to their archives, they aim to attract new visitors and increase their visibility.

They think that this proves it. They see digitization as a way to communicate with larger audiences and better promote their library or archive (Melchior, 2019).

AUGMENTED REALITY FOR DIGITAL ARCHIVE INVESTIGATION: THE FLITTING ROOM APPLICATION

There are constant temperature and humidity facilities at the Fashion Institute of Technology (FIT), where original sketches and drawings of Coco Channel, Jean Patou, and Halston are kept in stainless steel boxes. Researchers have to make an appointment to be able to examine them. The number of those who have access is limited. To increase accessibility and help deepen their study, Miyo Sandlin and Joseph Anderson created an augmented reality application, "The Fitting Room," that allows users to try on these historical garments to bring these sketches to life and attract researchers to take an interest in them. This chapter will present this application and analyse how technology bridges the gap between archival material and digitization (Sandlin and Anderson, 2021).

Researchers considering the FIT digital archive have been thinking about turning designs into hats and accessories that can be worn virtually. In the same way, the users can add a filter to their selfie photos. Using the digital image of the hat and Zappar's face monitoring application, they could quickly "wear" the hat on their head. The application developers believe that they have connected the private archival material for public use with the technology to increase the accessibility of the collection (Sandlin and Anderson, 2021). Based on this idea, the website https://fittingroom.fitnyc.edu/ was created where visitors can start AR filters from any camera device, such as smartphones, tablets, or laptops. The site contains additional educational information about the fashion sketches displayed, but the users need to click on the information icon to show them.

THE RELATIONSHIP BETWEEN ANALOG AND DIGITAL ARCHIVES AND THE ROLE OF THE FASHION HERITAGE CURATOR

In classical museums and archives, fashion belongs to the holders of the evidence material. However, the digital reproduction and the curator's comments make each object a digital fashion heritage. Of course, the second status of the thing depends directly on the first. The only difference is the story accompanying the digital archive, the curator's approach. Such efforts have existed in the past in classical museums. The curators of the fashion museums were anonymous, as were the other workers. Still, the influence of fashion editor Diane Vreeland, who organized costume shows at the Costume Institute of New York MET, made the curator the show's center piece. The curator "tells" the projected fashion stories, gradually transforming the digital representation from objective to conceptual, and they try to convey this to the Wear Culture and Europeana Fashion websites. When fashion records are digitized and accompanied by curators' interpretations, they acquire a kind of life different from the classical permanence of the natural, tangible object, but this differentiation is not radical; it is an extension of the former. Finally, for the preservation and care of fashion objects, protection is their primary institutional duty in the classical analog museums. At the same time, in the digitized archives, this is vaguer, as it is a consequence of the idea that knowledge leads to understanding, sympathy, and indirect care (Melchior, 2019).

Since 1970, archives' role as memory reservoirs and cultural promoter-activator has been recognized. Archives convey postmodern culture by preserving memory and its relation to history, representation, and cultural ties (Rossi, 2020). Therefore, museums are institutions for safeguarding and promoting preserved heritage. The digital age imposes, and users rethink, the nature of archives and their internal structure, judging the ways of cataloging used in the past. Here should emphasize the emergence of a new professional specialty in digital humanities, the "Digital" curator. His duties include preserving digital records and adding value throughout their life. In addition to digital archiving and preservation, it contains excellent functionality, data management, and adding value to the data by adding new sources of information to create new knowledge. The digital humanities bring together anthropologists, designers, and technologists to develop new types of expertise, challenging classical scientific distinctions and avoiding firm boundaries between different fields of study. Key features of digital archives are digitizing the collection, storage, continuous improvement, and maximum dissemination of its content on the Internet. The museum's idea is a source of creating new unpublished knowledge; it is always valid (Rossi, 2020).

COMPLEMENTARITY OF REAL AND VIRTUAL MUSEUM

Digital technology contributes to the performance of fashion dynamism, addressing the vacuum created by the body and the interactivity of experience. In most fashion shows of recent years, there has been a significant increase in film projections, which bring to life static mannequins, and there are interactive screens, such as the digital wall at the entrance of the MoMu in Antwerp. Many times digital technology is a critical element of a curator's strategy. For example, in the exhibition for Charles James (Chicago History Museum, 2011), 3D computed tomography was used to reveal the construction details and the intricate internal structure of James's "Tree" dress (1957), which otherwise could not be perceived by visual examination. Digital technologies have demonstrated design dynamics and created new ways of exploring clothing and body while enhancing visitor engagement. Video and photo tracking capabilities on smartphones and new tagging mechanisms will fundamentally transform the museum-visitor relationship (Loscialpo, 2016).

Digital technology offers access to different levels, and visitors gain the experience of visiting a mixed reality museum that meets needs and expectations not met in the classical museum. Mobile phones favor "nomadic" research, as visitors to the exhibition can search and extract information and analysis, constantly moving between physical exhibits and the Internet. An example of physical and digital complementarity is the Fashion Curation 13 exhibition in Moving Textiles: Digital Encounters (University of Creative Arts, Canterbury, 2014) which experimented with digital practices and explored ways of representing the body and historical clothing. Transparent screens (which can be seen from both sides) projected 3D fashion films along with the natural clothing exhibition, where the 3D digital image was rotated 360°. At the same time, visitors could interact with the digital installation and add comments and tags. This interactive feature was created to work in the physical space of the exhibition to create a "dialogue" with the physical collection. The different media and ways of communication push visitors into a dynamic relationship with the space and the exhibits. The development of physical and digital dimensions expands the exhibition outside the natural room. It allows access to potential visitors, i.e., creates a demand that can be met later. When digital technologies are used effectively, new areas of exploration are created (Loscialpo, 2016). Since 2000, museums have experimented with interactive technologies and media, pushing the boundaries between the material and the digital realm. The devices and technologies they sometimes use preferentially represent clothing, despite directly linking it to its proper form. This shows that they focus on the increased emphasis on the subject, the user experience, and the "looking" process (Henning, 2006).

CONCLUSION

The heritage of fashion is an essential resource for studying folklore and culture, so it is something unique to spread and must be accessible to all. There is a profound change in the early 2020s, where the fashion archives of museums and fashion houses, from static thanks to digitization, come to life and open fashion sketches and artificial skills become easily accessible, management and operational to transfer knowledge and add new value. Each element must be known in its origin, its tropical and temporal context, its evolution, and its correlation with similar to create new open knowledge. The rapid technological changes today transform the philosophy of museums and fashion shows, and they shift to the needs of the community of users of their sites. They try to build relationships with them to achieve total commitment and participation in the museum's activities, with a new user experience different from the direct on-site visit. This shift leads to participatory learning and collaborative situations for users and digital curators to create new content and value. Digital technologies have made the fashion heritage an asset and are trying to integrate it into the daily lives of the user community. Unlimited access to the fashion records brought by digitization and the internet help in knowledge with new forms of learning, in the management of their heritage to recognize the value of their brand.

Digital fashion collectors can use widely digitized software, such as Dublin Core and the Open Archive Initiative, to create databases and customize them with application profiles (such as Costume Core) specifically for clothing. It is beneficial to use metadata that explains any digital object, common controlled vocabulary, understood by the file organizers and the prospective users. The platforms Europeana Fashion and We Wear Culture present fashion in stories and narratives that create interest and add value to the presented digital objects. In these narratives, the designer and the garment's origin are projected, emphasizing the individual creators, degrading the practical use of fashion. It is presented as directed and does not consider how subcultures create fashion with their unique forms of clothing.

It is impossible to create and transfer knowledge about fashion if digital technology is not guided by a socio-cultural ideology that does not want to turn it into an end. Technology alone allows change, not change. Digital technologies have changed the transmission of knowledge about road heritage, processes - and design methodologies to add new meaning and values.

REFERENCES

Buchyczyk, M., Nicolescu, G., & Urdea, A. (2017). Forging Folklore, Disrupting Archives: Curatorial Explorations between Tradition and Innovation. *The Museum of the Romanian Peasant Anthropology Journal*, *22*, 129–147.

Calanca, D. (2020). Archivi digitali della moda e patrimonio culturale tra descrizione e integrazione. *ZoneModa Journal*, *10*(2), 11–25.

Capacete-Caballero, X., Caulfield-Sriklad, D., & McKay, F. (2013). Enhancing the Display of the Fashion Artefact through Digital Multi-media Approaches. In *Proceedings of the 1st International Conference on Digital Fashion* (pp. 336 - 345). Digital Fashion 2013 Secretariat.

Fiormonte, D., Numerico, T., & Tomasi, F. (2015). *The Digital Humanist: A Critical Inquiry*. Punctum Books.

Franceschini, M. (2019). Navigating Fashion: On the Role of Digital Fashion Archives in the Preservation, Classification and Dissemination of Fashion Heritage. *Critical Studies in Fashion & Beauty*, *10*(1), 69–90. doi:10.1386/csfb.10.1.69_1

Hall, S. (2017). Memories of style: Digitizing the Yorkshire Fashion Archive. *Art Libraries Journal*, *42*(3), 157–161. doi:10.1017/alj.2017.22

Healy, T. (2016). *Creating Custom Storage Forms for Charles James Masterpieces*. Retrieved from The MET: https://www.metmuseum.org/blogs/now-at-the-met/2016/custom-storage-forms-charles-james

Henning, M. (2006). *Museums, Media and Cultural Theory*. Open University Press.

Kirkland, A., Martin, K., Schoeny, M., Smith, K., & Strege, G. (2015). Sharing Historic Costume Collections Online. *Dress: The Journal of the Costume Society of America*, *41*(2), 107–127. doi:10.1080/03612112.2015.1130394

Lauterbach, K. (2017). *We wear culture: Discover why we wear what we wear with Google Arts & Culture*. Retrieved from Google Arts & Culture: https://blog.google/outreach-initiatives/arts-culture/we-wear-culture-discover-why-we-wear-what-we-wear/

Loscialpo, F. (2016). From the physical to the digital and back: Fashion exhibitions in the digital age. *International Journal of Fashion Studies*, *3*(2), 225–248. doi:10.1386/infs.3.2.225_1

Lou, T. (1998). Doing the Laundry? A Reassessment of Object-based Dress History. *Fashion Theory*, *2*(4), 337–358. doi:10.2752/136270498779476118

Martin, K., & Ko, H.-S. (2011). Imagining Historic Fashion: Digital Tools for the Examination of Historic Dress. In *2011 Second International Conference on Culture and Computing* (pp. 51 - 56). Los Alamitos: IEEE Computer Society.

Martin, M., & Vacca, F. (2018). Heritage Narratives in the Digital Era. *Research Journal of Textile and Apparel*, *22*(4), 335–351. doi:10.1108/RJTA-02-2018-0015

Melchior, M. (2019). Digital Fashion Heritage: Understanding Europeanafashion.eu and the Google Cultural institute's We Wear Culture. *Critical Studies in Fashion & Beauty*, *10*(1), 49–68. doi:10.1386/csfb.10.1.49_1

Pacault, M., & Patchett, M. (2018). The Last Plumassier: Storying Dead Birds, Gender and Paraffection at Maison Lemarié. *Cultural Geographies*, *25*(1), 123–134. doi:10.1177/1474474016673067

Rossi, V. (2020). Digital Humanities e Moda. *ZoneModa Journal*, *10*(2), 43–59.

Sanderhoff, M. (2014). Foreword. In Sharing is Caring (pp. 9 - 11). Statens Museum for Kunst.

Sandlin, M., & Anderson, J. (2021). *Fashion for All: Using Augmented Reality to Explore Digital Archives*. Online Searcher.

Schnapp, J. (2008). Animating the Archive. In D. Green (Ed.), *WebWise 2.0: The Power of Community* (pp. 45–48). Institute of Museum and Library Services.

Schnapp, J. (2015). *Digital humanities. Meet the Media Guru*. EGEA.

Steele, V. (1998). A Museum of Fashion Is More Than a Clothes-Bag. *Fashion Theory*, *2*(4), 327–335. doi:10.2752/136270498779476109

Steele, V. (2008). Museum Quality: The Rise of the Fashion Exhibition. *Fashion Theory*, *12*(1), 7–30. doi:10.2752/175174108X268127

Valtysson, B. (2011). EUROPEANA: The digital construction of Europe's collective memory. *Information Communication and Society*, *15*(2), 151–170. doi:10.1080/1369118X.2011.586433

Chapter 6
Hip Hop-Low Bap-Killah P. Songs Written for Fyssas Without Pavlos:
A Critical Review

Georgios Pasiopoulos
University of the Aegean, Greece

Georgios Katsadoros
University of the Aegean, Greece

ABSTRACT

One of the main research interests of modern folklore science concerns data related to social, economic, political and cultural contexts of each group whose members maintain a sense of community. Music has always provided such groups with a means of expression, collectivities but also of communication between artists and the public, as the songs' lyrics depict social realities and representations. Low bap emerged from Hip hop music. These two kinds of music, exhibiting several similarities and differences, have not been yet analyzed and studied from a folkloristic point of view. The assassination of Pavlos Fyssas, member of Low bap band, brought again Low bap and Hip hop music to the fore. Its impact on Greek music scene in general can be seen through songs written especially about this murder and captured on social media. The purpose of our study is the research and analysis of these songs' lyrics, as well as the audience's responses to them. Furthermore, this collective way of responding to a certain event seems to signify another case of a group, a folk one in essence, to express itself, but also to demonstrate its members' common traits, in a digital, folk again, environment

INTRODUCTION

Folklore science no longer deals only with rural people (Avdikos, 2009), but involves a wider range of topics and perspectives. Internet gave birth to a new field of research for folklorists as it created new

DOI: 10.4018/978-1-6684-4461-0.ch006

topics, new habits and new social and spiritual realities (Katsadoros, 2013). Nowadays, interest is focused on various groups, thus turning collectivity into a key feature (Avdikos, 2009). These groups sharing a common trait, as Dundes clearly mentioned (1965), essentially constitute a folk group.

Beyond its philological character, folklore material is studied in relation to a large amount of information concerning social, economic, political and cultural contexts, coming from a specific group, and so we have the transition from the simple classification, collection and cataloging to the study of cultural forms and processes, which provides us with an integrated framework of cultural production. Modern folklorists study cultural forms and processes in order to better understand this production.

The aforementioned folk groups determine the way their members regard their surroundings and bring forth a self-community relation. Several of these groups share music as a common trait and they exploit internet availability and fast transmission to communicate among themselves (Gkasouka & Foulidi, 2012). The material circulated, folkloric in essence, carries evidence of repetition and variation, dissipates or vanishes after time and should be studied by folklorists not to capture several singular instances but to reveal emerging patterns (Blank, 2018).

Songs express a variety of emotional states and so became a key aspect of folk literature (Meraklis, 1992), but sometimes also act as the connecting communication link between the artist and the audience, while at the same time offer to the latter "emotional answers" (Cook, 2007). Song lyrics often reveal social values, mythologies and legends, making them one of the richest sources we have for analyzing human behavior (McLeod, 1965).

Hip hop music with its basic characteristic features (Breakdance, Graffiti, DJing, MCing) represents the youth culture that developed during the 70s in New York City and then spread worldwide (Androutsopoulos, 2004). Hip hop is one of the most popular types of music worldwide and it is a performed in numerous languages (Mitchell, 2001). In Greece, Hip hop culture has now reached the third decade of its existence (Efthymiou & Stavrakakis, 2018). Low bap is a subgenre of Hip hop music scene with specific elements and branches.

Hip hop and Low bap came to the fore again after the murder of Pavlos Fyssas[1] in the area of Amfiali, in 2013. At the beginning of his career the victim was a representative of Low bap music scene and then he continued as an independent artist, however, always remaining in Hip hop musical pathways.

In what way the incident of the murder of a young artist can be depicted in song lyrics? How do artists convey to the audience the aspects and effects of this incident? This is particularly interesting, especially if we consider that songs reflect the average level of perception regarding social issues (Kimourtzis, 2019) and through them inner feelings and thoughts of artists and their audience can be expressed, such as joy or sorrow (Segalo, 2006).

The present research consists of two parts. The first part begins with a brief review, as we look back at the origins of Hip hop music scene in Greece and Low bap music scene which is one of its branches. Then, the connection of the victim, Pavlos Fyssas, with the specific music type and his emergence as an anti-fascist symbol after his murder, is examined. In the second part an analysis of the songs written for the specific incident and a lexicological analysis of their lyrics is attempted.

This paper aims to contribute to the research of the so far rather unexplored, from a Folklore point of view, Hip hop and especially of Low bap music phenomenon. At the same time, examining the lyrics of the songwriters, an attempt is made to identify attitudes and perceptions of a part of Greek society towards an incident that shocked young people and the domestic political scene, confirming that songs reflect public's opinion and views.

THE BIRTH OF HIP HOP AND RAP MUSIC SCENE IN GREECE

Rap and Hip hop music appeared for the first time on the Greek music scene in the early 1980s. This is certainly related to the new forms of communication developed at the same time, mainly through Hollywood movies[3] and MTV music channel (Dixon, 2000).

More specifically, in 1985, a new type of dance, called Breakdance , emerged, mainly as an autonomous means of expression and not as part of Hip hop culture (Vogiatzis, 2013). That's how it all started and the first amateur bands experimented on the new sound, at the beginning with English lyrics and then with Greek ones. A milestone in the development of Hip hop culture was the concert of the American Hip hop group Public Enemy at Katrakis Theater in Piraeus in 1992. About 2,500 fans of Hip hop music gathered there, where a virtual "gestation" of new music groups took place (Terzidis, 2003). Soon after this concert, new bands were born such as FF.C. (Fortified Concept), Active Member and Terror X crew. The signing of a contract between Active Member and the multinational company Warner Music, through which they released a number of albums in the 1990s and 2000s (Efthymiou et al., 2018), is considered a turning point for the popularity of Hip hop music in Greece.

At the same time, in Europe, Hip hop and Rap music was spreading rapidly. Starting from African-American communities in deprived areas of New York, protesting against the deteriorating economic and social living conditions (Tatum, 2010; Powell, 1991) it was adapted by diverse socio-political and cultural groups, such as North African immigrants in France, young people of the post-soviet Poland, polarized minorities in the former Yugoslav countries and political activists in Italy (Efthymiou et al., 2018; Mitchell, 2001).

In Greece, Rap and Hip hop music do not seem to be directly related to a mass defiance or reaction of a social group. It started with the introduction of elements from the African-American music scene and gradually adapted cultural elements which were enriched with local cultural and linguistic elements, creating a new distinct domestic artistic expression (Androutsopoulos, 2004).

In the following years, Hip hop music experienced many ups and downs and great controversies between bands . Nowadays, a decline of this kind of music is noted, along with the emergence of new ones, such as Trap[8].

THE CASE OF LOW BAP[9] MUSIC SCENE

Low bap[10] music emerged in 1995 as a "child" of the band *Active Member*, founded by Michalis Mitakidis (B.D.Foxmoor). The members decided to go in a different direction than the other bands of Hip hop music scene and "baptized" their music identifying the direct relationship between life and speech (Pasiopoulos, 2014). It seems that this decision came as an attempt to escape from the unquestioning adoption of American lifestyle[11] by other bands that promoted a way of living which had nothing to do with Greek society of the 90s and 2000s (Terzidis, 2003).

This separation, gradually generated rivalry and ghettoisation. A music movement which was born in Perama, a relatively isolated part of Attica, made its own way, driven by its founder[12]. In 2000, after the release of the album "Strange days, wonderful days" the band experienced universal acceptance and recognition. At the same time, an entire workshop was created based on Solomou Street, which included a bookstore, a record store, and even a cafe (Vogiatzis, 2013), a very innovative commercial idea for that time. In 2005, *Active Member* created their own record company, *Octagon*, intending to promote their songs without any intermediaries, while in 2006 they initiated the *No Sponsors* movement, organizing concerts without sponsors and ads. They were one of the first bands to allow free distribution of internet material through their website and expressed the view that they are not against the so-called music piracy (Tsapari, 2013), while they systematically avoided being a member of A.E.Π.Ι.[13]

In a short period of time, under the umbrella of Active member a number of bands were created as well as a huge and organized fan base with specific characteristics and behavior. Throughout all this course their lyrics continued to contain political messages, maintaining a critical attitude towards various social, political and cultural issues.

On the other hand, according to Papadimitriou (2015), criticism of Low bap music scene is focused mainly on 3 axes. Initially, it is claimed that bands took advantage of the area of Perama, presenting themselves as representatives of a counterculture of a "difficult" neighborhood, while many of their members didn't even live there. In addition, criticism is leveled at their anti-authoritarian mood, which is characterized as "lumpen". Furthermore, one could argue that Low bap bands from time-to-time participated in concerts of left-wing political parties (Sinaspismos), while they also made statements of support for others (ANTARSYA). Finally, the influence exerted on young people, as a musical movement, failed to express specific parts of the society, being unprepared to deal with political developments (Papadimitriou, 2015)[14].

THE DYNAMICS OF MUSIC, THE POPULARITY, THE SONG AS A SOURCE OF INFORMATION AND SOCIAL DATA

Low bap/ Hip hop music scene managed to communicate its music and to become popular among a large number of young people, exhibiting, as a characteristic element in lyrics, an obvious intense aggression and denunciation, mainly continuing on the tradition of the subculture of the working class (Bozinis, 2008).

Besides, the most popular bands started to become popular especially in the working-class neighborhoods of Athens[15]. In this way, Low bap / Hip hop scene, as a youth subculture, connected musically in various ways with the grassroots classes as happened with Hip hop in the United States years ago, starting from the black ghettos of New York (Abraham, 2015; Bozinis, 2008).

Consequently, Low bap and Hip hop youth subcultures were full of references, perceptions and experiences originating from the evaluative system of popular culture; they communicated to a wider audience a way of life and cultural values, which, in connection with the characteristics of everyday life in modern society, sought social justice especially compared to the upper classes (Bozinis, 2008).

Over time, this particular music genre, based on personal experiences of its representatives, denounced economic cruelty and consequent economic and social exclusions (Bozinis 2008), while at the same time it managed to become popular among student population and to raise an embankment against far-right rhetoric (Papadimitriou, 2015). Nevertheless, despite its great initial impact, Low bap also gradually followed fashion and lifestyle (Bozinis, 2008).

Song, in terms of communication, presuppose the existence of both a transmitter and a receiver. One party conveys the message and the other receives it. This process takes place at two levels, an "exterior" one, where the performer of the song addresses his audience (through live performance or a record) and an "interior" one through the lyrics, which is a way of communication between the protagonist referred in the lyrics and the receiver (Laing, 2016).

Recent scientific studies of disciplines such as Linguistics, Psycholinguistics and Text-linguistics identify a number of additional social and psychological factors involved in this communication process. These interrelated factors make the aforementioned simple scheme of the transmitter and receiver more complex, adding a number of parameters that are directly or indirectly related to the sociocultural environment (Bonidis, 2004). Therefore, song lyrics cannot be examined without taking into account their surrounding social environment, the receivers of the messages and the researcher himself with his cognitive and emotional background (Efthymiadou 2012).

Even more, songs have the ability to offer us a wealth of information about the time of their creation, to convey unique pictures of everyday life, to vividly capture social values and stereotypes and reveal hidden aspects of everyday life. Furthermore, songs can trigger a range of emotions, as they have the power to thrill us, to make us feel sad or happy, to entertain us, to motivate us or to increase our sexual desire and in general they can capture the emotions of an entire era. Basically, songs consist of lyrics, music and performance that together form an information and value system. In particular, the conversation between music and lyrics contributes significantly in conveying their meaning (Karamanolakis, 2019).

RESEARCH QUESTION

The present study starts with the following question: in what way is the assassination of Pavlos Fyssas reflected in related song lyrics? This aspect is particularly interesting if we take into account that songs, and consequently their lyrics, express common perceptions regarding social issues; this perception is spread in a broader audience that contributes to their acceptance (Kimourtzis, 2019). This makes songs part of folk literature which, just like folk songs in previous ages, stripped of their lyrical intention, offer a realistic depiction not only of the natural but also of the social and intellectual environment (Meraklis, 1992). Therefore, we study songs as a reflection of public opinion and perception.

ANALYSIS METHOD

Laswell states that the directions towards which the researcher can turn for the analysis of the quality research are the transmitter, the receiver, the message and its effect (Efthimiadoy, 2012).

For the present study, content analysis[16] was chosen, focusing mainly on "standard" references. (Bonidis 2004; Iosifidis, 2008). As "standard" one could consider some individuals, some characteristic expressions and extreme phrases, which seem to appear frequently in the sample material and are of special interest for our study (Bonidis, 2004). Furthermore, research results were presented through narrative discussion[17] (Creswell, 2011) and, through codification, basic issues emerging from data were categorized and analyzed, both within each category as well as among different ones.

The aim of our paper will be to study the obvious meaning (what is expressed) in the lyrics of songs referring to the assassination of Pavlos Fyssas, followed by their underlying one (how it is expressed). Moreover, utilizing the parameters of "channel" and "message", we will try at the same time to highlight the message and attempt an analysis of the intention of the transmitter (why) as well as the impact the message may have (Bonidis, 2004).

Table 1. A short presentation of the artists and the songs referring to the assassination of Pavlos Fyssas

NO	SINGER	SONG TITLE	LYRICS	MUSIC	TYPE	YEAR	VIEWS[17]
1	Quadir Lateef	Fuck Golden Dawn	Quadir Lateef	Quadir Lateef	Rap	2013	68.327
2	Rigas Skepetaris	They aimed at your heart	Rigas Skepetaris	Rigas Skepetaris	Reggae	2014	17.486
3	Imiskoumbria	----------	Imiskoumbria	Imiskoumbria	Rap	2013	---
4	Alkinoos Ioannidis	It will always dawn	Alkinoos Ioannidis	Alkinoos Ioannidis	Greek Entechno	2014	601.345
5	Stamatis Kraounakis/ Maria Panosian	You are my brother Pavlos Fissas	Stamatis Kraounakis	Stamatis Kraounakis	Greek Entechno	2014	13.259
6	Yperastikoi	Black Dawn	Yperastikoi	Yperastikoi .	Collaboration of artists	2014	261.467

THE SONGS UNDER STUDY[18] - A CRITICAL REVIEW

Our study material includes 6 songs that have been initially composed in response and essentially refer to the assassination of Pavlos Fyssas. Five of them include instrumental accompaniment and another one was sang a capella by the band of *Imiskoubria* during the joint press conference of all the bands of the field on Tuesday 24 September 2013 in the hall of E.Σ.H.E.A[18].

The unharmonious group of artists who were inspired by this incident is noteworthy, a black American rapper, a Greek reggae singer, two Greek artful (Entcehno) musicians and a collaboration of other musicians as well. This fact is indicative of the impact and effect the assassination had, surpassing the specific music field of Rap/Hip Hop music Fyssas belonged to. All of the songs were composed in the same year or the following one, attesting to the incident's impact.

The musicians wrote the lyrics themselves. What you write is what you feel, what you believe and what you relate to. That fact, in combination with a honest heartfelt performance, strengthens the bond between the audience and the song, which characterizes the attitude of the audience towards a large part of folk music (Laing, 2016).

In the first song, Quadir Lateef[19], a moderately popular Rapper in USA, uses several swear words to describe Golden Dawn party, which is obvious even in the title of the song "Fuck Golden Dawn". He calls them cowards and relates them to the world-famous racist organization "Ku Klux Klan". Moreover, he believes that the party is supported by the Greek government, since the latter does not take measures against it. The lyrics describe the hostile and aggressive attitude of Golden Dawn members towards social and religious groups (immigrants, homosexuals, Muslims, religiously devoted people). The rapper from Houston also challenges the fans of the fascist organization to come and confront him: he will wait for them with plenty of weapons in his hands, wanting to start a vendetta of long-running violent incidents. Finally, he calls the Greeks to stand up and take control because "you can't let racists and

Table 2.

Wanna go to war homie? Let the AK spray. Who the hell is Golden Dawn, the new KKK Supported by the Greek government, who let y'all stay Bunch of coward ass racists, Imma make y'all pay rest in peace Killah P, he was taken away, take the life of a man who has something to say you attack immigrants and the people who gay, you attack muslims, and the people who pray bunch of fascists, that's why I gotta spit in your face, y'all attack Killah P, it was 20 to 1! come attack Quadir Lateef, we got plenty of guns! I'm a soldier homie, see I was raised in the slum, it won't be a Golden Dawn if you ain't seen the sun; it's war! Could you wanna be the Ku Klux Klan I'm about to bring the ruckus like Wu Tang Clan catch you right at protest I won't let y'all stand, nigga!	Fuck Golden Dawn (x6) You wanna go to war homie? Bring it on. Fuck Golden Dawn (x6) I fear no man, bring it on Niggas- -cowards man. I don't understand this fake skinhead, this fake KKK wannabe, running around, getting at people man like y'all boys run things man the people, the people in Greece gotta stand up man the people in Greece gotta stand up man and form, and form a unit man and get right at them boys, man you gotta take the power back man can't let them people kill people man just walk around and tryna be racist and fascists man y'all do nothing about it man we gotta lock and load on them boys man that's the only way you're gonna get peace sometimes it takes war Quadir Lateef, rest in peace Killah P Who next? Yeah...

fascists kill people and wander around without doing nothing", while the song ends with the question "Who is going to be next?".

The following year, 2014, the song "They aimed at your heart" is a reggae song written by Rigas Skepetaris, with an indicative title that describes the stabbing scene. The song is more lyrical and in soft tones. Throughout his lyrics, the artist wonders what causes someone to commit violent acts and even a murder (how it is possible to be seduced by hate and death) and asks his audience not to act vengefully, not to forget but also not to be trapped into an endless cycle of violence and bloodshed. ("[…] No more blood, no more war and hate, we forgot the obvious and it became a riddle").

The next song was presented during the joint press conference of Hip hop and Low bap bands held in honor of Pavlos Fyssas. At this point, the audience is also encouraged not to continue the cycle of violence, but to respond to extreme violent actions with love and solidarity ("[…]terminate hate end darkness"). In fact, they created a mixed word with an English theme and a Greek suffix (Altogather-vosini - sense of togetherness) to emphasize its content. In addition, they believe that love and harmony are intertwined with this type of music.

In 2014, Alkinoos Ioannidis, a very popular artist in Greece with a loyal audience, also wrote a song in memory of Pavlos Fyssas with the title "It will always dawn". This song is the most popular of the previous ones since it reached 602,000 views[20] on YouTube. At the same time, the lyrics regarding the far-right rhetoric and practices appear to be the most optimistic. The artist insists that as long as there are people who will embrace similar authoritarian ideologies, there will also be democratic people who will react in every possible way, there will always be the "light" that will defeat the "darkness". You float, you fight and at the same time you become a lighthouse to shine for the others, ¯"even when knives

Table 3.

Σε σημαδέψαν στην καρδιά, γιατί δεν είχαν και ζηλέψαν. Στην πλάτη σου έβγαλες φτερά, κάπου ψηλά σε ταξιδέψαν. Και ρωτώ τι να 'ναι αυτό που το μυαλό τους κυριεύει; Το μίσος και ο θάνατος μα πως τους σαγηνεύει; Τίποτα δεν τελειώνει, τα χρόνια όσο περνάνε η ψυχή μου δυναμώνει και Το κάθε χέρι που ένα λουλούδι κόβει να ξέρει πως στη θέση του ένα νέο θα φυτρώνει. Πρέπει να πιάσουμε τα πράγματα νομίζω εξ αρχής, πρέπει να μάθεις και αν ξέχασες πρέπει να θυμηθείς. Μην ξεχαστείς, γίνε λυγμός της σιωπής, στα άδυτα της σκέψης σου πρέπει να βυθιστείς.	Δώσε αγάπη στο διπλανό και στον απέναντί σου, στους πάνω και στους κάτω σου και θα 'ρθουνε μαζί σου. Ότι δίνεις παίρνεις ποτέ μην το ξεχάσεις, βοήθησε όσο μπορείς τις σκέψεις κάνε πράξεις. Μάζεψε τα κομμάτια σου ότι έχει μείνει σώστο φτιάξε στο μήνυμά σου οχυρό και σ' όλους δώστο. Όχι άλλο αίμα, όχι πόλεμος και μίσος, το αυτονόητο ξεχάσαμε και έγινε γρίφος. Διαίρει και βασίλευε τα πάντα ένα κουμάντο στρατιωτάκια με υπερβάλλων ζήλο γίνονται κομάντο. Θέλουνε θύματα πάντα έξω και ασφάλεια στο μαντρί, μα η διαφορετικότητα έχει αξία μαγική.

Table 4.

Με ρούμι τεκίλα και άφθονη μπύρα κοιτάζοντας ψηλά την απόφαση μου πήρα. Τέρμα στον πόνο τέρμα στο μίσος, τέρμα στο σκοτάδι τέρμα στο ίσως. Ναι στο χαμόγελο για όλα τα παιδιά. Σήμερα σας δίνω της καρδιά μας τα κλειδιά.	Alltogetherνοσύνη, φτιάχνω νέα λέξη με τον Μπαμπινιώτη πλέον να τα έχει παίξει. Το Χιπ χοπ είναι κουλτούρα, είναι ένωση και ρίμα είναι κτήμα μας, είναι τοΥ δρόμοΥ ποίημα. Είναι εικόνα ποΥ περνά σαν αστραπή Κι ίσως κάποΥ εκεί ψηλά χαμογελάει ο Killah P.

Table 5.

Είσαι αδερφός μου Παύλο Φύσσα, Τώρα σε βλέπω απ' την αφίσα, Με την πληγή, η μνήμη που κρατάει μαχαίρι οπλίζει τώρα κι άλλο χέρι και καίει τη γη ζωές ζητάει να αποτελειώσει. Ο φασισμός πουλάει τη δόση. Κι ο καναπές την αγοράζει. Στις γειτονιές των ηττημένων	Το τέρας στέκεται στημένο. Σπίτια ρημάζει. Είσαι αδελφός μου Παύλο Φύσσα, αν είσαι αέρας τώρα φύσα. Να σηκωθούμε, με ένα ορφανό τραγούδι Παύλο. Το πλήρωσες εσύ το ναύλο. Χωρίς επιστροφή να πούμε. Είσαι αδελφός μας Παύλο Φύσσα, αν είσαι αέρας τώρα φύσα…

are out (…) It will always dawn (…) What is life, what's non-life and what lies between them[21] / a dim light[22] unborn in the heart of darkness".

In the next song, Stamatis Kraounakis, identifies himself with Pavlos Fyssas, his actions and life: "you are my brother Pavlos Fyssas". Technically, we should note that, in contrast with the rest of the songs, the lyrics are written in pair rhyme of the type AABCCB and not paired of the type AABB (Parisis & Parisis, 2015). From a semantic point of view, the action and the spread of Golden Dawn in city neighborhoods is due to the passive and inactive position of the average citizen who just sits comfortably on a couch without taking any action ¯ "fascism sells the dose and the couch buys it". Making a pun with the word "Fyssa" (means "blow" in Greek) and through the power involved in the sacrifice, encourages people to stand up against any similar incident or even to completely terminate such practices.

The last song was written by a collaboration of musicians with an obvious leftish ideological origin, under the name Yperastikoi, with the mocking title "Black Dawn", having a clear intention to exhibit the consequences of fascism in our daily life, which becomes gloomy and dark. Here, Pavlos Fyssas appears to be the third victim in a series of assassinations committed by far-right groups, such as the murders of Abdul Manan[25] and Sahjat Lukman : ¯ "Pavlos Fyssas, I have three wounds. (Alim) Abdul Manan, I count ten blades". "My torn vein, bleeding, looks at Sahjat Lukman". This song presents another version of fascism that we do not find in the other songs. More specifically, in the lyrics it is implied that Golden Dawn, as an organization and political party, appears to be born through the most fragile parts of urban

Table 6.

Αν έχεις δόντι του φονιά και γούστα ματωμένα. Αν μαύρισες τον ουρανό και θες να φας κι εμένα μέσα στη καταιγίδα… Θα γίνω αγκάθι στο λαιμό σου, σκόνη μες το μάτι, μέσα στ' αυτί σου ψίθυρος και σύγκρυο στην πλάτη, στη σιγουριά σου αγκίδα… Πάντα θα ξημερώνει. Σκοτάδι αν είσαι αφέγγαρο, λεπίδι δίχως πόνο, δύναμη δίχως όνειρο, ταξίδι δίχως δρόμο οργή χωρίς καθρέφτη…	Θα γίνω μέρα που θα 'ρθει κι άνοιξη στο λουλούδι μες στο γκρεμό σου αντίλαλος και πιο βαθύ τραγούδι στη μαχαιριά που πέφτει… Πάντα θα ξημερώνει. Τι είναι Ζωή, τι ειν' η Ζωή και τι τ' ανάμεσό τους. Ένα φωσάκι αγέννητο μες στην καρδιά του σκότους… Πάντα θα ξημερώνει.

Table 7.

<table>
<tr>
<td>Παρακάλια και ευχές δεν τρομάζουν τις οχιές.
Μαύρη Αυγή σέρνεται στη γη, φαρμακερό φίδι «αγκυλωτό».
Παύλο Φύσσα, τρεις πληγές φορώ.
(Αλίμ) Αμπντούλ Μάναν, δέκα αιχμές μετρώ.
Η σκισμένη φλέβα μου κοιτά,
μες στο αίμα τον Σαχτζάτ Λουκμάν.
Μαύρη Αυγή σέρνεται στη γη, φαρμακερό φίδι «αγκυλωτό».
Απ’ τη σάπια μήτρα των αστών,
Ρουπακιάδες, τάγματα φιδιών,
δουλικών του καπιταλισμού
που μισούν το δίκιο του λαού.</td>
<td>Το φασισμό πάτα στο λαιμό.
Του φασίστα χέρι αν σηκωθεί,
την πυγμή του καπιταλιστή
δοκιμάζει πάνω στο λαό,
που τον θέλει έρμο και σκυφτό.
Το φασισμό πάτα στο λαιμό.
Ο λαός μας όρθιος θα σταθεί,
στους αγώνες θα ατσαλωθεί,
θα τσακίσουμε το φασισμό,
του συστήματος γιο και φρουρό.
Παρακάλια και ευχές δεν τρομάζουν τις οχιές.</td>
</tr>
</table>

society and at the same time to be a tool of the capitalist system that is used against common people, its rights and freedoms with the sole purpose to control them in order to achieve its ultimate aspirations. Therefore, the leftist origin of the collaborated musician we mentioned above becomes obvious, since leftish rhetoric often makes references to this version of capitalism (Communist Review / Department of Economy of the Communist Party of Greece (KKE), Central Committee, 2018).

In conclusion, they encourage citizens, as was the case in other songs presented above, to stand up against fascists in order to get rid of fascism once and for all, as the pleas and wishes do not seem enough.

AN ATTEMPT OF CATEGORIZATION

The attempt of a classification-grouping based on some common characteristics through such a limited material for analysis, just six songs in total, makes any project particularly risky and daring. However, a number of terms and words included in these songs can make our classification effort, easier. Therefore, we suggest that these six songs fall into three different categories.

More specifically, in the first category, we placed songs with more aggressive and vengeful lyrics. The song of the American rapper Quadir Lateef and the collaboration of artists "Yperastikoi" can be included here. In these songs the predominance of "good" against "evil" will come only through the extermination of the "opponent". War seems inevitable and is presented as the only possible solution[25]. ¯ [Fuck Golden Dawn] "I make y' all pay (…) I' am a soldier homie (…) we got plenty of guns!", [Black Dawn] "press fascism down the throat" are some characteristic lyrics of these two songs.

In the second category, we placed songs of a more optimistic content ¯ [It will always dawn] "it will always dawn (…) I will be day and spring", ¯ [No title-*Imiskoumbria*] "let 's finish the hatred (…) say yes to smile", more specifically, the songs from *Imiskoumbria* and Alkinoos Ioannidis. The assassination of Pavlos Fyssas is no longer proposed as the trigger for a new cycle of violence, but more like a step for a new, more optimistic, beginning, where hatred, resentment and intolerance will no longer have a place in society and the "good" will emerge as the only viable option.

The third and last category, is that of encouraging and activating society against such unfortunate incidents. This includes the songs of Rigas Skepetaris and Stamatis Kraounakis. More specifically, their lyrics, apart from an optimistic view ¯ [They aimed at your heart] "no more blood and hatred (…) give love (…) "every hand that cuts a flower knows that in its place a new one will sprout", also include a feeling, a message to society to never forget who is responsible for such heinous acts ¯ "you have to learn

Table 8. Detailed presentation of typical words depicting perpetrator's side

WORD	NUMBER OF APPEARANCES	NUMBER OF SONGS WHERE THE WORD APPEEARS
Hate	4	3
Darkness	2	2
Death	1	2
Dead	1	2
Blood	3	3
War	5	2
Little soldiers	1	1
Cowards	3	1
Racists	2	1
Fascists	2	2
Attack	4	1
Pain	2	2
Gun-blade-knife	4	3
Snake - viper	4	1
Storm	1	1
Power	1	1
Cliff	1	1
Wound	1	1
Monster	1	1
Defeated	1	1

and if you forgot you have to remember (…) put thoughts into action (…) "you are my brother Pavlos Fyssas (…) If you are wind now blow and let's stand up". Oblivion is what feeds the hand of the "bad ones" and remembering is what will put an end to such extreme behaviors and ideologies.

Therefore, according to our semantic analysis, the categorization resembles a pendulum where on the one side we have an extremely aggressive point of view, on the other an extremely optimistic one and, in between, a more moderate view that considers the awakening of society as the more appropriate way to deal with such phenomena.

From the victim's side, as we have already given the definition, the referred words are more optimistic. The most frequently repeated words are: heart, flower, dawn-light and song, all of them related to the victim Pavlos Fyssas and his life.

Finally, it becomes obvious that song lyrics focus more on the perpetrator than on the victim. The number of the words attempting to describe the acts and practices of the perpetrator is larger than of those referring to the passive victim, which to some extent seems reasonable, if we consider that the motive for writing the songs is to stigmatize and condemn the act of murder.

Table 9. Detailed presentation of typical words depicting victim's side

WORD	NUMBER OF APPEARANCES	NUMBER OF SONGS WHERE THE WORD APPEARS
Spring	1	1
Flower	2	2
Poem	1	1
Smile	1	1
Dream	1	1
Diversity	1	1
Heart	4	3
Dawn	5	1
Light	1	1
Song	2	2
Air	1	1

OUTCOMES

Music has always been a pole of attraction and a means of expression for many people, especially young ones. Songs, through their lyrics, convey the experiences, the ways of expression and cultural values of popular culture. At the same time, based on music, collectivities are created that have the ability to send and spread messages to society. The assassination of Pavlos Fyssas is an incident that was deeply engraved in the collective memory of Greek society and is reflected in the lyrics of the songs that were written about it.

Online groups based on music have been formed for many decades now. Our search on the internet for songs related to this tragic event has indicated the existence of a folk group of people that not only like a specific kind of music, but also concern themselves with related issues and communicate with each other, pose questions, agree or disagree. Related *YouTube* video views exceeded 1,000,000[26], with the recorded comments to reflect views from each conflicting party, demonstrating that this incident, even after 7 years, seems to still generate controversy and extreme emotions that are evoked through dipoles (good ones - bad ones, freedom – fascism, peace – war) contained within the lyrics of the songs.

The six songs that refer to this incident may seem few, but we must also consider that this was the only single incident for the last decade that inspired artists to collaborate and compose a series of dedicated songs.

Finally, through the lyrics we can distinguish 3 different aspects, an obvious controversy, an emphasis to an optimistic side, rebirth and creation and a third one calling for vigilance and acting to prevent similar incidents in the future. It becomes clear that the study of songs constitutes a reliable tool in order to analyze society's view, providing us with a clear understanding of average perception and public opinion and this leads us to useful conclusions.

Limitations and Perspectives

The study at hand involved all songs composed and performed until early 2020 in response to a specific tragic event, the assassination of Pavlos Fyssas. Their small number, six, surely seems inadequate to provide safe general results concerning the way such an event is depicted in song lyrics. This research, essentially a first part of a broader one, is to be followed by another one recording, analyzing and categorizing Youtube users' comments on the specific songs. Similarly, related messages and graffiti painted on public walls would be of great research interest.

CONCLUSION

As Blank (2018) clearly states, "ephemeral digital folk culture underscores how individuals construct expressive repertoires, accumulate knowledge and mastery of folkloric forms, and meaningfully engage in vernacular discourse as part of a folk process aimed at quickly parsing through the onslaught of mass mediated information". Songs seem to condense the average perception regarding social issues and at the same time connect to society. Moreover, they transmit messages and receive feedback from society, maintaining a permanently open interdependence channel. The present paper presents an attempt to highlight this relationship, and to detect the impact and consequences of the assassination of Pavlos Fyssas in the Greek Hip hop/ Low bap music field, as Fyssas was more related with this scene, even though these songs belong to other music genres, such as Greek artistic song or reggae. However, such a small research sample fails to draw a more complete picture of the transmitted messages. In any case, it constitutes an initial research that will hopefully be extended. A following, wider, research in social media will allow us to further investigate other effects of this tragic incident such as related views and opinions, friendly or hostile, thus demonstrating a certain group's, a folk one in essence formed based on music preferences and digital literacy, response and notions.. In conclusion, it seems that songs with their lyrics can be a potential field for receiving research data and drawing important conclusions useful for folklore science, while lyrics reflect collectivities, social realities and representations.

REFERENCES

Abraham, I. (2015). Christian hip hop as pedagogy: A South African case study. *Journal of Beliefs & Studies*, *36*(3), 285–296. doi:10.1080/13617672.2015.1095518

Androutsopoulos, G. (2004). Ο ραψωδός που θέλεις να φτάσεις: Γλωσσικές πολιτισμικής οικειοποίησης στο ελληνόφωνο ραπ. Πρακτικά του 6ου Διεθνούς Συνεδρίου Ελληνικής Γλωσσολογίας (6th ICGL), Πανεπιστήμιο Κρήτης, Εργαστήριο Γλωσσολογίας [Lexical characteristics of Greek language]. Rethymno.

Avdikos, E. (2009). *Εισαγωγή στις σπουδές του λαϊκού πολιτισμού* [Lexical characteristics of Greek language]. Κριτική.

Blank, T. J. (2018). Folklore and the Internet: The Challenge of an Ephemeral Landscape. *Humanities (Washington)*, *7*(2), 50. https://doi.org/10.3390/h7020050

Bonidis, K. (2004). *Το περιεχόμενο του σχολικού βιβλίου ως αντικείμενο έρευνας: Διαχρονική εξέταση της σχετικής έρευνας και μεθοδολογικές προσεγγίσεις* [Lexical characteristics of Greek language]. Μεταίχμιο.

Bozinis, N. (2008). *Ροκ παγκοσμιότητα και Ελληνική τοπικότητα. Η κοινωνική ιστορία του ροκ στις χώρες της καταγωγής του και στην Ελλάδα* [Lexical characteristics of Greek language]. Νεφέλη.

Citizen Protection Ministry. (2005). Police operation "Πόλις"' [Lexical characteristics of Greek language]. Press release 02/12/2005. Athens.

Cook, N. (2007). *Music Performance Meaning*. Taylor & Francis Ltd.

Demetis, C. (2013). Hip Hop και Low bap δείχνουν τον δρόμο: Ενωμένοι ενάντια στον φασισμό για τον Παύλο Φύσσα [Lexical characteristics of Greek language], news247.gr. https://www.news247.gr/koinonia/hip-hop-kai-low-bap-deichnoyn-to-dromo-enomenoi-enantia-ston-fasismo-gia-ton-p-fyssa.6227946.html

Department of economy of the communist party of Greece (KKE), (2018). Χρυσή Αυγή – "Δεκανίκι" του Καπιταλισμού στην Ελλάδα. Κομμουνιστική Επιθεώρηση [Lexical characteristics of Greek language], (5), Athens: Σύγχρονη εποχή. https://www.komep.gr/m-article/XRYSI-AYGI-DEKANIKI-TOY-KAPITALISMOY-STIN-ELLADA/

Dixon, W. (2000). The new genre cinema. In W. Dixon (Ed.), *Film genre 2000* (pp. 1–13). State University Of New York Press.

Dundes, A. (1965). *The study of folklore*. Prentice-Hall.

Efthymiadou, X. A. (2012). *"Σε σένα μιλάω Νεοέλληνα": Οι νέοι τραγουδούν την εθνική ταυτότητα* [Lexical characteristics of Greek language]. (Unpublished postgraduate thesis). Αριστοτέλειο Πανεπιστήμιο Θεσσαλονίκης, Thessaloniki.

Eythimiou, A., & Stavrakakis, H. (2018). Rap in Greece: Gendered configurations of power in-between the rhymes. *Journal of Greek Media & Culture*, *4*(2), 205–222. doi:10.1386/jgmc.4.2.205_1

Gasouka, M., & Foulidi, X. (2012). *Σύγχρονοι ορίζοντες των λαογραφικών σπουδών* [Lexical characteristics of Greek language]. Ι. Σιδέρης.

Iosifidis, T. (2008). *Ποιοτικές μέθοδοι έρευνας στις κοινωνικές επιστήμες* [Lexical characteristics of Greek language]. Κριτική.

Karamanolakis, E. (2019). *Η μουσική: Η δεκαετία του '40 και το ρεμπέτικο τραγούδι. Από έργο τέχνης σε τεκμήριο του ιστορικού* [Lecture notes]. ΕΚΠΑ, Πρόγραμμα: Οι πηγές του ιστορικού-Ερευνώντας την Ελληνική ιστορία του 20ου αιώνα [Lexical characteristics of Greek language].

Katsadoros, G. (2013). Η επιστήμη της λαογραφίας στη σύγχρονη τεχνολογική εποχή. Η ηλεκτρονική προφορικότητα. In G. Kokkinos & M. Maskofoglou-Xionidou (Eds.), *Επιστήμες της εκπαίδευσης: από την ασθενή ταξινόμηση της παιδαγωγικής στη διεπιστημονικότητα και στον επιστημονικό υβριδισμό* [Lexical characteristics of Greek language]. (pp. 99–122). Ταξιδευτής.

Kimourtzis, P. (2016). Πτυχίο: Εισιτήριο, αλλά για ένα ακαθόριστο ταξίδι [Lexical characteristics of Greek language]. *Academia (Caracas)*, *14*, 141–160.

Laing, D. (2016). Λόγος και σημασία στο Πανκ Ροκ [Lexical characteristics of Greek language]. One chord wonders. Athens: Κουκκίδα.

Mayring, Ph. (2000). Qualitative Content analysis. *Forum Qualitative Social Research*, *1*(2), 20.

MCLeod, N. (1965). Review of The Anthropology of Music by Alan P. Merriam. *Anuario*, *1*, 127–130.

Meraklis, M. (1992). *Λαϊκή Τέχνη. (Ελληνική Λαογραφία. Τόμος Γ¢)* [Lexical characteristics of Greek language]. Οδυσσέας.

Mitchell, T. (2001). *Global Noise: Rap and Hip Hop Outside the USA*. Wesleyan University Press.

Nasopoulos, D. (2014). Η μνήμη απέναντι στη σκληρή καθημερινότητα [Lexical characteristics of Greek language]. Τα Νέα (September 13-14), p. 25.

Oliver, P. (1963). *The meaning of the blues.* New York: Collier books.

Papadimitriou, G. (2015, Ιανουάριος). Οι τρεις μύθοι του Low Bap [Lexical characteristics of Greek language]. *Unfollow,* σ. 104-111.

Parisis, G. & Parisis, N. (2015). *Λεξικό λογοτεχνικών όρων* [Lexical characteristics of Greek language]. Athens: ΟΕΔΒ, ΥΠ. ΠΑΙΔΕΙΑΣ-ΙΤΥΕ ΔΙΟΦΑΝΤΟΣ:

Pasiopoulos, G. (2014). *Η κοινωνική έκφραση και εκδήλωση μέσα από τη σύγχρονη μουσική: Το κίνημα Low Bap* [Lexical characteristics of Greek language] (Unpublished postgraduate thesis). Πανεπιστήμιο Αιγαίου, Παιδαγωγικό Τμήμα Δημοτικής Εκπαίδευσης, Rhodes.

Powell, C. (1991). Rap Music: An Education with a Beat from the Street. *The Journal of Negro Education*, *60*(3), 245–259.

Psara, M. (2017, September 20). Παύλος Φύσσας: Ο μουσικός που έγινε σύμβολο του αντιφασιστικού αγώνα [Lexical characteristics of Greek language]. https://www.news247.gr/afieromata/paylos-fyssas-o-moysikos-poy-egine-symvolo-toy-antifasistikoy-agona.6518566.html

Segalo, P. (2006). The psychological power of rap music in the healing of black communities. *Muziki*, *3*(1), 28–35. doi:10.1080/18125980608538781

Skaribas, G. (2016). *Άπαντες στίχοι 1936-1970* [Lexical characteristics of Greek language]. Νεφέλη.

Tatum, B. (2010). The link between rap music and youth crime and violence: A review of the literature and issues for future research. *The Justice Professional*, *11*(3), 339–353. doi:10.1080/1478601X.1999.9959513

Terzidis, C. (2003). *To hip hop δε σταματά* [Lexical characteristics of Greek language]. Athens: Οξύ.

Theodoridis, G. (2022 March 05). *(drama) "Euripides – Helen". https://www.poetryintranslation.com/theodoridisgeuripideshelen.php*

Tsapari, Ol. (2013). *No Sponsors - Χωρίς χορηγούς: Η Low Bap σκηνή του Περάματος ως παράδειγμα πολιτιστικής διαχείρισης* [Lexical characteristics of Greek language]. (Unpublished postgraduate thesis). Πανεπιστήμιο Ιωαννίνων, Ioannina.

Vogiatzis, T. (2013). Το ελληνικό hip hop στα '80s και στα '90s. [Lexical characteristics of Greek] In T. Vogiatzis (Ed.), *Hip hop: code of the streets* (pp. 14–21). Sonik.

ADDITIONAL READING

Bradley, L. (2001). *Bass culture: When reggae was king*. Penguin.

Chang, J. (2005). *Can't stop, won't stop. A history of the Hip-Hop generation*. St. Martin's Press.

Daloukas, M. (2012). *Ελληνικό Ροκ. Ιστορία της νεανικής κουλτούρας από τη γενιά του Χάους μέχρι το θάνατο του Παύλου Σιδηρόπουλου. 1945-1990* [Lexical characteristics of Greek language]. Άγκυρα.

Jeffries, M. P. (2010). *Thug Life: Race, Gender, and the Meaning of Hip Hop*. The University of Chicago Press.

Magiopoulos, T. (2013). Το ελληνικό hip hop στα '80s και στα '90s. Στο T. Βογιατζής (Επιμ.), [Lexical characteristics of Greek language]. Hip hop: code of the streets (σσ.14-21). Athens: Sonik.

Patsalidis, S. (2000). Η μουσική rap και η ιδεολογία της βίας και της αντίστασης. *Μουσικολογία*, [Lexical characteristics of Greek language]. (12-13), 189-205.

Reeves, M. (2008). *Somebody scream: rap music's rise to promince in the aftershock of black power*. Faber & Faber inc.

Sifaki, E., Stamou, A., & Papadopoulou, M. (2020). *Η ανάδυση ενός νέου κύματος στο σύγχρονο ελληνικό κινηματογραφό. Διαδικασίες καλλιτεχνικής παραγωγής, καθιέρωσης και επικοινωνίας στον κόσμο της τέχνης* [Lexical characteristics of Greek language]. EKKE.

ENDNOTES

1 Pavlos Fyssas was born in Keratsini, a neighborhood of Piraeus with high unemployment, whose residents are hardworking people who mainly work in the neighboring area of Perama, in construction field and in small craft businesses which are located in Schisto (Nasopoulos, 2014). Fyssas worked for a while in the shipbuilding and repair zone and became a member of the Trade Union of Metal Workers of Piraeus. At an early age he was involved in the Hip Hop music scene and during the first years of his music career he was member of the Low bap community (Vogiatzis, 2013) based in neighboring Perama and more specifically of the band *Kaka Mantata* from 1998 to 2001 along with Totem and Dj Longplay. In the music scene he became known by the nickname Killa P (Killer of the Past). He collaborated with several bands of the Hip Hop scene such as Imiskumbria and participated in concerts held in small venues with a targeted audience. The lyrics of his songs are of leftist ideology and in many cases self-referential, meaning that there is an inseparable relationship between lyrics and music, something very common in Hip Hop, "What I write is what I am" (Efthymiou et al., 2018). The songs deal with issues related to refugees, immigrants, the assassination of Alexandros Grigoropoulos as well as that of Carlo Giuliani, an

anti-globalization protester in Genoa. In 2013 he was killed by a Golden Dawn member in the area of Amfiali (more information about this incident can be found in the book "The Black Bible of Golden Dawn", in the chapter "Pogrom and Lynching" pp. 415-430). This incident had great impact in the Hip Hop music scene. Besides the fact that Golden Dawn's leading members were sent to trial, the bands of Greek Hip Hop/Low bap music scene were brought together, put aside their differences and held a joint press conference (Demetis, 2013). Furthermore, after this incident, anti-fascist lyrics prevailed in the songs of Rap bands and became a common point of reference for the rappers, which was added to the already intense controversy that triggered by the assassination of Alexandros Grigoropoulos and the operation under the name 'POLIS' carried out by the police within the context of the 2005 anti-crime policy (Efthymiou et al., 2018; Citizen Protection Ministry, 2005).

2 Right after his death, Pavlos Fyssas became a symbol of the anti-fascist struggle. Many demonstrations took place in various cities of Greece, such as Thessaloniki, Patras, Heraklion and Chania. Large protests also took place in the areas of Keratsini and Nikea. On September 25, 2013, a large anti-fascist protest was organized by the General Confederation of Greek Workers (GSEE) and the Civil Servants' Confederation (ADEDY), and then followed a protest march towards Mesogeion Street to the headquarters of Golden Dawn. Protests also took place in major cities in Europe such as Barcelona, Paris and Valencia by Greek students abroad (Psara, 2017). In 2014, a year after his assassination, a statue was erected at the site of the murder, which was vandalized several times by right-wing extremists who realize that it symbolizes the struggle against fascism. Alexis Tsipras, Greek Prime Minister at that time, in a post on social media referred to Pavlos Fyssas as a leading symbol against fascism, xenophobia and racism. Specifically, the post was: "September 18 is a day of pain for every democrat, a black page in the modern history of our country. The assassination of Pavlos Fyssas by the criminal neo-Nazi gang of Golden Dawn reminded us, in the most tragic way, where hate ideologies can lead and history has shown that such practices have been condemned definitively and irrevocably. Pavlos Fyssas is considered right now one of the most iconic symbols against fascism, xenophobia and racism. Attacks against refugees, immigrants, anti-fascists, such as the recent one against a member of SYRIZA Youth - but also against each one the neo-Nazis persecute because of his/her diversity, find us all strongly opposed. Condemnation of fascism crimes in our daily life, in education and work is a common responsibility we all have to take. The daily struggle for freedom and solidarity is a struggle for a society of mutual respect and progress for everyone" (posted by the Prime Minister Alexis Tsipras on September 18, 2018, retrieved from https://primeminister.gr/2018/09/18/20562, 02/01/2020).

3 Political concerns, black urban music, new visual styles more and more appear in Hollywood movies directed and written by artists such as Bill Duke, Spike Lee, Kasi Lemmons, Parnell Martin, John Singleton and George Tillman Jr. (Dixon, 2000).

4 The movies "Wild style" (1982) (Director: Charlie Ahearn-Stars: 'Lee' George Qiinores, Lady Pink, Fab 5 Freddy) https://www.imdb.com/title/tt0084904/ and "Beat street" (1984) (Director: Stan Lathan-Stars: Rae Dawn Chong, Guy Davis, Jon Chardiet) https://www.imdb.com/title/tt0086946/ also played an important role in the spread of this type of dance (IMDb.com).

5 Active Members were founded by Michalis Mitakidis (B.D. Foxmoor) in 1992 and the band's initial lineup included Nikitas Clint (X-ray) and Dimitris Konstantopoulos (Dj Booker).

6 The debut studio album of *Active Member*, released by *Warner Music*, entitled "To Megalo Kolpo" (The Big Game). Since then, 6 more albums were released, all of them by Warner Music (Terzidis, 2003).

7 The biggest controversy broke out between fans and bands of Hip Hop and Low bap music scene, which was a new genre of music with Active Member as the main representatives. In Greece, although quarrels between the bands did not escalate as those of the American music scene (with extreme incidents such as the murders of 2pac, Notorious B.I.G. etc.), they still managed to divide the scene into two sides: the music band of *Active Member* on the one and all the others on the other (Terzidis, 2003, p. 114).

8 A genre of music, a branch of Rap music, which is characterized by threatening lyrics and sound which incorporates double and triple divisions of time.

9 Low bap established a special style characterized by a slow, almost "singing" pronunciation with pauses in the accentuated bar. For more information cf. www.lowbap.com.

10 Opinions differ regarding the origin of the term "Low bap". On the one hand, the founder of the band believes that nothing special hides behind this name. On the other hand, there is a view that the reason was Boom bap style of music and the American rapper KRS-1, (Pasiopoulos, 2014).

11 A purely delinquent lifestyle where criminal activity coexists with the use and trafficking of addictive substances.

12 Many band members agree on this. For example, Nikos Vourliotis (Going Through) states: "We started all together as friends, but Active Member, and specifically Michalis, tried to lead. To become a mentor" (Terzidis, 2003).

13 Α.Ε.Π.Ι. (Ανώνυμη Εταιρεία Πνευματικής Ιδιοκτησίας - Hellenic Society for the Protection of Intellectual Property) was a Public Limited Company for the collective management of copyright in musical works with the aim of representing intellectual creators and beneficiaries of musical works. For an artist or group, withdrawal from this company resulted in the loss of future gains from third party exploitation of their products. On May 14, 2018, its operating license was revoked.

14 There are few, if any, reports on reviews related to the Low bap movement (Unfollow Magazine, January 2015, Issue 37).

15 We typically mention Active member in Perama, T.X.C. in Nea Ionia and Iraklio of Attica, Going Through in Agia Varvara.

16 Qualitative content analysis was introduced in the 1980s by Ph. Mayring, who argued that social sciences failed to provide a synthetical and systematic tool for analyzing qualitative material and that present [at the time] methods were incomplete, inconsistent, unilateral and mostly based on quantitative criteria (Mayring, 2000; Bonidis, 2004). Content analysis offers a method for researching and analyzing social communication, as well as its effects (Iosifidis, 2008).

17 Narrative discussion is utilized for presenting qualitative research outcomes and textual interpretation. It is where researchers present their findings in detail (Creswell, 2011).

18 Ένωση Συντακτών Ημερησίων Εφημερίδων Αθηνών (Association of Editors of Athens Daily Newspapers).

19 Quadir Lateef is an American Rapper from Houston. More information to be found on the artist's personal website: https://qlateef.com/.

20 More specifically 601,345 views on January 30, 2022.

21 There is an obvious parallelism regarding the lines of G. Seferis poem "Helen", "what is god, what isn't, what's in between?" (Theodoridis, G., (drama) "Euripides – Helen"). This is a translation

of line 1147 of the drama "Helen" written by the ancient Greek tragic poet Euripides, where the question arises "which man can answer the question what is God or what is non-God?". In this case "who can say what life is?".

22 This is a word used by G. Skaribas in his poem "the seagull". "farewell, at infinity's heart / my night seagull, you are leaving – like a ship, the night comes after you are gone, the silence, my room, a dim light (fosaki), a book" (Skaribas, 2016).

23 At 00:30 on Wednesday, May 12, 2011, unknown perpetrators stabbed and killed the 21-year-old Bangladeshi immigrant Alim Abdul Manan, at the intersection of Stratigou Kallari and Konstantinidis streets, in Kato Patisia, Athens. The murder was considered to be an act of racism and the perpetrators were never arrested.

24 On January 17, 2013, Sahjat Lukman was stabbed to death by two members of Golden Dawn in Petralona. The two perpetrators were arrested, brought before the prosecutor and were charged with intentional homicide, illegal possession of weapons, illegal carrying of weapons, illegal use of weapons but without the inclusion of racist motives in the charges.

25 These songs remind us of the subgenre of the black American street culture that at some point was integrated into the urban blues under the title "The dozens". It was an informal competition for whoever would use the most offensive lyrics against their opponents, in this case expressing a far-right ideology (Oliver, 1963).

26 If other videos of the same songs are included. For example, the song "It will always dawn" has almost 200,000 views.

Section 2

Digital Humanities, Education, Gamification, and Applications

Chapter 7
Digital Narrative as an Educational Tool for Cultural Heritage Teaching

Nikolaos Karantalis
University of Patras, Greece

Dimitrios Koukopoulos
University of Patras, Greece

George Koutromanos
https://orcid.org/0000-0002-8542-9329
National and Kapodistrian University of Athens, Greece

ABSTRACT

Our age is unquestionably characterized by the dominance of technology and digital media in all manifestations of human action. Inevitably, the debate over the use of these media becomes more intense in areas that are extremely important for the intellectual development of man, such as the field of culture and education. This reality leads educational systems to adapt curricula to new developments, so that digital media is now a key educational tool for many courses. Especially in the subject of history and especially of local history and folklore, digital storytelling can be the connecting link between the old and the new. This can be very helpful when the lesson plans are aimed at bringing students in touch with cultural heritage, both material and intangible. The present study aims to show that digital storytelling can be used creatively in teaching a local history and folklore course.

INTRODUCTION

The importance of teaching cultural heritage at all levels of education is now undeniable and is taken seriously in the planning of educational activities in many countries (López-Fernández et al., 2021; Potocnik, 2020; Goodarzparvari & Camejo, 2018). Emphasis is placed mainly on the student's contact

DOI: 10.4018/978-1-6684-4461-0.ch007

with cultural heritage through the humanities lessons and especially the history lesson. Study heritage among all:

... Facilitates the understanding of historical concepts and helps to understand the world in which we live, contributing to the multiple understanding of history and to the building of the three pillars of history education: History - Memory – Identity (Magro et al., 2014).

In the context of local history, contact with cultural goods and cultural heritage, tangible and intangible, is pedagogically important, as they are important learning tools for integration and application that make teaching less book-centered and livelier, giving meaning to learning (Mendes, 2009).

An important part of the teaching of local history aims at the student's contact with the folklore tradition and the sources from where the teacher can draw material that she/he will use in the development of the teaching plan. These are places such as folklore museums, folk art galleries, libraries, traditional settlements, etc. Lesson plans and assignments with educational material drawn from those areas are many and constantly increasing (Ferrara et al., 2013; Pinto & Ibañez-Etxeberria, 2018).

However, apart from the lessons that aim at the student's contact with the tangible cultural tradition, a corresponding interest must be given to the intangible cultural tradition. Fairy tales, folk legends and folk songs, still retain their aesthetic and pedagogical value, although they often seem outdated and foreign to the interests of students (Yalçınkaya 2015; Dagnino et al., 2017). In general, narration, which is a basic learning tool from infancy, is more difficult today to maintain its dynamics, under the influence of the image. Even historical narrative, as a key part of teaching history, seems to make it difficult for students. Having identified the problem, more and more often teachers across the spectrum of education are looking for ways of creating lesson plans, which will bring storytelling back to the center of the teaching, in a more modern way, even in lessons that are theoretically based on traditional teaching methods (Ramsey, 2017).

Despite the strong interest in educational plans for local history and the benefits it offers, this difficulty is easily accepted, due to the mentality of modern students and especially adolescents. Students today, being particularly familiar with digital technologies, often find that lessons in local history and tradition do not meet their interests (Akengin & Cendek, 2017). This reality is a challenge that the teacher can face with the help of technology and digital media. One such tool is digital storytelling. In matters of teaching local history with an emphasis on the promotion of folk tradition, tangible and intangible, there are many examples, where digital storytelling is at the heart of the educational process (Conrand, 2013).

Therefore, a need arises to implement teaching plans for the teaching of local history considering several challenges, like the reconnection of students with oral tradition and the fruitful use of technology based on the encouragement of students' initiative, cooperation, and creativity. Most researchers focus on the study of digital storytelling in subjects, like history, suggesting ways to use it didactically (Barsch, 2020; Ganino, 2015). However, there is no comprehensive research in the literature that focuses on the study of changing students' attitudes towards cultural tradition, when the course includes all three axes: intangible and tangible cultural heritage, local history, digital storytelling.

In this context a critical question arises: "To what extent can students' attitudes towards cultural heritage be changed through modern educational interventions?" Our initial goal is the investigation of the degree of student's familiarity with the basic terms (cultural heritage, local history, folklore). Then, through the teaching of a local history lesson using digital storytelling, we attempt to quantify with measurable data the changes in students' attitudes towards cultural heritage.

In this chapter, we intend to present a comprehensive lesson plan for the teaching of cultural heritage to secondary school students, based on the triptych of cultural heritage - local history - digital storytelling. The research plan includes a visit to the city's folklore museum, where students could take photos of museum objects and associate them later in the school lab with folk tales, historical, and fairytale figures, real events and legends of their place, creating an original digital story which could be shared online.

This research is based on a sample of 20 first-graders of a public school in Greece. The students live in a city, Ioannina, with a great cultural tradition and history, which allows quality research. On the one hand, we aim to examine the current situation in terms of students' knowledge and contact with cultural heritage, folklore, and local history, and on the other hand, we seek to examine whether, with the use of digital storytelling, there is a change in the motivation and interest of learning and the degree of students' familiarity to the above terms, so that there are improvements in educational planning.

The chapter follows the effort to investigate the relationship between education and cultural heritage, as it has been done in relevant studies (Röll & Meyer, 2020, Kokko & Kyritsi,2012, Boxtel et al., 2016, Jagielska-Burduk & Pszczyński, 2021). However, to the best of our knowledge this is the first time a study attempts to assess with measurable data through a comprehensive project of teaching local history the effect the digital storytelling has on students' re-approach towards cultural heritage.

This chapter is organized as follows: in Section 2 we briefly present the basic terms included in the research and we mainly examine their position in educational planning. Section 3 describes the used methodology. Section 4 presents the results and Section 5 discusses storytelling tools in the teaching of cultural heritage. Finally, in Section 6 we present the conclusions of the research.

BACKGROUND

Local History – Cultural Heritage – Digital Storytelling

In this chapter we will briefly present the basic terms mentioned in this article (cultural heritage, local history, digital storytelling). The purpose is not to cover the full range of concepts but focus on specific characteristic. We mainly want to focus on modern theories and find the coherent links that can connect local history, cultural heritage and digital storytelling in the educational process (Gizzi et al., 2019; López-Fernández et al., 2021; Okanovic et al., 2021).

Till now research efforts are limited to the teaching of cultural heritage using ICT. This study proposes to take into account the student's attitude towards cultural heritage and explore how this attitude can change. The important thing is the proposal of an educational approach that will involve students more actively, having also measurable results in terms of differentiating their attitude towards cultural heritage, after the completion of the course.

Local History

The lesson of local history is usually taught in the broader context of history. It is indicative that in the Greek educational system with the new curriculum the subject of local history is proposed essentially as a tool for consolidating history and not as an independent unit (http://iep.edu.gr/el/nea-ps-provoli). Nevertheless, one could argue that this is also a principle, in line with the principles for the teaching of history, as they are formulated in the statutory principles of the Council of Europe for the teaching of history (Council of Europe,2018). Local History is associated with the economic, political, moral, cultural aspects of a community (Walker,2015). Pierre Goubert (1971) uses the following definition for local history:

We shall talk local history that which concerns a village or a few villages, as small or a middle size town...or a geographical area not greater than a common provincial unit... (p.113)

Today, the importance of the local history lesson is undeniable. A key goal according to the history program of the Greek Institute of Educational Policy is for students to be able to:

become familiar with the history of their place and realize the contribution of their immediate environment to the general history by forming a complete personal social and national identity. (http://iep.edu.gr/el/nea-ps-provoli).

Respectively, in many countries, there are didactic proposals that aim to promote local history issues (Goksu & Somen, 2019; Schoeman & Visagie, 2014). However, the literature is limited, considering the importance of the subject. This is mainly because today local history is inextricably linked to the term cultural heritage. Such a connection obviously conceptually limits the framework, but a careful study may interpret this connection.

Local History and Cultural Heritage

Local history generally refers to the past of a narrowly geographically and demographically defined community. Undoubtedly, even in ethnically homogeneous countries, there are significant differences in terms of language, customs and traditions, economy, folklore traditions, legends, songs, etc. The holistic study of history may fail to address these local characteristics setting a threat to the community's identity. This possibility is now being addressed through the protection and promotion of cultural heritage in every way.

More specifically, according to ICOMOS:

Cultural Heritage is an expression of the ways of living developed by a community and passed on from generation to generation, including customs, practices, places, objects, artistic expressions and values. Cultural Heritage is often expressed as either Intangible or Tangible Cultural Heritage (ICOMOS, 2002).

The term "intangible" is used by UNESCO when referring to movable cultural heritage (paintings, sculptures, coins, manuscripts), immovable cultural heritage (monuments, sites, groups of buildings, etc.), and underwater cultural heritage such as shipwrecks, underwater ruins and cities (Kutut et al., 2021). The term "intangible" is more difficult to interpret, but in short, according to the UNESCO Declaration of 2003 intangible cultural heritage, is defined as:

The practices, representations, expressions, knowledge, skills - as well as the instruments, objects, artifacts and cultural spaces associated therewith - that communities, groups and, in some cases, individuals recognize as part of their cultural heritage" (UNESCO, 2003).

It is essentially a broad field that can holistically be included in the section of local history.

In any case, the importance of preserving cultural heritage is undeniable. Its role is important in the construction and reconstruction of political, moral, social, environmental, and religious history. It can be used in many ways and at different levels, from the field of protection of the special identity of communities to the economic development of an area. It can also give many opportunities to those who deal with it systematically, but also to the public itself (Nilson & Thorell, 2018). Cultural heritage is an inalienable human right and today it is threatened by many factors, such as wars, the ecological crisis and globalization (Cruz, 2017). This finding has mobilized many organizations for many years. The focus of this effort is based on the cooperation of the Member States with UNESCO. It also includes actions related to the protection, information, promotion, and utilization of cultural heritage around the world (Hoang, 2021; Nilson, 2018; De la Torre, 2014). Great importance is given to the contribution of technology in the promotion and protection of cultural heritage with the effective use of digital media (Niconova & Biryukova, 2017; Giglitto et al., 2019; Bentkowska & Mac Donald, 2017).

Education is the main tool for the protection and promotion of cultural heritage. In fact, this can be done in a bidirectional way where cultural heritage becomes a tool of education. It can, for example, be used in mathematics, language and environmental education, history. It is also linked with issues such as political education or the values and identity of the youth. Thus, it contributes to the creation of active citizens with social and communicational skills and the relationship of the individual with the environment and technologies (Gesche-Koning, 2018). Especially the contribution of new technologies to cultural education is a topical issue having multiple benefits. The application of ICTS in the field increases the number of monuments that the students can visit from a distance, even virtually, and enhances the communication and interaction between schools and organizations (Ott & Pozzi, 2011). The utilization of mobile devices, virtual reality, 3D illustrations is constantly increasing (Muenster 2022; Ocanovic et al., 2022).

Cultural Heritage and Digital Storytelling

Respectively creative, but without having been studied to the extent that it should be, is the role of digital storytelling. There are many different definitions of "Digital Storytelling," but in general, they all revolve around the idea of combining the art of telling stories with a variety of digital multimedia, such as images, audio, and video (Robin, 2011). The teacher can use the traditional core of storytelling and mobilize students' interest with the involvement of digital technology. This advantage of digital storytelling makes it one of the most effective educational tools today.

Especially in the field of cultural heritage, digital storytelling enables the student to visualize the intangible cultural heritage. Stories, legends, fairy tales, folk songs can mobilize the students' imagination, and this can be expressed through the creation of a digital narrative. There are several examples of such an educational process (Rizvic et al., 2020; Perouli, 2021; Vert, 2021). Also, in a similar context, digital storytelling is used in the history lesson where historical storytelling is transformed into digital by students with excellent results (Barsch, 2020; Peñalba et al., 2020). Through the process of digital storytelling in cultural heritage courses, students enhance creativity, collaboration, communication, and critical thinking (Liguori & Bakewell, 2019); they can better consolidate the story and the ways with which they can connect the present with the past of a place (López Salas, 2021) and they can announce their work more directly thus contributing actively to the promotion of the local cultural heritage (Rontani, 2012).

METHOD

The present research was designed based on the mixed research model, i.e., a combination of quantitative and qualitative research components. More specifically, "mixed methods research is the type of research in which a researcher or team of researchers combines elements of qualitative and quantitative research approaches (e.g., use of qualitative and quantitative viewpoints, data collection, analysis, inference techniques) for the broad purposes of breadth and depth of understanding and corroboration" (Johnson et al., 2007, p. 123).

Participants

The present study involved 20 students (10 boys and 10 girls), aged 15-16, from a Lyceum in the city of Ioannina, in Western Greece. The selection of students was based on the program of students who had to study in the same department. The students, while living in the same area of the city, show heterogeneity in terms of their origin, as well as learning heterogeneity (good-mediocre-weak).

Instruments

Data were collected through two questionnaires. Data collection was based on students' answers to specific closed-ended and open-ended questions. Students were given two questionnaires, one at the beginning and one at the end of the research to investigate whether there is a change in students' views about cultural tradition and their interest in the whole process. Specifically, the first questionnaire was given before the students' visit to the folklore museum of the city and aimed to collect data on their knowledge and experiences about the museum (Appendix 1). The first part of the questionnaire asked for information about the demographic characteristics of the students, such as gender and age. The second part consisted of six questions and asked students to answer through two dichotomous answers (YES / NO) if they: 1) know the term "folklore", 2) know that there is a folklore museum in the city, 3) have visited the folklore museum of the city, 4) have visited another folklore museum (outside their city), 5) know that museums have a website on the internet, and 6) have ever visited a museum website. The third part of the questionnaire consisted of four questions with which they were asked to state on a 5 / Likert scale (1 = Not at all, 2 = A little, 3 = Moderate, 4 = Very much, 5 = Too much) their agreement or disagreement whether: 1) they know what exhibits are in a folklore museum, 2) they find the visit to the folklore museum interesting, 3) they believe that they will better understand the history of the place after they visit the folklore museum, and 4) they believe that the visit to a museum on the internet is preferable to the physical presence. Finally, an open-ended question asked the students to express their expectations from the visit to the folklore museum that would take place in the coming days. Close-ended questions were selected to prioritise student preferences, while open-ended question allowed students to develop spontaneous answers.

The second questionnaire was given after the end of the teaching intervention in the computer lab and consists of four sections (Appendix 2). The first section was about the demographic characteristics of the students just like the first questionnaire given to them. The second section consisted of five questions. The first question was intended to collect data on the object that the students chose from the folklore museum to create their digital narrative. Students had to choose between different items (clothes, jewelry, weapon, household utensils, etc.). The second question was about the plot of the narrative they chose (folk song, folk tale, historical event, legend/folk history, other). The third question asked the students for information about the people they used in digital storytelling (e.g., people historical, anonymous, fictional, known from legends, traditions, folk songs). The fourth question asked for information on whether the digital narrative was related to the location of their area (e.g., monuments of their place, folklore traditions of the place) while the fifth question asked for information on the type of audiovisual material used in the narrative (e.g., audiovisual material from the visit to the museum, from the internet). The third section consisted of eight questions that aimed to examine the students' perceptions about their visit to the folklore museum and the learning process in which they participated. Their answers were on a 5 / Likert scale (1 = Not at all, 2 = A little, 3 = Moderate, 4 = Very much, 5 = Too much).

In addition to the questionnaires, one of the three researchers in this chapter kept notes on how the students worked, how they interacted with each other, and recorded their questions, queries, and comments about the digital narrative they created.

Procedure

The present research consists of three phases. In the first phase, students were divided into groups of four by random selection. They were given a parental consent form to participate in the research and then they were given the first questionnaire, before the start of the educational scenario. In the second phase, the students visited the city folklore museum. They had already been informed to bring with them devices for taking photos and videos. During the tour of the museum, the students photographed the objects that impressed them, discussed with the people in charge of the history of the exhibits and consulted the printed material that the museum provided. In the third phase, the students, in the computer lab of their school (see Figure 1), were involved in creating a digital narrative that was related to the exhibits that impressed them and to a local history and folklore. The students first searched the internet for material related to their museum experiences, saved photos, music, videos, and then created a digital story using Windows Movie Maker (https://www.winmoviemaker.com/). The duration of this phase was two weeks. In the fourth phase, at the end of the teaching intervention, the students were given the second research questionnaire.

Analysis

The data retrieved from the questionnaires were coded and analyzed in Excel (Microsoft Office 365). The analysis focused on the descriptive analysis and more specifically in the frequency and the percentages.

RESULTS

The results were obtained through qualitative and quantitative research conducted over a period of two weeks. It includes data from the introductory questionnaire, from the field study and the observation of students' work in real time, and from the final questionnaire that aims to identify any changes in students' perceptions.

Figure 1. Students in the computer lab

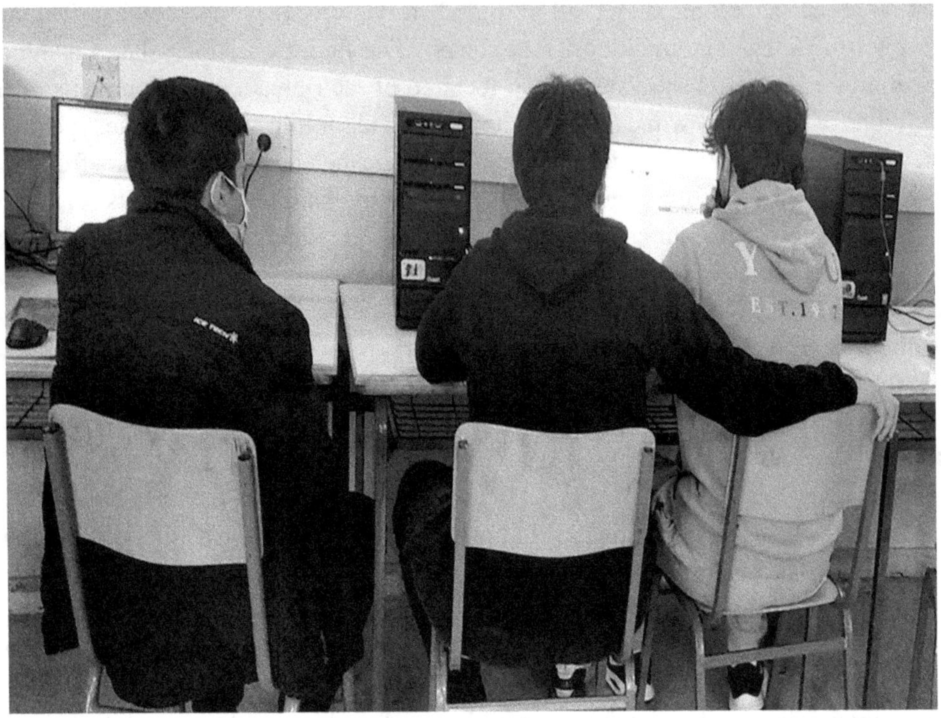

Exploring Students' Knowledge

The students' answers to the questionnaire before the visit to the folklore museum showed to a large extent that the degree of students' familiarity with the basic terms of the research was very small. More specifically, when asked if they knew the terms "cultural tradition" or "folklore", a large percentage of students (<80%) answered that they knew almost none of them, while the same percentage stated that they had not even heard them in the school environment. (Figure 2).

Half of the students were not even aware of the existence of a folklore museum in the city, while out of the 20 students in the survey, only two had visited this particular one or some other folklore museum. Few students answered that they know that folklore museums have a website (30%), while only one had visited such a website (Figure 3).

When asked openly about their expectations for a visit to the museum, most of the answers were one-word with a negative mood ("few", "none", "not many"), while only two students seemed excited about the upcoming visit.

After the Visit – Creation of a Digital Storytelling

The students were divided into five groups of four students and they created five digital stories by using the material that impressed them in the museum, the internet research for oral stories, folk legends - myths - fairy tales, historical events of local history, and audiovisual material (Figure 4).

Figure 2. Familiarity with the basic terms

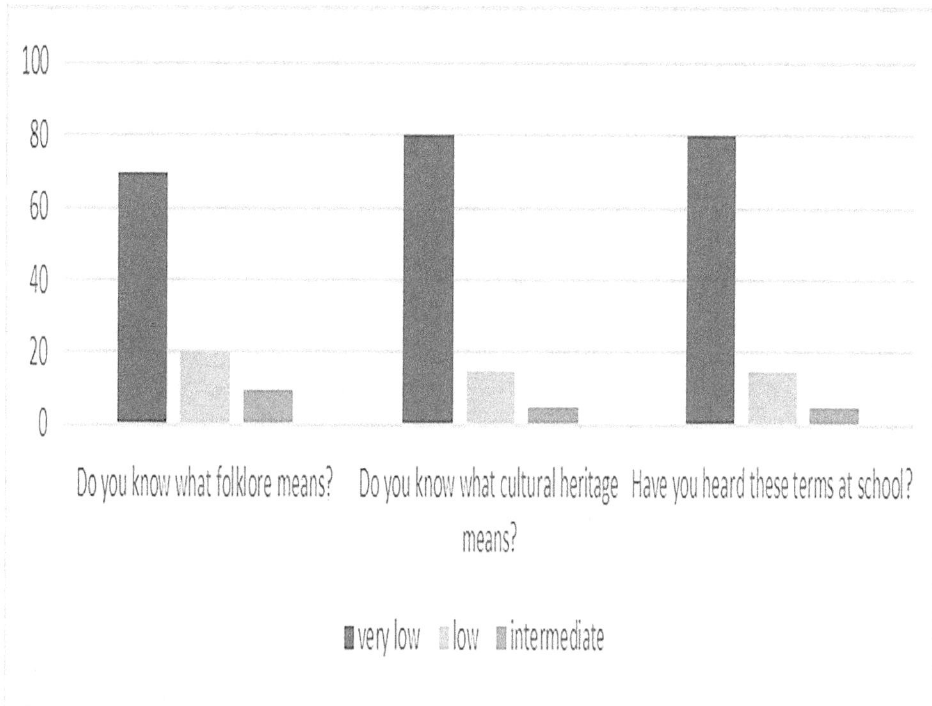

Figure 3. Familiarity with folk museums

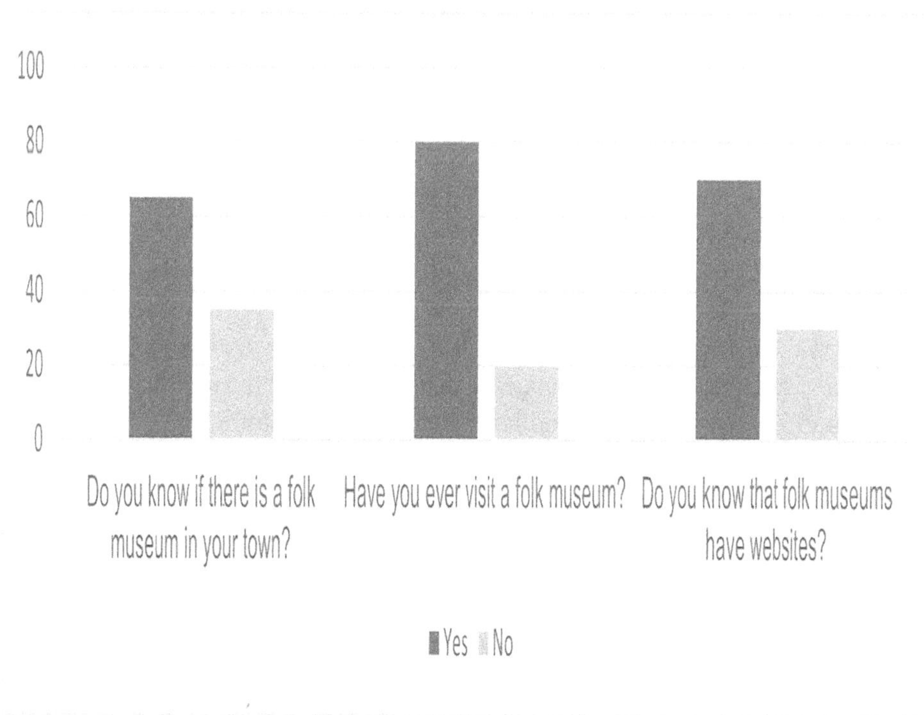

Figure 4. Screenshot from a students' digital narration

The first group worked using weapons and costumes and created a digital story having as central theme the story of Ali Pasha and the Greek young lady, Frosini, based on a folk song (https://bit.ly/36LA4Ef).

The second group created a digital story about the murder of a Turkish officer by robbers in a village in Epirus. Here, too, the weapons and amulets from the museum impressed them and combined them with a folk song that tells the story (https://bit.ly/3iAeIww).

The third group created a digital story regarding the custom of the wedding, inspired by the wedding costumes and jewelry in the museum (https://bit.ly/3LaROb3).

The fourth group based on household utensils and costumes created a digital story for the people of the area based on the story traditional polyphonic songs (https://bit.ly/3wB5OqO).

The fifth group, based on weapons, created a digital narrative based on the historical event of the siege of Souli by the Turks in 1823 (https://bit.ly/3wA7mkE).

Based on this work, questions were asked about the cultural heritage elements that the students used to create the digital narrative. The results showed that they were impressed by traditional costumes, weapons and to a lesser extent by jewelry and household utensils (Figure 5).

The students chose real historical events and less folk songs and folk tales. Some chose to combine them (Figure 6).

The students included in their story mainly historical figures and persons known from legends and folk traditions and less their own fictional heroes (Figure 7).

Finally, the students' digital story included audio-visual material mainly from the internet and the students' archive from the museum visit. There were, also, cases that they chose historical narrative and excerpts from testimonies (Figure 8).

Figure 5. Artifacts used to create the digital story

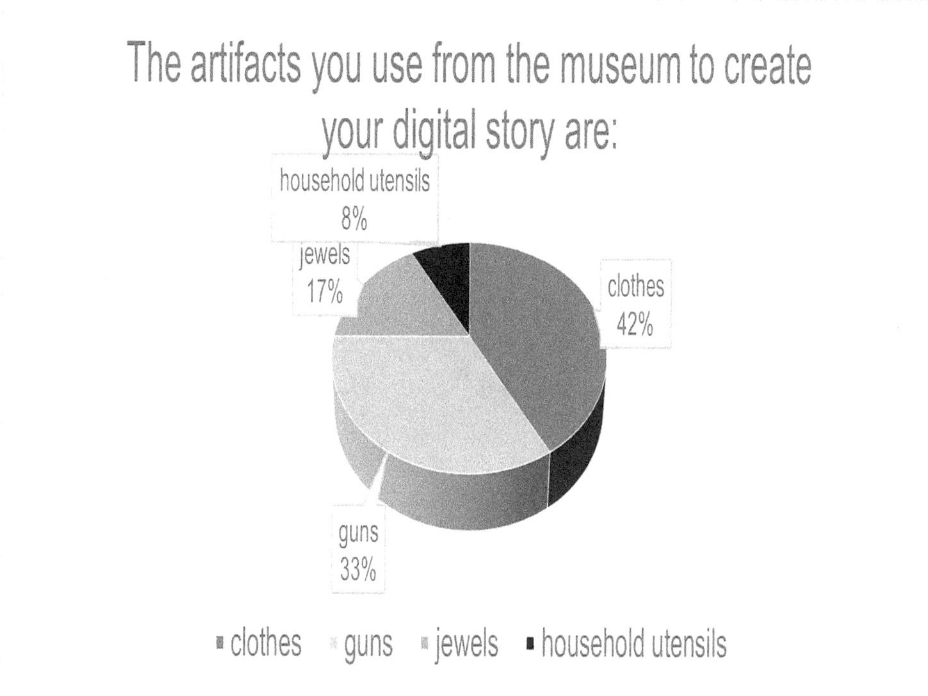

Figure 6. The plot was based on…

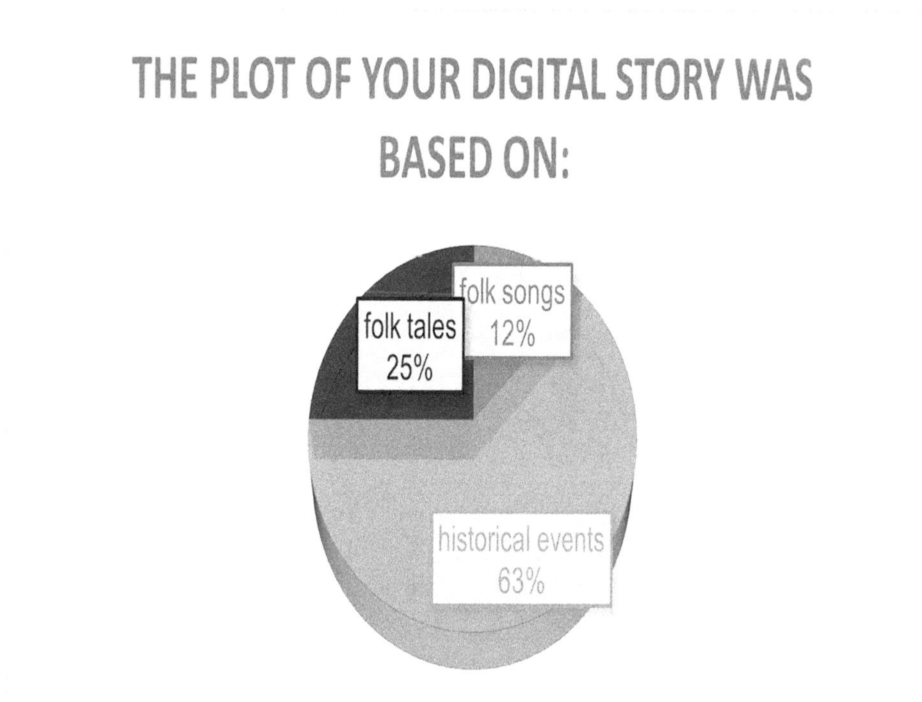

Figure 7. The digital story hero

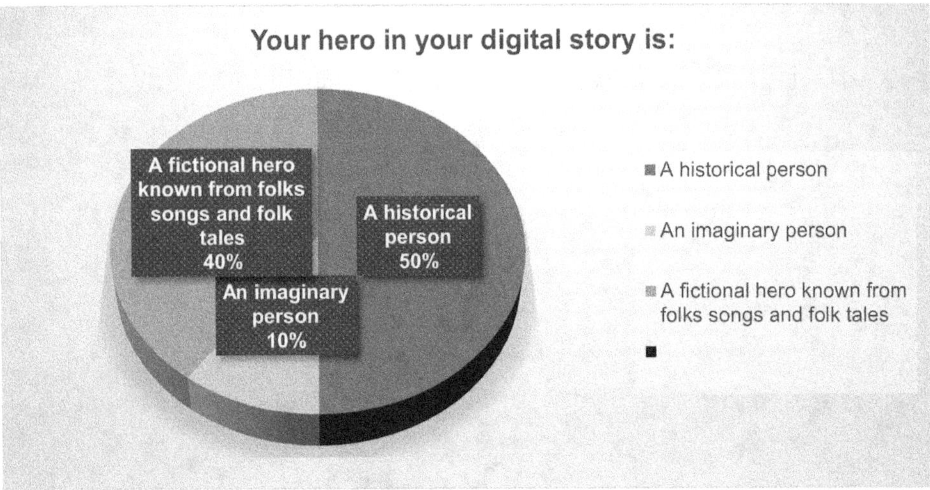

Figure 8. Your digital story includes…

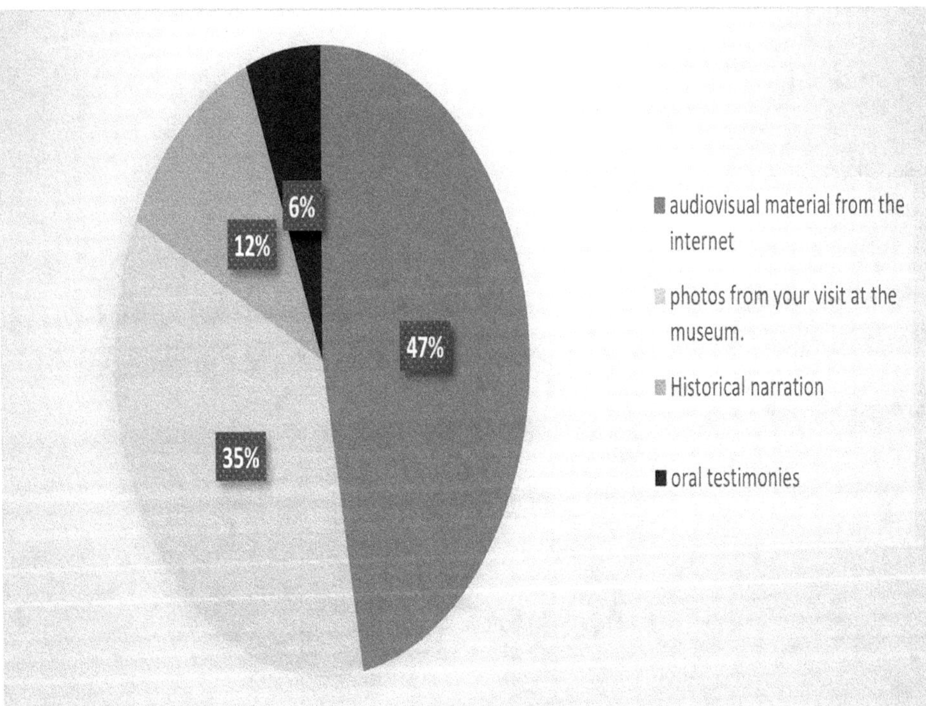

In the second group of questions, in the question concerning the students' impression by their visit to the folklore museum, the result was encouraging as the vast majority found it very or very interesting (Figure 9).

Figure 9. How interesting was the visit to the folklore museum?

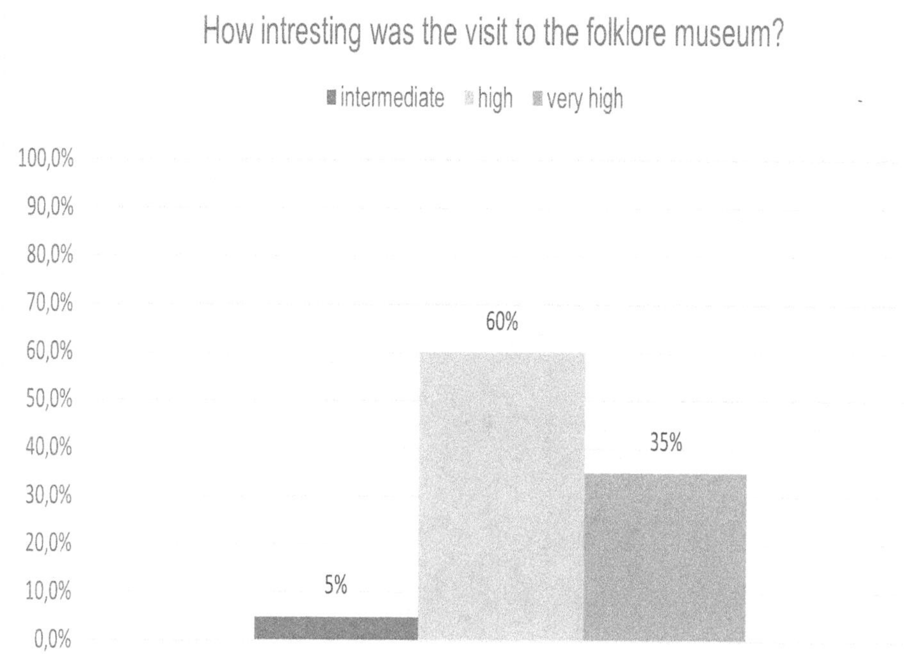

When asked how interesting the whole process was, the results were even more positive, as there were no negative judgments (Figure 10).

Regarding the material for the creation of the digital narrative, the students seem to have relied little on the museum website (Figure 11).

The material they photographed - videotaped in the folklore museum was used in a satisfactory degree (Figure 12)

Students also believed that they had the means to create digital storytelling (Figure 13).

Finally, almost all of them stated that the whole process helped them to better understand the local history and they would like to repeat it in other thematic sections (Table 14).

Students also recorded the pros and cons of the whole process. Specifically, most of them recorded as positive the knowledge they acquired, the fun and the team effort. As negative, they mentioned the limited space of research and the restrictions set by the measures against the pandemic

Students were given the opportunity in a short text to compare this teaching experience with corresponding lessons they had attended in the traditional way of teaching. Most insisted that the lesson was more interesting. More specifically, one student writes that "… digital storytelling makes the lesson more interesting, students are inspired and deal with the lesson better", while other noted that "… it is more interesting because we do not do everything from the book, but we also create, we do something with our imagination, find things, like images that we like ". Some find the process easier than classic storage. One student noted that "… learning history has become easier because it does not require memorization", while another view is that "… it is easier to search on your own, than to listen to the teacher delivering the lesson". Some students thought that in this way they worked more as a team "and

Figure 10. How interesting the whole process was?

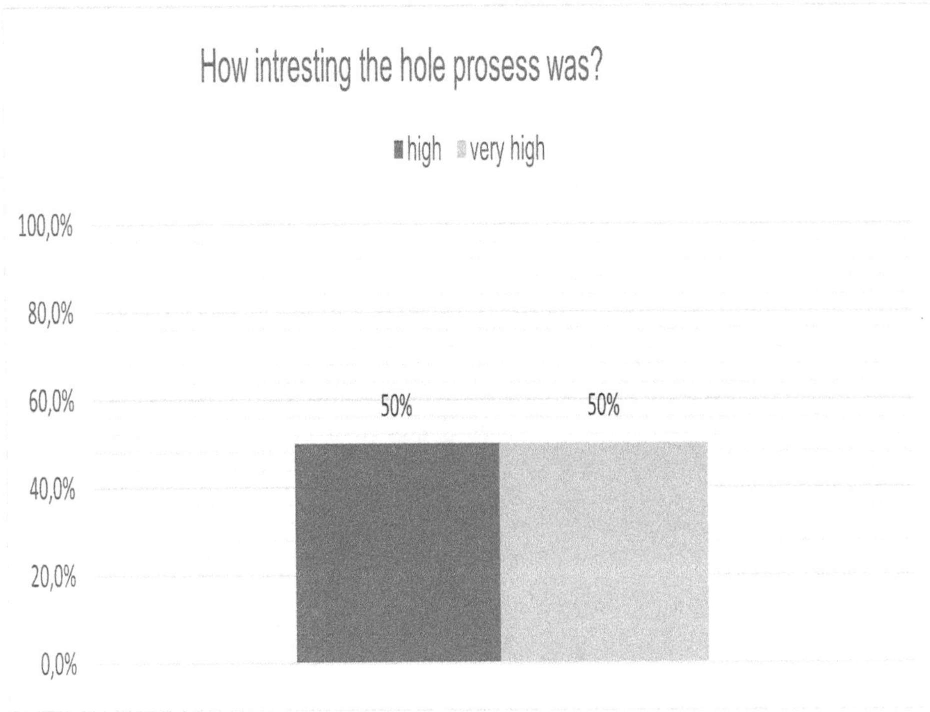

Figure 11. Did you use the museum's website?

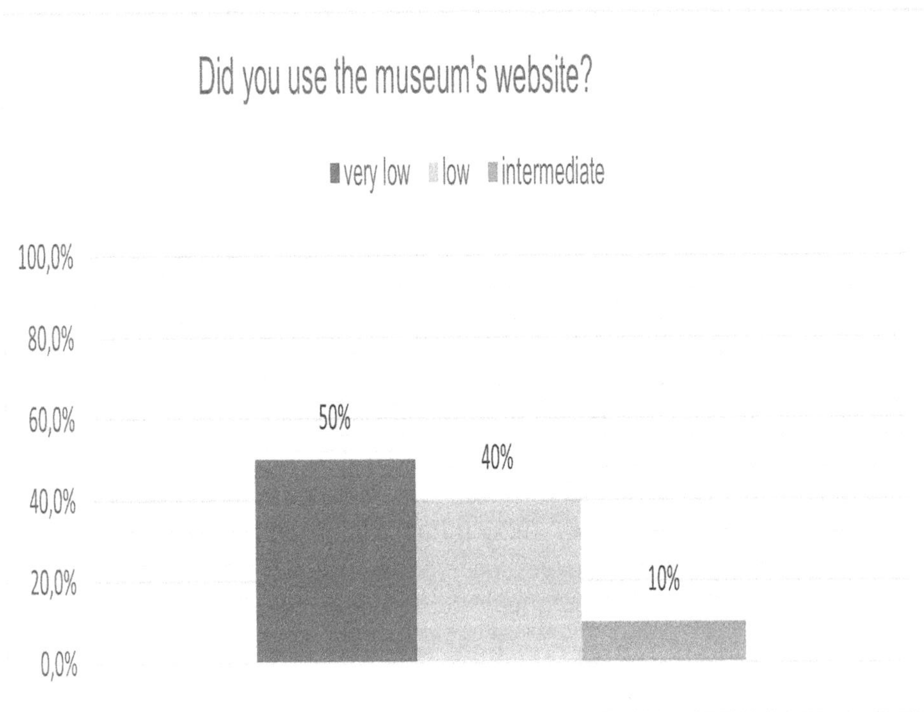

Figure 12. Did you use your own photos or video from your visit to the museum?

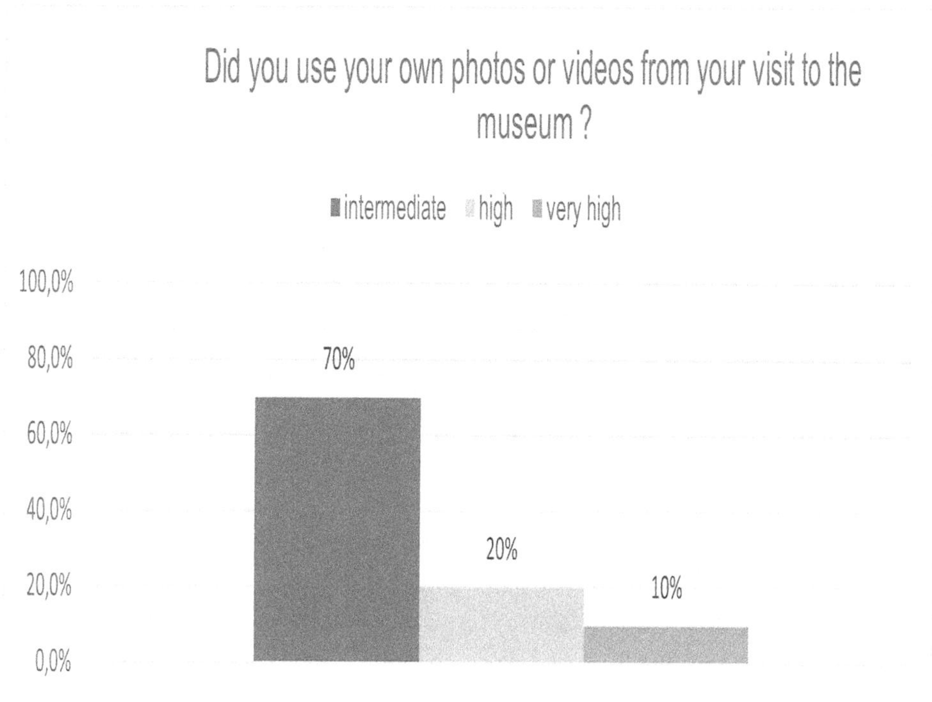

Figure 13. Did you have the right tools to create a digital narration?

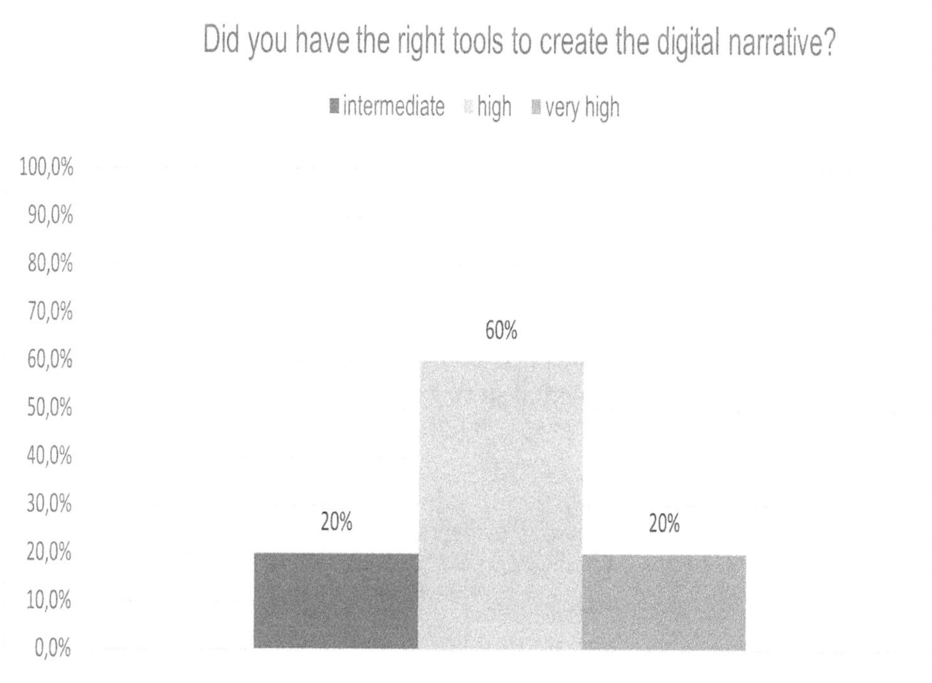

Figure 14. Evaluation of the process

that was a lot of fun". However, several students did not want to answer, while two replied that "they do not see any difference"

DISCUSSION

This paper was aiming to explore students' knowledge and interest in cultural tradition, whether it is easy to use digital storytelling as an educational tool in the teaching of cultural tradition, tangible and intangible, through the history lesson. Based on this, useful conclusions were drawn concerning the change of the students' perceptions about folklore and cultural heritage. To achieve this goal, we proceeded to the teaching of a complete lesson plan which included the experiential contact with tangible cultural heritage through the visit to a folklore museum and taking photos of all the artifacts impressed the students. This procedure triggered students to search for oral and written texts related to intangible cultural heritage and compose them in a digital story, based on historical narrative and fiction.

Table 1. Pros and cons

Positive	Negative
Knowledge	Limited research space
Fun	Measures against the pandemic
Teamwork	

The involvement of students in the whole process played an important role in the success of the educational scenario. Students selected and took photos in their digital story. Observing them in the museum, we found that they chose traditional costumes and weapons and to a lesser extent jewelry. Discussing their choices, they told us that these objects are more related to history and folk tales - songs. This was indeed understood in their digital stories, where they used these artifacts even combining them.

At the same time, in the online research in the computer room, students often wondered whether they should base their story on real events, historical narration or fictional stories from the folklore tradition. This shows that students often understand the distinction among these three elements and with the proper guidance and motivation they often surprise even themselves. Also, as teenagers, it seemed that they had no problem searching the material on the internet and composing it through a program, such as Windows Movie Maker.

Research has confirmed studies showing that digital storytelling can be an important educational motivator for students (Foelske, 2014, Yang & Wu, 2012, Grant & Bolin, 2016). However, it goes one step further as it shows that especially in the perspective of activating students in matters of cultural heritage, it plays a decisive role. Throughout this multi-layered work, we made sure to monitor the students' views and attitudes on the subject from the beginning to the end. Based on the quantitative and qualitative characteristics of the research, a significant change was observed in the relationship of students with the terms "cultural heritage" and "folklore". The initial questionnaire confirmed the distance they had from the folklore tradition and the challenges of the educational systems, in general, to bring students closer to the folklore tradition (Lopez-Fernadez et. al, 2021,Li,2019).

It thus strengthened the belief that initiatives are needed to suggest ways so that, through the educational process, the students can acquire an interest in cultural heritage. From the moment the lesson became experiential and involved digital technology, students became more familiar with such terms and came in better contact with local history. But beyond that, their whole attitude towards the lesson seems to have changed. While their expectations from the project were low and, initially, their general mood was negative, after completing the course, they described the whole process as interesting and fun. After all, the pleasure and interest in participating in the course is a key goal of the respective educational interventions and, in general, of every educational process (Samdal et al., 1998; Sezer & Can, 2020; Giggi et al., 2020).

Of course, there is a percentage of students who did not see any difference with the traditional teaching and did not seem to change their attitude towards the interest that the whole process aimed to cause them; this is a challenge for future educational interventions. Possibly, the observation of many students about the limited space of the research can give an explanation to their reluctance and their dissatisfaction. In fact, this can be combined with those who considered the measures for the pandemic, which impose restrictions on movement, as a negative element of the process.

These students obviously associate the cultural heritage with visiting mainly open spaces and monuments, like bridges, traditional settlements and temples, which they often encounter in their place. Therefore, it is worth to further research this aspect, utilizing and enriching corresponding proposals (Gizzi et al., 2019; Benetteti et al., 2021).

CONCLUSION

The purpose of this research effort was to investigate whether students' attitudes towards cultural heritage can be changed, if elements of cultural heritage, local history and digital storytelling are used in the educational process. Indeed, despite the small sample, it appeared that at the end of the lesson the students, both cognitively and emotionally, had overwhelmingly acquired a positive attitude towards the lesson.

We would say that the present research demonstrates the need for students to come into contact with the cultural heritage as a whole through educational experiential activities and with the help of digital media. The hitherto fragmentary approaches to the subject through small didactic interventions in subjects, such as history or literature, and with the traditional frontal-teacher-centered way of teaching, increase the students' distance from the cultural heritage. Continuing, relevant educational initiatives can lead to a more systematic and organized teaching of tangible and intangible cultural heritage based on the respect for the tradition, age and interests of students and the potential of the new digital era.

The lack of substantial contact with the local cultural tradition, especially in a place with a rich history, is a matter of concern. Students answered that they have not been taught the terms folklore and cultural heritage at school. This observation, although exaggerated, shows the need for education systems to implement more targeted policies. This means that teachers really need to be informed and trained on the subject, as many studies suggest (Potocnik, 2020; Gómez-Carrasco, 2020; Cuenca-Lopez et al., 2021). Opening schools to the community and teaching the local history lesson by co-teaching literature could also work positively.

But the main conclusion that emerges from the research is that the use of digital media plays a catalytic role in changing students' attitudes towards cultural heritage. Throughout the process students felt pleasure, because in a lesson that they did not have many expectations, they found many interesting things to explore. But this means that an educational action regarding such an issue requires time, freedom of movement and means. Possibly, it could function as a quarterly or semester program, in parallel with the history lesson, which would include visits to places of cultural interest, interviews, online research and digital storytelling. Thus, the students would have a better idea of the importance of preserving cultural heritage, recognize the common links between material and intangible cultural heritage, and feel like following it through digital storytelling.

Limitations

This research is essentially a pilot attempt to investigate a topic that has so far been studied piecemeal. We recognize that the sample is small, but the goal based on this is to proceed with the study by enriching it in a network of students in different cities. At the same time, there were difficulties due to the limitations set by the pandemic and the frequent absences of students, due to covid infection. Also, the selection of students had to be from one department because the teaching hours and the school curriculum did not give room for flexibility. However, these constraints can be envisaged in a future plan that will include more students, in different cities, taking advantage of the physical, but also the distant, collaboration of the students. It can also be extended to the study of the attitude of teachers who teach history, but also the points of the curricula that need to be redesigned in order to systematically teach cultural heritage.

REFERENCES

Akengin, H., & Cendek, M.,2017). A Study of Students' Opinions About History Subjects in the Social Studies Curriculum. *Journal of Literature and Art Studies*, *7*(10), 1347-1353.

Anagnostou, G., Chatziefstratiou, A., Peristeri, T., & Theofanellis, T. (2020). Suggestions on how to use Europeana for pedagogical purposes in order to promote Europe's cultural heritage. In *Proceedings of International Conference on Cultural Informatics, Communication & Media Studies* (*Vol. 1*, No.1). Academic Press.

Barsch, S. (2020). Does experience with digital storytelling help students to critically evaluate educational videos about history? *History Education Research Journal*, *17*(1), 67–80.

Benedetti, B., Abbondandolo, I., & Gaiani, M. (2021). The Origins of the Postgraduate Programs on Cultural Heritage Knowledge, Management, Conservation, and Communication in Italy: A Vision of the Past as Engine for the Next Future. *Heritage*, *4*, 2691–2720.

Bentkowska-Kafel, A., & Mac Donald, L. (Eds.). (2017). *Digital Techniques for Documenting and Preserving Cultural Heritage*. Arc Humanities Press. doi:10.2307/j.ctt1xp3w16

Boxtel, C., Grever, M., & Klein, S. (2016). Introduction: The Appeal of Heritage in Education. In Sensitive Pasts. Berghahn Books.

Conrad, S. (2013). Documenting local history: A case study in digital storytelling. *Library Review*, *62*, 459–471.

Costa, R. C. (2019). The place of the humanities in today's knowledge society. *Palgrave Communications*, *5*(1), 1–5.

Council of Europe. (2018). *Quality History Education in the 21 st Century. Principles and Guidelines.* https://rm.coe.int/prems-108118-gbr-2507-quality-history-education-web-21x21/16808eace7

Cruz, G.-R. C. (2017). Cultural heritage and the challenge of sustainability. *Philippine Political Science Journal*, *38*(1), 74–76.

Cuenca-López, J. M., Martín-Cáceres, M. J., & Estepa Giménez, J. (2021). Teacher training in heritage education: Good practices for citizenship education. *Humanit Soc Sci Commun*, *8*, 62.

De la Torre, E. M. (2014). Values in Heritage Conservation: A Project of The Getty Conservation Institute. *APT Bulletin: The Journal of Preservation Technology*, *45*(2/3), 19–24.

Dagnino, F. M., Pozzi, F., Cozzani, G., & Bernava, L. (2017). *Using Serious Games for Intangible Cultural Heritage (ICH). Education: A Journey into the Canto a Tenore Singing Style* [Paper presentation]. VISIGRAPP.

Davidson, C. N., & Goldberg, D. T. (2004). Engaging the Humanities. *Profession*, 42–62.

Ferrara, V., Macchia, A., & Sapia, S. (2013). Reusing Cultural Heritage Digital resources in teaching. In *Proceedings of Digital Heritage International Congress* (pp. 409-412). IEEE.

Foelske, M. (2014). *Digital storytelling: the impact on student engagement, motivation and academic learning*. Graduate Research Papers, 167. https://scholarworks.uni.edu/grp/167

Gesche-Koning, N. (2018). Research for CULT Committee – Education in Cultural Heritage. European Parliament, Policy Department for Structural and Cohesion Policies.

Gilead, T. (2017). Justifying the teaching of the humanities: A new economic approach. *Policy Futures in Education*, *15*(3), 346–359.

Giglitto, D., Ciolfi, L., Claisse, C., & Lockley, E. (2019). Bridging cultural heritage and communities through digital technologies: Understanding perspectives and challenges. In *Proceedings of the 9th International Conference on Communities and Technologies: Transforming communities* (pp. 81-91). ACM.

Gizzi, F. T., Biscione, M., Danese, M., Maggio, A., Pecci, A., Sileo, M., Potenza, M. R., Masini, N., Ruggeri, A., Sileo, A., & Mercurio, F. (2019). Students Meet Cultural Heritage: An Experience within the Framework of the Italian School-Work Alternation (SWA)—From Outcomes to Outlooks. *Heritage*, *2*(3), 1986–2016.

Goodarzparvari, P., & Camejo, F. C. B. (2018). Preservation of cultural heritage via education of children, utilizing visual communication: Persepolis as a case study. *Creative Education*, *9*, 141–151.

Goksu, M., & Somen, T. (2019). History teachers' views on using local history. *European Journal of Education Studies*. doi:10.46827/ejes.v0i0.2436

Gómez-Carrasco, C. J., Miralles-Martinez, P., Fontal, O., & Ibañez-Etxeberria, A. (2020). Cultural Heritage and Methodological Approaches—An Analysis through Initial Training of History Teachers (Spain–England). *Sustainability*, *12*(3), 933.

Goubert, P. (1971). Local History. *Daedalus*, *100*(1), 113–127.

Grant, N. S., & Bolin, B. L. (2016). Digital Storytelling: A Method for Engaging Students and Increasing Cultural Competency. *The Journal of Effective Teaching*, *16*, 44–61.

Hoang, K. (2021). The benefits of preserving and promoting cultural heritage values for the sustainable development of the country. E3S Web of Conferences (vol. 234). doi:10.1051/e3sconf/202123400076

Jagielska-Burduk, A., Pszczyński, M., & Stec, P. (2021). Cultural Heritage Education in UNESCO Cultural Conventions. *Sustainability*, *13*(6), 3548.

Johnson, B. R., Onwuegbuzie, A. J., & Turner, L. A. (2007). Toward a definition of mixed methods research. *Journal of Mixed Methods Research*, *1*, 112–133.

ICOMOS. (2002). *International Cultural Tourism Charter. Principles And Guidelines For Managing Tourism At Places Of Cultural And Heritage Significance*. ICOMOS International Cultural Tourism Committee.

Kokko, S., & Kyritsi, A. (2012). Cultural Heritage Education for Intercultural Communication. *International Journal of Heritage in the Digital Era*, *1*, 165–168.

Kutut, V., Lepkova, N., & Zrobe, S. (2021). Immovable Cultural Heritage Usage Modes: *Theoretical Approach. European Research Studies Journal*, *24*(1), 1136–1151.

López-Fernández, J. A., Medina, S., López, M. J., & García-Morís, R. (2021). Perceptions of Heritage among Students of Early Childhood and Primary Education. *Sustainability*, *13*, 10636.

Liguori, A., & Bakewell, L. (2019). Digital Storytelling in Cultural and Heritage Education: A Pilot Study as Part of the 'DICHE' Project. In *Advanced Studies in Museum Education*. ESI - Edizioni Scientifiche Italiane. https://hdl.handle.net/2134/38037

Li, S. (2019). Study on School Education's Inheritance of Folk Culture. In *Proceedings of International Conference on Reform, Technology, Psychology in Education* (pp. 295-299). Academic Press.

López Salas, E. (2021). A collection of narrative practices on cultural heritage with innovative technologies and creative strategies. *Open Research Europe, 1*(130). doi:10.12688/openreseurope.14178.1

Magro, G., De Carvalho, J. R., & Marcelino, M. J. (2014). *Improving History Learning through Cultural Heritage, Local History and Technology* [Paper Presentation]. *International Conference on Mobile Learning*.

Mehta, J. (2013). The Penetration of Technocratic Logic Into the Educational Field: Rationalizing Schooling From the Progressives to the Present. *Teachers College Record*, *115*(5), 1–36.

Mendes, J. A. (2009). *Estudos do Património*. Imprensa da Universidade de Coimbra.

Muenster, S. (2022). Digital 3D Technologies for Humanities Research and Education: An Overview. *Applied Sciences (Basel, Switzerland)*, *12*, 2426.

Nilson, T., & Thorell, K. (Eds.). (2018). *Cultural Heritage Preservation: The Past, the Present and the Future*. Halmstadt University. http://urn.kb.se/resolve?urn=urn:nbn:se:hh:diva-37317

Nikonova, A., & Biryukova, M. (2017). The Role of Digital Technologies in the Preservation of Cultural Heritage. *Muzeologia a Kulturne Dedicstvo*, *5*, 169–173.

Okanovic, V., Ivkovic-Kihic, I., Boskovic, D., Mijatovic, B., Prazina, I., Skaljo, E., & Rizvic, S. (2022). Interaction in eXtended Reality Applications for Cultural Heritage. *Applied Sciences (Basel, Switzerland)*, *12*, 1241.

Ott, M., & Pozzi, F. (2011). Towards a new era for Cultural Heritage Education: Discussing the role of ICT. *Computers in Human Behavior*, *27*, 1365–1371.

Pinto, H., & Ibañez-Etxeberria, A. (2018). Constructing historical thinking and inclusive identities: Analysis of heritage education activities. *History Education Research Journal*, *15*(2), 342–354.

Samdal, O., Nutbeam, D., Wold, B., & Kannas, L. (1998). Achieving health and educational goals through schools—A study of the importance of the school climate and the students' satisfaction with school. *Health Education Research*, *13*(3), 383–397.

Schoeman, S., & Visagie, C. (2014). Local history teaching in the Overberg region of the Western Cape: The case of the Elim Primary School. *Yesterday and Today*, 118-132.

Perouli, C. (2021). Digital Storytelling in the Museum: Bringing Cultural Heritage to Life. *Crossing Conceptual Boundaries*, *11*(1), 34–46.

Peñalba, E. H., Samaniego, C. R. C., & Romeros, M. A. (2020). Digital storytelling: a tool for promoting historical understanding among college students. *Research in Learning Technology, 28*. doi:10.25304/rlt.v28.234

Petti, L., Trillo, C., & Makore, C. (2019). Towards a Shared Understanding of the Concept of Heritage in the European Context. *Heritage, 2*, 2531–2544.

Plaza, O. (2004). Technology Education versus Liberal Arts Education? *The Journal of Technology Studies, 30*(1), 16–19.

Potocnik, R. (2020). Heritage preservation education: Teachers' preconceptions and teachers implementation in visual arts classes. *CEPS Journal, 10*(2), 49–76.

Ramsey, J. T. (2017). The Validity of Historical Narrative and Its Use in Teaching History. *Honors Projects, 67*. https://digitalcommons.spu.edu/honorsprojects/67

Rizvić, S., Boskovic, D., Okanovic, V., Sljivo, S., & Zukić, M. (2020). Interactive digital storytelling: Bringing cultural heritage in a classroom. *Journal of Computers in Education, 6*, 143–166.

Robin, B. (2011). The educational uses of digital storytelling. In *Proceedings of Society for Information Technology & Teacher Education International Conference* (pp. 709-716). Academic Press.

Röll, V., & Meyer, C. (2020). Young People's Perceptions of World Cultural Heritage: Suggestions for a Critical and Reflexive World Heritage Education. *Sustainability, 12*(20), 1–18.

Rontani, M. (2012). *Patrimonito: a visual storytelling of World Heritage from and for children* [Dissertation]. Malmö högskola/Kultur och samhälle.

Prompayuk, S., & Chairattananon, P. (2016). Preservation of Cultural Heritage Community: Cases of Thailand and Developed Countries. *Procedia: Social and Behavioral Sciences, 234*, 239–243.

Sezer, S., & Can, E. (2020). School Happiness: A Grounded Theory. *Educational Policy Analysis and Strategic Research, 15*(1), 44–62.

Sullivan, J. (2021). Transcending the Technocratic Mentality through the Humanities. *Religions, 12*, 676.

UNESCO. (2003). *Convention for the safeguarding of the intangible Cultural Heritage*. UNESCO.

Vert, S., Andone, D., Ternauciuc, A., Mihaescu, V., Rotaru, O., Mocofan, M., Orhei, C., & Vasiu, R. (2021). User Evaluation of a Multi-Platform Digital Storytelling Concept for Cultural Heritage. *Mathematics, 9*, 2678.

Walker, S. L. (2015). The Role of Local History in the Curriculum at a Rural, Southeastern Community College. *Walden Dissertations and Doctoral Studies*. 1233. https://scholarworks.waldenu.edu/dissertations/1233

Yalçınkaya, E. (2015). Creative Drama Study about Intangible Cultural Heritage: Turkish Wedding Traditions. *Creative Education, 6*, 22–31.

Yang, Y. C., & Wu, W. (2012). Digital storytelling for enhancing student academic achievement, critical thinking, and learning motivation: A year-long experimental study. *Computers & Education, 59*, 339–352.

ADDITIONAL READING

Campelo, A., Reynolds, L., Lindgreen, A., & Beverland, M. (Eds.). (2019). *Cultural Heritage*. Routledge.

Edmond, J. (Ed.). (2020). *Digital Technology and the Practices of Humanities Research*. Open Book Publishers.

Fisanick, C., & Stakeley, R. O. (2020). *Digital Storytelling as Public History: A Guidebook for Educators* (1st ed.). Routledge.

Floch, J., & Jiang S. (2015). One place, many stories digital storytelling for cultural heritage discovery in the landscape. *Digital Heritage*, 503-510.

Hood, C., & Reid, P. H. (2018). Social media as a vehicle for user engagement with local history: A case study in the north-east of Scotland. *The Journal of Documentation*, *74*(4), 741–762.

Kremers, H. (2020). *Digital Cultural Heritage*. Springer., doi:10.1007/978-3-030-15200-0

Stocchetti, M. (2016). *Storytelling and Education in the Digital Age*. https://www.peterlang.com/document/1067688

Stolare, M., Ludvigsson, D., & Trenter, C. (2021). The educational power of heritage sites. *History Education Research Journal*, *18*(2), 264–279.

Wu, J., & Chen, D. T. (2020). A systematic review of educational digital storytelling. *Computers & Education*, *147*. Advance online publication. doi:10.1016/j.compedu.2019.103786

KEY TERMS AND DEFINITIONS

Cultural Heritage: An expression of the ways of living developed by a community and passed on from generation to generation, including customs, practices, places, objects, artistic expressions, and values.

Digital Storytelling: The result of the combination of traditional storytelling with the use of multimedia technology.

Education: The process of receiving or giving systematic instruction, especially at a school or university.

Folklore: The traditional stories, customs, and habits of a specific community or nation.

Intangible Cultural Heritage: Are expressions, activities, knowledge and information, skills or techniques which constitute testimonies of traditional, folk, and literary culture.

Local History: The study of history in a geographically local context, that often concentrates on the local community.

Tangible Cultural Heritage: The material traces such as archaeological sites, historical monuments, artifacts, and objects that are significant to a community, a nation, or/and humanity.

APPENDIX 1

Table 2. Questionnaire 1

Questionnaire 1						
1. Answer yes or no to the following questions.						
	YES		NO			
Do you know the term "folklore"?						
Did you know that there is a folklore museum in the city						
Have you visited the folklore museum of the city?						
Have you visited a folklore museum?						
Did you know that museums have a website on the internet?						
Have you ever visited a museum website?						
2. Evaluate the following sentences by marking X in the corresponding box. Grading scale						
Very low	Low	Intermediate	High			Very High
1	2	3	4			5
	1	2	3	4	5	
1. Do you know what exhibits there are in a folklore museum?						
2. Do you find the visit to the folklore museum interesting?						
3. Do you think that you will better understand the history of the place after visiting the folklore museum?						
4. Do you think that visiting a museum online is preferable to being in the physical presence?						
3. What are your expectations from visiting the folklore museum?						

APPENDIX 2

Table 3. Questionnaire 2

Questionaire 2
i. Answer to the follow questions:
1. The digital storytelling plot you created was based on:
A. In a folk song
B. In a folk tale
C. In a historical event
D. In legend / folk history
E. Other
2. The digital story you created includes:
A. Historical figures
B. Anonymous, but real persons
C. Fantastic faces
D. Famous people from legends, traditions, folk songs
E. Other
3. The digital story you created
A. You relate to the history of your place
B. With the folklore traditions of your place
C. With the oral traditions of your place
D. With monuments of your place
E. With none of the above
4. The digital story you created which of the following is included
A. Audiovisual material from the visit to the museum
B. Audiovisual material from the internet
C. Excerpts from folk songs, legends, folk tales
D. Historical narrative
E. Testimonies
ii. Evaluate the following sentences according to this grading scale.

Very low	low	intemediate	high	Very high
1	2	3	4	5

1.Did you find the visit to the folklore museum interesting?
2. Did the visit to the folklore museum help you to get to know the history of the place better?
3. Did the exhibits you photographed help you create the digital narrative?
4. Did you use material from the museum website to create digital history?
5. Did you have the means to create digital storytelling?
6. Did you find the whole process interesting?
7. How easy did you find the whole process?
8. Did it help you understand the lesson?
iii. Briefly describe the pros and cons of this lesson.
iv. Briefly describe the differences you have identified from a history or literature lesson taught in the traditional way.

Chapter 8
Digital Media in Indigenous Language Education

Miguel A. Sanchez-Acevedo
https://orcid.org/0000-0002-0996-0038
Universidad de la Cañada, Mexico

Beatriz A. Sabino-Moxo
Universidad de la Cañada, Mexico

Jose A. Marquez-Dominguez
https://orcid.org/0000-0003-2552-2289
Universidad de la Cañada, Mexico

Carmen C. Martinez-Gil
Universidad de la Cañada, Mexico

ABSTRACT

Education has started a transformation by including digital media technologies to enhance the learning process. This transformation was accelerated by the COVID-19 pandemic, which paralyzed face-to-face classes and switched to distance education modalities through various platforms. Animation and storytelling have been the most influential digital tools to transmit knowledge; also, augmented reality has gained popularity in education. Indigenous languages are a cultural wealth and provide great philosophical and cultural value associated with linguistic diversity. This chapter describes different digital tools developed to teach Cuicateco, Mazateco, and Nahuatl, three indigenous languages spoken in Mexico; then, a usability study is described to evaluate the effectiveness of digital tools; finally, a case study is presented to evaluate the proposed methodology.

INTRODUCTION

In recent years, education has started a transformation by including digital media technologies to improve the learning process (Cannon, 2018). This transformation was accelerated by the COVID-19 pandemic,

DOI: 10.4018/978-1-6684-4461-0.ch008

which paralyzed face-to-face classes and switched to distance education modalities through various platforms such as the Internet, TV, radio, and smartphones (ECLAC-UNESCO, 2020). Animation (Strømme and Mork, 2021) and storytelling (Friskie, 2020; Maureen *et al.*, 2020) have been the most influential digital tools to transmit knowledge in a comprehensive way. Furthermore, augmented reality has gained popularity in education due to the advantage of displaying digital information over physical content (Abdinejad *et al.*, 2021; Bhagat *et al.*, 2021; Dreimane and Daniela, 2021; Zhang *et al.*, 2021). The inclusion of digital media in formal education opens the door to recover traditions that have been lost in indigenous communities (United Nations, 2017; Outakoski *et al.*, 2018).

Smartphones and tablets are the main information and communication technologies appropriated by indigenous communities (Rivoir and Morales, 2019). Most of the technology targeting indigenous languages is related to digital literacy focused on reading and writing skills (Li, Brar and Roihan, 2021). Digital content creation for indigenous communities has been concentrated in apps, websites, movies, music, video games, social media, coding, digital files, virtual reality, augmented reality, and artificial intelligence (Meighan, 2021).

Indigenous languages are a cultural wealth and provide great philosophical and cultural value associated with linguistic diversity; therefore, it is important to preserve them and avoid their disappearance (Del Carpio, 2014). In Mexico there are 68 indigenous languages, which have been classified into 11 linguistic families, of which 364 variants are diversified by regions or ethnic groups. Oaxaca is a state characterized by its great ethnic, cultural, and linguistic diversity, as well as the rich biodiversity of its territories; it is the Mexican entity where the largest number of ethnic groups reside: Amuzgos, Cuicatecos, Chatinos, Chinantecos, Chocholtecos, Chontales, Huaves, Ixcatecos, Mazatecos, Mixes, Mixtecos, Nahuas, Triquis, Zapotecos, Zoques and Afro-Mexicans (Castillo, 2018). La Cañada is one of the eight regions belonging to the state of Oaxaca and is made up of two districts: Cuicatlán, with 20 municipalities, and Teotitlán, with 25 municipalities; three indigenous languages are spoken in this region: Cuicateco, Mazateco, and Nahuatl.

The Cuicateco language has approximately 12,785 speakers in the municipalities of San Pedro Teutila, San Andrés Teotilalpam, San Francisco Chapulapa, Santa María Tlalixtac, San Pedro Sochiapam, Concepción Pápalo, Santa María Pápalo, San Juan Tepeuxila, Santos Reyes Pápalo, Valerio Trujano and San Juan Bautista Cuicatlán. Mazateco is spoken by 170,155 inhabitants of Huautla de Jiménez, San Bartolomé Ayautla, San Juan Coatzospam, Santa María Chilchotla, San Mateo Eloxochitlán de Flores Magón, San Francisco Huehuetlán, San Cristóbal, San Pedro Ocopetatillo, San Jerónimo Tecoatl, San José Tenango, Santiago Texcalcingo, San Lucas Zoquiapam, San Pedro Ixcatlán, Jalapa de Díaz, and San Miguel Soyaltepec (Carrera, 2011). Nahuatl has around 13,000 speakers in Santa María Teopoxco, Santiago Texcalcingo, Vigastepec, San Bernardino, and Capultitla (Summer Institute of Linguistics, 2021).

This chapter describes different digital tools developed to teach Cuicateco, Mazateco, and Nahuatl, three indigenous languages spoken in the Cañada region in the state of Oaxaca, Mexico (Figure 1); then a usability study is described to evaluate the effectiveness of digital tools; finally, a case study is presented to evaluate the proposed methodology.

BACKGROUND

Galdames *et al.* (2006) mention that there are different points to encourage teachers to reflect on the importance of teaching the indigenous language and how to help parents understand the benefits of

Figure 1. Indigenous languages spoken in the Cañada Region of Oaxaca, Mexico.

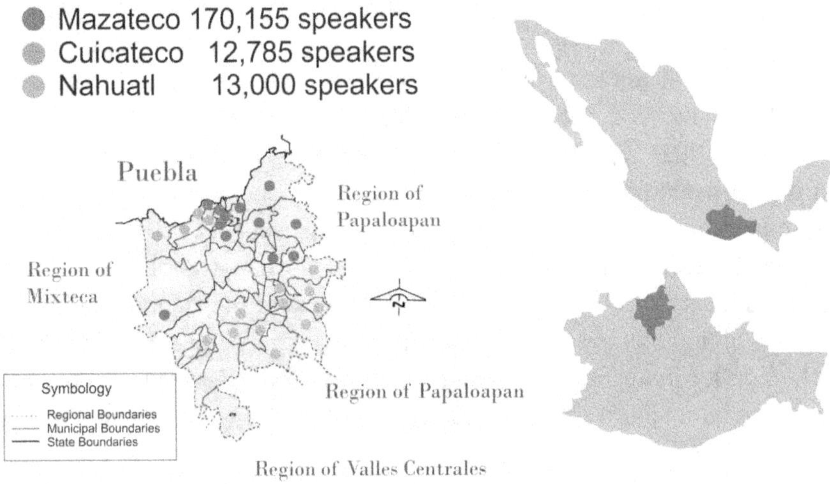

bilingual education. Children find it easier to learn if their native language is used in instruction and bilingualism provides a greater capacity to act with confidence and obtain one's own vision of the world; moreover, learning a second language using the native language produces better results

Two axes on which actions can be developed for the recovery and revitalization of indigenous languages are: basic linguistic and pedagogical training, this contributes to the sustainable development of local literacy and documentation capacities; promotion and development of a national linguistic and educational policy to improve the living conditions and respect for the human rights of indigenous communities (UNESCO, 2003).

To avoid the decrease of speakers of indigenous languages in Mexico, bilingual schools have been created, whose objective is the conservation of the local language, teaching pronunciation, writing, and the use of words in their cultural environment; private lessons or specialized courses have been generated, where native speakers contribute their knowledge of the language, giving rise to specializations; finally, web, mobile, and desktop applications have been created to rescue, preserve, and spread a native language in the learning process.

Among the tools developed for Nahuatl, Martínez-Gil *et al.* (2012) proposed a Nahuatl-Spanish translator. Muñoz-Garcia (2018) developed the application "Aprender Náhuatl" for users who wish to learn the Nahuatl language. Miron-Chacón *et al.* (2019) developed a web system that allows users to see and hear in real time the pronunciation, spelling, and meaning of words used in basic conversations.

In the case of Cuicateco, Valdez-Besares *et al.* (2016) developed a collaborative web application as a tool for learning the writing and pronunciation of indigenous languages, including Chatino, Chinanteco, Cuicateco, Huave, Mazateco, Mixe, Mixteco, Triqui, and Zapoteco.

For Mazatec, Armas (2020) presents an interactive book that uses Augmented Reality to view and listen content in Mazateco; this is used as a tool for teaching the Mazateco language to bilingual primary school students in the municipality of Huautla de Jiménez, Oaxaca. Valencia (2020) proposes an alternative for the rescue, conservation and dissemination of at least one variant of the Mazateco language consisting of a book and an Augmented Reality application where the identity of a community is identified through

Figure 2. a) use case diagram, b) class diagram, c) sequence diagram.

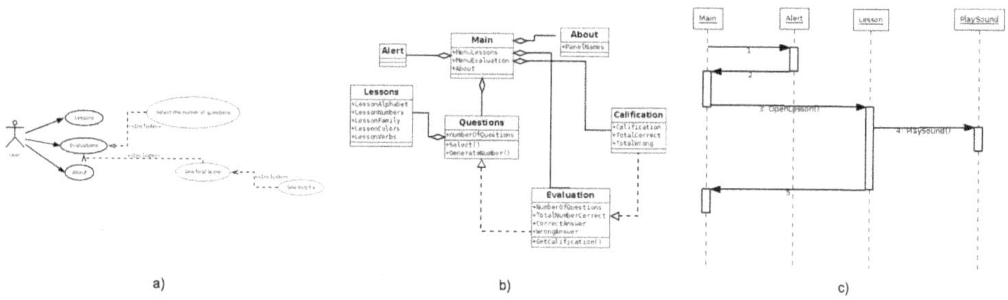

texts and images. Cresencio (2021) presents an application for mobile devices using Augmented Reality technology and printed material that complements the educational content in the Mazateco language; according to educational needs and the cultural context of indigenous education, incorporates themes of animals, fruits and vegetables, nature, numbers, objects, and body parts; this vocabulary collection is based on the book "Én yama Naxínní Lengua Mazateca Huautla de Jiménez, Oaxaca".

To learn a new language, it is usual to start by knowing the most common words or phrases and then gradually increase the knowledge of the vocabulary and grammar rules of this new language. A methodology to design and implement a bilingual software system to learn basic vocabulary of an indigenous language can be structured in five stages. The first stage is made up of two sub-phases: Educational Needs Analysis and User Analysis. In the second stage the formal requirements of the application are described. Stage three is subdivided into three sub-phases: Educational Design, Computational Design, and Interface Design. In Educational Design, the learning objectives are established for each lesson. In Computational Design, the internal structure of the software is modeled with UML, through use case diagrams (Figure 2a); a class diagram (Figure 2b) is used to show the structure of the system, and the interaction is modeled through a sequence diagram (Figure 2c).

USABILITY IN DIGITAL MEDIA ORIENTED TO EDUCATION IN INDIGENOUS LANGUAGES.

UCD is a methodology that places the user at the center of the design process, it is highly recommended for the development of products and services that must be simple and easy to use. UCD is considered a problem-solving process where designers analyze how users tend to use a product or service based on their real-world needs and behavior (Garreta and Mor, 2018; Lowdermilk, 2013). The stages of the UCD methodology are analysis, design, testing, and implementation (Figure 3).

Analysis

The documentation of the situation of the indigenous language in the context of education requires data collection techniques and instruments to identify the characteristics of the users, the different methods and methodologies used by teachers, the type of evaluation of student learning, and the technological tools used in the teaching of the indigenous language. To carry out this phase, the following activities

Figure 3. UCD methodology.

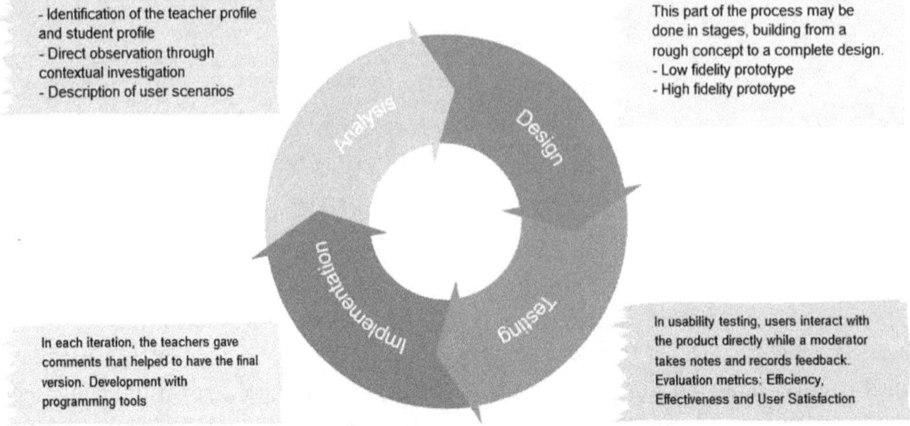

are recommended: identification of the teacher profile and student profile, direct observation through contextual investigation and description of user scenarios.

Identification of the Teacher Profile and Student Profile

In the profile of the teacher and the student, gender, age, academic level, and language proficiency are considered.

Direct Observation through Contextual Investigation

Direct observation allows observing various learning environments for the active and effective participation of students in the classroom as well as the techniques and tools in the teaching of the indigenous language. Some techniques to apply direct observation are work groups as a strategy for interaction and coexistence, interaction in the classroom speaking only in the indigenous language, singing groups in the indigenous language guided by the teacher, elaboration of drawings in the student's notebooks, spell aloud the indigenous language alphabet illustrated by the students and elaboration of models with paper, wood, reed, totomoxtle, cloth, plasticine.

Description of User Scenarios

The scenario technique consists of the description of a person or actor who uses a system or product in the context of daily use.

Design and Evaluation

After identifying the users and the context of use of a mobile application, the next phase of the DCU methodology is the design of the application. Initially, a low-fidelity prototype is drawn on paper, it is

Figure 4. Iterations to obtain the final prototype

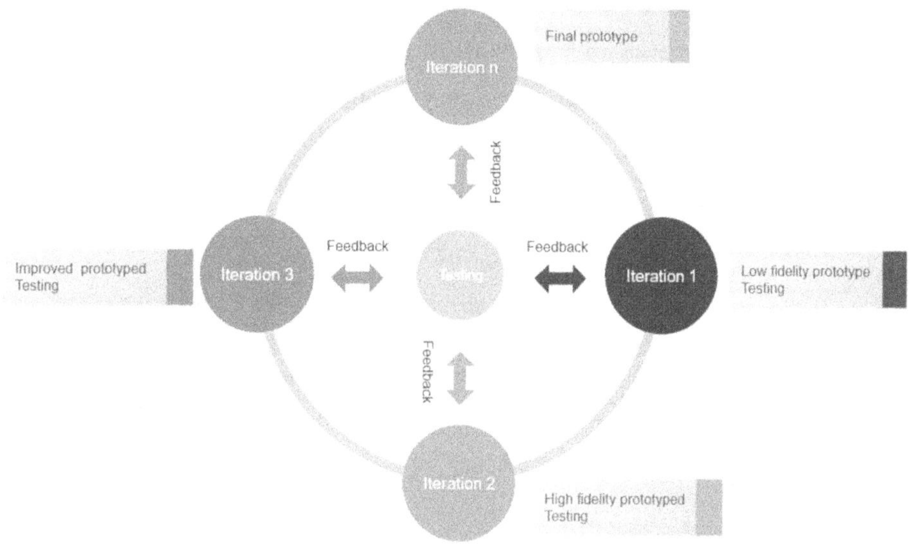

evaluated by users, and with the feedback received, the high-fidelity prototype is implemented considering the characteristics of the hardware of the teachers' mobile devices. In the second iteration, the functional prototype is evaluated to obtain user opinions; later the software improvements are implemented and evaluated in a last iteration. Through iterations a progressive improvement adapted to the needs of the users is obtained. In each iteration, the teachers give comments that help to have the final version. The evaluation considers the usability metrics: satisfaction, efficacy and efficiency.

Implementation

According to the methodology, n-iterations are performed to improve the design and implementation (Figure 4). The activities of each iteration are described below.

First Iteration

In this iteration, the assistance of the teachers is essential to guide the students in the use of the application, by considering difficulty to use the device, size of objects for proper appreciation, confusing background colors with the objects and sound volume.

Second Iteration

After making the improvements of the first iteration and obtaining the acceptance of the teachers and students, the following should be considered: the lighting of objects, the position of objects to improve the visual appearance and text location and background color.

Table 1. Teacher archetype.

<table>
<tr><td rowspan="4">Teacher
Name: Alma
Age: 30 years old
Profession: bilingual teacher</td><td colspan="2">About Alma
Alma is a teacher at the indigenous preschool education center, she has taught for 9 years. Together with her family, she lives in the indigenous community, she is passionate about teaching and is pleased to contribute to the rescue of the indigenous language.</td></tr>
<tr><td>Objective: to contribute to the rescue of mother tongues.</td><td>Technological devices used: computer, tablet, smartphone.</td></tr>
<tr><td>Specific objectives:
● Organize cultural activities for the dissemination of mother tongues.
● Use technology to document indigenous languages.
● Have various materials and contents for the teaching of mother tongues.</td><td>Personality: Kind, caring, organized, patient.</td></tr>
<tr><td colspan="2">Information needs:
To carry out her work, she considers it essential to have children's texts written in the indigenous language, audios with the pronunciation of words, phrases, children's songs, representations in drawings and models made with various materials.</td></tr>
</table>

Third Iteration

In the last iteration usability metrics should be analyzed: efficacy, efficiency, and satisfaction.

Testing

In the third stage of the DCU methodology, the software is evaluated with usability metrics: effectiveness, efficiency, and satisfaction. Effectiveness measures the percentage of success, it refers to the tasks that the user completes, when the percentage is greater than 78%, it is considered acceptable. Efficiency refers to the average time required to complete each task. The level of satisfaction can be obtained from questions that measure the user's general opinion about the usability of the software. If the result is less than 78%, more work is required on the design of the process or on the interface.

A CASE STUDY FOR VALIDATING THE PROPOSED METHODOLOGY

A bilingual school was elected to use a digital tool in the learning process of the indigenous language to evaluate its effectiveness. The first step of this stage was to obtain the profiles of the teacher and the student, for which a guided interview was conducted with the teachers and students at the school. Six teachers were identified, four women and two men in a range of 30 to 50 years. Regarding the academic level, one teacher has a bilingual linguistic profile, and the rest are bilingual educators. As for the students, the academic levels are first, second and third grade of preschool education, with ages from 3 to 5 years, on average there are 15 students per group.

After applying direct observation and contextual research it was identified that there is no work that links the use of digital tools in the teaching of the indigenous language or any other technological tool that complements current traditional teaching methods. From the collected data, a teacher archetype and user archetype were delineated; the archetypes are described in Table 1 and Table 2.

Then scenarios for teacher and student are defined:

Table 2. Student archetype.

<table>
<tr><td rowspan="4">Student
Name: Juan
Age: 5 years old
Grade: Preschool</td><td colspan="2">About Juan
Juan is a preschool student, currently in third grade. Juan's parents consider that speaking an indigenous language is a privilege and it is extremely important that his son learns and acquires the language in a formal learning environment such as school.</td></tr>
<tr><td>Objective: finish preschool education.</td><td>Technological gadgets that he knows how to use: Smartphone</td></tr>
<tr><td>Specific objectives:
● Have lots of friends to play with.
● Know how to sing children's songs in Spanish and in their mother tongue.</td><td>Personality: restless, curious, friendly</td></tr>
<tr><td colspan="2">Information needs: For their academic training, they receive the information provided by teachers, through the various teaching-learning methodologies.</td></tr>
</table>

Teacher Scenario: Every Wednesday the teacher wears typical community clothing and has prepared to teach the vocabulary of animals from the region in Spanish and the indigenous language. He has planned to use the recognition technique by instant visualization using a mobile application.

- At the table in front of the classroom, the teacher orders a collection of cards with the names of the animals, opens the mobile application and randomly selects a student.
- Teacher asks the student to choose a card of an animal that he likes and provides him with a mobile device with the application.
- Teacher invites the student to focus the camera of the mobile device towards the card to view a 3D model with animation of the animal and listen to the pronunciation in Spanish and the indigenous language.
- Teacher asks the student to leave the mobile device on the table and say aloud the name of the animal in the indigenous language.
- Teacher writes the word on the board, then she tells the students to pretend to write the letters of the word that was written on the board.
- Teacher asks to close her eyes and repeat the writing technique three times.
- Finally, the teacher asks to open her eyes and visualize the name of the animal written on the blackboard for five seconds, after this time the teacher deletes the word, and the student must write it in his notebook.
- The dynamic is repeated until the list of students is finished.

Student Scenario: the students arrive at school wearing typical clothing. In the classroom, the teacher tells them that they will learn and know some names of animals in the area. The analysis obtained will help to identify the needs of users to carry out their objectives.

Design and Evaluation

The design of the prototypes considered the information needs and characteristics of the hardware of the mobile devices that each teacher possesses. The first proposal was a low-fidelity prototype; after being accepted by the users, a high-fidelity prototype was made. The high-fidelity prototype was later evaluated in three iterations, achieving an evolutionary improvement until the final version was completed. The iterations performed are described below.

Improvements made in the first iteration: instead of a tablet, the use of a cell phone was proposed, to reduce the size of three-dimensional objects for better appreciation, a white background has been placed over 3D objects for better viewing and a speaker connected with Bluetooth technology was used to have a higher volume level.

Improvements made in the second iteration: place more lighting on three-dimensional objects, it uses a base to place the cards with marker recognition, which allows greater comfort when using the tool and placement of the name in three-dimensional text.

Improvements made in the third iteration: users agreed with the results of the second evaluation, no changes were made to the application in this iteration. The results of the usability tests are described in the next section.

Testing

Efficiency: The value of this metric was calculated with the percentages of the tasks carried out by the users, obtaining an effectiveness percentage of 80%. Because this result is greater than 78%, the software has reached the required percentage of effectiveness.

Efficiency: The efficiency in the time of carrying out the activities by all users was greater than 60%, which is why, according to some authors, this percentage is considered acceptable for the evaluated software.

Satisfaction: To measure this metric, the SUS (System Usability Scale) questionnaire was used, in addition, teachers were asked to rate the software on a scale of 1 to 10. The average score was 8.6, since above 7.0 the software was considered acceptable.

DISCUSSION

For many years the indigenous languages were abandoned, leaving many of them in a state of extinction. Fortunately, people have become aware of maintaining and recovering indigenous languages. Digital tools are useful to encourage and facilitate the teaching and learning process of indigenous languages.

Vocabulary is a fundamental element in the process of learning a language, an interactive software that helps in learning vocabulary is very useful in this process. The methodology proposed in this chapter aims to provide a systematic way of building vocabulary software to increase the efficiency of the learning process.

The ease of use of digital tools is essential to encourage their daily use; In addition, the usability of the application is of great value for the quality of learning. In this chapter, the User Centered Design Methodology was adapted to develop applications focused on the process of learning indigenous languages. Usability guarantees the effectiveness, efficiency and satisfaction of the digital tools applied in the classroom.

REFERENCES

Abdinejad, M., Talaie, B., Qorbani, H. S., & Dalili, S. (2021). Student perceptions using augmented reality and 3D visualization technologies in chemistry education. *Journal of Science Education and Technology*, *30*(1), 87–96. doi:10.100710956-020-09880-2

Armas, E. (2020). *Libro interactivo con realidad aumentada para la enseñanza de la lengua mazateca en primer grado de primaria* [Bachelor Thesis]. Universidad de la Cañada.

Bhagat, K. K., Yang, F. Y., Cheng, C. H., Zhang, Y., & Liou, W.-K. (2021). Tracking the process and motivation of math learning with augmented reality. *Educational Technology Research and Development*, *69*(6), 3153–3178. doi:10.100711423-021-10066-9

Cannon, M. (2018). *Digital Media in Education.* Macmillan., doi:10.1007/978-3-319-78304-8

Carrera, C. (2011). *Acercamiento gramatical a la lengua mazateca de Mazatlán de Villa de Flores Oaxaca*. INALI.

Castillo, M. C. (2018). Las identidades étnicas en Oaxaca. *Oaxaca Población Siglo XXI*, *41*, 23–40.

Cresencio, L. (2021). *Herramientas con realidad aumentada de apoyo en la enseñanza de la lengua materna mazateca de Huautla de Jiménez, Oaxaca* [Bachelor Thesis]. Universidad de la Cañada.

Del Carpio, K. B. (2014). *La importancia de las comunidades indígenas, sus lenguas y culturas*. Retrieved from https://web.archive.org/web/20210728084951/http://www.revista pueblos.org/blog/2014/12/06/la-importancia-de-las-comunidades-indigenas-sus-lenguas-y-culturas/ Consulted in December 2021.

Dreimane, S., & Daniela, L. (2021). Educational potential of augmented reality mobile applications for learning the anatomy of the human body. *Technology. Knowledge and Learning*, *26*(4), 763–788. doi:10.100710758-020-09461-7

ECLAC-UNESCO. (2020). *Education in the time of COVID-19*. United Nations.

Friskie, S. (2020). The healing power of storytelling: Finding identity through narrative. *The Arbutus Review*, *11*(1), 19–27. doi:10.18357/tar111202019324

Galdames, V., Walqui, A., & Gustafson, B. (2006). *Enseñanza de Lengua Indígena como Lengua Materna*. CDI.

Garreta, D., & Mor, P. (2018). *Diseño centrado en el usuario*. Universidad Oberta de Catalunya.

Li, J., Brar, A., & Roihan, N. (2021). The use of digital technology to enhace language and literacy skills for indigenous people: A systematic literature review. *Computers and Education Open*, *2*, 10035. doi:10.1016/j.caeo.2021.100035

Lowdermilk, T. (2013). *User-Centered Design*. O'Reilly Media, Inc.

Martínez-Gil, C. C., Zempoalteca-Pérez, A., Soancatl-Aguilar, V., Estudillo-Ayala, M. J., Lara-Ramírez, J. E., & Alcántara-Santiago, A. (2012). Computer systems for analysis of Nahuatl. *Research in Computing Science*, *47*(1), 11–16. doi:10.13053/rcs-47-1-1

Maureen, I. Y., van der Meij, H., & de Jong, T. (2020). Enhancing storytelling activities to support early(digital) literacy development in early childhood education. *International Journal of Early Childhood, 52*(1), 55–76. doi:10.100713158-020-00263-7

Meighan, P. J. (2021). Decolonizing the digital landscape: The role of technology in Indigenous language revitalization. *Alternative, 17*(3), 397–405. doi:10.1177/11771801211037672

Miron-Chacón, M. J., Angheven-Negrete, J. S., Juárez-Ibáñez, J. A., & Avendaño-Cortés, I. (2019). Development of the web system as a learning tool for Nahuatl in the Orizabense variant. In A. Marroquín, J. Olivares, P. Díaz, & L. Cruz (Eds.), *Mujeres en la tecnología*. ECORFAN.

Muñoz-Garcia, R. (2018). *Aplicación móvil para el aprendizaje de la lengua Náhuatl* [Master Thesis]. Universidad Autónoma de Guerrero.

Outakoski, H., Cocq, C., & Steggo, P. (2018). Strengthening indigenous languages in the digital age: Social media-supported learning in Sápmi. *Media International Australia, 169*(1), 21–31. doi:10.1177/1329878X18803700

Rivoir, A., & Morales, M. J. (2019). *Tecnologías digitales: miradas críticas de la apropiación en América Latina*. CLACSO. doi:10.2307/j.ctvt6rmh6

Strømme, T. A., & Mork, S. M. (2021). Student's conceptual sense-making of animations and static visualizations of protein synthesis: A sociocultural hypothesis explaining why animations may be beneficial for student learning. *Research in Science Education, 51*(4), 1013–1038. doi:10.100711165-020-09920-2

Summer Institute of Linguistics. (2021). *El Náhuatl del norte de Oaxaca*. Retrieved from https://mexico.sil.org/es/lengua_cultura/nahuatl/nahuatl-nhy

UNESCO. (2003). *Vitalidad y peligro de desaparición de las lenguas*. UNESCO.

United Nations. (2017). *State of the World's Indigenous Peoples: Education*. United Nations.

Valdez-Besares, J. G., Ronquillo-Jorge, A., Mendez-Gijon, F., López-Núñez, L., & Servín-Juárez, F. (2016). Aplicación web para recopilar, difundir y aprender lenguas originarias del sur de México: Una perspectiva desde los hablantes. *Salud y Administración, 3*(7), 19–31.

Valencia, F. (2020). *MÉ XI KUÉNA JMÍNI Libro con Realidad Aumentada para el rescate, conservación y difusión de la lengua mazateca de Huautla de Jiménez, Oaxaca* [Bachelor Thesis]. Universidad de la Cañada.

Zhang, Z., Li, Z., Han, M., Su, Z., Li, W., & Pan, Z. (2021). An augmented reality-based multimedia environment for experimental education. *Multimedia Tools and Applications, 80*(1), 575–590. doi:10.100711042-020-09684-x

Chapter 9
Enlivening a Young Adult Novel on Instagram:
Fostering Reading for Pleasure and Interest in Local History

Evangelia Efstratios Moula
Hellenic Open University, Greece

ABSTRACT

This chapter presents action research based on the transformational design of a young adult novel (Y.A.) into an alternate reality game (ARG) on Instagram and its implementation as an extra-curricular activity. The Y.A. novel, The Deer of Rhodes, by K. Stoforos, was selected according to specific criteria, among which of major importance was the smooth integration of local history elements in it. The action research explored the relationship between students' participation in the activity and their attitudes toward literature, their acquisition of certain historical knowledge, and the strengthening of their computational thinking. The assessment of the action research was based on the monitoring of the students' engagement during the implementation, the recording of their performance in embedded tests, and the statistical analysis of their responses in the questionnaire that was handed out after the implementation.

INTRODUCTION

In the postmodern era the boundaries between high and low culture have become blurred. The osmosis and intersection of the fields of culture, art and technology have created new hybrid forms, which question the whole conceptual edifice of modernism, with its institutions and established practices, including literature itself, the concept of aesthetic prestige and its criteria (Moula, 2013). The new digital reality influences radically and recasts the narrative theory (Moula 2010). Through multimodal expression, the traditional form and reception of literature changes and a new digital fiction emerges (Moula, 2019c) where a variety of innovative projects combine and enrich the written textual form with digital sources (Giannikopoulou & Fokiali, 2011). The narrative emancipates itself from its once dominant literary

DOI: 10.4018/978-1-6684-4461-0.ch009

conventions and the accompanying criticism, whose role was to safeguard and guarantee the canonical reception. The various media with their own cultural, semiotic and technological dimensions mark the developments in the field of narrative to varying degrees (Bal & Van Boheemen, 2009: xx).

The theoretical starting point of the transformation of the novel into an ARG was the commonly accepted assumption in the literary field of Humanities, that narrative, once monopolized by the literary writing, has been liberated from the literary conventions and has evolved into a dominant cultural attitude. What's more, the underlying philosophy of the transformation of the literary text into an ARG was the theory of multiliteracies, which legitimizes the intervention in a pre-existing project/artifact (designed) so as to create new derivative products in multimodal terms (redesigned). Design involves representation, reframing (integration into a new environment), recombination and hybridization, transforming the available resources, while the redesigned product never simply copies what is designed, but interprets it or sheds light on different aspects of it.

The fundamental distinction between literary texts and literature itself (Ingarden, 1973) served furthermore as the theoretical cornerstone of our experiment. On the one hand, literary texts are autonomous entities with material or intangible dimensions and on the other, literature is a heteronomous process and exists only activated through the consciousness of the reader, who receives it and animates it. At the same time, digital environments consist a challenge to our educational approaches in general and to literary reading in particular. Given, on the one hand that the preoccupation with the digital universe is causally linked to the decline of literary reading (Levine et al. 2007) and the indifference to the historical past, and on the other hand, young people's literary literacy rates are declining dramatically, this research aimed to explore the possibilities of harnessing digital space's advantages to achieve a positive attitude toward literature and history as well. The whole project aspired to cultivate through a playful - entertaining engagement of young people with literature, a more favorable response to literature (Thompson & McIlnay, 2019) and secondarily to history.

Even more, modern pedagogical theories and methodological trends which permeate the curricula and redefine the philosophy of literature teaching, shift the lesson's gravity center from the text to the reader. The process of responding to the literary text is prioritized, beyond the control of the understanding of the literary conventions and techniques (Kalogirou, 2004). Thus, today's literature teaching mainly aims at the aesthetic cultivation of students through experiential approaches and playful activities that inspire and motivate them and in general, cultivate their cultural literacy. Our project aimed at creating an affinity space, e.g. a virtual environment beyond the typical frame of a learning site, where students would participate voluntarily, interact and collaborate freely and critically around a common goal (Gee, 2017) .

The dynamic between literature, pleasure and play is highlighted, as the balanced combination of these factors can serve as an opening vestibule for the "more serious" literary reading of adult life.

With this action research, we aimed at the prospective reader type as a player (Appleyard, 1991) and as a performer (reader as interpreter), without underestimating the dimension of his / her identification with peer heroes (reader as hero and heroine). We have given priority to the fun side of literary reading (Poslaniec & Houyel, 2001), since voluntary participation in a playful, reading activity is a positive precondition for engaging and immersing oneself in the world of books.

The experiment of converting a literary text to an ARG on Instagram, with computational thinking as the main tool for the transformational design, aimed to test the effectiveness of this type of narrative in improving students' relationship with literature, reading for pleasure and local history. At the same time we aimed to investigate whether the integration of computational thinking into the plot is related to the students' liking or dislike for the activity.

BACKGROUND: ALTERNATE REALITY GAMES AS A WINDOW INTO NEW STORYWORLDS AND SOCIAL NETWORKS' EVOLVING ROLE IN EDUCATION

ARGs (Alternate reality games) is a relatively new category of storytelling, pervasive, transmedial, and playful, developed in online interactive environments but also utilizing real-world communication methods. As hybrids between story and game, they achieve immersion and encourage participatory storytelling, problem-solving, and action by the reader-player. The fact that they blur the boundaries between imagination and reality and are diffused in the real and virtual world, contributes to the enhancement of the learning experience (Stojanović et al., 2020; Stylianidou et al 2020).

Transemdia narrative refers to a process in which integral elements of a story are systematically dispersed across multiple distribution channels, forming story worlds, where characters, events, locations, and objects evolve in ways that are not possible in one-media narratives, so that they can create a unified and coordinated entertainment experience. Ideally, each medium creates a distinct and valuable contribution to storytelling. (Jenkins, 2007)

The phenomenon of the migration of imaginary elements of a narrative world in different texts causes the so-called radical intertextuality (Jenkins, 2011).

ARGs as a form of online transmedia storytelling, encourage players to take on missions to collect, interpret and reassemble fragments of a story, which are distributed across a variety of media, platforms, and locations (Bonsignore et al, 2013). Their pedagogical potentials and their implementation in education are not numerous but important (Moula, 2019a).

ARGs have nothing in common with most online games or video games of the past. One of their main goals is to disguise the fact that these are games, making the TINAG philosophy (this is not a game) their main principle (Szulborski, 2005: 7). To be more precise, they deliberately blur the boundaries between in-game and out-of-game experiences, and data can be provided to players in almost any form (Gosney, 2005: 2).

In addition, ARGs have, in principle, been designed as narrative vehicles (Martin et al., 2006), combining interaction with immersion. One way to capitalize on a narrative in an ARG is to reveal parts of it gradually, as a reward for achieving specific goals by reader-players (Bopp, 2008).

Alternate reality games are divided into 5 main categories, including the educational ones. In the early stages, the applications were mainly aimed at higher education, but from 2010 onwards they are significantly expanded to other educational levels (Moula, 2019a).

The alternate reality narration of a literary text is supposed to function as a "cultural activator" (Jenkins 2009), attracting and mobilizing the students' community to collaborate, formulate assumptions, process data, exchange reflections, solve problems, and decipher ambiguous or puzzling elements.

The digital environment chosen for the development of the action research was the social network Instagram.

Historically, mobile technologies and social media were originally used for entertainment, personal needs, and direct communication. Over time, these technologies have spread and conquered the business world, while today, the trend of their use in teaching is becoming more and more intense. Thus, while social media is considered by the vast majority as having the sole purpose of communicating between friends (Amichai-Hamburger &. Vinitzky, 2010), there is now significant evidence (Tess, 2013) that they can be used as tools to promote learning, to facilitate academic communication, to allow sharing and to get feedback among peers (Gallardo-Echenique et al., 2015).

The increasing number of surveys on the use of mobile devices and social media in education, intensified since 2005, reveals the growing interest of the academic community in the field (Manca, 2020; Greenhow & Chapman, 2020). Social interaction implicates emotional responses which become a powerful catalyst for learning (Meltzoff et al., 2009). Nevertheless, educators have been reluctant to engage with mobile learning, sometimes going to the other extreme of banning device use in class (Farley et al., 2015).

The most frequently analyzed social media used in the education process are: Facebook (Blair et al., 2014), Twitter, blogs (Michailidis et al., 2019), Instagram (Green et al., 2019; Carpenter et. al., 2019), and YouTube, which appear to be the most popular among young people (Al Bahrani et al., 2015). An important challenge for this action research was to examine whether mobile devices and social networks should not be considered a problem in the educational process, but a tool that can improve the quality of education provided.

The popularity of social networks in the last decade has gone through great fluctuations and subversions. According to the latest statistical measurements and the comparative analysis of recent years, Facebook's use among young people fell from 42% in 2012 to 2%, in the fall of 2020, Twitter from 27% to 3%, while Instagram from 12% rose to 25%, having previously reached its peak in 2014 with 30%. Its slight decline and stabilization are attributed to the emergence of new networks such as Snapchat in 2015 and Tiktok in 2019.

Instagram competitors in the multimedia social media landscape, Snapchat and Tiktok (Qiyang, & Jung, 2019) differ in their operating frame and their functions. Snapchat only supports content that is ephemeral and removed right after its emergence (Bayer et al. 2016). Transience, as its most prominent feature contrasts with the permanence of the communication content of older networks (boyd & Ellison 2007). On the other hand, Tiktok limits the type of posting to short videos, which are usually the trigger for a chain reaction of mimetic video responses (Zulli & Zulli, 2020). Despite the restrictive nature of the aforementioned networks, today the possibilities of their exploitation in education are also being investigated (Zhou, 2019).

However, it is evident by a quick glimpse at the key features of the most popular social networks among young people, that Instagram was the most suitable environment for the development of our project. It supports a variety of types of posts, permanent or temporary, with plenty of commenting options (icons, gifs), polls, image, and video editing, and live streaming.

The demands of the transmedial transposition of the literary text to a social network could not be met in the other two popular networks and in fact, the choice of Instagram was the only practically feasible, as out of the 19 participants only 2 students had a Facebook profile.

Even more, Instagram has already been used as a potential means for achieving learning goals (Arceneaux, 2018; Stojanović et al., 2019; Gonulal, 2019; Soviyah & Etikaningsih, 2018) and has proved its effectiveness, thanks to the flexibility of its features.

MAIN FOCUS OF THE CHAPTER: COMPUTATIONAL THINKING AND ITS INTERDISCIPLINARY DIMENSION

The importance of Computational Thinking (CT) and its interdisciplinary dimension have been supported by a large body of research, which examines CT's relationship with the teaching of a variety of subjects in education (Fessakis et al., 2019).

Such subjects are Mathematics (Barcelos & Silveira, 2012; Weintrop et al., 2016), Biology and Physics (Basu et al., 2013), Language and History (Lee, Martin & Apone, 2014), and even literature (de Paula et al., 2018). Although CT tends to be considered as a prerequisite for meeting the challenges of the future, only a small percentage of teachers know how to encourage it (Hsu et al., 2018). One of the most popular, current trends among educators to promote CT is the use of activities based on code learning and programming (Computational Thinking) (Barr & Stephenson, 2011), which is only one side of its potential.

Mannila et al. (2014) consider that CT is a term that covers a set of concepts and processes, from computer science that help to shape problems and their solutions in different disciplines. Similarly, Riley and Hunt (2014: 4) parallel the cognitive strategies of computational thinking with the way computer scientists think, without necessarily leading to computer programming (Sysło and Kwiatkowska (2013: 50). Most of the definitions refer to problem-solving, problem comprehension, and problem formulation (Wing, 2006; Liu and He, 2014; Saari & Hopkins, 2020).

Computational mentality (Isbell, et al., 2009) consists of 9 basic dimensions and corresponding areas of skills, such as data management (collection, analysis, and representation), problem deconstruction, subtraction, algorithmic logic and processes, automation, parallelism, and simulation. The skills and practices that emerge from computational thinking are also applied to the creative use of media, in their design and production, as well as programmatic logic is required at each stage of content enrichment and at the level of reflection (Jacob & Warschauer, 2018).

In recent research, from all the educational subjects that support the integration of computational thinking, literary studies have a very low percentage and mainly focus on data collection (Fessakis et al. 2018). This finding incited us to challenge the existing situation and explore the possibilities of computational thinking in literary education.

ACTION RESEARCH

The action research was conducted at the 2nd High School of Rhodes, in the school year 2020-21, during the pandemic and was addressed to 19 9th graders.

It was used as a communicative bridge for the members of the class, to maintain contact, to keep the spirit high in times of isolation and to offer them relaxation (Galvin & Greenhow, 2020). At the same time, it served as a vehicle for approaching a literary text out of the box, in an unconventional and alternative way and for the discovery of a local historical period of great importance.

Action research is the most appropriate way to examine one's own practice in order to check if it is as it should be and then improve it (McNiff et al., 1996). It seeks transformational change through the simultaneous process of action and research, which are intertwined with critical thinking.

This type of research allows the researcher to deal with more than one issue at a time. There is a central axis, about the main issue under investigation and around it,a series of concentric circles that concern secondary issues. So, the researcher deals with several problems, without losing sight of the core problem. In this way, he/she controls all the conditions that affect it, describes them in an inductive way, and tries to interpret the course of action, the stages, the process of change, and the consequences (Katsarou & Tsafos, 2014).

Thus, in this case, although the central issue was to attract students to an alternative and playful literary experience, which could serve as a "cultural attractor" to actual literary reading and to their local history, the students' response to the challenges and riddles interspersed in the narrative canvas and the development of their computational skills, such as problem-solving, logical reasoning, algorithmic thinking, and pattern matching, were also taken into account. In addition, the relationship between their level of participation and the various kinds of puzzles and problems, the dynamics of the exchange of messages and their content, and the acquisition of skills in specific digital environments were examined as well.

So we applied statistical hypothesis tests as follows:

1st null hypothesis: the participation in an ARG created by the transformation of a Y.A. novel doesn't affect positively students' attitudes toward literature.

1st alternative hypothesis: the participation in an ARG created by the transformation of a Y.A. novel affects positively students' attitudes toward literature.

2nd null hypothesis: the integration of local history in an ARG created by the transformation of a Y.A. novel doesn't play significant role in the acquisition of the corresponding knowledge.

2nd alternative hypothesis: the integration of local history in an ARG created by the transformation of a Y.A. novel plays significant role in the acquisition of the corresponding knowledge.

3rd null hypothesis: the integration of computational thinking into an ARG created by the transformation of a Y.A. novel does not contribute to the positive reception of the experience involved.

3rd alternative: the integration of computational thinking into an ARG created by the transformation of a Y.A. novel contributes to the positive reception of the experience involved.

4th null hypothesis: 4th null hypothesis: the social medium selected does not affect the participation experience and the level of participation.

4th alternative hypothesis: the social medium selected affects the participation experience and the level of participation.

REDESIGNING THE ORIGINAL LITERARY TEXT

The selected literary text takes place in the Dodecanese and specifically on the islands of Astypalea, Rhodes, and the rocky islet of Syrna. The well-known -from previous books- company of K. Stoforos, is meeting again: Antigone, Katerina, Zoe and Zenovia, Katerina and Zoe's parents, Michalis, Zenovia's father, and grandfather Lefteris, who needs to recover from the adventure in Kastoria with grandmother Zoe, are all going on vacation to Astypalea. Soon, other the rest of the old friends arrive, Jason and Savvas from Litochoro. They then meet Reno and Francesca and their parents from Southern Italy, who are on holiday but also on a specific mission. In a masterful way, the past of their new friends' relatives is connected to the history of the Dodecanese during the Italian occupation (an incredible love story, a shipwreck, diplomatic tricks, frauds, stolen antiquities, and snapshots from the National Resistance are interweaved). The Deer of Rhodes (an imaginary lost statue of the famous ancient sculptor Haris) is the unifying axis between yesterday and today. In the meantime, the company grows, has fun, develops bonds, and spends pleasant moments against the backdrop of the summertime landscape of the island, while their pursuers of the deer (Amelio and Juanos) follow them closely.

For the choice of the novel the place where the adventure evolves, the Dodecanese islands, played a major role. However, it was selected for a number of other qualities as well, such as his suitability for the age group that participated in the research, its genre, of adventure-mystery, which attracts young readers, but also its historical dimension with interesting local references. An outstanding feature of the young adult novel- series of K. Stoforos is the entwining of the well-documented historical facts with the present of his heroes, into exciting mysteries to be solved.

The basic axis of our intervention was on the time-level of the narrative. The constant flashbacks and the delivery of the narrative in the original text demanded the rearrangement of the narrative units with the help of computational thinking methodology.

Thus, after the decomposition of the narrative in its structural components, those that were not organically related to the main narrative axis were removed. Then, the remaining text was rearranged to support the seamless narrative flow and to reveal the causal sequencing of the narrative units. The process of abstraction, in which one distinguishes between important and less important information, is at the core of computational thinking (Wing, 2008).

Constant shifts in temporal view were avoided. This was made possible by replacing the third-person omniscient narrator of the text with the multifocal first-person narrative of the heroes-heroines, who succeeded one another. Even more, intertextual references to previous stories of the heroes were considered superfluous and avoided and The Deer of Rhodes was treated as an independent and self-contained narrative.

Besides, as there were many minor characters in the original text, whose even brief presence on Instagram would be confusing, burdening the participants with unnecessary information, it was decided that some of them should not appear at all. The characters for whom there was created a profile on Instagram were: Jason, Antigone, Francesca, Reno, grandfather Lefteris and Juanos (table 1). Savvas' twitter and Amelio's blog were also used in support. Since Facebook does not allow a visit to a profile if someone does not have an account, it was completely avoided. The designer of the action through her personal profile, interfered rarely, as an extra-diegetic narrator, violating the verisimilitude and the flow and provoking ontological transgressions with enjoyable and amusing extensions.

In the affinity space of the restricted group on Instagram, members were asked to search for information, to draw conclusions from fragmentary data, to make assumptions, to express their opinion, to make calculations, to resort to digital tools, to decrypt messages, and to solve problems which required inductive thinking, pattern matching, or algorithm application.

As mentioned earlier, in ARGs one way to promote the narrative is to reveal parts of it gradually, as a reward for the achievement of specific goals by the students (Bopp, 2008).

A common tactic was to reveal pieces of information that by themselves were not sufficient for meaning- making. So, students should make assumptions based on common sense or turn to the internet for help. For example, when "the Deer" group was initiated, in order for the students to understand the meaning of the group's name, they had to guess the latent parallelism between the statue of the Deer, with the statue of Sleeping Love (probably from Rhodes), whose route, lost in time ended up in the Metropolitan Museum of Art in New York. The puppetmaster (the researcher) of the game, to give an extra clue, uploaded additionally an official document from the Italian consulate, about the illicit trade in antiquities during the period of the Italian occupation of Dodecanese, under the administration of Ameglio. The students were supposed to guess that The Deer was also a stolen statue.

As the context of the action research suggests, the design deviated several times from the original one and was redefined according to the participants' response to an issue. Once the procedures were being condensed and some other times a freer commentary was allowed even if its operation was centrifugal. The retrospective narratives adapted to the economy of the medium were taken over by Reno and Francesca, as the past events directly or indirectly concerned their ancestors. At the same time, the events of the present, e.g. the fairytale festival, the everyday swimming in the Aegean Sea, and the romantic adventures of the kids were evolving. The love affairs of the protagonists aroused great interest to the students, as they participated in two polls for the desired result, which they even determined (thus, Jason chose Francesca as his girlfriend, while in the end, Antigone, unexpectedly, met a boy, who was about to be her boyfriend for the rest of the summer).

To enliven the historical background and urge students to get involved with it, primary sources from the Italian Occupation era were provided, like newspapers, which supported an explorative and experiential approach.

The narration was scattered with riddles in various cryptographic methods (Caesar, Pigpen, Morse, QR codes), augmented reality (ARUnite), and also others that required problem-solving, pattern recognition, deciphering, algorithm applying and other computational strategies to discover the hidden meaning. Also, GoogleMaps were used to locate certain places by their coordinates and to calculate distances and travel times, depending on the means of transportation the heroes used and its speed. Some other time, at a restaurant, the participants had to match patterns, between letters and ingredients, so that they could place the correct order to the waiter and proceed further ahead. A message written upside down required the use of a mirror to be read, while a locked file needed a password, which corresponded to the solution of an algorithm puzzle. At the critical point, where the heroes were in danger by the criminals, a double-digit number was sent to some members of the group separately. By combining the numbers according to an algorithm, the telephone number of the puppet-master would be formed. For the solution to this riddle, teamwork and collective intelligence had to be combined.

OUTCOMES

In the end of the implementation the first thing checked was the degree of the students' understanding of the plot. Scattered phrases with references to events from different time levels were distributed and the students had to rearrange them so as to recompose the narrative. The next step was to create a mindmap, serving as a kind of narrative plan.

The students' participation in the ARG cultivated a series of new media skills (Jenkins et al. (2006: 4) which intersect with the principles of computational thinking, as follows:

- the ability to interact with the environment in the form of problem-solving (play)
- the ability to adopt alternative identities and real-world modeling (simulation)
- the ability to collect and transform content from various media (data collecting),
- the ability to observe the environment and focus on important details (multitasking),
- the ability to interact with tools and take advantage of internet sources (distributed knowledge),
- the ability to activate logical reasoning for a common goal (collective intelligence)
- the critical ability and
- the ability to monitor the flow of information in multiple media (navigation)

The participants' responses to the questionnaire that was handed out to them, were collected and analyzed. In order to draw conclusions regarding the first hypothesis, the correlations between students' satisfaction from the experience with their desire to participate in a similar one in the future and with their intention of reading this one, or a similar book were checked.

In order to draw conclusions about the second and the third hypotheses, we took into account both the scores of students' in-game embedded tests, puzzles, and riddles, and their responses to specific questions from the questionnaire.

As far as it concerns the 4th hypothesis, a comparison was attempted between this action research and a previous similar one made by the researcher in terms of participation levels in the selected social network compared to the one that had been used before.

In the research participated 19 students. Two of them were not Instagram users (they had an inactive registration), while 2 others were occasional visitors and not regular users. So the target group consisted in fact of 15 people. Of the 15 players, 8 belonged to the devotees and interacted with almost every post, 2 belonged to the active players, who participated selectively but quite often, and the remaining 5 belonged to the curious browsers. Of the 8 dedicated players, 6 were boys.

The category of casual players did not even exist (see: igda, white paper, 2006, 45-47). To sum up, 53% of the participants were loyal players, a percentage, statistically significant compared to that of a previous similar experimental project (39%), which was mainly developed on Facebook (Moula, 2019b)

Examining the frequencies of the students' responses to the questionnaire, we received the following results (on the Likert scale, 1 equaled to "Not at all" and 5 to "Absolutely Yes").

- Did you find the transformation of the novel into an ARG on Instagram interesting? 4.33
- Was the behavior of the characters convincing in terms of their role in the narrative? 4.53
- Was the switching of characters and the multifocal narrative more interesting compared to a third-person omniscient narrator? 4.60
- Was it easy to follow the story through the posts? 3.87
- Are you able to recompose it in general? 3.13
- Did you like the intertwining of storytelling and riddles? 4.40
- Was the collaboration in the group helpful to solve the puzzles? 4.47
- Did you like the polls? 4.47
- Did you feel like you were part of the story? 3.90
- Had you ever before solved cryptographic riddles? 0,5
- Did you like the puzzles (cryptography, pattern matching, algorithms, etc.)? 4.30
- Had you ever before used QR, AR and google maps? 1,5
- Did you enjoy using digital tools to solve puzzles? 4.20
- Do you feel competent to use them again? 3,2
- Did the elements of local history included, warm up your interest in the story? 4.22
- Did you learn things you didn't know about local history? 4
- What was your degree of engagement in the action? 3.47
- Would you like to take part in a similar action again? 3.80
- Did the experience arouse your interest in reading the book? 3.53
- Did the experience aroused your curiosity to read a similar adventure book? 3.

Regarding the first hypothesis, we detected statistically significant correlations ($p < 0.05$) with a strong correlation index between the degree of interest caused by the transformation of the novel on Instagram with the persuasiveness of the characters (R = .747), with the ease of following the story (R. = .843), with the successful interaction of narrative and puzzles (R. = .839), with the desire to participate in a similar action (R = .855) and with their interest in reading the book (R = .857). All the above, with emphasis on the last two, support the alternative hypothesis, showing that participation in the ARG affected positively students' attitudes toward literature.

Concerning the second hypothesis the students answered that the narrative development in familiar landscapes in Rhodes and Dodecanese islands was a decisive factor for their interest in it (4,22). In addition, after collecting the results of the historical riddles and puzzles that were scattered throughout the canvas of the story, it was found out that they were 80 percent successfully answered. To crosscheck the permanence of the knowledge acquired, a corresponding test was delivered to the students one week later. The results were optimistic, showing only a slight decrease compared to the in-game results (68 percent of right answers). Once again, the alternative hypothesis was verified.

Regarding the third hypothesis, we found out that although 90% of the students had not previously been involved in computational reasoning, they did not have difficulty with the assignments of the cryptography, patterns' matching, or the algorithms. Even more, although 70% had never used the applications embedded in the story (QR, augmented reality, google maps), they found the missions intriguing and declared that they acquired new thinking and digital skills (62%). In addition, the desire to participate in a similar future action shows a very high correlation with the intertwining of narrative and puzzles (R = .893). Still, although the participants stated a moderate possibility of reconstructing the story after the completion of the action (3,13) when rearranging and connecting the events for the mindmap, they responded adequately. These findings prove the third alternative hypothesis valid.

Finally, by performing a simple linear regression to test the predictive relationships between variables, it was found that high interest in the transformation of the novel on Instagram is a predictor for the desire to participate in a similar future action (adjusted R2 = .711) and to read the book (adjusted R2 = .711). Also, the degree of immersion in the story is a prognostic factor for the desire to participate in a similar action (adjusted R2 = .647).

Regarding the 4th hypothesis, the alternative one was also verified. Comparing this implementation with a previous one by the same researcher, 2 years ago, the book reading prognosticwas now much stronger than in the previous project, where the R2 (with the degree of involvement as predictor factor) was just .227 while the participation desire in a similar action was .229.

CONCLUSION AND FUTURE RESEARCH DIRECTIONS

The choice of Instagram as the environment for the development of the ARG based on K. Stoforos' Y.A. novel, The Deer of Rhodes, proved itself to be more attractive for the participants, hence more effective than Facebook in the previous relevant research. The constant switching of the voices and the multifocal narrative, the sense of immersion in the story, the persuasiveness of the characters, the entanglement of narrative with puzzles, the interpolation of polls, the collaboration, but also the variety of missions in combination with the use of new digital tools, contributed to the positive reception of the action by the students. The local historical references and the familiar descriptions from local places enticed the interest of the participants. Their use as the background of the story or as part of the plot helped students absorb effortlessly the historical information.

The active engagement of the students and their interest was a major prognostic factor for the future reading of the book and for the participation in a similar action. Although the results from the processing of the questionnaire do not guarantee the cultivation of a more permanent positive attitude toward reading literature for pleasure, they serve, at least, as indications that the activity really created -as intended by its design- an intimacy and affinity space and that the ARG became a cultural attractor to literature, evoking a positive experience. Even more, local history, smoothly integrated into the plot and in embedded missions was an additional factor of interest and it was proved that the students acquired knowledge inadvertently and effortlessly.

As the Instagram environment favored the exchange of multimodal material, and the use of oral expressions or even slang, the group Instagram space turned into a field of friendly socializing, where the students expressed themselves uninhibitedly and they created gradually their own code of communication

However, the small sample of students who participated in the action research as well as the minimal research data for similar actions so far internationally, are limiting factors for the generalization of the conclusions. More research needs to be done in the future, including more students and different levels of education, in order to draw more reliable and solid conclusions.

REFERENCES

Al-Bahrani, A., Patel, D., & Sheridan, B. (2015). Engaging students using social media: The students' perspective. *International Review of Economics Education*, *19*, 36–50. doi:10.1016/j.iree.2015.06.001

Amichai-Hamburger, Y., & Vinitzky, G. (2010). Social network use and personality. *Computers in Human Behavior*, *26*(6), 1289–1295. doi:10.1016/j.chb.2010.03.018

Appleyard, J. A. (1991). *Becoming a reader: The experience of fiction from childhood to adulthood.* Cambridge University Press. doi:10.1017/CBO9780511527609

Arceneaux, P. C., & Dinu, L. F. (2018). The social mediated age of information: Twitter and Instagram as tools for information dissemination in higher education. *New Media & Society*, *20*(11), 4155–4176. doi:10.1177/1461444818768259

Barcelos, T. S., & Silveira, I. F. (2012, October). Teaching computational thinking in initial series an analysis of the confluence among mathematics and computer sciences in elementary education and its implications for higher education. In 2012 XXXVIII Conferencia Latinoamericana En Informatica (CLEI) (pp. 1-8). IEEE. doi:10.1109/CLEI.2012.6427135

Barr, V., & Stephenson, C. (2011). Bringing computational thinking to K-12: What is involved and what is the role of the computer science education community? *ACM Inroads*, *2*(1), 48–54. doi:10.1145/1929887.1929905

Basu, S., Dickes, A., Kinnebrew, J. S., Sengupta, P., & Biswas, G. (2013, May). CTSiM: A Computational Thinking Environment for Learning Science through Simulation and Modeling. In CSEDU (pp. 369-378). Academic Press.

Bayer, J. B., Ellison, N. B., Schoenebeck, S. Y., & Falk, E. B. (2016). 'Sharing the small moments: Ephemeral social interaction on Snapchat'. *Information Communication and Society*, *19*(7), 956–977. doi:10.1080/1369118X.2015.1084349

Blair, R., Millard, D., & Woollard, J. (2014). Perceptions of school children of using social media for learning. In *E-Learn: World Conference on E-Learning in Corporate, Government, Healthcare, and Higher Education* (pp. 227–237). Academic Press.

Bonsignore, E., Hansen, D., Kraus, K., Visconti, A., Ahn, J., & Druin, A. (2013, June). Playing for real: designing alternate reality games for teenagers in learning contexts. In *Proceedings of the 12th International Conference on Interaction Design and Children* (pp. 237-246). ACM. 10.1145/2485760.2485788

Bopp, M. M. (2008). Storytelling and motivation in serious games. In *Final Consolidated Research Report of the Enhanced Learning Experience and Knowledge Transfer–Project*. ELEKTRA. http://www.elektra-project.org/

boyd, d., & Ellison N. (2007). Social network sites: Definition, history, and scholarship. *Journal of Computer-Mediated Communication, 13*(1), 210–30.

Carpenter, J., Morrison, S., Craft, M., & Lee, M. (2019, March). Exploring how and why educators use Instagram. In Society for information technology & teacher education international conference (pp. 2686-2691). Association for the Advancement of Computing in Education (AACE).

Cope, B., & Kalantzis, M. (Eds.). (2000). *Multiliteracies: Literacy learning and the design of social futures*. Psychology Press.

de Paula, B. H., Burn, A., Noss, R., & Valente, J. A. (2018). Playing Beowulf: Bridging computational thinking, arts and literature through game-making. *International Journal of Child-Computer Interaction, 16*, 39–46. doi:10.1016/j.ijcci.2017.11.003

Fessakis, G., Komis, V., Mavroudi, E., & Prantsoudi, S. (2018). Exploring the scope and the conceptualization of Computational Thinking at the K-12 classroom level curriculum, In M. S. Khine (Ed.), Computational Thinking in the STEM Disciplines: Foundations and Research Highlights. Springer.

Gallardo-Echenique, E. E., Marqués Molías, L., & Bullen, M. (2015). Students in higher education: Social and academic uses of digital technology. *Int. J. Educ. Technol. High. Educ., 12*(1), 25–37. doi:10.7238/rusc.v12i1.2078

Galvin, S., & Greenhow, C. (2020). Educational networking: A novel discipline for improved K-12 learning based on social networks. In *Educational networking* (pp. 3–41). Springer. doi:10.1007/978-3-030-29973-6_1

Gee, J. P. (2017). Affinity Spaces and 21st Century Learning. *Educational Technology, 57*(2), 27–31.

Giannikopoulou, A., & Fokiali, E. (2013). In the networks of literature. Teaching in the age of the internet. In Educational planning issues. Social networks and school unit: Bridges and meanings (pp. 66-90). Interaction.

Gonulal, T. (2019). The use of Instagram as a mobile-assisted language learning tool. *Contemporary Educational Technology, 10*(3), 309–323. doi:10.30935/cet.590108

Green, C. A., McMillan, E., Munn, L., Sole, C., & Eady, M. J. (2020). Entering Their World: Using Social Media to Support Students in Modern Times. In *Putting Social Media and Networking Data in Practice for Education, Planning, Prediction and Recommendation* (pp. 15–28). Springer. doi:10.1007/978-3-030-33698-1_2

Greenhow, C., & Chapman, A. (2020). *Social distancing meet social media: digital tools for connecting students, teachers, and citizens in an emergency*. Information and Learning Sciences.

Hsu, T. C., Chang, S. C., & Hung, Y. T. (2018). How to learn and how to teach computational thinking: Suggestions based on a review of the literature. *Computers & Education*, *126*, 296–310. doi:10.1016/j.compedu.2018.07.004

Ingarden, R. (1973). *The literary work of art*. Northwestern University Press.

Isbell, C., Stein, L., Cutler, R., Forbes, J., Fraser, L., Impagliazzo, J., Proulx, V., Russ, S., Thomas, R., & Xu, Y. (2009). (Re)Defining Computing Curricula by (Re)Defining Computing. *ACM SIGCSE Bulletin*, *41*(4), 195–207. doi:10.1145/1709424.1709462

Jacob, S. R., & Warschauer, M. (2018). Computational thinking and literacy. *Journal of Computer Science Integration*, *1*(1). Advance online publication. doi:10.26716/jcsi.2018.01.1.1

Jenkins, H. (2006). *Convergence Culture: Where Old and New Media Collide*. New York University Press.

Jenkins, H., Purushotma, R., Weigel, M., Clinton K., & Robison, A. J. (2009). Confronting the challenges of participatory culture: Media education for the 21st century. MIT Press.

Kalogirou, T. (2004). Lector Ludens: reading as a game / games of reading. In A. Katsiki-Givalou (Ed.), *Literature today: aspects, revisions, perspectives*. Greek Letters.

Katsarou, E., & Tsafos, B. (2004). *From Research to Teaching. Educational action research*. Savvalas Publishing House.

Lee, I., Martin, F., & Apone, K. (2014). Integrating computational thinking across the K—8 curriculum. *ACM Inroads*, *5*(4), 64–71. doi:10.1145/2684721.2684736

Levine, L. E., Waite, B. M., & Bowman, L. L. (2007). Electronic Media Use, Reading, and Academic Distractability in College Youth. *Cyberpsychology & Behavior*, *10*(4), 560–566. doi:10.1089/cpb.2007.9990 PMID:17711365

Liu, B., & He, J. (2014). Teaching Mode Reform and Exploration on the University Computer Basic based on Computational Thinking Training in Network Environment. *Proceedings of the 9th International Conference on Computer Science & Education*, 59-62.

Manca, S. (2020). Snapping, pinning, liking or texting: Investigating social media in higher education beyond Facebook. *The Internet and Higher Education*, *44*, 100707. doi:10.1016/j.iheduc.2019.100707

Mannila, L., Dagiene, V., Demo, B., Grgurina, N., Mirolo, C., Rolandsson, L., & Settle, A. (2014). Computational thinking in K-9 education. In *Proceedings of the Working Group Reports of the 2014 on Innovation & Technology in Computer Science Education Conference*. ACM. 10.1145/2713609.2713610

McNiff, J., Lomax, P., & Whitehead, J. (1996). *You and Your Action Research Project*. Routledge, Hyde Publications. doi:10.4324/9780203281291

Michailidis, N., Kapravelos, E., & Tsiatsos, T. (2019). Examining the effect of interaction analysis on supporting students' motivation and learning strategies in online blog-based secondary education programming courses. *Interactive Learning Environments*, 1–12. doi:10.1080/10494820.2019.1678487

Moula, E. (2010). Literature and theory of narrative or how developments require new approaches. *I-Teacher*, *1*, 23-34.

Moula, E. (2013). New technologies and literature: the embarrassment in the face of the "new" or the age-old conflict between tradition and modernity with a new face? *I-Teacher*, *6*, 38-57. http://i-teacher.gr/files/6o_teyxos_i_teacher_9_2013.pdf

Moula, E. (2019a). Alternate reality games as an educational strategy in the age of media convergence. *I-Teacher*, *18*, 15-35.

Moula, E. (2019b). Alternate reality games and reading for pleasure: Research findings from the implementation of the transformation of the Young Adult Novel Leros' Code into an ARG. *EducatioNext, 2*, 80-111. http://educationext.gr/files/ednext_2o_teyxos_09_2019.pdf

Moula, E. (2019c). The Thousand and One Aspects of Digital Fiction and the Future of Reading. *I-Teacher*, *19*, 9-29.

Moula, E., & Malafantis, K. (2019). From Literature to Alternate Reality Games: Prerequisites, Criteria, and Limitations of a Young Adult Novel's Transformational Design for Educational Purposes. *Advances in Literary Study*, *7*(4), 224. https://www.scirp.org/journal/paperinformation.aspx?paperid=95937

Poslaniec, C., & Houyel, C. (2001). *Activités de lecture à partir de la littérature policière*. Hachette.

Qiyang, Z., & Jung, H. (2019). *Learning and Sharing Creative Skills with Short Videos: A Case Study of User Behavior in TikTok and Bilibili. International Association of Societies of Design Research (IASDR)* Design Revolution.

Riley, D. D., & Hunt, K. A. (2014). *Computational thinking for the modern problem Solver*. CRC Press. doi:10.1201/b16688

Saari, E. M., & Hopkins, G. (2020). Computational thinking–Essential and pervasive toolset. *Asian Journal of Assessment in Teaching and Learning*, *10*(1), 23–31. doi:10.37134/ajatel.vol10.1.3.2020

Soviyah, S., & Etikaningsih, D. R. (2018). Instagram use to enhance ability in writing descriptive texts. *Indonesian EFL Journal*, *4*(2), 32–38. doi:10.25134/ieflj.v4i2.1373

Stojanović, D., Bogdanović, Z., Despotović-Zrakić, M., Naumović, T., & Radenković, M. (2019). An approach to using Instagram in secondary education. *The 14th International Conference on Virtual Learning ICVL*, 247–253.

Stojanović, D., Bogdanović, Z., Petrović, L., Mitrović, S., & Labus, A. (2020). Empowering learning process in secondary education using pervasive technologies. *Interactive Learning Environments*, 1–14. doi:10.1080/10494820.2020.1806886

Stylianidou, N., Sofianidis, A., Manoli, E., & Meletiou-Mavrotheris, M. (2020). "Helping Nemo!"—Using Augmented Reality and Alternate Reality Games in the Context of Universal Design for Learning. *Education Sciences*, *10*(4), 95. doi:10.3390/educsci10040095

Sysło, M. M., & Kwiatkowska, A. B. (2013). Informatics for All High School Students: A Computational Thinking Approach. In I. Diethelm & R. T. Mittermeir (Eds.), *ISSEP 2013. LNCS* (Vol. 7780, pp. 43–56). Springer.

Tess, P. A. (2013). The role of social media in higher education classes (real and virtual) – A literature review. *Computers in Human Behavior*, *29*(5), A60–A68. doi:10.1016/j.chb.2012.12.032

Thompson, R., & McIlnay, M. (2019). Nobody wants to read anymore! Using a multimodal approach to make literature engaging. *Journal of English Language and Literature*, *7*, 21–40.

Wing, J. (2006). Computational Thinking. *Communications of the ACM*, *49*(3), 33–35. doi:10.1145/1118178.1118215

Wing, J. (2008) Computational thinking and thinking about computing. *Phil. Trans. R. Soc. A.*, *366*(1881), 3717–3725. www.igda.org/arg/whitepaper.html

Zhou, Q. (2019). *Understanding User Behaviors of Creative Practice on Short Video Sharing Platforms–A Case Study of TikTok and Bilibili* (Doctoral dissertation). University of Cincinnati.

Zulli, D., & Zulli, D. J. (2020). Extending the Internet meme: Conceptualizing technological mimesis and imitation publics on the TikTok platform. *New Media & Society*. doi:10.1177/1461444820983603

ADDITIONAL READING

Ensslin, A. (2014). *Literary Gaming*. MIT Press. doi:10.7551/mitpress/9450.001.0001

Gibbons, A. (2015). Creativity and multimodal literature. In *Routledge Handbook of Language and Creativity* (pp. 293–306). Routledge.

Moula, E., & Malafantis, K. (2021). *From literature to Digital Fiction*. Mainandros.

Pellicone, A., Bonsignore, E., Kaczmarek, K., Kraus, K., Ahn, J., & Hansen, D. (2017). Alternate reality games for learning: A frame by frame analysis. In A. Garcia & G. Niemeyer (Eds.), *Alternate Reality Games and the Cusp of Digital Gameplay* (pp. 78–105). Bloomsbury Academic.

Strehovec, J. (2014). The E-literary Text as an Instrument and a Ride. Novel Forms of Digital Literatureand the Expanded Concept of Reading. In M. Cornis-Pope (Ed.), *New Literary Hybrids in the age of Multimedia Expression. Crossing borders, crossing genres* (pp. 340–356). John Benjamins Publishing Company.

Susan, S., Ray, S., & Unsworth, J. (Eds.). (2016). *A New Companion to Digital Humnaities* (pp. 127–136). Wiley Blackwell.

Thompson, R., & McIlnay, M. (2019). Nobody wants to read anymore! Using a multimodal approach to make literature engaging. *Journal of English Language and Literature*, *7*, 21–40.

KEY TERMS AND DEFINITIONS

Alternate Reality Games: A relatively new category of storytelling, pervasive, transmedial, and playful, developed in online interactive environments but also utilizing real-world communication methods.

As hybrids between story and game, they achieve immersion and encourage participatory storytelling, problem-solving, and action by the reader-player. The fact that they blur the boundaries between imagination and reality and are diffused in the real and virtual world, contributes to the enhancement of the learning experience.

Computational Thinking: A set of problem-solving methods and practices that involve confronting problems and finding solutions in ways that a computer would also execute. The characteristics that define computational thinking are decomposition (taking a complex problem and breaking it down into a series of small, more manageable problems), pattern recognition/ data representation (detecting arrangements of characteristics or data that yield information about a given system or data set), generalization/ abstraction, (formulating general concepts from specific instances by abstracting common properties), and algorithms (a process or set of rules to be followed in calculations or other problem-solving operations or for accomplishing a task).

Cultural Activator: Any cultural artifact, happening or activity that provokes the active engagement of the recipients. Jenkins uses the term to define the aesthetic goals of convergence culture projects that serve first and foremost as "cultural attractors" by bringing people together, and then, as "cultural activators" by providing opportunities for participation.

Transformational Design: The transformation of the available meaning resources, by designing something new and using the old materials in relation to each other to create patterns of meaning in various contexts. This procedure results in the Redesigned (According to the multiliteracies theory of the New London Group, 2000).

Transmedia Narrative: The narrative that takes place across multiple platforms and formats using current digital technologies. The concept was introduced by Henri Jenkins in his seminal work Convergence Culture. In transmedia narratives all media contribute to extend, expand, or enrich the initial narrative.

APPENDIX

Table 1. The protagonists' profiles in Instagram

ıntigone	Frantzeska	Reno	Grandpa Lefteris	Tzouanos	Jason

Figure 1. An embedded poll

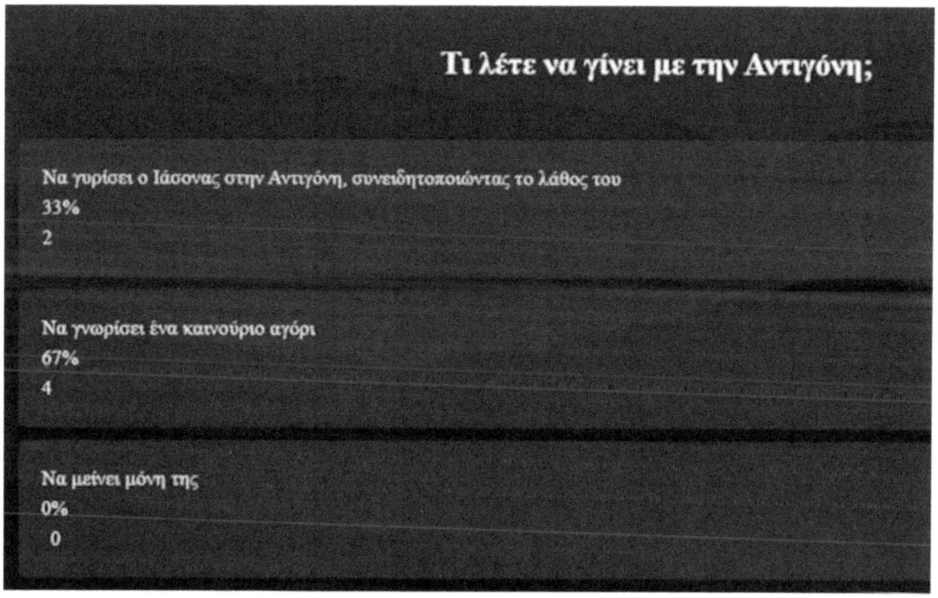

Table 2. Newspaper clips of the time

ΤΟ ΑΘΗΝΑΪΚΟΝ ΤΕΛΟΣ ΤΟΥ ΠΑΤΑΓΩΔΟΥΣ ΕΙΔΥΛΛΙΟΥ

Ο ΤΑΣΣΟΣ ΚΑΙ Η ΑΛΖΑ ΣΑΣ ΧΑΙΡΕΤΟΥΝ ΑΠΟ ΤΗΝ ΡΟΔΟ

Η ΑΝΑΧΩΡΗΣΙΣ ΤΩΝ ΑΠΟ ΤΟΝ ΑΕΡΟΛΙΜΕΝΑ ΤΟΥ ΜΕΓΑΛΟΥ ΠΕΥΚΟΥ

ΓΥΡΩ ΑΠΟ ΤΟ ΠΡΙΓΚΗΠΙΚΟΝ ΕΙΔΥΛΛΙΟΝ

ΤΑ ΑΥΣΤΗΡΑ ΕΘΙΜΑ ΤΟΥ ΒΑΣΙΛΕΙΟΥ ΤΟΥ ΙΡΑΚ

(Οἱ Ἰρακινοὶ θὰ ἐκδικηθοῦν τὴν ἐξωμότιδα πριγκήπισσαν;)

ΤΗΣ ΣΥΝΕΡΓΑΤΙΔΟΣ ΜΑΣ ΔΙΔΟΣ ΙΡΙΔ-Σ ΣΚΑΡΑΒΑΙΟΥ

Figure 2. A riddle based on computational thinking

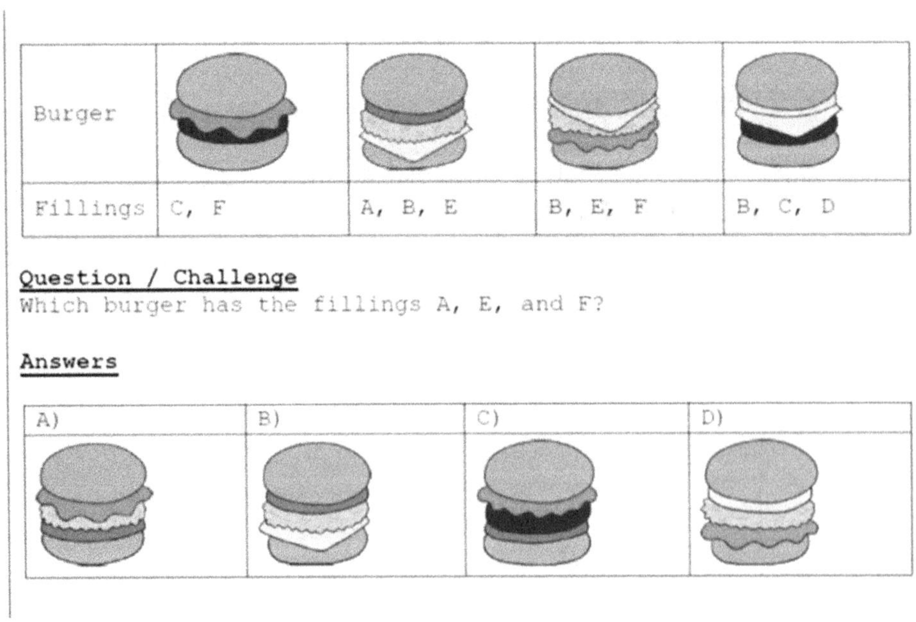

Chapter 10
Using Social Media as Learning Aids and Preservation:
Chinese Martial Arts in Hong Kong

Myra Yi Ching Mak
The University of Hong Kong, Hong Kong

Ada Yuen Mei Poon
https://orcid.org/0000-0002-4661-6439
The University of Hong Kong, Hong Kong

Dickson K. W. Chiu
https://orcid.org/0000-0002-7926-9568
The University of Hong Kong, Hong Kong

ABSTRACT

Chinese martial arts (Kungfu) is a popular cultural heritage, but its teaching and learning is very traditional. Social media have been increasingly used in education. The use of social media fosters a virtual learning environment for better interaction and helps effective and efficient learning. This research investigates how social media aids Kungfu learning and preservation and the factors affecting learners' behavioral intention. Semi-structured interviews with learners were conducted to obtain qualitative data. Many learners are currently using YouTube, Facebook, and WhatsApp to share videos, exchange learning materials, and communicate with teachers and classmates. Using social media helps preserve Kungfu in two ways—heritage protection and interest arousal—while face-to-face lessons are still highly valued. Recommendations are suggested to teachers, learners, martial arts associations, and the Hong Kong government accordingly.

DOI: 10.4018/978-1-6684-4461-0.ch010

INTRODUCTION

Driven by the rapid development of the Internet and mobile technologies, social media have been increasingly integrated into the toolboxes of most teachers and have also been broadly used in education (Ma, Chiu, & Tang, 2016; Zhang, Huang, Chiu, & Ho, 2015). The use of social media fosters a virtual learning environment for better interaction among teachers and learners and enables learners to learn more effectively and efficiently (Dong et al., 2021; Lei et al., 2021; Tse et al., 2022). Social media are now servings as aids and extensions to e-Learning, referring to learning with the support of electronic resources, which has become widespread as a social phenomenon (Zhang et al., 2015; Leung et al., in press). Thus, social media, which provides a collaborative virtual learning environment, have been increasingly adopted in education (Popescu, 2014; Lei et al., 2021). Social media-supported e-learning can improve collaboration by connecting people who share mutual desires and interests, encouraging active involvement, enhancing the variety and access to education, as well as unifying and sharing content (Lei et al., 2021; Leung et al., in press).

Chinese martial arts, also called Kungfu or Wushu, are popular Chinese cultural heritages. Teaching and learning Chinese martial arts have been very traditional. Transmission of the skills, techniques, and knowledge to the next generations is mainly based on personal contacts and oral communication between masters and learners (Lo et al., 2021). Consequently, establishing the "Master-disciple" bond is greatly significant in maintaining the continuity and stability of Chinese martial arts (Lo et al., 2019; 2021).

Although Chinese martial arts masters appear to be very traditional and conservative and may refuse to use advanced technology in assisting their teaching work, some Kungfu masters have recently applied social media and other technologies in their teaching (Lo et al., 2019; 2021). Chinese martial arts learning is about learning skills, techniques, and tacit knowledge, many of which cannot be effectively depicted with text or diagrams (International Guoshu Association, 2017). Thus, a collaborative learning environment and a community of practice supported by social media could facilitate effective Chinese martial arts learning (Lei et al., 2021). Besides, social media could also be an effective platform for preserving Chinese martial arts (International Guoshu Association, 2017; Lo et al., 2019). Therefore, this research aims to better understand the application of social media in Chinese martial arts learning and preserving Chinese martial arts.

LITERATURE REVIEW

Education and Training in Chinese Martial Arts

Chinese martial arts are sequences of fighting styles. Various styles of Chinese martial arts have been established over a long historical period in China and evolved into an extensive system covering various schools or sects. They can be classified by geographical locations, names of the creator and master, and training methods (Lo et al., 2021). Qigong, Wing Chun, Tai Chi, Wudang, and Shaolin are instances of the most outstanding and dominant styles of Chinese martial arts. The concept of "martial morality" is a crucial foundation that is an expression in social relation (external) and emotional mind (internal). Such concepts and often linked with Chinese history and myths, which arouse the younger generation's attention, especially through gaming and entertainment (He et al., 2022)

First, the core values of Chinese martial arts are virtue, trust, respect, morality, and humility. Second, Chinese Martial Arts' main concepts related to the emotional mind are courage, patience, endurance, perseverance, and will (Lo et al., 2021). Because of martial morality, martial arts are learned for self-defense and to help the general public. Martial artists are obliged to respect artists of other schools and should not be offensive in any situation. Martial morality is supported by martial artists and inherited from generation to generation (Lo et al., 2019; 2021). Basics, forms, applications, and weapons are the significant components of Chinese martial arts for preserving its original purpose of self-defense.

Traditionally, Chinese martial arts training is deep-rooted in the close affiliation between masters and learners in China (Lo et al., 2019; 2021). Besides, the masters published some special training manuals with text, images, and illustrations that allow readers to see how various martial arts may be practiced. In Hong Kong, martial arts schools and training clubs have been established to provide Chinese martial arts training with the increasing attractiveness of martial arts. The number of Chinese martial arts learners has been increasing. Besides, more students are encouraged by their parents to learn Chinese martial arts for better physical health and obtain a better portfolio for education (Zhou, 2019). Training classes have been organized to deliver Chinese martial arts learning experiences for students in schools as extracurricular activities. Discussion about integrating martial arts into the physical education curriculum took place a few years ago. Older literature on the cultural importance of martial arts and more traditional ways of passing them down is available in Mak (2019).

Social Media and Education

Social media are broadly defined as a diversity of web tools that serve as social communication channels dedicated to community-based input, interaction, content-sharing, and collaboration (Boyd & Ellison, 2007). As an outreach media for e-learning, social media can take along great opportunities for education and cultural sharing (Zhang et al., 2015). Social media can be successfully and effectively applied for technology-enhanced learning, and researchers indicated that there is increasing use of social media for teaching and learning (Lei et al., 2021; Leung et al., in press).

Yates (2007) examined and evaluated the RAT online project, which provides online learning resources for South African martial arts learners. Relating to martial arts learning, video sharing sites have made the exchange, distribution, and use of video quickly and broadly. As a result, social media stimulate a wider variety of capabilities and proficiency, enable collaborative learning methods, and empower the development of community and knowledge sharing for learners (Lei et al., 2021). Besides, social media enables learners to instantly and constantly connect with instructors and other learners (Dong et al., 2021). This feature promotes collaborative learning and allows authentic learning on the move anytime and anywhere (Yip et al., 2016; Leung et al., in press).

With the aid of social media, a collaborative learning environment can be established among peers and teachers to enhance learning performance (Lei et al., 2021) by providing immediate feedback and simultaneous conservation within and outside learning activities. Enhanced interaction is significant because it results in more effective learning and increases the possibility and opportunity of learning success (Dong et al., 2021). Besides interactivity, engagement is considered another crucial element contributing to collaborative learning, emphasizing the quantity of mental and physical effort a student puts into the learning experience (Ma et al., 2016). The application of social media in learning would increase students' motivation and participation in learning activities, and in turn, collaboration with peers and mutual influence, which raises students' overall satisfaction and learning performance (Lei et al., 2021).

Social media change the role of learners in the education process, and they are empowered as the primary stakeholders. They are offered different opportunities to accomplish and achieve their learning and create tailored resources and tools (Zhang et al., 2015; Lei et al., 2021). In a sense, learners can deliver information from various sources and select to filter, analyze, and cope with external information under the non-linear learning way (Ma et al., 2016). Moreover, informal learning tolerates learners to enlarge their ability and capacity for acquiring knowledge and understanding through associating with external resources. Hence individuals can sensibly improve and expand their capability and ability without constraint, and social media can ease learning to become more student-centered, encouraging students to interrelate, collaborate, and make individual choices (Lei et al., 2021; Zhang et al., 2015).

Referring to the above discussion, the application of social media in learning can enhance the advantages of e-learning, such as student-centered learning, self-paced learning, and unlimited access to knowledge. Moreover, social media reduces the disadvantage of asynchronous e-learning because it lacks immediate feedback. From e-learning to social learning, learning has become more synchronous with better interaction and connectivity, especially with the recent popularity and advancement in mobile technologies (Yip et al., 2020; Lei et al., 2021). Collaborative learning has been most frequently discussed in the issue of social media learning. The application of social media in learning realizes effective collaborative learning, which, in turn, promotes student satisfaction and learning performance (Dong et al., 2021; Leung et al., in press). In summary, student-centered learning, self-paced learning, social presence, and media richness also contribute to the positive outcomes of social media learning (Yip et al., 2020; Lei et al., 2021; Leung et al., in press).

Although social media application in learning has numerous advantages for learners, some teachers and learners may not be willing to adopt social media. Leung et al. (in press) pointed out that although the technology frequently changes, some learners still require structured support and content as well as recognized accreditation from traditional education institutions. Thus, these learners tend to follow the linear learning model to study as long as they are not confident enough to learn independently. Therefore, there is a need to research the factors influencing learners' intention to adopt social media in their learning, which may differ according to different disciplines and knowledge.

Preservation of Intangible Heritage and Social Media

Chinese martial arts (or Kungfu) have become a significant cultural heritage because of their emotional and sensitive value. They can bring a sense of identity and belonging to Chinese people and should be preserved for their offspring in the future (Lo et al., 2017). Documentation is one of the effective preservation measures for transmitting Chinese martial arts from generation to generation (Poorna, Mymoon, & Hariharan, 2014; Lo et al., 2021). Some martial arts associations show great concern for documenting Chinese martial arts before their disappearance and pursue the authorization of the United Nations Educational, Scientific and Cultural Organization's (UNESCO) intangible cultural heritage list due to the death of aging Kungfu masters (Lo et al., 2017; 2021).

Notably, it is not only to preserve the martial arts theoretically but is also essential to preserve authentic practice and techniques. The originality and talent of Kungfu masters should be captured precisely and preserved to minimize interpretation loss (Mak, 2019). It is indispensable to help the next generation understand Chinese martial arts and correctly gain skills and techniques. Focusing on the education and training of martial arts, the traditional transmission of techniques and knowledge to the next generations is mainly based on oral transmission and personal contact between masters and learners (Lo et al., 2021). Digital media can serve as an effective tool for achieving the above preservation objectives (Lo et al., 2017). The Hong Kong Martial Arts Living Archive is the effort of the International Guoshu Association (2017) to preserve Chinese martial arts by utilizing digital media, providing valuable 3D-recording documentation of masters' martial arts performances. Chinese martial arts learners can share the archive with social media, which creates a web-learning environment for martial arts learning and provides content for museum exhibitions (Lo et al., 2017).

The benefits of applying social media in Chinese martial arts learning do not only take account of the improved effectiveness of learning and teaching, but also consist of preserving valuable cultural heritage. Kungfu is recognized as one form of Chinese intangible cultural heritage (ICH). Cultural heritages are classified into three main categories: tangible, intangible, and natural heritage. Intangible heritages are those intangible attributes, for example, language and tradition, of a group or society inherited from past generations (Sullivan, 2015). Kungfu has distinctive heritage values and is worth preservation (Lo et al., 2017; 2021).

In 2003, UNESCO put forward the Convention for safeguarding the intangible cultural heritage (ICH) because social transformation and globalization began to pose hazardous threats to the preservation of the ICH based on oral transmission and traditional culture. Khalid and Chowdhury (2016) claimed that social media plays a vital role in preserving ICH. Social media provide the space for awareness-building, knowledge creation, and diffusion of innovations due to the increased affordability of mobile devices, literacy rate, education level, and adoption of Internet services (Yip et al., 2020; Dong et al., 2021; Lei et al., 2021). Severo and Venturini (2016) explored how digital methods, such as online data extraction, analysis, and visual presentation, outline the geographical distribution of ICH. "Web mapping" helps develop a better national preservation system. Besides, Pietrobruno (2013) suggested that YouTube can serve as an archive and safeguard multiple versions of heritage for documentation and records in video format. Individuals can produce and upload videos to YouTube. As a result, informal archives of cultural heritage in digital formats are created informally by individuals. For example, Pietrobruno (2013) explored whether social archiving can counter official heritage narratives and meet sustainability and development challenges and concluded that YouTube could accomplish the goal of safeguarding intangible cultural heritage as a final point.

Research Gap and Research Questions

Although social media have been increasingly utilized in various art disciplines, scant focus studies on the application of social media in the learning of Chinese martial arts. Therefore, it is necessary to understand how social media are currently used in Chinese martial arts learning to promote social media. Hence, we have the following research question:

RQ1: *How are social media used in Chinese martial arts learning?*

To encourage learners to use social media in their learning, it is necessary to explore motivating and engaging factors. With the knowledge of motivational factors increasing behavioral intention to use social media in Chinese martial arts learning, promotion campaigns could be designed to encourage the use of social media. Hence, we have the following research question:

RQ2*: What factors affect learners' behavioral intention to use social media in Chinese martial arts learning?*

Further, with the collaborative learning environment on social media for knowledge sharing, abundant visual and audio learning materials can be shared and promoted. Thus, the use of social media may help preserve Chinese martial arts. Hence, we have the following research question:

RQ3: *How can Social media help the preservation of Chinese martial arts?*

Research Methodology

The choice of research methods is strongly correlated with the research paradigm, which is a set of beliefs about the real world and knowledge sources. Hence, a research paradigm makes available a framework to understand the research problem, as well as the most appropriate ways of collecting and analyzing data (Saunders, Lewis, & Thornhill, 2012).

Interpretivism believes that people's subjective interpretations construct multiple realities. Valid knowledge is value-biased and is obtained by inductively interpreting multiple sources of qualitative information. The qualitative research approach is frequently adopted by interpretivism (Saunders et al., 2012). Qualitative studies aim to provide rich data about real-life people and situations and understand behavior in a broader context by collecting information from various sources.

Semi-structured interviews were arranged to collect qualitative data for gaining participants' insights (Mak, 2019) about using social media in Chinese martial arts learning and preservation. The interviews comprised three parts. Part A comprised five questions asking interviewees' background information about their Chinese martial arts learning. Part B comprised seven questions asking their opinions about the use of social media in Chinese martial arts learning. Part C comprised three questions, asking their opinions about the use of social media in preserving Chinese martial arts as a cultural heritage. The interview sessions were conducted about 30 to 45 minutes face-to-face. Every participant was asked the same set of open-end questions, but they were free to reflect on their insights and opinions.

Chinese Martial Arts learners in Hong Kong were recruited from local Chinese martial arts training clubs such as the Hong Kong Wushu Union and social networks like Facebook. Purposeful sampling was selected for choosing five learners with different backgrounds. All interviews were carried out independently in the chosen settings for participants to avoid the pressure on the interviewees.

Recordings were examined for their meaningful content through interpretation for qualitative data analysis of interviews. Transcription was the first step for analyzing the discourse before identifying the themes. After examining the data, common issues and concerns were identified, and then the respondents' views were summarized into diverse themes and categories, as stated by the research questions. The coding scheme, which aimed to indicate the idea or concept underpinning the theme, was established for applying to the collected data.

ANALYSIS AND FINDINGS

Background Information

Table 1 summarizes the first part of the interview about the interviewees' background. Interviewees have 1 to 10 years of learning experience, except interviewee 2, with 29 years of experience as a martial arts teacher. Two interviewees are learning Tai Chi and two learning Wing Chun, both being the most popular martial arts styles (Lo et al., 2021). Concerning the familiarity with social media, all of them are

Table 1. Background information of five interviewees

Interviewee	Style	Experience	Social media	Use in learning
1	Tai Chi	3 years	WhatsApp, YouTube	YouTube for watching videos
2	Bak Mei	29 years	WhatsApp, LINE, Facebook, YouTube	YouTube for uploading and sharing videos, Facebook & Forum for promotion and sharing materials
3	Wing Chun	3 years	WhatsApp, Facebook, Instagram	Instagram for sharing videos
4	Wing Chun	1 year	WhatsApp, Facebook, YouTube, LINE, Forum	YouTube for watching videos, Forum for sharing information and meeting more friends
5	Tai Chi	10 years	WhatsApp, Facebook	None

familiar with at least two kinds of social media. Particularly, Interviewee 4 claimed that he is familiar with five social media. WhatsApp, YouTube, and Facebook are the most popular social media. Almost all of them are at ease with at least two of these social media in their daily life.

Almost all interviewees have used social media to learn Chinese martial arts. Only Interviewee 5 said that she did not use social media in learning. Although WhatsApp is one of the most frequently used social media in their daily lives, interviewees did not use it for Chinese martial arts learning but just for communication with their teachers and classmates. They frequently use YouTube to share and watch martial arts videos, and Interviewee 3 uses Instagram to share videos. On the other hand, Interviewee 4 has been using forums for sharing information and meeting more friends. Besides, all interviewees use Facebook for promotion and sharing information and learning materials.

Table 2. Purposes, benefits, and barriers of using social media in Chinese martial arts learning

Interviewee	Teacher	Learner	Benefit	Barrier
1	Upload videos	Share videos	Convenience, memory recall, more effective	Busy, health problem
2	Promotion, organize activities	Share videos and information	Easy to access information, effective promotion	Busy
3	Upload videos	Communication with WhatsApp, share videos	Easier to learn, convenient, gain assistance	None
4	Upload videos, make announcements	Share videos	Have a chance to learn even busy, convenient, effective, memory recall	Wi-Fi access
5	Share videos	Share videos, communicate with WhatsApp	Memory recall, convenience, better communication, remote instruction	Health problem

Table 3. Cultural preservation of Chinese martial arts by using social media

Interviewee	Useful?	Cultural Preservation	Role of government
1	Yes	Make records	Financial funding, promotion, school curriculum
2	Not helpful in spirit and virtue transmission	Make records, Historical archives	Provide more venues, produce living archives
3	Not much	Arouse interest	Promotion, provide more activities
4	Yes	Protech heritage	Funding, provide more venues, arouse engagement
5	Yes	Make records	No idea

Using Social Media in Chinese Martial Arts Learning

Table 2 summarizes how social media has been used for teaching and learning and the benefits and barriers of using social media. Firstly, all interviewees said they were actively using social media and would continually use it. Hence, they intended to use social media in Chinese martial arts learning. Martial arts teachers usually use social media to release videos to learners for their reference. As a result, learners can view their demonstration videos via YouTube at home. Besides, teachers use social media to make announcements (e.g., class schedules), organize activities (e.g., learning classes and competitions), and promote their classes. Learners also recorded their individual videos during practice and shared them with classmates for comments. Besides, social media were also used for exchanging learning materials and activity information.

Interviewees perceived convenience and effectiveness as the main benefits of using social media in learning. Learners opined that they could watch demonstration videos repeatedly anywhere and anytime. They could learn and practice without attending any class when they were full of activity and busy. Learners could even record videos of their practicing martial arts to their teacher and classmates, so that teachers could instruct revisions remotely. Therefore, social media served them as tools for making learning more convenient. Besides, social media helped them recall memory by watching videos. Learners could access many learning materials for practicing and improving. Hence, learning has become more effective than before by using social media. On the other hand, insufficient time and health problems were the major barriers to inhibiting learners from learning martial arts. Interviewee 4 also claimed that no Wi-Fi-access was one of his hesitations to view the online video via Youtube outside due to concern of mobile Internet tariffs.

Using Social Media to Preserve Chinese Martial Arts

Table 3 summarizes the interviewees' opinions on whether using social media is useful for preserving Chinese martial arts, how the heritage can be preserved, and what the government can do.

Most of the interviewees reported that they thought social media were instrumental in making records and living archives of Chinese martial arts, such as great masters' demonstrations. Heritage can be better protected and preserved by making more records and living archives. However, not all interviewees thought using social media instrumental is a complete solution to preserving Chinese martial arts. For example, Interviewee 2 opined that the traditional spirit and virtue, the essential elements, could not be transmitted from generation to generation without "master-disciple" bone. Interviewee 3 claimed that social media are unhelpful in cultural preservation as numerous intangible heritage components cannot be preserved without human interaction and exchange. Therefore, he supposed social media are only beneficial in arousing interest from the general public so that they may subsequently engage in heritage preservation in their desired ways.

To preserve Chinese martial arts heritage, the interviewees suggested that the Hong Kong Government could provide financial funding and aid to support the preservation and more venues for people to engage in martial arts activities and training classes. Besides, the government could help promote the heritage and arouse the public's interest and engagement. In short, interviewees focused more on heritage protection by making video records and living archives.

DISCUSSION

Use of Social Media for Chinese Martial Arts Learning (RQ1)

Our results showed that martial arts learners were currently using YouTube, Facebook, and WhatsApp in their learning. YouTube was the most frequently used social media for sharing and watching martial arts videos. Facebook was usually used for sharing information such as class schedules and activity information. WhatsApp was used to communicate with teachers and learners. In this case, referring to the previous discussion, social media gained credibility, which is a trusted source of information and a platform for frequent interaction between instructors and students (Lei et al., 2021). Our findings are in line with the general usage of social media in education, providing students with the capability to acquire more valuable information and connect with online learning groups, providing a virtual learning environment and a community of practice (Alsuraihi, Almaqati, Abughanim & Jastaniah, 2016; Lei et al., 2021; Dong et al., 2021; Leung et al., 2022; Tse et al., 2022).

Factors Affecting Behavioral Intention to USE SOCIAL MEDIA (RQ2)

Our participants opined that YouTube, Facebook, and WhatsApp were easy to use, with more support in Hong Kong to facilitate using these social media (Cheung & Leung, 2016; Ma et al., 2016; Let et al., 2021; Leung et al., in press). Hence, learners have frequently used YouTube, Facebook, and WhatsApp in their learning. Besides, participants reflected that they would like to use social media in their learning because social media were convenient tools for sharing videos, other learning materials, and activity information (Zhang et al., 2015). Participants also opined that using social media made learning Chinese martial arts more effective, productive, and easier. As a result, performance expectancy is one of the significant factors affecting the intention to use social media in Chinese martial arts learning, which is similar to the opinions of music learners (Lei et al., 2021).

According to our findings, experiences for applying social media in dance and music education are decidedly appreciated and can also be used in Chinese martial arts learning due to their similarity. Martial arts and dancing strongly emphasize the holistic nature of actions and movements. Kavakli et al. (2004) indicated that the impressive outcomes for applying social media in dance education include growing the functionality and interactivity of the web learning environment, widening the scope of the learning resources offered, and the type of potential learners for setting up online dance learning community.

Preservation of Chinese Martial Arts (RQ3)

Social media can benefit from preserving Chinese martial arts in two directions. First, arousing interest and engagement in Chinese martial arts from the public, the younger generation, and foreigners overseas is similar to the contributions of museums (Lo et al., 2017). Second, social media can also help protect heritage assets by making video records and conducting research accordingly (Lazzeretti, Sartori, & Innocenti, 2015; Lo et al., 2021). Our findings identify video recording and living archives are useful for preserving Chinese martial arts. By doing so, martial arts heritage can be better protected and transmitted to the next generation. Interest arousal can also be achieved by using social media. In this connection, arousing public interest in Chinese martial arts is also a productive approach to preserve the heritage and maintain sustainability.

In line with this approach, a local example is the Hong Kong Martial Arts Living Archive (International Guoshu Association, 2017), which can be considered a great effort to preserve Chinese martial arts while also providing online resources for teaching and learning. Similar to viewing recorded dancing performances, learners can learn and preserve styles efficiently and effectively to accomplish the sustainability of dance styles (Khan, 2015). In this connection, social media is an effective measure to be used in cultural preservation widely.

RECOMMENDATIONS

Based on the research findings, recommendations are made to individual teachers and learners, martial arts clubs and associations, and the Hong Kong government, respectively.

Individual Teachers and Learners

Notably, social media are convenient tools to improve learning effectiveness and motivation (Ma et al., 2016). Chinese martial arts teachers are suggested to integrate social media in their curriculum and lessons to deliver further assistance to their learners. Thus, they can produce more videos systematically for teaching. They are correspondingly recommended to plan social media such as Facebook and WhatsApp to communicate teaching schedules, distribute learning materials, and give remote instruction and guidance to build up an effective learning community (Zhang et al., 2015; Ma et al., 2016; Lei et al., 2021).

On the other hand, learners can participate directly in their learning rather than inactively absorbing information to form a community of practice (Lei et al., 2021), watching videos online, commenting on social media, and interconnecting with their teachers and classmates more closely. They can also use social media to exchange and inspirit ideas and insights with classmates (Dong et al., 2021). Social media are technologies for creating a convenient online learning environment to facilitate effective learning for various art forms (Kavakli et al., 2004; Lo et al., 2017; Lei et al., 2021). Teachers and learners should devote more effort to using social media in teaching and learning. In this sense, deeper engagement and interaction are necessary to highlight better performance from all teachers and learners (Ma et al., 2016).

Martial Arts Clubs and Associations

Social media have increasingly been applied in Chinese martial arts teaching and learning. Many teachers have produced many videos to aid their teaching of students. However, individual teachers do not have sufficient resources to improve their teaching with social media aids (Zhang et al., 2015). Martial arts clubs and associations are recommended to take the lead and organize using social media to help Chinese martial arts learning, particularly those motions hard to be explained with text or diagrams alone. For example, they can develop martial arts learning system and provide technical support for using social media to the learner. They can also collect teaching videos from various masters to form a teaching library and archive. In parallel, it is essential to maintain the quality of teaching videos by setting up a quality control panel to minimize loss and misinterpretation. Further, with the decreasing costs, technological advancement, and success reported in dance preservation (Khan, 2015), grandmasters' three-dimensional scanning and motion capture would be the next step in archiving and cultural preservation (Lo et al., 2019).

Hong Kong Government

Chinese martial arts are valuable cultural heritage (Daly & Winter, 2012). The Hong Kong Government should take strong initiatives to promote martial arts and be responsible for preserving heritage. The government is recommended to provide adequate financial support to promote the campaign and arouse interest and engagement from the public. In the long run, the government is also urged to provide sustainable funds to support the production of martial arts archives and development for Chinese martial art. Besides, there is insufficient venues and training center for learners to practice martial arts in Hong Kong. Providing more suitable venues and simplifying the application procedure is also absolutely helpful.

Adding "Chinese Martial Arts" into the Curriculum of Physical Education of the primary and secondary schools can also contribute to preserving and bringing up Chinese martial arts. To engage the public in cultural heritage preservation, the government is advised to establish an Advisory Board to encourage public members to discuss and express their views on preservation issues. In parallel, public libraries and museums should pay efforts to carry out public education and publicity to arouse public interest by various means, such as organizing thematic talks and roving exhibitions (Theeboom, Zhu & Vertonghen, 2017; Lo et al., 2017; Deng et al., 2022). In this connection, the Home Affairs Bureau, Education Bureau, and the Leisure and Cultural Services Department in Hong Kong should cooperate and work out detailed policies for promotion and development in the future.

FUTURE RESEARCH DIRECTIONS

There may be some possible limitations in this study. Although limited generalizations can be made due to the relatively small sample size and sample bias, this serves as a pilot study for exploring this topic to address the lack of preceding research. This is still a significant opportunity to develop a new research typology, identify new gaps in the prior literature, and present the essential for further development in this topic. We plan more detailed studies on pedagogy and quantitative surveys of martial art learners and teachers, as well as other art forms. Besides, promotion aspects of social media not covered in this study are also on our research agenda (Cheng et al., 2020).

Besides, we are interested in an in-depth study focusing on the issue of martial arts becoming part of the secondary school physical education curriculum. Regarding the cultural preservation of Chinese martial arts, re-using social media data for research or heritage collections is another related topic to be explored. Technical issues related to digital preservation and record management, such as by what method to record, manage, and store the information and the potential risks and challenges in the archive, are also worth investigating in the future.

Due to the lockdown and gathering restrictions during the COVID-19 pandemic (Yu et al., 2022; Huang et al., 2021; 2022), venues for learning and practicing martial arts cannot be accessible. Thus, using social media to teach martial arts becomes the main choice, and students have to rely more on social media for informal or even formal learning. On the other hand, students have now been generally accustomed to social media for learning purposes. Besides, we are researching the use of social media in the teaching and learning on social media for other arts and formal academic subjects, especially under the impact of COVID-19.

CONCLUSION

The qualitative results in this study reveal that learners have emphasized the effectiveness and convenience of using social media. Performance expectancy refers to the extent to which social media can increase a learner's productivity and performance. Therefore, the interviewees of the qualitative study focused more on the influence of performance expectancy. The qualitative study has revealed that Chinese martial arts learners thought social media are useful in making valuable records and living archives and hence can protect the heritage. The interviewees also opined that social media could help arouse public interest and engagement and, hence, preserve the heritage. However, it seems the interviewees focused more on heritage protection than interest arousal.

Even though there are more or fewer limitations and obstacles expressed by martial arts learners, it is no doubt that the use of social media can help martial arts teaching and learning correspondingly. Sufficient resources on Youtube, Facebook, and Instagram create a new learning environment and content to increase the feasibility and accessibility of learning from home instead of face to face. Nevertheless, some teachers and students still choose the traditional ways to teach and learn martial arts as the irreplaceable foundation approach to preserve valuable Chinese culture and morality. All in all, social media has provided positive impacts and aids in martial arts learning and preservation.

ACKNOWLEDGMENT

This research is partially supported by the HKU Knowledge Exchange Fund KE-IP-2018/19-36 granted by the University Grants Committee.

REFERENCES

Alsuraihi, A., Almaqati, A., Abughanim, S., & Jastaniah, N. (2016). Use of social media in education among medical students in Saudi Arabia. *Korean Journal of Medical Education*, *28*(4), 343–354. doi:10.3946/kjme.2016.40 PMID:27907981

Boyd, D. M., & Ellison, N. B. (2007). Social network sites: Definition, history, and scholarship. *Journal of Computer-Mediated Communication*, *13*(1), 210–230. doi:10.1111/j.1083-6101.2007.00393.x

Cheng, W. W. H., Lam, E. T. H., & Chiu, D. K. W. (2020). Social media as a platform in academic library marketing: A comparative study. *Journal of Academic Librarianship*, *46*(5), 102188. doi:10.1016/j.acalib.2020.102188

Cheung, F., & Leung, W. (2016). Facebook users' habits in getting commercial information: A study on Hong Kong students. *Economics, Management, and Financial Markets*, *11*(3), 56–71.

Daly, P., & Winter, T. (2012). *Routledge handbook of heritage in Asia*. Routledge. doi:10.4324/9780203156001

Deng, W., Chin, G. Y.-l., Chiu, D. K. W., & Ho, K. K. W. (2022). (in press). Contribution of Literature Thematic Exhibition to Cultural Education: A Case Study of Jin Yong's Gallery. *Micronesian Educators*, *32*.

Dong, G., Chiu, D. K. W., Huang, P.-S., Lung, M. M., Ho, K. K. W., & Geng, Y. (2021). Relationships between Research Supervisors and Students from Coursework-based Master's Degrees: Information Usage under Social Media. *Information Discovery and Delivery*, *49*(4), 319–327. doi:10.1108/IDD-08-2020-0100

He, Z., Chiu, D. K. W., & Ho, K. K. W. (2022). Weibo Analysis on Chinese Cultural Knowledge for Gaming. In Z. Sun (Ed.), *Handbook of Research on Foundations and Applications of Intelligent Business Analytics* (pp. 320–349). IGI Global. doi:10.4018/978-1-7998-9016-4.ch015

Huang, P. S., Paulino, Y., So, S., Chiu, D. K. W., & Ho, K. K. W. (2021). Special issue editorial - COVID-19 pandemic and health informatics (part 1). *Library Hi Tech*, *39*(3), 693–695. doi:10.1108/LHT-09-2021-324

Huang, P.-S., Paulino, Y. C., So, S., Chiu, D. K. W., & Ho, K. K. W. (2022). Guest editorial: COVID-19 Pandemic and Health Informatics (Part 2). *Library Hi Tech*, *40*(2), 281–285. doi:10.1108/LHT-04-2022-447

International Guoshu Association. (2017). *Hong Kong Martial Arts Living Archive*. Retrieved from: https://www.fringebacker.com/en/projects/HK_Martial_Arts_Living/

Kavakli, E., Bakogianni, S., Damianakis, A., Loumou, M., & Tsatsos, D. (2004). *Traditional dance and e-learning: The WEBDANCE learning environment.* Paper presented at the International Conference on Theory and Applications of Mathematics and Informatics, Greece.

Khalid, S., & Chowdhury, S. A. (2016). Representation and Dissemination of Intangible Cultural Heritage of Bangladesh through Social Media. *Anatolia*, *29*(2), 194–203. doi:10.1080/13032917.2017.1414438

Khan, M. (2015). Archive to repertoire: Motion capture & motion sensing data for digital intangible heritage (DIH). *Digital Heritage*, *2*, 197–198. doi:10.1109/DigitalHeritage.2015.7419490

Lazzeretti, L., Sartori, A., & Innocenti, N. (2015). Museums and social media: The case of the Museum of Natural History of Florence. *International Review on Public and Nonprofit Marketing*, *12*(3), 267–283. doi:10.100712208-015-0136-5

Lei, S. Y., Chiu, D. K. W., Lung, M. M., & Chan, C. T. (2021). Exploring the Aids of Social Media for Musical Instrument Education. *International Journal of Music Education*, *39*(2), 187–201. doi:10.1177/0255761420986217

Leung, T. N., Hui, Y. M., Luk, C. K. L., Chiu, D. K. W., & Kevin, K. K. W. (in press). An Empirical Study on the Aid of Facebook for Japanese Learning. *Library Hi Tech*.

Lo, P., Chan, H. H. Y., Tang, A. W. M., Chiu, D. K. W., Cho, A., Ho, K. K. W., See-To, E., He, J., Kenderdine, S., & Shaw, J. (2019). Visualising and Revitalising Traditional Chinese Martial Arts – Visitors' Engagement and Learning Experience at the 300 Years of Hakka KungFu. *Library Hi Tech*, *37*(2), 273–292. doi:10.1108/LHT-05-2018-0071

Lo, P., Cheuk, M. K., Ng, C. H., Lam, S. K., & Chiu, D. K. W. (2021). 文武之道【下冊】:以拳入哲 [The Tao of Arts and Warriorship: The Philosophy of Fists]. Hong Kong: Systech Publications.

Ma, J., Chiu, D. K., & Tang, J. K. (2016). Exploring the Use of Social Media to Advance K12 Science Education. *International Journal of Systems and Service-Oriented Engineering*, *6*(4), 47–59. doi:10.4018/IJSSOE.2016100104

Mak, Y. C. M. (2019). *Application of social media in Chinese martial arts learning and preservation of Chinese martial arts in Hong Kong. HKU Theses Online.*

Miller, M. (2011). *YouTube for business: Online video marketing for any business*. Pearson Education.

Pietrobruno, S. (2013). YouTube and the social archiving of intangible heritage. *New Media & Society*, *15*(8), 1259–1276. doi:10.1177/1461444812469598

Poorna, R. L., Mymoon, M., & Hariharan, A. (2014). Preservation and protection of traditional knowledge–diverse documentation initiatives across the globe. *Current Science*, *107*(8), 1240–1246.

Popescu, E. (2014). Providing collaborative learning support with social media in an integrated environment. *World Wide Web (Bussum)*, *17*(2), 199–212. doi:10.100711280-012-0172-6

Saunders, M., Lewis, P., & Thornhill, A. (2012). *Research Methods for Business Students*. Pearson Education.

Severo, M., & Venturini, T. (2016). Intangible cultural heritage webs: Comparing national networks with digital methods. *New Media & Society*, *18*(8), 1616–1635. doi:10.1177/1461444814567981

Sullivan, A. M. (2015). Cultural Heritage & New Media: A Future for the Past. *J. Marshall Rev. Intell. Prop. L.*, *15*, 604.

Theeboom, M., Zhu, D., & Vertonghen, J. (2017). 'Wushu belongs to the world'. But the gold goes to China: The international development of the Chinese martial arts. *International Review for the Sociology of Sport*, *52*(1), 3–23. doi:10.1177/1012690215581605

Tse, H. L., Chiu, D. K., & Lam, A. H. (2022). From Reading Promotion to Digital Literacy: An Analysis of Digitalizing Mobile Library Services With the 5E Instructional Model. In A. Almeida & S. Esteves (Eds.), *Modern Reading Practices and Collaboration Between Schools, Family, and Community* (pp. 239–256). IGI Global. doi:10.4018/978-1-7998-9750-7.ch011

Yates, S. (2007). RAT online: Martial arts learning resources. *The Electronic Library*, *25*(5), 495–516. doi:10.1108/02640470710829505

Yip, K. H. T., Chiu, D. K. W., Ho, K. K. W., & Lo, P. (2020). Adoption of Mobile Library Apps as Learning Tools in Higher Education: A Tale between Hong Kong and Japan. *Online Information Review*, *45*(2), 389–405. doi:10.1108/OIR-07-2020-0287

Yu, P. Y., Lam, E. T. H., & Chiu, D. K. W. (2022, February 16). (in press). Operation management of academic libraries in Hong Kong under COVID-19. *Library Hi Tech*. Advance online publication. doi:10.1108/LHT-10-2021-0342

Zhang, Q., Huang, B., Chiu, D. K. W., & Ho, K. K. W. (2015). Learning Japanese through social network sites: A case study of Chinese learners' perceptions. *Micronesian Educators*, *21*, 55–71.

Zhang, X., Gao, Y., Yan, X., de Pablos, P. O., Sun, Y., & Cao, X. (2015). From e-learning to social-learning: Mapping development of studies on social media-supported knowledge management. *Computers in Human Behavior*, *51*, 803–811. doi:10.1016/j.chb.2014.11.084

Zhou, J. (2019, October). A Survey of the Value of Chinese Kung-fu on the Physical and Mental Health of College Students from the Perspective of Healthy China. In *2nd International Conference on Contemporary Education, Social Sciences and Ecological Studies (CESSES 2019)*. Atlantis Press. 10.2991/cesses-19.2019.92

KEY TERMS AND DEFINITIONS

Community of Practice: A group of people sharing a common concern of what they do and learn how to do it better with regular interactions.

Guoshu/Kungfu: A synomym for Chinese martial arts.

Martial Arts: Codified systems and combat traditions practiced for purposes such as self-defense, military, law enforcement competition, physical, mental, and spiritual development, entertainment, and intangible cultural heritage preservation.

Semi-Structured Interview: A qualitative research method commonly used in the social sciences: which is open (as opposed to a structured interview that is strict and does not allow diversion), allowing new ideas to be brought up according to the interviewee's responses, thus resulting in rich data.

Social Media: Interactive network technologies and digital channels that facilitate the creating and sharing of information, ideas, interests, images, videos, links, and other information.

Virtual Learning Environment (VLE): A commonly used web-based platform for learning that allows teachers to digitalize learning, for instance, offering assessments with feedback, learning resources in multiple formats, and the course structure and organizing activities for social interaction and communication in discussion forums, to students.

Chapter 11

Teaching Ancient Greek Theatre Through In-Game Exploration:
The Case of ThimelEdu

Anastasios Kristofer Barianos
https://orcid.org/0000-0001-6709-9250
Hellenic Mediterranean University, Greece

Ilias Logothetis
Hellenic Mediterranean University, Greece

Michail Kalogiannakis
https://orcid.org/0000-0002-9124-2245
University of Crete, Greece

Nikolas Vidakis
https://orcid.org/0000-0003-0726-8627
Hellenic Mediterranean University, Greece

ABSTRACT

Serious games are increasingly integrated into official learning settings due to their effectiveness as teaching tools, especially in cultural heritance. Despite extensive research on the field and a consensus on their value, there are few meticulous studies that evaluate serious games and their effect on knowledge in the long term. Literature describes a lot of games and their innovations, but few go on to perform a retrospective analysis to locate areas that should be solved in future games. In this chapter, a retrospective analysis of a serious game teaching about Ancient Greek Theater is performed, utilizing study results from experiments conducted with the game. The authors describe the experiments and the results procedures and present them along with their conclusions on how game design and development decisions affected those results. With the work presented in this chapter, the authors expect valuable insight to be unlocked for the improvement of future game designs for education.

DOI: 10.4018/978-1-6684-4461-0.ch011

INTRODUCTION

Culture is a major cornerstone of all societies, however small or large in scale. No society can include individuals that do not share common beliefs and practices. In essence, culture is the connective tissue of society, keeping historical connections to the past as a bonding element and a steppingstone for a common shaping of future developments and improvement of quality of life (Margetis et al., 2020). Culture, affected by economic and technological evolutions, changes shapes. In general terms, we can identify three distinct ages for culture, pre-industrial evolution, named Culture 1.0, postindustrial evolution, called Culture 2.0, and we are currently moving towards a new age, called Culture 3.0 (Papadakis, 2021; Sacco, 2011), in which users and producers of culture become one interchanging role, assumed by all individuals. This evolution results from the influence of information technologies, such as the web and video games. The scale of online platforms and their high connectivity have created new online communities. Cultural market dominance is increasingly challenged by the proliferation and expansion of a community of practice in which members interact on a non-market exchange paradigm (Sacco, 2011). This rapid segue to a new age for culture is influenced by the growth of information and communication technologies (ICTs) and their effect on many other aspects of life. This effect has spread widely to all aspects of life, including science, business, and lifestyle. Thus, new trends are created, and a new aspect of life emerges the digital life (Kapaniaris & Zampetoglou, 2021). While this rapid digitization is still challenging for some people, today's young adults, teenagers and children are highly familiarized and even emerged with the digital life. In many cases, they even feel safer in digital worlds, such as 3D virtual worlds, compared to reality (Cabiria, 2008; McKenna & Chughtai, 2020).Virtual worlds are usually used to simulate reality or create fictional worlds that we could only imagine until a few years ago. However, an interesting intersection of the two is to recreate past worlds so that we can experience history from a new perspective (Poultsakis, Papadakis, Kalogiannakis & Psycharis, 2021). The use of technologies, such as computer graphics, provides new digital tools that can facilitate a better understanding and exploration of history and civilization while also offering the possibilities for participation and dissemination of cultural heritage (Margetis et al., 2020; Ott & Pozzi, 2011). There is a wide consensus on the value of Cultural Heritage, which is also a prominent concern in international policy, with UNESCO playing a crucial role in identifying and assuring cultural protection. Governments, academia and independent organizations join forces to document, protect and make culture accessible, including archaeological sites, natural parks, museums, folk traditions, etc.) (Alivizatou-Barakou et al., 2017). Virtual Museums are the most prevalent case in utilizing contemporary technologies to provide interactive experiences in cultural heritage while utilizing state-of-the-art technologies to create new experiences and forms of studying and interacting with history (Marinos Ioannides & Davies, 2018). At the same time, educators are convinced of the benefits new technologies carry for students when utilized in the learning procedure (Kalogiannakis & Papadakis, 2007). Thus, educators are looking to transform their learning sessions and provide their students with the modern, digital tools that will create new opportunities through activities that would traditionally not be included in education, such as serious games which transform learning into playing with the additional benefits of rewarding, feedback, high engagement, and motivated students (Groh, 2012; Stewart et al., 2013). The intersection of game-based learning, 3D graphics, virtual worlds, narrative, and cultural heritage carries a high potential for exploration and learning of historical sites in a manner that is often difficult, or even impossible, through traditional means and must thus be utilized for the betterment of students understanding of history (Katsaris & Vidakis, 2021). Despite the wide acceptance of serious games as an effective educational tool, the crucial elements and how they affect knowledge absorption by students is still a subject explored by researchers. Therefore, the authors have created a serious game that allows players to explore the site of an ancient Greek theatre and have conducted studies to understand its effect on students' motivation and satisfaction and the effect on gained knowledge and comprehension of the topics included in the game. In this chapter, the authors will attempt to conduct a retrospective analysis and critique, as is often performed in the video games industry, of the serious game they created and the experimental studies that allowed them to have data for the retrospective analysis. This analysis aims to identify game elements crucial for knowledge gain and understand how serious games affect knowledge compared to traditional teaching methods (Barianos, Papadakis & Vidakis, 2022). As key indicators for the research, two research questions were formulated and will be investigated below:

RQ1: Can low satisfaction with specific game constituents negatively affect knowledge gain?

RQ2: Can game design drawbacks negatively affect student motivation in a classroom setting?

The initial concept for this game, called ThimelEdu (Vidakis et al., 2018), was designed in 2017. The initial version of the game was ready in 2018 when the first experimental study took place (Vidakis et al., 2020). Some further improvements were made to the game in 2019, creating a second version used in the second study (Papadakis et al., 2020). Through those studies, the authors were able to collect data on the satisfaction of users and the effect the game had on educational results in an official school setting.

BACKGROUND

Serious games are games with an explicit educational intent and goals (Abt, 1970) rather than enjoyment which is the primary goal of commercial games. Since the dawn of digital games in the mid 20th century, giant leaps of progress have been performed, moving from rudimentary graphics comprised of lines and dots to 3D virtual, photorealistic models and virtual worlds with limitless options for the players. In modern terminology, one could argue that serious games could be defined as the junction of eLearning, game-based learning, and video games. Games have been criticized as instructional tools due to the controversiality commercial video games also faced during the same period. However, it is now universally acknowledged that serious games have instructional value, and their potential is still being realized (Arnab et al., 2015; Bellotti et al., 2013; Connolly et al., 2012). As a result, the popularity of serious games is rising and especially in terms of the potential to create compelling and exciting learning experiences in educational games (Lai & Hwang, 2016). It is proven that serious games excite students and can improve engagement and learning in a constructivist manner, which is highly valued by educators (Kalogiannakis & Papadakis, 2019). A wide range of games and computer software is available to help students attain various educational objectives. Educational games for children, in particular, have been widely used to enhance learning in official (i.e., classroom) and unofficial settings. Through this utilization, Educators observed and investigated the possible influence of this new technology on their pupils, assisting them in learning more effectively in a dynamic setting. Game-Based Learning is supported and aided by technological advancements. Educators and students can readily share information (Lazarinis, Boididis, Kozanidis & Kanellopoulos, 2022).

Additionally, students have access to exercises and can commence a conversation or conduct additional research and elaborate on their assignments in an online setting (Dichev et al., 2013). An additional innovation in digital learning includes the gamification and ludification of education processes (Vidakis et al., 2019). Learning is transformed into play through mobile devices, 3D printing rewards, field teaching and feedback. Those techniques allow students to become more motivated and interested in the learning process while facilitating collaboration (De Grove et al., 2012). Furthermore, serious games are proven to be beneficial in the context of a complicated subject, such as climate change, due to their ability to increase the players' personal and emotional engagement (Rajanen & Rajanen, 2019), but also due to the purposeful abstraction through which the attention to fundamental components is strengthened, exposing underlying linkages and lead to a better, more spherical and deep knowledge of the topic as a whole, essentially converting complex issues into tangible ones, understandable by the students (Karakose et al., 2021).

Similarly to education, museums, and cultural assets in general, have seen value in digitizing processes. Especially during the last decade, the emergence of smart portable devices and multimedia techniques has been a catalyst for creating applications for museums, such as virtual tours and more (Kalochristianakis et al., 2016). Cultural heritage and history have been brought to a broader audience through digitization and the construction of virtual worlds, which provide immersive experiences from the past (Mortara et al., 2014). Virtual tours and digital museums offer specific audiences the option to study certain sites and reach previously unavailable or unreachable insights. Despite the value that such implementations provide, the experience created is passive. For more significant learning, a more active state is required. For that reason, serious games are better suitable since they can engage the audience with entertaining, fascinating, and educational content (Catalano et al., 2014). Several serious games and other digital media have been developed to aid in the learning of cultural heritage issues. Schools, museums, and archaeological sites are the primary consumers of these games. Even within such a specific category of serious games, such as Cultural Heritage games, there can be unique approaches to creating the digital experiences, depending on the nature of the culture expressed through the game. Such segregation can be defined between tangible and intangible Cultural Heritage, which have different needs when studied to implement a serious game. However, they also share some common steps, such as modelling (Doulamis et al., 2017). Some basic steps are shared in the design of cultural heritage games, regardless of the particular topic examined. Those steps include Data acquisition, Digitization and Visualization, Content Design and storytelling. (Marinos; Ioannides et al., 2017).

Dive in the Past

Dive in the Past (Cozza et al., 2021) is a serious game focused on the Cultural Heritage hidden underwater in the Mediterranean sea. In this game, users can explore factual representations of archaeological sites beneath the sea in three dimensions. The game engages tourists, regardless of their interest and experience in diving, in a virtual simulation of an exploratory dive to archaeological locations, through which they emerge with raised awareness and knowledge levels of the heritage located beneath humans' view. Figure 1 - Screenshots within the Dive in the Past game *(Cozza et al., 2021)* illustrate the view users experience as they approach a shipwreck.

HieroQuest

For many reasons, ancient Egypt is one of the distinctive cultures in historical studies. The innovation and complexity of the Egyptian language, as expressed through the Hieroglyphs, is a particular field of study with many challenges, yet a fascinating one. HieroQuest (Plecher et al., 2020) aims to propagate knowledge of hieroglyphs of the Middle Egyptian language through an immersive mobile serious game.

Figure 1. Screenshots within Dive in the Past game (Cozza et al., 2021)

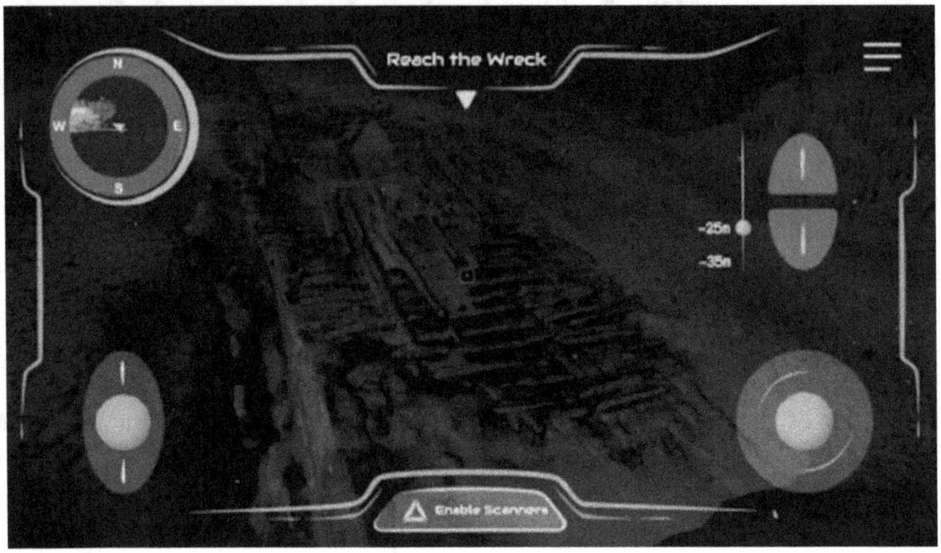

The game utilizes the story of the Shipwrecked Sailor, a text from the middle kingdom of Egypt, to teach fundamental and advanced topics of hieroglyph studies through a storytelling prism which keeps users engaged and facilitates learning. As seen in Figure 2 - HieroQuest gameplay, the game is created with 3D graphics and lets the user explore in the first person while looking for the hieroglyphs and their meanings, which some help from the game UI.

The Seafarers

Trading has been one of the most important catalysts for cultural interactions throughout history today. Seafaring has been very important to the Mediterranean area and played a significant role in trading and culture for all area people. For that reason, "The Seafarers" (Poullis et al., 2019), a serious game, was designed to engage the general public with the cultural heritage of maritime and the Mediterranean area. It explores data from shipwrecks and utilizes geospatial data, and the result is a turn-based strategy game where the player becomes a merchant commanding a vessel. Through the travels and explorations of the merchant, the user becomes accustomed to Mediterranean geography and culture, learning through a constructivist approach.

The gameplay can be seen in Figure 3 - Seafarers gameplay.

eShadow

In Greek Culture, shadow theatre is a tradition that continues to be popular and relevant to this day. The "eShadow"(Moraiti et al., 2016), (Christoulakis et al., 2013) is a collaborative platform featuring a collection of tools for the creation of digital shadow theatre productions that can also be shared and watched on the platform. A team developed it at the Technical University of Crete. It has a two-dimension interface that allows users to create their productions using existing or new puppets or watch a play

Figure 2. HieroQuest gameplay (Plecher et al., 2020)

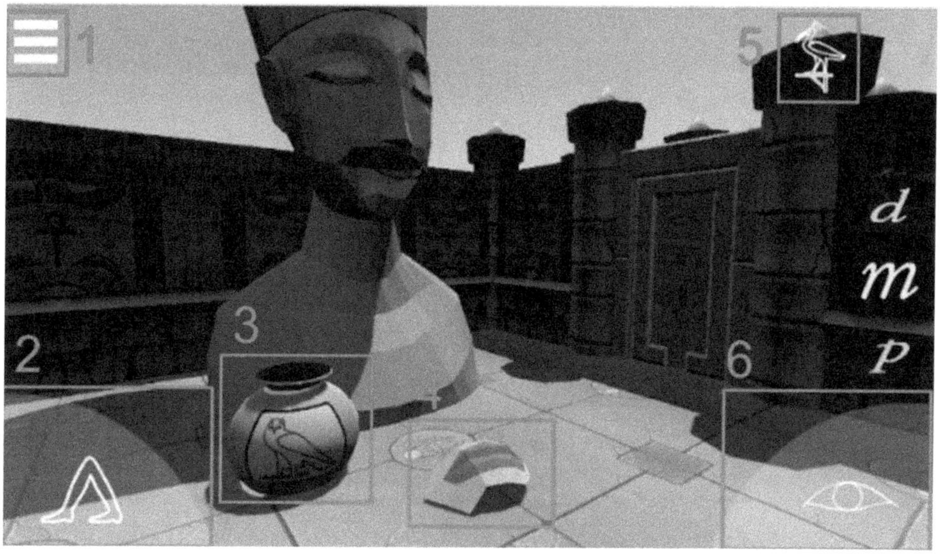

shared by other users. Figure 2 Creation Screen in eShadow *(Moraiti et al., 2016)* illustrates a view of the creation procedure.

Acropolis Virtual Tour

The Acropolis Virtual tour (Hellenic Ministry of Culture, 2017) is an online application that showcases the archaeological site in the Acropolis of Athens and allows users to take a digital tour around the premises, read information about the buildings and the history of Athens while watching high quality,

Figure 3. Seafarers gameplay (IMareCulture, n.d.)

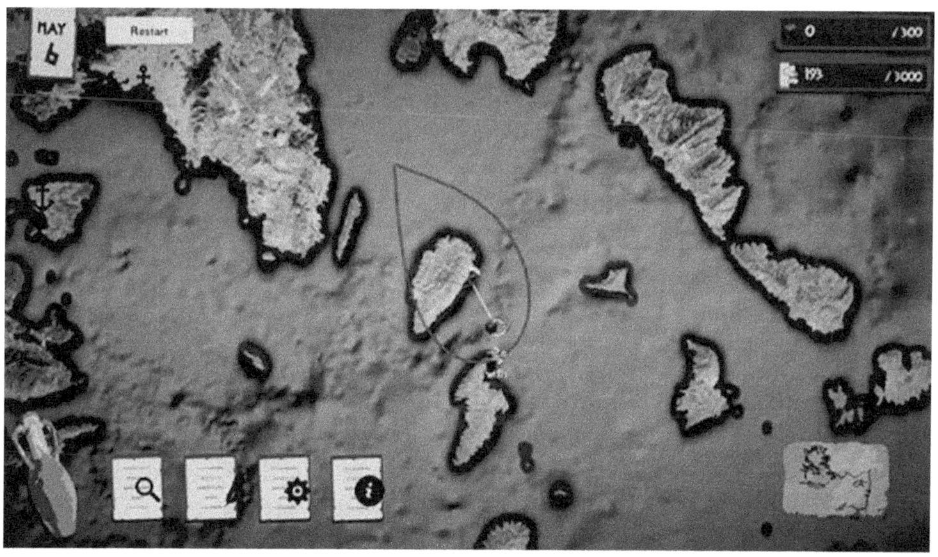

Figure 4. Creation screen in eShadow (Moraiti et al., 2016)

gigapixel pictures taken for this application, as well as panoramas. Additionally, an orthophoto map allows users to navigate between viewpoints, exploring multiple angles of each location. The way the images are presented to the users is illustrated in Figure 3 - Parthenon view in Acropolis Virtual Tour.

Figure 5. Parthenon view in Acropolis virtual tour

ThimelEdu

Interest and fascination with ancient theatre are vibrantly active with experts of many fields and amateurs, despite the thousands of years since the inception and original play productions. The reasons behind each interest and the topics focused on can be very versatile, including history, culture, philosophy, costumes, architecture, sound, art, and more. Despite the broad enthusiasm, little has been done to make ancient theatre studies more attractive to children and distinguish it from the written word they study in school. Engaging students in art, theatre, ancient architecture, and tools is challenging for any teacher. Mainly if the lessons are limited to literary studies of the subject, as they usually are. Due to the nature of the topic, the inability to access physical theatre sites and reproduce situations or environments for experiential learning within the classroom often leads to a tedious learning process revolving around books. It causes disinterest in students (Gonzalez et al., 2007). Although a thorough study has been conducted, only a few educational games were found with a relative topic. However, none could cover cultural, societal, and historical knowledge about the Greek ancient theatre as an event and location.

For this reason, the authors decided to create an interactive digital game with a 3D representation of Ancient Theater, where students are free to roam and discover architecture, tools, and subjects of interest at their own pace. Additional technological innovations have been integrated with the game, such as adaptability for students with special needs through the IOLAOS Platform (Vidakis & Charitakis, 2018), Learning analytics using Experience API (Rustici Software, n.d.) and dynamic content capabilities. These provide elevated levels of experience for the students while also allowing educators to unlock valuable insights into their learning sessions, students' experiences, and ultimately efficiency in learning. ThimelEdu was created as a single-player, first-person instructional game in a 3D virtual world. Players are tasked with exploring an ancient theatre through free roam within an ancient theatre site, discovering architectural elements and tools of the construct and learning facts and taking quizzes about each discovery. The environment is created with a playful yet accurate representation, as the target audience is elementary school students. The game content is flexible, leveraging IOLAOS user profiles and game personalization techniques to cater to user preferences and learning styles. The same setting is also available through in-game menus for users who are not satisfied with the settings IOLAOS has created or those who do not wish to use the IOLAOS platform. Those settings are categorized into visual, movement and font settings. ThimelEdu is designed to be used as a teaching aid in the classroom. Hence there are no pre-defined play situations. The game's goal is to find historic theatre relics hidden throughout the world and interact with them to learn more about them.

Furthermore, during the player's engagement with these artefacts, quizzes are provided to them. Figure 4 - ThimelEdu 3D World illustrates the world as the players experience it. Fundamental game constituents and characteristics include the educational material, evaluation procedure, learning analytics, multilingualism, English and Greek included so far, a Heads-Up Display with information about score and a mini-map, and finally, the menu from which many settings can be customized, on top of the automated IOLAOS profiling. Navigation is achieved through one of the most common techniques for first and third-person games, a combination of the keyboard (W-A-S-D or arrow keys) for movement and mouse for aim.

Educational Material

The majority of games have static, pre-designed educational material. Because ThimelEdu's primary purpose is education, an agile module to manage the game's content has been built to handle all different types of data in-game customization successfully. Students of different ages or educational capabilities receive different informative material and quizzes in practice. The infrastructure allows further factors to be considered, such as difficulty levels, previous score history, and more. However, for the moment, the educational material available is not enough for such levels of personalization. All instructional content is given in a conversation box containing articles, images, and other material regarding the

Figure 6. ThimelEdu 3D world

interacting object. Different types of information are presented on different tabs. With infinite material study time, the user can switch between tabs as many times as needed. Real-time view modifications are possible through buttons that handle font properties such as size. The entirety of the information window is showcased in Figure 4 - Information Dialogue, where we can see images provided for the topic of "Thimele", an informative text, and arrows to navigate between more pictures and texts, as well as the view modification buttons.

Figure 7. Information dialogue

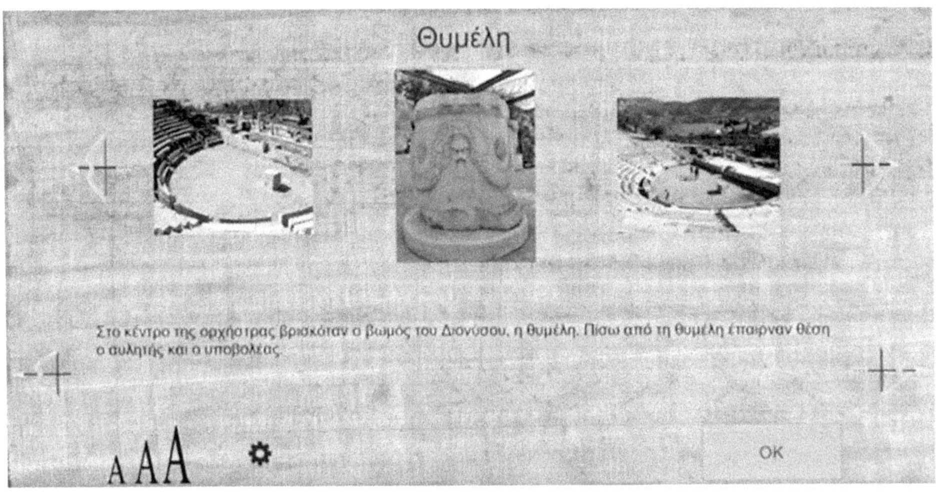

Evaluation

Evaluation of the students' learning is equally important. Therefore an evaluation mechanism in the form of quizzes that already have been mentioned is also included. Like the informative elements, Quizzes

Figure 8. Quiz, correct and wrong answer

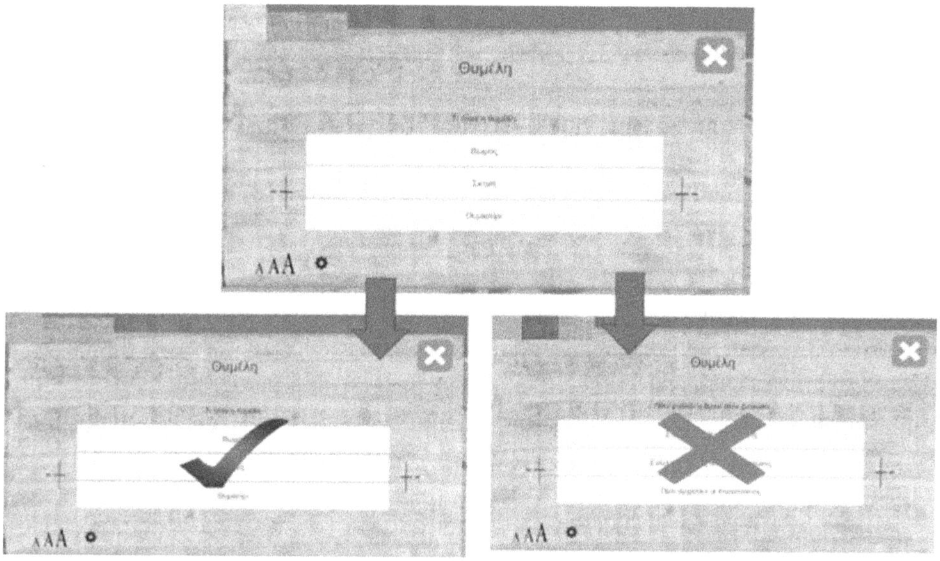

are provided within a dialogue box. Questions are always multiple-choice, with either two (true-false), three or four possible answers, depending on the grade and difficulty level selected by the IOLAOS profiling, as described above for the educational material. For each artefact, there might be multiple questions. Thus the dialogue may be comprised of multiple tabs. When an answer is selected, the focus is automatically switched to the next unanswered question tab. Players can quit the quiz and return later by pressing the exit button. Upon answering, visual and audible feedback is offered to indicate success or failure and the appropriate score points are awarded. The scoring system is based on a straightforward incremental approach where is a valid question provided one point on the scale. Wrong questions do not decrease awarder points.

Additionally, a special prize is awarded when all questions of an artefact are answered correctly on the first try. The game is concluded when the score equals the number of questions in the game, and the unique gifts serve as a reward for the player's expertise. The dialogue and the visual feedback for correct or wrong answers are presented in Figure 5 - Quiz, Correct and Wrong Answer. Additional fundamental game constituents and characteristics include the multilingualism, English and Greek included so far, a Heads-Up Display with information about score and a mini-map, and finally, the menu from which many settings can be customized, on top of the automated IOLAOS profiling.

Learning Analytics

Learning Analytics is a collection of data regarding the play session of each user. The activity in an e-Learning environment is described and retraced through this data. Such data is utilized to gain insights into the learning procedure as experienced by the user (Chaudy et al., 2014). Through learning analytics, game developers can evaluate the effectiveness of their games and locate any shortcomings that can be improved. In contrast, educators can evaluate their students in a more spherical and inclusive way than they would be able to with observation alone. Therefore, learning analytics were deemed crucial and was included in ThimelEdu through the xAPI specification, storing data about each action a user can take within the game, such as reading texts, answering questions, discovering artefacts, and more. From this data, visualization can be created to study specific exciting elements of the learning procedure. Additional analysis can also be done, allowing better evaluation of students and the game itself. It is an invaluable tool that needs detailed design and implementation but can yield valuable information.

STUDIES AND RESULTS

Two separate studies were conducted to evaluate ThimelEdu as an educational tool. The first study (Vidakis et al., 2020) explored the satisfaction and engagement of students with the game. The second study (Papadakis et al., 2020) was designed to appraise the learning procedure by examining a group of students taught through a game approach against a control group taught through traditional techniques. Both studies offered positive feedback and uncovered some issues that need to be addressed.

Student Satisfaction Evaluation

To assess user satisfaction, an experiment was designed and carried out during an event two consecutive years, in 2018 and 2019, in Heraklion Crete. In this event, schools would visit the Cultural Center of Heraklion, where multiple technological innovations were displayed for the students to see and learn more about. It is calculated that approximately 600 students aged 7-19 years old visited the event during the two years the experiment was conducted. The experiment ran for two days each year, from 10 a.m. to 5 p.m., and the educational sessions lasted approximately 10–15 minutes for each student. The flow of students visiting the ThimelEdu exhibit depended on the arrival schedule of schools and the time available for each school. Of the approximated number of 600 visitors for both years, 67 agreed to provide their anonymous answers to questionaries for the study. The procedure for the experiment was the same between the two years and followed a 4-step procedure.

1. A short overview of Greek Ancient Theatre
2. Game overview. Description of the game, including navigation, interactions, sequence of events, etc.
3. Play ThimelEdu
4. Fill out the surveys

The survey questionnaires, designed to evaluate the user experience from the gameplay, educational content, and the effectiveness of the process, were given to the students after 10-15 minutes of play sessions. The questions provided covered topics about the educational content, navigation, controls and gameplay in the 3D world, the level of complexity of interaction with 3D objects, etc. Each response is rated on a scale of 1 to 5, with one indicating “bad” and five indicating “outstanding”. Students selected their responses depending on their perception of the game. The complete list of questions is presented in Table 1 - Survey questions.

For the second year of the experiment, Learning Analytics was enabled as a way to cross-examine our survey results. Through the learning analytics, interaction-based events were recorded in a Learn-

Table 1. Survey questions

Question	Abbreviation
Are you satisfied with the educational material (Text/Images)	Q1
Was the examination procedure (questions) satisfactory?	Q2
Are you satisfied with the game's navigation controls (keyboard/mouse)?	Q3
Do you find the map an easy-to-use navigation tool?	Q4
How hard were the games\navigation?	Q5
Are you satisfied with the interaction with the 3D graphics?	Q6
Do you think the game environment has a high ease of use?	Q7
How satisfied are you with the game's graphics?	Q8

ing Record Store in the form of "Who-Did-What" statements. The specific interaction statements are presented in Table 2- Interaction statements (2019 only).

Table 2. Interaction statements (2019 only)

Who	Did	What	Abbreviation
Player/Student	Accessed	ThimelEdu	S1
Player/Student	Exited	ThimelEdu	S2
Player/Student	Interacted	Dynamic Generated	S3
Player/Student	Completed	Dynamic Generated	S4
Player/Student	Answered (true)	Dynamic Generated	S5
Player/Student	Answered (false)	Dynamic Generated	S6

Responses

After both years of the experiment, the surveys were collected, parsed, and analyzed into the following summaries. A total number of students and their gender, as presented in Table 3 - Sample overview, average responses by year and gender, as presented in Table 4 - Question responses by year and gender, and, finally, averages by age group and year, as presented in Table 5 - Averages by age group and year. The game was gender-neutral; therefore, it was interesting to analyze whether answers were influenced by gender, which is why all analysis includes gender as a filter.

Research Findings

From the statistical analysis conducted on the results described in the above tables, multiple shortcomings of the game are identified, especially in navigation and aesthetics. In more detail, from Table 4 - Question responses by year and gender, it can be deduced that Q5 and Q8 show dissatisfaction with the navigation within the 3D environment and the graphics. Additionally, Table 5 - Averages by age group and year, show the same trends regarding questions Q5 and Q8 across all age groups. Furthermore, the average

Table 3. Sample overview

Year	Boys	Girls	Total
2018	27	11	38
2019	20	9	29
Both Years	47	20	67

Table 4. Question responses by year and gender

	2018		2019	
Questions	**Boys**	**Girls**	**Boys**	**Girls**
Q1: educational material satisfaction	4.48	4.36	4.5	3.5
Q2: Exam Procedure	4.55	4.54	4.33	3.16
Q3: Nav. controls	4.25	4.72	4.08	3
Q4: Map tool	4.22	4.54	4.08	2.66
Q5: Game Overall Nav.	3.18	2.54	2.16	3
Q6: 3D graphics Interaction	4.25	4.63	3.9	3.1
Q7: ease of use	4.11	4.45	3.54	2.6
Q8: game's graphics	3.96	4.5	3	3

of each question in the 2019 (second year) iteration is significantly lower than the 2018 one for multiple age groups, spanning the entire range between 10 and 18 years of age. This drop-in averages could not be explained by cross-examination with the Learning Analytics data or by any other reason deducted through the data collected, leading the authors to conclude that further improvements and studies must be conducted to pinpoint the game's problems and solve them.

Table 5. Averages by age group and year

	2018						2019				
	Age groups						Age groups				
Questions	**7-9**	**10-12**	**13-15**	**16-18**	**19+**		**7-9**	**10-12**	**13-15**	**16-18**	**19+**
Q1: educational material satisfaction	5	4.52	4.11	4.33	4.57		-	3.6	4.1	3.33	4.5
Q2: Exam Procedure	5	4.64	4.11	4.33	4.85		-	3.2	3.88	3.33	4.5
Q3: Nav. controls	5	4.35	4	4.66	4.71		-	3.2	3.33	3.33	5
Q4: Map tool	5	4.35	4	3.66	4.71		-	3.2	3.44	2.66	4.5
Q5: Game Overall Nav.	1.5	3.23	3	1.33	3.57		-	2.2	2.22	0.66	3
Q6: 3D graphics Interaction	5	4.64	3.55	4.66	4.42		-	2.2	3.33	3.33	4.5
Q7: ease of use	4	4.17	4	3.66	4.85		-	1.8	2.88	2.66	5
Q8: game's graphics	4.5	4.41	3.1	2.66	4.42		-	1.4	3	2.0	4.5

Learning Procedure Evaluation

This study aimed to compare a conventional teaching method to a game-based approach and analyze whether the second approach aids knowledge retention by students. While evaluating the impact of the two teaching methods on the learning outcomes for the students, a co-examination of the effect of additional parameters, such as gender and age was also undertaken. For this study, two hypotheses were investigated.

H1: The initial knowledge of the two groups will increase significantly after the intervention.

H2: The knowledge of students taught ancient theatre elements with the 'traditional' approach is significantly less than that of students taught ancient theatre elements with a game and is not affected by factors such as gender.

This research took place in a public high school during the 2018-2019 school year, between January and April 2019. The research sample comprised 22 students (8 males, 14 females) who were ethically and linguistically homogeneous from the city of Heraklion, prefecture of Crete, Greece. At the measurement time, the student's ages ranged from 17 to 17,5 years (M=210 months, SD = 4,7 months). In the final experimental sample, only students who completed both rounds of testing (pre-test and post-test) were included. All measures regarding consent, confidentiality and data usage requirements were meticulously met, both orally and in writing, though informing school staff, students and parents about the study's aims and their choice to refrain from participation. Naturally, university ethical guidelines were also followed. Throughout the instructional intervention, a common set of ethical standards was adopted.

Experiment Design

The experiment designed to verify the research hypotheses was based on two groups, the experimental and control groups, and included 3 phases. A pre-experimental control was conducted to measure the dependent variable in phase A. In phase B, the experimental phase, a teaching intervention took place, where the independent variable manipulation was performed. Lastly, in phase C, the post-experimental control phase, the control of the dependent variable was conducted.

There were two stages of the research procedure. The pilot test of the game and the creation ad evaluation of the questionnaires took place in the first stage that spanned from September to December of 2018. The pre-experimental, experimental teaching intervention and post-experimental evaluation procedures were included in the second stage. This stage lasted m January to May of 2019. Assignations into one of two groups were random, and both groups followed the same curriculum with the same teacher. The teaching was supplemented by structured research on the web (WebQuest) for the control group, while the experiment group was introduced to a serious thematic game, ThimelEdu, presented above.

A questionnaire was expressly administered for the study, assessing student performance pre and post the educational intervention. In short, the questionnaire attempts to identify elements of the ancient theatre, including architectural elements and their roles, such as the "orchestra", the "thimele", and more. A few questions about each element are scattered across the test.

Research Findings

The study's main goal was to examine how students' performance in ancient theatre knowledge is affected after being taught using a serious thematic game. To evaluate the performance, questionnaires were used. Using a dependent (paired samples) t-test, both groups were compared in terms of their previous knowledge on the topic, using a questionnaire created for this experiment, which was answered pre and post-experimental intervention. The results of the t-test analysis are displayed in Table 6 - t-test per group analysis. Through this analysis, the authors concluded that the knowledge of both groups increased after the teaching intervention. However, there is a statistically significantly different in the performance between the two groups, with the experimental group achieving higher levels of knowledge. Additional study investigations for another factor that might affect the performance concluded that neither age nor gender has a statistically significant effect on ancient theatre knowledge. Both hypotheses were verified through the experiment. Both groups significantly increased their knowledge after the intervention (H1). The two groups had a significant difference in performance, with the experimental group achieving higher statistical scores of knowledge.

Table 6. T-test per group analysis

			M	SD	*t-test(df=10)*
Game-Based Approach	Knowledge	Pre-test	9.64	2.84	-7.49, p=0.000
		Post-test	21.45	4.44	
			M	**SD**	***t-test(df=10)***
Traditional Approach	Knowledge	Pre-test	9.91	4.85	=6.34, p=0.000
		Post-test	15.00	4.41	

FUTURE RESEARCH DIRECTIONS

Game-based learning aspires to develop educational processes beyond tradition that engage students and transform the educational process into a more effective, exciting and engaging procedure. Students directly interact with the educational content (Kalogiannakis et al., 2020; Mawas et al., 2019). This is especially true in Cultural Heritage, where interaction with artefacts from the past is crucial but often impossible. Experiential learning can allow complex knowledge to emerge from simple digital materials as it would work with actual, physical objects. With the popularity and availability that technologies such as Augmented and Virtual have recently achieved, is it now more than ever possible to create emerging and engaging experiences in historical situations and places which were impossible until just a few years ago? With materials being the centre of any archaeological research as well as the centre of students' attention and curiosity, it is imperative that attention is given to the recreation of historical artefacts, locations and situations in a digital 3D matter as the best means to preserve and distribute historical and folklore artefacts and knowledge, detached from strict geographical confines.

CONCLUSION

Serious games have been overwhelmingly proven to offer high educational value to the learning process. It is critical to use novel teaching methods in the classroom to facilitate learning, and serious games are one of the most suited candidates for such interventions. Especially in areas of Cultural Heritage, serious games offer further benefits due to the nature of the studied subjects that are often hard to convey to students without facilitation from digital means (Papadakis, Kalogiannakis, Sifaki & Vidakis, 2018). The authors aimed to create a serious game to deliver game-based and experiential learning on a topic with geographical restrictions and academic difficulties that disallow experiential learning in any other form. With this endeavour, the authors aimed to revisit the serious game and experimental studies, combining the outcomes to understand further implications regarding game elements and knowledge gained through serious digital games. Previous research on the game proved that educational value was added in the cases where the game was utilized in teaching procedures, proving its value for education. However, the research also surfaced multiple shortcomings and limitations of the game, highlighting paths for improvements that need to be addressed. The game was designed with a lot of modalities and capabilities in an attempt to be flexible and adapt to user needs; however, from the satisfaction study, it was concluded that users are dissatisfied with the game navigation, ease of use and graphics, three of the principal axes that the game aimed to make as good and personalized as possible.

Additionally, the authors could not explain a significant statistical drop in satisfaction between the two iterations of the study, demonstrating shortcomings and limitations in the research that must be addressed in the future. Additionally, learning analytics was successfully integrated into the game from a technical perspective, but they were not adequately utilized in research. Learning analytics is a valuable and promising tool for tracking student behaviour within serious games during the educational process. The presence of learning analytics can greatly assist critical decision-making regarding student behaviour and needs. There is value for the betterment of the entire educational process from learning analytics. For those reasons, the authors shall consider those capabilities and functionalities when designing future experiments so that a better value can be drawn and insights from a complex perspective are unlocked.

Furthermore, none of the findings through the research conducted was validated through delayed post-test. Thus, knowledge gained was not measured for retention or satisfaction in a longer-term setting. Overall, the results of the experiments were positive, showcasing user satisfaction and a gain in knowledge regarding ancient Greek theatre. Further conclusions were drawn through this retrospective of the studies. For both research questions, RQ1 and RQ2, there is no evidence that low satisfaction or game design drawbacks have negatively affected students' learning or motivation in the classroom setting. Knowledge gain was high compared to traditional teaching methods, and students were motivated by the game (Zourmpakis, Papadakis & Kalogiannakis, 2022). However, it is possible that even better results would be possible with a game more appealing to the students.

Additionally, the drawbacks detected through the studies are significant, despite not negating the positive effects the game has on engagement, motivation, education, and comprehension of the subject. However, they shine a light on often overlooked game design issues and techniques that failed their cause. With the wisdom gained through these procedures, the authors have reconsidered the goals and techniques they use in game design and development, aiming to create experiences with a higher level of satisfaction that will ultimately engage students even more and create a better platform for learning and knowledge retention.

ACKNOWLEDGMENT

This research received no specific grant from any funding agency in the public, commercial, or not-for-profit sectors.

REFERENCES

Abt, C. C. (1970). *Serious Games*. doi:10.1109/VS-GAMES.2009.8

Alivizatou-Barakou, M., Kitsikidis, A., Tsalakanidou, F., Dimitropoulos, K., Giannis, C., Nikolopoulos, S., Al Kork, S., Denby, B., Buchman, L., Adda-Decker, M., Pillot-Loiseau, C., Tillmane, J., Dupont, S., Picart, B., Pozzi, F., Ott, M., Erdal, Y., Charisis, V., Hadjidimitriou, S., . . . Grammalidis, N. (2017). Intangible Cultural Heritage and New Technologies: Challenges and Opportunities for Cultural Preservation and Development. In Mixed Reality and Gamification for Cultural Heritage (pp. 129–158). Springer International Publishing. doi:10.1007/978-3-319-49607-8_5

Arnab, S., Lim, T., Carvalho, M. B., Bellotti, F., De Freitas, S., Louchart, S., Suttie, N., Berta, R., & De Gloria, A. (2015). Mapping learning and game mechanics for serious games analysis. *British Journal of Educational Technology*, *46*(2), 391–411. doi:10.1111/bjet.12113

Barianos, A., Papadakis, A., & Vidakis, N. (2022). Content manager for serious games: Theoretical framework and digital platform. *Advances in Mobile Learning Educational Research, 2*(1), 251-262. doi:10.25082/AMLER.2022.01.009

Bellotti, F., Kapralos, B., Lee, K., Moreno-Ger, P., & Berta, R. (2013). Assessment in and of serious games: An overview. *Advances in Human-Computer Interaction*, *2013*, 1–11. Advance online publication. doi:10.1155/2013/136864

Cabiria, J. (2008). Virtual World and Real World Permeability: Transference of Positive Benefits for Marginalized Gay and Lesbian Populations. *Journal of Virtual Worlds Research*, *1*(1). Advance online publication. doi:10.4101/jvwr.v1i1.284

Catalano, C. E., Luccini, A. M., & Mortara, M. (2014). Guidelines for an effective design of serious games. *International Journal of Serious Games*, *1*(1). Advance online publication. doi:10.17083/ijsg.v1i1.8

Chaudy, Y., Connolly, T., & Hainey, T. (2014). Learning Analytics in Serious Games: A Review of the Literature. *Ecaet 2014*.

Christoulakis, M., Pitsiladis, A., Moraiti, A., Moumoutzis, N., & Christodoulakis, S. (2013). EShadow : A Tool for Digital Storytelling Based on Traditional Greek Shadow Theatre. *Fdg 2013*.

Connolly, T. M., Boyle, E. A., Macarthur, E., Hainey, T., & Boyle, J. M. (2012). A systematic literature review of empirical evidence on computer games and serious games. *Computers & Education*, *59*(2), 661–686. doi:10.1016/j.compedu.2012.03.004

Cozza, M., Isabella, S., Di Cuia, P., Cozza, A., Peluso, R., Cosentino, V., Barbieri, L., Muzzupappa, M., & Bruno, F. (2021). Dive in the Past: A Serious Game to Promote the Underwater Cultural Heritage of the Mediterranean Sea. *Heritage*, *4*(4), 4001–4016. doi:10.3390/heritage4040220

De Grove, F., Bourgonjon, J., & Van Looy, J. (2012). Digital games in the classroom? A contextual approach to teachers' adoption intention of digital games in formal education. *Computers in Human Behavior*, *28*(6), 2023–2033. doi:10.1016/j.chb.2012.05.021

Dichev, C., Dicheva, D., Agre, G., & Angelova, G. (2013). Current practices, trends and challenges in k-12 online learning. *Cybernetics and Information Technologies*, *13*(3), 91–110. doi:10.2478/cait-2013-0028

Doulamis, N., Doulamis, A., Ioannidis, C., Klein, M., & Ioannides, M. (2017). Modelling of Static and Moving Objects: Digitizing Tangible and Intangible Cultural Heritage. In *Mixed Reality and Gamification for Cultural Heritage* (pp. 567–589). Springer International Publishing. doi:10.1007/978-3-319-49607-8_23

Gonzalez, J. L., Cabrera, M. J., & Gutierrez, F. L. (2007). Using videogames in special education. *Lecture Notes in Computer Science*, *4739*, 360–367. doi:10.1007/978-3-540-75867-9_46

Groh, F. (2012). Gamification: State of the Art Definition and Utilization. *Proceedings of the 4th Seminar on Research Trends in Media Informatics*, 39–46. http://fold.it

Hellenic Ministry of Culture. (2017). *Acropolis Virtual Tour*. Hellenic Ministry of Culture. http://acropolis-virtualtour.gr/index.html

iMareCulture. (n.d.). Retrieved February 27, 2022, from https://imareculture.eu/downloads/project-tools/seafarers-game/

Ioannides, M., Magnenat Thalmann, N., & Papagiannakis, G. (2017). *Mixed Reality and Gamification for Cultural Heritage*. Springer International Publishing. doi:10.1007/978-3-319-49607-8

Ioannides, M., & Davies, R. (2018). ViMM - Virtual Multimodal Museum: a Manifesto and Roadmap for Europe's Digital Cultural Heritage. *2018 International Conference on Intelligent Systems (IS)*, 343–350. doi:10.1109/IS.2018.8710556

Kalochristianakis, M., Vonorta, H., Stamoulias, A., Lakka, E., Kontakis, K., & Malamos, A. (2016). Experiential educational environments for cultural heritage. *2016 International Conference on Telecommunications and Multimedia, TEMU 2016*, 6–11. doi:10.1109/TEMU.2016.7551907

Kalogiannakis, M., & Papadakis, S. (2007). The dual form of further education of educators in ICT: technological and pedagogical training. In C. Constantinou, Z. Zacharias, & M. Papaevripidou (Eds.), *8th International Conference On Computer Based Learning in Science* (pp. 265–276). Academic Press.

Kalogiannakis, M., & Papadakis, S. (2019). Evaluating pre-service kindergarten teachers' intention to adopt and use tablets into teaching practice for natural sciences. *International Journal of Mobile Learning and Organisation*, *13*(1), 113. https://doi.org/10.1504/IJMLO.2019.096479

Kalogiannakis, M., Papadakis, S., & Dorouka, P. (2020). Tablets and apps for promoting robotics, mathematics, STEM education and literacy in early childhood education. *International Journal of Mobile Learning and Organisation*, *14*(2), 255. https://doi.org/10.1504/IJMLO.2020.10026334

Kapaniaris, A., & Zampetoglou, G. (2021). Visual programming for the greation of digital shadow play performance using mobile devices in times of Covid-19. *Advances in Mobile Learning Educational Research*, *1*(2), 162-170. doi:10.25082/AMLER.2021.02.010

Karakose, T., Polat, H., & Papadakis, S. (2021). Examining Teachers' Perspectives on School Principals' Digital Leadership Roles and Technology Capabilities during the COVID-19 Pandemic. *Sustainability*, *13*(23), 13448. https://doi.org/10.3390/su132313448

Katsaris, I., & Vidakis, N. (2021). Adaptive e-learning systems through learning styles: A review of the literature. *Advances in Mobile Learning Educational Research, 1*(2), 124-145. doi:10.25082/AMLER.2021.02.007

Lai, C. L., & Hwang, G. J. (2016). A self-regulated flipped classroom approach to improving students' learning performance in a mathematics course. *Computers & Education, 100*, 126–140. https://doi.org/10.1016/j.compedu.2016.05.006

Lazarinis, F., Boididis, I., Kozanidis, L., & Kanellopoulos, D. (2022). An adaptable multi-learner serious game for learning cultural heritage. *Advances in Mobile Learning Educational Research, 2*(1), 201-215. doi:10.25082/AMLER.2022.01.004

Margetis, G., Apostolakis, K. C., Ntoa, S., Papagiannakis, G., & Stephanidis, C. (2020). X-Reality Museums: Unifying the Virtual and Real World Towards Realistic Virtual Museums. *Applied Sciences (Basel, Switzerland), 11*(1), 338. https://doi.org/10.3390/app11010338

Mawas, N. E., Truchly, P., Podhrasky, P., & Muntean, C. (2019). The effect of educational game on children Learning experience in a Slovakina School. *CSEDU 2019 - Proceedings of the 11th International Conference on Computer Supported Education.*

McKenna, B., & Chughtai, H. (2020). Resistance and sexuality in virtual worlds: An LGBT perspective. *Computers in Human Behavior, 105*, 106199. https://doi.org/10.1016/j.chb.2019.106199

Moraiti, A., Moumoutzis, N., Christoulakis, M., Pitsiladis, A., Stylianakis, G., Sifakis, Y., Maragoudakis, I., & Christodoulakis, S. (2016). Playful creation of digital stories with eShadow. *2016 11th International Workshop on Semantic and Social Media Adaptation and Personalization (SMAP)*, 139–144. doi:10.1109/SMAP.2016.7753399

Mortara, M., Catalano, C. E., Bellotti, F., Fiucci, G., Houry-Panchetti, M., & Petridis, P. (2014). Learning cultural heritage by serious games. *Journal of Cultural Heritage, 15*(3), 318–325. https://doi.org/10.1016/j.culher.2013.04.004

Ott, M., & Pozzi, F. (2011). Towards a new era for Cultural Heritage Education: Discussing the role of ICT. *Computers in Human Behavior, 27*(4), 1365–1371. https://doi.org/10.1016/j.chb.2010.07.031

Papadakis, S. (2021). Advances in Mobile Learning Educational Research (A.M.L.E.R.): Mobile learning as an educational reform. *Advances in Mobile Learning Educational Research, 1*(1), 1-4. doi:10.25082/AMLER.2021.01.001

Papadakis, S., Kalogiannakis, M., Sifaki, E., & Vidakis, N. (2018). Evaluating Moodle use via Smart Mobile Phones. A case study in a Greek University. *EAI Endorsed Transactions on Creative Technologies, 5*(16).

Papadakis, S., Trampas, A., Barianos, A., Kalogiannakis, M., & Vidakis, N. (2020). Evaluating the Learning Process: The "ThimelEdu" Educational Game Case Study. *Proceedings of the 12th International Conference on Computer Supported Education*, 290–298. doi:10.5220/0009379902900298

Plecher, D. A., Herber, F., Eichhorn, C., Pongratz, A., Tanson, G., & Klinker, G. (2020). HieroQuest - A Serious Game for Learning Egyptian Hieroglyphs. *Journal on Computing and Cultural Heritage*, *13*(4), 1–20. https://doi.org/10.1145/3418038

Poullis, C., Kersten-Oertel, M., Benjamin, J. P., Philbin-Briscoe, O., Simon, B., Perissiou, D., Demesticha, S., Markou, E., Frentzos, E., Kyriakidis, P., Skarlatos, D., & Rizvic, S. (2019). Evaluation of "The Seafarers": A serious game on seaborne trade in the Mediterranean sea during the Classical period. *Digital Applications in Archaeology and Cultural Heritage*, *12*, e00090. https://doi.org/10.1016/j.daach.2019.e00090

Poultsakis, S., Papadakis, S., Kalogiannakis, M., & Psycharis, S. (2021). The management of Digital Learning Objects of Natural Sciences and Digital Experiment Simulation Tools by teachers. *Advances in Mobile Learning Educational Research, 1*(2), 58-71. doi:10.25082/AMLER.2021.02.002

Rajanen, D., & Rajanen, M. (2019). Climate change gamification: A literature review. *CEUR Workshop Proceedings*, *2359*, 253–264.

Rustici Software. (n.d.). *Experience API*. Retrieved January 26, 2018, from https://xapi.com/overview/

Sacco, P. L. (2011). *Culture 3.0: A new perspective for the EU 2014-2020 structural funds programming*. Academic Press.

Stewart, J., Lizzy, I., Van Looy, J., Mariën, I., All, A., Schurmans, D., Willaert, K., De Grove, F., Jacobs, A., & Misuraca, G. (2013). *The Potential of Digital Games for Empowerment and Social Inclusion of Groups at Risk of Social and Economic Exclusion: Evidence and Opportunity for Policy*. doi:10.2791/88148

Vidakis, N., Barianos, A., Trampas, A., Papadakis, S., Kalogiannakis, M., & Vassilakis, K. (2019). Generating Education in-Game Data: The Case of an Ancient Theatre Serious Game. In *Proceedings of the 11th International Conference on Computer Supported Education - Volume 1*. CSEDU. DOI: doi:10.5220/0007810800360043

Vidakis, N., Barianos, A., Xanthopoulos, G., & Stamatakis, A. (2018). Cultural Inheritance Education Environment: The Ancient Theater Game ThimelEdu. *12th European Conference on Games Based Learning, ECGBL 2018*, 730–740.

Vidakis, N., Barianos, A. K., Trampas, A. M., Papadakis, S., Kalogiannakis, M., & Vassilakis, K. (2020). Game Raw Data Collection and Visualization in the Context of the "ThimelEdu". Educational Game. https://doi.org/10.1007/978-3-030-58459-7_30

Vidakis, N., & Charitakis, S. (2018). Designing the Learning Process. *Proceedings of the 10th International Conference on Subject-Oriented Business Process Management - S-BPM One '18*, 1–11. doi:10.1145/3178248.3178254

Zourmpakis, A.-I., Papadakis, St., & Kalogiannakis, M. (2022). Education of Preschool and Elementary Teachers on the Use of Adaptive Gamification in Science Education. *International Journal of Technology Enhanced Learning*, *14*(1), 1–16.

Chapter 12
Gamification Techniques Capitalizing on State-of-the-Art Technologies

Ilias Logothetis
Hellenic Mediterranean University, Greece

Anastasios Kristofer Barianos
https://orcid.org/0000-0001-6709-9250
Hellenic Mediterranean University, Greece

Alexandros Papadakis
Hellenic Mediterranean University, Greece

Eirini Christinaki
https://orcid.org/0000-0001-5785-1509
KU Leuven, Belgium

Orestis Charalampakos
Hellenic Mediterranean University, Greece

Iraklis Katsaris
Hellenic Mediterranean University, Greece

Michail Kalogiannakis
https://orcid.org/0000-0002-9124-2245
University of Crete in Greece, Greece

Nikolas Vidakis
https://orcid.org/0000-0003-0726-8627
Hellenic Mediterranean University, Greece

ABSTRACT

Teachers incorporate gamification techniques and game-based learning (GBL) into the learning material rapidly. Technological advancements on the world wide web have essentially assisted GBL as it has allowed the creation of many educational platforms and applications. Despite these web applications' advancements, technology has more to offer than a just website, moving into virtual worlds, enhancing the real world with digital content and artefacts, using users' geolocation to navigate them into learning material around their physical world, and gathering, processing, and analysing information about the users with the purpose to better adjust the information provided to them. The collaboration between gamification techniques and modern technologies are explored to showcase the possibilities this merger can give. Applications using state-of-the-art technologies and gamification techniques tend to increase engagement and motivation of students, increase their soft skills, and develop a positive perspective towards learning and education.

DOI: 10.4018/978-1-6684-4461-0.ch012

INTRODUCTION

Students are quickly bored with the traditional learning methods, and most of them do not appreciate paper books and long text studying. Students seek interactive and fast-paced content to intrigue their attention and boost their interest. Therefore, Gamification techniques are essential to spark the students' interest and keep them motivated and engaged with the learning material. The goal of gamification in education is to use the motivational power of video games in the classroom (Ahmad, Migniot, and Dipanda, 2019). Teachers achieve motivation by changing students' gaming involvement into an instructional context that intends to influence students' behaviour and encourage the completion of learning objectives (Vidakis et al., 2014). Goals related to knowledge acquisition and the old teaching model are being transferred to a new method outlined in previous decades by the educational community. The use of knowledge and the construction of a pleasant classroom environment for enhanced creativity are two of the main goals of this innovative method (Mahayuddin and Saif 2020). Students may stimulate curiosity through discussion, investigation, and experimentation, making learning more enjoyable.

Traditional teaching methods do not make substantial use of new technologies, causing students to lose interest in school. While students are accustomed to working and being engaged in environments with a wide range of stimuli in their daily lives, the traditional school remains a place with limited options (Mahayuddin and Saif 2020). A transition to a new model is required to make learning more creative and engaging by incorporating new visual learning modes (Huang, Chen, and Chou, 2016). Students can increase their thinking and concentration (Schechter et al., 2015) around a topic by playing, a fun and engaging way to achieve particular learning goals (Téllez Alarcia & Iturriaga Barco, 2014). Students' engagement aids them in achieving a range of goals outside of learning, such as improved awareness and a deeper understanding of the subject (Chu and Hung 2015).

As a result of technological advancements in software and hardware and particularly significant advances in the performance of smart devices, our daily lives have been adapted to the utilization of such devices (Papadakis, 2021). One of the many areas where these technological breakthroughs are gradually becoming apparent is education (Kapaniaris & Zampetoglou, 2021). Virtual worlds that offer immersive experiences, Augmented Reality (AR) applications that superimpose virtual content into the physical world and general applications utilizing touchscreens, cameras, or head-mounted devices are expected to diversify instruction in the coming years (Radu, 2014).

AR technology is compatible with and may be used in conjunction with gamification, and Game-Based Learning (GBL) approaches to improve educational processes. It can also help learners with their studies' cognitive and motivational aspects. In this book chapter, the authors aim to show how gamification techniques and GBL approaches can be combined with modern Information and Communications Technologies (ICT) to provide an enhanced learning experience that is best suited to the needs and requirements of students. The expectations are that combining the two will increase learners' interest and motivation in the subjects they are studying.

BACKGROUND

Gamification

Gamification can be defined as the attempt to incorporate game elements and principles into a non-game context, thus offering game-like experiences to intensify user engagement (Deterding et al., 2011). Gamification is based on the instincts and desires of the user, and such instincts include competition, mastery, a sense of victory and more. Common strategies for gamification include rewarding systems to make the user feel a sense of progression, completion, and competition to lure them into engagement with learning. Common game design elements widely used and adopted are awarding points and badges, providing performance information through leaderboards and graphs, and giving depth into the content through meaningful stories, avatars, and teammates to engage users in collaboration. The following paragraphs describe the most frequently used gamification techniques to understand better where and how it is appropriate to use each one.

Points

Points are elements rewarded to a user upon completing a task and are commonly employed to measure progress or performance (Brewer et al., 2013). Studies (Alomari, Al-Samarraie, and Yousef, 2019) indicate that point-based systems can motivate students as they crave the rewards from engagement in learning activities. Points make students feel challenged (Davis et al., 2018; Diniz et al., 2017; Wang & Lieberoth, 2016) as they represent their progress. Points can be of many forms depending on the reason they are invoked. As the points acquisition can be an essential element of students' participation in learning activities, this promotes student-centred learning (Hew et al., 2016).

Badges

Badges are a rewarding system awarded to individuals to represent achievements earned from a gamified activity (Seaborn and Fels 2015). Like point-based systems, badges also aid motivation and performance advancement (Suh, Wagner, and Liu, 2018). Social interaction between learners is another aspect in which the badges help strengthen (Ding, Er, and Orey 2018). They indicate the possession of achievement and allow individuals to become members of badge owners. Furthermore, badges can influence one's decisions as the selection of challenges and pathways can be made based on the rewarding badge (Wang and Sun 2011).

Leaderboards

Leaderboards are used to rank users among others based on specific criteria, measuring the success rate within a learning activity. It is a competitive process that aims to increase motivation (Seaborn and Fels 2015) and performance as they try to place themselves in the higher ranks on the leaderboard. While leaderboards can have positive effects, it is crucial to note that for a learner, ranking among the lower positions on the leaderboard can have the opposite effects (Werbach and Hunter 2015). Engagement in learning activities is also increased through leaderboards (Burguillo, 2010) as learners can feel pressure to increase their scores and ascend the ranking ladder of the leaderboard.

Performance Graphs

Performance graphs measure users' performance, but in contrast to leaderboards, it is measured not against other users but based on their performance during the game (Sailer et al., 2017). This can serve as an evaluation metric for the users over time and allow them to improve. Sailer et al. (2017) report that this technique drives users to master a task based on their criteria based on motivation theory.

Levels

Levels serve as a ranking or measure system for an individual's advancement through certain stages, based on activities and challenges to move onto the next stage. It is commonly accepted that lower levels represent low difficulty, while higher levels demand more time and effort to complete (Nah et al., 2014). This technique can increase motivation as learners can focus on the task at hand and pursue the solution in contemplation of completing the level (Butler & Bodnar, 2017; Diniz et al., 2017; Kim, Rothrock, and Freivalds, 2016; Mekler et al., 2017). Levels assist in setting goals leading to a smooth performance improvement.

Meaningful Stories

This technique attempts to bring meaning into otherwise simple tasks and questions to complete a goal. Adding a story to an activity can be as simple as forging a compelling title or even building a complete storyline as those found in role-playing games (Kapp, 2012). Meaningful stories can increase the motivation and interest of users as a compelling story can intrigue one's interest.

Progress Bar

Progress bars, like most gamification techniques, have been used mainly to increase the motivation and engagement of learners in an activity as they can track their progression. Another use of progress bars is to measure the contribution of each member within a group activity and better visualize their overall involvement (Ding et al., 2018; Roosta, Taghiyareh, and Mosharraf, 2016).

Avatars

Avatars usually represent the users inside the gamified environment (Werbach and Hunter 2015), created or selected by them. They can be from simple images to 3D models, and their goal is to serve as an alternative identity within the gamified environment with that the user will interact through it(Annetta, 2010).

Teammates

This technique mainly seeks to bolster cooperation within a group, addressing users into teams with the requirement to work together to achieve a common goal. (Werbach and Hunter 2015).

Game-Based Learning

In contrast to gamification, game-based learning employs a game as a means of instruction, allowing users to learn by playing. In game-based learning, the player is assigned tasks to complete, and the points or levels are just an extra element of the game, and they do not act as the primary motivational engine for the user (Poultsakis, Papadakis, Kalogiannakis & Psycharis, 2021). Through game-based learning, learners can develop soft skills such as leadership, team and time management, as they are called to solve problems to advance through the game (Sousa and Rocha 2017; Katsaris & Vidakis, 2021). Game-based learning promotes enjoyable conditions that lead learners to be more creative (Mahayuddin and Saif 2020). There are three perspectives on game-based learning theory (Sousa and Rocha 2017). The first perspective identifies the learning as a result of playing a game. In this approach, learning is perceived through game technologies (Gee, 2003; Prensky, 2003). The second perspective considers pedagogical theories and game technologies and believes that the learning is achieved not only through the game but also through complementary activities completed along with the game (Barianos, Papadakis & Vidakis, 2022). The third perspective utilizes game mechanics and gamifies the learning process, focussing on innovating the learning experience through game design ideas (Kapp, 2012).

Criticism

Although gamification offers many positive aspects to learning, some reports support the opinion that gamification can also produce adverse effects (Lazarinis, Boididis, Kozanidis & Kanellopoulos, 2022). These negative effects can be due to some users' unfamiliarity with the gamified content (Ding et al., 2018). Furthermore, it can be unmotivating as users get frustrated or lose confidence when their performance is lower than desired (Vidakis et al., 2019). Additionally, studies on gamification in online training and GBL suggest that users can develop negative feelings, poor relationships, and anxiety while collecting points and rewards rather than focusing on the learning content itself (Alabbasi, 2018). Another study in GBL shows that the students can ignore the learning material to win the game (Guribye, Wake, and Wasson 2014). Nadolny et al. (2017) study the effects of game mechanics in academic grades to present which mechanics are more effective in each grade and which are not (Nadolny et al., 2017).

STATE-OF-THE-ART TECHNOLOGIES AND FRAMEWORKS

Technology can act as a medium to deliver educational content to learners in an intriguing and more personalized way. Technology has been rapidly evolving in recent years, and youngsters are more comfortable using it. Advancements in communication, collaboration, sharing content, and more are some contributions that technology has offered (Saleem, Noori, and Ozdamli 2022). Education has also started adapting to a technological approach to take advantage of these new capabilities, gamification elements, and gaming concepts (Bouchrika et al., 2021). This section presents state-of-the-art technologies combined with gamification techniques to achieve an elevated learning experience.

Extended Reality in Education

Extended reality is an umbrella term that holds technologies like Augmented Reality (AR), Virtual Reality (VR), Mixed Reality (MR), and, more broadly, any combination of real-virtual environments. Such technologies allow users to completely immerse themselves in a virtual world and interact with the artificially created environment. This can be a great benefit because educators can create virtual content as field trips and allow students to experience and explore the environment in places that would otherwise be difficult or impossible to visit (Cheng and Tsai 2020). Through MR and AR, a combination of the natural and virtual world, it is achieved the ability to enrich the physical world with virtual 3D objects, images, or sounds. This added material displayed in the real world can help students understand many laborious topics as they can see their effects in real-time and interact with them (Cai et al., 2017; Laine et al., 2016). A distinguished advantage and one of the reasons that AR is highly adopted in education is the low cost of the required devices. The only requirement for such technology to run is a relatively new smart device.

Location-Based Games

Location-based games (LBG) push users to move to pre-defined locations of interest to complete tasks and advance in-game (Lehmann, 2012). LBGs rely mainly upon the global positioning system (GPS) to locate places or users' positions. These games are targeted toward mobile devices as they require the constant movement of the user. The leading premise of these games is that players integrate information and physical activities that occur in the real world, particularly in educationally valuable locations such as historic city centres (Papadakis et al., 2020). LBGs can serve both academic and pedagogical purposes. Such games (Vidakis, Syntychakis, Kostantinos Kalafatis, et al. 2015) are ludic and blend learning with enjoyment. The properties of such games reinforce the capacity to engage users in meaningful indoor and outdoor learning activities (Wijers, Jonker, and Drijvers 2010). LBGs combination with AR is a very intriguing topic as a user can move into a location and experience the history of the place through AR.

Physical Hand Interaction and Natural User Interfaces (NUI)

Physical hand interaction and Natural User Interfaces provide an alternative way of interacting with digital content in XR environments. Users have the freedom to use their hands, similar to how they complete everyday tasks. This enables a more natural interaction without using different devices such as a keyboard and mouse, which alone require further training or familiarization to operate (Christinaki, Vidakis, and Triantafyllidis 2014). There are many techniques to achieve such interaction. All of them depend on recognizing and tracking the user's hands, a task that is a very challenging problem in the scientific community. Devices for tracking the hands alone, such as Leap Motion, have been developed, as have devices capable of tracking the entire human body, such as Microsoft Kinect. A modern approach to this problem incorporates machine learning and computer vision algorithms to track the hands through an RGB or RGB-D camera (Ahmad et al., 2019).

Personalize Content and Content Builders

It is important to note, especially as the world is moving toward digitization, that there is an increasing necessity for frameworks and platforms that assist educators or teachers in creating digital educational material and guide them throughout the process to ensure that the desired outcome is served (Vidakis et al., 2020). Furthermore, such platforms and frameworks have the potential to gather information about users, for example, their preferences and performance. This information can be processed to provide more personalized content to the user. The ability of information retrieval from educational platforms is an essential aspect of education as the student can receive educational content that represents the methods and format that can better understand and perceive (Vidakis, Syntychakis, Konstantinos Kalafatis, et al. 2015).

RESEARCH

This chapter presents various existing research employing gamification techniques and game-based learning to enhance the learning experience. The purpose of the applications is to furnish an appealing environment for the users to learn the material. To achieve this, technologies such as AR, the creation of virtual worlds, location-based techniques, and alternative means of interaction. Such means of interaction involve those of physical hand-virtual object interaction using a Kinect device or by recognizing a hand through an RGB camera. The authors created the applications in this section to provide alternative methods for learners to explore topics excitingly and engagingly. These applications consider the gamification above technics and utilize state-of-the-art technologies and hardware to deliver educational content.

Heraklion Fortification Gates LBG

The fortification gates of Heraklion are part of the Venetian Walls of the city, and they are among the best-preserved gates in Europe and comprise one of the main attractions in the city. The "Heraklion Fortification Gates LBG" (Vassilakis et al., 2018) application implements AR and GPS technologies to prompt users to explore Heraklion city enjoyably. The basic flow of the gamified application (Figure 1) when a user downloads and opens the application is to wait for the application to find the user's location from GPS and give navigation instructions for a specific location. While the user searches for the location, the application displays information concerning this location on the smart device's screen.

Upon arrival at the location, the user must scan the area to find a pattern that will present a 3D object on the screen in an AR environment setting. When the pattern is found, a multiple-choice question (Figure 2) will also be displayed on the screen that the user has to answer. Finally, the user is asked to take a selfie before moving to the following location. When all places are visited, the user can see the correct answers to the previously asked questions and the selfies captured.

The application was developed using the Unity3D Game Engine (Unity n.d.) and the Vuforia5 (Vuforia n.d.) library to enable AR functionality and execution for smart devices. The GPS method was used for the user's position as it offers high accuracy. A flow diagram of the application is shown in Figure 3. The application is built on "Search and Find", a typical build pattern in Location-based games. The application gives instructions to navigate the users to specific locations.

Figure 1. Example flow through the screens of the application

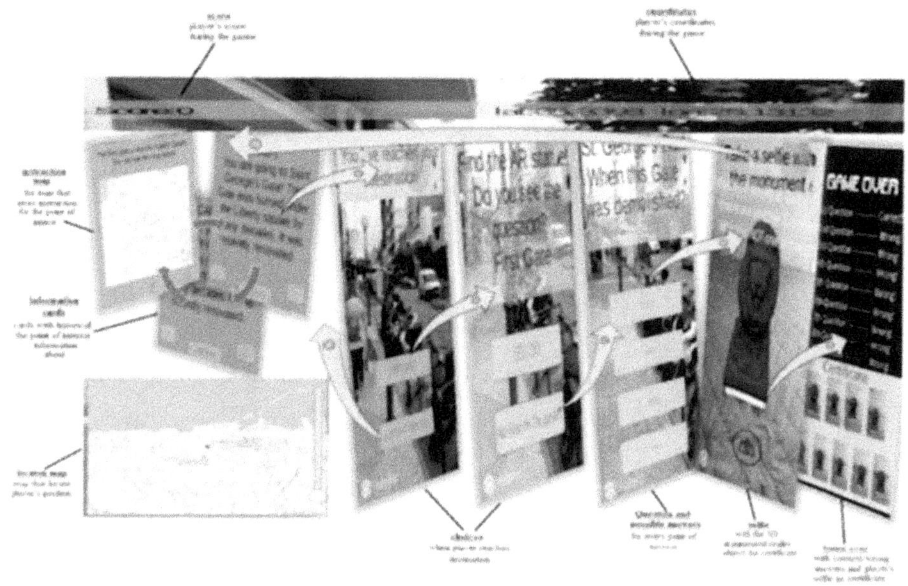

While the user searches for the following location, the information presented to the user has various forms, such as text, videos, and images about this point of interest. Switching between instructions about the location and the information presentations is available during the searching process. When the player reaches the location, a notification indicating the arrival is triggered, and the user has to search for the pattern or select to abandon the search (Figure 4). If the user does not wish to search for the pattern, a uestionn is shown immediately instead of the 3D object. After answering the question, the user can take a selfie at the point with the AR object regardless of the previous choice of searching for it or not. For each correct answer, the user is awarded one point added on a simple scoring system and with none if the answer is wrong. Additionally, the user loses a point if he does not find the AR object.

Figure 2. From left to right: quiz question with AR, quiz question without AR, selfie with the 3D object, the final score

Figure 3. Flow diagram

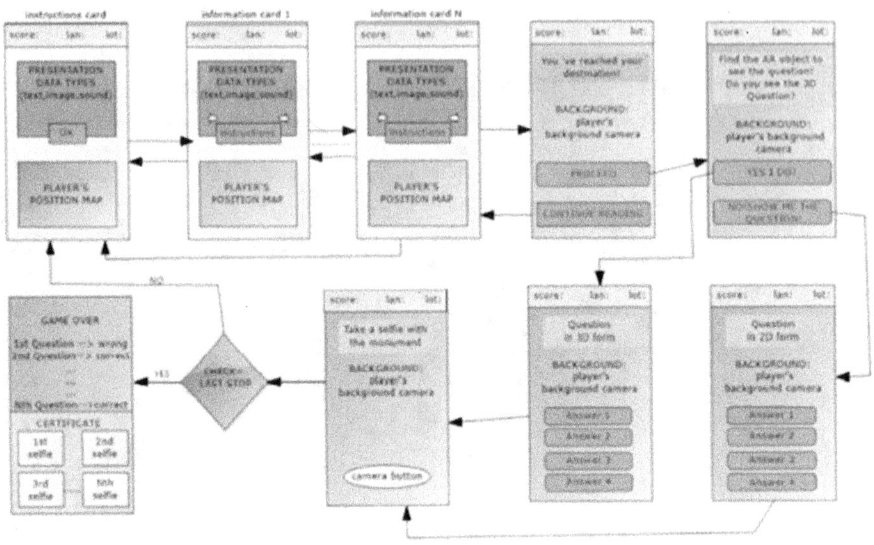

Figure 4. Navigation & information presentation and select whether to search for the object or proceed to the question

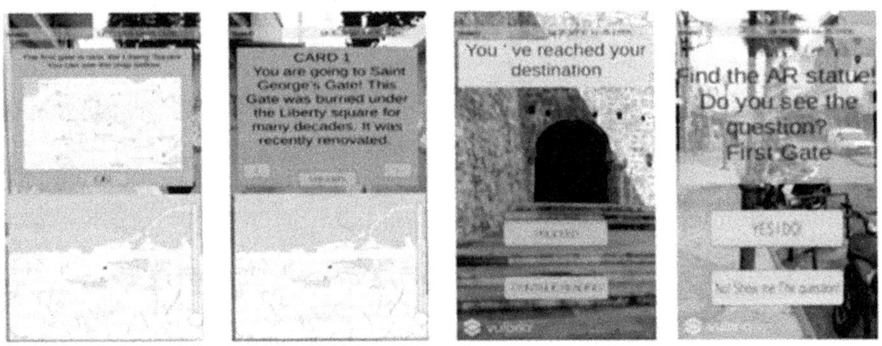

A Novel Educational Game for teaching Emotion Identification Skills to Preschoolers with Autism Diagnosis

Aiming to aid children with Autistic Spectrum Disorder (ASD) in recognizing and learning about emotions, a gesture-based serious game is proposed (Christinaki et al., 2014). The game is played on a computer using physical interaction for navigation and interaction within the game. The game includes traditional methodologies, visual support, positive reinforcement, and reward. To offer a comfortable environment for children with minimal distractions, the game environment is simple with a white background, context coloured in black and grayscale stimuli. Instructions are given at the beginning of the game to let the

Figure 5. Instruction Page sample

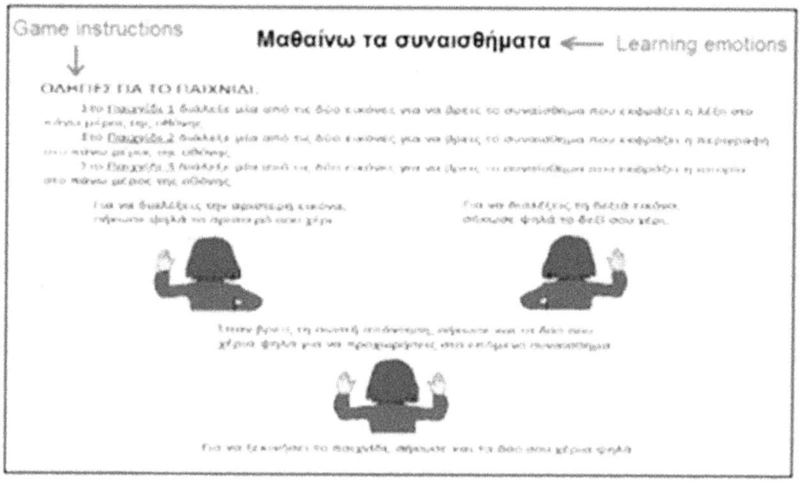

children know what and how to complete the tasks. The instructions are given both in text and audio (Figure 5). The child can start the game when the instructions are well understood.

There are three levels of increasing difficulty. The first level (Figure 6) aims to teach the children to associate emotions between texts and images. The second level recognizes emotions from their description and facial features. The third level steps further into understanding emotions and aims to teach the children to identify why an emotion can occur in various scenarios. This is provided as social stories. These levels aim to issue recognition, matching, observation, understanding, and generalization of facial emotions; these elements are extracted from Kolb's learning and Piaget's cognitive models.

The images used for the game are taken from the California Facial Expressions (CAFE) (M. N. Dailey n.d.) dataset and comprise 15 grayscale pictures of male and female faces. The emotions selected for this game are those of happiness, sadness, anger, fright, and surprise, as those are the most possible for children at a young age to recognize. The game uses Microsoft Kinect for the physical interaction within the game as it can track movement and offers reliable results in skeleton tracking. It provides a Software Development Kit (SDK) compatible with the C# programming language. The game was implemented using C# within XNA Game Studio with the addition of XNA libraries for the graphics.

The game offers a natural user interface controlled by hand gestures removing the need for a keyboard and a mouse. All the interaction needed for the game is performed with three actions: choosing the left or right image or continuing to the next. The gestures for these actions are related to the action itself, meaning that for choosing the left or right image, the player needs to move the corresponding hand above the head, and for the following image action, it is required to raise both hands above the head.

While the game is in progress, it informs the player about the correct and incorrect selections by visual and audio feedback, rewarding the player with a "Bravo" and changing the colour of the image into green or cheering to try again, saying ", Try again" and changing the colour of the image into red upon a wrong selection.

Figure 6. First level example (wrong selection)

ThimelEdu

A complementary tool for teaching ancient theatre architecture (Vidakis et al., 2018) was created to trigger students' interest in the topic by providing an alternative to the traditional methods. This approach allows a student to experience a 3D world with an ancient theatre and the landscape around it. The navigation in this virtual world is in first-person and supports a single player, meaning that a user is interacting in the environment alone without other users. While in this world, the user can roam freely to explore ancient theatre artefacts located around the world and interact with them to acquire more information about them and their role in the ancient theatre. Additionally, the user is called to complete quizzes during the interaction process.

The virtual world is created in Unity 3D Game Engine and designed to support adaptably personalized and customizable content through the IOLAOS's framework and API (Vidakis et al., 2014).

The main interface of this application remains simple (Figure 7), showing only necessary information to the user, such as a mini-map that shows the points of interest around the ancient theatre, the score of the user, a helper menu, and the user's information. The points of interest are shown in three different colours (Figure 8) that annotate the state of the point; blue if the point is not visited yet, green if it is visited and the quiz is completed correctly, and red if the quiz outcome was wrong.

The information presented to users during their interaction with the various artefacts inside the world is designed to handle many forms of data. A dialogue box on the screen holds all the necessary information about an artefact in the available forms of data, such as articles, images, and other media. The ability to switch between each available media for the artefact and study it for as long as the user requires (Figure 9) is supported. Furthermore, real-time text adjustments are supported to enable the user to customize the size and style of the text.

A similar dialogue box is displayed for the quizzes about an artefact (Figure 10). These quizzes include questions of "True/False" or multiple-choice nature. Upon answering a question, the user gets visual and audio feedback that notifies the user if the answer was correct or wrong. For answering correct questions,

Figure 7. Graphical user interface: mock-up (left), In-Game main window (right)

Figure 8. In-game maps

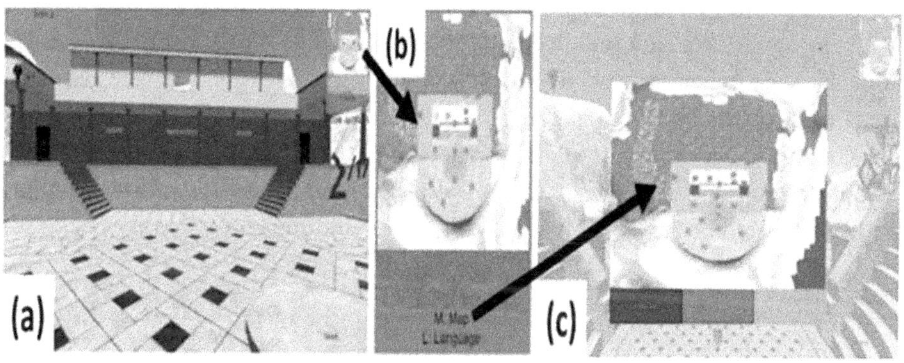

Figure 9. Dialog box showing information about artefacts

Figure 10. Dialog box for quiz questions

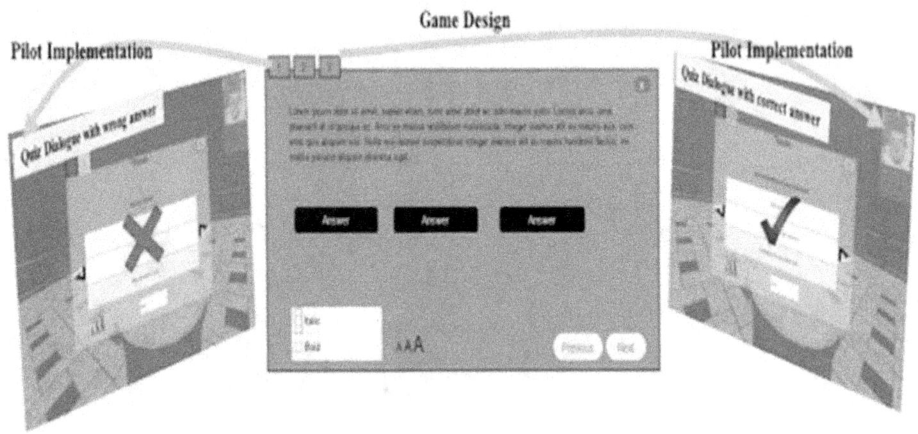

the user is awarded points that are added together to form a simple incremental scoring system. When the user answers all the questions correctly, the application ends, and rewards are provided to the user as a recognition of the acquired knowledge.

At the start of the application, automatic customization based on the user is triggered. There are three possible options: No customization when the user is a guest, aka there is no profile about this user; User with no preferences when the user has a partially completed profile through the IOLAOS platform; Full customization when the user has a complete profile through IOLAOS platform. There are also more customization options for users to tweak, offering a better game experience. Such customizations include shadows visibility, the field of view, brightness, text colour and more.

The Word Hangman Game

Another application aiming at the development of students' vocabulary around specific topics (recycling and covid19) and increasing their creativity by storytelling using the previously learned vocabulary was developed utilizing AR, GBR and gamification techniques to capture the attention of learners with this alternative presentation of the classic word game of hangman (Logothetis et al., 2021). For this application, technologies such as AR and physical interaction with virtual objects are incorporated to make the content more enjoyable and encourage the students to engage with the learning material actively.

The development is based on a custom tool created in Unity3D Game Engine and Python to facilitate the development of applications in AR environments and physical interaction. The tool's architecture is shown in Figure 11; it is separated into two modules, one that handles the hand recognition and one that provides components to create the desired application. The usage of sockets achieves the communication between the two components. As the name suggests, the "Hand Tracking Module" is responsible for recognizing where the hand is located in an image and sending the points that the hand is located to the "Unity Module". The "Unity Module" offers components such as a virtual hand visualization and functionality, gesture definitions, actions that can be taken using the hand, collision detection and other utility components like image acquisition through the device's camera.

Figure 11. Toolset architecture

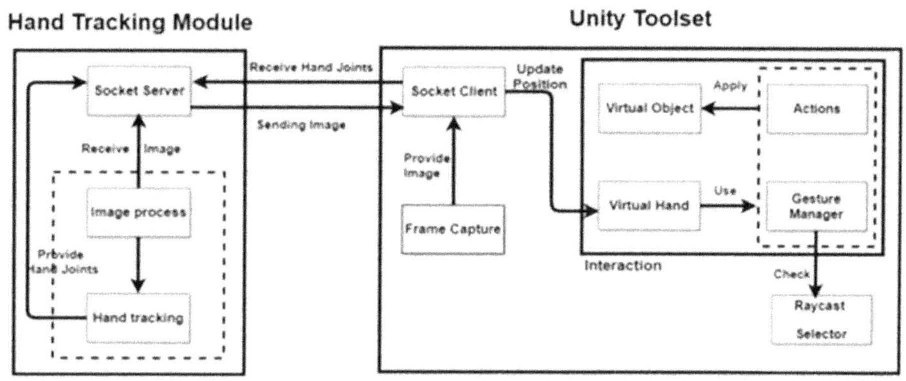

To bring off the goals of the application, two tasks are created. The first task involves the classic word game of hangman and is intended to support language learning, while the second aims to increase students' creativity by storytelling. The word hangman game is separated into five levels with increasing difficulty and contains a word that the student has to find. The word's first letter is filled from the beginning to navigate the student towards the possible answer. The rest of the letters are presented with the underscore symbol that indicates the number of letters the word contains. A set of letters are provided below the word to guess so the student can "grab" with their hands (Figure 12) and move into the correct position.

When the student completes the word, an image with the word is displayed on the screen (Figure 13), and the game moves on to the next level. The next word is of increased difficulty regarding the letters the words contain.

To correctly guess the word, the student has five tries, and as extra assistance, an image showing the object describing the word is displayed to the student after two wrong letter placements. The option to retry the level is provided additionally to encourage the student to try again and complete all five levels in the end. If the retry option is selected, the letters available to the student for placement are more accessible as extra help.

The student correctly guesses each word, and the student is awarded a card (Figure 14) with an image describing the word found. The goal is for the students to complete all levels because with the progression through levels, the student can better understand the game's topics. The completion of five levels is

Figure 12. Letter grab and movement

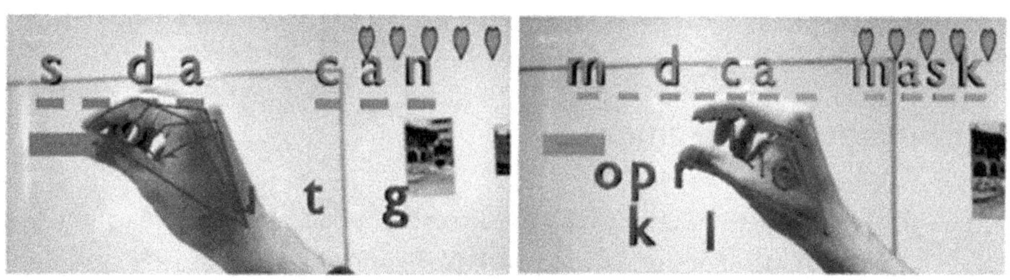

Figure 13. Completed word

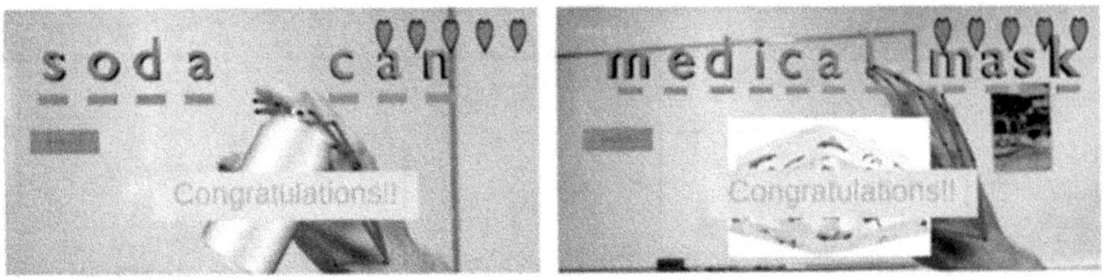

also essential because these cards will be used on the second task of the application; thus, each student should be awarded five cards by the end of the first task.

Figure 14. Rewarded paper cards

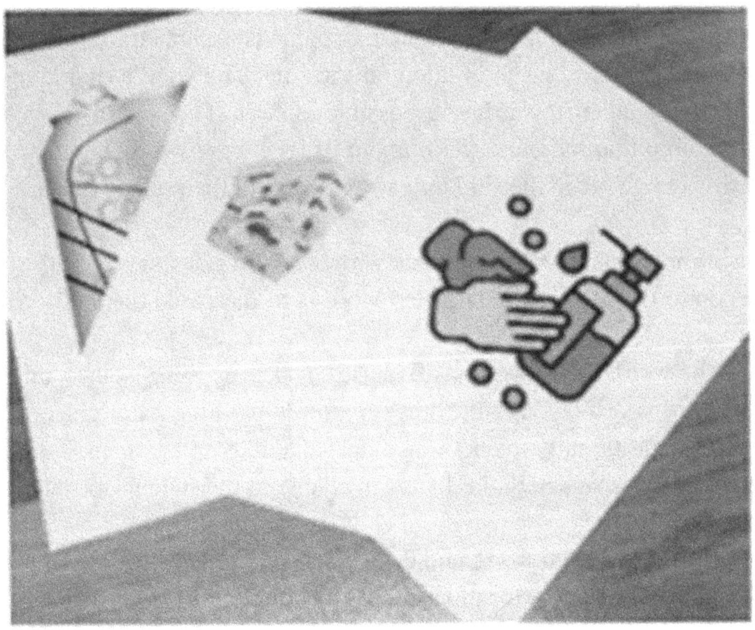

The second task calls the students to place the cards previously collected around the classroom and create a story. While storytelling, the student can move around the cards with a mobile device and scan the cards to display a 3D virtual object of the item displayed in the card (Figure 15).

Concealing Education into Games

It is essential to be able to support someone that wants to create educational games and learning environments in general. To this end, developing a framework focusing on enhancing serious games' effective-

Figure 15. 3D objects during the storytelling process

ness for learners, educators, and parents is fundamental. The Open Authorable Digital Adaptive and Ludic platform (Vidakis, Syntychakis, Konstantinos Kalafatis, et al. 2015) implements a framework that seeks to codify educational methods, learning styles and the generation of educational games based on the requirements and skills and learning goals.

The overall architecture of the platform is shown in Figure 16. The modules of the Open Authorable Digital Adaptive and Ludic platform are the following:

1. **Abstract Educational Game Model – Protocol (AEGM-P):** This module is responsible for holding the guidelines on how a serious game prototype should be created. It utilizes the functionality of the other modules to be of service in the corresponding role, for example, personalizing the

Figure 16. Open authorable digital adaptive and ludic platform architecture

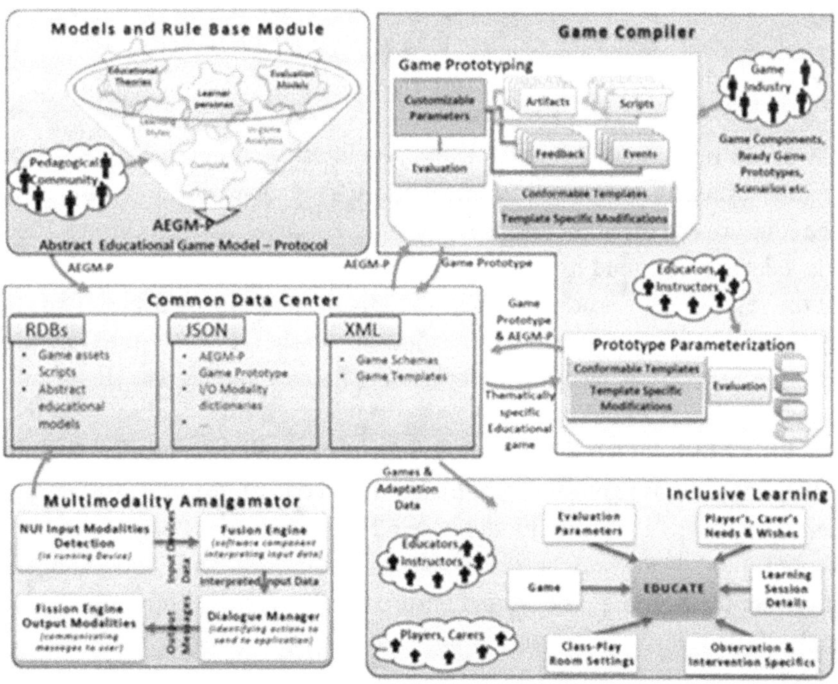

Figure 17. Game compiler module rewarding scenes

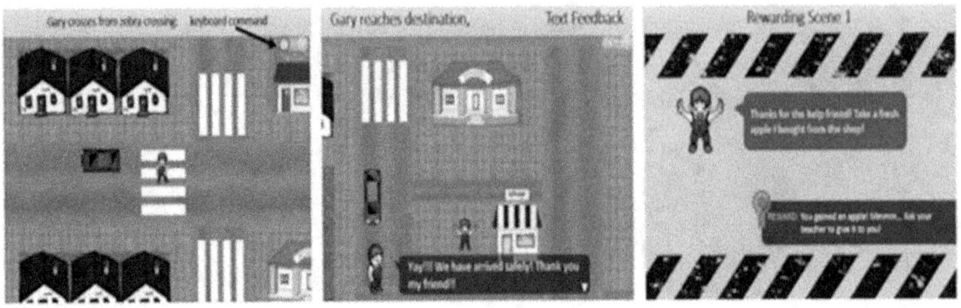

content of learners and adjusting the game specifications to match the educational standards of an individual.

2. **Common Data Center:** Responsible for holding the data of the platform. It can support various data storing formats like RDBs, OWL and JSON.
3. **Multimodality Amalgamator (MA):** This component detects the user's device so it can adapt to different inputs and produce the correct output for the user.
4. **Models and Rule Base Module (MRB):** Within this module are contained services to store, retrieve and modify through an API and a graphical user interface (GUI), information such as Learning styles, pedagogical methods, and cognitive limitations. The API allows modifications on run time, while the GUI offers a simple environment for the educator to add new material through four simple steps. Progressing through these steps, the educator defines the basic information such as name, description and learning styles, and information about which elements of the selected learning styles will be included. Evaluation, feedback, rewards, and penalty data are recorded based on the selections made on educational theories and learning styles. Finally, information about the target group is stored to better personalize the game's content, therefore serving a formal learning process.

Education – Training Session Module (ETS): Handles the functionality for the real-life session configuration. Services for observation, intervention and evaluation of the session are also included in this module. The educator can manage the learning session based on the target group's necessities through this module. The educator can send invitations to individuals upon the initiation of a session. After the initialization of the session, the session manager is responsible for the distribution of the game data and the communication between the invited students and the teacher. If not limited by the educator, each user can have different controls depending on the devices accessing the game (Figure 17 and Figure 18).

5. **Game Compiler Module (GC):** The contribution of this module is services for creating prototypes and personalizing serious games in compliance with the learning and user preferences. These two services are assigned to a separate module each. Figure 16 Game designers and educators use the game prototype module to yield their proposals and game prototypes. Tools are employed to guide the game creator through the process and ensure that the chosen options provided by the AEGM – P are not violated during the creation phase by prompting the creator to make changes if the content is not in compliance with a rule. The creator can adjust the background colour, characters,

Figure 18. Sample gameplay scenario

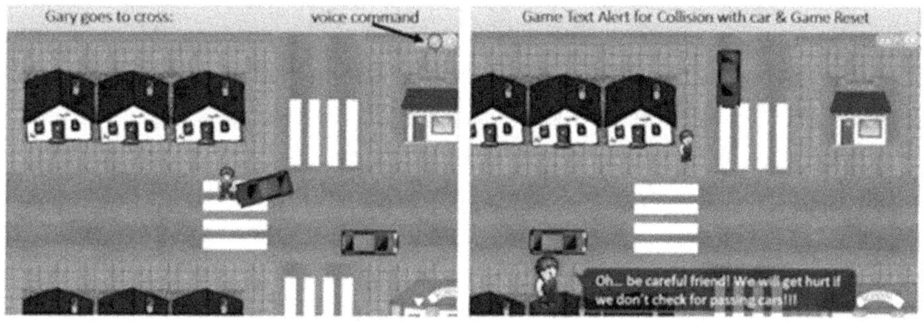

rewarding and evaluation systems, items and characters, and the game's general rules. I stored all this information in JSON format inside the CDC module to be available to be referenced in the future. After the prototype creation, the creator can always modify it to make it more suitable to the needs of the target users. The actual game can take shape when the prototype is customized correctly based on the AEGM – P. The creator uses an interface that makes the process within a few simple steps (Figure 19). Finally, the evaluation and rewarding systems are defined.

Figure 19. Game compiler module scene creation

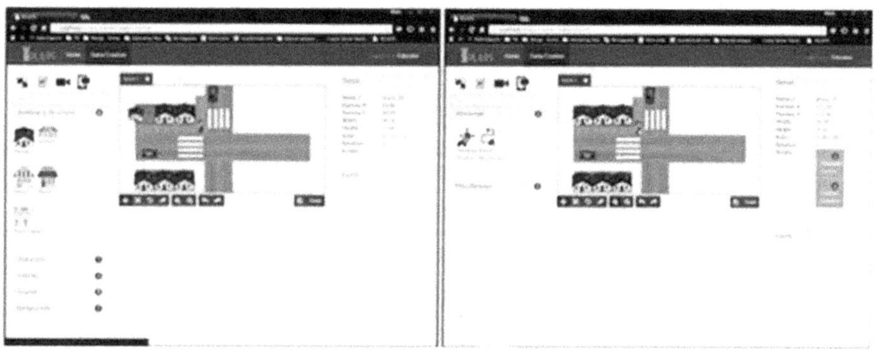

STUDIES AND RESULTS

The Word Hangman Game

A field study involving the transformed word hangman game into an AR game enriched with a second task, the task of storytelling, drawing inspiration from the words correctly completed from the previous step. The study involved 36 students, both boys and girls, who traditionally played the game using pen and paper, and the new version utilizes AR and physical hand interaction. The study shows that the students playing the game using modern technology enhance their involvement within the class, and learning goals are fulfilled enjoyably.

In detail, remarkable differences were observed in the task of storytelling. The students using technology developed their imagination further. They used the previously acquired cards, placed them around the classroom, and could actively present their story to their classmates. The collaboration between students strengthened as they started having conversations and expressing their thoughts about the subjects. A significant factor for their increased involvement, as observed, is the rewarding of the cards on the game's first task. In terms of vocabulary development, both the traditional and the AR games were the same result. The only difference between the two ways was the students' excitement about playing the game using AR.

Students that played the AR game presented a slightly better understanding of the topics of recycling and Covid 19. Students' awareness improved, and they started to suggest actions about the improvement of recycling and ways to better protect themselves and society in general from viruses. They also were more accepting of following the protocol about Covid 19 and were more precautious when using disinfectants and with their hygiene.

Educational Game for Teaching Emotion Identification Skills

This study explored interaction techniques that seek to eliminate the distraction introduced by interaction devices that require attention to operate. The focus falls on NUI devices to enhance engagement and effectiveness in learning task completion. This study explores the advantages of NUI devices and their impact on player involvement and performance. Moreover, it observes how such games can aid users' emotional state and their effects on their learning abilities. Finally, the player's cooperation behaviour is reviewed concerning the environment during the engagement with the game. A survey conducted throughout sessions was separated into five main sections. These sections include the emotional state, surroundings, the game, instructor acknowledgement before the session, and the game interaction.

The study's results show that NUI devices can improve the player's involvement, thus enhancing the overall learning process. Despite the environment changes, despite it being known that even small changes can seriously affect the game experience and process when using NUI devices, minor to no effect was observed. This confirms that such devices can offer an upgraded learning process. On the other hand, the player's emotional state can seriously affect the learning process, and such games cannot conquer this barrier.

DISCUSSION

Through this research, gamification techniques combined with modern technologies were presented in pursuit of enhancing the learning experience and increasing the engagement of learners (Papadakis, Kalogiannakis, Sifaki, & Vidakis, 2018). Merging technology with gamification techniques can produce compelling results that are capable of intriguing one's interest. Moreover, the authors present insights on how to combine gamification techniques and state-of-the-art technologies and what the resulting applications resemble. The experimental studies support the literature hypothesis that such techniques can increase students' motivation and engagement and help them develop soft skills such as this teamwork and collaboration (Zourmpakis, Papadakis & Kalogiannakis, 2022).

In detail, rewarding students for completing tasks increase their motivation and engagement. The reward can be relative to the theme of the task. This way, rewards gain meaning and let students process the learning material longer. Another exciting outcome of gamification and GBL is that the students can stay focused on the subject for more extended periods and external distractions have lower effects than traditional teaching techniques. Students and young people are attracted to technology alone can increase their interest. Using technology in the right way can offer great possibilities for learning, such as these virtual field trips to remote places or the simulations of complex devices. The utilization of technology has to be guided to not deviate from the educational purposes of the application. For this reason, guidelines and tools to assist educators and creators of educational material in creating such applications should be developed and explored.

REFERENCES

Ahmad, A., Migniot, C., & Dipanda, A. (2019). Hand Pose Estimation and Tracking in Real and Virtual Interaction: A Review. *Image and Vision Computing*, *89*, 35–49. doi:10.1016/j.imavis.2019.06.003

Alomari, I., Al-Samarraie, H., & Yousef, R. (2019). The Role of Gamification Techniques in Promoting Student Learning: A Review and Synthesis. *Journal of Information Technology Education*, *18*(08), 2019. doi:10.28945/4417

Annetta, L. A. (2010). The 'I's' Have It: A Framework for Serious Educational Game Design. *Review of General Psychology*, *14*(2), 105–113. doi:10.1037/a0018985

Barianos, A., Papadakis, A., & Vidakis, N. (2022). Content manager for serious games: Theoretical framework and digital platform. *Advances in Mobile Learning Educational Research*, *2*(1), 251–262. doi:10.25082/AMLER.2022.01.009

Bouchrika, I., Harrati, N., Wanick, V., & Wills, G. (2021). Exploring the Impact of Gamification on Student Engagement and Involvement with E-Learning Systems. *Interactive Learning Environments*, *29*(8), 1244–1257. doi:10.1080/10494820.2019.1623267

Brewer, R., Anthony, L., Brown, Q., Irwin, G., Nias, J., & Tate, B. (2013). Using Gamification to Motivate Children to Complete Empirical Studies in Lab Environments. In *Proceedings of the 12th International Conference on Interaction Design and Children, IDC '13*. Association for Computing Machinery. 10.1145/2485760.2485816

Burguillo, J. C. (2010). Using Game Theory and Competition-Based Learning to Stimulate Student Motivation and Performance. *Computers & Education*, *55*(2), 566–575. doi:10.1016/j.compedu.2010.02.018

Butler & Bodnar. (2017). *Establishing the Impact That Gamified Homework Portals Can Have on Students' Academic Motivation*. Academic Press.

Cai, S., Chiang, F.-K., Sun, Y., Lin, C., & Lee, J. J. (2017). Applications of Augmented Reality-Based Natural Interactive Learning in Magnetic Field Instruction. *Interactive Learning Environments*, *25*(6), 778–791. doi:10.1080/10494820.2016.1181094

Cheng, K.-H., & Tsai, C.-C. (2020). Students' Motivational Beliefs and Strategies, Perceived Immersion and Attitudes towards Science Learning with Immersive Virtual Reality: A Partial Least Squares Analysis. *British Journal of Educational Technology*, *51*(6), 2140–2159. doi:10.1111/bjet.12956

Christinaki, E., Vidakis, N., & Triantafyllidis, G. (2014). A Novel Educational Game for Teaching Emotion Identification Skills to Preschoolers with Autism Diagnosis. *Computer Science and Information Systems*, *11*(2), 723–743. doi:10.2298/CSIS140215039C

Chu, H.-C., & Hung, C.-M. (2015). Effects of the Digital Game-Development Approach on Elementary School Students' Learning Motivation, Problem Solving, and Learning Achievement. *International Journal of Distance Education Technologies*, *13*(1), 87–102. doi:10.4018/ijdet.2015010105

Dailey, M. N., Cottrell, G. W., & Reilly, J. (n.d.). *California Facial Expressions*. CAFE.

Davis, K., Sridharan, H., Koepke, L., Singh, S., & Boiko, R. (2018). Learning and Engagement in a Gamified Course: Investigating the Effects of Student Characteristics. *Journal of Computer Assisted Learning*, *34*(5), 492–503. doi:10.1111/jcal.12254

Deterding, S., Sicart, M., Nacke, L., O'Hara, K., & Dixon, D. (2011). Gamification. Using Game-Design Elements in Non-Gaming Contexts. In CHI '11 Extended Abstracts on Human Factors in Computing Systems, CHI EA '11. Association for Computing Machinery. doi:10.1145/1979742.1979575

Ding, L., Er, E., & Orey, M. (2018). An Exploratory Study of Student Engagement in Gamified Online Discussions. *Computers & Education*, *120*, 213–226. doi:10.1016/j.compedu.2018.02.007

Diniz, G. C., Graciotto Silva, M. A., Gerosa, M. A., & Steinmacher, I. (2017). Using Gamification to Orient and Motivate Students to Contribute to OSS Projects. *2017 IEEE/ACM 10th International Workshop on Cooperative and Human Aspects of Software Engineering (CHASE)*. 10.1109/CHASE.2017.7

Gee, J. P. (2003). What Video Games Have to Teach Us about Learning and Literacy. *Computers in Entertainment*, *1*(1), 20. doi:10.1145/950566.950595

Hew, K. F., Huang, B., Kai, W. S. C., & Chiu, D. K. W. (2016). Engaging Asian Students through Game Mechanics: Findings from Two Experiment Studies. *Computers & Education*, *92–93*, 221–236. doi:10.1016/j.compedu.2015.10.010

Huang, T.-C., Chen, C.-C., & Chou, Y.-W. (2016). Animating Eco-Education: To See, Feel, and Discover in an Augmented Reality-Based Experiential Learning Environment. *Computers & Education*, *96*, 72–82. doi:10.1016/j.compedu.2016.02.008

Kapaniaris, A., & Zampetoglou, G. (2021). Visual programming for the greation of digital shadow play performance using mobile devices in times of Covid-19. *Advances in Mobile Learning Educational Research*, *1*(2), 162–170. doi:10.25082/AMLER.2021.02.010

Kapp, K. M. (2012). *The Gamification of Learning and Instruction: Game-Based Methods and Strategies for Training and Education*. John Wiley & Sons.

Katsaris, I., & Vidakis, N. (2021). Adaptive e-learning systems through learning styles: A review of the literature. *Advances in Mobile Learning Educational Research*, *1*(2), 124–145. doi:10.25082/AMLER.2021.02.007

Kim, Rothrock, & Freivalds. (2016). The Effects of Gamification on Engineering Lab Activities. *2016 IEEE Frontiers in Education Conference (FIE)*.

Laine, T. H., Nygren, E., Dirin, A., & Suk, H.-J. (2016). Science Spots AR: A Platform for Science Learning Games with Augmented Reality. *Educational Technology Research and Development*, *64*(3), 507–531. doi:10.100711423-015-9419-0

Lazarinis, F., Boididis, I., Kozanidis, L., & Kanellopoulos, D. (2022). An adaptable multi-learner serious game for learning cultural heritage. *Advances in Mobile Learning Educational Research*, *2*(1), 201–215. doi:10.25082/AMLER.2022.01.004

Lehmann, L. A. (2012). *Location-Based Mobile Games*. Academic Press.

Logothetis, I., Papadourakis, G., Katsaris, I., Katsios, K., & Vidakis, N. (2021). Transforming Classic Learning Games with the Use of AR: The Case of the Word Hangman Game. In P. Zaphiris & A. Ioannou (Eds.), *Learning and Collaboration Technologies: Games and Virtual Environments for Learning* (pp. 47–64). Springer International Publishing. doi:10.1007/978-3-030-77943-6_4

Mahayuddin, Z. R., & Saif, A. F. M. S. (2020). Augmented Reality Based AR Alphabets towards Improved Learning Process in Primary Education System. *Journal of Critical Reviews*, *7*(19), 514–521.

Mekler, E. D., Brühlmann, F., Tuch, A. N., & Opwis, K. (2017). Towards Understanding the Effects of Individual Gamification Elements on Intrinsic Motivation and Performance. *Computers in Human Behavior*, *71*, 525–534. doi:10.1016/j.chb.2015.08.048

Nah, F. F.-H., Zeng, Q., Telaprolu, V. R., Ayyappa, A. P., & Eschenbrenner, B. (2014). Gamification of Education: A Review of Literature. *International conference on HCI in business*. 10.1007/978-3-319-07293-7_39

Papadakis, S. (2021). Advances in Mobile Learning Educational Research (A.M.L.E.R.): Mobile learning as an educational reform. *Advances in Mobile Learning Educational Research*, *1*(1), 1–4. doi:10.25082/AMLER.2021.01.001

Papadakis, S., Kalogiannakis, M., Sifaki, E., & Vidakis, N. (2018). Evaluating Moodle use via Smart Mobile Phones. A case study in a Greek University. *EAI Endorsed Transactions on Creative Technologies, 5*(16).

Papadakis, S., Trampas, A., Barianos, A., Kalogiannakis, M., & Vidakis, N. (2020). Evaluating the Learning Process: The "ThimelEdu" Educational Game Case Study. In *Proceedings of the 12th International Conference on Computer Supported Education* - Volume 2. CSEDU. 10.5220/0009379902900298

Poultsakis, S., Papadakis, S., Kalogiannakis, M., & Psycharis, S. (2021). The management of Digital Learning Objects of Natural Sciences and Digital Experiment Simulation Tools by teachers. *Advances in Mobile Learning Educational Research*, *1*(2), 58–71. doi:10.25082/AMLER.2021.02.002

Prensky, M. (2003). Digital Game-Based Learning. *Computers in Entertainment*, *1*(1), 21. doi:10.1145/950566.950596

Radu, I. (2014). Augmented Reality in Education: A Meta-Review and Cross-Media Analysis. *Personal and Ubiquitous Computing*, *18*(6), 1533–1543. doi:10.100700779-013-0747-y

Roosta, F., Taghiyareh, F., & Mosharraf, M. (2016). Personalization of Gamification-Elements in an e-Learning Environment Based on Learners' Motivation. *2016 8th International Symposium on Telecommunications (IST)*. 10.1109/ISTEL.2016.7881899

Sailer, M., Hense, J. U., Mayr, S. K., & Mandl, H. (2017). How Gamification Motivates: An Experimental Study of the Effects of Specific Game Design Elements on Psychological Need Satisfaction. *Computers in Human Behavior*, *69*, 371–380. doi:10.1016/j.chb.2016.12.033

Saleem, A. N., Noori, N. M., & Ozdamli, F. (2022). Gamification Applications in E-Learning: A Literature Review. *Technology, Knowledge and Learning*, *27*(1), 139–159. doi:10.100710758-020-09487-x

Schechter, R., Macaruso, P., Kazakoff, E. R., & Brooke, E. (2015). Exploration of a Blended Learning Approach to Reading Instruction for Low SES Students in Early Elementary Grades. *Computers in the Schools*, *32*(3–4), 183–200. doi:10.1080/07380569.2015.1100652

Seaborn, K., & Fels, D. I. (2015). Gamification in Theory and Action: A Survey. *International Journal of Human-Computer Studies*, *74*, 14–31. doi:10.1016/j.ijhcs.2014.09.006

Sousa, M. J., & Rocha, Á. (2017). Game Based Learning Contexts for Soft Skills Development. *World Conference on Information Systems and Technologies*. 10.1007/978-3-319-56538-5_92

Suh, A., Wagner, C., & Liu, L. (2018). Enhancing User Engagement through Gamification. *Journal of Computer Information Systems*, *58*(3), 204–213. doi:10.1080/08874417.2016.1229143

Téllez Alarcia & Iturriaga Barco. (2014). Videojuegos y aprendizaje de la historia: La saga Assassin's Creed. *Contextos Educativos, 17*.

Unity. (n.d.). Retrieved March 11, 2022 (https://unity.com/)

Vassilakis, K., Charalampakos, O., Glykokokalos, G., Kontokalou, P., Kalogiannakis, M., & Vidakis, N. (2018). Learning History Through Location-Based Games: The Fortification Gates of the Venetian Walls of the City of Heraklion. In A. L. Brooks, E. Brooks, & N. Vidakis (Eds.), *Interactivity, Game Creation, Design, Learning, and Innovation* (pp. 510–519). Springer International Publishing. doi:10.1007/978-3-319-76908-0_49

Vidakis, Christinaki, Serafimidis, & Triantafyllidis. (2014). *Combining Ludology and Narratology in an Open Authorable Framework for Educational Games for Children: The Scenario of Teaching Preschoolers with Autism Diagnosis*. Academic Press.

Vidakis, N., Barianos, A. K., Trampas, A. M., Papadakis, S., Kalogiannakis, M., & Vassilakis, K. (2020). Game Raw Data Collection and Visualization in the Context of the "ThimelEdu" Educational Game. In H. C. Lane, S. Zvacek, & J. Uhomoibhi (Eds.), *Computer Supported Education. CSEDU 2019. Communications in Computer and Information Science* (Vol. 1220). Springer. doi:10.1007/978-3-030-58459-7_30

Vidakis, N., Barianos, K. A., Xanthopoulos, G., & Stamatakis, A. (2018). Cultural Inheritance Educational Environment: The Ancient Theatre Game Thimeledu. *Proceedings of the European Conference on Games-Based Learning*, 730–39.

Vidakis, N., Syntychakis, E., Kalafatis, K., Christinaki, E., & Triantafyllidis, G. (2015). *Ludic Educational Game Creation Tool: Teaching Schoolers Road Safety. Academic Press.*

Vidakis, N., Syntychakis, E., Kalafatis, K., Varhalamas, P., & Triantafyllidis, G. (2015). Concealing Education into Games. *Proceedings of the European Conference on Games-Based Learning*, 554–63.

Vidakis, N., Barianos, A., Trampas, A., Papadakis, S., Kalogiannakis, M., & Vassilakis, K. (2019). Generating Education in-Game Data: The Case of an Ancient Theatre Serious Game. In *Proceedings of the 11th International Conference on Computer Supported Education - Volume 1*. CSEDU. doi:10.5220/0007810800360043

Vuforia. (n.d.). *Vuforia Engine Developer Portal*. Retrieved March 11, 2022 https://developer.vuforia.com/

Wang, A. I., & Lieberoth, A. (2016). The Effect of Points and Audio on Concentration, Engagement, Enjoyment, Learning, Motivation, and Classroom Dynamics Using Kahoot. *European conference on games based learning*, 20.

Wang, H., & Sun, C.-T. (2011). Game Reward Systems: Gaming Experiences and Social Meanings. DiGRA Conference, 114.

Werbach, K., & Hunter, D. (2015). *The Gamification Toolkit: Dynamics, Mechanics, and Components for the Win*. University of Pennsylvania Press.

Wijers, M., Jonker, V., & Drijvers, P. (2010). MobileMath: Exploring Mathematics Outside the Classroom. *ZDM*, *42*(7), 789–799. doi:10.100711858-010-0276-3

Zourmpakis, A.-I., Papadakis, St., & Kalogiannakis, M. (2022). Education of Preschool and Elementary Teachers on the Use of Adaptive Gamification in Science Education. *International Journal of Technology Enhanced Learning*, *14*(1), 1–16. doi:10.1504/IJTEL.2022.120556

Section 3

Digital Humanities: Online Communities, Digital Storytelling, Libraries, and Museums

Chapter 13
A Methodological Guide for the Study of Online Communities

Alkistis Dalkavouki
National Technical University of Athens, Greece

ABSTRACT

The chapter will instruct readers into the fundamentals of online social research, filling a vital, instructional gap in the literature. After a summary of the theoretical path towards digital ethnography and a description of the discipline's overall strengths, the chapter will begin a practical breakdown of the research planning and execution processes. This will follow the following steps: preparation and entrée, sample design, quantitative and qualitative methods of data collection, and ethical considerations. All the above will be informed by the researcher's own experience and will be geared towards under- or post-grad anthropology and ethnography students with some experience with online spaces.

INTRODUCTION

Digital research is becoming increasingly popular in a variety of fields –folklore included–and yet it often appears confusing to the uninitiated. Despite digital ethnography and its methodologies becoming more widespread in recent years, instructions for them are either too broad –e.g., in dedicated manuals– or too narrow –e.g., focusing on specific categories or aspects of research. The solution is the proposal of a general roadmap for younger researchers, which is what this chapter aims to be.

As disciplines, ethnography and folklore studies have abandoned traditional fieldwork in a single site; the Internet, in particular, has offered tantalizing opportunities for study. Researchers can use the new tools at their disposal to discover new cultural worlds, observe small populations discreetly and connect their findings to even greater patterns of activity. However, this can prove chaotic for newcomers. Moreover, basic research templates do exist for traditional ethnography, but they have yet to be proposed for online research, except for individual pieces of advice.

This chapter will provide a general guideline for research into online communities, by consolidating its general theoretical background with a practical breakdown and additional suggestions. This proposal aims to fill the lack of sources for digital humanities studies and ethnographic research with digital media

DOI: 10.4018/978-1-6684-4461-0.ch013

and data, as it has yet to be systematized, thus fitting with the publication's intended use as a teaching manual or teaching enrichment material for digital humanities. It will be supported by an example research project which used online ethnographic methodologies to study an online culture. The chapter will be best suited for under- or post-grad students who have some familiarity with online spaces and etiquette. In particular, those studying anthropology and ethnography and with some knowledge of ethnographic fieldwork will benefit the most.

LITERATURE REVIEW

The following section will outline two topics: the evolution of the fieldwork on the Internet; and how the discipline has adapted to those changes. The first part will discuss how both changes within ethnography and the realization of some of its features made it ideal for online research. The second part will detail some fundamental changes, as well as the problems that have arisen for younger researchers.

The Theoretical Underpinnings of Online Research

This examination shall start with an overview of the theoretical underpinnings of online research, beginning with the very idea of the field and how it gradually changed. According to traditional definitions, the discipline aims to capture the "social meanings and ordinary activities" of people in "naturally occurring settings", which are commonly referred to as "the field" (Brewer, 2000). In practice, the researcher usually remained in a single-site location and reconstructed greater social frames from that experience. However, by the mid-1980s, scientists who wished to investigate more complex systems felt restrained. Thus, anthropology began to expand from single-sited to multi-sited fieldwork and observe more complex systems and interactions by the 1990s (Marcus, 1995). This was further accelerated by the Internet. Its emergence as a viable place of human interaction made it worthy of scientific interest and analysis (Kozinets et al., 2010), and it introduced a variety of new fields and methodological complexities (Wittel, 2000). The result is a complex field in need of new or modified research approaches.

At the same time, ethnography processes several traits that are uniquely suited to online spaces. As a discipline, it is known for the following: its qualitative, flexible, and context-sensitive approaches to cultural phenomena; its use of "thick description", which allows for the researcher's immersion and excavation of deep insights into specific cultural words; and the production of descriptive and analytical results alike. Moreover, close interaction with the research subjects is encouraged, to the point that the first identification of the community being studied is often followed by the researcher interacting with it and gaining "participant experience"[1] (Walstrom, 2004). The capture and analysis of these acts allow for an authentic, "enhanced cultural understanding, the confirmation of interpretation, and new opportunities to recast the research enterprise as collaboration rather than appropriation". The process can also be transparent by sharing the findings with the studied community for its benefit (Kozinets, Dolbec & Earley, 2014, p. 266), as well as by practicing "reflexivity", with the researcher aiming "to explore the ways in which [their] involvement with a particular study influences, acts upon and informs such research" (Nightingale & Cromby, 1999, p. 228). Finally, ethnography is extremely versatile, having been used to study a diverse array of subject matter, from pop culture fandoms (Reijnders, 2011) to communities of ill (Kleinman, 1992) and stigmatized (Collumbien et al., 2009) people.

Digital Ethnography: Adaptations and Approachability

With the addition of new considerations for ethical practice, cultural entrée, and data preparation (Kozinets, Dolbec & Earley, 2014), the discipline has adapted to become better suited theoretically and practically for the Internet, even with some resistance. Although various names have been proposed for the new methodology –the one used in this chapter will be "digital ethnography" (Murthy, 2008)[2]–, the result is the same: a toolset for the cultural analysis of online community data (Kozinets et al., 2010) resulting fast and discreet research, merging the traits of traditional ethnography with new ways of choosing field sites and collecting data, as well as new ethical considerations (Beaulieu, 2004). Even if members of the scientific community were slow to acknowledge its legitimacy (Kaur-Gill & Dutta, 2017) and there is a danger of missing out on the parallel component of "real-life" interactions, online ethnography is used with increasing regularity, combining ethnography's qualities with new responsibilities, "maintaining the cultural quality of the social media phenomenon through the careful consideration of the researcher's own role and social intelligence throughout the process of online social scientific research" (Kozinets, Dolbec & Earley, 2014, p. 275).

That said, the way these adaptations are communicated to new scientists can be problematic. Recent literature on online research follows one of two paths: they either constitute general manuals (Cleland, Dixon & Kilvington, 2019; Salmons, 2021) or zoom in on specific topics –e.g., focusing exclusively on aspects like qualitative methods (Bonfim, 2021), the ethical dimension of research (Chan et al., 2020) or any combination of specialized issues (Lester, 2020). As a result, there are few existing guidelines for young researchers who are interested in the field and its methodologies. This issue will be addressed in the next part, with the proposal of a plan for online research.

NET-WORKING: A BREAKDOWN OF ONLINE RESEARCH

This chapter's main focus is a step-by-step guideline for designing and executing an online ethnographic research methodology, with an emphasis on advice and examples. All parts are organized as follows: firstly, a summary of how the relevant topic has been discussed in the literature is presented; after that, a practical approach to the issues raised is elaborated on. The latter is done using a single study of an online pop culture fandom and its interactions with workers of its respective official cultural franchise[3] (Dalkavouki, 2018) as an example. The chapter will consider the process to start before final fieldwork and end with data collection, with special mention of proper research ethics online.

Fieldwork Preparation

Theoretical Overview

Before the *de facto* research work can begin, some preparatory steps need to be taken. The "traditional" ethnographic procedures of choosing a topic –often after an extensive literature review–, posing research questions/hypotheses, and sampling (Leavy, 2017) are still practiced and followed, but one needs to be aware of how the Internet can shape them. However, all processes and the subsequent project can be dramatically influenced by the scope and size of the group or phenomenon under study: a single topic can spawn multiple communities in different sites (Correll, 1995), and the size of one such community can complicate or simplify the social dynamics observed within it (Zhivov, Scheepers & Stockdale, 2011). An unclear definition of the studied community and data collecting strategies can, therefore, overwhelm the researcher (Garcia et al., 2009).

Thus, before embarking on the research proper, one must be sure that they are grasping the studied community and cultural context to avoid these problems; this is a prerequisite that began with traditional ethnography, but, with researchers now choosing their field sites and carefully planning their introductions (Kozinets et al., 2010), it has changed in its online counterpart. One of the most widely-used processes is "lurking", "a form of online reconnaissance – to gain information on the community before making the entrée" (Kozinets, Dolbec & Earley, 2013). It is often considered an important way of initial contact with a community (Shoham, 2004); it should, however, lead to further interactions with it, as there is a possibility of missing less visible pieces of the observed phenomenon (Beaulieu, 2004). As a result, the researcher enters a specific cultural space smoothly but also after some personal introspection (Cherny, 1999), like in any ethnographic research project. This initial, preparatory practice –which may include the observation of virtual spaces and the consumption of important cultural texts– will not only aid the researcher in narrowing the focus of their project into a manageable state and avoid "data overload" (Garcia et al., 2009) but also raise the chance of a successful entrée.

Practical Application

The above were actualized in the sample project as follows. The researcher was already aware of American comics production through literature and had personal experience with fandom culture[4]; choosing a general topic and some key research questions was quite easy. For the thesis in question and after an additional literature review period, the choice was narrowed down to a commercial yet relatively niche, multi-media cultural franchise with a stable pop-cultural presence and renewed fan interest due to certain recent successful titles. This would allow for a comparative qualitative study of the evolution of the property's culture from both the official and the amateur viewpoint over the last decade of production. Its cult status would also ensure that both populations were small enough to study, even if exact numbers were difficult to obtain.

However, preparing for engaging with that fandom entailed understanding their specific sub-culture; this was achieved both through "traditional" ethnographic preparation and lurking. The groundwork for the project included an extensive non-participant observation period. The researcher lurked through multiple virtual spaces frequented by the subjects: franchise-centric forums, fan fiction archives, social media platforms, fan-maintained encyclopedias and sites, etc. This proved vital in understanding facets of their culture, from their social hierarchy, composition, and rituals to their perception of the brand's history, as well as their specialized codes of communication and vocabulary. It also led to discovering the specific online spaces and social media platforms that subjects frequented the most, and thus narrowed the scope of the research. As new issues of the comic were released and more media were discussed with fans and professional creators alike, entrée proved to be a continuous and successful process, as it helped communicate with subjects later. In the end, this preparatory period provided an overall view of the subject matter's history, culture, and community before the researcher ventured into the more recent iteration's production and reception.

Lurking, in particular, was useful in improving the project in multiple ways. Firstly, an old, long-running fan art project was discovered, which would help in gathering data on the past synthesis of the fandom and if/how it has shifted in later years. Secondly, through it, it was discovered that multiple, prolific and current comics creatives –artists in particular– had previously been fans and contributed to amateur projects. Thirdly, through contact with individual fans as interlocutors[5], the researcher was able to determine the second population's size –about 10,000 to 20,000 active fans– and discover a link to the official side of content production –community members had the contact information of prolific artists and offered them to help the project. As a result, a final methodology was formulated: the creation of a quantitative sample of official creatives and fans to examine their geographic spread and demographic makeup, and the collection of descriptive, qualitative insights to complement and explain them, possibly from interviews. The above were paramount in locking down even more specific themes for study –the evolution of the official workforce and the fandom, as well as the relationship between the two–, focusing on specific research questions –how the official workforce changed, what its relationship with the fandom is and what factors affect one's transition from amateur to professional– and calculating an examined sample to get a complete picture of the fandom -talked about in more detail in the next part.

Sample Design and Subject Discovery

Theoretical Overview

After the preparatory period, the researcher needs to design a sample and discover specific subjects, a process that can get chaotic on the Internet; the first of the two tasks, and especially the creation of a statistically significant sample (Knoke & Yang, 2007), is the more standardized of the two and has been covered in extensively in other sources. The researcher begins by narrowing down a selection pool and describing the elements they wish to study. From them, two populations are defined, a general one and a study one; the latter will be used to draw the sample. Its number can vary greatly: it can sometimes be predetermined, or depend on the methodology used –quantitative research favors larger sample sizes, and the opposite is true of qualitative methods–, as well as the researcher's available time and budget. Usually, a few inputs –population size, confidence level, margin of error– are inserted in online sample size calculators; moreover, depending on the researcher's knowledge about the sample, additional methods can be used to design a sampling strategy –i.e., probability and purposeful sampling (Leavy, 2017). That said, although there are factors that affect the sample size –the depth and nature of the research topic, how homogeneous the studied population is, the depth of the analysis/interpretation attempted, and practical concerns–, there are no standard rules dictating the exact sample size. The researchers have to individually justify their choices in their texts (Roller & Lavrakas, 2015). This procedure continues until saturation, which happens when there are no more insights from additional data (Coffey, 1999).

One way of generating a representative sample, especially if that concerns a hard-to-reach population (Faugier & Sargeant, 1997), is the snowball technique. It has been described as an ascending methodology, a strategy "elaborated at a community or local level and specifically adapted to the study of selected social groups" which employs "selective and intensive" data collection (Van Meter, 1990). In its classic iteration, the methodology proceeds as follows. The researcher spots and communicates with a group of key interlocutors with certain desired characteristics called the "source" or "seed"; they, in turn, reach out to their own social networks for similar subjects and respondents. The same process is repeated with the new group of individuals, for as many stages as is needed. Though part of a larger group of link-tracing methodologies (Spreen, 1992) taking advantage of the (assumed) bonds between an initial sample and a target population (Atkinson & Flint, 2001), this approach is inspired by the image of a snowball rolling down a hill (Everitt & Howell, 2005) and "contact tracing", the process in which "one individual names all other individuals who were associated with a specific event" (Sadler et al., 2010) in public health; it has also been historically used to study underprivileged (Whyte, 2012), criminalized and stigmatized individuals (Kaplan, Korf, & Sterk, 1987; McNamara, 1994).

The traditional snowball technique processes significant upsides: it is inexpensive, relatively unobtrusive yet incisive, chain-referral and dependent on community knowledge and bonds, can combine qualitative and quantitative research practices, and follow the dynamic evolution of a phenomenon (Atkinson & Flint, 2001; Sadler et al., 2010), while also being capable of producing internationally comparable data (Avico et al., 1988). However, a few factors make it labor-intensive, unpredictable, and even prohibitive: the need for insider knowledge to locate the first batch of participants, usually from people in positions of authority or proximity to the examined population (Groger, Mayberry & Straker, 1999); its dependence on the initial research questions asked of the "seeds" (Atkinson & Flint, 2001); and the possibility of suspicion and hostility on the part of the subjects. Lastly, the method entails that trust is established between themselves and the studied community (Faugier & Sargeant, 1997).

The snowball technique's usefulness has only increased with its adaptation to online spaces. Some of those improved characteristics include a greater emphasis on communicating with the subjects (even personally); a broader definition of sources and collaborating with formal or informal "group leaders" (Sadler et al., 1998; Sadler et al., 2006); and easier networking and recruitment processes via targeted e-mails at individuals, institutions or official groups at social media platforms (Bowen, Williams & Horvath, 2004). These changes help overcome the traditional methodology's most egregious disadvantages: the generation of small (Atkinson & Flint, 2001), non-random, and demographically unbalanced samples biased towards upper-class, highly-educated individuals and their peers (Magnani et al., 2005); the omission of "isolates", people not connected to any network(s) discovered by the research (Van Meter, 1990) or facing geographical, transportation and financial barriers (Fahrenwald & Stabnow, 2005); the possible high refusal rate of participation due to the absence of a prior relationship with the community; the inability to spot whether the sample is "saturated" –when it offers no new information– or not (Sadler et al., 2010); and the amount of time and effort it takes to execute by a single researcher (Faugier & Sargeant, 1997). The above, therefore, have made the method ideal for spotting subjects, particularly when it is informed by the previous lurking.

Practical Application

The aforementioned framework of sample creation proceeded as follows for the example project. It was decided that the focus of the research would be on the franchise's online fandom, for convenience of access and study. Thanks to lurking, the researcher spotted the forums and social media platforms with the greatest concentrations of fans, and thus targeted them for a survey that examined the fandom's current demographic and geographic profile. The population size had already been determined by communicating with an initial group of interlocutors. As a result, the number of necessary survey answers was calculated to represent it, which was lowered from about 370 to 300 individuals due to a lack of budget. The online poll was circulated widely over the different platforms with the aid of the aforementioned interlocutors for a few weeks. The poll closed when the answers began to get saturated and repetitive, at 300 completed surveys.

Furthermore, although pop culture fans do not constitute a vulnerable group by this trait alone, they are narrowly defined and thus nearly indistinguishable from the rest of the populous; as a result, an online variation of the snowball technique would have to be used to uncover them. The initial source was a popular weekly podcast hosted by fans, which was spotted during the aforementioned lurking phase. The researcher reached out to two members of the team and asked for their collaboration in circulating the survey, to which they agreed. In turn, they pointed toward more individuals, who circulated the poll on social media platforms to bring more attention to it. The last survey question was the optional choice to participate in an interview –in more detail below–, where all interested parties would leave their contact information –i.e. their e-mail address. The final number of survey and interview participants was large enough to be considered statistically sufficient for the studied community, and thus no additional statistical manipulation was needed (Knoke & Yang, 2007).

Data Collection

Theoretical Overview

This part of the research involves the creation or collection of content by the researcher; it can be split into two very general methodologies –qualitative and quantitative–, but some very basic principles apply to both of them. Whichever methodologies are followed –writing fieldwork observations, conducting interviews, collecting other documents (Corbin & Strauss, 2008), or conducting experiments and creating surveys respectively (Leavy, 2017)– should be thorough. Subsequent data analysis, which should be grounded in them, can be performed in ways that are similar to those of "traditional" ethnography and sociology (Corbin & Strauss, 2008). However, it should be noted that several standard methods of collecting evidence or unpacking meaning –e.g., content analyses– (Leavy, 2017) have also been adapted to online standards, and so might require a different approach.

For this, two types of data have to be introduced and defined before moving forward: archival and field note data. The first is used to describe anything the researcher can gather online that was not a product of their involvement. They are used to create a "cultural baseline" for the subject matter and uncover the community's state before the researcher's incursion. The second type concerns notes created by the researcher directly throughout the project, and specifically to record the research, reflect upon it and analyze it. As such, those notes "document the journey of the netnographer from an outsider to an inside cultural member" (p. 268). They can also take any media form –text, image, audio, video, etc. This note-keeping should start as early as possible and continue throughout the duration of the project (Kozinets, Dolbec & Earley, 2013). Their usability as data can differ based on which methodology one chooses –quantitative or qualitative–, but both types are invaluable in completing an online ethnographic project.

What is also noteworthy is the possible variance and volume of the collected data and its impact on the research. Firstly, one has to keep in mind not to diffuse the conversation about a given topic into multiple spaces (Correll, 1995) or risk being incapable of following it. Furthermore, since the ethnographer's field can now include blog-like spaces, wikis, and social media sites, all of which have unique background research requirements (Kozinets, 2010), the availability of tools for automatically saving, sorting, classifying, and archiving media is tempting, but not advisable. While the use of management software –for downloading, classifying, or analyzing– can be incredibly useful, especially in cases of large amounts of data, it is up to the researcher to carefully define the scope of their project and exercise critical thinking (Corbin & Strauss, 2008). Nevertheless, data management should always be a concern, regardless of one's chosen methodology.

The first major branch of methodology worth examining is that of quantitative methods. "Traditional" methodologies such as experiments and surveys (Leavy, 2017) can be executed online with little alteration (Collins, Evans & Gorman, 2010; Murthy, 2008), and established online methodologies like data mining[6] can also be employed (Injadat, Salo & Nassif, 2016). What truly distinguishes online ethnography, however, is the ability to observe an online community without participating in it through freely available and public data. This requires rigorous note-taking –on both the observable materials and the researcher's own thoughts, in any form that suits the researcher and the project– and its frequent re-organization (Myers, 1999), as well as constant inspections, to manage the volume of data (Kozinets, 2010). Dedicated software can make downloading, classifying, and labeling data easier. However, since critical thinking and decision-making are paramount to the success of this process, its complete automation is inadvisable (Corbin & Strauss, 2008).

Similarly, several "traditional" qualitative methods are extensively used, from the in-depth interview to thick description (Van Dijk, 2001; Mack et al., 2005); the first one will be briefly analyzed first. The interview is a data collection technique with an open-ended and semi-structured (pre-planned yet conversational) format that can be applied to a variety of tasks. Its main use is for the comprehension and interpretation of a correspondent's feelings and opinions on a given subject. The interview is often recorded and complemented with the researcher's written notes, which can point to the interviewee's reactions or posit further questions (Mack et al., 2005). One way of conducting them is by following the subsequent seven-step template: thematizing (deciding on the purpose of the interviews and the key pieces of information wanted); designing (drafting an interview guide with questions and accompanying comments); interviewing (the process itself, which also includes explaining its context to the participants and easing them into the experience); transcribing (writing all spoken words and reactions down and producing a text); analyzing (re-reading the aforementioned and identifying discreet themes); verifying (confirming how credible the information stated in the text is); and reporting (distributing the results of the process via a report) (Kvale, 1996). Although the process can be long and demanding on the part of the researcher, the result is a deeper understanding of the subject matter, as well as starting topics for further research.

Online ethnography has also impacted the interview as a tool, allowing researchers to conduct it from a distance; the new name proposed for this tool is the "e-interview". Although the term is often used to describe e-mail correspondence (Bampton & Cowton, 2002), it can be used to refer to all interviews conducted through the Internet. This has impacted the tool in several ways, from the means of contacting subjects (Fast, 2012) to the complexity of online interactions –private/public, synchronous/asynchronous, over different geographic locations/time zones, with two or more contributors (Ruhleder, 2000), over different spaces and using different formats –text, image, audio, video, etc. The e-interview has many advantages over its traditional form: it can be faster and more economical; it connects geographically and socially distant subjects and allows for the inclusion of participants with schedule and face-to-face communication difficulties; it captures certain types of data; it makes the formulation of follow-up questions easier. At the same time, e-interviews require all parties to be willing and technology-literature to participate, a "limited register for communication", and the creation of backup files (Bampton & Cowton, 2002).

The full process for conducting efficient e-interviews, as outlined by Meho (2006), begins with an individual invitation to participants. This takes the form of an e-mail with an effective subject line. In it, the researcher should introduce themselves, offer background information on their project, highlight safety measures, and provide incentives for participation –e.g., a copy of the project's results. If the interview is to be conducted through a written questionnaire, instructions and deadlines should be included and the queries should be as clear and interesting as possible. If possible, this process should be flexible enough to accommodate discussions of related disclosures that could lead to new insights. If, after its completion, the researcher has follow-up questions, those should be issued fast, and new questions could be created for the next interviewees. The process can be supplemented with the following steps: creating and mailing a recruitment letter explaining the project's context and the participants' rights –more details in the next section (Fast, 2012); asking for the subject's explicit permission to record their words before transcribing them word for word (Bryman, 2004); and citing conversations and e-mails with an interviewee in the case of additional correspondence (Dodds, 2006).

Two other forms of e-interview are also worth describing: live chat via messaging and live interview via an online connection. The first is a synchronous and surprisingly sophisticated mode of communication despite its assumed brevity, particularly thanks to the frequent use of acronyms, emoticons, and specially formatted text (Shepherd, 2003). This mode has added advantages: it allows the participants more power, as they can delve into sensitive topics with less pressure and interrupt the interview whenever they wish; the conversation it creates can be more dynamic and spontaneous; and it can be more easily transcribed or looked over in preparation for follow-up research. As a result, specific researchers have advocated for its wider use as a tool (Fontes & O'Mahony, 2008). The second format is live calling, which shares many traits with phone interviews and sometimes has the added benefit of inspecting body language through a video camera (Kozinets, Dolbec & Earley, 2014). Both methods provide valuable data and can be incorporated into many research schemes, although the researcher should be at least superficially familiar with the technology first through a few trials.

Finally, thick description deserves a mention for its usefulness in unpacking meaning. It is a particular method of critical discourse analysis, defined as "a type of discourse analytical research that primarily studies the way social power abuse, dominance, and inequality are enacted, reproduced, and resisted by text and talk in the social and political context" by Van Dijk (2001, p. 354). According to its theory, "culture is not a power, [...] it is a context, something within which they [construable signs, symbols] can be intelligibly-that is, thickly-described" (Geertz, 1973, p. 14). The method can still be done by hand, with researchers identifying meaningful ideas and looking for the ways people make sense of them. However, recent papers have proposed its use in Big Data analysis, either by analyzing a small subset of data or by using statistical techniques for qualitative insights (Shaffer, 2018).

Practical Application

In the project used as an example, the quantitative component of the research included the creation of three distinct samples: one for the "official" comics creators who were discovered through credits in the publisher's main line of books with the characters at two distinct moments; one for the property's fans in the past, as gauged through the aforementioned popular fan art project; and one for the franchise's current fandom, through an online survey. The data obtained from them included their country of residence, gender, and previous experience with the property, following the example of Norcliffe and Rendace (2003). To discover those individuals' identities, the researcher indexed 364 issues of comics, 664 fan-made comic strips, and 300 answered surveys; this was performed manually, as the data volume was manageable by one individual. The first sample's data was cataloged and tracked through online sources, general –publically available databases, social media– and specific to this group –personal websites, wikis– alike. The second group was collected similarly, while the third submitted their information through a survey created on Google forms. All textual information and additional field notes were compiled in an Excel spreadsheet, to make both calculations and thematic summarizing and updating easier. The entire process was completed in about three weeks.

Finally, qualitative data was obtained via e-interviews with fans and official artists. The first group was invited through the survey, by completing its final, optional choice. Each participant would enter their e-mail address on the space provided and wait for a specified date and time, to avoid diffusing the conversation into the multiple online spaces and platforms where the poll had been circulated. These people received a massive message containing a detailed yet friendly recruitment letter. The second group was reached through the initial source via specialized e-mail messages. The interview process was similar for both of them: dates, times, and interview formats were decided individually to accommodate all subjects' needs and took place over a period of six weeks; concessions were made for delayed responses, the interviewees' harsh working schedules, and sick subjects who needed time to recover. What differed were the individual questions, influenced by the initial literature review and the lurking period for both groups: the fans were asked about their gender, place, and language use, while the professional artists were inquired as to their (in)formal training in the arts, financial survival and relationship to fandom; their relationship to the property and each other was a common theme. Before each interview, the subjects were asked to consent to be recorded; all agreed. These interviews –especially the ones in video or voice format- were transcribed, compiled, and summarized. Field notes were also included, reconstructing the conversation, describing reactions, and noting thoughts for the later part of the process/next interviews. Finally, the interviews were thematized and the insights gained from each piece were reconstructed into general concepts and viewpoints.

Ethical Considerations

Theoretical Overview

Last but not least, two intertwined topics need to be highlighted: ethics and academic transparency. The former is a long-time concern of traditional ethnography (Gorbach et al., 2009), and the latter has placed increased emphasis on integrity and the enrichment of the studied community through specific moral commitments, particularly in collaborative ethnography projects (Lassiter et al., 2004). The issue is also discreet from discussions of online safety (Rode, 2009), which should also be a concern for the researcher.

Both the specific nature of the data in question and their importance in the broader research have to be sorted out. Although what is private information is contextual (Bansal, Zahedi & Gefen, 2016), commonly discussed variables include: name, location, and address (Reyes, 2018); age, gender/sexual orientation, and race (Gray, 2012); political opinion (Wang & Liu, 2021), health (Sik, 2021) and criminal status (Contreras, 2019). Moreover, the issue is two-fold: both the researcher (Livia, 1999) and the subjects (Claudot et al., 2009) require protection. It becomes apparent that protecting the private information of ethnography participants, particularly if any of them belong to a vulnerable group –e.g., the LGBTQ+ community (Gorbach et al., 2009)– is of paramount importance in contemporary online research (Markham & Buchanan, 2012).

At the same time, this can function both as a safety measure and as an opportunity to make the research approachable and transparent. A researcher who builds trust with their subjects, clearly defines the ways the collected material will be used, and shares vital information and concerns with them can gain even greater insights into the cultural world they are studying, as those people will not be afraid of sharing insights (Faugier & Sargeant, 1997). One such way is by providing incentives to participants, such as a copy of the results of the project (Meho, 2006). In the end, a preoccupation with ethical and safe research is beneficial for all parties, especially the individuals the project is about.

This aspect of the research is also difficult to approach due to it being one of the least standardized. There is a lack of definitive privacy guidelines in online research, although both general and specialized rule proposals –such as for "seeds" and invitees of the "snowball technique"– do exist and are worth investigating before engaging with subjects directly (Claudot et al., 2009; Markham & Buchanan, 2012). Specific ethnographic tools, such as the e-interview, have inspired more thorough discussions on privacy and consent during and after the process (Kozinets, Dolbec & Earley, 2014), and such insights should be incorporated into future projects. That said, given that most proposals can become easily dated as the Internet changes rapidly, researchers are encouraged to inspect the latest literature on the subject and communicate clearly with the subjects.

Practical Application

The following paragraphs outline some practical strategies for protecting the identities of everyone involved with an ethnographic project, beginning with the participants. Firstly, during the aforementioned quantitative data collection phase, a few gaps cropped up in the listings; almost all of them were from fan writers who either preferred to keep their information private or had deleted accounts in the years between their participation and the research. These omissions were considered acceptable, as spending time to unearth old data would have been extremely time-consuming and perhaps unpleasant for the individuals themselves.

This concern with privacy and courtesy extended into the next phase of data collection. Details on how the subjects would remain anonymous –by having their answers aggregated– and how the data would be subsequently used were outlined both in the survey and the recruitment letter before the interviews. Moreover, before the start of the latter, the subjects were asked to consent to be recorded and agree to the publication of excerpts. Since some interviewees disclosed details of their private lives and others belonged to the LGBTQ+ community, their identities had to be protected. The closeness of the community and the repetition of online handles across platforms also made publishing any of them potentially dangerous; no legal or user name was displayed, and interviewees only had their self-described gender, age, and country of residence published, except for the visible, eponymous artists. If they wished for any of these identifiers to not be shown in the thesis had their request fulfilled. Finally, in the cases when massive e-mails needed to be sent to a large number of subjects, all recipients remained hidden from one another using the "carbon copy" alternative allowed in messaging platforms. All subjects were approached in a casual yet respectable and knowledgeable manner; any issues that arose were discussed and solved with their input.

Measures were also taken to protect the researcher's identity. Before even beginning to approach any subject, the researcher created a dedicated e-mail account and new personal pages on social media platforms, to avoid using their personal data and having to abandon the accounts in the case of a leak and/or cyberstalking. When they started contacting the first potential "seeds", they introduced themselves by both outlining their academic career and good intentions. One such piece of evidence was the usage of the term "aca-fan", a "hybrid creature which is part fan and part academic", who shares the passion of both groups and wants to bridge them (Jenkins, 2018). Moreover, following Livia (1999) and Hine's (2000) observations regarding gender, the researcher was presented in as non-threatening and neutral a way as possible. After some suggestions from the sources, full names[7] were shortened to ambiguous nicknames, and most correspondences were signed with initials. In case of any misgendering on the part of the interviewees, the mistake was approached humorously and used as a springboard for more conversation.

Finally, some measures of transparency and approachability are mentioned below. The researcher's interests and the project's aims were explained to the initial "seeds" thoroughly, in the prologue to the circulated survey and the recruitment letter for the interviews. Moreover, the researcher tried to be playful with the subjects: each interviewee was allowed to ask the researcher one question –about their academic or fan interests– in return, as a reversal of roles and proof of "fanhood". Finally, a digital copy of the final text was used as a participation incentive, an admission of transparency, and an effort to improve the studied community. The researcher remained engaged, approachable, and transparent throughout the entire process, especially when answering questions.

CONCLUSION

This chapter suggested a basic template for folklore research on the Internet and thus filled a void in the literature. It systematized aspects of online ethnography research, particularly by offering practical advice to interested young researchers. Starting from the structure of "traditional" ethnography, new –or adapted– tools were introduced and broader topics were broached. However, it falls on the individual researcher to remain engaged and updated about this ever-changing field. Aspects like online embedded reality games (Alavesa & Xu, 2020) and modern forms of communication through video platforms like TikTok (Schellewald, 2021) have not been mentioned but are already studied with new methodologies. This text should serve as a basic guideline for online research, but its future update is inevitable.

ACKNOWLEDGMENT

This research received no specific grant from any funding agency in the public, commercial, or not-for-profit sectors.

REFERENCES

Aipperspach, R., Rattenbury, T. L., Woodruff, A., Anderson, K., Canny, J. F., & Aoki, P. (2006). *Ethno-mining: integrating numbers and words from the ground up* (Technical Report No. UCB/EECS-2006-125). Electrical Engineering and Computer Sciences University of California at Berkeley. http://citeseerx.ist.psu.edu/viewdoc/download?doi=10.1.1.173.8069&rep=rep1&type=pdf

Alavesa, P., & Xu, Y. (2020). Unblurring the boundary between daily life and gameplay in location-based mobile games, visual online ethnography on Pokémon GO. *Behaviour & Information Technology*, 1–13. doi:10.1080/0144929X.2020.1825810

Atkinson, P., & Hammersley, M. (1994). Ethnography and participant observation. In N. K. Denzin & Y. S. Lincoln (Eds.), *Handbook of Qualitative Research* (pp. 248–261). SAGE Publications.

Atkinson, R., & Flint, J. (2001). Accessing hidden and hard-to-reach populations: Snowball research strategies. *Social Research Update*, *33*(1), 1–4. https://sru.soc.surrey.ac.uk/SRU33.PDF

Avico, U., Kaplan, C., Korczak, D., & Van Meter, K. (1988). *Cocaine Epidemiology in Three European Community Cities: a pilot study using a snowball sampling methodology*. European Communities Health Directorate.

Bampton, R., & Cowton, C. J. (2002). The E-Interview. *Forum Qualitative Social Research*, *3*(2). Advance online publication. doi:10.17169/fqs-3.2.848

Bansal, G., Zahedi, F. M., & Gefen, D. (2016). Do context and personality matter? Trust and privacy concerns in disclosing private information online. *Information & Management*, *53*(1), 1–21. doi:10.1016/j.im.2015.08.001

Beaulieu, A. (2004). Mediating ethnography: Objectivity and the making of ethnographies of the internet. *Social Epistemology*, *18*(2-3), 139–163. doi:10.1080/0269172042000249264

Bonfim, L. (2021). Spanning the boundaries of qualitative grounded theory methods: Breaking new grounds into the new online era. *RAUSP Management Journal*, *55*(4), 491–509. doi:10.1108/RAUSP-04-2019-0061

Bowen, A., Williams, M., & Horvath, K. (2004). Using the Internet to Recruit Rural MSM for HIV Risk Assessment: Sampling Issues. *AIDS and Behavior*, *8*(3), 311–319. doi:10.1023/B:AIBE.0000044078.43476.1f PMID:15475678

Brewer, J. (2000). *Ethnography*. Open University Press.

Bruckman, A. (2006). Teaching students to study online communities ethically. *Journal of Information Ethics*, *15*(2), 82–98. doi:10.3172/JIE.15.2.82

Bryman, A. (2004). *Social Research Methods*. Oxford University Press.

Chan, S. C., Joosse, P., Martin, S. J., & Tian, X. (2020). Ethnography in Calamitous Times. *Etnografia e ricerca qualitativa*, *13*(2), 175-184. doi:10.3240/97803

Cherny, L. (1999). *Conversation and Community: Chat in a Virtual World*. University of Chicago Press.

Claudot, F., Alla, F., Fresson, J., Calvez, T., Coudane, H., & Bonaïti-Pellié, C. (2009). Ethics and observational studies in medical research: Various rules in a common framework. *International Journal of Epidemiology*, *38*(4), 1104–1108. doi:10.1093/ije/dyp164 PMID:19336436

Cleland, J., Dixon, K., & Kilvington, D. (2019). *Online Research Methods in Sport Studies*. Routledge. doi:10.4324/9780367809300

Coffey, A. (1999). The ethnographic self: Fieldwork and the representation of identity. *Sage (Atlanta, Ga.)*.

Collins, H., Evans, R., & Gorman, M. E. (2010). Trading Zones and Interactional Expertise. In M. E. Gorman (Ed.), *Trading Zones and Interactional Expertise* (pp. 7–23). The MIT Press. doi:10.7551/mitpress/9780262014724.003.0002

Collumbien, M., Qureshi, A. A., Mayhew, S. H., Rizvi, N., Rabbani, A., Rolfe, B., Verma, R. K., Rehman, H., & Naveed-i-Rahat. (2009). Understanding the context of male and transgender sex work using peer ethnography. *Sexually Transmitted Infections*, *85*(Suppl 2), ii3–ii7. doi:10.1136ti.2008.033571 PMID:19307348

Contreras, R. (2019). Transparency and Unmasking Issues in Ethnographic Crime Research: Methodological Considerations. *Sociological Forum*, *34*(2), 293–312. doi:10.1111ocf.12498

Corbin, J. M., & Strauss, A. L. (2008). *Basics of Qualitative Research: Techniques and Procedures for Developing Grounded Theory*. SAGE Publications. doi:10.4135/9781452230153

Correll, S. (1995). The ethnography of an electronic bar: The lesbian cafe. *Journal of Contemporary Ethnography*, *24*(3), 270–298. doi:10.1177/089124195024003002

Dalkavouki, A. (2018). *Now and On Earth: The evolving geography of pop culture production and consumption. The case of the "Transformers" comics* [Master's thesis, National Technical University of Athens, Athens, Greece]. DSpace NTUA.

Dodds, K. (2006). Popular geopolitics and audience dispositions: James Bond and the internet movie database (IMDb). *Transactions of the Institute of British Geographers*, *31*(2), 116–130. doi:10.1111/j.1475-5661.2006.00199.x

Everitt, B. S., & Howell, D. (2005). Encyclopedia of Statistics in Behavioral Science. John Wiley & Sons. doi:10.1002/0470013192

Fahrenwald, N. L., & Stabnow, W. (2005). Sociocultural Perspective on Organ and Tissue Donation among Reservation-Dwelling American Indian Adults. *Ethnicity & Health*, *10*(4), 341–354. doi:10.1080/13557850500168826 PMID:16191731

Fast, K. (2012). *More than Meets the Eye: Transmedial Entertainment as a Site of Pleasure, Resistance and Exploitation* [Doctoral dissertation, Karlstad University, Karlstad, Sweden]. Digitala Vetenskapliga Arkivet.

Faugier, J., & Sargeant, M. (1997). Sampling hard to reach populations. *Journal of Advanced Nursing*, *26*(4), 790–797. doi:10.1046/j.1365-2648.1997.00371.x PMID:9354993

Fayyad, U., Piatetsky-Shapiro, G., & Smyth, P. (1996). Knowledge discovery and data mining: Towards a unifying framework. In E. Simoudis, J. Han, & U. Fayyad (Eds.), *KDD'96: Proceedings of the Second International Conference on Knowledge Discovery and Data Mining* (pp. 82–88). AAAI Press.

Fontes, T. O., & O'Mahony, M. (2008). In-depth interviewing by Instant Messaging. *Social Research Update*, *53*(2), 1–4. https://sru.soc.surrey.ac.uk/SRU53.pdf

Garcia, A. C., Standlee, A. I., Bechkoff, J., & Cui, Y. (2009). Ethnographic Approaches to the Internet and Computer-Mediated Communication. *Journal of Contemporary Ethnography*, *38*(1), 52–84. doi:10.1177/0891241607310839

Geertz, C. (1973). *The Interpretation of Cultures: Selected Essays*. Basic Books, Inc.

Gold, R. L. (1958). Roles in Sociological Field Observations. *Social Forces*, *36*(3), 217–223. doi:10.2307/2573808

Gorbach, P. M., Murphy, R., Weiss, R. E., Hucks-Ortiz, C., & Shoptaw, S. (2009). Bridging Sexual Boundaries: Men Who Have Sex with Men and Women in a Street-Based Sample in Los Angeles. *Journal of Urban Health*, *86*(1), 63–76. doi:10.100711524-009-9370-7 PMID:19543837

Gray, K. L. (2012). Deviant bodies, stigmatized identities, and racist acts: Examining the experiences of African-American gamers in Xbox Live. *New Review of Hypermedia and Multimedia*, *18*(4), 261–276. doi:10.1080/13614568.2012.746740

Groger, L., Mayberry, P., & Straker, J. (1999). What We Didn't Learn Because of Who Would Not Talk to Us. *Qualitative Health Research*, *9*(6), 829–835. doi:10.1177/104973299129122180

Hine, C. (2000). *Virtual Ethnography*. SAGE Publications. doi:10.4135/9780857020277

Injadat, M., Salo, F., & Nassif, A. B. (2016). Data mining techniques in social media: A survey. *Neurocomputing*, *214*, 654–670. doi:10.1016/j.neucom.2016.06.045

Isomäki, H., & Silvennoinen, J. (2013). Online ethnographies. In P. Isaías & M. B. Nunes (Eds.), *Information systems research and exploring social artifacts: Approaches and methodologies* (pp. 124–141). IGI Global. doi:10.4018/978-1-4666-2491-7.ch007

Jenkins, H. (2018). *Who The &%&# Is Henry Jenkins? Confessions of an Aca-Fan*. Henry Jenkins. http://henryjenkins.org/aboutmehtml

Junker, B. (1960). *Field Work*. University of Chicago Press.

Kaplan, C. D., Korf, D., & Sterk, C. (1987). Temporal and Social Contexts of Heroin-Using Populations An Illustration of the Snowball Sampling Technique. *Journal of Mental and Nervous Disorders*, *175*(9), 566–574. doi:10.1097/00005053-198709000-00009 PMID:3655783

Kaur-Gill, S., & Dutta, M. J. (2017). Digital Ethnography. In J. Matthes, C. S. Davis, & R. F. Potter (Eds.), *The International Encyclopedia of Communication Research Methods* (pp. 1–10). John Wiley & Sons, Inc. doi:10.1002/9781118901731.iecrm0271

Kleinman, A. (1992). Local Worlds of Suffering: An Interpersonal Focus for Ethnographies of Illness Experience. *Qualitative Health Research*, *2*(2), 127–134. doi:10.1177/104973239200200202

Knoke, D., & Yang, S. (2007). *Social Network Analysis: Quantitative Applications in the Social Science*. SAGE Publications.

Kozinets, R. V. (2010). *Netnography: Doing Ethnographic Research Online*. SAGE Publications.

Kozinets, R. V., De Valck, K., Wojnicki, A. C., & Wilner, S. J. (2010). Networked Narratives: Understanding Word-of-Mouth Marketing in Online Communities. *Journal of Marketing*, *74*(2), 71–89. doi:10.1509/jm.74.2.71

Kozinets, R. V., Dolbec, P. Y., & Earley, A. (2014). Netnographic Analysis: Understanding Culture Through Social Media Data. In U. Flick (Ed.), *The SAGE Handbook Of Qualitative Data Analysis* (pp. 262–276). SAGE Publications. doi:10.4135/9781446282243.n18

Kuhlmann, A. (1992). Collaborative Research among the Kickapoo Tribe of Oklahoma. *Human Organization, 51*(3), 274–283. doi:10.17730/humo.51.3.k3n65x64t5nx36x5

Kvale, S. (1996). *InterViews: An Introduction to Qualitative Research Interviewing. Academic Press.*

Lassiter, L. E., Goodall, H., Campbell, E., & Johnson, M. N. (2004). *The Other Side of Middletown: Exploring Muncie's African American Community*. AltaMira Press.

Leavy, P. (2017). *Research Design: Quantitative, Qualitative, Mixed Methods, Arts-Based, and Community-Based Participatory Research Approaches*. The Guilford Press.

Lester, J. N. (2020). Going Digital in Ethnography: Navigating the Ethical Tensions and Productive Possibilities. *Cultural Studies« Critical Methodologies, 20*(5), 414-424. doi:10.1177/1532708620936995

Livia, A. (1999). Doing Sociolinguistic Research on the French Minitel. *The American Behavioral Scientist, 43*(3), 422–435. doi:10.1177/00027649921955353

Mack, N., Woodsong, C., MacQueen, K. M., Guest, G., & Namey, E. (2005). *Qualitative Research Methods: A Data Collector's Field Guide*. Family Health International.

Magnani, R., Sabin, K., Saidel, T., & Heckathorn, D. (2005). Review of sampling hard-to-reach and hidden populations for HIV surveillance. *AIDS (London, England), 19*(Suppl 2), S67–S72. doi:10.1097/01.aids.0000172879.20628.e1 PMID:15930843

Marcus, G. E. (1995). Ethnography in/of the World System: The Emergence of Multi-Sited Ethnography. *Annual Review of Anthropology, 24*(1), 95–117. doi:10.1146/annurev.an.24.100195.000523

Markham, A., & Buchanan, E. (2012). *Ethical decision-making and Internet research: Version 2.0*. Association of Internet Researchers. https://wwwcs.uwstout.edu/ethicscenter/upload/aoirethicsprintablecopy.pdf

McNamara, R. P. (1994). *The Times Square Hustler: Male Prostitution in New York City*. Praeger.

Meho, L. I. (2006). E-mail interviewing in qualitative research: A methodological discussion. *Journal of the American Society for Information Science and Technology, 57*(10), 1284–1295. doi:10.1002/asi.20416

Murthy, D. (2008). Digital Ethnography: An Examination of the Use of New Technologies for Social Research. *Sociology, 42*(5), 837–855. doi:10.1177/0038038508094565

Myers, M. D. (1999). Investigating Information Systems with Ethnographic Research. *Communications of the Association for Information Systems, 2*(1), 23. doi:10.17705/1CAIS.00223

Nightingale, D., & Cromby, J. (1999). *Social Constructionist Psychology: A Critical Analysis of Theory and Practice*. Open University Press.

Norcliffe, G., & Rendace, O. (2003). New Geographies of Comic Book Production in North America: The New Artisan, Distancing, and the Periodic Social Economy. *Economic Geography, 79*(3), 241–263. doi:10.1111/j.1944-8287.2003.tb00211.x

Powdermaker, H. (1966). *Stranger and Friend: The Way of an Anthropologist*. W. W. Norton.

Reijnders, S. (2011). Stalking the Count: Dracula, Fandom and Tourism. *Annals of Tourism Research, 38*(1), 231–248. doi:10.1016/j.annals.2010.08.006

Reyes, V. (2018). Three models of transparency in ethnographic research: Naming places, naming people, and sharing data. *Ethnography*, *19*(2), 204–226. doi:10.1177/1466138117733754

Rode, J. A. (2009). Digital parenting: designing children's safety. In A. F. Blackwell (Ed.), *People and Computers XXIII Celebrating People and Technology* (pp. 244–251). British Informatics Society Limited.

Roller, M. R., & Lavrakas, P. J. (2015). *Applied Qualitative Research Design: A Total Quality Framework Approach*. Guilford Press.

Ruhleder, K. (2000). The Virtual Ethnographer: Fieldwork in Distributed Electronic Environments. *Field Methods*, *12*(1), 3–17. doi:10.1177/1525822X0001200101

Sadler, G. R., Lee, H. C., Lim, R. S. H., & Fullerton, J. (2010). Recruitment of hard-to-reach population subgroups via adaptations of the snowball sampling strategy. *Nursing & Health Sciences*, *12*(3), 369–374. doi:10.1111/j.1442-2018.2010.00541.x PMID:20727089

Sadler, G. R., Nguyen, F., Doan, Q., Au, H., & Thomas, A. G. (1998). Strategies for Reaching Asian Americans With Health Information. *American Journal of Preventive Medicine*, *14*(3), 224–228. doi:10.1016/S0749-3797(97)00067-6 PMID:9569224

Sadler, G. R., York, C., Madlensky, L., Gibson, K., Wasserman, L., Rosenthal, E., Barbier, L., Newman, V. A., & Tso, C. (2006). Health parties for African American study recruitment. *Journal of Cancer Education*, *21*(2), 71–76. doi:10.120715430154jce2102_6 PMID:17020516

Said, E. W. (1989). Representing the Colonized: Anthropology's Interlocutors. *Critical Inquiry*, *15*(2), 205–225. doi:10.1086/448481

Salmons, J. E. (2021). Doing Qualitative Research Online. *Sage (Atlanta, Ga.)*.

Schellewald, A. (2021). Communicative Forms on TikTok: Perspectives From Digital Ethnography. *International Journal of Communication*, *15*, 21. https://ijoc.org/index.php/ijoc/article/view/16414

Shaffer, D. W. (2018). Epistemic network analysis: Understanding learning by using big data for thick description. In F. Fischer, C. E. Hmelo-Silver, S. R. Goldman, & P. Reimann (Eds.), *International Handbook of the Learning Sciences* (pp. 520–531). Routledge. doi:10.4324/9781315617572-50

Shepherd, N. (2003). Interviewing online: Qualitative research in the network(ed) society. In *AQR Qualitative Research Conference*, 16-19 July, 2003, *Sydney, Australia*. Association for Qualitative Research.

Shoham, A. (2004). Flow experiences and image making: An online chat-room ethnography. *Psychology and Marketing*, *21*(10), 855–882. doi:10.1002/mar.20032

Sik, D. (2021). From Lay Depression Narratives to Secular Ritual Healing: An Online Ethnography of Mental Health Forums. *Culture, Medicine and Psychiatry*, *45*(4), 751–774. doi:10.100711013-020-09702-5 PMID:33372246

Spreen, M. (1992). Rare populations, hidden populations, and link-tracing designs: What and why? *Bulletin of Sociological Methodology. Bulletin de Methodologie Sociologique*, *36*(1), 34–58. doi:10.1177/075910639203600103

Van Dijk, T. A. (2001). Critical Discourse Analysis. In Handbook of Discourse Analysis (pp. 352-371). Blackwell.

Van Meter, K. (1990). Methodological and Design Issues: Techniques for Assessing the Representatives of Snowball Samples. In E. Y. Lambert (Ed.), *The Collection and Interpretation of Data from Hidden Populations* (pp. 31–43). U.S. Department of Health and Human Services.

Varis, P. (2016). Digital Ethnography. In A. Georgakopoulou & T. Spilioti (Eds.), *The Routledge Handbook of Language and Digital Communication* (pp. 55–68). Routledge.

Walstrom, M. K. (2004). Ethics and engagement in communication scholarship: Analyzing public, online support groups as researcher/participant experiencer. *Virtual Research Ethics: Issues and Controversies*.

Wang, D., & Liu, S. (2021). Doing Ethnography on Social Media: A Methodological Reflection on the Study of Online Groups in China. *Qualitative Inquiry*, *27*(8-9), 977–987. doi:10.1177/10778004211014610

Whyte, W. F. (2012). *Street Corner Society: The Social Structure of an Italian Slum*. University of Chicago Press.

Wittel, A. (2000). Ethnography on the move: From field to net to internet. *Forum Qualitative Sozialforschung/Forum: Qualitative. Social Research*, *1*(1). Advance online publication. doi:10.17169/fqs-1.1.1131

Zhivov, J., Scheepers, H., & Stockdale, R. (2011). Facebook-The Final Frontier For TV Fandom: A Lurker's Perspective. In *ACIS 2011 Proceedings*. Association for Information Systems.

ADDITIONAL READING

Baker, S. (2013). Conceptualising the use of Facebook in ethnographic research: As tool, as data and as context. *Ethnography and Education*, *8*(2), 131–145. doi:10.1080/17457823.2013.792504

Gosling, S. D., Vazire, S., Srivastava, S., & John, O. P. (2004). Should We Trust Web-Based Studies? A Comparative Analysis of Six Preconceptions About Internet Questionnaires. *The American Psychologist*, *59*(2), 93–104. doi:10.1037/0003-066X.59.2.93 PMID:14992636

Hine, C. (2020). *Ethnography for the internet: Embedded, embodied and everyday*. Routledge. doi:10.4324/9781003085348

McKenna, K. Y., & Bargh, J. A. (1998). Coming out in the age of the Internet: Identity "demarginalization" through virtual group participation. *Journal of Personality and Social Psychology*, *75*(3), 681–694. doi:10.1037/0022-3514.75.3.681

Norris, P. (2001). *Digital Divide: Civic Engagement, Information Poverty, and the Internet Worldwide*. Cambridge University Press. doi:10.1017/CBO9781139164887

Sade-Beck, L. (2004). Internet Ethnography: Online and Offline. *International Journal of Qualitative Methods*, *3*(2), 45–51. doi:10.1177/160940690400300204

Sloan, L., & Quan-Haase, A. (2017). *The SAGE Handbook of Social Media Research Methods*. SAGE Publications.

KEY TERMS AND DEFINITIONS

Digital Ethnography: The adaptation of the discipline of ethnography to online environments.

E-Interview: An interview conducted online for research purposes.

Internet Culture: The beliefs, modes of communication, and values of individuals and groups interacting on the Internet. It can differ between various sub-groups.

Lurking: A method of obtaining information and familiarizing oneself with an online culture. It involves observing a given space without interfering in it.

Research Ethics: The preoccupation and measures taken to protect the safety and dignity of all participants in research. They can include anonymizing of all participants, asking for their consent in recording and publicizing their words, and helping them in understanding the research context.

Snowball Technique: A method of sample design. It begins with locating a starting group ("seed") and using their contacts within a community to locate more individuals with similar desired traits. It has been adapted to online environments.

Thick Description: A method of cultural analysis. It involves describing a given topic, sight, or event in great detail, in order to understand how meaning and social dynamics are produced within it.

ENDNOTES

1 Despite being a very widely used term in ethnography, "participant observation" is difficult to conceptualize. It is broadly defined as "observation carried out when a researcher is playing an established participant role in a scene studied" (Aktinson & Hammersley, 1994, p. 248). However, there are nuances in the observant-participant dichotomy. A fourfold typology is preferred instead: complete observer, observer as participant, participant as observer, and complete participant (Gold, 1958; Junker, 1960).

2 Other terms include "netnography" (Kozinets, Dolbec & Earley, 2014) and "netography" (Myers, 1999). For a comparative overview of some of the most popular ones, see Isomäki & Silvennoinen (2013).

3 In more detail, the project examined how two populations invested in the "Transformers" cultural franchise –the workers producing official comics for the brand and its fans– changed over the course of ten years. The changes pertained to their gender, country of residence, culture, and relationship to fan culture. It was discovered that the two groups interact rather closely and that certain individuals from the fandom become professional creators.

4 Textual engagement is also par for the course in "traditional" ethnographic preparation. During planning for the example project, the researcher consumed several important texts in the cultural franchise's history. Since the focus of the project was on comic books, all stories from the then-current publisher's lineup, as well as select pieces from influential past iterations and other tie-in

series, were tracked down and read. A selection of other multi-media tie-ins was also included in that body of work.

5 This concern with the state of the studied population is indicative of a broader shift in the way the discipline views the subjects. The first name used by anthropology to refer to individuals providing the researcher with knowledge in the field was "informants"; the researchers' main motivation for engaging with them was not to aid them, but to collect data from them (Powdermaker, 1966). However, this was changed by the mid-1980s post-modern turn; now, the discipline places a much bigger emphasis on reciprocity and collaboration with the studied communities (Kuhlmann, 1992). Amongst other things, the term "informants" was abandoned for the much more inclusive "interlocutors", although there are separate discussions to be made about its usage and political weight (Said, 1989).

6 "Data mining" is a sub-discipline of computer science, and is defined as "the non-trivial process of identifying valid, novel, potentially useful, and ultimately understandable patterns in data" (Fayyad et al., 1996, p. 83). Since then, ethnographers have used data mining in research, even creating new methodologies that bridge the two like "ethnomining" (Aipperspach et al., 2006). However, the amount of data can be overwhelming and ultimately unhelpful, and ethnographers are warned to exercise caution (Varis, 2016).

7 It has to be noted that this proved easier with the researcher's obscure, non-Anglophone name, which most English speakers asked could either not identify or considered masculine in terms of gender.

Chapter 14
Recent Digitalization Development of Buddhist Libraries: A Comparative Case Study

Xin Sun
The University of Hong Kong, Hong Kong

Dickson K. W. Chiu
https://orcid.org/0000-0002-7926-9568
The University of Hong Kong, Hong Kong

Cheuk Ting Chan
Independent Musician, Hong Kong

ABSTRACT

This study investigates the adaption and digitalization development of Buddhist libraries in the current mobile computing age and proposes a three-level pyramid model of Buddhist library digitalization. The cases studied include the functions, missions, and objectives of the Yunlin Buddhist Library in Lingyin Temple, Mainland China; the Luminary Buddhist Institute Library in Taiwan; and the Buddhist Digital Resource Center (BDRC) in America. In particular, their path of development, objectives, achievements, and obstacles are analyzed. This case study provide some examples for maintaining digital Buddhist databases and physical Buddhist libraries in these temples for sustainable development.

INTRODUCTION

Buddhist library originates from Buddhist Sutra Mansions. Collections are organized in simple rules for monks, Buddhists, and scholars to read and learn. The construction funds are mainly received from governments and individual donations. Collections include different physical formats such as books

DOI: 10.4018/978-1-6684-4461-0.ch014

issued by states, carved works by monks and Buddhists, commodity books purchased from the market, and scattered preservation selected from various sources. Traditionally, physical media include paper, stone, and Bayeux tree trunks (Huang, 2011b). Research on collection management, communication, openness, and preservation of Buddhist libraries could be traced to these Buddhist Sutra Mansions.

However, limited by time, technology, and lack of standards, vast Buddhist collections keep the traditional ways of management (Huang, 2011a). Master Taixu (1889-1947) was one of the most famous eminent monks in modern China. He devoted all his life to reforming modern Chinese Buddhism, actively promoting the establishment of modern Chinese Buddhism libraries, and thus became one of the most remarkable founders. In 1932, master Taixu founded the World Buddhist Center Library in Wuchang and opened resources to the public, a milestone in library development history (Li, 2014). Table 1 provides a glimpse of some early Chinese Buddhist libraries (Zhuo, 2012a; 2012b).

Table 1. Earlier Buddhist libraries in China

Establish	Name	Collection	Service
1930	Shanghai Buddhist Bookstore	Physical works	Open to distant readers
1932	World Buddhist Center Library	Physical works	Open to public
1940	Dalun Law Library	Physical works	Termly openness
1942	Shanghai Buddhist Institute Library	Physical works	Internal openness
1946	Shanghai Buddhist Youth Association Library	Physical works	Open to public
1948	Xingci Middle School Library	Physical works	Internal openness

Table 2. Digital Buddhist library in China

Establish	Name	Collection	Service
2000	Guangdong Zhongshan Library Buddhist Branch	Physical works & digital works	Modernized, automated management
2007	Emei Mount Buddhist Library	Physical works & digital works	Advanced digital management, local area network
2008	Hangzhou Library Buddhist Branch	Physical works & digital works	Present Buddhist culture with digitalized West Lake scenery
2009	Yangzhou Jianzhen Library	Physical works & digital works	Digital preservation of research paper

In the digital age, Buddhist culture spreads and communicates on a higher horizon with more advanced infrastructure and approaches. Buddhist preservations in digital formats have emerged, and the functions and services of Buddhist libraries have expanded gradually. Table 2 shows some examples. The appearance of Buddhist libraries provides convenience for people to read Buddhist classics, improves Buddhism's study standard, and expands Buddhism's influence.

Besides, many Buddhist libraries collect not only classics but also relevant research works, playing an active role in inheriting traditional culture and popularizing knowledge. At present, the development of the Buddhist libraries has to exceed the physical boundary, playing an essential role in social-cultural

Table 3. Different types of libraries in the digital age

Name	Location	Form	Functions
Buddhist Digital Resource Center (BDRC)	Massachusetts	Database	Knowledge Base, a free public-accessible database offering easy searchability of Buddhist works; and the Digital Library. Preserve and disseminate all Buddhist literary traditions that remain endangered due to precarious social and environmental factors (Hartley, Sep 2007).
Luminary Buddhist Institute Library (LBIL)	Taiwan	Database & physical library	Open-shelf reading; database of Buddhist works, library operation, and professional classification; own publications; multiple advanced retrieval systems; collaborative projects; workshops.
Yunlin Buddhist Library (YBL)	Hangzhou	Physical library	Open-shelf reading; modernized and automated operation system; preservation of physical works; collaborative projects; workshops.

services. Public and university libraries have been involved in constructing the temples' libraries, leading to a brighter future for Buddhist monastery libraries with more reach and influence. Nowadays, integrated Buddhist collections are distributed in professional databases and physical libraries. Table 3 summarizes the three representative cases selected for this study.

It is necessary to induct a development model of Buddhist libraries, clarifying their structure and mission and making them more adaptive to the mobile digital age. The following research questions summarize the objective of this study.

RQ1: What are the main stages of Buddhist libraries' digitalization development?

RQ2: What are the main characteristics and services provided by Buddhist libraries at different stages?

RQ3: What are the challenges in developing digitalization for Buddhist libraries?

According to the induction and comparison of Yunlin Buddhist Library (YBL) in Lingyin Temple, Mainland China, to the Luminary Buddhist Institute Library (LBIL) in Taiwan and Buddhist Digital Resource Center (BDRC) in America as cases, this study proposes a three-level pyramid model of Buddhist library digitalization. During the development process, key problems are identified and evaluated to provide relevant suggestions for future development.

Literature Review

With comprehensive access to preserving and using digital resources in the digital age (Chung and Chiu, 2016; Lo et al., 2019), studies on preserving and using Buddhist collections emerged at the beginning of the 21st century (Wittern, 2000). Changes in communication facilities have significantly improved the accessibility of global Buddhism resources for studies. Buddhist libraries supported by databases and other online services have become a trend. Today's Buddhist library has various characteristics that illustrate its advancement. First is the diversification of construction from a single temple to multiple cooperators, including public libraries and universities. Secondly, the scope of service has expanded from monks and Buddhists to the public. Third, digitalization plays a key role. Forth, standard classification has become universal in China (Chen & Xu, 2010).

There are some case studies based on Buddhist libraries, such as Jiming Temple Library in Nanjing (Huixu, 2016), Jianzhen Library in Yangzhou (Shen, 2014), and Hanshan Temple in Suzhou (Zhang, 2010). These studies illustrate the history and contribution of temples' collections, giving suggestions for improving future running and appealing to more public attention. Besides constructing digital and physical collections, some scholars, such as Shiyongxin (2012) and Zhuo (2012b), focus on the library's conservation function and preservation of endangered works. Since Buddhist libraries have become more multifunctional and digitalized with large collections, establishing professional classification standards has become a popular research topic for better management, preservation, retrieval, and usage (Zhou, 2005; Dong, 2015; Bai, 2008; Zeng, 2012).

As for other Western theological libraries, digitalization is also a major trend. For example, the Admont Abbey Library and the Abby Library of Sain Gall librarians mentioned in their interviews that they have been digitizing their large historical collections (Lo, Cho, and Chiu, 2017, Chapter 26, 27). Many other libraries with large ancient and rare book collections also have various digitalization projects ongoing, and overall results are generally positive (Cho et al., 2017). As for international studies on Buddhism-related digitalization, Bingenheimer (2020) provided an excellent bibliography. Jiang et al. (2020) provide plenty of recent information on the management of various libraries, archives, and museums from a cultural perspective.

However, previous studies of Buddhist libraries are mainly focused on two directions. On the one hand, they introduce the detailed conditions of a particular temple's library, demonstrating the digitalization measurements. On the other hand, they suggest future development at a macro level of all Buddhist libraries. However, there is still a gap in mastering an explicit knowledge of this field. Buddhist libraries should be classified into different tiers with diverse responsibilities and objectives. To increase the efficiency of collection utilization and avoid the redundant efforts of digitalization, a simplified running model is proposed for reference. Besides, previous methods of improvement should also be compared and evaluated.

METHODOLOGY

This study aims to analyze the structure of Buddhist libraries, including a pyramid of organizations and the structure inside a library. It analyzes Buddhist databases and physical libraries of different scales, content, founders, objectives, and functions. Therefore, applying an inductive approach is appropriate in this research. An inductive approach summarizes various theories from specific observations for bottom-up reasoning. This approach aims at making conclusions out of multiple aspects and evidence. The benefit of an inductive approach is that researchers can often get inspiration and new thoughts from inductive reasoning (Bryman & Bell, 2015).

This study used the qualitative research method that provides in-depth data (Cresswell, 2003). Data were collected by in-depth document analysis and application from a specific library. A series of steps in a qualitative study include designing research questions, collecting data, and analyzing data (Verd, 2004) to help understand and compare digital Buddhist libraries. Then, the collaborative and integrated data were analyzed comprehensively and demonstrated clearly.

The thematic framework method (Richards, 2017) is an analytical method based on forms to ensure the rigor and transparency of the data collection and analysis process. Therefore, it is considered a more mature qualitative data analysis approach widely used (Lo, Chiu, & Cho, 2017). For this research, the theme is Buddhist libraries in the digital age. Different libraries are organized by diverse management methods with different founders, history, collections, values, missions, and development stages. The information should be gathered from all kinds of documents and organized in a common form for systematic analysis.

Documentary analysis is necessary to master the basic condition of Buddhist libraries in the digital age. As comprehensive as possible, typical Buddhist libraries should be involved in the comparison process. From the official websites, articles, and other resources, documents could be collected and re-organized into a clear format. Therefore, one of the objectives of this research, a multiple-leveled framework of Buddhist libraries, could be summarized.

This research adopts data collection methods due to the characteristics of its topic, object, resources, and other aspects. First, the sample of the research objective was a small group including monks and managers in some organizations. Second, as documents did not adequately reflect some of the operations and problems, this research applied semi-structured interviews of specific Buddhist libraries to get in-depth information. Questions were designed with changeable order and open discussion. The interviewees were managers of Yunlin Buddhist Library of Lingyin Temple in Hangzhou, Venerable Wenhai, and Venerable Huiyang. The interviews aim to know detailed information about the library development process and evaluate the effect of innovative actions on library development. Notably, the Yunlin Buddhist Library is one of the most advanced and superior physical Buddhist libraries with its book classification in China and applied offline training for Buddhist librarians, which is considered an innovation (Zhou, 2005).

Data analysis is an important step in research. Guided by the inductive method, qualitative analysis organizes all the valid information by content-coding forms designed according to existing documents and supplemented by detailed inquiry (Gibson and Brown, 2009). Besides, interviews were transcribed, confirmed, and organized into a clear word format with valid information. Then, tables and charts are applied to help analyze the structure and operation of these Buddhist libraries.

This paper chooses Yunlin Buddhist Library (YBL) as the primary case to compare with the Buddhist Digital Resource Center (BDRC) and Luminary Buddhist Institute Library (LBIL), which are comparable organizations to investigate the current development condition of Buddhist library digitalization.

On July 7th, 2018, the Chinese Buddhist Library Association was founded in YBL, Lingyin Temple, in Hangzhou, China. This association was raised by 14 leading Buddhist libraries and cooperated by 46 libraries, with more than 100 representatives. At the establishment meeting, these representatives communicated the situation that Buddhist libraries were facing together and decided to seek opportunities for further development in the digital age. For training a group of qualified librarians in Buddhist libraries, the association raised description courses, inviting teachers from external organizations to teach monks. The curriculum included Chinese Library Classification and Yunlin Buddhist Book Classification that monks could directly apply to their daily work. After training, learners were given certificates offered by the National Library of China and Linyin Temple. To conclude, Yunlin Buddhist Library could be regarded as a key advanced Buddhist library raised by the temple and supported by all sectors of society. It also has been very active in seeking opportunities to cooperate with other organizations.

This study interviewed two leading managers of YBL, Venerable Huiyang and Venerable Wenhai, to learn more about the operation process of their library. For future development, there are significant potentials as well as many obstacles. This study further compares two other organizations, BDRC and LBIL, summarizing their experience and giving suggestions for Buddhist library digitalization at different levels.

CASE BACKGROUND

Yunlin Buddhist Library (YBL)

YBL was established in 2003 as an internal library in Lingyin Temple. Yunlin is another name for this temple given by Emperor Kangxi of the Qing dynasty. As early as the time of Emperor Daoguang, Qing dynasty, a governor of Zhejiang province and a famous scholar Ruanyuan founded the Linyin Book Collection, which could be considered the earliest public (Buddhist) library in China. Although it is quite different from today's Yunlin Buddhist Library in many dimensions, the rebuild of this book collection aims to resume the function of these Buddhism books, benefiting the Buddhists who visit this temple, giving them abundant precious experience and knowledge.

The collection of YBL can be divided into three parts, books, journals, audio, and video materials. Books are mainly about Buddhism and some about social science as a supplement. This library has as many as 12 kinds of Tibetan sutras and some English, Japanese, Korean, and Thai Buddhist classics. Books on social sciences related to Buddhism include classics about philosophy, history, literature, and art at home and abroad. There are more than 60 Buddhist magazine titles and 46 other journals. Audio and video materials are mainly tapes, CDs, and VCDs, including Buddhism music, sutra recitation, lectures, etc.

YBL has adopted the fourth edition of the Chinese Library Classification to organize its collection. Besides, YBL adopts the 1996 edition of the Buddhist Book Classification proposed by the LBIL in Taiwan as a reference and comes up with extensions and modifications, establishing their new classification called the Yunlin Buddhist Book Classification. The original 32 categories are expanded to more than 500 for more accurate classification of Buddhist collections.

YBL adopts the Author Sort Number Management System for books of the same category. The creation and utilization of sort numbers have a substantial connection with the library cataloging and circulation department work. Its validity affects the veracity of bibliography data and collection circulation directly (Jingtao & Qingyi, 2002). YBL's Author Sort Number System has multiple advantages. First, it keeps the tradition, gathering the same author's publications together. Second, it is a relatively simple and short number to facilitate computerization, making it convenient for archiving and access.

Since its establishment, YBL has applied an advanced management philosophy to facilitate large collections, qualified services, convenient access, and effective management. First, the library employs experienced librarians and researchers to design the library, collaborating with the two monks selected from the temple to learn daily operations. Then, the library bought Interlib, an integrated computerized management system complying with the CNMARC (China Machine-Readable Catalogue) format, to automate various library operations, including purchasing, description, circulation, retrieval, etc.

Buddhist Digital Resource Center (BDRC)

BDRC (https://legacy.tbrc.org/) is a non-profit organization dedicated to finding, archiving, preserving, and using worldwide Buddhist resources. Its mission is to keep the ancient treasure and wisdom in the Buddhism world and spread the. BDRC has cooperated with Zhejiang University Buddhist Resource and Research Center, raising a mobile application named BDRC Lib, offering retrieval function and digital resources for users. In the meantime, Zhejiang University will work with Harvard University to run Buddhist Universal Digital Archive, providing an encyclopedic digital Buddhist library with the current 18957 files of precious archives in the BDRC database.

Zhejiang University Buddhist Resource and Research Center is the first organization in China that combines Buddhist resources preservation, integration, and academic research. BDRC supports various kinds of retrieval access and languages. For users' convenience, it supports offline search for users without the Internet to download the resources later. According to the introduction from Professor He, the director of BDRC, the China-US cooperation team is in charge of technology development. The US side is led by the South Asia division of East Asian languages and civilizations department at Harvard University. The China side is led by Zhejiang University Library and BRDC.

Luminary Buddhist Institute Library (LBIL)

The Luminary Buddhist Institute was founded in 1980 to enrich Buddhist education resources and established its library in 1982. The early collections were mainly donated by external Buddhists, resulting in a comprehensive but random collection that varies by time. Finding books became very hard with the increasing collection size since there was no logical classification. So LBIL developed management policies in 2010 and aims for education, providing quality materials for Buddhist learners. The policies include short, middle, and long-term objectives, collection standards, purchase plans, donation management process, and book elimination criteria. LBIL has been the most established professional Buddhist library in Taiwan. At the Chinese Buddhist Library Association meeting, LBIL shared its development and management experiences with other Buddhist libraries. LBIL's official website has established a comprehensive database with a user-friendly interface (http://www.gaya.org.tw/library/) to provide diversified retrieval methods covering internal and external journals and Buddhist scriptures. It even includes a consortium catalog cooperating with ten Buddhist libraries and organizations.

Case Analysis of YBL

To better understand today's different types of Buddhist libraries, Table 4 provides enriched descriptions of these cases, summarizing their resources and business and showing significant differences among these Buddhist libraries. Their missions have played a decisive role in the operation and development direction. To some extent, the foundations supporting the running of these libraries have also affected the programs libraries could participate in. YBL's development comprises several key elements compared to other organizations, as discussed in the following subsections.

Missions

YBL is founded in Hangzhou, Mainland China. The Chinese Buddhist Library Association regards it as an advanced example and a communication center for Buddhist Librarians. The missions of this library comprise two parts. On a macro level, it aims at becoming a platform for Buddhist Libraries nationwide to lead and communicate with each other and advocate innovation and cooperation. A reflection is its training courses in cataloging, which have attracted librarians from many other temples. On a technology level, YBL has its professional objectives as a leader of Buddhist libraries. For example, the Yunlin Buddhist Book Classification is modified according to domestic information needs and is widely adopted in Mainland China. YBL will also provide open access to the public in the future.

Table 4. Comparison of three Buddhist libraries

	Yunlin Buddhist Library (YBL)	Buddhist Digital Resource Center (BDRC)	Luminary Buddhist Institute Library (LBIL)
Region	Hangzhou, China	Cambridge, Ma (USA) Hangzhou (China) New Deli (India) Bangkok (Thailand) Munich (Germany)	Taiwan
Form	Physical Buddhist library	Buddhist Database	Educational organization
Resources	12 collections of Tibetan sutras, English, Japanese, Korean, Thai Buddhist classics, more than 60 Buddhist magazines (domestic and international), 46 other journals, tapes, CDs, and VCDs, including Buddhist music, sutra recitation, lectures, etc.	Over 15,000,000 scanned pages, catalogs, and e-texts from Buddhists worldwide. In the China branch, Europe, America, and Japan databases	63 domestic journals, 481 international journals (more than 300 Buddhist journals), Taiwan Buddhist journals in the 1940s and 1950s, Doctoral and Master's dissertations on Buddhism, and other resources.
Functions	• Internal reading • Classics preservation • Classification guidance for other libraries • Training volunteers help the Buddhist library • Description courses open to Buddhist libraries	• Digitally preserve Buddhist texts • Archive and restore original contexts • Online retrieval with tags of metadata • Offline access with "Digital Library Drives." • Data application interfaces (APIs), direct access to the XML content of the library	• External reading • Buddhist books consult • Online retrieval with tags of metadata • Training volunteers helping Buddhist library • Extension education of Buddhist resources • Buddhist library management guidance
Technology Contribution	• Yunlin Buddhist Book Classification • 2018 Revised edition of Yunlin Buddhist Book Classification	• Mobile application of BDRC	• Buddhist Book Classification • Compilation of Buddhist Degree Dissertation 1963-2000, 2000-2006 • Union Catalog of Buddhist collections in Taiwan • [REMOVED HYPERLINK FIELD] Information Management for Buddhist Libraries (quarterly) • Network Buddhist Resource e-paper • Conference brochures and assembly materials
Cooperation	• Help Hangzhou Buddhist college in collection purchase	• Partner with Harvard University's Digital Repository Service (DRS) about long-term storage • Partner with the Lamas' Lineage & Legacy Project (LLLP) to sustain traditional texts • Fragile Palm Leaves Foundation, Orient Foundation of Arts and Culture, Indian Council for cultural relations • Zhejiang University, Central University of Tibetan Studies, University of Virginia	• Interlibrary cooperation for more convenient usage of Buddhist books
Funding partners	Yunlin Foundation	Khyentse Foundation, Gruber Foundation, The Robert H. N. Ho Family Foundation	Gaya Hill Foundation
Objectives	• Spread Buddhism with precious classics • Develop Buddhist culture regionally • Help Buddhist learners and readers use the resources • Enrich and standardize Buddhist books classification	• Preserve precious Buddhist literature • Provide open access to the public to deliver Buddhism culture • Keep digitalization with respect to the original contexts of Buddhist culture • Build a logical system to tag all preserved resources • Develop the efficiency of the retrieval and usage of resources	• Provide open access to Buddhist literature to the public • Catch up with the need for academic research • Develop interlibrary cooperation • Offer online consult service of high quality • Educate management talents for Buddhism libraries • Being an all-rounded Buddhism center

Key Development Projects

YBL is originally a physical library with classic Buddhism collections in various formats, mainly book series, journals, and videos. Since it is a library from the Qing dynasty, the preservation work of precious Buddhism classics is YBL's main business. Besides, this library's operation has changed flexibly to adapt to the digital age.

First, enhancing the classification scheme is a hard but meaningful project. A group of experts with expert knowledge of Buddhist books oversaw this project to better fulfill the needs of archiving Buddhist books, more efficient management, and utilization. They studied the 1996 edition of Buddhist Book Classification proposed by LBIL, finding it very practical and satisfying the basic professional needs. However, extensions and adaptions were necessary because the LBIL scheme could not be applied directly to book management due to the cultural and political differences between Mainland and Taiwan.

Another contribution of YBL is its leading position in other Buddhist organizations, including temples and educational institutes. As Venerable Huiyang introduced, YBL donated a series of Buddhist books to Hangzhou Buddhist College over these years. Hangzhou Buddhist College is an educational organization approved by the people's Republic of China State Bureau of Religious Affairs, founded by The Buddhist Association of Hangzhou. The donation improves the quality of Buddhism education and culture. YBL develops many communication and exchange opportunities for Buddhist organizations throughout China, especially Buddhist libraries.

According to Venerable Huiyang and Venerable Wenhai, YBL has various supports from different partners and donators. Lingyin Temple provides audit reports of Yunlin Foundation to society for reference every year. In 2018, donation income amounted to nearly 2.4 million yuan (1 USD=6.5 CNY approximately). YBL also receives some government support as well. However, the purchase of books and other resources collections, operation costs, and building maintenance of YBL all rely on donations.

In addition, Venerable Guangquan Hangzhou established the Yunlin Foundation under Linyin Temple in 2014 registered in the Municipal Civil Affairs Bureau for being a responsible member of society, spreading Buddhist culture, and charity participation,

Support

Apart from financial support, professional and technical support is necessary for YBL's daily operation. According to Venerable Huiyang and Venerable Wenhai, professors from the National Library of China and Zhejiang Library come to YBL every year to advise on the development projects and other operational logistics. The Chinese Buddhist Library Association also introduce other professors to implement training courses for managers in Lingyin Temple and other temples in the province.

Pyramid of Buddhist Libraries (RQ1)

To answer RQ1, Figure 1 depicts our three-stage pyramid model of Buddhist libraries, with increasing new objectives, activities, and services. The model is designed based on the development experience of the three cases compared in this study.

Stage 1 is the physical library which has been developed for over a thousand years. Despite recent technological advancements, physical libraries remain indispensable, as readers may still prefer physical books due to different reading needs (Wang et al., 2016; Ding et al., 2021). Less used books can be stored

Figure 1. Pyramid of Buddhist libraries

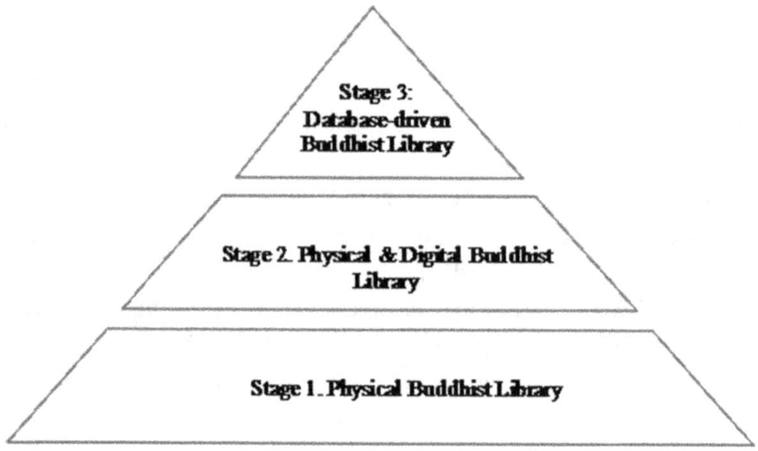

in remote storage, keeping the book information in a traditional OPAC for reasonable access (Wong & Chiu, 2023; Chung & Chiu, 2016). The main traditional contribution is to provide high-quality learning materials for monks and benefit local education institutes with Buddhist resources.

Stage 2 is a mixed physical and digital library where digitalization occurs. The digitalization process is very long and costly for Buddhist libraries because of the large volume of Buddhist scriptures and literature. However, digitalization facilitates easy access, searching, and information preservation (Mak et al., 2022; Lo, Cho, & Chiu, 2017). Internal and external Venerables may create content, such as sermon videos and audio to enrich the collections (Cheung et al., 2021). This stage starts building a larger database for storing diversified Buddhist resources in different formats to form a shared platform readily sharable among different libraries, forming consortia (Wong & Chiu, 2023). Moreover, many readers may access digitalized materials concurrently, anytime, anywhere, with mobile or desktop devices, bringing many conveniences as many religious libraries are quite remote and libraries may be locked down during the COVID-19 pandemic (Yu et al., in press; Huang et al.; 2021; 2022). With such an infrastructure, Buddhist libraries may start to provide reference and consultation services in the field of Buddhism culture.

Stage 3 is a database-driven Buddhist library, providing digital formats of Buddhist resources, including books and other materials. This stage can be reached after finishing most of the digitalization work, and library consortia are well developed with trust and smooth cooperation. As Buddhist rare and old books are valuable assets and significant cultural heritage, and some may even have religious value, many such precious books highlight individual Buddhist libraries' unique collections and should still be physically preserved (Lo, Cho, & Chiu, 2017). This stage can provide well-organized collections with scientific catalogs and descriptions for future generations' convenience. Further collaborations with researchers to analyze religious texts to discover further knowledge and wisdom is also possible with the huge amount of digitalized information in the databases (Okunlaya et al., in press).

BUDDHIST LIBRARY CHARACTERISTICS AT DIFFERENT STAGES (RQ2)

Table 5 summarizes Buddhist libraries' characteristics at the three different phases of digitalization with progressively increasing objectives, primary business processes, challenges, cooperation opportunities, and contributions. Based on the development experience explained by the two YBL managers, YBL was established in Stage 1 from a physical Buddhist library, started digitalization in Stage 2, and is currently in Stage 3, focusing on a database-driven catalog and digitalized collection. Notably, this does not mean old valuable collections with historical value should be abandoned. Many older objectives and activities remain but with less emphasis, e.g., accepting donations of valuable rare Buddhist books and preserving them both physically and digitally. Compared YBL with two other major Buddhist libraries, they all are very similar in their current objectives, situation, and services, reflecting a globalized knowledge-driven community even in a religious domain.

DISCUSSION – OBSTACLES AND SUGGESTIONS (RQ3)

To spread Buddhism culture and cultivate more Buddhists worldwide, Buddhist libraries still have a long way to go. Even with clear objectives, Buddhist libraries still face human resources, cost, and efficiency problems, especially regarding the potential value of the collections and the digital databases. This section discusses RQ3 about the challenges and possible solutions for the digitalization of Buddhist libraries.

The first problem is collection management, including cataloging and descriptions (Lo, Cho, & Chiu, 2017). For special libraries, cataloging cannot be done by simply using the information from sources like the National Library of China or WorldCat. Many Buddhist books are thread-bound rare books that need manual cataloging. The monks need more training from specialized library professors for descriptions and cataloging. Current cataloging work of collections and digitalized content, to some extent, is done by external experts voluntarily.

Most published collections have little necessity to be scanned considering previous usage frequencies, but rather for preservation and easy access (Wong & Chiu, 2023). Advanced retrieval approaches for users to access these resources may be the next step if a library decides to maintain its unique collections. However, this process requires library experts with more professional knowledge of Buddhism, such as the expertise in extracting keywords and classification. In the meantime, image scanning may be adopted. However, full-text scanning, which is useful for better searching, subsequent computer analyses, and research, requires a huge devotion to proofreading the text, though related scientific research has constantly been improving (Ma et al., 2020; Liu et al., 2022).

Due to limited human resources, there is a need to determine whether the full texts should be scanned or just a description, as well as the digitalization priority. Volunteers and interns can be recruited to solve some of the human resources requirements (Yau et al., in press; Li & Chiu, in press). Also, some current databases are still preliminary, and the retrieval methods are relatively simple. With many other technical and management difficulties, professional librarians may be hired to manage these libraries when the budget permits (Lo, Cho, & Chiu, 2017; Chapter 27). To summarize, digitalization is an integrated and complicated project once committed. In addition, copyright is another important issue. Full-text scanning sometimes may infringe copyright and need negotiations with copyright owners.

Table 5. Comparing the three stages of Buddhist library digitalization

	1. Physical Buddhist library	2. Physical & Digital Buddhist library	3. Database-driven Buddhist library
Objectives	• Provide abundant physical collections to users with smooth circulation services • Preserve precious Buddhist classics and external donations • Develop own unique collections	• Provide books, journals, audios, videos, and other physical collections • Offer retrieval access for users to find collections, • Act as a professional library of Buddhism subject	• Provide digital format of Buddhist resources, including books and other materials.
Business Processes	• Purchase books, journals, and other publications • Apply catalog and description from national libraries • Enrich the classification of Buddhist books • Design friendly reading environments • Keep scientific collection management with suitable physical and chemical conditions	• Purchase books, journals, and other publications • Apply catalog and description from national libraries • Enrich the classification of Buddhist books • Build databases for the collections • Provide different retrieval approaches to the texts	• Explore different Buddhism resources • Archive physical materials selected • Scan the physical materials • Cataloging and description for database • Provide retrieval approaches for users • Solve the copyright issues
Cooperation	• With education institute to build Buddhist collection • With other temples to help monks read Buddhist classics	• Provide books, journals, audio and videos, and other physical collections to users • Offer retrieval access for users to find collections • Act as a professional library of Buddhism subjects.	• With Buddhist research organizations in different regions to find and acquire special local collections • With different media to better spread and use the database • With technological teams to design diverse retrieval accesses, websites, and mobile applications
Challenges	• Scientifically design the venue for both archiving and reading • Keep the environment suitable for precious materials • Find out the unique value of the library	• Purchase books, journals, and other publications • Apply catalog and description from national libraries • Enrich the classification of Buddhist books • Build databases for the collections • Provide different retrieval approaches to the texts	• Low utilization of digital format for published books • The massive cost of various scan machines and human resources • How could users search for specific collections • How to catalog the collections logically • Develop the exploration of the database's value
Contributions	• Donations from all sectors of society • Provide high-quality learning materials for monks • Develop the opportunities for communication among temples • Benefit local education institutes with Buddhist resources	• With other libraries to build union catalogs for interlending • With other Buddhist libraries, to avoid massive repetitive digitalization work • With internal and external Venerables to make sermon videos and audios to enrich the collections • With a larger scale database-driven Buddhist library to upload the resources to a shared platform • Provide consultation service in the field of Buddhism culture	• Preserve precious Buddhism culture • Low the cost of maintaining Buddhist collections for learners, researchers, and Buddhists worldwide • Well organize the collections by scientific catalogs and descriptions for future generations' convenience • Collaborate with researchers to analyze religious texts to discover further knowledge and wisdom

CONCLUSIONS AND LIMITATIONS

This study has investigated the adaption and digitalization development of Buddhist libraries in the current mobile computing age and proposes a three-level pyramid model of Buddhist library digitalization through a case study of YBL. Notably, due to the tremendous size of Buddhist sutras and other related work, the collections and other digitalization efforts need advanced database support for Open Public Access Catalog (OPAC)(Chung & Chiu, 2016). Human resources, operation, and maintenance costs are substantial also due to the enormous collection size.

Digitalized Buddhist resources would contribute much to the education and popularization of Buddhist traditional religion, values, and ethics. Buddhist libraries may consider deploying outrearch activities to the next generation in schools with the help of educational institutes or NGOs based on digitalized resources and media created (Tse et al., 2022). Also, digitalized materials may contribute to cultural game development to outreach to the younger generation (He et al., 2022). Further promotion of Buddhist knowledge and library services can be carried out through social media to reach the mass public (Lam et al., in press).

The main limitation of this study is its scope within only the field of Chinese Buddhist libraries. For example, BDRC was established in America with branches in other places such as India, Thailand, and Germany. Further studies should be carried out on the situations, services, and contributions of non-Chinese Buddhist resources, and other theological libraries worldwide (Lo, Cho, & Chiu, 201u7).

REFERENCES

Bai, H. (2008). Problems of the Catalog of Chinese Buddhism Books. *Journal of Peking University*, *45*(1), 142–145.

Bingenheimer, M. (2020). *Digitization of Buddhism*. Oxford University Press.

Chen, L., & Xu, J. (2010). The Analysis of Buddhism Library Construction in Mainland China. *Journal of Academic Libraries*, *28*(2), 19–23.

Cheung, T. Y., Ye, Z., & Chiu, D. K. W. (2021). Value chain analysis of information services for the visually impaired: A case study of contemporary technological solutions. *Library Hi Tech*, *39*(2), 625–642. doi:10.1108/LHT-08-2020-0185

Chung, A. C. W., & Chiu, D. K. (2016). OPAC Usability Problems of Archives: A Case Study of the Hong Kong Film Archive. *International Journal of Systems and Service-Oriented Engineering*, *6*(1), 54–70. doi:10.4018/IJSSOE.2016010104

Ding, S. J., Lam, E. T. H., Chiu, D. K. W., Lung, M. M., & Ho, K. K. W. (2021). Changes in reading behavior of periodicals on mobile devices: A comparative study. *Journal of Librarianship and Information Science*, *53*(2), 233–244. doi:10.1177/0961000620938119

Dong, Y. (2015). The Transmutation of the Category of B94 Buddhism in Chinese Library Classification. *Hebei Sci-Tech Library Journal*, *28*(5), 41–43.

Hartley, L. (2007). Tibetan Buddhist Resource Center (TBRC) Knowledge Base and Digital Library. *College & Research Libraries*, *68*(5), 446.

He, Z., Chiu, D. K. W., & Ho, K. K. W. (2022). Weibo Analysis on Chinese Cultural Knowledge for Gaming. In Z. Sun (Ed.), *Handbook of Research on Foundations and Applications of Intelligent Business Analytics* (pp. 320–349). IGI Global. doi:10.4018/978-1-7998-9016-4.ch015

Huang, J. (2011a). On Openness of the Ancient Chinese Buddhist Sutra Mansions. *Library and Information Service*, *55*(9), 138–142.

Huang, J. (2011b). A Study on the Ancient Chinese Buddhist Sutra Mansions. *Library & Information*, *55*(3), 139–144.

Huang, P. S., Paulino, Y., So, S., Chiu, D. K. W., & Ho, K. K. W. (2021). Special Issue Editorial - COVID-19 Pandemic and Health Informatics (Part 1). *Library Hi Tech*, *39*(3), 693–695. doi:10.1108/LHT-09-2021-324

Huang, P.-S., Paulino, Y. C., So, S., Chiu, D. K. W., & Ho, K. K. W. (2022). Guest editorial: COVID-19 Pandemic and Health Informatics Part 2. *Library Hi Tech*, *40*(2), 281–285. doi:10.1108/LHT-04-2022-447

(2016). Huixu. (2016). Talks on Construction of Digital Archives and Library in Buddhist Temples. *Archives and Construction*, (9), 81–84.

Jiang, T., Lo, P., Cheuk, M. K., Chiu, D. K. W., Chu, M. Y., Zhang, X., Zhou, Q., Liu, Q., Tang, J., Zhang, X., Sun, X., Ye, Z., Yang, M., & Lam, S. K. (2019). **文化新語:兩岸四地傑出圖書館、檔案館及博物館傑出工作者訪談** [New Cultural Dialog: Interviews with Outstanding Librarians, Archivists, and Curators in Greater China]. Hong Kong: Systech Publications.

Jingtao, S., & Qingyi, Z. (2002). Library Sort Number Management System. *Computer Systems& Applications*, *2002*(11), 127–130.

Lam, A. H. C., Chiu, D. K. W., & Ho, K. K. W. (in press). Instagram for student learning and library promotions? A quantitative study using the 5E Instructional Model. *Aslib Journal of Information Management*.

Li, H. (2014). History of Master Taixu Establishing World Buddhist Center Library. *Mt Wutai Researches*, *2014*(S1), 44–47.

Li, K. K., & Chiu, D. K. W. (2021, December 23). A Worldwide Quantitative Review of the iSchools' Archival Education. *Library Hi Tech*. Advance online publication. doi:10.1108/LHT-09-2021-0311

Liu, X. (2022). *Chinese Buddhist Literature Database and Image Text Extraction Algorithm. In International Conference on Cognitive based Information Processing and Applications (CIPA 2021)* (pp. 122-127). Springer.

Lo, P., Chan, H. H. Y., Tang, A. W. M., Chiu, D. K. W., Cho, A., Ho, K. K. W., See-To, E., He, J., Kenderdine, S., & Shaw, J. (2019). Visualising and Revitalising Traditional Chinese Martial Arts – Visitors' Engagement and Learning Experience at the 300 Years of Hakka KungFu. *Library Hi Tech*, *37*(2), 273–292. doi:10.1108/LHT-05-2018-0071

Lo, P., Chiu, D. K. W., & Cho, A. (2017). *Inside the World's Major East Asian Collections: One Belt, One Road, and Beyond*. Chandos Publishing.

Lo, P., Cho, A., & Chiu, D. K. W. (2017). *World's Leading National, Public, Monastery and Royal Library Directors – Leadership, Management, Future of Libraries*. De Gruyter.

Ma, L., Long, C., Duan, L., Zhang, X., Li, Y., & Zhao, Q. (2020). Segmentation and recognition for historical Tibetan document images. *IEEE Access: Practical Innovations, Open Solutions*, *8*, 52641–52651. doi:10.1109/ACCESS.2020.2975023

Mak, M. Y. C., Poon, A. Y. M., & Chiu, D. K. W. (2022). Using Social Media as Learning Aids and Preservation: Chinese Martial Arts in Hong Kong. In S. Papadakis & A. Kapaniaris (Eds.), *The Digital Folklore of Cyberculture and Digital Humanities*. IGI Global.

Okunlaya, R. O., Syed Abdullah, N., & Alias, R. A. (2022, March 07). (in press). Artificial intelligence (AI) library services innovative conceptual framework for the digital transformation of university education. *Library Hi Tech*. Advance online publication. doi:10.1108/LHT-07-2021-0242

Richards, T. (2017). Thematic framework of online review research. *International Journal of Contemporary Hospitality Management*, *29*(1), 307–354. doi:10.1108/IJCHM-11-2015-0664

Shen, X. (2014). Jianzhen Library: Analysis on the Cultural Features of the Biggest Buddhist Library in China. *Sci-Tech Information Development & Economy*, *2014*(17), 77–78.

(2012). Shiyongxin. (2012). Talks on Preservation of Ancient Books in Buddhist Temple. *Religions In China*, (6), 64–65.

Tse, H. L., Chiu, D. K., & Lam, A. H. (2022). From Reading Promotion to Digital Literacy: An Analysis of Digitalizing Mobile Library Services With the 5E Instructional Model. In A. Almeida & S. Esteves (Eds.), *Modern Reading Practices and Collaboration Between Schools, Family, and Community* (pp. 239–256). IGI Global. doi:10.4018/978-1-7998-9750-7.ch011

Wang, P., Chiu, D. K. W., Ho, K. K., & Lo, P. (2016). Why read it on your mobile device? Change in reading habit of electronic magazines for university students. *Journal of Academic Librarianship*, *42*(6), 664–669. doi:10.1016/j.acalib.2016.08.007

Wittern, C. (2000). Buddhist Studies in the Digital Age. *Chung-Hwa Buddhist Journal*, *2000*(13), 321–351.

Wong, S. W. S., & Chiu, D. K. W. (2023). (in press). Re-examining the value of remote academic library storage in the mobile digital age: A comparative study. *Portal (Baltimore, Md.)*, *23*(1).

Yau, A., Chiu, D. K. W., Nakamura, Y., & Li, K. K. (in press). Quantitative Comparison of LIS Programs Accredited by ALA and CILIP. *Library Hi Tech*.

Yu, P. Y., Lam, E. T. H., & Chiu, D. K. W. (2022, February 16). Operation management of academic libraries in Hong Kong under COVID-19. *Library Hi Tech*. Advance online publication. doi:10.1108/LHT-10-2021-0342

Zeng, Y. (2012). Wang Wenshan: The Founder of the Classification of Chinese Modern Buddhist Classics. *Journal of The Sichuan Society for Library Science*, *2012*(5), 79–80.

Zhang, Z. (2010). Talks from Past to Present of Buddhist Book Collection in Ancient Chinese Temple. *Library Theory and Practice*, *2010*(4), 96–98.

Zhou, Z. (2005). The Attempt of Buddhist Library to Use Chinese Library Classification — the Compilation of Yunlin Buddhist Library Classification. *Journal of the China Society of Indexers*, *3*(3), 37–39.

Zhuo, G. (2012a). A Preliminary Study on the Development of Buddhist Temple Libraries in China. *Ascent*, *31*(4), 161–164.

Zhuo, G. (2012b). Views on the Construction of Tibetan Buddhist Temple Library. *Library Work and Study*, *31*(9), 81–83.

KEY TERMS AND DEFINITIONS

Digitalization: A process of moving the libraries to provide services digitally, using digital technologies to alter the mode of library services and enhance the quality of services to users in the case of libraries.

Online Public Access Catalog (OPAC): An online database of materials held by a library, group of libraries, archives, musuems, or other information organization.

Special Libraries: A type of library providing information resources and services specialized and restricted to a particular group of clientele, normally small in size. Examples include museum libraries, law libraries, theological libraies, and libraries for students with special education needs.

Yunlin Buddhist Library: A religious librry established in 2003 as an internal library in Lingyin Temple, a Buddhist temple in Hangzhou, China.

Chapter 15
Museum Digital Activities During the Pandemic:
Art as a Communicative Experience

Eirini Sifaki
https://orcid.org/0000-0002-8342-3898
University of Thessaly, Greece

ABSTRACT

The COVID-19 pandemic and the consequent instability of the health crisis rapidly transformed the cultural landscape and the way the public experiences the museum. Recent research suggests that museums saw a rise in online activity, shifting traditional audience profiles and challenging museums to find ways of accommodating new forms of engagement. This chapter highlights the central role of online cultural content in broadening social access, enhancing the museum experience, and consolidating a new form of communication with audiences in the digital environment. Building from cultural theory, the author then focus on cultural creation during the COVID-19 pandemic confinement focusing on an innovative, creative project organized by the National Museum of Contemporary Art in Athens (EMST). Finally, these vernacular forms of cultural expression converse with digital folklore research, hoping to fuel the discussions within the digital humanities related to the worlds of art, its social influences, and reception.

INTRODUCTION

The adverse situation of the global health crisis accelerated the digital transformation in the cultural sector. It opened the way to extensive use of digital media by cultural institutions that offered their content online during the pandemic. The experience of visiting a museum, attend to an exhibition, or watching a play or a film in a public space was limited by having access to online cultural content, making the internet the default form of engagement. Cultural institutions were therefore forced to accelerate their digital practices and processes and make sharp modifications to their programming, using a wide variety of activities drawing on existing resources, including digitized collections and social media, and the creation of new digital content, such as virtual exhibitions, curatorial talks, and virtual tours of

DOI: 10.4018/978-1-6684-4461-0.ch015

galleries. As a result, user participation and engagement emerged as a main priority and concern for the institutions to continue to exercise their mission and social role and discover new means to stay present in their constituents' lives.

Recent surveys and research suggest that museums saw a rise in engagement and changed traditional audience proðles, challenging museums to ðnd ways of accommodating new forms of engagement to survive and thrive in the post-pandemic environment. Therefore, from an audience development perspective, the shift to digital-only participation brings the potential for new and diversified audiences to encounter cultural institutions' collections and artworks.

However, the main concern raised within the scope of digital humanities is related to issues of cultural traditions and digital folklore produced by the cultural elites and authorities. How do cultural institutions fulfill their multiple societal roles as organic entities that link creation, experience, and meaning? And more importantly, what are audiences and individual users doing with the cultural content once they have access to it? What forms of expression emerge from these creative activities?

This chapter highlights the central role of online cultural content in broadening social access, enhancing the museum experience, and consolidating a new form of communication with audiences. We explore how the pandemic has changed the ways museums and cultural institutions provide access to public collections, consider the early and ongoing challenges they face, and the impacts on the type of cultural traditions they produce. Building from cultural theory, which aims to explain the nature of culture and its implications for social life, we focus on cultural creation during the confinement period and its aftermath. Individual, felt experience with arts involvement is a rare gift offered to researchers in their quest to critically explore how culture shapes human action and relates to society. Our analysis focuses on valuable empirical material produced by health professionals during the pandemic. This creative material of vernacular expression was chosen among digital cultural activities on offer during the confinement period for its creative and social character. "EMST for Health" was organized by the National Museum of Contemporary Art (EMST) to bring health professionals into a creative dialogue with contemporary art and function as relief in that period and as a tool for negotiating fear, responsibility, and fatigue. Participants approached and communicated with the various artists' works from different perspectives and modes of expression. The phase of creation and expression was indeed the core project's intention to reduce the intensity and fatigue through art and open a window to dream and creative expression. Participants then engaged with selected artworks of the EMST collection (paintings, installations, videos, sculptures) chosen by the curators and sent randomly to participants to produce their creations. Their involvement with different works of art resulted in producing rich textual and visual material (short texts, poems, photographs, paintings, objects, and artifacts), which comprises their thoughts, feelings, and experience with the work of art in that particular period. In this light, we consider this specific collection of artistic/cultural creations the repository of recorded communication that allows us to explore the cultural traditions and digital folklore produced by the cultural elites and authorities' emergent forms of expression and individual experiences.

Finding adequate theoretical vocabularies and grammars to capture and critically address these shifting realities in Greece and beyond is a challenge in cultural theory. In this study, we undertake an ethnographic approach to the subject in cultural analysis. This interdisciplinary practice – proposed and developed by cultural theorist Mieke Bal (2009), resists the tendency to use cultural objects as illustrations of a pre-existing argument or theoretical scheme. It calls instead for intimate engagement with the object of study through close readings that are always attentive to the object's situatedness: the context of its making and the multiple other shifting contexts in which it is called to function and in which it intervenes.

Various mini-methodologies to use Bal's terminology, concepts and tools guide our engagement with the cultural object. All online material and the organization's official discourse on the web were scrutinized and analysed to produce contextual real-world knowledge about issues of cultural traditions and digital folklore produced by the cultural elites and authorities. To illuminate the process through which particular cultural articulations are forged by cultural institutions and in order to discuss the validity of theoretical concepts and models, we decided to conduct a semi-structured interview with the two educational curators who created the project. Field research would allow us to understand their aspirations as cultural managers better, the project's context and intentions, their experiences of the process (designing and implementing cultural actions and programs), and this project's impact. The interview guide included questions that resulted from our research questions and our empirical findings. It included conceptual questions regarding the role and the benefits of museum's activities to society, their experiences as creators and recipients of the creative activities, and the intrinsic benefits of involvement and the creative process, but also generic questions about EMST's role and mission and technical questions regarding the design and implementation of the specific project. We then performed a qualitative content analysis to encounter the cultural texts, in this case with the analysis of the textual and visual material (short texts, poems, photographs, paintings, objects, and artifacts) produced by the project EMST for health participants.

MUSEUM'S PARTICIPATORY STRATEGIES IN THE DIGITAL AGE

Museums constitute rich participatory ecosystems that promote knowledge, understanding of their cultural context, and different kinds of benefits for individuals, communities, and societies. Museum's mission has changed over the years while its core activities are aligned with a participatory experience and anthropocentric character. However, social interaction is also inherent to museum practices, while cultural activities enhance learning, aesthetic experiences, and sociability. In this light, the first digital interactive applications that sought to provide a richer and more engaging experience for visitors were strongly criticized for prioritizing the individual user while overturning the inherent social potential of museums for co-participation and cooperation. The digital shift has led to the development of a promising research area looking for ways to enhance the digital social dimension of museums to meet their purposes and missions in general (Vayanou, Katifori, Chrysanthi & Antoniou, 2020).

As Ruttkay and Benysei (2018) point out, we are experiencing the renaissance of museums through the digital age. Undoubtedly, enhancing the digital environment offers museums the opportunity to achieve visibility, extroversion, and sustainability (Bertacchini & Morando, 2013). For museums, their cultural content is the source of long-term social value and the "recyclable raw materials" of the information and knowledge society (Ross, Economou & Anderson, 1998). Digital technology opens up new perspectives and expectations for the way visitors interact with the museum. As technology is constantly evolving, so is art. The constant exploration and experimentation of new forms of communication, of a more interactive and two-way nature, is another challenge for museums (Carayannis, Bast & Campbell, 2018).

Along with the digital shift in technology, there has also been a change in narration (storytelling), with user experience, commitment, and co-creation taking a central place in the design and implementation of museum services. Of particular importance is the use of new technologies in the display and communication of museums, opening communication channels not only with the existing public but also with potential visitors - users on an interactive level (Akker & Legend, 2016). The most crucial advantage that new technologies offer is undoubtedly interactivity. Through digital technology in the museum space, until now, ordinary visitors have become active participants in the museum (Rey & Casado-Neira, 2013), thus enhancing their two-way communication with the museum. The creation of participatory culture and the democratization of knowledge (Sylaiou, Basiouka, Patias, & Stylianidis, 2013) remains a focal point of these advancements.

According to Ruttkay and Benyei (2018), the digital communication strategy of a museum should have a long-term character and use digital media to achieve specific communication goals. Equally important is the ongoing accessibility that extends beyond online visits by encouraging discussion-building communities and further reflection. Their experience, however, their involvement and critical evaluation can have a dynamic impact on the museum since they lay the foundations of the museum's digital "edifice" (O'Brien & Toms, 2008).

Therefore, a museum's digital communication strategy is vital to promote its cultural content and communicate its benefits to the general public. It also contributes to the enrichment of the experience gained by the visitor - user through digital aesthetic stimuli he receives, enhances the museum's visibility to an international audience through the messages it spreads, and encourages the creation of virtual communities. Virtual participants and users give life and voice to the museum and develop initiatives and innovative actions with a human-centered character. Quality metrics and online marketing research can offer a deep understanding of the needs and preferences to enable museums/ cultural organizations to understand and quickly respond to their digital visitor's expectations, implementing an effective anthropocentric design for their cultural actions. Digital media and the practices they choose to adopt, their promotion on social media, and the enhancement of their digital environment offer a great advantage, especially since 2020 when the pandemic plagued the world.

MUSEUM COMMUNICATION DURING THE PANDEMIC

Digital Transformations in the Cultural Sector

The outbreak of the Covid-19 pandemic in late 2019 has affected every aspect of society. Countries had to find a delicate balance between protecting public health, minimizing economic and social disruption, and respecting human rights (Magliacani & Sorrentino, 2021). The evolving pandemic manifested itself as a total social event that disrupted socio-economic, political, and cultural institutions and spread to every aspect of daily life locally, nationally, and globally (Demertzis & Eyeman, 2020).

This new crisis surpassed all known precedents, suddenly interrupting the flow of everyday life and bringing the citizens to a rupture with what, until then, they considered facts. As a result, national governments have taken many restrictive measures to limit the spread of coronavirus and protect the supreme good of public health and human life. These measures included closing borders, banning travel, suspending the operation of retail, catering, and training units, and introducing compulsory distance education and teleworking. The imposed state of lockdown and consequent social isolation has led to space-time compression, plunging millions of citizens into a climate of uncertainty and anxiety, cultivating feelings of sadness and fear of an uncharted world. The negative impact of isolation on mental health suggests the importance of interaction between citizens and with important sites where cultural heritage plays a critical social role. The pandemic highlighted how the size of space and the intervention between people determine profound changes in the personal, social, and economic spheres and consequently in the way of life (Europa Nostra, 2020). Demertzis and Eyeman (2020) note that the combination of health, economic and humanitarian crises may develop into a cultural trauma that determines individual and collective identity.

As an integral part of society, culture has found itself in an unexpected situation, while the viability of museums and cultural organizations has been and continues to be a vivid topic of discussion. The cultural landscape was the first to suffer the effects of the pandemic and the protection measures for public health. The appearance of the first epidemic in Greece on 26 February 2020 initially led to the cancellation of carnival celebrations and the gradual adoption of horizontal restrictive measures such as the closure of schools on 10 March and all other public gathering places on 13 March.

The country, having a weak national health system due to the previous economic crisis and an aging population, went into a state of lockdown on 23 March 2020. Taking individual responsibility was at the forefront of the information campaign conducted on social media under the auspices of the social message: "we stay home." This supernatural situation soon extended to any form of individual or collective artistic activity, affecting the endemic fragile ecosystem of cultural life. The disruption of the processes and functions of the cultural sector has led to the paralysis of the national and global cultural and artistic industry, disrupting the social system and revealing structural components of the disease of the cultural sector (Micheli, 2020). Furthermore, the sharp decline in the supply and demand of tourism affected economically and socially communities and plunged artists and those employed in culture into a state of extreme economic and social instability (Unesco, 2020a). The Ministry of Culture harmonized with the world cultural policy and imposed a universal ban on visiting all places of cultural interest (museums, galleries, cinemas, archeological sites).

Museums, which relied heavily on the number of visitors for their income, faced a severe problem of financial viability. Therefore, the Ministry of Culture has launched a series of horizontal and development measures to mitigate the economic consequences of the pandemic, enhance the viability of cultural organizations, and support artists and those employed in the cultural sector, investing more than 100 million euros in the cultural sector. In addition, for the first time, the fundamental forces of culture have been transparently mapped so that practical political and financial tools can be established (Ministry of Culture and Sports, 2020a). At the same time, the Ministry of culture addressed a special invitation to create and distribute digital cultural material, original or conversion of an existing one, aiming at the possibility of remote access in the context of finding alternative ways of cultural production and innovative means of cultural expression (Ministry of Culture and Sports, 2020b).

According to the Unesco report (2020b), the impact of the suspension of museums is not only economic but also social, as museums play a vital role in society. They are not just "utensils" of works and artifacts but meeting places, knowledge exchange, and social networking that strengthen the local and regional creative economy, promote education and creativity, enhance social cohesion and act as carriers of collective memory. In addition, they promote tourism, which is a critical factor in sustainable economic development at a local and national level, which will help overcome the crisis in the future (Unesco, 2020b).

The Reaction of Cultural Organizations and the Change in the Museum Experience

The covid-19 pandemic and the consequent instability of the health crisis rapidly transformed the cultural landscape and the way the public experiences the museum as the condition of physical presence is no longer a choice. However, museums have shown remarkable resilience and developed immediate reflexes to maintain an active, experiential relationship with visitors and attract new audiences instead of usual practices (Tranta et al., 2021). Furthermore, cultural institutions have turned to harness their inexhaustible digital resources, trying to perpetuate artistic creativity and reduce the impact on a beleaguered culture, acting as start-ups and strengthening their digital strategies. Their main focus was to maintain their contacts and consolidate the public through the internet and social media (Orlandi 2020: 57).

As part of their communication extroversion, museums have utilized their existing resources to reach a more comprehensive online audience, such as their digitized collections, website, and social media accounts. In addition, they also offer free old and new content such as virtual tours, online exhibitions, curatorial speeches, archival material, e-books, podcasts, microsites, virtual tours in artists' houses, live streaming artistic performances, webinars, and experiential workshops. As a result, museums have been transformed from spaces for people to spaces of people (Janes, & Sandell, 2019). The open and interactive situation of new media also helps to expand the concept of a participatory museum (Simon, 2010). The openness and activeness created by new media increase the number of users and enhance the stable management of museums because it increases the opportunity for user participation.

Furthermore, in the context of participatory culture, they asked users to share their representations of famous works of art using everyday household items. In contrast, they shared museum stories and collections through widespread hashtags, such as #MuseumFumsHome, #M, #ClosedButOpen, #ClosedButActive, and #ArTyouReady, which disseminate information and engage users in an enhanced dialogue (Europeana pro n.d.).

Museums have been synchronized with the new condition of the home education process, offering creative ways for students to learn and socialize. Such activities include online training programs, competitions, quizzes, virtual treasure hunts, and recreational activities that have served as a cohesive family home for as long as they had to stay at home. Unesco has recorded more than eight hundred individual digital actions from museums and galleries in response to the pandemic (Unesco 2020b). The European Commission supported the creation of the Creatives Unite digital platform. Cultural initiatives and good museum practices are gathered, while the Ministry of Culture hosts museum organizations' digital actions and entertainment proposals. The digital transformation is emerging by the European Council as a vital pillar of the recovery and resilience mechanism for tackling the economic and social difficulties posed by the pandemic (EKT 2021).

The museum space is considered an environment of calm and mental rehabilitation. Therefore, the museums used their therapeutic action to virtually connect their visitors, acting as an "antidote" to sadness and personal isolation. After all, this tactic has been applied since 2018, when the French-speaking Medical Association of Canada, in collaboration with the Museum of Fine Arts in Montreal, prescribed free museum visits to its patients (Kara & Sungur, 2021). Furthermore, museums extended their social role and responded to the community's needs by offering free masks and gloves to hospitals, even operating as vaccination centers, such as the American Museum of Natural History and the Castello di Rivoli Museum in Rome. Recording and collecting the social and material culture of the incarceration experience as part of their function of building cultural resilience and protecting the cultural heritage of their communities (Cobley et al., 2020). Due to the available free time, art and culture generally functioned as a way of escape and an opportunity for individual and collective improvement (Magliacani & Sorrentino, 2020).

NEMO's following up survey in January 2021 recorded a digital boom, with 93% of museums increasing or launching online services during the pandemic, while more than 75% reported they had either increased their activities in social media or started video content creation. In addition, according to Agostino et al. (2020) research, museums conduct their activities based on the feedback they collect from social networks.

Also, 40% of museum personnel were redeployed to digital services, with 80% working from home, using communication tools such as zoom, Microsoft Teams, and Skype. The majority of the largest museums (81%) increased their digital capabilities, while only 47% of the smaller museums, indicating the lack of resources and digital skills and the need for support for a complete digital transition. Digital activities in social media were ranked as the most popular followed by educational videos (42%) and virtual tours (28%), which are more experiential and multimodal than linear (NEMO 2022c, Cobley et al. 2020). The cultural sector was twice "quarantined" since the first lockdown began on 13 March 2020 and ended in the summer of the same year. In Greece, museums opened on 15 June. The second forced lockdown was applied without consultation and stricter measures on 07 November. The downward trend of the epidemiological curve allowed the restart of museum organizations on 14 May 2021 (International Museum Day), in compliance with strict safety and health measures for the protection of visitors and their staff (Magliacani & Sorrentino, 2020). After the first opening of the museums, there was a decrease in visitors between 25-and 75% due to the decline of global tourism, reduced capacity, and restrictive measures. At the same time, the online traffic remained mainly at the same levels.

However, 40% of the museums did not follow the evolution of their online traffic, indicating the lack of a digital framework and reliable measurement and evaluation methods (NEMO, 2022c). The digital boom highlights the creativity and adaptability of the cultural sector in crises while highlighting some structural weaknesses in terms of resources, digital staff skills, communication, and the quality of cultural content on offer (ICOM, 2020a).

In addition, increased online activity has changed traditional visitor profiles, re-examining issues of audience segmentation, motivation, and interaction, and challenging museums to find ways to accommodate new forms of engagement in order to survive and thrive in the post-pandemic environment (Noehrer et al., 2021). Museums have increased their online presence and changed the content of cultural material transmitted through digital channels, which have evolved from communication tools to tools for disseminating knowledge.

The first type is the educational approach, where a one-way relationship is developed with the user through telling a story or an interview with a curator. The second approach involves asynchronous interaction, where the user receives information. However, it either does not require participation or requires an asynchronous response. Finally, the third approach consists of contemporary interaction, where the museum and the user interact simultaneously, as in the case of real-time educational initiatives (Agostino et al., 2020). In particular, contemporary interaction is a crucial element that strengthens the social context of cultural experiences (Vayanou et al., 2020). Through the pandemic, museums used digital platforms to offer object experiences, cognitive experiences, introspection experiences, and social experiences (Kara & Sungur, 2021), combining Pine & Gilmore's four spheres of experience.

According to Foucault (1966), museums are places of heterotopia. These places contain other places and other times, emphasizing the contribution of the organization of the space in shaping the museum visit experience (Tranta et al., 2021). Simon (2010) provides a theoretical approach to how digital technologies are reshaping the communication structure of museums in an information environment where the boundaries between the physical and online worlds become blurred. The experience and knowledge of the collection accessible in the online exhibition space, i.e., outside the original time and space, is reconstructed and enhanced with multimedia content used as an additional information field. The complementary narrative expands the involvement of the interested viewer, strengthening the level of the spiritual bond between him and the exhibition (Resta et al., 2021). Users act as ad hoc recipients and co-producers of cultural content, having the right to use, reuse and share information (Michelis, 2020).

Expanding the knowledge and experience of the interface improves the quality of the services offered, expands the use, and creates added cultural value. Furthermore, a new interface outside the exhibition room can complement the existing service, enabling a wider diverse audience to use it. Therefore, the use of digital media contributes to the retention of users and the interactive engagement of a potential audience as a critical tool for enhancing the sustainable competitiveness of museums (Resta et al., 2021).

Therefore, the pandemic is triggered by museums' efforts to use more effective means of communication to attract users amid a changing social context. In light of these recent changes, user involvement in museum management and the subsequent expansion of experience are expected to add value, creating a solid momentum of change for museum institutions and emphasizing digital innovation (Choi & Kim, 2021). Based on the initial literature review, the evolving pandemic served as both a threat and an opportunity to reconsider the rationalization of museum functions, the inclusion of new audiences, and the changing business models, highlighting the need for more investment and innovation in digital strategies. Furthermore, digital engagement is at the core of museum communication practices, directly linked to the competitiveness of museums (Noehrer et al., 2021).

Examples of Adoption of Good Communication Practices by Museums

Despite the challenges, many cultural institutions continued to function as sources of resilience and support for their communities, developing original and creative online initiatives to provide access to culture under restrictive measures (Unesco, 2020b). For example, in response to the stressful situation caused by the pandemic crisis, the History Museum of London, in strategic partnership with the Museum of Dreams of Canada, has created the digital version of an oral history program that seeks to capture Londoners' dreams by recording their personal experiences during the pandemic.

The Guardians of Sleep program is part of the museum's broader work to study the impact of the Collecting Covid pandemic, exploring ways to deal with stress in times of crisis. According to the museum's head of digital services, the work seeks to record and tell the personal stories of Londoners throughout the pandemic, allowing them to document a shared experience so that future generations can better understand it. Participants were invited to chat with psychosocial experts via zoom, while the collected material was examined to be included in the museum's permanent collection (Charr, 2021).

The Museo del Prado in Madrid wanted to take advantage of this period to present the invisible side of the museum by promoting the series "Video en directo" on social networks (Facebook, Instagram) and its official channel on YouTube. The videos present selected works in a dialectical format with the curators, custodians, or experts from all fields, delving into critical aspects of the permanent collection. Penetrating the invisible world of the museum, they highlight works of art found in the warehouse and reveal ways of preservation and details that go unnoticed during the physical visit. At the same time, they conduct live chats every Friday at noon, where the curators answer questions posed by the public throughout the week.

In the same context, the Museum of Modern Art (Moderna Museet) in Stockholm organizes live tours every Thursday (Sofa Tours) published on its official website and Facebook page. Users can ask questions about art at the museum staff from the comfort of their couch. The videos are stored and re-broadcast on Facebook and the museum's channel on YouTube, while related podcasts are also available.

The methods regularly used by the administrators of museum organizations to attract the public through participatory actions have become widespread. One of the most innovative activities that were quickly rebroadcast through social media and encouraged international participation in the Getty Challenge was implemented by the Getty Museum in Los Angeles in collaboration with the Rijksmuseum (Amsterdam), the Metropolitan Museum (New York), and (St. Petersburg), with the initial inspiration of an Instagram account from Amsterdam, called "Between Art and Quarantine."

The Getty Museum posted the challenge on its Twitter page, urging restricted users to display famous works of art using everyday household materials and post their photos on social media (Figures 2, 3, 4). This imaginative project received a spectacular response (viral), while in addition to individuals, the challenge was recaptured by other cultural institutions, such as the National Museum of Arts of Romania (https://art.art/blog/between-art-and-quarantine).

The Rijksmuseum State Museum created the video series "Rijksmuseum from Home," which proved to be very popular with the public. It took viewers to the museum administrators' homes to share stories about their favorite museum exhibits. In addition, the museum offered an interactive 360-degree virtual tour of the Gallery of Honor, its most iconic gallery, and live TikTok tours. The Masterpieces Up Close tour allows the public to get up close and personal with some of the museum's most famous works of art while incorporating game play elements for participants over the age of nine to discover hidden keys found inside the gallery (Richardson, 2021).

An excellent example of understanding the current issue of modern social isolation due to a pandemic was the creation of videos based on the Anne Frank Diary from the Anne Frank Museum in Amsterdam. These videos aimed to understand the audience's experience of Anna's confinement and isolation and deepen their own experiences due to social distancing and confinement. Comments in a recent video diary suggest that the audience gains strength through emotional identification. Some say that the then inclusion of Anne Frank has had a strong emotional impact on the world throughout the pandemic (Kist, 2020).

Similarly, the International Slavery Museum (www.liverpoolmuseums.org.uk/international-slavery-museum), based in Liverpool, England, encouraged understanding of COVID-19's recent experiences by posting @migrant_artist_mutual_aid on Instagram, which brought together user isolation experiences. The museum states that from all the answers collected, the word "power" stands out among all, which is not at all surprising. "Our spirit will not be broken!" This Instagram post defines isolation as a collective experience and encourages a sense of shared resilience. Such examples show that through digital cultural actions, the public can understand the experience of isolation and raise intense concerns about personal roles and social responsibility in the post-Covid era (Kist, 2020).

Greek museums took advantage of the pandemic period and the suspension of the operation of their natural spaces to enhance their digital environments and actions. The Greek government, during the pandemic, presented through its website (covid19.gov.gr/draseis-politismou/) a variety of digital activities of various museums that were free to the public.

The National Archaeological Museum (EAM) has launched its digital transformation program with a plan for its completion in 2023, aiming to strengthen its communication services to the public. In addition, by updating its website (www.namuseum.gr) it managed to reach 1,500,000 online visitors. In addition to the documentation and digitization of its exhibits, the Archaeological Museum of Piraeus

Figure 1. Cycladic. Marble [Male Harp Player of the Early Spedos Type, 2700–2300 B.C]. © The J. Paul Getty Museum. Recreation via Facebook DM by Irena Ochódzka with canister vacuum, Retrieved from https://www.getty.edu/news/getty-artworks-recreated-with-household-items-by-creative-geniuses-the-world-over/

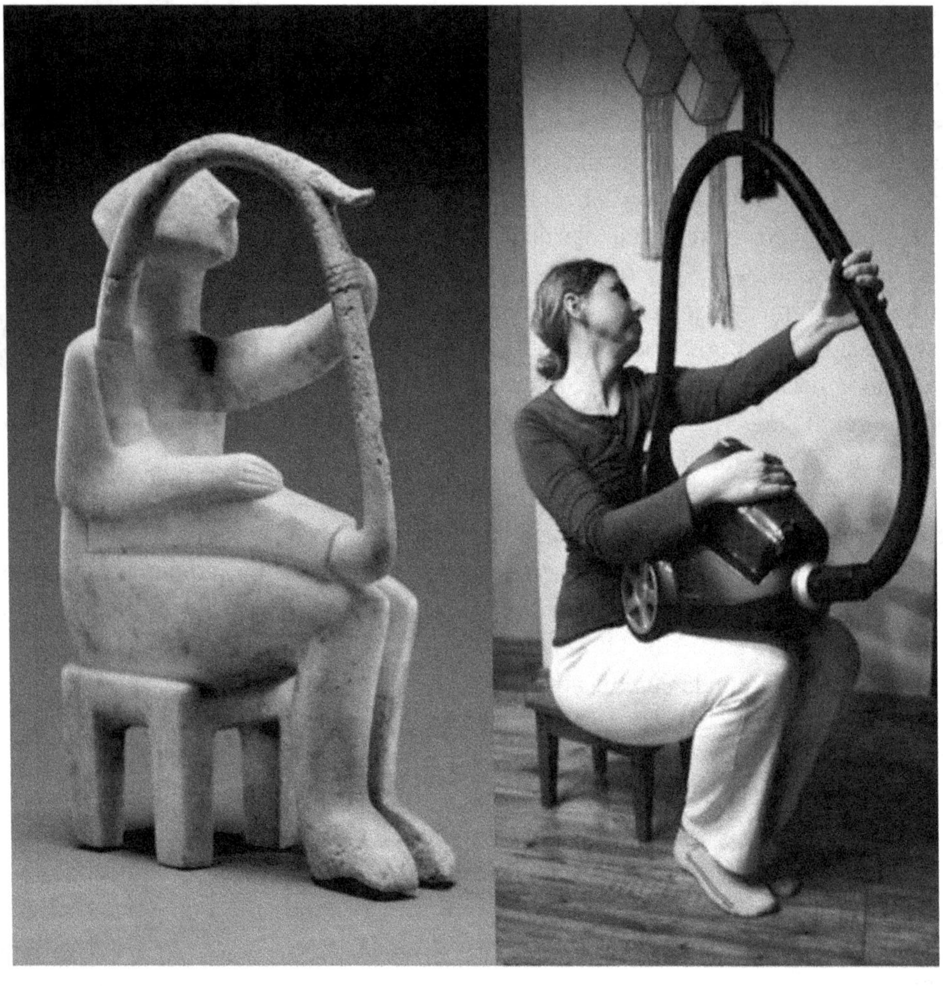

led the digital exhibition "2,500 years from Salamis and Thermopylae" organized under the auspices of the Museum Directorate of the Ministry of Culture.

The Museum of the History of Greek Costume of the Lyceum of Greek Women asked the online public to send anything related to the period of confinement, such as handmade masks, works of art, sketches, clothing, improvised inventions, or objects related to personal experiences virus. The museum's purpose was to collect the "Objects of the pandemic" for the formation of a unique collection in order to create a real-time memory bank. Furthermore, the preservation of material evidence from the pandemic era would be used for future study and scientific readings of how the world experienced the change in its daily life.

The Benaki Museum utilized its cultural stock and produced a new one, offering a virtual tour of its collections and an audio tour in six languages. During its suspension period, the museum's staff's desire to be close to its audience led to implementing "Close-Ups" digital action. It concerns an original series of short and comprehensive videos presenting the objects of its collection through its narration scientific director and curators of the museum. The series attempts to shed light on museum objects through the stories they tell and the stories of the people associated with them. The concept of proximity, which indicates the title of the digital action, urges the public to closely see the details of the museum objects to stay close to the museum itself, motivating the physical visit at the beginning of its reopening.

As part of the SNF Nostos festival, the Stavros Niarchos Foundation Cultural Center (SNFCC) invited children and teenagers aged 6 to 17 to participate in the interactive Minecraft Challenge game to imagine and build their version of an entire or selected section of the SNFCC. Participants could participate in the challenge either through their electronic device using Minecraft software or unplugged with their building materials. The purpose of the digital action was to encourage children to browse online at the SNFCC sites, be inspired by them, and create a fantastic world with the contribution of technology.

The mentioned digital actions bring a double benefit to the communication strategy of the international and domestic museum organizations. On the one hand, their increased presence on social media increases their visibility and enhances their reputation. However, on the other hand, they act according to the feeling of being socially responsible, especially in times of crisis, giving them added value (Guboglo, 2020).

Among all the digital cultural activities on offer, one that attracted our attention for its creative and social character was the "EMST for Health", organized by the National Museum of Contemporary Art (EMST). This cultural action wanted to honor the health workers for their valuable work and the tireless support they offer to the community.

The National Museum of Contemporary Art Athens: An Inclusive Museum Opens to Society and Contemporary Culture

The National Museum of Contemporary Art Athens (EMST) was founded in 1997 as a non-profit Legal Entity by Private Law, supervised and subsidized by the Hellenic Ministry of Culture and Sports. The museum began its operation in 2000 when it acquired the first artworks in its collection, and the first temporary exhibition took place. From 2003 until 2008, the EMST held exhibitions and activities at the Athens Concert Hall, the Athens School of Fine Arts, and public spaces.). In May 2015, the museum moved to its permanent location. The following year, the museological and museographical studies were approved by the Council of Museums of the Ministry of Culture and Sports. From October 2016 until January 2019, EMST operated the temporary exhibition spaces, educational programs, screening room, and the museum shop (https://www.emst.gr/en/the-museum/history). In addition, it presented many exhibitions and other activities in this context, including conferences, publishing presentations, film, dance and musical performances, and promotions.

As an official national patron and supporter of contemporary art in Greece, EMST collects, exhibits, preserves, researches, and interprets the art of our time in the broader global, historical and interdisciplinary context. The museum's mission statement mentions the general objectives of most contemporary art organizations. These include the preservation and promotion of works of art by Greek and foreign artists, with a focus on the history of contemporary art and works of various movements of contemporary artistic production, the promotion of aesthetic cultivation and artistic education of the public, the development of scientific research regarding the history and theory of contemporary art and contemporary artistic creation and the support and accommodation of art historians and theorists that specialize in museology (https://www.emst.gr/en/the-museum/mission). However, a particular corporate identity emerges when wandering around the museum's exhibitions, either in the natural space or in the digital environment, encountering the collection, studying the exhibition practices and the choices of artworks and its activities. Equal access to art for all, elimination of social exclusion, and enabling social inclusion could be the motto of EMST. An anthropocentric museum, open to society, embracing with its collaborations, synergies, and projects different social groups and especially vulnerable ones. For instance, the innovative program EMST Without Borders launched in 2009 includes collaborations and synergies with social groups and not-for-profit organizations such as Rehabilitation Centers Against Drug Abuse, Elderly Care Units, immigrant groups, the Academic Support and Accessibility Unit for Students with Disabilities of the Athens School of Fine Art, Schools of Intercultural Education and Second Chance Schools in Detention Centers. Acknowledging its social role and the need to respond to the specific requirements of different target groups, EMST adopts a participatory approach in the design and implementation of its projects: educational, recreational, experiential, interdisciplinary, and interactive.

EMST addresses the public from an activist and multicultural perspective, open to exploration, facilitating artistic and creative exchanges and prospects on contemporary culture. A culture that seems to be in constant search and negotiation, creating counter-narratives fueled from below. After many years of nomadic course with many administrative difficulties and two years of headless operation with transitional managers, in February 2020, EMST opened fully operational to the public. However, in just three weeks, in March 2020, the operation of all cultural venues was suspended due to the first lockdown in Greece. Despite all the adversity and the fact that the museum was forced to close temporarily shortly after its opening, it managed to remain active online by inviting the public to meet and participate in its digital activities, facilitating artistic dialogue (with its works of art), participatory activities and creation. EMST responded immediately and quickly adapted to the new situation that emerged from the rise of Covid - 19. In the first lockdown, there was an immediate self - organization to maintain the established dynamics with this digital organization of each person in charge of his home.

Regarding the essential elements of EMST's digital communication strategy, its central keystone is always the content. EMST's digital strategy promotes its identity as a living organization and enables a friendly and easy online visit. Another keystone of the museum's digital communication strategy is the constant monitoring of the cultural landscape and the adaptation to new emerging realities to the needs of the museum and the public in terms of enhancing EMST's communication with the public through digital content implemented during the confinement period. Especially during the first lockdown, people showed a great need to engage in creative ways from home and participate in the collective effort to deal with confinement. This was enabled by bringing forth new interpretations of the EMST collection's works with the public's active participation.

EMST managed to keep the public's interest active through its digital actions, engaging in a two-way dialogue. During the second lockdown, the museum's website was upgraded to make it friendlier, more accessible, and more manageable. In addition, EMST exploited social media and managed to increase user engagement continuously. Two more applications (Smartify and EMSTapp) are constantly being improved to meet better the needs of the museum and its contact and communication with the public. Some participatory digital activities also took place as the museum's communications manager considered it extremely important for the museum to have an excellent digital presence despite the difficulties and build an image that would showcase EMST and reflect its identity as a multifaceted cultural contemporary art organization. According to the museum's education curator, EMST designed interactive programs that activated physical participation, sought public involvement, and emphasized vulnerable groups (EMST 2021).

Figure 2. Yorgos Gyparakis. (1998). Nocturnal Landscape, Sculptural Installation]. © National Museum of Contemporary Art Athens (EMST). Athens, Greece.

Art as a Communicative Experience: Close Encounters with the Project EMST for Health

«Art reveals, entertains, excites, activates our creativity, and turns us into dreamers, fighters, or travelers. In the difficult period we are going through due to the Covid-19 pandemic, art can offer some relief, liberate us, and, above all, unite us» (https://www.emst.gr/en/category/emst-for-health). In these words, EMST for health curators communicated the project's ambitions/intentions to the public. Along these lines, the virtues of artistic creation and its receptive qualities are linked to broader social benefits.

Our goal in this section is to outline those hidden meanings, these expressive realities, and how they interiorize the participant's experiences during the social isolation period imposed by the pandemic. It should be acknowledged that our analysis in this section has its origins in different disciplines and contexts. However, the main insights are based on John Dewey's classic and influential work Art as Experience ([1934] 1980) and McCarthy's synthetic analysis of art as a communicative process (pp. 39-52). Looking into this valuable empirical material, we aspire to explicate contemporary cultural works and historicize, contextualize, and theorise on them. We will attempt to answer the main research questions: What are audiences and individual users doing with the cultural content once they have access to it? What forms of expression emerge from these creative activities, and what does it tell us about the historical understanding of lived experiences?

During the period December 2020- to February 2021 and following a relevant invitation from social media, the museum sent by email to interested participants a work of art from the permanent museum collection in the form of an electronic card, requesting their response to the artistic stimulus in any communicative form they desired. The program's purpose was to bring health professionals into a creative

Figure 3. Kimsooja. (2017). Bottari. [Installation]. © National Museum of Contemporary Art Athens (EMST). Athens, Greece.

dialogue with contemporary art. As a result, they can be relieved of their busy daily life and express themselves creatively.

Twenty-eight participations by health professionals of different backgrounds were the outcome of this innovative online cultural action. Their names and professional status are either mentioned under the generative title "EMST for health participations" or their more specific job title. These include nurses in intensive care Covid clinic, social workers, doctors, attending first anesthesiologists, systemic therapists and members of drug addiction prevention, pneumonologist - Intensive care specialist, mental health activities coordinators, art therapists, Coordinating Director (Greek) NHS, anesthesiologist, rehabilitation doctor, nurse, psychiatrist - psychotherapist, radiodiagnostic doctor, and a pharmacist. They live and work in Athens and other Greek cities but come from abroad (Elisabeth Ioannides, education curator at EMST, interview with the author 20/04/2022). According to the curators, the choice of artworks sent to participants was utterly random. "Our collection has many works, so we chose about 20 works and sent it to participants, trying to include various them" (Elisabeth Ioannides, education curator at EMST, interview with the author 20/04/2022). All were individual participations except for one group participation from the addiction treatment center, Kethea Epirus.

Now that the groups are gone and we are left as units,

how will the colors unfold, how will the knot be untied?

Figure 4. Maria Alexandri. (2021). Untitled. EMST for health participations. Retrieved from https://www.emst.gr/en/emst-for-health/maria-alexandri

Now that the groups are gone and we are left as units,

how will the colors unfold, how will the knot be untied?

Figure 5. Beatrice Andreotti. (2021). War refugee [Drawing]. EMST for health participations. Retreived from https://www.emst.gr/en/emst-for-health/beatrice-andreotti

A first objective finding is that most participants (18 out of 28) engaged with more than one artwork. Thirteen participants asked for a second card depicting a work of art from the museum's collections, two participants asked for a third card, and three asked for a fourth card. Participants approached and communicated with the various artists' works from different perspectives and modes of expression. The phase of creation and expression was indeed the core project's intention to reduce the intensity and fatigue through art and open a window to dream and creative expression. Participants then engaged with selected artworks of the EMST collection (paintings, installations, videos, sculptures) chosen by the curators and sent randomly to participants to produce their creations. Their involvement with different works of art resulted in producing rich textual and visual material (short texts, poems, photographs, paintings, objects, and artifacts). Writing was the preponderant mode of expression resulting in 30 responses. These responses comprised different types of creative writing such as short texts, phrases, prose, poems, and

Figure 6. Nikos Kessanlis. (1965). Restany [painting]. © National Museum of Contemporary Art Athens (EMST). Athens, Greece.

even song lyrics and lyrics from other poems. Through language, they reflected on the cultural contexts and meaning of the selected pieces. On the other hand, non-verbal artistic expressions such as drawings, paintings, photographs, and collages, connect more with the formal qualities of the artworks.

Seventeen responses included photographs of different types, both analog and digital such as smartphones, polaroids, etc. In some cases, photos accompanied a short text or poem explaining their associations with the artwork. In other cases, they display intermediality regarding discourses and modalities of representation of other photographs or recall their own past experiences. Other forms of artistic creation incorporated photographs into a collage (5 in total) using different materials and experimenting with the original artwork. In two instances, participants reprocessed digitally the original artwork created through mixed media art with additional or alternative narrations. Finally, realistic art is displayed through 7 paintings and three drawings, connecting with the formal and discursive qualities of the artwork that inspired them. This creative and discursive engagement with the various artworks functioned in different ways. Through our extended reading and thematic analysis of the artworks, we have identified two main categories that guide the interpretation of the produced vernacular material. They also respond to

Figure 7. Jones Evie. (2021). The path back to normality [painting]. EMST for health participations. Retrieved from https://www.emst.gr/en/emst-for-health/evie-jones

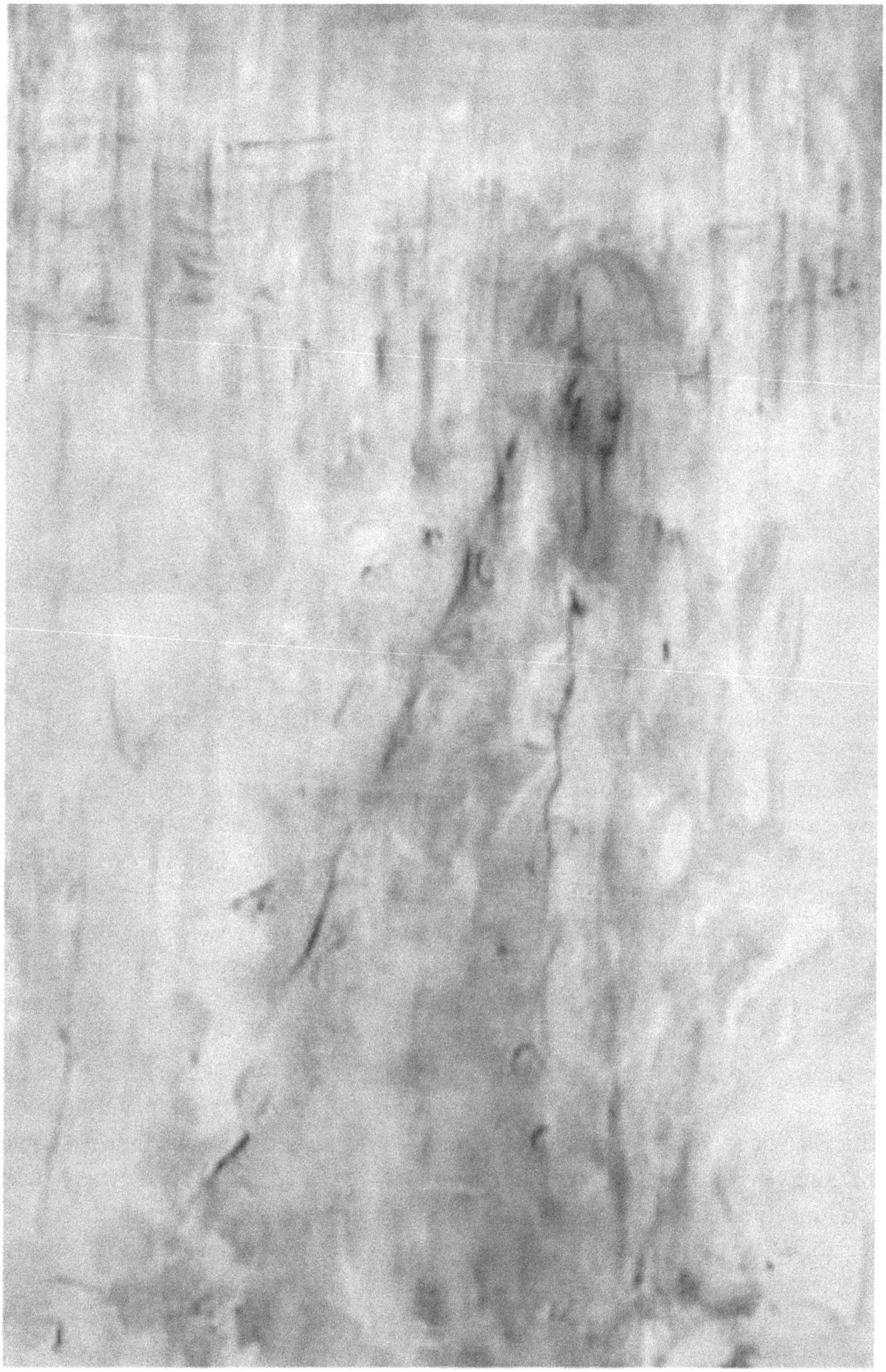

our third research question related to the forms of expression that emerge from these creative activities

Figure 8. Xenofon Tsoukalis. (2021). Sesamum Indicum. EMST for health participations. Retrieved from https://www.emst.gr/en/emst-for-health/tsoykalis-xenofon

and their subsequent effects/repercussions on the historical understanding of lived experiences. At the base of both categories, we can discern an internal process reflecting the thoughts and inner feelings that the work of art brought out.

Artistic creation is one of the most complex and mysterious activities of human consciousness and is only partly intelligible, even to those who have experienced it directly (McCarthy et al. 2004, p. 39). Accounts of the creative process generally agree that the artist draws on a highly developed capacity for vivid experiencing the world (including one's inner, private world). The artist, painter, writer, or composer often starts with an experience that is a kind of discovery. The second capacity is the ability to express this unique experience through a particular medium. As Joyce Cary, the Irish novelist, puts it, "the creative process is a kind of translation, not from one language into another, but one state of existence into another, from the receptive into the creative, from the purely sensuous impression into the purely reflective and critical act" (cited by McCarthy et al. 2004, p. 41). In the act of expression, the artist makes inner reality public and therefore communicable to others. The material he or she works with—whether language, image, sound, or movement—is not raw material but, rather, a public system of symbolic meaning developed and refined by generations of use and thus shaped by the society in which the artist develops. Engaging with the medium, the artist moves back and forth between his or her vision and the perspective of the imagined audience in the process of protracted labor. What is completed becomes an object in the physical world, which others can encounter and explore (McCarthy et al. 2004, p. 41). This encounter with art becomes enriched by reflection: the aesthetic experience is not limited to passive reception—it typically stimulates curiosity, questioning, and the search for explanation (McCarthy et al. 2004, p. 41). We can discern different levels and modes of engagement with the various works of art. In this first categorization, the creative responses present common characteristics regarding

Figure 9. Francis Alÿs. (2008). Camgun #84. [Installation]. © National Museum of Contemporary Art Athens (EMST). Athens, Greece.

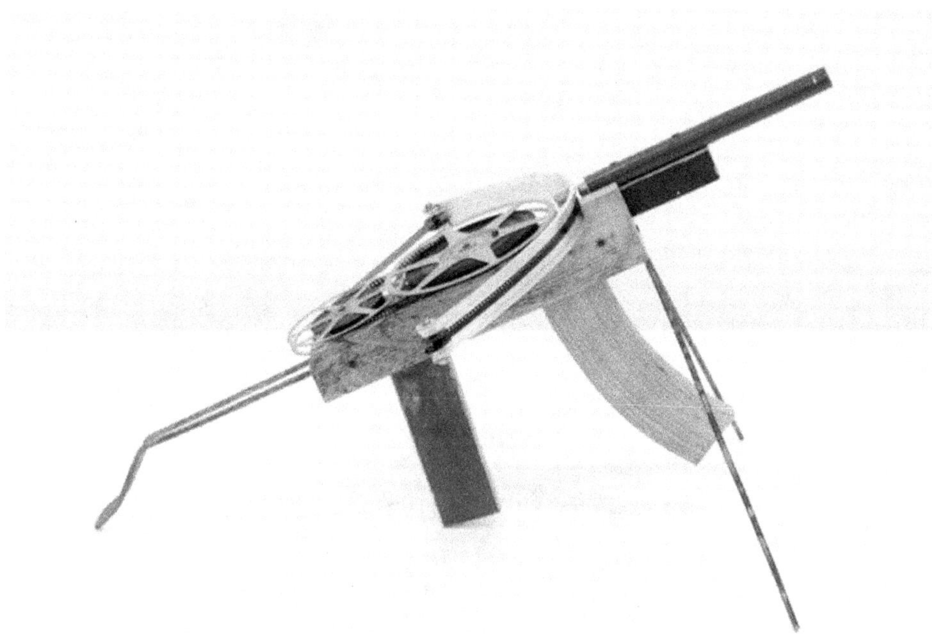

the mode of addressing the work of art that inspired them. In their approach, participants open a direct dialogue with the works of art. At times this dialogue is realized through interpretation, responding to the cultural contexts of the selected pieces. In others, a conversation with the work of art occurs through a discursive dialogue with its main subject, idea, or feeling.

Furthermore, finally, participants make more personal associations inspired by its conceptual or formal qualities. The participant's creative responses to the works of art offered a personal interpretation of their function and purpose, connecting with the artworks' material, conceptual and cultural significance. Interpretation of the selected pieces was not only a standard step in the appreciation process but also reflected a need to delve into the meaning of motifs, signs, and symbols used in work. In the second category of our analysis, participants' creative responses to the works of art are connected mainly with their formal qualities. Experimentation and reprocessing led to the production of original artworks. Mixed media were also used in response to two installations (Francis Alÿs, Camgun #84 and George Lappas', Mappemonde) that resulted in two artifacts, incorporating different elements to create a new discourse. An eloquent sculptural installation titled *Manipulations-Antispectacular*, by Theodoros (Papadimitriou) in 1974, also known as "anti-spectacular screens," inspired a participant to produce a 35-sec video that linked to the formal qualities of the work of art articulating a comment about vulnerability and courage.

Involvement with Art during the Pandemic: A Captivating and Liberating Experience

Unlike most human communication, which occurs through formalized discourse, art communicates through direct experience. At the heart of the participant's responses is lived experience, expressed as a kind of interpretation, questioning, revelation, or sense. In its way, each art form is capable of calling us

Figure 10. Beatrice Andreotti. (2021). Untitled [Installation]. EMST for health participations. Retrieved from https://www.emst.gr/en/emst-for-health/beatrice-andreotti

out of ourselves and stimulating rapt involvement. This attitude/stance demands continuous attention to what is happening each here and now as if everything of significance is happening. In contrast, everything that happens turns a leaf of time. I think of it as an experience of continuous presentness," says Cavell ([1969] 2002, p. 322). Encountering the works of art stimulated them by communicating something akin to what the artist envisioned by drawing upon their faculties of discovery and eliciting their emotions.

The cultural managers-curators of the project described it as an invigorating experience from the participant's perspective and very fulfilling on their part. "The words they later sent us in personal emails are staggering about what this process represented for them. Some people wrote in their emails that the Christmas period was challenging, and the fact that they could go and create helped them a lot. The feedback was amazing" (Elisabeth Ioannides, education curator at EMST, interview with the author 20/04/2022).

Some participants also appeared in the newspapers and shared their experiences and feelings from this encounter with art during the Covid-19 pandemic. In our view, their discourse and the thoughts they unfold are particularly elucidating about the lived experience. "The invitation of EMST for the interaction of health professionals with works of its permanent collection was a good occasion to meet the “elsewhere” of art within the prolonged confinement during the pandemic,” says Elias Vlachos, psychiatrist, Associate of the Psychiatric Clinic of EKPA (Vlachos, Elias, psychiatrist, interview to Vasiliadou, 2021). Petros Zezos is a pharmacist and one of the participants who requested and received more than one artwork. “I was informed about the action of EMST through the museum’s Instagram account when the area where I work was in the “deep red” and my need to connect with people against the isolation of the days was vital” (Zezus Petrito, pharmacist, interview to Vasiliadou, 2021).

Maria Alexandri is a nurse at “Aretaio” hospital. “Death, disease, decay are there; they exist as philosophical concepts and as a frightening reality. The unique reality for every patient who is also a mother, daughter, wife, sister or just a person who, as someone recently confessed to me, feels being ‘deconstructed’ by cancer,” she says. “These people at times do not need anything unnecessary next to them, only clarity and substantial help for their physical and mental needs. As a health professional, I have to face them with courage and sometimes admit my inadequacy. Philosophy and poetry are, without exaggeration, the only weapons I have. These shield me and lead me to the patient believing that I can help. Museums have been places of hospitality for me, where I have often resorted to seeking relief/ consolation. The EMST invitation was finally an opportunity for the expression” (Alexandri Maria, nurse, interview with Vasiliadou, 2021). “I started conversing with the work of Haris Epaminondas when I could not communicate and open up to anyone. It was not only the restriction of social contacts and the confinement that I had to negotiate, like everyone else but also my new work environment: a newly established Covid Intensive Care Unit”, says Anna Bitha, a nurse in ICU Covid. (Bitha Anna, nurse, interview with Vasiliadou, 2021). “At the same time, the war rhetoric that accompanied Covid-19 (in the media), the discourse of war, of heroes, of the front line, was an aggravating factor in my thinking and psychosynthesis. My conversation with the statuette of Haris Epaminondas, found in Africa as an exhibit at the Museum of Contemporary Art, served as a way out. Capturing my thoughts and feelings, I felt a consolation. After all, what I present to be or what others want me to be - a hero - is not me, like the statuette that takes another form in its new environment?” she wonders. (Bitha Anna, nurse, interview with Vasiliadou, 2021) “The work of George Gyparakis helped me to share experiences and discover other truths. Painful but also liberating. The difficulties and changes that lead to maturity and are reflected in the project are included in every transition process. Is not our present highly transient? Instead of talking about a return to normalcy, shouldn’t we talk about painless ways to move into the post-Covid era? In the end, both projects were for me a means of communication and at the same time a weapon of negotiation of fear, anger, anxiety, responsibility, fatigue in this so fluid age that we live in” (Bitha Anna, nurse, interview to Vasiliadou, 2021).

[.....] Take me wherever you want,

away from the darkness,

light me up and turn Hades into ashes.

Take me wherever you want,

as if I were a lost sleepwalker.

Erase the yesterday from my memory

Figure 11. Dimitris Tzamouranis, (2001) Sleepwalker [Painting]. © National Museum of Contemporary Art Athens (EMST). Athens, Greece.

and teach me how to love.

(Lavrentis Machairitsas, Ypnovatis, lyrics by L. Dimopoulou)

https://www.emst.gr/emst-gia-tin-ygeia/karanika-elli

Anchored in historical time and, particularly, the momentum of the Covid 19, pandemic confinement, and inspired by contemporary art, participants' artistic creations regard the attainment and fusion of historical self-consciousness generating the all-encompassing vantage point, not of individual consciousness, but humanity.

SOLUTIONS AND RECOMMENDATIONS

Rather than a "finished product," artistic creation is process-oriented, an act that provides an opportunity for communication and expression. In this context, the established boundaries between artist and public, art space and public or digital space, are eliminated so that people feel free to enter and become engaged in the artistic action. This extends the role of the participatory museum (Simon, 2010) beyond its natural space into the digital world as a living lab. Art can provide a powerful instance for participatory practice and create meaning in this place. When possible, artists and curators should make a conscious effort to respond to the needs of different social groups who may have an interest in creativity and art.

Figure 12. Katerina Veneri (2021). Untitled [photograph]. EMST for health participations. Retrieved from https://www.emst.gr/en/emst-for-health/veneri-katerina

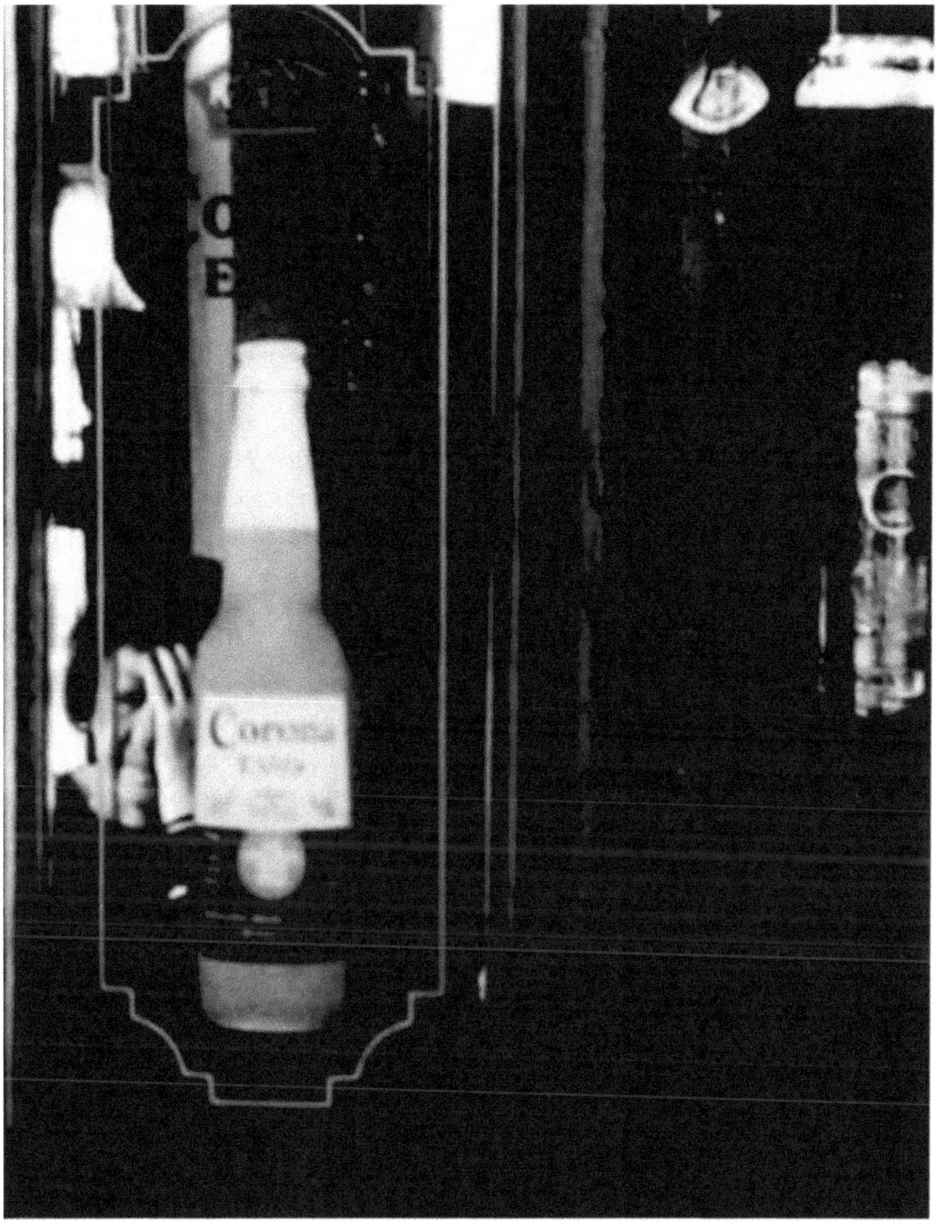

Consequently, museums could expand social discourse boundaries and issues. This can be seen as an attempt to retain and create existing users while enhancing the museums' capacity and making them more visible in the social context. With the close cooperation between museums and the public, the value of such connections becomes more critical. For example, participants in a museum's product production process, who know the museum well, could become active in promoting other users in that they produced it. Additionally, the differentiation of social discourse through users' perspectives changes the museum as a platform for communication and contributes to social integration (Choi & Kim, 2021). By strengthening their anthropocentric perception – shifting the interest from objects to people-, organizations now aim to have the visitors play an active role in shaping the meanings of an exhibition or other cultural activity (Stamatakis & Sifaki, 2020).

FUTURE RESEARCH DIRECTIONS

In this light, future research should provide a critical examination of the practices known as community or participatory arts, encompassing a field of work defined as incorporating active, creative collaboration between artists and people in a range of communities involving digital technology and associated forms. This will create an archive that will document work, content, and practices for further expansion and different critical openings that would otherwise be ephemeral. Future research should ideally focus on individual participants' and communities' views and experiences on the process of art involvement. Additionally, a closer reading of the produced material would provide meaningful insights regarding the historical understanding of lived experiences. For example, Raymond Williams's notion of "structure of feeling" (1954) focuses on how people negotiate their historical situatedness, entrenched in the flux of the present. This theoretical framework would be of particular interest vis-à-vis a more in-depth analysis of such digital actions and creative content.

CONCLUSION

The prevalence of the pandemic has pushed museums to highlight their adaptive character and dynamics through their digital environment (Orlandi, 2020). Strengthening their online presence following the suspension of their physical function to protect public health was a vital issue. The amplification of digital communication services of the museums was at the forefront, thus investing in maintaining communication with the large public. Furthermore, museums sought new communication channels with online visitors to maintain two-way digital communication with their audience. Therefore, new technologies and digital media have contributed significantly to maintaining the relationship between the museum and the public active, primarily encouraging cultural awareness and empathy with a broader audience through their active participation.

However, Crooke (2020) points out that museums should take into account that the term "digital participation" does not mean the actions and activities created for the public but the set of actions and media used by the museum and the digital strategy that follows, as they attract the public to participate actively. A museum is a place where visitors explore particular aspects of their identity by communicating and sharing experiences with other visitors. Such social needs and values of online visitors have greatly influenced museums' practices, media, and digital technology during the pandemic period. They aimed to contribute to the museum's social dimension, reduce the feeling of isolation, and turn innovation into a pillar of their sustainability. As a result, museums have been transformed from cultural information providers into social and cultural networking platforms (Choi & Kim, 2021).

Faced with the growing risk of cultural fragmentation, museums have proven that even when closed, they can function as spaces for a creative exchange of views and social cohesion, transforming the concept of social coexistence (Tranta et al., 2021). From a public policy perspective, the response of cultural organizations and international institutions to the Covid-19 pandemic's impact on the cultural sector put forward the notion of culture as a unifying force to promote dialogue and solidarity and lay the foundations for resilience in future crises. Unesco underlines the need to gain cultures' rightful place in various policies, both as a critical sector and as a source of rejuvenation and innovation for forging a more sustainable world (Unesco, 2020a). From this point of view, museums play an essential role in cultural and social life. This may be possible because museums are potent catalysts for ushering social changes in their communities. In addition, even though museums are generally deðned as non-proðt permanent institutions, they contribute to the social economy. The number of visitors/users has a huge potential for the future growth of local communities and, therefore, helps the sustainable management of museums.

The National Museum of Contemporary Art in Athens (EMST) undeniably fulfills its multiple missions in various ways. Utilizing art and culture to cultivate empathy, promote social inclusion, respect for diversity, intercultural dialog, peaceful coexistence, and other humanitarian values. Whereas participation from a broad social spectrum depends on several factors such as cultural strategies and politics of inclusion, involvement with the arts may impact social relations if it encourages participants to become actively involved in an understanding of the surrounding world (Grammatikopoulou 2017, p. 55). The digital action "EMST for health" we have taken as a case study in this chapter, taken together, forms the unique contributions of the arts to individual lives and collective experience. Far from being isolated from everyday experience, the arts, through their communicative power, enhance individual engagement with the world in ways that have personal benefits and create the fabric of shared values and meanings. We consider these forms of creation as affective elements of consciousness, emotions, moods, and atmospheres as historical and social phenomena. These vernacular forms of cultural expression emanating from established cultural institutions' digital strategies converse with digital folklore research, hoping to fuel the discussions within the Digital Humanities related to the worlds of art, its social influences, and reception.

ACKNOWLEDGMENT

I want to thank the educational curators of the National Museum of Contemporary Art Athens (EMST), Marina Tsekou and Elisabeth Ioannides, for providing a compelling intellectual discussion during our interview. Kassiani Benou, Athina Ioannou, and other personnel from EMST also provided assistance and technical help. Special thanks to the editors of this book, Stamatis Papadakis and Alexandros Kapaniaris, and the reviewers for providing feedback on the research and their valuable comments. This research received no specific grant from any funding agency in the public, commercial, or not-for-profit sectors.

REFERENCES

Agostino, D., Arnaboldi, M., & Lampis, A. (2020). Italian state museums during the Covid-19 crisis: From onsite closure to online openness. *Museum Management and Curatorship*, *35*(4), 362–372. doi:10.1080/09647775.2020.1790029

Akker, C. V. D., & Legene, S. (2016). *Museums in a digital culture: how art and heritage become meaningful*. Amsterdam University Press.

Bal, M. (2009). Working with concepts. *European Journal of English Studies, 13*(1), 13–23. doi:10.1080/13825570802708121

Bertacchini, E., & Morando, F. (2013). The future of museums in the digital age: New models for access to and use digital collections. *International Journal of Arts Management, 15*(2), 60–72.

Carayannis, E. G., Bast, G., & Campbell, D. F. (2018). Conclusion: The Museum of the Future and the Future of Museums. In G. Bast, E. G. Carayannis, & D. F. J. Campbell (Eds.), *The Future of Museums* (pp. 145–148). Springer. doi:10.1007/978-3-319-93955-1_13

Cavell, St. (1969/2002). *Must We Mean What We Say?* Cambridge University Press.

Charr, M. (2021,01 January). Museum of London collects Covid dreams. *Museum next*. Retrieved from https://www.museumnext.com/article/museum-of-london-collects-covid-dreams/

Cobley, J., Gaimster, D., So, S., Gorbey, K., Arnold, K., Pouliot, D., ... Jiang, M. (2020). Museums in the Pandemic: A Survey of Responses on the Current Crisis. *Museum Worlds, 8*(1), 111–134. doi:10.3167/armw.2020.080109

Crooke, E. (2020). Communities, change, and the COVID-19 crisis. *Museum & Society, 18*(03), 305–310. doi:10.29311/mas.v18i3.3533

Demertzis, N., & Eyerman, R. (2020). Covid-19 as cultural trauma. *American Journal of Cultural Sociology, 8*(3), 428–450. doi:10.105741290-020-00112-z PMID:32929388

EKT. (2021). Digital Transformation of Greek Enterprises. In *2020: The impact of the COVID-19 pandemic.* Athens: National Documentation Center. Retrieved from https://metrics.ekt.gr/node/500

Europeana Pro. (n.d.). *Mapping digital initiatives during Covid-19.* Retrieved from https://pro.europeana.eu/post/mapping-museum-digital-initiatives-during-covid-19

Grammatikopoulou, Ch. (2017). Breathing Art. Art as an Encompassing and Participatory Experience. In C. Van den Akker & S. Legêne (Eds.), *Museums in a Digital Culture* (pp. 41–56). Amsterdam University Press. doi:10.1515/9789048524808-005

Guboglo, A. (2020). Digital Museology Under Test: Challenges and Opportunities for Russian Museums. *Museum & Society, 18*(3), 311–313. doi:10.29311/mas.v18i3.3552

Janes, R. R., & Sandell, R. (2019). *Museum activism.* Routledge. doi:10.4324/9781351251044

Kara, N., & Sungur, A. (2021). Re-creating the Museum Space: Distance Learning in Museums during Covid-19 Lockdown. *Psychology and Education, 58*(3), 2989–2995.

Kist, C. (2020). Museums, challenging heritage, and social media during COVID-19. *Museum & Society, 18*(3), 345–348. doi:10.29311/mas.v18i3.3539

Magliacani, M., & Sorrentino, D. (2020). *Italian University Museums at Time of Covid-19 Lockdown: How to restore a "Sense of Normalcy"*. Research Square, Retrieved from., doi:10.21203/rs.3.rs-53886/v1

McCarthy, K. F., Ondaatje, E. H., Zakaras, L., & Brooks, A. (2004). *Gifts of the Muse: Reframing the debate about the benefits of the arts.* Rand Corporation.

Micheli, A. (2020). Culture in «restriction». The cultural experience of the imaginary and the actual space. *Epitheorese Koinonikon Ereunon*, *154*, 75–88. doi:10.12681/grsr.23230

Ministry of Culture and Sports. (2020a). *Measures to support culture and its employees*. Retrieved from: https://www.culture.gov.gr

Ministry of Culture and Sports. (2020b). *Special invitation of Digital Culture from the Ministry of Culture and Sports*. Retrieved from: https://www.culture.gov.gr/el/Information/SitePages/view.aspx?nID=3181

NEMO. (2022a). *Survey on the impact of the COVID-19 situation on museums in Europe. Final findings and Recommendations*. Retrieved from: https://www.ne-mo.org/fileadmin/Dateien/public/NEMO_documents/Final_Findings_and_Recommendations_CVOID19_12.05.2020.pdf

NEMO. (2022b). *Survey on the impact of the COVID-19 situation on museums in Europe*. Final Report. Retrieved from https://www.ne-mo.org/fileadmin/Dateien/public/NEMO_documents/NEMO_COVID19_Report_12.05.2020.pdf

NEMO. (2022c). *Follow-up survey on the impact of the COVID-19 pandemic on museums in Europe*. Final Report. January 2021. Retrieved from https://www.ne-mo.org/fileadmin/Dateien/public/NEMO_documents/NEMO_COVID19_FollowUpReport_11.1.2021.pdf

Noehrer, L., Gilmore, A., & Jay, C. (2021). The impact of COVID-19 on digital data practices in museums and art galleries in the UK and the US. *Humanit Soc. Science Communication*, *8*, 236.

Nostra, E. (2020). *Covid-19 & Beyond. Challenges and Opportunities for Cultural Heritage*. Retrieved from https://www.europanostra.org/wp-content/uploads/2020/10/20201014_COVID19_Consultation-Paper_EN.pdf

O'Brien, H. L., & Toms, E. G. (2008). What is user engagement? A conceptual framework for defining user engagement with technology. *Journal of the American Society for Information Science and Technology*, *59*(6), 938–955. doi:10.1002/asi.20801

Orlandi, S.-D. (2020). Museums Web Strategy at the Covid -19 Emergency Times. Digicult. *Scientific Journal on Digital Cultures*, *5*(1), 57–66.

Resta, G., Dicuonzo, F., Karacan, E., & Pastore, D. (2021). The impact of virtual tours on museum exhibitions after the onset of Covid-19 restrictions: Visitor engagement and long term perspectives. *Scientific Research and Information Technology*, *11*(1), 151–166.

Rey, F. B., & Casado-Neira, D. (2013). Participation and technology: Perception and public expectations about the use of ICTs in museums. *Procedia Technology*, *9*, 697–704. doi:10.1016/j.protcy.2013.12.077

Richardson, J. (2021). *Museums in Lockdown: Rijksmuseum*. Museum next. Retrieved from https://www.museumnext.com/article/rijksmuseum-covid-lockdown/

Ross, S., Economou, M., & Anderson, J. (1998). Funding Information and Communications Technology in the Heritage Sector: Policy Recommendations to the Heritage Lottery Fund. Project Report, University of Glasgow.

Ruttkay, Z., & Bényei, J. (2018). Renewal of the Museum in the Digital Epoch. In G. Bast, E. G. Carayannis, & D. F. J. Campbell (Eds.), *The Future of Museums* (pp. 101–116). Springer. doi:10.1007/978-3-319-93955-1_10

Simon, N. (2010). *The participatory museum*. Museum 2.0.

Stamatakis, V., & Sifaki, E. (2020). Quality evaluation and quality metrics in the cultural sector. *International Journal of Teaching and Case Studies, 11*(4), 317–343. doi:10.1504/IJTCS.2020.112743

Sylaiou, S., Basiouka, S., Patias, P., & Stylianidis, E. (2013). The volunteered geographic information in archaeology. ISPRS Annals of the Photogrammetry. *Remote Sensing and Spatial Information Sciences, 2*, 301–306.

Tranta, A., Alexandri, E., & Kyprianos, K. (2021). Young people and museums in the time of covid-19. *Museum Management and Curatorship, 36*(6), 632–648. doi:10.1080/09647775.2021.1969679

UNESCO. (2020a). *Online meeting of Ministers of Culture. The Covid-19 pandemic's impact on the cultural sector and the public policy response*. Retrieved from: https://unesdoc.unesco.org/ark:/48223/pf0000373601?posInSet=2&queryId=N-b0ed0ac3-17b2-4ff2-8829-40910f877942

UNESCO. (2020b). *Museums around the World in the face of COVID-19*. UNESCO Report. Retrieved from: https://unesdoc.unesco.org/ark:/48223/pf0000373530/PDF/373530eng.pdf.multi

Vasiliadou, M. (2021). *The art, "medicine" for doctors and nurses*. Kathimerini. Retrieved from https://www.kathimerini.gr/culture/561321304/i-techni-farmako-gia-giatroys-kai-nosileytes/

Vayanou, M., Katifori, A., Chrysanthi, A., & Antoniou, A. (2020). Cultural Heritage and Social Experiences in the Times of COVID 19. In *Proceedings of AV I 2CH 2020: Workshop on Advanced Visual Interfaces and Interactions in Cultural Heritage (AV I 2CH 2020). New York:* ACM.

Williams, R., & Orrom, M. (1954). Preface *to Film. Film* Drama Limited.

ADDITIONAL READING

Bishop, C. (2012). Art*ificial Hells. Participatory Art and the Politics of Spectatorship.* Verso.

Boletsi, M., Houwen, J., & Minnaard, L. (Eds.). (2020). *Languages of Resistance, Transformation, and Futurity in Mediterranean Crisis-Scapes: From Crisis to Critique*. Palgrave Mcmillan. doi:10.1007/978-3-030-36415-1

Burgess, J. (2006). Hearing ordinary voices: Cultural studies, vernacular creativity and digital storytelling. *Continuum J Media Cult Stud, 20*(2), 201–214. doi:10.1080/10304310600641737

de Seta, G. (2020). Digital Folklore. In J. Hunsinger, M. Allen, & L. Klastrup (Eds.), *Second International Handbook of Internet Research*. Springer. doi:10.1007/978-94-024-1555-1_36

Ioannidou, E. (2020). Spectres of Greekness at the Time of Corona. *Journal of Greek Media and Culture, 6*(2), 295–300. doi:10.1386/jgmc_00020_1

Kyprianos, K., Sifaki, E., & Bantimaroudis, P. (2020). Digital gatekeepers and website visitors of the Acropolis Museum: Revisiting gatekeeping theory in the cultural domain. *Museum Management and Curatorship*, *35*(4), 409–423. doi:10.1080/09647775.2019.1630851

Papanikolaou, D. (2021). *Weird Wave. A Cinema of Biopolitics*. Edinburgh University Press. doi:10.1515/9781474436335

Sifaki, E., & Papadopoulou, M. (2015). Advertising Modern Art. A Semiotic Analysis of Posters used to communicate about the Turner Prize Award. *Visual Communication*, *14*(4), 457–484. doi:10.1177/1470357215593850

Chapter 16
Cultural Heritage Redesigned Through Digital Storytelling

Tharrenos Bratitsis
https://orcid.org/0000-0003-4257-2755
University of Western Macedonia, Greece

ABSTRACT

In this chapter, digital storytelling is examined as means of cultural heritage preservation by focusing on personal attachment to stories themselves. In the contemporary digital society, stories are being told and they are being told differently. Thus, digital storytelling is becoming a significant part of social life and seems to be imposing a trend in humanitarian issues. This chapter attempts to examine the issue through a brief literature review on the connection of digital storytelling and cultural heritage. Examples of small-scale studies conducted within academic theses (mainly postgraduate) or funded projects are utilized in order to record the telling or retelling cultural stories, whether in everyday life or in more formal contexts, such as museum visits. Overall, the aim of the chapter is to reach an understanding of how short stories can redefine the way we perceive cultural elements, following the current societal trends for speed and increased interaction.

INTRODUCTION

There is no doubt that humans live in a digital society. Over the past couple of decades, Information and Communication Technologies (ICTs) have been integrated in everyday life, affecting and enhancing many aspects of it. In this context, children are born in a media-dominated society which allows them to interact with a variety of information from a very young age. Information is exchanged often through stories, in multiple contexts.

Nowadays, the way stories are conveyed has changed significantly. For example, Social Networks have redefined the concept of stories, altering significantly people's perception of many aspects of cultural capital, including language, history, education, societal issues, etc. Digitalization is a part of everyday life. Each person produces large amounts of digital material, including photos and videos capturing moments of interaction with cultural elements. On the other hand, people interact with huge amounts

DOI: 10.4018/978-1-6684-4461-0.ch016

of information constantly. One could wonder if an average person nowadays actually has the patience or the time to review long texts or videos. Speed and compaction seem to characterize daily interactions.

Cultural heritage is the heritage of tangible and intangible heritage assets of a group or community that is inherited from past generations. Not all heritages of past generations are "heritage"; rather, heritage is a product of selection by society (Logan, 2007). Cultural heritage includes the sites, things, and practices a society regards as old, important, and worthy of conservation. It is currently the subject of increasing popular and scholarly attention worldwide, and its conceptual scope is expanding (Brumann, 2015). As a term, cultural heritage has two constituents: a tangible and in intangible one. The former includes all sorts of artefacts (e.g. monuments, books, artworks) and the latter refers to tradition, language, preserved knowledge, etc. Others also mention a third constituent, that of natural heritage which is connected to the flora, fauna and landscape-related elements (Sullivan, 2016).

The diversity of cultural heritage elements lead to various capital preservation strategies and techniques, with storytelling being one of them. Combining the aforementioned perspectives, the question of how would that affects cultural capital preservation could be raised. As information passes by, what is really captured and processed, what is really affecting cultural cultivation? This chapter reflects upon the idea of utilizing Digital Storytelling (DS) as means of cultural heritage preservation by focusing on personal attachment to stories themselves. How is this issue being addressed currently? What seem to be the next steps in the corresponding research? What has not yet been examined?

(DIGITAL) STORYTELLING

For thousands of years, stories have been the medium for teaching principles and moral values (Brady, 1997). At the same time, they were means of entertainment, education, preservation of cultural heritage and formation of moral values. Especially while written language had not appeared yet, storytelling was the only way to transmit culture, values and history of a social group (Egan, 1989).

One can find many definitions of what storytelling is in the literature. One of the most accurate is that of Kim & Ball-Rokeach (2006), according to whom Storytelling is the interactive art of using words and actions to reveal images and elements of a story, while enhancing the recipient's imagination. In this way they describe a dynamic and ever-changing relationship between the teller, the story and the audience. Miller (2008) describes story as a series of real or fictional events in which causality is somehow entangled.

As a word, it comprises of two elements; story and telling. Story, corresponds to the story itself which has a specific structure, is classified into genres and has commonly accepted structural elements and characteristics that have been extensively studied and recorded in the literature. Telling, describes the connection between the teller and the audience, but not only. It also involves the space and time in which the telling itself takes place, but also the space and time in which the actual story takes place. These space-time can coincide or differ significantly. For example, one can today tell a story that will take place on another planet in a few thousand years or a story that took place in a different part of the earth a few thousand years ago.

Thus, the teller presents the story utilizing verbal and non-verbal communication, gestures, grimaces, in order to enchant the listeners. He/she "listens" to the reactions of the audience, in order to react appropriately and to keep their interest at a high level. The listeners are active recipients who experience the story in their own way depending on their prior experiences, they immerse themselves in it and are alert throughout its duration. Storytelling is therefore characterized as a collaborative and creative action / activity. In addition, it is important to distinguish between the term storytelling and the term narration or narrative, which are often misused in place of each other. The noticeable difference is that storytelling is this dynamic event mentioned above, while narration often refers to the detached and static form of transmitting of transferring an existing story (e.g., someone accurately tells an incident or retells a story in the form of a reading by a written text).

Storytelling in the form described above has existed essentially since humans existed as intelligent beings. Thus, one can study both the well-known stories and the philosophical quests about storytelling and story structure by Aristotle, Homer and other ancient Greeks. Recorded stories in the form of papyrus have been found in ancient Egypt. Until the discovery of typography that allowed the most systematic recording, retelling and preservation of stories, there were oral narratives of various social and ethnic groups, masterpieces such as the Gilgamesh Epic, the Nibelungenlied and 1001 Nights and other stories which integrate historical, cultural and other elements. At the same time, the Bards and the Troubadours used to function as messengers and news conveyors through their stories in the form of songs. Of course, by carefully examining what story means, as mentioned above, in fact the first recorded storytelling approaches of man in the form of cave paintings about 50,000 years ago.

But storytelling is also a daily habit for every person. It is used to describe thoughts, memories, reflections, but also everyday life itself. It is considered by many (eg Pedersen, 1995) as a teaching tool that contributes to the inquiry approach of learning (Bruner, 1990). Storytelling has always been an important learning technique because it can provide better understanding through specific examples related to one's experiences, rather than through abstract descriptions and generalizations (Frenzel et al., 2004). It helps the individual to form a more organized perception of the world (Friedberg, 1994).

Vygotsky (1976) stated that the socio-cultural context in which one grows and exists influences the way one learns, while learning takes place through a process of internalization and a process of externalization of knowledge. Examining his approach a more closely, one can see the involvement of the storytelling in these processes. Thus internalization occurs when one tries to explain the world to oneself and externalization occurs when one tries to explain it to someone else. In both cases, the fundamental meaning is the meaning given to the actions of the individual. Similar to this statement, Schank (1990) in her work of "Tell Me a Story". Narrative and Intelligence» reflects upon Vygotsky's (1978) view of stories as means of connecting with prior knowledge and improving memory differently. Abrahamson (1998) also consider that stories are used to provide meaning to experiences.

Particularly in education, storytelling is an important tool that contributes to children's cognitive development as it gives them the opportunity to analyze and explain (Bruner, 1990), to interpret (Gudmundsdottir, 1995), to organize and enhance their memory (Schank, 1999) and explore using different perspectives (McEwan & Egan, 1995). At the same time, it contributes to the understanding of ideas and properties, to comparison, to the drawing of conclusions and to generalization (Banyard & Hayes, 1997), and finally to the cultivation of creative and critical thinking. In combination with modern technology, storytelling can potentially be utilized in all situations, including formal, non-formal and informal education, but also work environments (Bratitsis, 2014).

Digital storytelling (DS) is a trend that appeared about 25 years ago and is gaining momentum over the past decade. DS is the combination of traditional oral narration with multimedia material and telecommunication tools and is characterized as an emerging art form (Lathem, 2005; Robin & McNeil, 2012). In digital stories, storytelling is often interactive. At the same time, the variety of multimedia elements (text, graphics, video, recorded narration and music) makes them more attractive and interesting.

In education, DS is essentially a modern teaching approach that seems to enhance students' engagement with the cognitive load and activate their emotional interest (Smeda et al., 2014). Storytelling can be made interactive through technology, in a way that enhances learning and understanding and develops students' critical thinking and problem-solving skills (Moutafidou & Bratitsis, 2013; Pitler, 2006; Smeda et al., 2014).

In essence, DS is an art form that combines different types of multimedia material to create a short story. The stories created in this way are utilized at all levels and in almost all cognitive objects, in different ways (Bratitsis, 2015).

There are many tools available for DS, many of which are free to use. Digital stories are usually in the form of a short video, but are not limited to this. This includes comics in digital format, elaborate infographics, special type animations (in the form of whiteboards, talking characters such as avatars or animated characters), interactive presentations and other forms that combine modern technologies (e.g. Augmented or Virtual Reality). One could therefore argue that the use of digital technology to shape and transmit a story, hence becoming a form of digital storytelling, occurs when educational robots are programmed for this purpose.

In this vein, DS is considered as a medium for bringing especially young children in contact with the cultural capital of the society they live and grow in, thus contributing in the preservation of cultural heritage, as discussed at the end of this chapter.

Ingredients and Structure of Good Stories (Classic or Digital)

Studying the literature one will come across many parameters mentioned as key components of a good story and many suggestions for the structure of a good story. Some typical examples, possibly the most common components are listed below and explained very briefly.

Point of View: refers to the way one perceives a situation, a phenomenon, anything. There are many kinds of possible perspectives on a story, depending on whether it is viewed by the heroes of the story, the narrator or the audience. Overall, however, the central point of view is one and determines the central idea of the story. It defines the reality that the narrator tries to communicate to the audience and thus serves all the points of the story. It fully clarifies the purpose of the story, as it is connected to the central hero's point of view (usually). It explains who (first, second, third person or dialogue) tells the story and why. Finally, it develops the emotional approach that the story follows.

Dramatic Question: Essentially it is usually an event or person that disrupts the initial balance that is presented at the introduction to the story. This imbalance explains the narrator's motivation, raises a question that needs to be answered or a goal that needs to be achieved. It often reveals the very reason for the story.

Emotional Approach: a good story often covers the whole emotional spectrum (from comedy to drama) so as to be balanced. This approach is good to be guided by plausibility, as the goal is to significantly influence the audience and provoke an emotional reaction.

Voice: the narrator has the opportunity to use the gift of voice. Adjusting its features such as rhythm, tone, hue and intensity can give emotional emphasis, define or modify the pace of the story, create patterns. Voice comprehension determines speech comprehension and can be connected in different ways.

Rhythm, Tone, Tempo: these parameters relate to the evolution of the story and all the audio information it contains. They differ from the corresponding ones mentioned in the voice element. In good stories the pace, tone and tempo of the sound background can captivate the listener, stimulate the senses and cause reflexive movements. Overall, they create a sense of space, time, but also affect the normal functions of the listener, such as breathing rate, heart rate, etc.

Narrative Structure: there are various story structures proposed in the literature, such as the Aristotelian structure, the pyramid of Gustav Freytag, the journey of Joseph Campbell's hero, and the list of beats proposed by Blake Snyder. Some of the proposed narrative structures best serve specific areas (eg cinema). In the case of DS, the Freytag pyramidal structure is often, if not always used. But all story structures have great similarities, consisting of an initial state, a final state, a fact that upsets the initial balance and the description of an evolutionary path to the final state.

Audience: The target audience is an important issue that needs to be addressed. The answer to this question determines how a message is narrated or retransmitted. Often, it even determines the style or content of the story. Typically, Vygotsky (1978) states that storytelling is a fundamental practice of learning, as aforementioned. In the processes of internalization and externalization that he describes, respectively, the mental models or shapes (Piaget, 1952) of the individual are created or utilized in order to make sense of the interaction with the environment. Given that the main goal of storytelling is to convey and understand messages, one realizes how important it is for the narrator to understand in depth his audience, in order to understand how this can make sense of the story to be told.

Immersion, Connection and Engagement: the stories have been described as magical by many experts in the field. It's very typical of Ben Haggerty, a professional performance storyteller, who in an interview during his tour for Mr Sandmann - bringer of dreams & nightmares states (in free translation): "Or is the power of these things. You can get lost in a story. You can lead others wherever you want, whether they want to or not " (Haggerty, 2013). So the goal is for the story to capture as well as to "take in" the listener (Meadows, 2003), involving him/her to its actual evolvement. This can be achieved by offering to the listener elements of attachment or connection, elements in which he/she can recognize something of him/herself or his/her experiences.

Backstory: It refers to the reason for the existence of the story, to the reason why it is worth to be told. It is the journey of history, the path of its evolution, the trigger for the story itself.

Respectively, for a good digital story the basic elements are seven, as suggested by the Center for Digital Storytelling (https://www.storycenter.org/) and the co-founder of the DS field, Joe Lambert (Lambert, 2012). These are: point of view, dramatic question, emotional content, the gift of the voice, the power of the sound background, economy and pace. It is noticeable that five of the seven elements are common to those mentioned in the literature as elements of a good story of any kind. The unique characteristics of DS are reflected in the two differentiated elements.

Specifically the soundtrack refers to all kinds of sound information can be integrated into a digital story (e.g. music background, sound effects). This information is related to the perception of visualized information and the (mental) mood of the story. The same image for example can be decoded by the viewer differently if it is accompanied by a romantic melody, than if it is accompanied by a scary melody. Usually the sound effects enhance the story and the background music enhances the creation of an emotional context and mood for watching the story. All of this is related to one of the fundamental differences between DS and other storytelling genres, that of the strong emotional component that governs digital stories. The main goal of DS is the particularly enhanced emotional engagement (as far as possible on a personal level) of the viewer with the story, something that is often achieved through identification elements (mentioned above) that offer components of the story to the viewer.

The economy refers to another fundamental feature of DS, that of the short duration of digital stories. The latter usually range between 2 and 5 minutes, with a few exceptions. For example, a story may be

6 or 7 minutes long, but by no means does it exceed that length. In such a case it begins to go beyond the scope of the DS and falls under other categories (e.g. short movies) that are distinguished by different characteristics and development techniques. Thus, in the case of DS, the creator must be precise, replace as many words with images as possible, and use musical backgrounds and audiovisual effects to highlight the story.

CULTURAL HERITAGE

Cultural Heritage (CH) is a term that can be at the same time simple and complex. Analysing the term, the second constituent is "Heritage" which refers to some kind of property, something that is inherited, passed down from previous to future generations. The first constituent refers to culture, which does not directly reflect to materialistic elements such as money or property, but to other abstract concepts such as values, traditions and customs. Cultural heritage implies something that brings together a community and defines the sense of belonging to it, differentiating the members of that community to those of other communities. It represents history and identity, the bond to the past, the present, and the future (Khan Academy, n.d.).

The CH are the cultural resources of an area such as language and customs of the residents but also resources and activities as for instance: fine arts, literature, history, music, dancing, shopping and sports facilities (Schuh et al., 2018). "CH is, in its broadest sense, both a product and a process, which provides societies with a wealth of resources that are inherited from the past, created in the present and bestowed for the benefit of future generations. Most importantly, it includes not only tangible, but also natural and intangible heritage" (Unesco, 2014). Heritage as a notion is important for culture and development, as it is practically the cultural capital of societies and in a sense it is what defines them and differentiates from other societies. According to Unesco (2014), "CH can also enrich social capital by shaping an individual and collective sense of belonging, which helps supporting social and territorial cohesion.". For that, it is important to preserve it, as it is directly connected to community and societal resilience, also facilitating diversity acceptance through understanding of social bonds.

Resilience is also connected to sustainability which requires "*...finding the right balance between benefiting from cultural heritage today and preserving its 'fragile wealth' for future generations*" (Unesco, 2014). This reveals that for properly preserving CH it is not only important to look at the past but also build on it, in relation to the present, and prepare for the future. "*Indeed, the understanding of heritage must be such that the collective memories of the past, and the traditional practices with their social and cultural functions, are constantly revised and updated in the present, thus allowing each society to relate to current issues and to maintain their sense, meaning and functioning in the future.*" (Unesco, 2014).

Thus, CH is the heritage of tangible and intangible heritage assets of a group or community that is inherited from past generations. Not all heritages of past generations are "heritage"; rather, heritage is a product of selection by society (Logan, 2007). Cultural heritage includes the sites, things, and practices a society regards as old, important, and worthy of conservation. It is currently the subject of increasing popular and scholarly attention worldwide, and its conceptual scope is expanding (Brumann, 2015). As a term, cultural heritage has two constituents: a tangible and in intangible one. The former includes all sorts of artefacts (e.g. monuments, books, artworks) and the latter refers to tradition, language, preserved knowledge, etc. Others also mention a third constituent, that of natural heritage which is connected to the flora, fauna and landscape-related elements (Sullivan, 2016).

According to Nuzzaci (2020), CH has ton taken on the same meaning over time. It has seen both the term heritage and that of culture change. Reflecting on the tangible and intangible aspects of CH, she concludes that CH "*…is an open concept today, as it is now evident that culture is a dynamic process, which reflects every component of life in the present and in the past. In all its aspects, it affirms in a tangible way that every man, every group or social practice is also a cultural outcome*". Reflecting on Dewey's (1916) theory about the interpretation of reality, Nuzzaci (2020) comes to the conclusion that "*Culture is therefore constantly evolving and depends largely on the interpretations that its representatives give; it can be said, in fact, the ability that allows to constantly and precisely extend the range of perceptions of its meanings*". Thus, CH is directly connected to meaning making out of its elements, despite of them being tangible or intangible, by contemporary citizens. These meaning can preserve or alter (even completely distort) the cultural capital that was built in the past.

On one hand, meaning making is connected to communication and, as already mentioned, to storytelling. In fact it is a fundamental concept within the storytelling approach which in the case of DS is also connected to multimodality and digital technologies that define today's society. On the other hand, it is connected to social practices and the construction of identities (Levi-Strauss, 1980). The latter are constructed through views of the past, but with influences of the present. Identity is not merely an individual attribute, but it is also understood as a part of a wider structure, a social one which is projected on the individual's reality. For Herskovitz (1948), culture is a construct that describes the total body of beliefs, behaviors, knowledge, sanctions, values and objectives, which distinguish the way people live: what they have, do and think (Nuzzaci, 2020).

Education is tightly connected to culture. As Vygotsky (1976) stated, the way an individual learns is directly affected by the sociocultural environment in which he/she lives in. As a child being educated is also a member of a society, he/she constructs an identity which derives from his/her past (culture of origin) and present (culture of the community of residence). Thus, the child's identity is a complex construction which, especially nowadays with migration becoming something common and widespread, is dynamically related to the localized but also the global conditions and becoming a multi-factoral concept. On the other hand, In the World Declaration on Education for all, the United Nations (1990) clearly highlighted the significance of the cultural factor as element of identity construction by stating that a child does not only need to "know how to read and write in the mother tongue which strengthens identity and cultural heritage", but also that all "the tools and channels of information available, communications and social action must be used to contribute to transmit essential knowledge and to inform and educate" (Nuzzaci, 2020). According to the European Commission (2018), cultural education is of high importance for the building of a resilient community; children need to be culturally competent, meaning that they should be aware of their heritage, be able to utilize it, work towards enhancing it and be able to understand it in multiple ways. The latter is directly connected to Multiliteracy which is, in turn, connected to meaning making (as discussed in the last section of the chapter).

Concluding, in order to have CH, education focusing in younger ages is important. Considering that DS has lately become a fundamental teaching approach, also in younger ages, this chapter seeks to understand the way CH and DS can be connected.

Overall, the above discussion highlights the foundation that school education from a very young age can provide to CH. The key concept seems to be meaning making, as already discussed. As Nuzzaci (2020) states, "*the school is the institution that mediates entry into culture.*", even though the process of becoming an encultured human being has been already initiated in the family context earlier in time.

Figure 1. The connection between culture, education and cultural heritage
Source: Nuzzaci (2020)

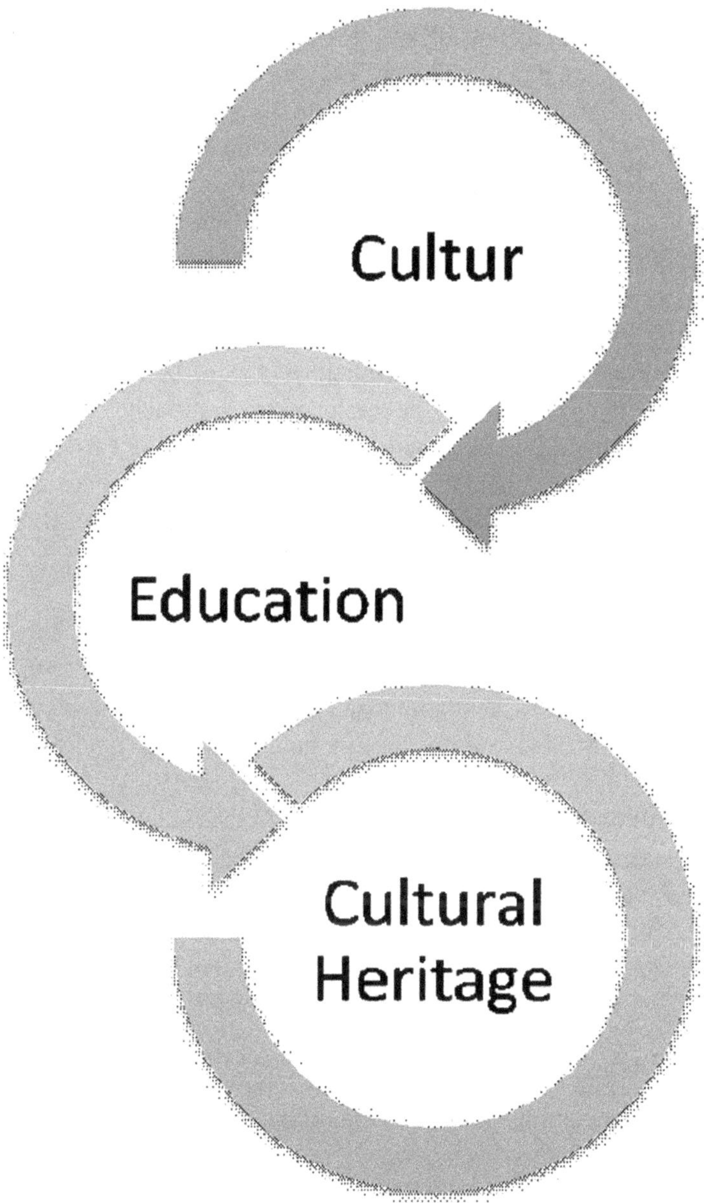

DIGITAL STORYTELLING AND CULTURAL HERITAGE

In the literature there are several works that connect DS and CH. Although the aim of this chapter is not to conduct a detailed literature review on the field, some indicative works will be discussed in this section in order to highlight the current status.

One of the main ways of integrating DS or plain storytelling in CH related activities is through story-based events and activities within cultural institutions such as museums. Bedford (2001) states that "*...museums can be considered as natural storytellers*". In fact, as institutions they try to make their exhibits appealing and engaging to an increasing variety of audiences while also nurturing their role in conservation, interpretation, education, and outreach (Rousou et al., 2015). For that reason they try to utilize multimodal mechanisms related to storytelling in the form of presentations, augmented reality information, etc. In this sense, DS is one of the ways that museums utilize in order to attract visitors and facilitate a better visiting experience (Trichopoulos et al., 2022).

In some cases such DS applications are merely multimedia rich presentation that do not actually present a story in the sense of having a concrete story structure as described in the corresponding section of this chapter. Such an example is the CHATS project (Trichopoulos et al., 2022), in which audio files are used for augmenting art pieces (in this case a famous painting) in order to provide a media-rich experience to visitors. In their literature review, Trichipoulos et al. (2022) identified 26 DS application over a 10-year span, which all integrated DS in the implemented approaches at various levels. CHESS (Pujol et al., 2012) was one of them, regarding audio stories for exhibits of the Acropolis Museum in Athens, also involving 3d model via augmented reality. In the EMOTIVE project (Katifori et al., 2018), a story authoring tool for creating digital stories for mobile devices was designed. Similar approaches mainly focus on a guiding experience for visitors within a museum (Hampson et al., 2013; Han et al., 2014; Tsekeridou et al., 2014).

Other contemporary technologies, such as virtual reality and 360° videos have been utilized for integrating DS (e.g. Karuzaki, et al., 2021; Rizvic et al., 2019; Edler et al, 2019; Walmsley & Kersten, 2020). The digital material in these cases the digital material is produced are highly interactive, focusing on a rich experience for the visitors of a museum. Overall, interactive DS is gaining momentum over the past few years, making its way also in the classroom (Rizvic et al., 2019).

Floch & Jiang (2015) focus on places that people visit in their everyday lives, which are directly connected to their cultural capital. They applied DS by collecting stories deriving from memories through a mobile application called "stedr". The core aim of their study was to engage younger people as users of traditional culture by involving them in stories' collection of this kind.

Furthermore, Casillo et al. (2021) designed a recommender system for DS for presenting multimodal material on a mobile device for visitors on physical sites and not restricted in an organization, such as a museum.

Overall, it is evident that most of the approaches which integrate DS for CH related to multimodal material of an interactive form, in combination with tangible material and/or mobile devices.

TOWARDS A NEW APPROACH IN EDUCATION

Reflecting on the previous sections of this chapter, one concrete conclusion can be made. The key concept is making meaning out of tangible and intangible artifacts of the environment. On one hand, DS as it was discussed in the corresponding sections is all about meaning making and meaning conveying in an experiential manner, fully immersing the recipient of the story in it. On the other hand, CH is also connected to meaning making out of the world in the past and the present in order to understand the future. This meaning making is also connected to identity construction which is a key element of an individual's character but also the resilience of society as a whole.

What was also evident in the previous sections is that the existing approaches and tools that connect DS and CH mainly concern multimodal material for presenting information, not always in a pure storytelling format but in most cases in an interactive format. Furthermore, although it is mentioned that children hold a significant role in CH and are being enculturated from a very young age, hence they are under-represented in the corresponding literature and research as stakeholders of DS-based tools. Of course museums are organizations that are also addressing children through educational visits, but is that enough?

In this chapter meaning making was mentioned often. It is also a key aspect of Multiliteracy. The later is the ability to identify, interpret, create, and communicate meaning across a variety of visual, oral, corporal, musical and alphabetical forms of communication (The New London Group, 1996; Cope and Kalantzis, 2000). As a term, beyond a linguistic notion of literacy it also involves the awareness of the social, economic and wider cultural factors that frame communication itself around these different semiotic channels. Awareness, in turn, is about understanding and in this case it refers to the world and its societal or cultural attributes, as already discussed earlier in this chapter. Contemporary pedagogy which focuses on multiliteracies is to create the conditions for citizens and prepare them for being capable of facing today's challenges, being able of critical understanding the community context they live in (Cope & Kalantzis, 2006) or of collaborating and negotiating with others who are different to themselves in order to forge a common interest (Cope & Kalantzis, 2015). For Binkley et al. (2012), multiliteracy is highly significant for children in their attempt to become active citizens through education. Thus it is important for building an understanding of a cultural capital that will guide then through their life as such.

Multiliteracies are related to multimodality for diverse forms of expression making use of the available ICTs, as opposed to the monomodal typical approaches, deprived from the creativity brought by diversity. Multiliteracies offer variability of meaning making in different cultural, social or domain-specific contexts without the language to focus on the national language via utilising multimodal tools. As such, multiliteracies are directly related to citizenship education (e.g. EACEA, 2012; European Commission, 2013).

Consequently, young learners can identify and transfer the identified patterns of cross-cultural meaning exchange within countries. Multiliteracies are also connected to the multimodal ways of meaning exchange and making via written-linguistic modes of meaning interface with oral, visual, audio, gestural, tactile and spatial patterns of meaning.

Multiliteracy is connected to multimodality, the freedom to use any medium and tool to create meaning in the new technologies' world. As such, the oral and textual language format has lost its pivotal importance. Meaning is now shaped with more semiotic means, evident in the multimodal meaning expression using diverse media and tools.

DS is an ideal approach for cultivating multiliteracy competences. The preparation of young children to participate successfully in a world of increasing social, cultural, ethnic, and linguistic diversity requires the inclusion of multiple literacies and modes for making meaning. As already mentioned, students are now living in a digital era and are surrounded by huge amounts of information, transmitted through various, multimodal semiotic channels. Within such an environment, communication itself has been altered. Furthermore, young children are a very under-represented population in the literature and corresponding research regarding CH. Also, it is not far from true to claim that young children are not considered as bearers of CH in their early years, in a stereotypical perception of people on how society functions. The fact that they are under aged leads often to a deprived perception of their societal role.

The author of this chapter has significant work on DS application in real teaching settings, in real classrooms. All the approaches are different from the ones mentioned in this chapter for CH in the sense that they strictly follow a typical story structure (mainly Freytag's Pyramid) which incorporates a main character, a setting and a story evolvement. These stories focus significantly on the elements of attachment or connection, as explained in the corresponding section of this chapter, which are offered to the children as recipients of the digital stories. This allows for them to build new perspectives in an experiential and reflective way.

Furthermore, children already carry a cultural capital from their families, before entering the educational system. Thus, they are already CH bearers and as such they are able to express themselves in relation to cultural issues. Research has shown that DS is an ideal way for them to express themselves and convey meaning in a multimodal way. During the past year, the author of this chapter has been working on how to guide young children (mainly aged 4-10 years old) in constructing digital stories for building messages to be shared with the world (peers, parents, teachers, etc.) in order to communicate their meaning of the world and the problems they might face. The latter are directly connected to cultural elements from the past and also the present (e.g. migration, tradition, language, diversity) which definitely affect the reformulation of the cultural capital they will bear to the future as active citizens. In this process, they can gain a better understanding of the world and start making decisions about potential problems that they face now of might face in the future. Towards this direction, the idea of creating repositories of digital stories from children for children has been raised and is being examined.

Thus, concluding this chapter aims at making a definite statement. Children are as much CH bearers and/or constituent as the adults. Since they are under-represented in corresponding research but one could also claim that they are underestimated and CH constituents, it is important that they raise their voice in society from their early years. This can be dome through DS, which provides them the opportunity to share their perspective of the cultural capital they are provided with, while building their social identity. Future research on this are seems very intriguing and should be pursued.

REFERENCES

Bedford, L. (2001). Storytelling: The Real Work of Museums. *Curator: Mus. J.*, *44*(1), 27–34. doi:10.1111/j.2151-6952.2001.tb00027.x

Brady, M. K. (1997). Ethnicfolklore. In T. A. Green (Ed.), *Folklore: An encyclopedia of beliefs, customs, tales, music, and art* (pp. 237–244). ABC-CLIO.

Bratitsis, T. (2016). A digital storytelling approach for fostering empathy towards autistic children. Lessons learned. In *7th International Conference on Software Development and Technologies for Enhancing Accessibility and Fighting Infoexclusion (DSAI 2016)-Special Track "Learning Technologies in Special Education"* (pp. 301-308). ACM. 10.1145/3019943.3019987

Bratitsis, T. (2017). Contextualized educators' training: The case of digital storytelling. In P. Anastasiades & N. Zaranis (Eds.), *Research on e-Learning and ICT in Education: Technological, Pedagogical and Instructional Perspectives* (pp. 31–43). Springer. doi:10.1007/978-3-319-34127-9_3

Bratitsis, T., Bardanika, P., & Ioannou, M. (2017). Science education and augmented reality content: The case of the water circle. In *Proceedings of the 17th IEEE International Conference on Advanced Learning Technologies - ICALT 2017* (pp. 485-489). IEEE.

Bratitsis, T., Kotopoulos, T., & Mandila, K. (2011) Kindergarten children as story Makers: The effect of the digital medium. In F. Xhafa, L. Barolli, & M. Köppen (Eds.), *Proceedings of the IEEE 3rdInternational Conference On Intelligent Networking and Collaborative Systems - INCoS 2011* (pp. 84-91). 10.1109/INCoS.2011.108

Bratitsis, T., & Mantellou, M. (2019). Utilizing digital storytelling for teaching mathematics. The case of vertical subtraction with borrowing. In G. Koutromanos & L. Galani (Eds.), *Proceedings of the 6th Panhellenic Scientific Conference "Integration and Use of ICTs in the Teaching Process"* (pp. 422-432). Academic Press.

Bratitsis, T., & Ziannas, P. (2015). From early childhood to special education: Interactive digital storytelling as a coaching approach for fostering social empathy. *Procedia Computer Science*, *67*, 231–240. doi:10.1016/j.procs.2015.09.267

Brumann, C. (2015). Cultural Heritage. In J. Wright (Ed.), *International Encyclopedia of the Social & Behavioral Sciences* (pp. 414–419). Elsevier Ltd. doi:10.1016/B978-0-08-097086-8.12185-3

Bruner, J. (1990). *Acts of meaning*. Harvard University Press.

Burmark, L. (2004). Visual presentations that prompt, flash & transform. *Media and Methods*, *40*(6), 4–5.

Casillo, M., Conte, D., Lombardi, M., Santaniello, D., & Valentino, C. (2021). Recommender System for Digital Storytelling: A Novel Approach to Enhance Cultural Heritage. In A. Del Bimbo, R. Cucchiara, S. Sclaroff, G. M. Farinella, T. Mei, M. Bertini, H. Jair Escalante, & R. Vezzan (Eds.), *Pattern Recognition. ICPR International Workshops and Challenges. ICPR 2021*. Springer. doi:10.1007/978-3-030-68787-8_22

Edler, D., Keil, J., Wiedenlübbert, T., Sossna, M., Kühne, O., & Dickmann, F. (2019). Immersive VR Experience of Redeveloped Post-industrial Sites: The Example of "Zeche Holland" in Bochum-Wattenscheid. *KN-J. Cartogr. Geogr. Inf*, *69*(4), 267–284. doi:10.100742489-019-00030-2

Egan, K. (1989). Memory, imagination, and learning: connected by the story. *The Docket: Journal of the New Jersey Council for the Social Studies*, 9-13.

Floch, J., & Jiang, S. (2022). *One place, many stories digital storytelling for cultural heritage discovery in the landscape. 2015 Digital Heritage*. doi:10.1109/DigitalHeritage.2015.7419566

Frenzel, K., Müller, M., & Sottong, H. (2004). *Storytelling. Das Harun-al-Raschid-Prinzip*. Hanser.

Friedberg, R. (1994). Storytelling and Cognitive Therapy with Children. *Journal of Cognitive Psychotherapy*, *8*(3), 209–217. doi:10.1891/0889-8391.8.3.209

Gakhar, S., & Thompson, A. (2007.) Digital storytelling: Engaging, communicating, and collaborating. In R. Carlsen, & D. A. Willis (Eds.), *Proceedings of Society for Information Technology and Teacher Education International Conference 2007* (pp. 607-612). Chesapeake, VA: AACE.

Gudmundsdottir, S. (1995). The narrative nature of pedagogical content knowledge. In H. McEwan & K. Egan (Eds.), *Narrative in Teaching, Learning, and Research*. Teachers College Press.

Haggerty, B. (2013). *Mr Sandmann, bringer of dreams & nightmares.* Available online at https://www.youtube.com/watch?v=gtnrB75MKlY

Hampson, C., Bailey, E., Munnelly, G., Lawless, S., & Conlan, O. (2013). Dynamic Personalisation for Digital Cultural Heritage Collections. *Proceedings of the UMAP.*

Han, K., Shih, P. C., Rosson, M. B., & Carroll, J. M. (2014). Enhancing community awareness of and participation in local heritage with a mobile application. In *Proceedings of the Proceedings of the 17th ACM conference on Computer supported cooperative work & social computing* (pp. 1144–1155). 10.1145/2531602.2531640

Karuzaki, E., Partarakis, N., Patsiouras, N., Zidianakis, E., Katzourakis, A., Pattakos, A., Kaplanidi, D., Baka, E., Cadi, N., Magnenat-Thalmann, N., Rings, C., Tasiopoulou, E., & Zabulis, X. (2021). Realistic Virtual Humans for Cultural Heritage Applications. *Heritage, 4*(4), 4148–4171. doi:10.3390/heritage4040228

Katifori, A., Roussou, M., Perry, S., Drettakis, G., Vizcay, S., & Philip, J. (2018). The EMOTIVE Project-Emotive Virtual Cultural Experiences through Personalized Storytelling. *Proceedings of the Workshop on Cultural Informatics Research and Applications co-located with the International Conference on Digital Heritage, CIRA@EuroMed 2018.*

Khan Academy. (n.d.). *What is Cultural Heritage?* Retrieved 1/2/2022 from https://www.khanacademy.org/humanities/special-topics-art-history/arches-at-risk-cultural-heritage-education-series/arches-beginners-guide/a/what-is-cultural-heritage

Kim, Y. C., & Ball-Rokeach, S. J. (2006). Community Storytelling Network, Neighborhood Context, and Civic Engagement: A Multilevel Approach. *Human Communication Research, 32*(4), 411–439. doi:10.1111/j.1468-2958.2006.00282.x

Korosidou, E., & Bratitsis, T. (2019). *Infusing Multimodal Tools and Digital Storytelling in Developing Vocabulary and Intercultural Communicative Awareness of Young EFL Learners* (Vol. 11899). Lecture Notes in Computer Science. Springer. doi:10.1007/978-3-030-34350-7_19

Lambert, J. (2012). Digital storytelling cookbook. Digital Diner Press.

Lathem, S. A. (2005). Learning communities and digital storytelling: new media for ancient tradition. In C. Crawford, R. Carlsen, I. Gibson, K. McFerrin, J. Price, R. Weber & D. A. Willis (Eds.), *Proceedings of Society for Information Technology & Teacher Education International Conference 2005* (pp. 2286-2291). Chesapeake, VA: AACE.

Logan, W. S. (2007). Closing Pandora's Box: Human Rights Conundrums in Cultural Heritage. In H. Silverman & D. Fairchild Ruggles (Eds.), *Cultural heritage and human rights* (pp. 33–52). Springer. doi:10.1007/978-0-387-71313-7_2

McEwan, H., & Egan, K. (Eds.). (1995). *Narrative in teaching, learning, and research.* Teacher's College Press.

Meadows, M. S. (2003). *Pause & Effect: The Art of Interactive Narrative.* New Riders.

Melliou, K., Moutafidou, A., & Bratitsis, T. (2015). 'Children's rights': Using digital storytelling and visible thinking approaches to create a narrative video in the early childhood classroom. *International Journal of Electronic Governance*, *7*(4), 333–348.

Miller, C. H. (2008). *Digital Storytelling: A Creator's Guide to Interactive Entertainment* (2nd ed.). Elsevier.

Peck, J. (1989). Using storytelling to promote language and literacy development. *The Reading Teacher*, *43*(2), 138–141.

Pedersen, E. (1995). Storytelling and the art of teaching. *English Teaching Forum*, *33*(1).

Piaget, J. (1952). *The origins of intelligence in children*. International University Press. doi:10.1037/11494-000

Pitler, H. J. (2006). Viewing technology through three lenses. *Principal*, *85*(5), 38–42.

Pujol, L., Roussou, M., Poulou, S., Balet, O., Vayanou, M., & Ioannidis, Y. (2012). Personalizing interactive digital storytelling in archaeological museums: The CHESS project. *Proceedings of the 40th annual conference of computer applications and quantitative methods in archeology*.

Rizvic, S., Boskovic, D., Bruno, F., Petriaggi, B., Sljivo, S., & Cozza, M. (2019). Actors in VR storytelling. In *Proceedings of the 2019 11th International Conference on Virtual Worlds and Games for Serious Applications (VS-Games)* (pp. 1–8). Academic Press.

Robin, B. R. (2008). Digital Storytelling: A Powerful Technology Tool for the 21st Century Classroom. *Theory into Practice*, *47*(3), 220–228. doi:10.1080/00405840802153916

Robin, B. R., & McNeil, S. G. (2012). What educators should know about teaching digital storytelling. *Digital Education Review*, *22*, 37–51.

Roussou, M., Pujol, L., Katifori, A., Chrysanthi, A., Perry, S., & Vayanou, M. (2015). The Museum as Digital Storyteller: Collaborative Participatory Creation of Interactive Digital Experiences. *Proceedings of the Annual Conference of Museums and the Web: MW2015*.

Schank, R. C. (1999). *Dynamic memory revisited*. Cambridge University Press. doi:10.1017/CBO9780511527920

Schuh, T. M., Agapito, D., & Pinto, P. (2018). "España Verde": Tourism Destination Image among German Facebook Users. In J. Rodrigues, C. Ramos, P. Cardoso, & C. Henriques (Eds.), *Handbook of Research on Technological Developments for Cultural Heritage and eTourism Applications* (pp. 284–311). IGI Global. doi:10.4018/978-1-5225-2927-9.ch014

Smeda, N., Dakich, E., & Sharda, N. (2014). The effectiveness of digital storytelling in the classrooms: A comprehensive study. *Smart Learning Environments*, *1*(1), 1–21. doi:10.118640561-014-0006-3

Sullivan, A. M. (2016). Cultural Heritage & New Media: A Future for the Past. J. Marshall Rev. Intell. *Prop*, *15*, 604.

Tsekeridou, S., Tsetsos, V., Chalamandaris, A., Chamzas, C., Filippou, T., & Pantzoglou, C. (2014). iGuide: Socially-enriched mobile tourist guide for unexplored sites. *Proceedings of the Hellenic Conference on Artificial Intelligence*. 10.1007/978-3-319-07064-3_52

UNESCO. (2014). *Culture For Development Indicators - Methodology Manual*. United Nations Educational, Scientific and Cultural Organization.

Vygotsky, L. S. (1978). *Mind in society: The development of higher psychological processes*. Harvard University Press.

Walmsley, A. P., & Kersten, T. P. (2020). The Imperial Cathedral in Königslutter (Germany) as an Immersive Experience in Virtual Reality with Integrated 360° Panoramic Photography. *Applied Sciences (Basel, Switzerland)*, *2020*(10), 1517. doi:10.3390/app10041517

ADDITIONAL READING

Borissova, V. (2018). Cultural heritage digitization and related intellectual property issues. *Journal of Cultural Heritage*, *34*, 145–150. doi:10.1016/j.culher.2018.04.023

Farazis, G., Thomopoulos, C., Bourantas, C., Mitsigkola, S., & Thomopoulos, S. (2019). Digital approaches for public outreach in cultural heritage: The case study of iGuide Knossos and Ariadne's Journey. *Digital Applications in Archaeology and Cultural Heritage*, *15*, e00114. doi:10.1016/j.daach.2019.e00126

Psomadaki, O., Dimoulas, C., Kalliris, G., & Paschalidis, G. (2018). Digital storytelling and audience engagement in cultural heritage management: A collaborative model based on the Digital City of Thessaloniki. *Journal of Cultural Heritage*, *36*, 12–22. doi:10.1016/j.culher.2018.07.016

Vrettakis, E., Kourtis, V., Katifori, A., Karvounis, M., Lougiakis, C., & Ioannidis, Y. (2019). Narralive – Creating and experiencing mobile digital storytelling in cultural heritage. *Digital Applications in Archaeology and Cultural Heritage*, *15*, e00114. doi:10.1016/j.daach.2019.e00114

KEY TERMS AND DEFINITIONS

Cultural Heritage: Are the cultural resources of an area such as language and customs of the residents but also resources and activities as for instance: fine arts, literature, history, music, dancing, shopping, and sports facilities.

Cultural Property: Includes the physical, or "tangible" cultural heritage, such as artworks.

Digital Storytelling: Is the combination of traditional, oral narration with multimedia and communication tools combining different types of multimedia material, including images, text, video clips, audio narration and music to tell a short story on a particular topic or theme.

Intangible Cultural Heritage: Consists of non-physical aspects of a particular culture, more often maintained by social customs during a specific period in history.

Multiliteracy: Is the ability to identify, interpret, create, and communicate meaning across a variety of visual, oral, corporal, musical and alphabetical forms of communication.

Natural Heritage: Is an important part of a society's heritage, encompassing the countryside and natural environment, including flora and fauna (biodiversity), as well as geological elements (geodiversity).

Compilation of References

(2012). Shiyongxin. (2012). Talks on Preservation of Ancient Books in Buddhist Temple. *Religions In China*, (6), 64–65.

(2016). Huixu. (2016). Talks on Construction of Digital Archives and Library in Buddhist Temples. *Archives and Construction*, (9), 81–84.

Abdinejad, M., Talaie, B., Qorbani, H. S., & Dalili, S. (2021). Student perceptions using augmented reality and 3D visualization technologies in chemistry education. *Journal of Science Education and Technology*, *30*(1), 87–96. doi:10.100710956-020-09880-2

Abraham, I. (2015). Christian hip hop as pedagogy: A South African case study. *Journal of Beliefs & Studies*, *36*(3), 285–296. doi:10.1080/13617672.2015.1095518

Abt, C. C. (1970). *Serious Games*. doi:10.1109/VS-GAMES.2009.8

Aeronovitch, D. (2010). *Voodoo Histories: The role of the Conspiracy Theory in Shaping Modern History*. Riverhead Books.

Agostino, D., Arnaboldi, M., & Lampis, A. (2020). Italian state museums during the Covid-19 crisis: From onsite closure to online openness. *Museum Management and Curatorship*, *35*(4), 362–372. doi:10.1080/09647775.2020.1790029

Ahmad, A., Migniot, C., & Dipanda, A. (2019). Hand Pose Estimation and Tracking in Real and Virtual Interaction: A Review. *Image and Vision Computing*, *89*, 35–49. doi:10.1016/j.imavis.2019.06.003

Aipperspach, R., Rattenbury, T. L., Woodruff, A., Anderson, K., Canny, J. F., & Aoki, P. (2006). *Ethno-mining: integrating numbers and words from the ground up* (Technical Report No. UCB/EECS-2006-125). Electrical Engineering and Computer Sciences University of California at Berkeley. http://citeseerx.ist.psu.edu/viewdoc/download?doi=10.1.1.173.8069&rep=rep1&type=pdf

Akengin, H., & Cendek, M.,2017). A Study of Students' Opinions About History Subjects in the Social Studies Curriculum. *Journal of Literature and Art Studies*, *7*(10), 1347-1353.

Akker, C. V. D., & Legene, S. (2016). *Museums in a digital culture: how art and heritage become meaningful*. Amsterdam University Press.

Alavesa, P., & Xu, Y. (2020). Unblurring the boundary between daily life and gameplay in location-based mobile games, visual online ethnography on Pokémon GO. *Behaviour & Information Technology*, 1–13. doi:10.1080/0144929X.2020.1825810

Al-Bahrani, A., Patel, D., & Sheridan, B. (2015). Engaging students using social media: The students' perspective. *International Review of Economics Education*, *19*, 36–50. doi:10.1016/j.iree.2015.06.001

Alivizatou-Barakou, M., Kitsikidis, A., Tsalakanidou, F., Dimitropoulos, K., Giannis, C., Nikolopoulos, S., Al Kork, S., Denby, B., Buchman, L., Adda-Decker, M., Pillot-Loiseau, C., Tillmane, J., Dupont, S., Picart, B., Pozzi, F., Ott, M., Erdal, Y., Charisis, V., Hadjidimitriou, S., . . . Grammalidis, N. (2017). Intangible Cultural Heritage and New Technologies: Challenges and Opportunities for Cultural Preservation and Development. In Mixed Reality and Gamification for Cultural Heritage (pp. 129–158). Springer International Publishing. doi:10.1007/978-3-319-49607-8_5

Alomari, I., Al-Samarraie, H., & Yousef, R. (2019). The Role of Gamification Techniques in Promoting Student Learning: A Review and Synthesis. *Journal of Information Technology Education, 18*(08), 2019. doi:10.28945/4417

Alsuraihi, A., Almaqati, A., Abughanim, S., & Jastaniah, N. (2016). Use of social media in education among medical students in Saudi Arabia. *Korean Journal of Medical Education, 28*(4), 343–354. doi:10.3946/kjme.2016.40 PMID:27907981

Amichai-Hamburger, Y., & Vinitzky, G. (2010). Social network use and personality. *Computers in Human Behavior, 26*(6), 1289–1295. doi:10.1016/j.chb.2010.03.018

Anagnostou, G., Chatziefstratiou, A., Peristeri, T., & Theofanellis, T. (2020). Suggestions on how to use Europeana for pedagogical purposes in order to promote Europe's cultural heritage. In *Proceedings of International Conference on Cultural Informatics, Communication & Media Studies* (*Vol. 1*, No.1). Academic Press.

Androutsopoulos, G. (2004). Ο ραψωδός που θέλεις να φτάσεις: Γλωσσικές πολιτισμικής οικειοποίησης στο ελληνόφωνο ραπ. Πρακτικά του 6ου Διεθνούς Συνεδρίου Ελληνικής Γλωσσολογίας (6th ICGL), Πανεπιστήμιο Κρήτης, Εργαστήριο Γλωσσολογίας [Lexical characteristics of Greek language]. Rethymno.

Annetta, L. A. (2010). The 'I's' Have It: A Framework for Serious Educational Game Design. *Review of General Psychology, 14*(2), 105–113. doi:10.1037/a0018985

Appleyard, J. A. (1991). *Becoming a reader: The experience of fiction from childhood to adulthood.* Cambridge University Press. doi:10.1017/CBO9780511527609

Arceneaux, P. C., & Dinu, L. F. (2018). The social mediated age of information: Twitter and Instagram as tools for information dissemination in higher education. *New Media & Society, 20*(11), 4155–4176. doi:10.1177/1461444818768259

Armas, E. (2020). *Libro interactivo con realidad aumentada para la enseñanza de la lengua mazateca en primer grado de primaria* [Bachelor Thesis]. Universidad de la Cañada.

Arnab, S., Lim, T., Carvalho, M. B., Bellotti, F., De Freitas, S., Louchart, S., Suttie, N., Berta, R., & De Gloria, A. (2015). Mapping learning and game mechanics for serious games analysis. *British Journal of Educational Technology, 46*(2), 391–411. doi:10.1111/bjet.12113

Atkinson, P., & Hammersley, M. (1994). Ethnography and participant observation. In N. K. Denzin & Y. S. Lincoln (Eds.), *Handbook of Qualitative Research* (pp. 248–261). SAGE Publications.

Atkinson, R., & Flint, J. (2001). Accessing hidden and hard-to-reach populations: Snowball research strategies. *Social Research Update, 33*(1), 1–4. https://sru.soc.surrey.ac.uk/SRU33.PDF

Avdikos, E. (2009). *Εισαγωγή στις σπουδές του λαϊκού πολιτισμού* [Lexical characteristics of Greek language]. Κριτική.

Avico, U., Kaplan, C., Korczak, D., & Van Meter, K. (1988). *Cocaine Epidemiology in Three European Community Cities: a pilot study using a snowball sampling methodology.* European Communities Health Directorate.

Bacon, J. (2011). *The Digital Folklore Project: Tracking the Oral Tradition on the World Wide Web* (MA thesis). East Tennessee State University. https://dc.etsu.edu/etd/1398

Bai, H. (2008). Problems of the Catalog of Chinese Buddhism Books. *Journal of Peking University, 45*(1), 142–145.

Bailey, M. Z. (2011). All the Digital Humanists Are White, All the Nerds Are Men, but Some of Us Are Brave. *Journal of Digital Humanities*, *1*(1), 9-12.

Bal, M. (2009). Working with concepts. *European Journal of English Studies*, *13*(1), 13–23. doi:10.1080/13825570802708121

Bampton, R., & Cowton, C. J. (2002). The E-Interview. *Forum Qualitative Social Research*, *3*(2). Advance online publication. doi:10.17169/fqs-3.2.848

Bansal, G., Zahedi, F. M., & Gefen, D. (2016). Do context and personality matter? Trust and privacy concerns in disclosing private information online. *Information & Management*, *53*(1), 1–21. doi:10.1016/j.im.2015.08.001

Barcelos, T. S., & Silveira, I. F. (2012, October). Teaching computational thinking in initial series an analysis of the confluence among mathematics and computer sciences in elementary education and its implications for higher education. In 2012 XXXVIII Conferencia Latinoamericana En Informatica (CLEI) (pp. 1-8). IEEE. doi:10.1109/CLEI.2012.6427135

Barianos, A., Papadakis, A., & Vidakis, N. (2022). Content manager for serious games: Theoretical framework and digital platform. *Advances in Mobile Learning Educational Research*, *2*(1), 251–262. doi:10.25082/AMLER.2022.01.009

Barr, V., & Stephenson, C. (2011). Bringing computational thinking to K-12: What is involved and what is the role of the computer science education community? *ACM Inroads*, *2*(1), 48–54. doi:10.1145/1929887.1929905

Barsch, S. (2020). Does experience with digital storytelling help students to critically evaluate educational videos about history? *History Education Research Journal*, *17*(1), 67–80.

Basu, S., Dickes, A., Kinnebrew, J. S., Sengupta, P., & Biswas, G. (2013, May). CTSiM: A Computational Thinking Environment for Learning Science through Simulation and Modeling. In CSEDU (pp. 369-378). Academic Press.

Bauman, Z. (2006). *Liquid Fear*. Polity Press.

Bayer, J. B., Ellison, N. B., Schoenebeck, S. Y., & Falk, E. B. (2016). 'Sharing the small moments: Ephemeral social interaction on Snapchat'. *Information Communication and Society*, *19*(7), 956–977. doi:10.1080/1369118X.2015.1084349

Beaulieu, A. (2004). Mediating ethnography: Objectivity and the making of ethnographies of the internet. *Social Epistemology*, *18*(2-3), 139–163. doi:10.1080/0269172042000249264

Bedford, L. (2001). Storytelling: The Real Work of Museums. *Curator: Mus. J.*, *44*(1), 27–34. doi:10.1111/j.2151-6952.2001.tb00027.x

Bellotti, F., Kapralos, B., Lee, K., Moreno-Ger, P., & Berta, R. (2013). Assessment in and of serious games: An overview. *Advances in Human-Computer Interaction*, *2013*, 1–11. Advance online publication. doi:10.1155/2013/136864

Benedetti, B., Abbondandolo, I., & Gaiani, M. (2021). The Origins of the Postgraduate Programs on Cultural Heritage Knowledge, Management, Conservation, and Communication in Italy: A Vision of the Past as Engine for the Next Future. *Heritage*, *4*, 2691–2720.

Bentkowska-Kafel, A., & Mac Donald, L. (Eds.). (2017). *Digital Techniques for Documenting and Preserving Cultural Heritage*. Arc Humanities Press. doi:10.2307/j.ctt1xp3w16

Bertacchini, E., & Morando, F. (2013). The future of museums in the digital age: New models for access to and use digital collections. *International Journal of Arts Management*, *15*(2), 60–72.

Bhagat, K. K., Yang, F. Y., Cheng, C. H., Zhang, Y., & Liou, W.-K. (2021). Tracking the process and motivation of math learning with augmented reality. *Educational Technology Research and Development*, *69*(6), 3153–3178. doi:10.100711423-021-10066-9

Bingenheimer, M. (2020). *Digitization of Buddhism*. Oxford University Press.

Blair, R., Millard, D., & Woollard, J. (2014). Perceptions of school children of using social media for learning. In *E-Learn: World Conference on E-Learning in Corporate, Government, Healthcare, and Higher Education* (pp. 227–237). Academic Press.

Blank, T. (2012). Pattern in the Virtual Folk Culture of Computer-Mediated Communication. In T. Blank (Ed.), *Folk Culture in the Digital Age* (pp. 1–24). Utah State University Press. doi:10.7330/9780874218909.c00

Blank, T. J. (2009). *Folklore and Internet: Vernacular Expression in the Digital World*. State University Press Logan. doi:10.2307/j.ctt4cgrx5

Blank, T. J. (2009b). Toward a Conceptual Framework for the Study of Folklore and the Internet. In T. J. Blank (Ed.), *Folklore and the Internet: Vernacular Expression in a Digital World* (pp. 1–20). Utah State University Press. doi:10.2307/j.ctt4cgrx5.4

Blank, T. J. (2012). *Folk Culture in the Digital Age: The Emergent Dynamics of Human Interaction*. Utah State University Press. doi:10.7330/9780874218909

Blank, T. J. (2013). *The Last Laugh: Folk Humor, Celebrity Culture, and Mass-Mediated Disasters, in the Digital Age*. University of Wisconsin Press.

Blank, T. J. (2018). Folklore and the Internet: The Challenge of an Ephemeral Landscape. *Humanities (Washington)*, *7*(2), 50. https://doi.org/10.3390/h7020050

Bodner, J., Welch, W., & Brodie, I. (2021). *COVID-19 Conspiracy Theories QAnon, 5G, the New World Order and Other Viral Ideas*. McFarland & Company, Inc., Publishers Press.

Bonfim, L. (2021). Spanning the boundaries of qualitative grounded theory methods: Breaking new grounds into the new online era. *RAUSP Management Journal*, *55*(4), 491–509. doi:10.1108/RAUSP-04-2019-0061

Bonidis, K. (2004). *Το περιεχόμενο του σχολικού βιβλίου ως αντικείμενο έρευνας: Διαχρονική εξέταση της σχετικής έρευνας και μεθοδολογικές προσεγγίσεις* [Lexical characteristics of Greek language]. Μεταίχμιο.

Bonsignore, E., Hansen, D., Kraus, K., Visconti, A., Ahn, J., & Druin, A. (2013, June). Playing for real: designing alternate reality games for teenagers in learning contexts. In *Proceedings of the 12th International Conference on Interaction Design and Children* (pp. 237-246). ACM. 10.1145/2485760.2485788

Bopp, M. M. (2008). Storytelling and motivation in serious games. In *Final Consolidated Research Report of the Enhanced Learning Experience and Knowledge Transfer–Project*. ELEKTRA. http://www.elektra-project.org/

Bouchrika, I., Harrati, N., Wanick, V., & Wills, G. (2021). Exploring the Impact of Gamification on Student Engagement and Involvement with E-Learning Systems. *Interactive Learning Environments*, *29*(8), 1244–1257. doi:10.1080/10494820.2019.1623267

Bowen, A., Williams, M., & Horvath, K. (2004). Using the Internet to Recruit Rural MSM for HIV Risk Assessment: Sampling Issues. *AIDS and Behavior*, *8*(3), 311–319. doi:10.1023/B:AIBE.0000044078.43476.1f PMID:15475678

Boxtel, C., Grever, M., & Klein, S. (2016). Introduction: The Appeal of Heritage in Education. In Sensitive Pasts. Berghahn Books.

boyd, d., & Ellison N. (2007). Social network sites: Definition, history, and scholarship. *Journal of Computer-Mediated Communication, 13*(1), 210–30.

Boyd, D. M., & Ellison, N. B. (2007). Social network sites: Definition, history, and scholarship. *Journal of Computer-Mediated Communication, 13*(1), 210–230. doi:10.1111/j.1083-6101.2007.00393.x

Bozinis, N. (2008). *Ροκ παγκοσμιότητα και Ελληνική τοπικότητα. Η κοινωνική ιστορία του ροκ στις χώρες της καταγωγής του και στην Ελλάδα* [Lexical characteristics of Greek language]. Νεφέλη.

Brady, M. K. (1997). Ethnicfolklore. In T. A. Green (Ed.), *Folklore: An encyclopedia of beliefs, customs, tales, music, and art* (pp. 237–244). ABC-CLIO.

Bratitsis, T. (2016). A digital storytelling approach for fostering empathy towards autistic children. Lessons learned. In *7th International Conference on Software Development and Technologies for Enhancing Accessibility and Fighting Infoexclusion (DSAI 2016)-Special Track "Learning Technologies in Special Education"* (pp. 301-308). ACM. 10.1145/3019943.3019987

Bratitsis, T., & Mantellou, M. (2019). Utilizing digital storytelling for teaching mathematics. The case of vertical subtraction with borrowing. In G. Koutromanos & L. Galani (Eds.), *Proceedings of the 6th Panhellenic Scientific Conference "Integration and Use of ICTs in the Teaching Process"* (pp. 422-432). Academic Press.

Bratitsis, T., Bardanika, P., & Ioannou, M. (2017). Science education and augmented reality content: The case of the water circle. In *Proceedings of the 17th IEEE International Conference on Advanced Learning Technologies - ICALT 2017* (pp. 485-489). IEEE.

Bratitsis, T. (2017). Contextualized educators' training: The case of digital storytelling. In P. Anastasiades & N. Zaranis (Eds.), *Research on e-Learning and ICT in Education: Technological, Pedagogical and Instructional Perspectives* (pp. 31–43). Springer. doi:10.1007/978-3-319-34127-9_3

Bratitsis, T., Kotopoulos, T., & Mandila, K. (2011) Kindergarten children as story Makers: The effect of the digital medium. In F. Xhafa, L. Barolli, & M. Köppen (Eds.), *Proceedings of the IEEE 3rdInternational Conference On Intelligent Networking and Collaborative Systems - INCoS 2011* (pp. 84-91). 10.1109/INCoS.2011.108

Bratitsis, T., & Ziannas, P. (2015). From early childhood to special education: Interactive digital storytelling as a coaching approach for fostering social empathy. *Procedia Computer Science, 67*, 231–240. doi:10.1016/j.procs.2015.09.267

Brednich, R. (2001). *Where They Originated... Some Contemporary Legends and Their Literary Origins.* Paper presented at ISCLR Congress, Melbourne, Australia. https://www.folklore.ee/folklore/vol20/legends.pdf

Brewer, J. (2000). *Ethnography.* Open University Press.

Brewer, R., Anthony, L., Brown, Q., Irwin, G., Nias, J., & Tate, B. (2013). Using Gamification to Motivate Children to Complete Empirical Studies in Lab Environments. In *Proceedings of the 12th International Conference on Interaction Design and Children, IDC '13.* Association for Computing Machinery. 10.1145/2485760.2485816

Bronner, S. J. (2009). Digitizing and Virtualizing Folklore. In Folklore and the Internet: Vernacular Expression in α Digital World. Utah State University Press. doi:10.2307/j.ctt4cgrx5.5

Brown, M. (1989). Women, Folklore and Feminism. *Journal of Folklore Research, 26*(3), 259–264.

Bruckman, A. (2006). Teaching students to study online communities ethically. *Journal of Information Ethics, 15*(2), 82–98. doi:10.3172/JIE.15.2.82

Brumann, C. (2015). Cultural Heritage. In J. Wright (Ed.), *International Encyclopedia of the Social & Behavioral Sciences* (pp. 414–419). Elsevier Ltd. doi:10.1016/B978-0-08-097086-8.12185-3

Bruner, J. (1990). *Acts of meaning*. Harvard University Press.

Bryman, A. (2004). *Social Research Methods*. Oxford University Press.

Buchyczyk, M., Nicolescu, G., & Urdea, A. (2017). Forging Folklore, Disrupting Archives: Curatorial Explorations between Tradition and Innovation. *The Museum of the Romanian Peasant Anthropology Journal*, *22*, 129–147.

Budka, Ph. (2011). *From Cyber to Digital Anthropology to an Anthropology of the Contemporary?* https://pdfs.semanticscholar.org/ac2c/2652a560a824eb5c1a919058e13154382376.pdf

Burguillo, J. C. (2010). Using Game Theory and Competition-Based Learning to Stimulate Student Motivation and Performance. *Computers & Education*, *55*(2), 566–575. doi:10.1016/j.compedu.2010.02.018

Burmark, L. (2004). Visual presentations that prompt, flash & transform. *Media and Methods*, *40*(6), 4–5.

Butler & Bodnar. (2017). *Establishing the Impact That Gamified Homework Portals Can Have on Students' Academic Motivation*. Academic Press.

Butter, M., & Knight, P. (2018). The History of Conspiracy Theory Research. A Review and Commentary. In J. E. Uscinski (Ed.), *Conspiracy Theories and the People Who Believe Them*. Oxford University. doi:10.1093/oso/9780190844073.003.0002

Cabiria, J. (2008). Virtual World and Real World Permeability: Transference of Positive Benefits for Marginalized Gay and Lesbian Populations. *Journal of Virtual Worlds Research*, *1*(1). Advance online publication. doi:10.4101/jvwr.v1i1.284

Cai, S., Chiang, F.-K., Sun, Y., Lin, C., & Lee, J. J. (2017). Applications of Augmented Reality-Based Natural Interactive Learning in Magnetic Field Instruction. *Interactive Learning Environments*, *25*(6), 778–791. doi:10.1080/10494820.2016.1181094

Calanca, D. (2020). Archivi digitali della moda e patrimonio culturale tra descrizione e integrazione. *ZoneModa Journal*, *10*(2), 11–25.

Campion-Vincent, V. (2007). Rumors and Urban Legends. *Diogenes*, *54*(1), 162–199. doi:10.1177/0392192107073437

Cannon, M. (2018). *Digital Media in Education*. Macmillan., doi:10.1007/978-3-319-78304-8

Capacete-Caballero, X., Caulfield-Sriklad, D., & McKay, F. (2013). Enhancing the Display of the Fashion Artefact through Digital Multi-media Approaches. In *Proceedings of the 1st International Conference on Digital Fashion* (pp. 336 - 345). Digital Fashion 2013 Secretariat.

Carayannis, E. G., Bast, G., & Campbell, D. F. (2018). Conclusion: The Museum of the Future and the Future of Museums. In G. Bast, E. G. Carayannis, & D. F. J. Campbell (Eds.), *The Future of Museums* (pp. 145–148). Springer. doi:10.1007/978-3-319-93955-1_13

Carpenter, J., Morrison, S., Craft, M., & Lee, M. (2019, March). Exploring how and why educators use Instagram. In Society for information technology & teacher education international conference (pp. 2686-2691). Association for the Advancement of Computing in Education (AACE).

Carrera, C. (2011). *Acercamiento gramatical a la lengua mazateca de Mazatlán de Villa de Flores Oaxaca*. INALI.

Casillo, M., Conte, D., Lombardi, M., Santaniello, D., & Valentino, C. (2021). Recommender System for Digital Storytelling: A Novel Approach to Enhance Cultural Heritage. In A. Del Bimbo, R. Cucchiara, S. Sclaroff, G. M. Farinella, T. Mei, M. Bertini, H. Jair Escalante, & R. Vezzan (Eds.), *Pattern Recognition. ICPR International Workshops and Challenges. ICPR 2021*. Springer. doi:10.1007/978-3-030-68787-8_22

Castillo, M. C. (2018). Las identidades étnicas en Oaxaca. *Oaxaca Población Siglo XXI*, *41*, 23–40.

Catalano, C. E., Luccini, A. M., & Mortara, M. (2014). Guidelines for an effective design of serious games. *International Journal of Serious Games*, *1*(1). Advance online publication. doi:10.17083/ijsg.v1i1.8

Cavell, St. (1969/2002). *Must We Mean What We Say?* Cambridge University Press.

Chan, S. C., Joosse, P., Martin, S. J., & Tian, X. (2020). Ethnography in Calamitous Times. *Etnografia e ricerca qualitativa*, *13*(2), 175-184. doi:10.3240/97803

Charr, M. (2021,01 January). Museum of London collects Covid dreams. *Museum next*. Retrieved from https://www.museumnext.com/article/museum-of-london-collects-covid-dreams/

Chaudy, Y., Connolly, T., & Hainey, T. (2014). Learning Analytics in Serious Games: A Review of the Literature. *Ecaet 2014*.

Cheng, K.-H., & Tsai, C.-C. (2020). Students' Motivational Beliefs and Strategies, Perceived Immersion and Attitudes towards Science Learning with Immersive Virtual Reality: A Partial Least Squares Analysis. *British Journal of Educational Technology*, *51*(6), 2140–2159. doi:10.1111/bjet.12956

Cheng, W. W. H., Lam, E. T. H., & Chiu, D. K. W. (2020). Social media as a platform in academic library marketing: A comparative study. *Journal of Academic Librarianship*, *46*(5), 102188. doi:10.1016/j.acalib.2020.102188

Chen, L., & Xu, J. (2010). The Analysis of Buddhism Library Construction in Mainland China. *Journal of Academic Libraries*, *28*(2), 19–23.

Cherny, L. (1999). *Conversation and Community: Chat in a Virtual World*. University of Chicago Press.

Cheung, F., & Leung, W. (2016). Facebook users' habits in getting commercial information: A study on Hong Kong students. *Economics, Management, and Financial Markets*, *11*(3), 56–71.

Cheung, T. Y., Ye, Z., & Chiu, D. K. W. (2021). Value chain analysis of information services for the visually impaired: A case study of contemporary technological solutions. *Library Hi Tech*, *39*(2), 625–642. doi:10.1108/LHT-08-2020-0185

Christinaki, E., Vidakis, N., & Triantafyllidis, G. (2014). A Novel Educational Game for Teaching Emotion Identification Skills to Preschoolers with Autism Diagnosis. *Computer Science and Information Systems*, *11*(2), 723–743. doi:10.2298/CSIS140215039C

Christoulakis, M., Pitsiladis, A., Moraiti, A., Moumoutzis, N., & Christodoulakis, S. (2013). EShadow : A Tool for Digital Storytelling Based on Traditional Greek Shadow Theatre. *Fdg 2013*.

Chu, H.-C., & Hung, C.-M. (2015). Effects of the Digital Game-Development Approach on Elementary School Students' Learning Motivation, Problem Solving, and Learning Achievement. *International Journal of Distance Education Technologies*, *13*(1), 87–102. doi:10.4018/ijdet.2015010105

Chung, A. C. W., & Chiu, D. K. (2016). OPAC Usability Problems of Archives: A Case Study of the Hong Kong Film Archive. *International Journal of Systems and Service-Oriented Engineering*, *6*(1), 54–70. doi:10.4018/IJSSOE.2016010104

Cichocka, A., Marchlewska, M., & Golec de Zavala, A. (2016). Does self-love or self-hate predict conspiracy beliefs? Narcissism, self-esteem and the endorsement of conspiracy theories. *Social Psychological & Personality Science*, *7*(2), 157–166. doi:10.1177/1948550615616170

Citizen Protection Ministry. (2005). Police operation "Πόλις" [Lexical characteristics of Greek language]. Press release 02/12/2005. Athens.

Clarke, St. (2002). Conspiracy Theories and Conspiracy Theorising. *Philosophy of the Social Sciences*, *32*(2), 131–150. doi:10.1177/004931032002001

Claudot, F., Alla, F., Fresson, J., Calvez, T., Coudane, H., & Bonaïti-Pellié, C. (2009). Ethics and observational studies in medical research: Various rules in a common framework. *International Journal of Epidemiology*, *38*(4), 1104–1108. doi:10.1093/ije/dyp164 PMID:19336436

Cleland, J., Dixon, K., & Kilvington, D. (2019). *Online Research Methods in Sport Studies*. Routledge. doi:10.4324/9780367809300

Cobley, J., Gaimster, D., So, S., Gorbey, K., Arnold, K., Pouliot, D., ... Jiang, M. (2020). Museums in the Pandemic: A Survey of Responses on the Current Crisis. *Museum Worlds*, *8*(1), 111–134. doi:10.3167/armw.2020.080109

Coffey, A. (1999). The ethnographic self: Fieldwork and the representation of identity. *Sage (Atlanta, Ga.)*.

Collins, H., Evans, R., & Gorman, M. E. (2010). Trading Zones and Interactional Expertise. In M. E. Gorman (Ed.), *Trading Zones and Interactional Expertise* (pp. 7–23). The MIT Press. doi:10.7551/mitpress/9780262014724.003.0002

Collumbien, M., Qureshi, A. A., Mayhew, S. H., Rizvi, N., Rabbani, A., Rolfe, B., Verma, R. K., Rehman, H., & Naveed-i-Rahat. (2009). Understanding the context of male and transgender sex work using peer ethnography. *Sexually Transmitted Infections*, *85*(Suppl 2), ii3–ii7. doi:10.1136ti.2008.033571 PMID:19307348

Connolly, T. M., Boyle, E. A., Macarthur, E., Hainey, T., & Boyle, J. M. (2012). A systematic literature review of empirical evidence on computer games and serious games. *Computers & Education*, *59*(2), 661–686. doi:10.1016/j.compedu.2012.03.004

Conrad, S. (2013). Documenting local history: A case study in digital storytelling. *Library Review*, *62*, 459–471.

Contreras, R. (2019). Transparency and Unmasking Issues in Ethnographic Crime Research: Methodological Considerations. *Sociological Forum*, *34*(2), 293–312. doi:10.1111ocf.12498

Cook, N. (2007). *Music Performance Meaning*. Taylor & Francis Ltd.

Cope, B., & Kalantzis, M. (Eds.). (2000). *Multiliteracies: Literacy learning and the design of social futures*. Psychology Press.

Corbin, J. M., & Strauss, A. L. (2008). *Basics of Qualitative Research: Techniques and Procedures for Developing Grounded Theory*. SAGE Publications. doi:10.4135/9781452230153

Correll, S. (1995). The ethnography of an electronic bar: The lesbian cafe. *Journal of Contemporary Ethnography*, *24*(3), 270–298. doi:10.1177/089124195024003002

Costa, R. C. (2019). The place of the humanities in today's knowledge society. *Palgrave Communications*, *5*(1), 1–5.

Council of Europe. (2018). *Quality History Education in the 21 st Century. Principles and Guidelines.* https://rm.coe.int/prems-108118-gbr-2507-quality-history-education-web-21x21/16808eace7

Cozza, M., Isabella, S., Di Cuia, P., Cozza, A., Peluso, R., Cosentino, V., Barbieri, L., Muzzupappa, M., & Bruno, F. (2021). Dive in the Past: A Serious Game to Promote the Underwater Cultural Heritage of the Mediterranean Sea. *Heritage*, *4*(4), 4001–4016. doi:10.3390/heritage4040220

Cresencio, L. (2021). *Herramientas con realidad aumentada de apoyo en la enseñanza de la lengua materna mazateca de Huautla de Jiménez, Oaxaca* [Bachelor Thesis]. Universidad de la Cañada.

Crooke, E. (2020). Communities, change, and the COVID-19 crisis. *Museum & Society*, *18*(03), 305–310. doi:10.29311/mas.v18i3.3533

Cruz, G.-R. C. (2017). Cultural heritage and the challenge of sustainability. *Philippine Political Science Journal*, *38*(1), 74–76.

Cuenca-López, J. M., Martín-Cáceres, M. J., & Estepa-Giménez, J. (2021). Teacher training in heritage education: Good practices for citizenship education. *Humanit Soc Sci Commun*, *8*, 62.

Dagnino, F. M., Pozzi, F., Cozzani, G., & Bernava, L. (2017). *Using Serious Games for Intangible Cultural Heritage (ICH). Education: A Journey into the Canto a Tenore Singing Style* [Paper presentation]. VISIGRAPP.

Dailey, M. N., Cottrell, G. W., & Reilly, J. (n.d.). *California Facial Expressions*. CAFE.

Dalkavouki, A. (2018). *Now and On Earth: The evolving geography of pop culture production and consumption. The case of the "Transformers" comics* [Master's thesis, National Technical University of Athens, Athens, Greece]. DSpace NTUA.

Daly, P., & Winter, T. (2012). *Routledge handbook of heritage in Asia*. Routledge. doi:10.4324/9780203156001

Davidson, C. N., & Goldberg, D. T. (2004). Engaging the Humanities. *Profession*, 42–62.

Davis, K., Sridharan, H., Koepke, L., Singh, S., & Boiko, R. (2018). Learning and Engagement in a Gamified Course: Investigating the Effects of Student Characteristics. *Journal of Computer Assisted Learning*, *34*(5), 492–503. doi:10.1111/jcal.12254

De Grove, F., Bourgonjon, J., & Van Looy, J. (2012). Digital games in the classroom? A contextual approach to teachers' adoption intention of digital games in formal education. *Computers in Human Behavior*, *28*(6), 2023–2033. doi:10.1016/j.chb.2012.05.021

De la Torre, E. M. (2014). Values in Heritage Conservation: A Project of The Getty Conservation Institute. *APT Bulletin: The Journal of Preservation Technology*, *45*(2/3), 19–24.

de Paula, B. H., Burn, A., Noss, R., & Valente, J. A. (2018). Playing Beowulf: Bridging computational thinking, arts and literature through game-making. *International Journal of Child-Computer Interaction*, *16*, 39–46. doi:10.1016/j.ijcci.2017.11.003

Dégh, L. (1994). *American Folklore and the Mass Media*. Indiana University Press.

Del Carpio, K. B. (2014). *La importancia de las comunidades indígenas, sus lenguas y culturas*. Retrieved from https://web.archive.org/web/20210728084951/http://www.revista pueblos.org/blog/2014/12/06/la-importancia-de-las-comunidades-indigenas-sus-lenguas-y-culturas/ Consulted in December 2021.

Demertzis, N., & Eyerman, R. (2020). Covid-19 as cultural trauma. *American Journal of Cultural Sociology*, *8*(3), 428–450. doi:10.105741290-020-00112-z PMID:32929388

Demetis, C. (2013). Hip Hop και Low bap δείχνουν τον δρόμο: Ενωμένοι ενάντια στον φασισμό για τον Παύλο Φύσσα [Lexical characteristics of Greek language], news247.gr. https://www.news247.gr/koinonia/hip-hop-kai-low-bap-deichnoyn-to-dromo-enomenoi-enantia-ston-fasismo-gia-ton-p-fyssa.6227946.html

Deng, W., Chin, G. Y.-l., Chiu, D. K. W., & Ho, K. K. W. (2022). (in press). Contribution of Literature Thematic Exhibition to Cultural Education: A Case Study of Jin Yong's Gallery. *Micronesian Educators*, *32*.

Department of economy of the communist party of Greece (KKE), (2018). Χρυσή Αυγή – "Δεκανίκι" του Καπιταλισμού στην Ελλάδα. Κομμουνιστική Επιθεώρηση [Lexical characteristics of Greek language], (5), Athens: Σύγχρονη εποχή. https://www.komep.gr/m-article/XRYSI-AYGI-DEKANIKI-TOY-KAPITALISMOY-STIN-ELLADA/

Deterding, S., Sicart, M., Nacke, L., O'Hara, K., & Dixon, D. (2011). Gamification. Using Game-Design Elements in Non-Gaming Contexts. In CHI '11 Extended Abstracts on Human Factors in Computing Systems, CHI EA '11. Association for Computing Machinery. doi:10.1145/1979742.1979575

Diamantaki, K. (2003). Internet Communities. An electronic public sphere? In *The digital challenge: Media and democracy*. Academic Press.

Dichev, C., Dicheva, D., Agre, G., & Angelova, G. (2013). Current practices, trends and challenges in k-12 online learning. *Cybernetics and Information Technologies*, *13*(3), 91–110. doi:10.2478/cait-2013-0028

Dimitriou, S. (2017). Social Development and Power Relations. The Methodology of the Human Sciences. Athens: Alexandria.

Ding, L., Er, E., & Orey, M. (2018). An Exploratory Study of Student Engagement in Gamified Online Discussions. *Computers & Education*, *120*, 213–226. doi:10.1016/j.compedu.2018.02.007

Ding, S. J., Lam, E. T. H., Chiu, D. K. W., Lung, M. M., & Ho, K. K. W. (2021). Changes in reading behavior of periodicals on mobile devices: A comparative study. *Journal of Librarianship and Information Science*, *53*(2), 233–244. doi:10.1177/0961000620938119

Diniz, G. C., Graciotto Silva, M. A., Gerosa, M. A., & Steinmacher, I. (2017). Using Gamification to Orient and Motivate Students to Contribute to OSS Projects. *2017 IEEE/ACM 10th International Workshop on Cooperative and Human Aspects of Software Engineering (CHASE)*. 10.1109/CHASE.2017.7

Dixon, W. (2000). The new genre cinema. In W. Dixon (Ed.), *Film genre 2000* (pp. 1–13). State University Of New York Press.

Dodds, K. (2006). Popular geopolitics and audience dispositions: James Bond and the internet movie database (IMDb). *Transactions of the Institute of British Geographers*, *31*(2), 116–130. doi:10.1111/j.1475-5661.2006.00199.x

Dong, G., Chiu, D. K. W., Huang, P.-S., Lung, M. M., Ho, K. K. W., & Geng, Y. (2021). Relationships between Research Supervisors and Students from Coursework-based Master's Degrees: Information Usage under Social Media. *Information Discovery and Delivery*, *49*(4), 319–327. doi:10.1108/IDD-08-2020-0100

Dong, Y. (2015). The Transmutation of the Category of B94 Buddhism in Chinese Library Classification. *Hebei Sci-Tech Library Journal*, *28*(5), 41–43.

Douglas, K. (2021). COVID-19 conspiracy theories. *Group Processes & Intergroup Relations*, *24*(2), 270–275. doi:10.1177/1368430220982068

Douglas, K. M., Sutton, R. M., Callan, M., Dawtry, R., & Harvey, A. (2016). Someone is pulling the strings: Hypersensitive agency detection and belief in conspiracy theories. *Thinking & Reasoning*, *22*(1), 57–77. doi:10.1080/13546783.2015.1051586

Douglas, K. M., Sutton, R. M., & Cichocka, A. (2017). The psychology of conspiracy theories. *Current Directions in Psychological Science*, *26*(6), 538–542. doi:10.1177/0963721417718261 PMID:29276345

Douglas, K. M., Uscinski, J. E., Sutton, R. M., Cichocka, A., Nefes, T., Ang, C. S., & Deravi, F. (2019). Understanding conspiracy theories. *Political Psychology*, *40*(S1), 3–35. doi:10.1111/pops.12568

Doulamis, N., Doulamis, A., Ioannidis, C., Klein, M., & Ioannides, M. (2017). Modelling of Static and Moving Objects: Digitizing Tangible and Intangible Cultural Heritage. In *Mixed Reality and Gamification for Cultural Heritage* (pp. 567–589). Springer International Publishing. doi:10.1007/978-3-319-49607-8_23

Dreimane, S., & Daniela, L. (2021). Educational potential of augmented reality mobile applications for learning the anatomy of the human body. *Technology. Knowledge and Learning*, *26*(4), 763–788. doi:10.100710758-020-09461-7

Dundes, A. (1965). *The study of folklore*. Prentice-Hall.

Dundes, A. (1980). *Interpreting Folklore*. Indiana University Press.

Dundes, A. (2005). Folkloristics in the Twenty-First Century (AFS Invited Presidential Plenary Address, 2004). *Journal of American Folklore*, *118*, 385–408.

Dynel, M. (2021). COVID-19 memes going viral: On the multiple multimodal voices behind face masks. *Discourse & Society*, *32*(2), 175–195. doi:10.1177/0957926520970385

ECLAC-UNESCO. (2020). *Education in the time of COVID-19*. United Nations.

Edler, D., Keil, J., Wiedenlübbert, T., Sossna, M., Kühne, O., & Dickmann, F. (2019). Immersive VR Experience of Redeveloped Post-industrial Sites: The Example of "Zeche Holland" in Bochum-Wattenscheid. *KN-J. Cartogr. Geogr. Inf*, *69*(4), 267–284. doi:10.100742489-019-00030-2

Efthymiadou, X. A. (2012). *"Σε σένα μιλάω Νεοέλληνα": Οι νέοι τραγουδούν την εθνική ταυτότητα* [Lexical characteristics of Greek language]. (Unpublished postgraduate thesis). Αριστοτέλειο Πανεπιστήμιο Θεσσαλονίκης, Thessaloniki.

Egan, K. (1989). Memory, imagination, and learning: connected by the story. *The Docket: Journal of the New Jersey Council for the Social Studies*, 9-13.

EKT. (2021). Digital Transformation of Greek Enterprises. In *2020: The impact of the COVID-19 pandemic*. Athens: National Documentation Center. Retrieved from https://metrics.ekt.gr/node/500

Ellis, B. (2001). A Model for Collecting and Interpreting World Trade Centre Disaster Jokes. *Newfolk: New Directions in Folklore, 5*, 1-10. https://scholarworks.iu.edu/journals/index.php/ndif/article/view/19881/25963

Escobar, A., Hess, D., Licha, I., Sibley, W., Strathern, M., & Sutz, J. (1994). Welcome To Cyberia: Notes on the Anthropology of Cyberculture. *Current Anthropology*, *35*(June), 211–231. doi:10.1086/204266

Europeana Pro. (n.d.). *Mapping digital initiatives during Covid-19*. Retrieved from https://pro.europeana.eu/post/mapping-museum-digital-initiatives-during-covid-19

Everitt, B. S., & Howell, D. (2005). Encyclopedia of Statistics in Behavioral Science. John Wiley & Sons. doi:10.1002/0470013192

Eythimiou, A., & Stavrakakis, H. (2018). Rap in Greece: Gendered configurations of power in-between the rhymes. *Journal of Greek Media & Culture*, *4*(2), 205–222. doi:10.1386/jgmc.4.2.205_1

Fahrenwald, N. L., & Stabnow, W. (2005). Sociocultural Perspective on Organ and Tissue Donation among Reservation-Dwelling American Indian Adults. *Ethnicity & Health*, *10*(4), 341–354. doi:10.1080/13557850500168826 PMID:16191731

Fast, K. (2012). *More than Meets the Eye: Transmedial Entertainment as a Site of Pleasure, Resistance and Exploitation* [Doctoral dissertation, Karlstad University, Karlstad, Sweden]. Digitala Vetenskapliga Arkivet.

Faugier, J., & Sargeant, M. (1997). Sampling hard to reach populations. *Journal of Advanced Nursing*, *26*(4), 790–797. doi:10.1046/j.1365-2648.1997.00371.x PMID:9354993

Fayyad, U., Piatetsky-Shapiro, G., & Smyth, P. (1996). Knowledge discovery and data mining: Towards a unifying framework. In E. Simoudis, J. Han, & U. Fayyad (Eds.), *KDD'96: Proceedings of the Second International Conference on Knowledge Discovery and Data Mining* (pp. 82–88). AAAI Press.

Fenster, M. (2008). Conspiracy Theories: Secrecy and Power in American Culture. University of Minneapolis Press.

Ferrara, V., Macchia, A., & Sapia, S. (2013). Reusing Cultural Heritage Digital resources in teaching. In *Proceedings of Digital Heritage International Congress* (pp. 409-412). IEEE.

Fessakis, G., Komis, V., Mavroudi, E., & Prantsoudi, S. (2018). Exploring the scope and the conceptualization of Computational Thinking at the K-12 classroom level curriculum, In M. S. Khine (Ed.), Computational Thinking in the STEM Disciplines: Foundations and Research Highlights. Springer.

Fine, G. A., & Ellis, B. (2010). *The Global Grapevine: Why Rumors of Terrorisms, Immigration and Trade Matter*. Oxford University Press. doi:10.1093/acprof:oso/9780199736317.001.0001

Fini, A. (2019). The technological dimension of a Massive Open Online Course: The case of the CCK08 course tools. *International Review of Research in Open and Distance Learning*, *10*(5). Advance online publication. doi:10.19173/irrodl.v10i5.643

Fiormonte, D., Numerico, T., & Tomasi, F. (2015). *The Digital Humanist: A Critical Inquiry*. Punctum Books.

Floch, J., & Jiang, S. (2022). *One place, many stories digital storytelling for cultural heritage discovery in the landscape. 2015 Digital Heritage*. doi:10.1109/DigitalHeritage.2015.7419566

Foelske, M. (2014). *Digital storytelling: the impact on student engagement, motivation and academic learning*. Graduate Research Papers, 167. https://scholarworks.uni.edu/grp/167

Fontes, T. O., & O'Mahony, M. (2008). In-depth interviewing by Instant Messaging. *Social Research Update*, *53*(2), 1–4. https://sru.soc.surrey.ac.uk/SRU53.pdf

Foulidis, X. (2015). *New horizons in Greek Folklore Studies: The internet as a field of production, dissemination and educational utilization of Popular Culture* [Doctoral Thesis]. University of the Aegean.

Franceschini, M. (2019). Navigating Fashion: On the Role of Digital Fashion Archives in the Preservation, Classification and Dissemination of Fashion Heritage. *Critical Studies in Fashion & Beauty*, *10*(1), 69–90. doi:10.1386/csfb.10.1.69_1

Frenzel, K., Müller, M., & Sottong, H. (2004). *Storytelling. Das Harun-al-Raschid-Prinzip*. Hanser.

Friedberg, R. (1994). Storytelling and Cognitive Therapy with Children. *Journal of Cognitive Psychotherapy*, *8*(3), 209–217. doi:10.1891/0889-8391.8.3.209

Friskie, S. (2020). The healing power of storytelling: Finding identity through narrative. *The Arbutus Review*, *11*(1), 19–27. doi:10.18357/tar111202019324

Fuchs, C. (2021). *Bill Gates Conspiracy Theories as Ideology in the Context of the COVID-19 Crisis. In Communicating COVID-19*. Emerald Publishing Limited. doi:10.1108/978-1-80117-720-720211007

Gakhar, S., & Thompson, A. (2007.) Digital storytelling: Engaging, communicating, and collaborating. In R. Carlsen, & D. A. Willis (Eds.), *Proceedings of Society for Information Technology and Teacher Education International Conference 2007* (pp. 607-612). Chesapeake, VA: AACE.

Galdames, V., Walqui, A., & Gustafson, B. (2006). *Enseñanza de Lengua Indígena como Lengua Materna*. CDI.

Gallardo-Echenique, E. E., Marqués Molías, L., & Bullen, M. (2015). Students in higher education: Social and academic uses of digital technology. *Int. J. Educ. Technol. High. Educ.*, *12*(1), 25–37. doi:10.7238/rusc.v12i1.2078

Galvin, S., & Greenhow, C. (2020). Educational networking: A novel discipline for improved K-12 learning based on social networks. In *Educational networking* (pp. 3–41). Springer. doi:10.1007/978-3-030-29973-6_1

Garcia, A. C., Standlee, A. I., Bechkoff, J., & Cui, Y. (2009). Ethnographic Approaches to the Internet and Computer-Mediated Communication. *Journal of Contemporary Ethnography, 38*(1), 52–84. doi:10.1177/0891241607310839

Garreta, D., & Mor, P. (2018). *Diseño centrado en el usuario*. Universidad Oberta de Catalunya.

Gasouka, M. (2017). *Ethnography, Internet and Folklore Studies. European Journal of Social Sciences*. Available online at www.oapub.org/soc

Gasouka, M., Arvanitidou, Z., Foulidi, X., & Raptou, E. (2012). Folklore Research and its New Challenges: From the Ethnography to Netnografy. *Mediterranean Journal of Social Sciences, 3*(8), 111–116.

Gasouka, M., & Foulidi, X. (2012). *Contemporary Horizons of Folklore Studies. Conceptual Framework, Research, Gender, Internet, School [Σύγχρονοι ορίζοντες των λαογραφικών σπουδών. Εννοιολογικό πλαίσιο, έρευνα, φύλο, διαδίκτυο, σχολείο]*. I. Sideris.

Gasouka, M., & Foulidi, X. (2012). *Contemporary Horizons of Folklore Studies-Conceptual Framework, Research, Gender, Internet, School*. Sideris.

Gasouka, M., & Foulidi, X. (2012). *New horizons of folklore studies - Conceptual framework, research, gender, internet, school*. Sideris Publications.

Gasouka, M., & Foulidi, X. (2012). *Σύγχρονοι ορίζοντες των λαογραφικών σπουδών* [Lexical characteristics of Greek language]. I. Σιδέρης.

Gasouka, M., & Foulidi, X. (2017). *Aspects of ethnographic research in folklore studies. Feminist Ethnography - Internet Ethnography [Όψεις Εθνογραφικής Έρευνας στις Λαογραφικές Σπουδές. Φεμινιστική Εθνογραφία- Διαδικτυακή Εθνογραφία]*. Papazisis.

Gasouka, M., & Foulidi, X. (2017). *Aspects of Ethnographic Research in Folklore Studies. Feminist Ethnography, Internet Ethnography*. Papazisis.

Gee, J. P. (2003). What Video Games Have to Teach Us about Learning and Literacy. *Computers in Entertainment, 1*(1), 20. doi:10.1145/950566.950595

Gee, J. P. (2017). Affinity Spaces and 21st Century Learning. *Educational Technology, 57*(2), 27–31.

Geertz, C. (1973). *The Interpretation of Cultures: Selected Essays*. Basic Books, Inc.

Gesche-Koning, N. (2018). Research for CULT Committee – Education in Cultural Heritage. European Parliament, Policy Department for Structural and Cohesion Policies.

Giannikopoulou, A., & Fokiali, E. (2013). In the networks of literature. Teaching in the age of the internet. In Educational planning issues. Social networks and school unit: Bridges and meanings (pp. 66-90). Interaction.

Giglitto, D., Ciolfi, L., Claisse, C., & Lockley, E. (2019). Bridging cultural heritage and communities through digital technologies: Understanding perspectives and challenges. In *Proceedings of the 9th International Conference on Communities and Technologies: Transforming communities* (pp. 81-91). ACM.

Gilead, T. (2017). Justifying the teaching of the humanities: A new economic approach. *Policy Futures in Education, 15*(3), 346–359.

Gizzi, F. T., Biscione, M., Danese, M., Maggio, A., Pecci, A., Sileo, M., Potenza, M. R., Masini, N., Ruggeri, A., Sileo, A., & Mercurio, F. (2019). Students Meet Cultural Heritage: An Experience within the Framework of the Italian School-Work Alternation (SWA)—From Outcomes to Outlooks. *Heritage, 2*(3), 1986–2016.

Goksu, M., & Somen, T. (2019). History teachers' views on using local history. *European Journal of Education Studies*. doi:10.46827/ejes.v0i0.2436

Gold, R. L. (1958). Roles in Sociological Field Observations. *Social Forces*, *36*(3), 217–223. doi:10.2307/2573808

Goldzwig, S. R. (2002). Conspiracy Rhetoric at the Dawn of New Millennium: A Response. *Western Journal of Communication*, *66*(4), 492–506. doi:10.1080/10570310209374751

Gómez-Carrasco, C. J., Miralles-Martinez, P., Fontal, O., & Ibañez-Etxeberria, A. (2020). Cultural Heritage and Methodological Approaches—An Analysis through Initial Training of History Teachers (Spain–England). *Sustainability*, *12*(3), 933.

Gonulal, T. (2019). The use of Instagram as a mobile-assisted language learning tool. *Contemporary Educational Technology*, *10*(3), 309–323. doi:10.30935/cet.590108

Gonzalez, J. L., Cabrera, M. J., & Gutierrez, F. L. (2007). Using videogames in special education. *Lecture Notes in Computer Science*, *4739*, 360–367. doi:10.1007/978-3-540-75867-9_46

Goodarzparvari, P., & Camejo, F. C. B. (2018). Preservation of cultural heritage via education of children, utilizing visual communication: Persepolis as a case study. *Creative Education*, *9*, 141–151.

Gorbach, P. M., Murphy, R., Weiss, R. E., Hucks-Ortiz, C., & Shoptaw, S. (2009). Bridging Sexual Boundaries: Men Who Have Sex with Men and Women in a Street-Based Sample in Los Angeles. *Journal of Urban Health*, *86*(1), 63–76. doi:10.100711524-009-9370-7 PMID:19543837

Goubert, P. (1971). Local History. *Daedalus*, *100*(1), 113–127.

Graeupner, D., & Coman, A. (2017). The dark side of meaning-making: How social exclusion leads to superstitious thinking. *Journal of Experimental Social Psychology*, *69*, 218–222. doi:10.1016/j.jesp.2016.10.003

Grammatikopoulou, Ch. (2017). Breathing Art. Art as an Encompassing and Participatory Experience. In C. Van den Akker & S. Legêne (Eds.), *Museums in a Digital Culture* (pp. 41–56). Amsterdam University Press. doi:10.1515/9789048524808-005

Grant, N. S., & Bolin, B. L. (2016). Digital Storytelling: A Method for Engaging Students and Increasing Cultural Competency. *The Journal of Effective Teaching*, *16*, 44–61.

Gray, K. L. (2012). Deviant bodies, stigmatized identities, and racist acts: Examining the experiences of African-American gamers in Xbox Live. *New Review of Hypermedia and Multimedia*, *18*(4), 261–276. doi:10.1080/13614568.2012.746740

Green, C. A., McMillan, E., Munn, L., Sole, C., & Eady, M. J. (2020). Entering Their World: Using Social Media to Support Students in Modern Times. In *Putting Social Media and Networking Data in Practice for Education, Planning, Prediction and Recommendation* (pp. 15–28). Springer. doi:10.1007/978-3-030-33698-1_2

Greenhow, C., & Chapman, A. (2020). *Social distancing meet social media: digital tools for connecting students, teachers, and citizens in an emergency*. Information and Learning Sciences.

Groger, L., Mayberry, P., & Straker, J. (1999). What We Didn't Learn Because of Who Would Not Talk to Us. *Qualitative Health Research*, *9*(6), 829–835. doi:10.1177/104973299129122180

Groh, F. (2012). Gamification: State of the Art Definition and Utilization. *Proceedings of the 4th Seminar on Research Trends in Media Informatics*, 39–46. http://fold.it

Guboglo, A. (2020). Digital Museology Under Test: Challenges and Opportunities for Russian Museums. *Museum & Society*, *18*(3), 311–313. doi:10.29311/mas.v18i3.3552

Gudmundsdottir, S. (1995). The narrative nature of pedagogical content knowledge. In H. McEwan & K. Egan (Eds.), *Narrative in Teaching, Learning, and Research.* Teachers College Press.

Haggerty, B. (2013). *Mr Sandmann, bringer of dreams & nightmares.* Available online at https://www.youtube.com/watch?v=gtnrB75MKlY

Hall, S. (2017). Memories of style: Digitizing the Yorkshire Fashion Archive. *Art Libraries Journal, 42*(3), 157–161. doi:10.1017/alj.2017.22

Hampson, C., Bailey, E., Munnelly, G., Lawless, S., & Conlan, O. (2013). Dynamic Personalisation for Digital Cultural Heritage Collections. *Proceedings of the UMAP.*

Han, K., Shih, P. C., Rosson, M. B., & Carroll, J. M. (2014). Enhancing community awareness of and participation in local heritage with a mobile application. In *Proceedings of the Proceedings of the 17th ACM conference on Computer supported cooperative work & social computing* (pp. 1144–1155). 10.1145/2531602.2531640

Hartley, L. (2007). Tibetan Buddhist Resource Center (TBRC) Knowledge Base and Digital Library. *College & Research Libraries, 68*(5), 446.

Healy, T. (2016). *Creating Custom Storage Forms for Charles James Masterpieces.* Retrieved from The MET: https://www.metmuseum.org/blogs/now-at-the-met/2016/custom-storage-forms-charles-james

Heft, A., & Buehling, K. (2022). Measuring the diffusion of conspiracy theories in digital information ecologies. *Convergence*, 1–22. doi:10.1177/13548565221091809

Hellenic Ministry of Culture. (2017). *Acropolis Virtual Tour.* Hellenic Ministry of Culture. http://acropolis-virtualtour.gr/index.html

Henning, M. (2006). *Museums, Media and Cultural Theory.* Open University Press.

Hew, K. F., Huang, B., Kai, W. S. C., & Chiu, D. K. W. (2016). Engaging Asian Students through Game Mechanics: Findings from Two Experiment Studies. *Computers & Education, 92–93*, 221–236. doi:10.1016/j.compedu.2015.10.010

He, Z., Chiu, D. K. W., & Ho, K. K. W. (2022). Weibo Analysis on Chinese Cultural Knowledge for Gaming. In Z. Sun (Ed.), *Handbook of Research on Foundations and Applications of Intelligent Business Analytics* (pp. 320–349). IGI Global. doi:10.4018/978-1-7998-9016-4.ch015

Hine, C. (2000). *Virtual Ethnography.* SAGE Publications. doi:10.4135/9780857020277

Hoang, K. (2021). The benefits of preserving and promoting cultural heritage values for the sustainable development of the country. E3S Web of Conferences (vol. 234). doi:10.1051/e3sconf/202123400076

Hofstadter, R. (1996). *The Paranoid Style in American Politics and Other Essays.* Harvard University Press. (Original work published 1965)

Howard, R. G. (2008). Electronic Hybridity: The Persistent Processes of the Vernacular Web. *Journal of American Folklore, 121*(480), 192–218. doi:10.1353/jaf.0.0012

Hsu, T. C., Chang, S. C., & Hung, Y. T. (2018). How to learn and how to teach computational thinking: Suggestions based on a review of the literature. *Computers & Education, 126*, 296–310. doi:10.1016/j.compedu.2018.07.004

Huang, J. (2011a). On Openness of the Ancient Chinese Buddhist Sutra Mansions. *Library and Information Service, 55*(9), 138–142.

Huang, J. (2011b). A Study on the Ancient Chinese Buddhist Sutra Mansions. *Library & Information, 55*(3), 139–144.

Huang, P. S., Paulino, Y., So, S., Chiu, D. K. W., & Ho, K. K. W. (2021). Special issue editorial - COVID-19 pandemic and health informatics (part 1). *Library Hi Tech*, *39*(3), 693–695. doi:10.1108/LHT-09-2021-324

Huang, P.-S., Paulino, Y. C., So, S., Chiu, D. K. W., & Ho, K. K. W. (2022). Guest editorial: COVID-19 Pandemic and Health Informatics (Part 2). *Library Hi Tech*, *40*(2), 281–285. doi:10.1108/LHT-04-2022-447

Huang, T.-C., Chen, C.-C., & Chou, Y.-W. (2016). Animating Eco-Education: To See, Feel, and Discover in an Augmented Reality-Based Experiential Learning Environment. *Computers & Education*, *96*, 72–82. doi:10.1016/j.compedu.2016.02.008

Hubert, L. D. (2003). *The Internet*. Kritiki Publications.

ICOMOS. (2002). *International Cultural Tourism Charter. Principles And Guidelines For Managing Tourism At Places Of Cultural And Heritage Significance*. ICOMOS International Cultural Tourism Committee.

iMareCulture. (n.d.). Retrieved February 27, 2022, from https://imareculture.eu/downloads/project-tools/seafarers-game/

Ingarden, R. (1973). *The literary work of art*. Northwestern University Press.

Injadat, M., Salo, F., & Nassif, A. B. (2016). Data mining techniques in social media: A survey. *Neurocomputing*, *214*, 654–670. doi:10.1016/j.neucom.2016.06.045

International Guoshu Association. (2017). *Hong Kong Martial Arts Living Archive*. Retrieved from: https://www.fringebacker.com/en/projects/HK_Martial_Arts_Living/

Ioannides, M., & Davies, R. (2018). ViMM - Virtual Multimodal Museum: a Manifesto and Roadmap for Europe's Digital Cultural Heritage. *2018 International Conference on Intelligent Systems (IS)*, 343–350. doi:10.1109/IS.2018.8710556

Ioannides, M., Magnenat Thalmann, N., & Papagiannakis, G. (2017). *Mixed Reality and Gamification for Cultural Heritage*. Springer International Publishing. doi:10.1007/978-3-319-49607-8

Iosifidis, T. (2008). *Ποιοτικές μέθοδοι έρευνας στις κοινωνικές επιστήμες* [Lexical characteristics of Greek language]. Κριτική.

Isbell, C., Stein, L., Cutler, R., Forbes, J., Fraser, L., Impagliazzo, J., Proulx, V., Russ, S., Thomas, R., & Xu, Y. (2009). (Re)Defining Computing Curricula by (Re)Defining Computing. *ACM SIGCSE Bulletin*, *41*(4), 195–207. doi:10.1145/1709424.1709462

Isomäki, H., & Silvennoinen, J. (2013). Online ethnographies. In P. Isaías & M. B. Nunes (Eds.), *Information systems research and exploring social artifacts: Approaches and methodologies* (pp. 124–141). IGI Global. doi:10.4018/978-1-4666-2491-7.ch007

Jacob, S. R., & Warschauer, M. (2018). Computational thinking and literacy. *Journal of Computer Science Integration*, *1*(1). Advance online publication. doi:10.26716/jcsi.2018.01.1.1

Jagielska-Burduk, A., Pszczyński, M., & Stec, P. (2021). Cultural Heritage Education in UNESCO Cultural Conventions. *Sustainability*, *13*(6), 3548.

Janes, R. R., & Sandell, R. (2019). *Museum activism*. Routledge. doi:10.4324/9781351251044

Jenkins, H. (2018). *Who The &%&# Is Henry Jenkins? Confessions of an Aca-Fan*. Henry Jenkins. http://henryjenkins.org/aboutmehtml

Jenkins, H., Purushotma, R., Weigel, M., Clinton K., & Robison, A. J. (2009). Confronting the challenges of participatory culture: Media education for the 21st century. MIT Press.

Jenkins, H. (2006). *Convergence Culture: Where Old and New Media Collide*. New York University Press.

Jiang, T., Lo, P., Cheuk, M. K., Chiu, D. K. W., Chu, M. Y., Zhang, X., Zhou, Q., Liu, Q., Tang, J., Zhang, X., Sun, X., Ye, Z., Yang, M., & Lam, S. K. (2019). 文化新語:兩岸四地傑出圖書館、檔案館及博物館傑出工作者訪談 [New Cultural Dialog: Interviews with Outstanding Librarians, Archivists, and Curators in Greater China]. Hong Kong: Systech Publications.

Jingtao, S., & Qingyi, Z. (2002). Library Sort Number Management System. *Computer Systems & Applications*, *2002*(11), 127–130.

Johnson, B. R., Onwuegbuzie, A. J., & Turner, L. A. (2007). Toward a definition of mixed methods research. *Journal of Mixed Methods Research*, *1*, 112–133.

Jolley, D., Douglas, K. M., & Sutton, R. M. (2018). Blaming a few bad apples to save a threatened barrel: The system-justifying function of conspiracy theories. *Political Psychology*, *39*(2), 465–478. doi:10.1111/pops.12404

Jones, S. (1997). *Virtual Culture*. Sage Publications.

Junker, B. (1960). *Field Work*. University of Chicago Press.

Kalochristianakis, M., Vonorta, H., Stamoulias, A., Lakka, E., Kontakis, K., & Malamos, A. (2016). Experiential educational environments for cultural heritage. *2016 International Conference on Telecommunications and Multimedia, TEMU 2016*, 6–11. doi:10.1109/TEMU.2016.7551907

Kalogiannakis, M., & Papadakis, S. (2007). The dual form of further education of educators in ICT: technological and pedagogical training. In C. Constantinou, Z. Zacharias, & M. Papaevripidou (Eds.), *8th International Conference On Computer Based Learning in Science* (pp. 265–276). Academic Press.

Kalogiannakis, M., & Papadakis, S. (2019). Evaluating pre-service kindergarten teachers' intention to adopt and use tablets into teaching practice for natural sciences. *International Journal of Mobile Learning and Organisation*, *13*(1), 113. https://doi.org/10.1504/IJMLO.2019.096479

Kalogiannakis, M., Papadakis, S., & Dorouka, P. (2020). Tablets and apps for promoting robotics, mathematics, STEM education and literacy in early childhood education. *International Journal of Mobile Learning and Organisation*, *14*(2), 255. https://doi.org/10.1504/IJMLO.2020.10026334

Kalogirou, T. (2004). Lector Ludens: reading as a game / games of reading. In A. Katsiki-Givalou (Ed.), *Literature today: aspects, revisions, perspectives*. Greek Letters.

Kapaniaris, A. (2008). *Digitization, Documentation and Promotion of Greek Culture: The Case of the Archive "Dimitrios G. Kaslas"* [Diploma Thesis]. Hellenic Open University.

Kapaniaris, A., & Gasouka, M. (2016). Folk culture and digitally enriched books (Enriched e-books): Designing learning resources for education using the internet. In Internet cultures. Pedio.

Kapaniaris, A., & Varvounis, M. (2019c). Folklore on the road to distance education (e-learning). *Folklore, Bulletin of the Hellenic Folklore Society*, *44*.

Kapaniaris, A., & Varvounis, M. (2019d). The experience of distance education (e-learning) in the field of Folklore: The evaluation, the first conclusions, the proposals and the new developments. *Folklore, Bulletin of the Hellenic Folklore Society*, *44*.

Kapaniaris, A., Varvounis, M. (2019c). Folklore on the road to distance education (e-learning). *Folklore, Bulletin of the Greek Folklore Society*, *44*.

Kapaniaris, A., Varvounis, M. (2019d). The experience of distance education (e-learning) in the field of Folklore: The evaluation, the first conclusions, the proposals and the new developments. *Folklore, Bulletin of the Greek Folklore Society, 44*.

Kapaniaris, A. (2020). *Digital Folklore and Education: Enriched Media and Innovative Approaches to the Teaching of Popular Culture*. Pedio.

Kapaniaris, A. (2022). The meeting of digital storytelling with popular culture and education in the field of digital folklore. In M. Varvounis, G. Katsadoros, & A. Kapaniaris (Eds.), *People, genders, identities, cultures. Folklore and gender approaches*. Gonis.

Kapaniaris, A., Gasouka, M., & Varvounis, M. (2019). E-learning program: «Introduction to the science of Folk Culture»: Evaluation of the semester course. *World Wide Journal of Multidisciplinary Research and Development*, *5*(5), 24–34.

Kapaniaris, A., Gasouka, M., & Varvounis, M. (2019). E-learning program: «Introduction to the science of Folk Culture»: Evaluation of the semester course: «Contemporary Horizons of Folklore Studies, (Gender, Internet, and Education). *World Wide Journal of Multidisciplinary Research and Development*, *5*(5), 24–34.

Kapaniaris, A., & Varvounis, M. (2019). Social networking and communication tools in archive ethnography: Tools for collecting, displaying and recording material or digital research notebooks? *WWJMRD*, *5*(5), 11–18.

Kapaniaris, A., & Varvounis, M. (2019a). Design and implementation of e-learning programs in folklore, ethnography and history: Following the Logic of the Mass Open Internet Courses (MOOC). *World Wide Journal of Multidisciplinary Research and Development*, *5*(1), 22–29.

Kapaniaris, A., & Varvounis, M. (2019a). Design and implementation of e-learning programs in folklore, ethnography, and history: Following the Logic of the Mass Open Internet Courses (MOOC). *World Wide Journal of Multidisciplinary Research and Development*, *5*(1), 22–29.

Kapaniaris, A., & Varvounis, M. (2019b). E-Learning Program «Introduction to the Science of Folk Culture»: Evaluation of the course. *World Wide Journal of Multidisciplinary Research and Development*, *5*(5), 1–10.

Kapaniaris, A., & Varvounis, M. (2019b). E-Learning Program «Introduction to the Science of Folk Culture»: Evaluation of the course: «Introduction to the Science of Folk Culture. *World Wide Journal of Multidisciplinary Research and Development*, *5*(5), 1–10.

Kapaniaris, A., & Varvounis, M. (2022). E-Learning program "Introduction to the Science of Folk Culture": Evaluation of the three-year program. In S. Papadakis & A. Kapaniaris (Eds.), *The Digital Folklore of Cyberculture and Digital Humanities*. IGI Global.

Kapaniaris, A., & Zampetoglou, G. (2021). Visual programming for the greation of digital shadow play performance using mobile devices in times of Covid-19. *Advances in Mobile Learning Educational Research*, *1*(2), 162–170. doi:10.25082/AMLER.2021.02.010

Kapaniaris, G. A. (2020). *Digital Folklore and Education, Enriched Media and Innovative Approaches to the Didactics of Folk Culture*. Pedio.

Kaplan, C. D., Korf, D., & Sterk, C. (1987). Temporal and Social Contexts of Heroin-Using Populations An Illustration of the Snowball Sampling Technique. *Journal of Mental and Nervous Disorders*, *175*(9), 566–574. doi:10.1097/00005053-198709000-00009 PMID:3655783

Kapp, K. M. (2012). *The Gamification of Learning and Instruction: Game-Based Methods and Strategies for Training and Education*. John Wiley & Sons.

Karakose, T., Polat, H., & Papadakis, S. (2021). Examining Teachers' Perspectives on School Principals' Digital Leadership Roles and Technology Capabilities during the COVID-19 Pandemic. *Sustainability, 13*(23), 13448. https://doi.org/10.3390/su132313448

Karamanolakis, E. (2019). *Η μουσική: Η δεκαετία του '40 και το ρεμπέτικο τραγούδι. Από έργο τέχνης σε τεκμήριο του ιστορικού* [Lecture notes]. ΕΚΠΑ, Πρόγραμμα: Οι πηγές του ιστορικού-Ερευνώντας την Ελληνική ιστορία του 20ου αιώνα [Lexical characteristics of Greek language].

Kara, N., & Sungur, A. (2021). Re-creating the Museum Space: Distance Learning in Museums during Covid-19 Lockdown. *Psychology and Education, 58*(3), 2989–2995.

Karsenti, T. (2013). What the research says. *International Journal of Technologies in Higher Education.*

Karuzaki, E., Partarakis, N., Patsiouras, N., Zidianakis, E., Katzourakis, A., Pattakos, A., Kaplanidi, D., Baka, E., Cadi, N., Magnenat-Thalmann, N., Rings, C., Tasiopoulou, E., & Zabulis, X. (2021). Realistic Virtual Humans for Cultural Heritage Applications. *Heritage, 4*(4), 4148–4171. doi:10.3390/heritage4040228

Katifori, A., Roussou, M., Perry, S., Drettakis, G., Vizcay, S., & Philip, J. (2018). The EMOTIVE Project-Emotive Virtual Cultural Experiences through Personalized Storytelling. *Proceedings of the Workshop on Cultural Informatics Research and Applications co-located with the International Conference on Digital Heritage, CIRA@EuroMed 2018.*

Katsadoros, G. (2013). The science of folklore in the modern technological age. Electronic orality [Η επιστήμη της λαογραφίας στη σύγχρονη τεχνολογική εποχή. Η ηλεκτρονική προφορικότητα]. In Education Sciences. From the weak classification of Pedagogy to interdisciplinarity and scientific hybridization [Επιστήμες της εκπαίδευσης. Από την ασθενή ταξινόμηση της Παιδαγωγικής στη διεπιστημονικότητα και στον επιστημονικό υβριδισμό]. Αθήνα: Παιδαγωγικό Τμήμα Δημοτικής Εκπαίδευσης Πανεπιστημίου Αιγαίου και Ταξιδευτής.

Katsadoros, G. (2013). The science of folklore in the modern technological age. *Electronic Orality. Education Sciences. From the weak classification of Pedagogy to interdisciplinarity and scientific hybridization*, 99-122.

Katsadoros, G., & Gotzageorgiou, A. (2010). Primary education and folklore. The collection of cultural material through the school practice. An example from Kremasti, Rhodes. *Proceedings of the* 1st Panhellenic Conference with international participation, Local Communities & Higher Education Institutions: Coexistence for Sustainable Development.

Katsadoros, G., & Nounanaki, A. (2021). The image of the Pontians in digital folklore: The case of memes. *Popular Tradition of Pontus: from the Past to the Present. Proceedings of the International Scientific Conference of Folklore*, 389-432.

Katsadoros, G. (2013). Η επιστήμη της λαογραφίας στη σύγχρονη τεχνολογική εποχή. Η ηλεκτρονική προφορικότητα. In G. Kokkinos & M. Maskofoglou-Xionidou (Eds.), *Επιστήμες της εκπαίδευσης: από την ασθενή ταξινόμηση της παιδαγωγικής στη διεπιστημονικότητα και στον επιστημονικό υβριδισμό* [Lexical characteristics of Greek language]. (pp. 99–122). Ταξιδευτής.

Katsaris, I., & Vidakis, N. (2021). Adaptive e-learning systems through learning styles: A review of the literature. *Advances in Mobile Learning Educational Research, 1*(2), 124–145. doi:10.25082/AMLER.2021.02.007

Katsarou, E., & Tsafos, B. (2004). *From Research to Teaching. Educational action research.* Savvalas Publishing House.

Kaur-Gill, S., & Dutta, M. J. (2017). Digital Ethnography. In J. Matthes, C. S. Davis, & R. F. Potter (Eds.), *The International Encyclopedia of Communication Research Methods* (pp. 1–10). John Wiley & Sons, Inc. doi:10.1002/9781118901731.iecrm0271

Kavakli, E., Bakogianni, S., Damianakis, A., Loumou, M., & Tsatsos, D. (2004). *Traditional dance and e-learning: The WEBDANCE learning environment.* Paper presented at the International Conference on Theory and Applications of Mathematics and Informatics, Greece.

Khalid, S., & Chowdhury, S. A. (2016). Representation and Dissemination of Intangible Cultural Heritage of Bangladesh through Social Media. *Anatolia, 29*(2), 194–203. doi:10.1080/13032917.2017.1414438

Khan Academy. (n.d.). *What is Cultural Heritage?* Retrieved 1/2/2022 from https://www.khanacademy.org/humanities/special-topics-art-history/arches-at-risk-cultural-heritage-education-series/arches-beginners-guide/a/what-is-cultural-heritage

Khan, M. (2015). Archive to repertoire: Motion capture & motion sensing data for digital intangible heritage (DIH). *Digital Heritage, 2*, 197–198. doi:10.1109/DigitalHeritage.2015.7419490

Kim, Rothrock, & Freivalds. (2016). The Effects of Gamification on Engineering Lab Activities. *2016 IEEE Frontiers in Education Conference (FIE).*

Kimourtzis, P. (2016). Πτυχίο: Εισιτήριο, αλλά για ένα ακαθόριστο ταξίδι [Lexical characteristics of Greek language]. *Academia (Caracas), 14*, 141–160.

Kim, Y. C., & Ball-Rokeach, S. J. (2006). Community Storytelling Network, Neighborhood Context, and Civic Engagement: A Multilevel Approach. *Human Communication Research, 32*(4), 411–439. doi:10.1111/j.1468-2958.2006.00282.x

Kirkland, A., Martin, K., Schoeny, M., Smith, K., & Strege, G. (2015). Sharing Historic Costume Collections Online. *Dress: The Journal of the Costume Society of America, 41*(2), 107–127. doi:10.1080/03612112.2015.1130394

Kist, C. (2020). Museums, challenging heritage, and social media during COVID-19. *Museum & Society, 18*(3), 345–348. doi:10.29311/mas.v18i3.3539

Kleinman, A. (1992). Local Worlds of Suffering: An Interpersonal Focus for Ethnographies of Illness Experience. *Qualitative Health Research, 2*(2), 127–134. doi:10.1177/104973239200200202

Knoke, D., & Yang, S. (2007). *Social Network Analysis: Quantitative Applications in the Social Science*. SAGE Publications.

Kokko, S., & Kyritsi, A. (2012). Cultural Heritage Education for Intercultural Communication. *International Journal of Heritage in the Digital Era, 1*, 165–168.

Konstantopoulou, Ch. (2011). *Symbols, Archetypes and phobias. Introduction to the sociology of the imaginary* [Σύμβολα, Αρχέτυπα και φοβίες. Εισαγωγή στην κοινωνιολογία του φαντασιακού]. Αθήνα: Εκδόσεις Παπαζήση.

Korosidou, E., & Bratitsis, T. (2019). *Infusing Multimodal Tools and Digital Storytelling in Developing Vocabulary and Intercultural Communicative Awareness of Young EFL Learners* (Vol. 11899). Lecture Notes in Computer Science. Springer. doi:10.1007/978-3-030-34350-7_19

Kozinets, R. V. (2010). *Netnography: Doing Ethnographic Research Online.* SAGE Publications.

Kozinets, R. V. (2020). *Netnography: The Essential Guide to Qualitative Social Media Research.* Sage. doi:10.4324/9781003001430

Kozinets, R. V., De Valck, K., Wojnicki, A. C., & Wilner, S. J. (2010). Networked Narratives: Understanding Word-of-Mouth Marketing in Online Communities. *Journal of Marketing, 74*(2), 71–89. doi:10.1509/jm.74.2.71

Kozinets, R. V., Dolbec, P. Y., & Earley, A. (2014). Netnographic Analysis: Understanding Culture Through Social Media Data. In U. Flick (Ed.), *The SAGE Handbook Of Qualitative Data Analysis* (pp. 262–276). SAGE Publications. doi:10.4135/9781446282243.n18

Krawczyk-Wasilewska, V. (2016). *Folklore in the Digital Age: Collected Essays*. University of Łodź.

Kuhlmann, A. (1992). Collaborative Research among the Kickapoo Tribe of Oklahoma. *Human Organization*, *51*(3), 274–283. doi:10.17730/humo.51.3.k3n65x64t5nx36x5

Kutut, V., Lepkova, N., & Zrobe, S. (2021). Immovable Cultural Heritage Usage Modes: *Theoretical Approach. European Research Studies Journal*, *24*(1), 1136–1151.

Kvale, S. (1996). *InterViews: An Introduction to Qualitative Research Interviewing. Academic Press.*

Lai, C. L., & Hwang, G. J. (2016). A self-regulated flipped classroom approach to improving students' learning performance in a mathematics course. *Computers & Education*, *100*, 126–140. https://doi.org/10.1016/j.compedu.2016.05.006

Laine, T. H., Nygren, E., Dirin, A., & Suk, H.-J. (2016). Science Spots AR: A Platform for Science Learning Games with Augmented Reality. *Educational Technology Research and Development*, *64*(3), 507–531. doi:10.100711423-015-9419-0

Laing, D. (2016). Λόγος και σημασία στο Πανκ Ροκ [Lexical characteristics of Greek language]. One chord wonders. Athens: Κουκκίδα.

Lam, A. H. C., Chiu, D. K. W., & Ho, K. K. W. (in press). Instagram for student learning and library promotions? A quantitative study using the 5E Instructional Model. *Aslib Journal of Information Management*.

Lambert, J. (2012). Digital storytelling cookbook. Digital Diner Press.

Lantian, A., Muller, D., Nurra, C., & Douglas, K. M. (2017). "I know things they don't know!": The role of need for uniqueness in belief in conspiracy theories. *Social Psychology*, *48*(3), 160–173. doi:10.1027/1864-9335/a000306

Lassiter, L. E., Goodall, H., Campbell, E., & Johnson, M. N. (2004). *The Other Side of Middletown: Exploring Muncie's African American Community*. AltaMira Press.

Lathem, S. A. (2005). Learning communities and digital storytelling: new media for ancient tradition. In C. Crawford, R. Carlsen, I. Gibson, K. McFerrin, J. Price, R. Weber & D. A. Willis (Eds.), *Proceedings of Society for Information Technology & Teacher Education International Conference 2005* (pp. 2286-2291). Chesapeake, VA: AACE.

Lauterbach, K. (2017). *We wear culture: Discover why we wear what we wear with Google Arts & Culture*. Retrieved from Google Arts & Culture: https://blog.google/outreach-initiatives/arts-culture/we-wear-culture-discover-why-we-wear-what-we-wear/

Lazarinis, F., Boididis, I., Kozanidis, L., & Kanellopoulos, D. (2022). An adaptable multi-learner serious game for learning cultural heritage. *Advances in Mobile Learning Educational Research*, *2*(1), 201–215. doi:10.25082/AMLER.2022.01.004

Lazzeretti, L., Sartori, A., & Innocenti, N. (2015). Museums and social media: The case of the Museum of Natural History of Florence. *International Review on Public and Nonprofit Marketing*, *12*(3), 267–283. doi:10.100712208-015-0136-5

Leavy, P. (2017). *Research Design: Quantitative, Qualitative, Mixed Methods, Arts-Based, and Community-Based Participatory Research Approaches*. The Guilford Press.

Lee, I., Martin, F., & Apone, K. (2014). Integrating computational thinking across the K—8 curriculum. *ACM Inroads*, *5*(4), 64–71. doi:10.1145/2684721.2684736

Lehmann, L. A. (2012). *Location-Based Mobile Games*. Academic Press.

Lei, S. Y., Chiu, D. K. W., Lung, M. M., & Chan, C. T. (2021). Exploring the Aids of Social Media for Musical Instrument Education. *International Journal of Music Education*, *39*(2), 187–201. doi:10.1177/0255761420986217

Lester, J. N. (2020). Going Digital in Ethnography: Navigating the Ethical Tensions and Productive Possibilities. *Cultural Studies« Critical Methodologies*, *20*(5), 414-424. doi:10.1177/1532708620936995

Leung, T. N., Hui, Y. M., Luk, C. K. L., Chiu, D. K. W., & Kevin, K. K. W. (in press). An Empirical Study on the Aid of Facebook for Japanese Learning. *Library Hi Tech.*

Levine, L. E., Waite, B. M., & Bowman, L. L. (2007). Electronic Media Use, Reading, and Academic Distractability in College Youth. *Cyberpsychology & Behavior*, *10*(4), 560–566. doi:10.1089/cpb.2007.9990 PMID:17711365

Li, S. (2019). Study on School Education's Inheritance of Folk Culture. In *Proceedings of International Conference on Reform, Technology, Psychology in Education* (pp. 295-299). Academic Press.

Lialina, O., & Espenschied, D. (Eds.). (2009). *Digital Folklore. To Computers Users with Love and Respect*. Merz & Solitude.

Liguori, A., & Bakewell, L. (2019). Digital Storytelling in Cultural and Heritage Education: A Pilot Study as Part of the 'DICHE' Project. In *Advanced Studies in Museum Education*. ESI - Edizioni Scientifiche Italiane. https://hdl.handle.net/2134/38037

Li, H. (2014). History of Master Taixu Establishing World Buddhist Center Library. *Mt Wutai Researches*, *2014*(S1), 44–47.

Li, J., Brar, A., & Roihan, N. (2021). The use of digital technology to enhace language and literacy skills for indigenous people: A systematic literature review. *Computers and Education Open*, *2*, 10035. doi:10.1016/j.caeo.2021.100035

Li, K. K., & Chiu, D. K. W. (2021, December 23). A Worldwide Quantitative Review of the iSchools' Archival Education. *Library Hi Tech*. Advance online publication. doi:10.1108/LHT-09-2021-0311

Liu, A. (2012). Where is Cultural Criticism in the Digital Humanities? In M. K. Gold (Ed.), *Debates in the Digital Humanities*. U of Minnesota P. doi:10.5749/minnesota/9780816677948.003.0049

Liu, B., & He, J. (2014). Teaching Mode Reform and Exploration on the University Computer Basic based on Computational Thinking Training in Network Environment. *Proceedings of the 9th International Conference on Computer Science & Education*, 59-62.

Liu, X. (2022). *Chinese Buddhist Literature Database and Image Text Extraction Algorithm. In International Conference on Cognitive based Information Processing and Applications (CIPA 2021)* (pp. 122-127). Springer.

Livia, A. (1999). Doing Sociolinguistic Research on the French Minitel. *The American Behavioral Scientist*, *43*(3), 422–435. doi:10.1177/00027649921955353

Lo, P., Cheuk, M. K., Ng, C. H., Lam, S. K., & Chiu, D. K. W. (2021). 文武之道【下冊】:以拳入哲 [The Tao of Arts and Warriorship: The Philosophy of Fists]. Hong Kong: Systech Publications.

Logan, W. S. (2007). Closing Pandora's Box: Human Rights Conundrums in Cultural Heritage. In H. Silverman & D. Fairchild Ruggles (Eds.), *Cultural heritage and human rights* (pp. 33–52). Springer. doi:10.1007/978-0-387-71313-7_2

Logothetis, I., Papadourakis, G., Katsaris, I., Katsios, K., & Vidakis, N. (2021). Transforming Classic Learning Games with the Use of AR: The Case of the Word Hangman Game. In P. Zaphiris & A. Ioannou (Eds.), *Learning and Collaboration Technologies: Games and Virtual Environments for Learning* (pp. 47–64). Springer International Publishing. doi:10.1007/978-3-030-77943-6_4

Lo, P., Chan, H. H. Y., Tang, A. W. M., Chiu, D. K. W., Cho, A., Ho, K. K. W., See-To, E., He, J., Kenderdine, S., & Shaw, J. (2019). Visualising and Revitalising Traditional Chinese Martial Arts – Visitors' Engagement and Learning Experience at the 300 Years of Hakka KungFu. *Library Hi Tech*, *37*(2), 273–292. doi:10.1108/LHT-05-2018-0071

Lo, P., Chiu, D. K. W., & Cho, A. (2017). *Inside the World's Major East Asian Collections: One Belt, One Road, and Beyond*. Chandos Publishing.

Lo, P., Cho, A., & Chiu, D. K. W. (2017). *World's Leading National, Public, Monastery and Royal Library Directors – Leadership, Management, Future of Libraries*. De Gruyter.

López Salas, E. (2021). A collection of narrative practices on cultural heritage with innovative technologies and creative strategies. *Open Research Europe, 1*(130). doi:10.12688/openreseurope.14178.1

López-Fernández, J. A., Medina, S., López, M. J., & García-Morís, R. (2021). Perceptions of Heritage among Students of Early Childhood and Primary Education. *Sustainability, 13*, 10636.

Loscialpo, F. (2016). From the physical to the digital and back: Fashion exhibitions in the digital age. *International Journal of Fashion Studies, 3*(2), 225–248. doi:10.1386/infs.3.2.225_1

Lou, T. (1998). Doing the Laundry? A Reassessment of Object-based Dress History. *Fashion Theory, 2*(4), 337–358. doi:10.2752/136270498779476118

Lowdermilk, T. (2013). *User-Centered Design*. O'Reilly Media, Inc.

Macek, J. (2005). Defining Cyberculture. In P. Binková, J. Volek, & N. Masaryk (Eds.), *Média a realita* (Vol. 2, pp. 35–65). University Press.

Mack, N., Woodsong, C., MacQueen, K. M., Guest, G., & Namey, E. (2005). *Qualitative Research Methods: A Data Collector's Field Guide*. Family Health International.

Magliacani, M., & Sorrentino, D. (2020). *Italian University Museums at Time of Covid-19 Lockdown: How to restore a "Sense of Normalcy"*. Research Square, Retrieved from., doi:10.21203/rs.3.rs-53886/v1

Magnani, R., Sabin, K., Saidel, T., & Heckathorn, D. (2005). Review of sampling hard-to-reach and hidden populations for HIV surveillance. *AIDS (London, England), 19*(Suppl 2), S67–S72. doi:10.1097/01.aids.0000172879.20628.e1 PMID:15930843

Magro, G., De Carvalho, J. R., & Marcelino, M. J. (2014). *Improving History Learning through Cultural Heritage, Local History and Technology* [Paper Presentation]. *International Conference on Mobile Learning*.

Mahayuddin, Z. R., & Saif, A. F. M. S. (2020). Augmented Reality Based AR Alphabets towards Improved Learning Process in Primary Education System. *Journal of Critical Reviews, 7*(19), 514–521.

Ma, J., Chiu, D. K., & Tang, J. K. (2016). Exploring the Use of Social Media to Advance K12 Science Education. *International Journal of Systems and Service-Oriented Engineering, 6*(4), 47–59. doi:10.4018/IJSSOE.2016100104

Mak, M. Y. C., Poon, A. Y. M., & Chiu, D. K. W. (2022). Using Social Media as Learning Aids and Preservation: Chinese Martial Arts in Hong Kong. In S. Papadakis & A. Kapaniaris (Eds.), *The Digital Folklore of Cyberculture and Digital Humanities*. IGI Global.

Mak, Y. C. M. (2019). *Application of social media in Chinese martial arts learning and preservation of Chinese martial arts in Hong Kong. HKU Theses Online.*

Ma, L., Long, C., Duan, L., Zhang, X., Li, Y., & Zhao, Q. (2020). Segmentation and recognition for historical Tibetan document images. *IEEE Access: Practical Innovations, Open Solutions, 8*, 52641–52651. doi:10.1109/ACCESS.2020.2975023

Manca, S. (2020). Snapping, pinning, liking or texting: Investigating social media in higher education beyond Facebook. *The Internet and Higher Education, 44*, 100707. doi:10.1016/j.iheduc.2019.100707

Mannila, L., Dagiene, V., Demo, B., Grgurina, N., Mirolo, C., Rolandsson, L., & Settle, A. (2014). Computational thinking in K-9 education. In *Proceedings of the Working Group Reports of the 2014 on Innovation & Technology in Computer Science Education Conference*. ACM. 10.1145/2713609.2713610

Marcus, G. E. (1995). Ethnography in/of the World System: The Emergence of Multi-Sited Ethnography. *Annual Review of Anthropology*, *24*(1), 95–117. doi:10.1146/annurev.an.24.100195.000523

Margetis, G., Apostolakis, K. C., Ntoa, S., Papagiannakis, G., & Stephanidis, C. (2020). X-Reality Museums: Unifying the Virtual and Real World Towards Realistic Virtual Museums. *Applied Sciences (Basel, Switzerland)*, *11*(1), 338. https://doi.org/10.3390/app11010338

Markham, A., & Buchanan, E. (2012). *Ethical decision-making and Internet research: Version 2.0*. Association of Internet Researchers. https://wwwcs.uwstout.edu/ethicscenter/upload/aoirethicsprintablecopy.pdf

Martin, K., & Ko, H.-S. (2011). Imagining Historic Fashion: Digital Tools for the Examination of Historic Dress. In *2011 Second International Conference on Culture and Computing* (pp. 51 - 56). Los Alamitos: IEEE Computer Society.

Martínez-Gil, C. C., Zempoalteca-Pérez, A., Soancatl-Aguilar, V., Estudillo-Ayala, M. J., Lara-Ramírez, J. E., & Alcántara-Santiago, A. (2012). Computer systems for analysis of Nahuatl. *Research in Computing Science*, *47*(1), 11–16. doi:10.13053/rcs-47-1-1

Martin, M., & Vacca, F. (2018). Heritage Narratives in the Digital Era. *Research Journal of Textile and Apparel*, *22*(4), 335–351. doi:10.1108/RJTA-02-2018-0015

Maureen, I. Y., van der Meij, H., & de Jong, T. (2020). Enhancing storytelling activities to support early(digital) literacy development in early childhood education. *International Journal of Early Childhood*, *52*(1), 55–76. doi:10.100713158-020-00263-7

Mawas, N. E., Truchly, P., Podhrasky, P., & Muntean, C. (2019). The effect of educational game on children Learning experience in a Slovakina School. *CSEDU 2019 - Proceedings of the 11th International Conference on Computer Supported Education.*

Mayring, Ph. (2000). Qualitative Content analysis. *Forum Qualitative Social Research*, *1*(2), 20.

McAuley, A., Stewart, B., Siemens, G., & Cormier, D. (2010). *The MOOC model for digital practice*. University of Prince Edward Island through the Social Sciences and Humanities Research Council's "Knowledge Synthesis Grants on the Digital Economy".

McCarthy, K. F., Ondaatje, E. H., Zakaras, L., & Brooks, A. (2004). *Gifts of the Muse: Reframing the debate about the benefits of the arts*. Rand Corporation.

McClelland, Br. (2000). Online Orality: The Internet, Folklore, and Culture in Russia. In L. B. Lengel (Ed.), *Culture and Technology in New Europe: Civic Discourse in Transformation in Post-Communist Nations* (pp. 179–191). Ablex.

McEwan, H., & Egan, K. (Eds.). (1995). *Narrative in teaching, learning, and research*. Teacher's College Press.

McKenna, B., & Chughtai, H. (2020). Resistance and sexuality in virtual worlds: An LGBT perspective. *Computers in Human Behavior*, *105*, 106199. https://doi.org/10.1016/j.chb.2019.106199

MCLeod, N. (1965). Review of The Anthropology of Music by Alan P. Merriam. *Anuario*, *1*, 127–130.

McNamara, R. P. (1994). *The Times Square Hustler: Male Prostitution in New York City*. Praeger.

McNiff, J., Lomax, P., & Whitehead, J. (1996). *You and Your Action Research Project*. Routledge, Hyde Publications. doi:10.4324/9780203281291

Meadows, M. S. (2003). *Pause & Effect: The Art of Interactive Narrative*. New Riders.

Meho, L. I. (2006). E-mail interviewing in qualitative research: A methodological discussion. *Journal of the American Society for Information Science and Technology*, *57*(10), 1284–1295. doi:10.1002/asi.20416

Mehta, J. (2013). The Penetration of Technocratic Logic Into the Educational Field: Rationalizing Schooling From the Progressives to the Present. *Teachers College Record*, *115*(5), 1–36.

Meighan, P. J. (2021). Decolonizing the digital landscape: The role of technology in Indigenous language revitalization. *Alternative*, *17*(3), 397–405. doi:10.1177/11771801211037672

Mekler, E. D., Brühlmann, F., Tuch, A. N., & Opwis, K. (2017). Towards Understanding the Effects of Individual Gamification Elements on Intrinsic Motivation and Performance. *Computers in Human Behavior*, *71*, 525–534. doi:10.1016/j.chb.2015.08.048

Melchior, M. (2019). Digital Fashion Heritage: Understanding Europeanafashion.eu and the Google Cultural institute's We Wear Culture. *Critical Studies in Fashion & Beauty*, *10*(1), 49–68. doi:10.1386/csfb.10.1.49_1

Melliou, K., Moutafidou, A., & Bratitsis, T. (2015). 'Children's rights': Using digital storytelling and visible thinking approaches to create a narrative video in the early childhood classroom. *International Journal of Electronic Governance*, *7*(4), 333–348.

Mendes, J. A. (2009). *Estudos do Património*. Imprensa da Universidade de Coimbra.

Meraklis, M. (1992). *Λαϊκή Τέχνη. (Ελληνική Λαογραφία. Τόμος Γ¢)* [Lexical characteristics of Greek language]. Οδυσσέας.

Michael, G. V. (2009). Homo Interneticus or Folklore and the Internet. Folklore, Bulletin of the Hellenic Folklore Society, 291-305.

Michailidis, N., Kapravelos, E., & Tsiatsos, T. (2019). Examining the effect of interaction analysis on supporting students' motivation and learning strategies in online blog-based secondary education programming courses. *Interactive Learning Environments*, 1–12. doi:10.1080/10494820.2019.1678487

Micheli, A. (2020). Culture in «restriction». The cultural experience of the imaginary and the actual space. *Epitheorese Koinonikon Ereunon*, *154*, 75–88. doi:10.12681/grsr.23230

Miller, C. H. (2008). *Digital Storytelling: A Creator's Guide to Interactive Entertainment* (2nd ed.). Elsevier.

Miller, M. (2011). *YouTube for business: Online video marketing for any business*. Pearson Education.

Ministry of Culture and Sports. (2020a). *Measures to support culture and its employees*. Retrieved from: https://www.culture.gov.gr

Ministry of Culture and Sports. (2020b). *Special invitation of Digital Culture from the Ministry of Culture and Sports*. Retrieved from: https://www.culture.gov.gr/el/Information/SitePages/view.aspx?nID=3181

Miron-Chacón, M. J., Angheven-Negrete, J. S., Juárez-Ibáñez, J. A., & Avendaño-Cortés, I. (2019). Development of the web system as a learning tool for Nahuatl in the Orizabense variant. In A. Marroquín, J. Olivares, P. Díaz, & L. Cruz (Eds.), *Mujeres en la tecnología*. ECORFAN.

Mitchell, T. (2001). *Global Noise: Rap and Hip Hop Outside the USA*. Wesleyan University Press.

Moraiti, A., Moumoutzis, N., Christoulakis, M., Pitsiladis, A., Stylianakis, G., Sifakis, Y., Maragoudakis, I., & Christodoulakis, S. (2016). Playful creation of digital stories with eShadow. *2016 11th International Workshop on Semantic and Social Media Adaptation and Personalization (SMAP)*, 139–144. doi:10.1109/SMAP.2016.7753399

Mortara, M., Catalano, C. E., Bellotti, F., Fiucci, G., Houry-Panchetti, M., & Petridis, P. (2014). Learning cultural heritage by serious games. *Journal of Cultural Heritage*, *15*(3), 318–325. https://doi.org/10.1016/j.culher.2013.04.004

Moula, E. (2010). Literature and theory of narrative or how developments require new approaches. *I-Teacher*, *1*, 23-34.

Moula, E. (2013). New technologies and literature: the embarrassment in the face of the "new" or the age-old conflict between tradition and modernity with a new face? *I-Teacher*, *6*, 38-57. http://i-teacher.gr/files/6o_teyxos_i_teacher_9_2013.pdf

Moula, E. (2019a). Alternate reality games as an educational strategy in the age of media convergence. *I-Teacher*, *18*, 15-35.

Moula, E. (2019b). Alternate reality games and reading for pleasure: Research findings from the implementation of the transformation of the Young Adult Novel Leros' Code into an ARG. *EducatioNext*, *2*, 80-111. http://educationext.gr/files/ednext_2o_teyxos_09_2019.pdf

Moula, E. (2019c). The Thousand and One Aspects of Digital Fiction and the Future of Reading. *I-Teacher*, *19*, 9-29.

Moula, E., & Malafantis, K. (2019). From Literature to Alternate Reality Games: Prerequisites, Criteria, and Limitations of a Young Adult Novel's Transformational Design for Educational Purposes. *Advances in Literary Study*, *7*(4), 224. https://www.scirp.org/journal/paperinformation.aspx?paperid=95937

Muenster, S. (2022). Digital 3D Technologies for Humanities Research and Education: An Overview. *Applied Sciences (Basel, Switzerland)*, *12*, 2426.

Muñoz-Garcia, R. (2018). *Aplicación móvil para el aprendizaje de la lengua Náhuatl* [Master Thesis]. Universidad Autónoma de Guerrero.

Murthy, D. (2008). Digital Ethnography: An Examination of the Use of New Technologies for Social Research. *Sociology*, *42*(5), 837–855. doi:10.1177/0038038508094565

Myers, M. D. (1999). Investigating Information Systems with Ethnographic Research. *Communications of the Association for Information Systems*, *2*(1), 23. doi:10.17705/1CAIS.00223

Nah, F. F.-H., Zeng, Q., Telaprolu, V. R., Ayyappa, A. P., & Eschenbrenner, B. (2014). Gamification of Education: A Review of Literature. *International conference on HCI in business*. 10.1007/978-3-319-07293-7_39

Nasopoulos, D. (2014). Η μνήμη απέναντι στη σκληρή καθημερινότητα [Lexical characteristics of Greek language]. Τα Νέα (September 13-14), p. 25.

NEMO. (2022a). *Survey on the impact of the COVID-19 situation on museums in Europe. Final findings and Recommendations.* Retrieved from: https://www.ne-mo.org/fileadmin/Dateien/public/NEMO_documents/Final_Findings_and_Recommendations_CVOID19_12.05.2020.pdf

NEMO. (2022b). *Survey on the impact of the COVID-19 situation on museums in Europe*. Final Report. Retrieved from https://www.ne-mo.org/fileadmin/Dateien/public/NEMO_documents/NEMO_COVID19_Report_12.05.2020.pdf

NEMO. (2022c). *Follow-up survey on the impact of the COVID-19 pandemic on museums in Europe.* Final Report. January 2021. Retrieved from https://www.ne-mo.org/fileadmin/Dateien/public/NEMO_documents/NEMO_COVID19_FollowUpReport_11.1.2021.pdf

Nightingale, D., & Cromby, J. (1999). *Social Constructionist Psychology: A Critical Analysis of Theory and Practice.* Open University Press.

Nikonova, A., & Biryukova, M. (2017). The Role of Digital Technologies in the Preservation of Cultural Heritage. *Muzeologia a Kulturne Dedicstvo*, *5*, 169–173.

Nilson, T., & Thorell, K. (Eds.). (2018). *Cultural Heritage Preservation: The Past, the Present and the Future*. Halmstadt University. http://urn.kb.se/resolve?urn=urn:nbn:se:hh:diva-37317

Noehrer, L., Gilmore, A., & Jay, C. (2021). The impact of COVID-19 on digital data practices in museums and art galleries in the UK and the US. *Humanit Soc. Science Communication*, *8*, 236.

Norcliffe, G., & Rendace, O. (2003). New Geographies of Comic Book Production in North America: The New Artisan, Distancing, and the Periodic Social Economy. *Economic Geography*, *79*(3), 241–263. doi:10.1111/j.1944-8287.2003.tb00211.x

Nostra, E. (2020). *Covid-19 & Beyond. Challenges and Opportunities for Cultural Heritage*. Retrieved from https://www.europanostra.org/wp-content/uploads/2020/10/20201014_COVID19_Consultation-Paper_EN.pdf

O'Brien, H. L., & Toms, E. G. (2008). What is user engagement? A conceptual framework for defining user engagement with technology. *Journal of the American Society for Information Science and Technology*, *59*(6), 938–955. doi:10.1002/asi.20801

Okanovic, V., Ivkovic-Kihic, I., Boskovic, D., Mijatovic, B., Prazina, I., Skaljo, E., & Rizvic, S. (2022). Interaction in eXtended Reality Applications for Cultural Heritage. *Applied Sciences (Basel, Switzerland)*, *12*, 1241.

Okunlaya, R. O., Syed Abdullah, N., & Alias, R. A. (2022, March 07). (in press). Artificial intelligence (AI) library services innovative conceptual framework for the digital transformation of university education. *Library Hi Tech*. Advance online publication. doi:10.1108/LHT-07-2021-0242

Oliver, P. (1963). *The meaning of the blues*. New York: Collier books.

Önnerfors, A. (2021). Conspiracy theories and COVID-19: The mechanisms behind a rapidly growing societal challenge. The Swedish Civil Contingencies Agency (MSB).

Oring, E. (2013). Thinking through Tradition. In Tradition in the Twenty-First Century: Locating the Role of the Past in the Present. Utah State University Press. doi:10.7330/9780874218992.c01

Orlandi, S.-D. (2020). Museums Web Strategy at the Covid -19 Emergency Times. Digicult. *Scientific Journal on Digital Cultures*, *5*(1), 57–66.

Ott, M., & Pozzi, F. (2011). Towards a new era for Cultural Heritage Education: Discussing the role of ICT. *Computers in Human Behavior*, *27*, 1365–1371.

Outakoski, H., Cocq, C., & Steggo, P. (2018). Strengthening indigenous languages in the digital age: Social media-supported learning in Sápmi. *Media International Australia*, *169*(1), 21–31. doi:10.1177/1329878X18803700

Pacault, M., & Patchett, M. (2018). The Last Plumassier: Storying Dead Birds, Gender and Paraffection at Maison Lemarié. *Cultural Geographies*, *25*(1), 123–134. doi:10.1177/1474474016673067

Papadakis, S., Kalogiannakis, M., Sifaki, E., & Vidakis, N. (2018). Evaluating Moodle use via Smart Mobile Phones. A case study in a Greek University. *EAI Endorsed Transactions on Creative Technologies, 5*(16).

Papadakis, S., Trampas, A., Barianos, A., Kalogiannakis, M., & Vidakis, N. (2020). Evaluating the Learning Process: The "ThimelEdu" Educational Game Case Study. *Proceedings of the 12th International Conference on Computer Supported Education, 2*, 290-298. https://www.scitepress.org/Link.aspx?doi=10.5220/0009379902900298

Papadakis, S. (2021). Advances in Mobile Learning Educational Research (A.M.L.E.R.): Mobile learning as an educational reform. *Advances in Mobile Learning Educational Research*, *1*(1), 1–4. doi:10.25082/AMLER.2021.01.001

Papadakis, S., Trampas, A., Barianos, A., Kalogiannakis, M., & Vidakis, N. (2020). Evaluating the Learning Process: The "ThimelEdu" Educational Game Case Study. *Proceedings of the 12th International Conference on Computer Supported Education*, 2, 290-298. 10.5220/0009379902900298

Papadimitriou, E., Kapaniaris, A., Zisiadis, D., & Kalogirou, E. (2013). *Digital Storytelling in Kindergarten: An alternative tool in children's way of expression*. Mediterranean Center of Social and Educational Research, MCSER Publishing.

Papadimitriou, G. (2015, Ιανουάριος). Οι τρεις μύθοι του Low Bap [Lexical characteristics of Greek language]. *Unfollow,* σ. 104-111.

Parisis, G. & Parisis, N. (2015). *Λεξικό λογοτεχνικών όρων* [Lexical characteristics of Greek language]. Athens: ΟΕΔΒ, ΥΠ. ΠΑΙΔΕΙΑΣ-ΙΤΥΕ ΔΙΟΦΑΝΤΟΣ:

Pasiopoulos, G. (2014). *Η κοινωνική έκφραση και εκδήλωση μέσα από τη σύγχρονη μουσική: Το κίνημα Low Bap* [Lexical characteristics of Greek language] (Unpublished postgraduate thesis). Πανεπιστήμιο Αιγαίου, Παιδαγωγικό Τμήμα Δημοτικής Εκπαίδευσης, Rhodes.

Peck, J. (1989). Using storytelling to promote language and literacy development. *The Reading Teacher*, *43*(2), 138–141.

Pedersen, E. (1995). Storytelling and the art of teaching. *English Teaching Forum, 33*(1).

Peñalba, E. H., Samaniego, C. R. C., & Romeros, M. A. (2020). Digital storytelling: a tool for promoting historical understanding among college students. *Research in Learning Technology, 28*. doi:10.25304/rlt.v28.234

Perouli, C. (2021). Digital Storytelling in the Museum: Bringing Cultural Heritage to Life. *Crossing Conceptual Boundaries*, *11*(1), 34–46.

Petridis, P. A. (2011). *Digital Records and Exchange Practices: An Anthropological Approach to Peer-to-Peer Networks*. Panteion University of Social and Political Sciences.

Petti, L., Trillo, C., & Makore, C. (2019). Towards a Shared Understanding of the Concept of Heritage in the European Context. *Heritage*, *2*, 2531–2544.

Piaget, J. (1952). *The origins of intelligence in children*. International University Press. doi:10.1037/11494-000

Pietrobruno, S. (2013). YouTube and the social archiving of intangible heritage. *New Media & Society*, *15*(8), 1259–1276. doi:10.1177/1461444812469598

Pinto, H., & Ibañez-Etxeberria, A. (2018). Constructing historical thinking and inclusive identities: Analysis of heritage education activities. *History Education Research Journal*, *15*(2), 342–354.

Pitler, H. J. (2006). Viewing technology through three lenses. *Principal*, *85*(5), 38–42.

Plaza, O. (2004). Technology Education versus Liberal Arts Education? *The Journal of Technology Studies*, *30*(1), 16–19.

Plecher, D. A., Herber, F., Eichhorn, C., Pongratz, A., Tanson, G., & Klinker, G. (2020). HieroQuest - A Serious Game for Learning Egyptian Hieroglyphs. *Journal on Computing and Cultural Heritage*, *13*(4), 1–20. https://doi.org/10.1145/3418038

Poorna, R. L., Mymoon, M., & Hariharan, A. (2014). Preservation and protection of traditional knowledge–diverse documentation initiatives across the globe. *Current Science*, *107*(8), 1240–1246.

Popescu, E. (2014). Providing collaborative learning support with social media in an integrated environment. *World Wide Web (Bussum)*, *17*(2), 199–212. doi:10.100711280-012-0172-6

Popper, K. R. (1945). *The open society & its enemies*. Routledge.

Porter, C. (2006). A Typology of Virtual Communities: A Multi-Disciplinary Foundation for Future Research. *Journal of Computer-Mediated Communication, 10*(1), 3. doi:10.1111/j.1083-6101.2004.tb00228.x

Poslaniec, C., & Houyel, C. (2001). *Activités de lecture à partir de la littérature policière*. Hachette.

Potocnik, R. (2020). Heritage preservation education: Teachers' preconceptions and teachers implementation in visual arts classes. *CEPS Journal, 10*(2), 49–76.

Poullis, C., Kersten-Oertel, M., Benjamin, J. P., Philbin-Briscoe, O., Simon, B., Perissiou, D., Demesticha, S., Markou, E., Frentzos, E., Kyriakidis, P., Skarlatos, D., & Rizvic, S. (2019). Evaluation of "The Seafarers": A serious game on seaborne trade in the Mediterranean sea during the Classical period. *Digital Applications in Archaeology and Cultural Heritage, 12*, e00090. https://doi.org/10.1016/j.daach.2019.e00090

Poultsakis, S., Papadakis, S., Kalogiannakis, M., & Psycharis, S. (2021). The management of Digital Learning Objects of Natural Sciences and Digital Experiment Simulation Tools by teachers. *Advances in Mobile Learning Educational Research, 1*(2), 58–71. doi:10.25082/AMLER.2021.02.002

Powdermaker, H. (1966). *Stranger and Friend: The Way of an Anthropologist.* W. W. Norton.

Powell, C. (1991). Rap Music: An Education with a Beat from the Street. *The Journal of Negro Education, 60*(3), 245–259.

Prensky, M. (2003). Digital Game-Based Learning. *Computers in Entertainment, 1*(1), 21. doi:10.1145/950566.950596

Prompayuk, S., & Chairattananon, P. (2016). Preservation of Cultural Heritage Community: Cases of Thailand and Developed Countries. *Procedia: Social and Behavioral Sciences, 234*, 239–243.

Psara, M. (2017, September 20). Παύλος Φύσσας: Ο μουσικός που έγινε σύμβολο του αντιφασιστικού αγώνα [Lexical characteristics of Greek language]. https://www.news247.gr/afieromata/paylos-fyssas-o-moysikos-poy-egine-symvolo-toy-antifasistikoy-agona.6518566.html

Pujol, L., Roussou, M., Poulou, S., Balet, O., Vayanou, M., & Ioannidis, Y. (2012). Personalizing interactive digital storytelling in archaeological museums: The CHESS project. *Proceedings of the 40th annual conference of computer applications and quantitative methods in archeology.*

Qiyang, Z., & Jung, H. (2019). *Learning and Sharing Creative Skills with Short Videos: A Case Study of User Behavior in TikTok and Bilibili. International Association of Societies of Design Research (IASDR)* Design Revolution.

Radu, I. (2014). Augmented Reality in Education: A Meta-Review and Cross-Media Analysis. *Personal and Ubiquitous Computing, 18*(6), 1533–1543. doi:10.100700779-013-0747-y

Rajanen, D., & Rajanen, M. (2019). Climate change gamification: A literature review. *CEUR Workshop Proceedings, 2359*, 253–264.

Ramsey, J. T. (2017). The Validity of Historical Narrative and Its Use in Teaching History. *Honors Projects, 67*. https://digitalcommons.spu.edu/honorsprojects/67

Reijnders, S. (2011). Stalking the Count: Dracula, Fandom and Tourism. *Annals of Tourism Research, 38*(1), 231–248. doi:10.1016/j.annals.2010.08.006

Resta, G., Dicuonzo, F., Karacan, E., & Pastore, D. (2021). The impact of virtual tours on museum exhibitions after the onset of Covid-19 restrictions: Visitor engagement and long term perspectives. *Scientific Research and Information Technology, 11*(1), 151–166.

Reyes, V. (2018). Three models of transparency in ethnographic research: Naming places, naming people, and sharing data. *Ethnography, 19*(2), 204–226. doi:10.1177/1466138117733754

Rey, F. B., & Casado-Neira, D. (2013). Participation and technology: Perception and public expectations about the use of ICTs in museums. *Procedia Technology*, *9*, 697–704. doi:10.1016/j.protcy.2013.12.077

Richardson, J. (2021). *Museums in Lockdown: Rijksmuseum.* Museum next. Retrieved from https://www.museumnext.com/article/rijksmuseum-covid-lockdown/

Richards, T. (2017). Thematic framework of online review research. *International Journal of Contemporary Hospitality Management*, *29*(1), 307–354. doi:10.1108/IJCHM-11-2015-0664

Riley, D. D., & Hunt, K. A. (2014). *Computational thinking for the modern problem Solver.* CRC Press. doi:10.1201/b16688

Risam, R. (2019). Beyond the margins: Intersectionality and the digital humanities. In B. Bordalejo & R. Risam (Eds.), *Intersectionality in Digital Humanities.* Arc Humanities Press. doi:10.2307/j.ctvs32szz.7

Rivoir, A., & Morales, M. J. (2019). *Tecnologías digitales: miradas críticas de la apropiación en América Latina.* CLACSO. doi:10.2307/j.ctvt6rmh6

Rizvic, S., Boskovic, D., Bruno, F., Petriaggi, B., Sljivo, S., & Cozza, M. (2019). Actors in VR storytelling. In *Proceedings of the 2019 11th International Conference on Virtual Worlds and Games for Serious Applications (VS-Games)* (pp. 1–8). Academic Press.

Rizvić, S., Boskovic, D., Okanovic, V., Sljivo, S., & Zukić, M. (2020). Interactive digital storytelling: Bringing cultural heritage in a classroom. *Journal of Computers in Education*, *6*, 143–166.

Robin, B. (2011). The educational uses of digital storytelling. In *Proceedings of Society for Information Technology & Teacher Education International Conference* (pp. 709-716). Academic Press.

Robin, B. R. (2008). Digital Storytelling: A Powerful Technology Tool for the 21st Century Classroom. *Theory into Practice*, *47*(3), 220–228. doi:10.1080/00405840802153916

Robin, B. R., & McNeil, S. G. (2012). What educators should know about teaching digital storytelling. *Digital Education Review*, *22*, 37–51.

Rode, J. A. (2009). Digital parenting: designing children's safety. In A. F. Blackwell (Ed.), *People and Computers XXIII Celebrating People and Technology* (pp. 244–251). British Informatics Society Limited.

Roller, M. R., & Lavrakas, P. J. (2015). *Applied Qualitative Research Design: A Total Quality Framework Approach.* Guilford Press.

Röll, V., & Meyer, C. (2020). Young People's Perceptions of World Cultural Heritage: Suggestions for a Critical and Reflexive World Heritage Education. *Sustainability*, *12*(20), 1–18.

Rontani, M. (2012). *Patrimonito: a visual storytelling of World Heritage from and for children* [Dissertation]. Malmö högskola/Kultur och samhälle.

Roosta, F., Taghiyareh, F., & Mosharraf, M. (2016). Personalization of Gamification-Elements in an e-Learning Environment Based on Learners' Motivation. *2016 8th International Symposium on Telecommunications (IST).* 10.1109/ISTEL.2016.7881899

Ross, S., Economou, M., & Anderson, J. (1998). Funding Information and Communications Technology in the Heritage Sector: Policy Recommendations to the Heritage Lottery Fund. Project Report, University of Glasgow.

Rossi, V. (2020). Digital Humanities e Moda. *ZoneModa Journal*, *10*(2), 43–59.

Roussou, M., Pujol, L., Katifori, A., Chrysanthi, A., Perry, S., & Vayanou, M. (2015). The Museum as Digital Storyteller: Collaborative Participatory Creation of Interactive Digital Experiences. *Proceedings of the Annual Conference of Museums and the Web: MW2015.*

Ruhleder, K. (2000). The Virtual Ethnographer: Fieldwork in Distributed Electronic Environments. *Field Methods, 12*(1), 3–17. doi:10.1177/1525822X0001200101

Rustici Software. (n.d.). *Experience API.* Retrieved January 26, 2018, from https://xapi.com/overview/

Ruttkay, Z., & Bényei, J. (2018). Renewal of the Museum in the Digital Epoch. In G. Bast, E. G. Carayannis, & D. F. J. Campbell (Eds.), *The Future of Museums* (pp. 101–116). Springer. doi:10.1007/978-3-319-93955-1_10

Saari, E. M., & Hopkins, G. (2020). Computational thinking–Essential and pervasive toolset. *Asian Journal of Assessment in Teaching and Learning, 10*(1), 23–31. doi:10.37134/ajatel.vol10.1.3.2020

Sacco, P. L. (2011). *Culture 3.0: A new perspective for the EU 2014-2020 structural funds programming.* Academic Press.

Sadler, G. R., Lee, H. C., Lim, R. S. H., & Fullerton, J. (2010). Recruitment of hard-to-reach population subgroups via adaptations of the snowball sampling strategy. *Nursing & Health Sciences, 12*(3), 369–374. doi:10.1111/j.1442-2018.2010.00541.x PMID:20727089

Sadler, G. R., Nguyen, F., Doan, Q., Au, H., & Thomas, A. G. (1998). Strategies for Reaching Asian Americans With Health Information. *American Journal of Preventive Medicine, 14*(3), 224–228. doi:10.1016/S0749-3797(97)00067-6 PMID:9569224

Sadler, G. R., York, C., Madlensky, L., Gibson, K., Wasserman, L., Rosenthal, E., Barbier, L., Newman, V. A., & Tso, C. (2006). Health parties for African American study recruitment. *Journal of Cancer Education, 21*(2), 71–76. doi:10.120715430154jce2102_6 PMID:17020516

Said, E. W. (1989). Representing the Colonized: Anthropology's Interlocutors. *Critical Inquiry, 15*(2), 205–225. doi:10.1086/448481

Sailer, M., Hense, J. U., Mayr, S. K., & Mandl, H. (2017). How Gamification Motivates: An Experimental Study of the Effects of Specific Game Design Elements on Psychological Need Satisfaction. *Computers in Human Behavior, 69*, 371–380. doi:10.1016/j.chb.2016.12.033

Saleem, A. N., Noori, N. M., & Ozdamli, F. (2022). Gamification Applications in E-Learning: A Literature Review. *Technology, Knowledge and Learning, 27*(1), 139–159. doi:10.100710758-020-09487-x

Salmons, J. E. (2021). Doing Qualitative Research Online. *Sage (Atlanta, Ga.).*

Samdal, O., Nutbeam, D., Wold, B., & Kannas, L. (1998). Achieving health and educational goals through schools—A study of the importance of the school climate and the students' satisfaction with school. *Health Education Research, 13*(3), 383–397.

Sanderhoff, M. (2014). Foreword. In Sharing is Caring (pp. 9 - 11). Statens Museum for Kunst.

Sandlin, M., & Anderson, J. (2021). *Fashion for All: Using Augmented Reality to Explore Digital Archives.* Online Searcher.

Saunders, M., Lewis, P., & Thornhill, A. (2012). *Research Methods for Business Students.* Pearson Education.

Schank, R. C. (1999). *Dynamic memory revisited.* Cambridge University Press. doi:10.1017/CBO9780511527920

Schechter, R., Macaruso, P., Kazakoff, E. R., & Brooke, E. (2015). Exploration of a Blended Learning Approach to Reading Instruction for Low SES Students in Early Elementary Grades. *Computers in the Schools*, *32*(3–4), 183–200. doi:10.1080/07380569.2015.1100652

Schellewald, A. (2021). Communicative Forms on TikTok: Perspectives From Digital Ethnography. *International Journal of Communication*, *15*, 21. https://ijoc.org/index.php/ijoc/article/view/16414

Schnapp, J. (2008). Animating the Archive. In D. Green (Ed.), *WebWise 2.0: The Power of Community* (pp. 45–48). Institute of Museum and Library Services.

Schnapp, J. (2015). *Digital humanities. Meet the Media Guru*. EGEA.

Schoeman, S., & Visagie, C. (2014). Local history teaching in the Overberg region of the Western Cape: The case of the Elim Primary School. *Yesterday and Today*, 118-132.

Schuh, T. M., Agapito, D., & Pinto, P. (2018). "España Verde": Tourism Destination Image among German Facebook Users. In J. Rodrigues, C. Ramos, P. Cardoso, & C. Henriques (Eds.), *Handbook of Research on Technological Developments for Cultural Heritage and eTourism Applications* (pp. 284–311). IGI Global. doi:10.4018/978-1-5225-2927-9.ch014

Seaborn, K., & Fels, D. I. (2015). Gamification in Theory and Action: A Survey. *International Journal of Human-Computer Studies*, *74*, 14–31. doi:10.1016/j.ijhcs.2014.09.006

Segalo, P. (2006). The psychological power of rap music in the healing of black communities. *Muziki*, *3*(1), 28–35. doi:10.1080/18125980608538781

Severo, M., & Venturini, T. (2016). Intangible cultural heritage webs: Comparing national networks with digital methods. *New Media & Society*, *18*(8), 1616–1635. doi:10.1177/1461444814567981

Sezer, S., & Can, E. (2020). School Happiness: A Grounded Theory. *Educational Policy Analysis and Strategic Research*, *15*(1), 44–62.

Shaffer, D. W. (2018). Epistemic network analysis: Understanding learning by using big data for thick description. In F. Fischer, C. E. Hmelo-Silver, S. R. Goldman, & P. Reimann (Eds.), *International Handbook of the Learning Sciences* (pp. 520–531). Routledge. doi:10.4324/9781315617572-50

Shahsavari, S., Holur, P., Tangherlini, T. R., & Roychowdhury, V. (2020). Conspiracy in the time of corona: Automatic detection of covid-19 conspiracy theories in social media and the news. *Journal of Computational Social Science*, *3*(2), 279–317. doi:10.100742001-020-00086-5 PMID:33134595

Shen, X. (2014). Jianzhen Library: Analysis on the Cultural Features of the Biggest Buddhist Library in China. *Sci-Tech Information Development & Economy*, *2014*(17), 77–78.

Shepherd, N. (2003). Interviewing online: Qualitative research in the network(ed) society. In *AQR Qualitative Research Conference*, 16-19 July, 2003, *Sydney, Australia*. Association for Qualitative Research.

Shoham, A. (2004). Flow experiences and image making: An online chat-room ethnography. *Psychology and Marketing*, *21*(10), 855–882. doi:10.1002/mar.20032

Sik, D. (2021). From Lay Depression Narratives to Secular Ritual Healing: An Online Ethnography of Mental Health Forums. *Culture, Medicine and Psychiatry*, *45*(4), 751–774. doi:10.100711013-020-09702-5 PMID:33372246

Simon, N. (2010). *The participatory museum*. Museum 2.0.

Skaribas, G. (2016). *Άπαντες στίχοι 1936-1970* [Lexical characteristics of Greek language]. Νεφέλη.

Smeda, N., Dakich, E., & Sharda, N. (2014). The effectiveness of digital storytelling in the classrooms: A comprehensive study. *Smart Learning Environments*, *1*(1), 1–21. doi:10.118640561-014-0006-3

Smith, P. (1997). Contemporary Legend. In Th. A. Green (Ed.), *Folklore: An Encyclopedia of belief, customs, tales, music and art* (pp. 493–495). ABC-CLIO.

Sofos, A., Kostas, A., & Parashou, V. (2015). *Online distance learning - From theory to practice*. Association of Greek Academic Libraries – National Technical University of Athens.

Sousa, M. J., & Rocha, Á. (2017). Game Based Learning Contexts for Soft Skills Development. *World Conference on Information Systems and Technologies*. 10.1007/978-3-319-56538-5_92

Soviyah, S., & Etikaningsih, D. R. (2018). Instagram use to enhance ability in writing descriptive texts. *Indonesian EFL Journal*, *4*(2), 32–38. doi:10.25134/ieflj.v4i2.1373

Spreen, M. (1992). Rare populations, hidden populations, and link-tracing designs: What and why? *Bulletin of Sociological Methodology. Bulletin de Methodologie Sociologique*, *36*(1), 34–58. doi:10.1177/075910639203600103

Stamatakis, V., & Sifaki, E. (2020). Quality evaluation and quality metrics in the cultural sector. *International Journal of Teaching and Case Studies*, *11*(4), 317–343. doi:10.1504/IJTCS.2020.112743

Steele, V. (1998). A Museum of Fashion Is More Than a Clothes-Bag. *Fashion Theory*, *2*(4), 327–335. doi:10.2752/136270498779476109

Steele, V. (2008). Museum Quality: The Rise of the Fashion Exhibition. *Fashion Theory*, *12*(1), 7–30. doi:10.2752/175174108X268127

Stewart, J., Lizzy, I., Van Looy, J., Mariën, I., All, A., Schurmans, D., Willaert, K., De Grove, F., Jacobs, A., & Misuraca, G. (2013). *The Potential of Digital Games for Empowerment and Social Inclusion of Groups at Risk of Social and Economic Exclusion: Evidence and Opportunity for Policy*. doi:10.2791/88148

Stojanović, D., Bogdanović, Z., Despotović-Zrakić, M., Naumović, T., & Radenković, M. (2019). An approach to using Instagram in secondary education. *The 14th International Conference on Virtual Learning ICVL*, 247–253.

Stojanović, D., Bogdanović, Z., Petrović, L., Mitrović, S., & Labus, A. (2020). Empowering learning process in secondary education using pervasive technologies. *Interactive Learning Environments*, 1–14. doi:10.1080/10494820.2020.1806886

Strathern, M. (1987). An Awkward Relationship: The Case of Feminism and Anthropology. *Journal of Women in Culture and Society*, *12*(2), 288–292. doi:10.1086/494321

Strømme, T. A., & Mork, S. M. (2021). Student's conceptual sense-making of animations and static visualizations of protein synthesis: A sociocultural hypothesis explaining why animations may be beneficial for student learning. *Research in Science Education*, *51*(4), 1013–1038. doi:10.100711165-020-09920-2

Stylianidou, N., Sofianidis, A., Manoli, E., & Meletiou-Mavrotheris, M. (2020). "Helping Nemo!"—Using Augmented Reality and Alternate Reality Games in the Context of Universal Design for Learning. *Education Sciences*, *10*(4), 95. doi:10.3390/educsci10040095

Suh, A., Wagner, C., & Liu, L. (2018). Enhancing User Engagement through Gamification. *Journal of Computer Information Systems*, *58*(3), 204–213. doi:10.1080/08874417.2016.1229143

Sullivan, A. M. (2015). Cultural Heritage & New Media: A Future for the Past. *J. Marshall Rev. Intell. Prop. L.*, *15*, 604.

Sullivan, A. M. (2016). Cultural Heritage & New Media: A Future for the Past. J. Marshall Rev. Intell. *Prop*, *15*, 604.

Sullivan, J. (2021). Transcending the Technocratic Mentality through the Humanities. *Religions*, *12*, 676.

Summer Institute of Linguistics. (2021). *El Náhuatl del norte de Oaxaca*. Retrieved from https://mexico.sil.org/es/lengua_cultura/nahuatl/nahuatl-nhy

Sylaiou, S., Basiouka, S., Patias, P., & Stylianidis, E. (2013). The volunteered geographic information in archaeology. ISPRS Annals of the Photogrammetry. *Remote Sensing and Spatial Information Sciences*, *2*, 301–306.

Sysło, M. M., & Kwiatkowska, A. B. (2013). Informatics for All High School Students: A Computational Thinking Approach. In I. Diethelm & R. T. Mittermeir (Eds.), *ISSEP 2013. LNCS* (Vol. 7780, pp. 43–56). Springer.

Taguieff, P. A. (2016). Court traité de complotologie. Paris: Fayard.

Tatum, B. (2010). The link between rap music and youth crime and violence: A review of the literature and issues for future research. *The Justice Professional*, *11*(3), 339–353. doi:10.1080/1478601X.1999.9959513

Téllez Alarcia & Iturriaga Barco. (2014). Videojuegos y aprendizaje de la historia: La saga Assassin's Creed. *Contextos Educativos, 17.*

Terzidis, C. (2003). *To hip hop δε σταματά* [Lexical characteristics of Greek language]. Athens: Οξύ.

Tess, P. A. (2013). The role of social media in higher education classes (real and virtual) – A literature review. *Computers in Human Behavior*, *29*(5), A60–A68. doi:10.1016/j.chb.2012.12.032

Theeboom, M., Zhu, D., & Vertonghen, J. (2017). 'Wushu belongs to the world'. But the gold goes to China: The international development of the Chinese martial arts. *International Review for the Sociology of Sport*, *52*(1), 3–23. doi:10.1177/1012690215581605

Theodoridis, G. (2022 March 05). *(drama) "Euripides – Helen". https://www.poetryintranslation.com/theodoridisgeuripideshelen.php*

Thomas, L. V. (1978). *Civilisation et Divagation*. Payot.

Thompson, R., & McIlnay, M. (2019). Nobody wants to read anymore! Using a multimodal approach to make literature engaging. *Journal of English Language and Literature*, *7*, 21–40.

Thompson, T. (2012). Netizens, Revolutionaries, and the Inalienable Right to the Internet. In T. Blank (Ed.), *Folk Culture in the Digital Age* (pp. 46–59). Utah State University Press. doi:10.7330/9780874218909.c02

Tranta, A., Alexandri, E., & Kyprianos, K. (2021). Young people and museums in the time of covid-19. *Museum Management and Curatorship*, *36*(6), 632–648. doi:10.1080/09647775.2021.1969679

Tsapari, Ol. (2013). *No Sponsors - Χωρίς χορηγούς: Η Low Bap σκηνή του Περάματος ως παράδειγμα πολιτιστικής διαχείρισης* [Lexical characteristics of Greek language]. (Unpublished postgraduate thesis). Πανεπιστήμιο Ιωαννίνων, Ioannina.

Tse, H. L., Chiu, D. K., & Lam, A. H. (2022). From Reading Promotion to Digital Literacy: An Analysis of Digitalizing Mobile Library Services With the 5E Instructional Model. In A. Almeida & S. Esteves (Eds.), *Modern Reading Practices and Collaboration Between Schools, Family, and Community* (pp. 239–256). IGI Global. doi:10.4018/978-1-7998-9750-7.ch011

Tsekeridou, S., Tsetsos, V., Chalamandaris, A., Chamzas, C., Filippou, T., & Pantzoglou, C. (2014). iGuide: Socially-enriched mobile tourist guide for unexplored sites. *Proceedings of the Hellenic Conference on Artificial Intelligence*. 10.1007/978-3-319-07064-3_52

Turkle, S. (1995). Life on the screen: identity in the age of the Internet. New York: Simon & Schuster.

Tzimogiannis, A. (2017). *E-Learning, Theoretical Approaches, and Educational Designs*. Athens: Kritiki Publication.

UNESCO. (2003). *Convention for the safeguarding of the intangible Cultural Heritage*. UNESCO.

UNESCO. (2003). *Vitalidad y peligro de desaparición de las lenguas*. UNESCO.

UNESCO. (2014). *Culture For Development Indicators - Methodology Manual.* United Nations Educational, Scientific and Cultural Organization.

UNESCO. (2020a). *Online meeting of Ministers of Culture. The Covid-19 pandemic's impact on the cultural sector and the public policy response*. Retrieved from: https://unesdoc.unesco.org/ark:/48223/pf0000373601?posInSet=2&queryId=N-b0ed0ac3-17b2-4ff2-8829-40910f877942

UNESCO. (2020b). *Museums around the World in the face of COVID-19*. UNESCO Report. Retrieved from: https://unesdoc.unesco.org/ark:/48223/pf0000373530/PDF/373530eng.pdf.multi

United Nations. (2017). *State of the World's Indigenous Peoples: Education*. United Nations.

Unity. (n.d.). Retrieved March 11, 2022 (https://unity.com/)

Valdez-Besares, J. G., Ronquillo-Jorge, A., Mendez-Gijon, F., López-Núñez, L., & Servín-Juárez, F. (2016). Aplicación web para recopilar, difundir y aprender lenguas originarias del sur de México: Una perspectiva desde los hablantes. *Salud y Administración*, *3*(7), 19–31.

Valencia, F. (2020). *MÉ XI KUÉNA JMÍNI Libro con Realidad Aumentada para el rescate, conservación y difusión de la lengua mazateca de Huautla de Jiménez, Oaxaca* [Bachelor Thesis]. Universidad de la Cañada.

Valtysson, B. (2011). EUROPEANA: The digital construction of Europe's collective memory. *Information Communication and Society*, *15*(2), 151–170. doi:10.1080/1369118X.2011.586433

Van Dijk, T. A. (2001). Critical Discourse Analysis. In Handbook of Discourse Analysis (pp. 352-371). Blackwell.

Van Meter, K. (1990). Methodological and Design Issues: Techniques for Assessing the Representatives of Snowball Samples. In E. Y. Lambert (Ed.), *The Collection and Interpretation of Data from Hidden Populations* (pp. 31–43). U.S. Department of Health and Human Services.

Van Prooijen, J.-W., & Douglas, K. M. (2017). Conspiracy theories as a part of history: The role of societal crisis situations. *Memory Studies*, *10*(3), 323–333. doi:10.1177/1750698017701615 PMID:29081831

Van Prooijen, J.-W., Douglas, K. M., & de Inocencio, C. (2018). Connecting the dots: Pattern perception predicts belief in conspiracies and the supernatural. *European Journal of Social Psychology*, *48*(3), 320–335. doi:10.1002/ejsp.2331 PMID:29695889

Varis, P. (2016). Digital Ethnography. In A. Georgakopoulou & T. Spilioti (Eds.), *The Routledge Handbook of Language and Digital Communication* (pp. 55–68). Routledge.

Varvounis, A., & Kapaniaris, A. (2021). Folklore on the road to distance education (e-learning). *Folklore*, *44*(4), 75–96.

Varvounis, M., & Kapaniaris, A. (2019). Archival ethnography & interpretations in the digital environment: 'conversing' with the archives of the 'Pelioritians in Egypt': The planning of a long-term research [Αρχειακή εθνογραφία & αναγνώσεις σε ψηφιακό περιβάλλον: «συνομιλώντας» με τα αρχεία των «Πηλιορειτών εν Αιγύπτω»: Ο σχεδιασμός μιας μακροχρόνιας έρευνας]. *Εκκλησιαστικός Φάρος Επιστημονικόν Θεολογικόν Περιοδικόν Σύγγραμμα του Πατριαρχείου Αλεξάνδρας και πάσης Αφρικής. Τόμος ΠΖ΄-ΠΗ΄*, (2018-2019), 113–146.

Vasiliadou, M. (2021). *The art, "medicine" for doctors and nurses*. Kathimerini. Retrieved from https://www.kathimerini.gr/culture/561321304/i-techni-farmako-gia-giatroys-kai-nosileytes/

Vassilakis, K., Charalampakos, O., Glykokokalos, G., Kontokalou, P., Kalogiannakis, M., & Vidakis, N. (2018). Learning History Through Location-Based Games: The Fortification Gates of the Venetian Walls of the City of Heraklion. In A. L. Brooks, E. Brooks, & N. Vidakis (Eds.), *Interactivity, Game Creation, Design, Learning, and Innovation* (pp. 510–519). Springer International Publishing. doi:10.1007/978-3-319-76908-0_49

Vayanou, M., Katifori, A., Chrysanthi, A., & Antoniou, A. (2020). Cultural Heritage and Social Experiences in the Times of COVID 19. In *Proceedings of AV I 2CH 2020: Workshop on Advanced Visual Interfaces and Interactions in Cultural Heritage (AV I 2CH 2020). New York:* ACM.

Vert, S., Andone, D., Ternauciuc, A., Mihaescu, V., Rotaru, O., Mocofan, M., Orhei, C., & Vasiu, R. (2021). User Evaluation of a Multi-Platform Digital Storytelling Concept for Cultural Heritage. Mathemati*cs, 9, 2678.*

Vidakis, Christinaki, Serafimidis, & Triantafyllidis. (2014). Combinin*g Ludology and Narratology in an Open Authorable Framework for Educational Games for Children: The Scenario of Teaching Preschoolers with Autism Diagnosis. Academi*c Press.

Vidakis, N., & Charitakis, S. (2018). Designing the Learning Process. Proceed*ings of the 10th International Conference on Subject-Oriented Business Process Management - S-BPM One '18, 1–11.* doi:10.1145/3178248.3178254

Vidakis, N., Barianos, A. K., Trampas, A. M., Papadakis, S., Kalogiannakis, M., & Vassilakis, K. (2020). Game Raw Data Collection and Visualization in the Context of the "ThimelEdu". Educational Game. https://doi.org/10.1007/978-3-030-58459-7_30

Vidakis, N., Barianos, A., Trampas, A., Papadakis, S., Kalogiannakis, M., & Vassilakis, K. (2019). Generating Education in-Game Data: The Case of an Ancient Theatre Serious Game. Proc*eedings of the 11th International Conference on Computer Supported Education, 1, 36*-43. doi:10.5220/0007810800360043

Vidakis, N., Barianos, A., Trampas, A., Papadakis, S., Kalogiannakis, M., & Vassilakis, K. (2019). Generating Education in-Game Data: The Case of an Ancient Theatre Serious Game. Proc*eedings of the 11th International Conference on Computer Supported Education, 1, 36*-43. https://link.springer.com/chapter/10.1007/978-3-030-58459-7_30

Vidakis, N., Barianos, A. K., Trampas, A. M., Papadakis, S., Kalogiannakis, M., & Vassilakis, K. (2020). Game Raw Data Collection and Visualization in the Context of the "ThimelEdu" Educational Game. In H. C. Lane, S. Zvacek, & J. Uhomoibhi (Eds.), Com*puter Supported Education. CSEDU 2019. Communications in Computer and Information Science (*Vol. 1220). Springer. doi:10.1007/978-3-030-58459-7_30

Vidakis, N., Barianos, A., Xanthopoulos, G., & Stamatakis, A. (2018). Cultural Inheritance Education Environment: The Ancient Theater Game ThimelEdu. 12*th European Conference on Games Based Learning, ECGBL 2018,* 730–740.

Vidakis, N., Barianos, K. A., Xanthopoulos, G., & Stamatakis, A. (2018). Cultural Inheritance Educational Environment: The Ancient Theatre Game Thimeledu. P*roceedings of the European Conference on Games-Based Learning,* 730–39.

Vidakis, N., Syntychakis, E., Kalafatis, K., Christinaki, E., & Triantafyllidis, G. (2015). *Ludic Educational Game Creation Tool: Teaching Schoolers Road Safety. Academic Press.*

Vidakis, N., Syntychakis, E., Kalafatis, K., Varhalamas, P., & Triantafyllidis, G. (2015). Concealing Education into Games. *Proceedings of the European Conference on Games-Based Learning*, 554–63.

Vogiatzis, T. (2013). Το ελληνικό hip hop στα '80s και στα '90s. [Lexical characteristics of Greek] In T. Vogiatzis (Ed.), *Hip hop: code of the streets* (pp. 14–21). Sonik.

Vuforia. (n.d.). *Vuforia Engine Developer Portal*. Retrieved March 11, 2022 https://developer.vuforia.com/

Vygotsky, L. S. (1978). *Mind in society: The development of higher psychological processes*. Harvard University Press.

Walker, S. L. (2015). The Role of Local History in the Curriculum at a Rural, Southeastern Community College. *Walden Dissertations and Doctoral Studies*. 1233. https://scholarworks.waldenu.edu/dissertations/1233

Walmsley, A. P., & Kersten, T. P. (2020). The Imperial Cathedral in Königslutter (Germany) as an Immersive Experience in Virtual Reality with Integrated 360° Panoramic Photography. *Applied Sciences (Basel, Switzerland)*, *2020*(10), 1517. doi:10.3390/app10041517

Walstrom, M. K. (2004). Ethics and engagement in communication scholarship: Analyzing public, online support groups as researcher/participant experiencer. *Virtual Research Ethics: Issues and Controversies*.

Wang, H., & Sun, C.-T. (2011). Game Reward Systems: Gaming Experiences and Social Meanings. DiGRA Conference, 114.

Wang, A. I., & Lieberoth, A. (2016). The Effect of Points and Audio on Concentration, Engagement, Enjoyment, Learning, Motivation, and Classroom Dynamics Using Kahoot. *European conference on games based learning*, 20.

Wang, D., & Liu, S. (2021). Doing Ethnography on Social Media: A Methodological Reflection on the Study of Online Groups in China. *Qualitative Inquiry*, *27*(8-9), 977–987. doi:10.1177/10778004211014610

Wang, P., Chiu, D. K. W., Ho, K. K., & Lo, P. (2016). Why read it on your mobile device? Change in reading habit of electronic magazines for university students. *Journal of Academic Librarianship*, *42*(6), 664–669. doi:10.1016/j.acalib.2016.08.007

Werbach, K., & Hunter, D. (2015). *The Gamification Toolkit: Dynamics, Mechanics, and Components for the Win*. University of Pennsylvania Press.

Wernimont, J., & Losh, E. (2018). Introduction. In Bodies of Information: Intersectional Feminism and the Digital Humanities (pp. ix-xxvi). University of Minnesota Press.

Whyte, W. F. (2012). *Street Corner Society: The Social Structure of an Italian Slum*. University of Chicago Press.

Wijers, M., Jonker, V., & Drijvers, P. (2010). MobileMath: Exploring Mathematics Outside the Classroom. *ZDM*, *42*(7), 789–799. doi:10.100711858-010-0276-3

Williams, R., & Orrom, M. (1954). *Preface to Film*. Film Drama Limited.

Wing, J. (2008) Computational thinking and thinking about computing. *Phil. Trans. R. Soc. A.*, *366*(1881), 3717–3725. www.igda.org/arg/whitepaper.html

Wing, J. (2006). Computational Thinking. *Communications of the ACM*, *49*(3), 33–35. doi:10.1145/1118178.1118215

Wittel, A. (2000). Ethnography on the move: From field to net to internet. *Forum Qualitative Sozialforschung/Forum: Qualitative. Social Research*, *1*(1). Advance online publication. doi:10.17169/fqs-1.1.1131

Wittern, C. (2000). Buddhist Studies in the Digital Age. *Chung-Hwa Buddhist Journal*, *2000*(13), 321–351.

Wong, S. W. S., & Chiu, D. K. W. (2023). (in press). Re-examining the value of remote academic library storage in the mobile digital age: A comparative study. *Portal (Baltimore, Md.)*, *23*(1).

Yalçınkaya, E. (2015). Creative Drama Study about Intangible Cultural Heritage: Turkish Wedding Traditions. *Creative Education*, *6*, 22–31.

Yang, Y. C., & Wu, W. (2012). Digital storytelling for enhancing student academic achievement, critical thinking, and learning motivation: A year-long experimental study. *Computers & Education*, *59*, 339–352.

Yates, S. (2007). RAT online: Martial arts learning resources. *The Electronic Library*, *25*(5), 495–516. doi:10.1108/02640470710829505

Yau, A., Chiu, D. K. W., Nakamura, Y., & Li, K. K. (in press). Quantitative Comparison of LIS Programs Accredited by ALA and CILIP. *Library Hi Tech.*

Yip, K. H. T., Chiu, D. K. W., Ho, K. K. W., & Lo, P. (2020). Adoption of Mobile Library Apps as Learning Tools in Higher Education: A Tale between Hong Kong and Japan. *Online Information Review*, *45*(2), 389–405. doi:10.1108/OIR-07-2020-0287

Yu, P. Y., Lam, E. T. H., & Chiu, D. K. W. (2022, February 16). (in press). Operation management of academic libraries in Hong Kong under COVID-19. *Library Hi Tech.* Advance online publication. doi:10.1108/LHT-10-2021-0342

Zeng, Y. (2012). Wang Wenshan: The Founder of the Classification of Chinese Modern Buddhist Classics. *Journal of The Sichuan Society for Library Science*, *2012*(5), 79–80.

Zhang, Q., Huang, B., Chiu, D. K. W., & Ho, K. K. W. (2015). Learning Japanese through social network sites: A case study of Chinese learners' perceptions. *Micronesian Educators*, *21*, 55–71.

Zhang, X., Gao, Y., Yan, X., de Pablos, P. O., Sun, Y., & Cao, X. (2015). From e-learning to social-learning: Mapping development of studies on social media-supported knowledge management. *Computers in Human Behavior*, *51*, 803–811. doi:10.1016/j.chb.2014.11.084

Zhang, Z. (2010). Talks from Past to Present of Buddhist Book Collection in Ancient Chinese Temple. *Library Theory and Practice*, *2010*(4), 96–98.

Zhang, Z., Li, Z., Han, M., Su, Z., Li, W., & Pan, Z. (2021). An augmented reality-based multimedia environment for experimental education. *Multimedia Tools and Applications*, *80*(1), 575–590. doi:10.100711042-020-09684-x

Zhivov, J., Scheepers, H., & Stockdale, R. (2011). Facebook-The Final Frontier For TV Fandom: A Lurker's Perspective. In *ACIS 2011 Proceedings*. Association for Information Systems.

Zhou, Q. (2019). *Understanding User Behaviors of Creative Practice on Short Video Sharing Platforms–A Case Study of TikTok and Bilibili* (Doctoral dissertation). University of Cincinnati.

Zhou, J. (2019, October). A Survey of the Value of Chinese Kung-fu on the Physical and Mental Health of College Students from the Perspective of Healthy China. In *2nd International Conference on Contemporary Education, Social Sciences and Ecological Studies (CESSES 2019).* Atlantis Press. 10.2991/cesses-19.2019.92

Zhou, Z. (2005). The Attempt of Buddhist Library to Use Chinese Library Classification — the Compilation of Yunlin Buddhist Library Classification. *Journal of the China Society of Indexers*, *3*(3), 37–39.

Zhuo, G. (2012a). A Preliminary Study on the Development of Buddhist Temple Libraries in China. *Ascent*, *31*(4), 161–164.

Zhuo, G. (2012b). Views on the Construction of Tibetan Buddhist Temple Library. *Library Work and Study*, *31*(9), 81–83.

Zourmpakis, A.-I., Papadakis, St., & Kalogiannakis, M. (2022). Education of Preschool and Elementary Teachers on the Use of Adaptive Gamification in Science Education. *International Journal of Technology Enhanced Learning*, *14*(1), 1–16.

Zulli, D., & Zulli, D. J. (2020). Extending the Internet meme: Conceptualizing technological mimesis and imitation publics on the TikTok platform. *New Media & Society*. doi:10.1177/1461444820983603

About the Contributors

Stamatios Papadakis has been a postdoctoral researcher in Educational Technology, with an emphasis on mobile learning, at the Department of Preschool Education at the University of Crete, Greece, since 2016. He has graduated from the Department of Informatics, Athens University of Economics and Business, Athens, Greece. In 2006 he completed a master's degree (M.Ed.) in Pre-school Education and Educational Design at the University of Aegean, Rhodes, Greece, at the School of Humanities, Department of Pre-school Education. In 2016, he completed a PhD at the University of Crete, Department of Education in Rethymnon, Greece. He has worked as an adjunct Lecturer in Education teaching Didactics in Programming (2017-2018) at the Department of Computer Sciences, School of Sciences and Engineering at the University of Crete, Greece. Since 2017 he has worked as an adjunct Lecturer in Education teaching Informatics (2017-2018) at the Department of Preschool Education, School of Education, University of Crete, Greece. He has worked in several international and national computational thinking and pedagogy projects, of Pre-K to 16 Education. His scientific and research interests include the study of mobile learning, especially on the use of smart mobile devices and their accompanying mobile applications (apps) in Preschool and Primary Education, focusing on the development of Computational Thinking and students' understanding of numbers. Furthermore, he currently investigates how a STEM learning approach influences learning achievement through a context-aware mobile learning environment in the preschool classroom and explains the effects on preschoolers' learning outcomes.

Alexander Kapaniaris was born in Zagora and has two children. He works as an IT teacher in the Secondary Education and he is a Regional Coordinator of Educational Work of Computer Science of Thessaly. His basic degree is as an IT Engineer of the Technological Institute of Computer Engineering and Information of Athens and is a graduate of the department of "Studies in Greek Culture" of the Faculty of Humanities of the Greek Open University and a graduate of the School of pedagogical of PATES / S.E.L.E.T.E. of Thessaloniki. He also has MSc degrees on the topics of "Graphic Arts - Multimedia" from the Greek Open University and Modern Learning Environments & Production of Teaching Material of University of Thessaly (Department of Education). Since 2017, he has been a PhD of Folk Culture, Education and ICT, of the University of the Aegean (Department of Early Childhood Education and Educational Planning). He has completed two post doctorate researches in the Department of History and Ethnology, Democritus University of Thrace. He has published and has participated in Greek and international conferences as a rapporteur and a judge and his research interests include the E/H educational technology, internet addiction, pedagogical applications, educational software, ICT, cultural informatics, digitizing historical archives, local history and folk culture. He has authored books on the teaching use of ICT in education and the digital school, on civilization and education. He is currently teaching in the Greek Open University in postgraduate level the course "Digital Storytelling in education". He also teaches at the Hellenic Open University in the Department of Greek Culture the course Public and Private Life in Greece (Folk Studies).

* * *

Zoi Arvanitidou holds a Ph.D. in "Folklore, Gender and Fashion", an M. Ed. in "Gender and the new Educational and Working Environments of the Information Society", a BA in "Studies in Greek Civilization" and a BA in "Fashion Design". She is also a certified trainer and examiner for vocational training. She is skilled and experienced in adult education and training, information and communication technologies in education and training, fashion design, folklore, fashion and gender analysis, qualitative research and surveying, sociology, social and gender identity. On top of the above, she also has numerous personal and team publications in proceedings' volumes and journals related to gender, identity, dressing, subcultures, and education as well as two published books on Fashion Design.

Anastasios Barianos was born in Danderyd, Stockholm Sweden. He received a BSc in Informatics Engineering from the Technological Educational Institute of Crete in 2018. Currently, he is a post graduate student in Informatics and Multimedia at the Technological Educational Institute of Crete. Since 2016 he is a member and research assistant at Natural Interactive LEarning Games Lab (NILE-lab).

Cheuk Ting Chan received the degree of Bachelor of Arts in Music at The Chinese University of Hong Kong in 1995, and Master of Arts in Music Education at the Hong Kong Baptist University in 2007. She was the concertmaster of the Hong Kong Youth Chinese Orchestra 1991-1995, and was a freelance musician of the Hong Kong Chinese Orchestra 1994-1997. She has also been a music teacher for over 20 years. Her research interest is in music education and Buddhist studies.

Orestis Charalampakos holds a Master's degree in 'Informatics & Multimedia' from the Hellenic Mediterranean University. He is working as a senior software engineer, specialized in web application design and development.

Dickson K. W. Chiu received the B.Sc. (Hons.) degree in Computer Studies from the University of Hong Kong in 1987. He received the M.Sc. (1994) and the Ph.D. (2000) degrees in Computer Science from the Hong Kong University of Science and Technology (HKUST). He started his own computer consultant company while studying part-time. He has also taught at several universities in Hong Kong. His teaching and research interest is in Library & Information Management, Service Computing, and E-learning with a cross-disciplinary approach, involving library and information management, e-learning, e-business, service sciences, and databases. The results have been widely published in around 300 international publications (most of them have been indexed by SCI/-E, SSCI, and EI, such as top journals MIS Quarterly, Computer & Education, Government Information Quarterly, Decision Support Systems, Information Sciences, Knowledge-Based Systems, Expert Systems with Application, Information Systems Frontiers, IEEE Transactions, including many taught master and undergraduate project results and around 20 edited books. He received a best paper award in the 37th Hawaii International Conference on System Sciences in 2004. He is an Editor (-in-chief) of Library Hi Tech, a prestigious journal indexed by SSCI (impact factor 2.357). He is the Editor-in-chief Emeritus of the International Journal on Systems and Service-Oriented Engineering (founding) and International Journal of Organizational and Collective Intelligence, and serves in the editorial boards of several international journals. He co-founded several international workshops and co-edited several journal special issues. He also served as a program committee member for around 300 international conferences and workshops. Dr. Chiu is a Senior Member of both the ACM and the IEEE, and a life member of the Hong Kong Computer Society. According to Google Scholar, he has over 5,000 citations, h-index 37, i-10 index 109, ranked worldwide 1st in "LIS," "m-learning," and "e-services."

Eirini Christinaki is a postdoctoral researcher in the Research Group Ophthalmology (Biomedical Sciences - Department of Neurosciences) at KU Leuven (Belgium). She holds a B.Sc in Applied Informatics & Multimedia, a M.Sc in Informatics & Multimedia, both from TEI of Crete (Greece), and a PhD in Computer Science from University of Essex (UK). During her undergraduate studies, she has participated in the development of Serious Games in the areas of intervention and education for children with autism. Since then, she conducts multidisciplinary research at the intersection of computer science and medicine. Her current research focuses on the quest for retinal biomarkers for neurodegenerative diseases and includes the study of various retinal imaging techniques coupled with AI-based analysis for the early detection and clinical follow-up of patients with Alzheimer's disease.

Alkistis Dalkavouki is a Ph.D. candidate in the Department of Geography and Regional Planning of the National Technical University of Athens. She attended the International Konitsa Summer School in Anthropology, Ethnography, and Comparative Folklore of the Balkans in 2014 and has since been studying the subject in conjunction with the rest of her studies. She graduated from the Aristotle University of Thessaloniki (Department of Rural and Surveying Engineering) in 2016. She received her Master's title from the interdepartmental "Architecture –Space Planning" program of the National Technical University of Athens' School of Architecture in 2018. Her diploma thesis focused on the geographic and demographic evolution of the workers and culture of American comic books through the bidirectional relationship between professionals and amateurs. To complete it, she utilized methods of digital ethnography. Her academic experience includes participating in international conferences and contributing auxiliary work for the Department of Geography and Regional Planning.

Maria Gasouka has completed her PhD in Folklore and Gender. She is a Professor Emerita in the Department of Science Education and Educational Design in the Aegean University, in the field of "Gender and Folklore". She is also a Member of the scientific group of design and implementation of the post-graduate studies program of the Aegean University's "Gender and New Educational and Working Environment, in the Information Society", offered through distance learning. Maria Gasouka is the Chairwoman of the Scientific Committee of the Cypriot Equality Observatory. Along with being a researcher, trainer and coordinator of E.C., she is associated with Initiatives and Programmes in Mainstreaming and Equal Opportunity issues. She has published various editions like "Sociological Approaches to Gender-Authority and Hierarchy Issues, Athens 1998", "Women's Political Speech". Also "Texts on the Left Wing and Gender, Athens 1999", "On Folklore and Folk Culture Gendering Sociology vol.I (2006) and vol.II (2008)", "Aspects of Feminist Research. Feminist Ethnography-Internet Ethnography (2007)", "Thoughts and Notes on the Issues of Reconciliation of Work and Family Life in Europe. The Experience of Cyprus, New York, 2010 (with Maria Kokkinou)", "Aspects of Gender and Discrimination (2021)" etc.

Rea Kakampoura is Associate Professor of Folklore Studies at the Department of Primary Education, National and Kapodistrian University of Athens. She is the Director of the Postgraduate Programme "Social Sciences and Humanities in Education" and the Director of the Laboratory of Social Sciences at the Department of Primary Education. Her research interests include aspects of cultural heritage and its management through formal and non-formal education (schools, museums, cultural institutions), digital folklore and biographical approach. She has founded the "Archive of Life Stories" at the Department of Primary Education which consists of over 800 life story interviews. She has been Coordinator or member of the Research team of several national and international research programs (e.g. "Critical Heritages (CoHERE): Performing and Representing Identities in Europe"/ HORIZON 2020). She has published 5 books and edited books and more than 50 papers in international and national refereed journals as well as in international and national peer-reviewed conference proceedings. She is a member of the Greek National Scientific Committee for the Safeguarding of Intangible Cultural Heritage (UNESCO) and also a member of several Scientific Committees (Museum of Greek Folk Musical Instruments, member of the Board of the Hellenic Folklore Society, etc.)

Michail Kalogiannakis is an Associate Professor in the Department of Preschool Education at the University of Crete and Associate Tutor at School of Humanities at the Hellenic Open University. He has graduated from the Physics Department of the University of Crete and continued his postgraduate studies at the University Paris 7-Denis Diderot (D.E.A. in Didactic of Physics), University Paris 5-René Descartes-Sorbonne (D.E.A. in Science Education) and received his PhD degree at the University Paris 5-René Descartes-Sorbonne (PhD in Science Education). His research interests include science education in the early childhood, science teaching and learning, e-learning, the use of ICT in education, distant and adult education. He has published many articles in international conferences and journals and has served on the program committees of numerous international conferences.

Nikolaos Karantalis was born in Agrinio, Greece, in 1976. He received the bachelor diploma in Greek Philology in 2000, the MA in creative writing in 2018 and since 2020 he is PhD student in the department of History and Archaeology at the University of Patras. His current research interests include digital storytelling, intangible cultural heritage, intelligent cultural environments, and education. He currently works as a teacher in a secondary school in Greece.

George Katsadoros is Associate Professor of Folklore at the Department of Primary Education of the University of the Aegean. His main research interests include the diffusion and distribution of folkloric genres through modern media and their appliance in Education. He has taken part and acted as a referee in many congresses and journals and has published several works in Greece and abroad.

Iraklis Katsaris works as a teacher in the Greek Ministry of education and concurrently working as PhD candidate at the Hellenic Mediterranean University Department of Electrical and Computer Engineering. Iraklis was born in Thessaloniki, Greece. He received a Bachelor of Education at the Department of Primary Level Education, Democritus University of Thrace in 2009,and an MSc in Sociology, Department of Sociology, University of the Aegean in 2017. Since 2020 he has been a member and researcher at Natural Interactive LEarning Games Lab (NILE-lab). His research interest are focused on Adaptive Educational Systems, Intelligent Tutoring Systems, Theories in Education, Blended learning, Serious Games, Game Based Learning and Gamification.

Dimitrios Koukopoulos is an Associate Professor at the Department of History and Archaeology (University of Patras, Greece) and Adjunct Lecturer at the School of Science and Technology (Hellenic Open University, Greece). He is an author of more than 70 papers in well-known international journals (TCS, TOCS, JPDC, JECR, IJACI, Heritage, JAISE) and conferences (SPAA, HiPC, DISC, EuroMed, Digital Heritage). His major fields of study cover cultural technology, algorithms, and trustworthy multimedia networks. He participated as a researcher in many EU funded projects. He has served as a member of program committee in various conferences and as a reviewer in many journals. He is an editor of a handbook for applications in cultural heritage environments published by IGI.

George Koutromanos is an Assistant Professor of Information Communication Technologies (ICT) in Education at the Department of Primary Education of the National and Kapodistrian University of Athens. He holds a Bachelor degree in Education, an MSc degree in Computers in Education (National and Kapodistrian University of Athens) and two PhD degrees in ICT in Education (one from National and Kapodistrian University of Athens and one from Kings' College London, University of London). His current research interests include: The impact of ICT on education, the development and evaluation of computer-assisted learning materials, the flipped learning, the use of augmented reality in education, the use of mobile games in formal and informal learning environments and the use of drones in education. He has published over 110 papers in English and Greek journals, edited volumes and conference proceedings.

Ilias Logothetis studied Applied Informatics and Multimedia in the Computer Engineering Department of the Technical University of Crete in Heraklion and received his MSc degree in Applied Informatics and Multimedia from the Computer Engineering Department of the Hellenic Mediterranean University (HMU). He is now a PhD candidate at the Hellenic Mediterranean University (HMU). His research is focused on Extended Reality (XR) and its uses in education. His interest is in the effect of educational methods in XR and creating tools that assist the creation of educational content.

Myra Yi Ching Mak received the MSc degree in Library and Information Management in 2019 at The University of Hong Kong. Her research interest in social media and cultural education.

José Márquez-Domínguez is a Professor-Researcher at the University of La Cañada since 2008, he obtained a Master's degree in Computer Science at the Autonomous University of Puebla. He currently participates in different research projects as well as in conferences, he has written and collaborated in the publication of refereed and indexed articles, book chapters and two books. The areas of interest are Pattern Recognition, Information Retrieval, Augmented Reality, Technology in Education, Medical Informatics, Computer Graphics and Application of Information Systems.

Carmen Martínez-Gil received the B.S. degree in computer science from the Benemérita Universidad Autónoma de Puebla (BUAP) in 2001, and the M.S. and Ph.D. degrees in computer science from the Instituto Nacional de Astrofísica, Óptica y Electrónica (INAOE), Puebla, Mexico, in 2004 and 2008, respectively. She worked as a professor at the Instituto Tecnológico Superior de Atlixco (ITSA) y la Universidad de la Sierra Juárez (UNSIJ). Since 2008, she has been a full-time Professor at the Universidad de la Cañada (UNCA). Her main research interests include Machine Learnig and Computational Linguistics.

Evangelia Moula is a Philologist, Ph.D. in children's literature, Postdoc researcher on Literature in digital space. Author of various educational and academic books with publications in Greek and international journals. Research interests: contemporary cultural resources in education, such as comics, digital environments, social networks, in the light of critical literacy.

Vidakis Nikolas's Current Position is Associate Professor at the Hellenic Mediterranean University (HMU), School of Engineering, Department of Electrical and Computing Engineering, Crete, P.O Box: 71500, Profile Summary: Dr. Nikolaos Vidakis was born in Heraklion, Crete and is an Associate Professor at the Department of Electrical and Computer Engineering (ECE) of the Hellenic Mediterranean University (ELMEPA) with the subject "Technologies of Interactive Learning Software". He holds a PhD from the Technical University of Vienna, Austria titled: "Supporting Task-Based and User-Oriented Design and Implementation for Interactive Systems". He received a Bachelor of Science degree in "Computing in Business" from Northumbria University in Newcastle, England in 1993. In the past he worked at (TU-WIEN Austria), the Minoan Lines ANE (Heraklion) and the TEI-Crete. During his work at the Technical University of Vienna, the Minoan Lines ANE and the TEI-Crete he participated in various research & technological - development projects which were mostly funded by the European Union. In the curriculum of the ECE department of the engineering school of ELMEPA, he is the academic responsible for the courses: "Software Technology", "Data and Information Visualization Systems", "Game Design and Development" and "Flexible Software Development". In the Postgraduate Program "Informatics Engineering" of the ECE department he is the academic responsible for the course: "Advanced Software Engineering and Big Data Modeling. Up to today, he has supervised more than 30 postgraduate theses, more than 80 undergraduate theses and over 60 student internships in the above subjects. He is the Scientific Responsible of the research team "Laboratory of Natural Interactive Educational Games and Environments (NILE)" which operates under the ELMEPA research laboratory "Laboratory of Artificial Intelligence and Systems Engineering". He was a member of the iSTLab research laboratory from 2006 to 2016. He has participated as a lead researcher in several European and National R&D programs. He has organized and participated in the organization of international conferences and workshops. At the same time, he has participated as a reviewer and member of organizing committees in various international scientific conferences and journals. He has authored several publications in international scientific books, journals, and conferences, which have received more than 400 heterogeneous citations. His research interests include: Software Engineering, Games-based learning, Inclusive design, Educational Virtual environments / ecosystems, Assistive technologies, Interaction techniques, Multimodal Sensing and Natural User Interfaces, Serious Games, and applications as well as their applications in education. In recent years he has developed an extensive network of universities and partnerships, mainly through the execution of projects and project proposals, in the areas of Software Technology, Pedagogical Learning, Comprehensive Design, Educational Virtual Environments / Systems, Technical Supports, multimodal detection and physical user interfaces and serious games and applications. Some of these partners are University of Crete, Institute of Technology and Research (ITE), University of the Aegean, Regional Directorate of Primary and Secondary Education of Crete (RDPSEC), University of Nottingham Trent (NTU), United Kingdom. Kepler Universität Linz (JKU), Austria, University of Aalborg (AAU), Denmark, Fraunhofer Institute for Intelligent Analysis and Information Systems, Germany, Legendary Games, SMEs, UK, Serious Games Solutions GmbH, SMEs, Germany, University of Reading (UK), UK, BSD, SME, Italy, LightAct, SME, Slovenia, OpenGroup, CO-OP, Italy, Fondazione Stella Maris (FSM), Institute, Italy, Universidad de Sevilla, (USA), Spain, IES Caura, (CAU), Spain, Buenaventura

Media, SMEs, Spain. **Aphrodite-Lidia Nounanaki** is a graduate of the Department of Sociology of Panteion University. She holds a Master's degree on "Folklore and Culture" from the Department of Primary Education, National and Kapodistrian University of Athens. For her postgraduate studies she received a scholarship from the State Scholarship Institute. She also holds a PhD on Folklore Studies from the Department of Primary Education of the National and Kapodistrian University of Athens. Her theses is on "Greek contemporary Legends on the Internet". She has participated in research programs as a member of the Laboratory of Social Sciences at the same Department. She was also a member of the scientific group in documenting the G.A. Megas' digital archive manuscripts of the Hellenic Folklore Society. She has also participated in various Greek and international conferences and publications. Her research interests revolve around digital folklore, focusing on the diffusion of forms of modern popular culture through the internet and new such forms resulting in the digital world. Aspects of modern popular culture she is researching on is digital humour (e.g., memes), but mainly issues concerning the metaphysical (e.g. ghost lore), the scary (e.g. creepypasta) and narrative genres reflecting the fearsome perception of the modern world (e.g., contemporary legends, conspiracy theories), that is the occult and its diffusion through the internet.

Alexandros Papadakis was born in Heraklion, Greece. He received a BSc in Informatics Engineering from the Technological Educational Institute of Crete in 2018. Also received MSc in Informatics and Multimedia at the Hellenic Mediterranean University. Since 2018 he is member of Natural Interactive ELearning Games Lab (NILE-lab). He is working as a game developer with focus on serious games and game-based learning, game design and game development, software analysis, design, and development.

George Pasiopoulos is a primary school teacher and a PhD candidate at the Department of Primary Education at the University of the Aegean (Rhodes) in Folklore. He has completed two postgraduate courses and has been awarded three scholarships, including the "Panagiotis Sevastelis" scholarship of the University of the Aegean. His research interests, in addition to general educational and folklore issues, include youth subcultures, focusing on the Low bap music movement based in the area of Perama (Piraeus). He has taken part and acted as a referee in several scientific conferences of university institutions in Greece.

Ada Poon received the MSc degree in Library and Information Management in 2020 at The University of Hong Kong. Her research interest is in social media and cultural education.

Beatriz Sabino-Moxo is a full-time Professor-Researcher at the Universidad de la Cañada, attached to the Computer Science Degree, is a member of the Applied Computational Technology academic body. She has published various scientific articles, book chapters and books, and also works as a reviewer of scientific articles in journals of national and international impact. Since 2013, she has been recognized as a Desirable Profile accredited by the Undersecretary of Higher Education. Her areas of interest are: Digital Image Processing, Medical Informatics, Augmented Reality and Bioinformatics.

Miguel Angel Sanchez Acevedo has been a research professor at the Universidad de la Cañada since 2015. He obtained a PhD from the Popular Autonomous University of the State of Puebla. He is part of the Academic Body of Applied Computational Technology, of the Public Health and ARN-SUNEO Research groups. He currently directs the Intelligent and Distributed Systems Laboratory and the research groups: Innovation in Nutritious Food Products and Environmental Surveillance Network. His areas of interest are: Intelligent and Distributed Systems, Data Science and Rural Economy.

Eirini Sifaki is an associate professor in cultural theory and criticism at the department of language and intercultural studies, University of Thessaly. She holds a Phd in information and communication sciences from the University Paris 3 – Sorbonne Nouvelle. She has participated in various Greek and European research projects on cultural communication, education and research ethics. In 2016, she was the principal investigator of a research project on Contemporary Greek Cinema funded by the European Parliament. She also serves as an independent ethics expert of the DG Research and Innovation of the European Commission. Eirini is also the co-editor of two books: City and Cinema: Theoretical and Methodological Approaches, Athens, Nissos (in Greek) and World Film Locations Athens, London, Intellect. She is also the co-author of "The emergence of a New Wave in contemporary Greek cinema: Processes of artistic production, legitimization and communication in the art world" an open access book published by the National Center for Social Research, Greece. Her research interests and her publications involve issues on cultural theory, film studies and cultural communication.

Xin Sun obtained her degree of Master of Science in Library and Information Management from the University of Hong Kong in 2019. Her current research interests are digital preservation and special libraries.

Emmanouil Varvounis was born in 1966 on Samos, Greece, where he completed his primary and secondary education. He was a student of the Section for History and Archaeology of the Philosophical School of the University of Athens (1983 – 1988) and of the University of Athens Theological School. He specialized in folklore and in 1991 was awarded a doctorate in folklore by the Department of Primary Education of the University of Athens. During the period 1996 – 1997, he did post-doctoral research at the Université Catholique de Louvain (Louvain – la – Neuve) in Belgium. Since 1992 he has taught folklore in the Department of History and Ethnology of the Democritus University of Thrace, where he is today a Professor and Department Chairman. He is a member of many learned societies in Greece and abroad, such as the Hellenic Folklore Society, in Athens, of which he is also a member of the Administrative Committee, the British Folklore Society, of London, and the American Folklore Society, of Washington. He is the author of many works, some independent studies and some published in collective volumes. His works have been translated and published in English, French, Spanish, Italian, German, Serbian, Turkish, Russian, Georgian, Arabic, Armenian, Latin and Bulgarian. In March, 2005, His Beatitude the Ecumenical Patriarch Vartholomaios honoured him with the rank of 'Master Protector of Letters of the Great Holy Church of Christ'. In 2007, Priest and Patriarch of Alexandria and All Africa Theodoros II honoured him with the rank of 'Master Keeper of the Archives' of the Patriarchal Throne of Alexandria. In February 2011, His Beatitude the Patriarch of Jerusalem Theophilos III proclaimed him 'Crusader of the All-Holy Tomb'. In December 2011, he was awarded a prize by the Academy of Athens, in January of 2011 he was awarded the Gold Medal for the Arts and Sciences and in 2012 the Great Gold Cross of the International Albert Schweitzer Organization. In 2012 he was awarded an Honorary Doctorate by St. Stephen Harding University, North Carolina. He is Corresponding Member of the Accadeia Costantina (Rome, 2013), the Accademia Bonifaciana (Milan, 2014), Honorary Member of the Norman Academy (France, 2014), of the REAL Academia de Buenas Letras (Barcelona, 2015), of and a Regular Member of the International Academy of Social Sciences (Florida, 2015). He is an Accedemico d'Onore of the

Real Academia Sancti Ambrosii Martyris of Portugal (2016). He is also an Honorary Doctor of Letters (LL. Doctorate, Doctor of Letters) of the Theological College and Seminary, St. Stephen Harding University (2014) and Honorary Doctor of Theology (DD, Doctor of Divinity) of the St. Seraphim School of Orthodox Theology (2015). In 2015, he was awarded the 'Great Prize' by the Institute of Pedagogical Studies and Applications for his academic work and for his contribution to the international spread and study of Greek culture. He was also awarded the 15th International Giuseppe Sciacca Prize in 2017 and in the same year made an Honorary Professor of the Department of Classical and Modern Greek Philology (Departamentul de Filologie Clasica şi Neogreacă) of the University of Bucharest. He has been awarded many state and Church decorations for his educational and social work. He is married and the father of two sons.

Index

H

I

K

L

M

N

O

P

Q

R

S

T

U

V

Y

www.ingramcontent.com/pod-product-compliance
Lightning Source LLC
LaVergne TN
LVHW080015210926
848481LV00011B/3027